HONOUR AND DUTY

HONOUR AND DUTY

The Memoirs of
Countess Ilona Edelsheim Gyulai
Widow of Stephen Horthy, Vice-Regent of Hungary

Purple Pagoda Press Ltd

English edition first published 2005 by
Purple Pagoda Press Ltd.
43 St Anne's Crescent
Lewes
East Sussex BN7 1SD
UK

Originally published in Hungarian in two volumes:
Gróf Edelsheim Gyulai Ilona
Horthy István kormányzóhelyettes özvegye
Becsüet és kötelesség 1 1918–1944
Published by EÚROPA KÖNYVKIADÓ, Budapest, 2000

Gróf Edelsheim Gyulai Ilona
Horthy István, kormányzóhelyettes özvegye
Becsüet és kötelesség 2 1945–1988
Published by EÚROPA KÖNYVKIADÓ, Budapest, 2002

ISBN: 0-9550022-0-6

Typesetting in Sabon by Leonard Hurd

Printed in Great Britain by Hobbs the Printers Ltd,
Totton, Hampshire, UK.

Dedication

I dedicate my memoirs in the first place with everlasting love and gratitude to my husband Stephen Horthy and his parents, 'Miklóspapa' and 'Magdamama', who showed me a shining example – among other things – in their sense of duty, their love of work, truth and justice; and to my one and only beloved son Sharif Stephen Horthy, who always shares everything with me, and whose opinion and help I value.

I wrote this book – the story of the eighty years I have lived – for my descendants, so that they may know the truth and, at the very least, not have to ponder the veracity of writings that have been influenced by Nazi and Communist slander campaigns.

It is therefore meant for:

My five grandchildren: Leonard István, Helena Linda, Henry, Manuela and Stewart Miklós.

My eleven great-grandchildren: Loren, Garrett, Dexter, Mattea, Rosabel, Lailani, Rhyland, Harley, Berenice, Lenita and Marvela.

My ten godchildren: Magdi Darányi Kienast, Paul Esterházy, András Kállay, Victor Makovits, Migui Pap, Deana Moore, Henrietta Monteverde Andersen, Victor Martins, Osanna Andujar and Isabel Rogers.

Acknowledgments

I wrote my book partly in English and partly in Hungarian. For the Hungarian–English translations grateful thanks go to Anna Nilsen, who had already perfectly translated the book *The Tragic Death of Flight Lieutenant István Horthy*, edited by me. My thanks also go to Ilona Stemler (of the Hungarian National Museum) for her reliable and outstanding help with the published photographs.

Last but not least, my grateful thanks go to Manuela Mackenzie who helped me reduce the two Hungarian volumes into one, and edited my book with enthusiasm and professionalism.

Contents

Contents

Historical Note

From before the sixteenth century Hungary's fate had been entwined with that of Austria and the Habsburgs, the dynasty that long reigned over both countries. The relationship between the two was far from easy: the Austrian overlords, ruling from Vienna, saw themselves as absolute monarchs over their empire, whereas Hungarians held that their kingdom – as symbolised by the holy crown of Hungary's first king, Saint Stephen – existed as a distinct entity in its own right. In their eyes, on taking the Coronation Oath the King undertook to rule in accordance with the constitution of the Hungarian kingdom. In the mid-nineteenth century these diverging views came to a head when, after losing an ill-fated war for independence, Hungary was proclaimed to be no more than a province of Austria and suffered direct and oppressive rule from the Habsburg Court in Vienna.

This changed only when Austria encountered a series of military defeats in other parts of the Empire. From 1867, as a result of the agreement known as the Compromise, the Austrian Empire and Hungary became two halves of the 'Austro-Hungarian Monarchy'. Under this dual monarchy both countries still had the same ruler, Francis Joseph I (1848-1916), and also shared the same currency, foreign and defence policies; but internal affairs were managed by the separate government of each state.

By the end of World War I, Francis Joseph had been succeeded by his nephew Charles I (as Austrian Emperor; Charles IV as Hungarian King). Losing the war engendered a wave of revolutionary reaction, with much loss of life and property, and led to the disintegration of the Habsburg Empire: Hungary and other states declared their independence, and Charles abdicated as Emperor in November 1918.

This was a time of deep unrest and instability. In Hungary, the first independent People's Republic was headed by the progressive aristocrat Mihály Károlyi, but his tenure was short lived. He had disbanded the Hungarian army, and Yugoslavia, Romania and Czechoslovakia invaded and occupied much land inside Hungary's borders. By March 1919, having failed on the military and domestic fronts, Károlyi handed power over to the Socialist Party of Hungary.

This Communist government, led by Béla Kún, lasted only 133 days. During that time the Hungarian Red Army achieved some military successes against the incursions from neighbouring states, but the Communist's policy of nationalising the large estates, compulsorily requisitioning food products to supply the cities, and the appalling atrocities perpetrated against any opposition, alienated all levels of Hungarian society. The Allies – France and particularly Britain – had no wish to see a Bolshevik-controlled Hungary; therefore Hungarian politicians led by Count István Bethlen, Count Julius Károlyi and Archduke Joseph (son of King Charles IV), were supported by Britain to organise an opposition government, based at Szeged.

Miklós Horthy of Nagybánya was the person to whom Count Bethlen turned to form his National Army. Born in 1868, Miklós Horthy belonged to an old family of Hungarian landowners. He entered the Austro-Hungarian Navy, and from 1909 to 1914 was aide-de-camp to Emperor Francis Joseph. During the war he had distinguished himself greatly, and had been appointed commander in chief of the fleet. Now he became commander in chief of the National Army. Showing considerable skill in negotiations, both with the Allied forces and with the Rumanians who had occupied Budapest, Admiral Horthy eventually entered the capital city at the head of his soldiers on 16 November 1919.

In 1920, in the aftermath of the conflict, a new government was formed. The parliament's first task was to clarify points of constitutional law. It was agreed that the crowned King, Charles IV, had not relinquished his sovereignty in 1918 when he resigned from taking part in conducting affairs of the state; the kingship should therefore be seen as remaining, if dormant. But Archduke Joseph, who had been named Regent by Charles in August 1919, had immediately been forced to resign by the French – their premier, George Clemenceau, being determined to destroy any vestige of Habsburg power. The Allies now again made it clear that under no circumstances would they approve any re-instatement of the Habsburgs, as this would be seen as a threat, not only by them but also by the newly formed Czechoslovakia and the other surrounding states. These countries, no longer part of the original Austrian Empire, had no intention of giving up their recently acquired lands. It was therefore decided, as had happened on two previous occasions in Hungarian history, to appoint a Regent of State. By an overwhelming majority – 131 to 10 – the parliament voted to elect Admiral Miklós Horthy to the dignity of Regent.

The monarchy was thus maintained, but an interregnum set in. Twice in the following year, King Charles attempted to regain his throne. He unexpectedly entered Hungary from his exile in Switzerland, first in March and then in October 1921, but he failed on both occasions. On orders from the Allies, a Dethronement Act abrogated his rights. The English authorities banished him to Madeira, where he died the following year.

Hungary remained a constitutional monarchy in which the powers of head of state rested with the Regent. The legislative power remained, as before 1918, with a parliament made up of two assemblies: the upper house, which included representatives of the church, the nobility and the general population; and the house of deputies, which was elected by universal suffrage. Miklós Horthy remained as head of state until 1944 when, after the German invasion of Hungary, he and his immediate family were arrested and imprisoned in Bavaria.

For further reading:
> *History of Hungary* by Denis Sinor. London,
> George Allen & Unwin Ltd (1959) (reprinted 1976)
> *Hungary, A Short History* by C. A. Macartney Chicago, Aldine (1962)
> (By the same author: *October Fifteenth: a History of Modern Hungary 1925–1945*, Edinburgh, University Press (1961))

Foreword

Consider a young girl, born in the last year of the First World War, in the centre of Europe, indeed, in the centre of the Austro-Hungarian monarchy, very soon to break up and disappear. Yet she is blessed with a happy childhood, in the midst of a very old family of noblemen and noblewomen. She is beautiful.

Her native Hungary has been mutilated, a state designating itself as a kingdom but one without a king, at its head a Regent, a former admiral but now without a navy; an old gentleman, whose son falls in love with her. They marry in the first year of the Second World War. A year later they have a son. Another year later her husband is made vice-regent of the nation.

This is 1942, the middle of World War Two. Hungary, well-nigh inevitably, is an ally of Hitler's Germany. The Regent (and his son) are not happy with this. He tries not to accord with many of Hitler's wishes. His daughter-in-law grows to love him. Now she is a nurse on the Russian front. Her husband is a flyer with the Hungarian air arm. His plane crashes; he dies. There is some reason to think of German sabotage; in any event, Hitler and the Germans are pleased to have gotten rid of him. His widow, in the Regent's palace, is at work helping all kinds of refugees, including Hungarian Jews. Then Hitler chooses to occupy Hungary. The Regent is stunned but, here and there, he manages to resist. His young daughter-in-law is with him, involved in doing many things, managing secret radios. They decide to save their country by announcing an armistice with the Allies. The Germans drive into the palace compound, arrest the Regent, his wife, his daughter-in-law and her son. They are interned in a castle in Germany.

The war ends, but they are not free yet. Eventually they leave for Portugal. She is a young widow, continuing to live with her in-laws. A British officer falls in love with her. They are married. Decades pass. She lives to be present at the re-burial of her beloved parents-in-law in their once country place in her native country.

What a story this is. She was a participant in great and tragic historic events. She recounts them with a modesty that is more than charming. She is addicted to reconstructions and to corrections to what to her seem misreadings of history. She is insistent but never shrill. Her good heart and affectionate good nature breathe through her pages. Her intelligence colours her writing. Many of her pages are reflections of a now vanished world; indeed, vanished forever. In a way the purpose of her book is a portrait less of its writer than of her husband and of his parents. It has signs of what Goethe once called 'die Herrlichkeit des Herzens': the courtesy of the heart. Her life, of which this book is a residue, is that of a triumph of character.

This is a memoir of an extraordinary woman.

John Lukacs

Preface

Easter Sunday 1994

The day has finally come – I never imagined that it would – when I am beginning to write down the story of my life. It has taken much persuasion by my husband, my son, friends and others, to whom my answer had always been: 'So many books have been written about that part of the Second World War, why another one? Besides which, you know that I am not a writer.' But gradually I began to feel a responsibility, mainly towards my family, and especially to my five grandchildren and ever-growing number of great-grandchildren.

When they become interested, who will be able to tell them the truth, and how will they be able to discern what is true and what is false? So many untruths inspired by political trends and hatred have been written about my country, and especially about members of the Horthy family. Now I am the only survivor of those last years, and particularly of the dramatic final days in the Royal Palace in Budapest, and even the little that I can contribute may also be of value to those historians who search for the truth.

I also have the feeling that by writing I might now discover more for myself about my life. In thinking about past events I already notice how clearly I remember my childhood; but for the most turbulent years of the 1940s, when so much happened, details have fallen away. I noticed things but they did not stick. Now, at the age of seventy-six, I notice and remember all sorts of details that enchant me, like the sun shining through palm trees with all the colours changing from gold to light and dark greens. Trees, flowers, birds, all delight me. This, I suppose, is the advantage of age: paying more attention to detail, being able to stop and truly enjoy without feeling that it is wasting time.

So now, after everything that I have lived through, I count myself extremely fortunate to be able to write 'my story' in my present situation. I have my own writing room – you could call it a working room, or a spiritual recollection room – but whatever it is, to me it is a very peaceful, quiet place, where I look out onto the most beautiful, three-terraced garden, full of blooming shrubs, bougainvilleas, hibiscus, oleanders and lantanas. In the first few months of the year the mimosa trees bloom and transform the place into blazing gold. There is constant birdsong; and from where I am writing I have a breathtaking view of the Atlantic Ocean in the distance.

In order to be able to write, I feel I must first make an effort to understand myself – which is not at all easy. Now that I am in my old age, I can see that at birth I was given two very valuable characteristics and two unfortunate ones. The first positive element is not being afraid, possessing an inner certainty. Mind you, there is no merit in this, as it is not courage. Courage as I understand it is overcoming fear. If there is no fear, there is no need for courage. The second is an ability to see the good side of things; easily forgetting the disagreeable, the offences and so on, and remembering what is good and pleasant. I have found this to be very useful and rewarding.

If I am right in my assessment, the first of the two more negative aspects of my nature is a lack of imagination, a failure to seek wider knowledge, a conviction that I have no talents of my own; while the second is being too easily adaptable – even at the risk of being smothered – a trait I inherited from both my parents. It was only thanks to God's help and illumination that I was able to save myself from this dangerous abyss.

I will do my best to be honest and write down what I clearly remember. All my life I have loved the truth, even if sometimes it has been painful. I can cope with upheavals and tragedies as long as I know the facts. My diaries will help me to follow the sequence of events. From 1942 onwards, each of these diaries contains five years of short daily notes I wrote down about the day's events. The earlier ones are lost, as they were left behind when the German Gestapo took us away from Hungary.

In this book I hope to convey my experiences to you as sincerely as I possibly can; I leave it to you to judge their veracity for yourself and trust your own inner conviction about them.

We all have to find things out for ourselves; and I feel that I am incredibly lucky to have been given an ability to understand which goes back to my early years. I used to ask myself what was the most important thing in life, and the answer seemed to be to understand why we are in this world and what happens when we leave it. So, just as I sought out people who liked to do the things I liked to do, such as riding, improvising at the piano, or skiing, I thought I ought also to seek out the company of people who knew more about such things than I did. But how to find them? I did not know. Until one day – much later, in 1958, through my son – I met people who could show me the answer to this fundamental need. But let us start at the beginning.

Part One

1

The Beginning

I was born in Budapest, in my father's house, 12 Dísz Square, on Buda Hill in the old part of the city. It was 14 January 1918 – a critical time for the whole of Europe. The First World War was nearing its end, and the Austro-Hungarian Empire was breaking up. I was my parent's third daughter and a real disappointment to my father, who would have liked a son. Apparently I was an agreeable-looking baby, and so my father – after finally deciding to look at me – admitted that at least he had a pretty daughter.

These were hard times for the people in the city, and food was difficult to come by. My mother had no milk to give me and it was almost impossible to buy any. I was told that the first solid food I was given was noodles with poppy-seeds (a popular dish in Hungary). Maybe this is why dishes made with poppy-seeds later became my favourite food.

The situation in the country was deteriorating rapidly. In 1919 Hungary was declared a Soviet Republic and the proletarian dictatorship was established. Naturally I do not remember this myself, but I was told that the first clear word I spoke – to my parents' horror – was 'elvtárs' (comrade). I do not mind the fact that it was my first word, just as long as it is not my last!

It is scarcely remembered, and I wonder if it was ever generally understood outside my country, that Hungary never wished to enter the First World War. When the Austro-Hungarian Parliament took the decision to declare war, the only one who openly and officially opposed it was the Hungarian prime minister, Count István Tisza. But as part of the Austro-Hungarian Empire we had no choice. After the war, the Trianon Treaty of 1920, which we signed under duress, then deprived Hungary of two-thirds of her former territory.

It hardly bears thinking about. It was and remains a blatant injustice, contrary to all the rules of democracy. Surrounding countries were paid off with chunks of Hungary, in some of these areas the rights and particularly the culture of the Hungarians living there being systematically stamped out and crushed.

Before the First World War, the population of Hungary (without Croatia) was over 18 million – Trianon left us 7.5 million; the country covered 283,000 square kilometres – they left us 92,000. Hungary lost 71 per cent – more than two-thirds – of its original territory, whereas they took only 10 per cent of Germany. They removed our forests, coal, salt and other minerals, and the sources of our rivers, which now entered our country from outside our territory. This is how Europe showed its gratitude to the Hungarian 'buffer-state' that had defended it from the Turks and Tartars at great cost to itself.

Anyone hearing this would rightly ask what Hungary's great sin could have been, to be so severely punished? Whatever anyone can say, I will never understand it and therefore cannot give a reason for it. Was it because we do not belong to either the Slav or the German country-groups? Was this why the victorious powers rewarded their allies with Hungarian territory? US General H. H. Bandholtz (American head of the Inter-Allied Military Commission) wrote in his diary in 1920:

> While we shall all be glad to be homeward bound, yet we cannot but feel some regrets at leaving Hungary. Personally, I came here rather inclined to condone or extenuate much of the Rumanian procedure, but their outrageous conduct in violation of all international law, decency and humane considerations, has made me become an advocate of the Hungarian cause.
>
> Turning over portions of Hungary, with its civilised and refined population, will be like turning over Texas and California to the Mexicans. The great Powers of the Allies should hang their heads in shame for what they allowed to take place in this country after an armistice. It would be just as sensible to insist also that Switzerland, on account of her mixed French, German, and Italian population, be subdivided into three states, as to insist upon the illogical ethnographic subdivision and distribution of the territory and people of old Hungary. It is simply another case of the application of long-range theory as against actual conditions.
>
> The Hungarians certainly have many defects, at least from an American point of view, but they are so far superior to any of their neighbors that it is a crime against civilisation to continue with the proposed dismemberment of this country.

It is tragic that both the note sent to the powers engaged in the war by the US President, Mr Thomas Woodrow Wilson, in which he set forth his ideas about a just peace treaty involving self-determination and plebiscites, and the later efforts of Lord Rothermere – the owner of the English newspaper the *Daily Mail* – to bring 'Justice for Hungary', were ignored because it was not in the interest of the powers which had won the First World War to change the borders laid down at Trianon.

All this has been widely written about and I only want to give a taste of what I felt – and still feel – about it to those who do not know.

Despite being humiliated, dismembered and downtrodden, after Trianon, Hungary enjoyed an almost miraculous recovery. An enormous amount of work was accomplished under the leadership of Admiral Miklós Horthy and the governments appointed by him, so that order and peace could reign in the country.

What was this new Hungary like? We were surrounded by hostile countries. A multiple-party political system prevailed, although the Social Democratic Party was subject to a number of restrictions and the Communist Party was forbidden, being considered subversive because it sought to overthrow the existing social system. There were functioning upper and lower houses of Parliament, and freedom of the press.

Trianon also profoundly affected my own family. The country estate belonging to the family of my father, Count Leopold Edelsheim Gyulai, was near the village of Felső Elefánt (Upper Elephant) in the district of Nyitra in the north of Hungary, and this area was ceded to Czechoslovakia under the treaty.

It was here that my parents moved after I was born, having decided it would be safer than living in Budapest. When, in 1920, my father suddenly found that his home was in Czechoslovakia instead of Hungary, he had to adapt himself to a completely new situation. From then onwards we were Czechoslovakian citizens, but Hungarian nationals, and this was officially written into every population census.

Also, land reform was immediately implemented in Czechoslovakia. Before the First World War the Felső Elefánt estate had covered 2,840 acres of arable and pastureland and 4,260 acres of woodland. The Czech government's land reform cut the arable land owned by the estate by three-quarters. Fortunately, the woodland was allowed to remain intact.

The truth is that I was never really interested in my ancestry, but in later years my son and friends asked me so many questions about it that I finally became interested myself. So first I will describe what I knew of my maternal grandparents, before telling you what I learnt from my father about his forebears, and which I am sure is correct.

My mother's parents were Count Tódor (Theodore) Pejacsevich, who died in 1928, and his wife, born Baroness Lilla Vay. Grandfather Tódor was a unionist Croat politician and served eighteen years as lord lieutenant in Eszék. He was also chairman of the Serb-Croat coalition, Governor of Croatia, Slavonia and Dalmatia, and minister without portfolio in the government of Croatia, Slavonia and Dalmatia. He was said to be an outstanding administrator, friendly to everyone, and to possess a good sense of humour.

I remember him less well than my grandmother because he had died before my sister Myro and I paid our visits to Grandmother in Nasice, but I know from the family that in the summer of 1914 Grandfather Tódor went to take the waters in Vichy in France, and was there when the First World War broke out. The French immediately interned him, until in 1916 he was allowed to go home in exchange for the release of a few Serbian generals.

Grandmother Lilla was a remarkable personality. She could sing and play the piano, and was also a talented actress, appearing in many charity performances in her youth. When I knew her she had beautiful thick white hair, held in a large, loose bun on top of her head. She had three small snow-white Maltese terriers, two of which she trained to perform various tricks. One 'sang' quietly when she played pianissimo on the piano, and howled loudly when she played fortissimo. For the other she played a waltz, and when she said 'Waltzing, waltzing,' the small dog got up onto its hind legs and started turning round and round. The third dog was hopelessly lacking in talent.

Grandmother entertained us with her sense of humour, her honesty, and her many stories. But the most interesting story was her own great tragedy. She underwent a major operation in which her uterus and ovaries were removed – at that time the doctors took out everything at the same time – the after-effect of which was that she became deranged and was locked up in a mental institution. As her condition slowly improved she was transferred to a home in the country, where she had her own room but was under constant supervision because she was still a little confused.

She was well enough to know that she was being kept confined and thought she would never be allowed back home, so she decided to commit suicide. A railway line passed not far from the house, and she often heard the trains passing. So when everyone was asleep she put her coat over her nightdress, found the key to the front door, and quietly crept out. She found the track and lay on her front between the rails (not across them), and waited for a train to arrive: dawn was breaking when suddenly she heard it coming. She was petrified with fear and could not move. The rolling stock in those days had large wheels and rode high above the track, so the train passed over her; all that happened was that the chains connecting the twelve carriages hit her hard on the bottom, bang ... bang ... bang ... twelve times. It was very painful and she started bleeding. Suddenly the train ground very noisily to a stop. The driver had seen something lying on the track and had stopped the train. In fright Grandmother rolled down the embankment and hid in a wheat field. She heard men walking along the track, but as they did not find anything, the train continued its journey and Grandmother crept back to the house.

Although a decided failure as a suicide attempt, it seems she had given herself some shock therapy, and after that she made a complete recovery.

In our house in Budapest there was a portrait (painted by Kriehuber in 1830) of Ignácz Gyulai, with an inscription in German: 'Ignatz, Count Gyulai, Governor of Croatia, Field Marshal General, Commanding Upper and Lower Austria'. His son, Ferencz Gyulai, married a Baroness Edelsheim, and when their son – named Ignácz after his grandfather – died as a young boy, Ferencz adopted his nephew Baron Leopold Edelsheim, my great-grandfather. This is how our family names were joined and became Edelsheim Gyulai; the title of Count was later given to him by the Emperor. The perfectly preserved, gold-decorated documents of the name change and the bestowal of the title, with the Emperor's personal signature, were found after the Second World War amid debris in the cellar of our house in Budapest, and are now in my possession.

My great-grandfather is certainly worth talking about. I lived for seventy-six years without anyone ever telling me any real details about him, but now, ever since I decided to write about him, I can hardly believe the amount of information that has come to me about this amazing man. I have been receiving articles, old letters and photographs from completely unexpected sources. First a young man in Slovakia found our family crypt lying in ruins in the woods, and saw my great-grandfather's name and the marble relief behind his tomb, on which he is shown riding into battle with his sword drawn. This helpful young man made it his hobby to find out everything about him. He went to public libraries and so on, and found a lot of documents; and when he discovered my address, he sent them all to me.

Then a collector went to the Hungarian National Museum and offered to sell them old letters and papers dating from 1630 to the First World War. They had been found in a cellar, somewhere in Budapest. The head of the museum department knows me and, seeing that all these documents were about my family, she bought them all. I happened to visit her a week later and found a vast range of articles, photographs and letters about my great-grandfather and his beautiful wife Friderika. How on earth can these things have survived two wars and forty-three years of Communist rule?

Here then is a brief summary, distilled from the huge amount of material that was found and also from the little my father told me about my great-grandfather:

'He was the army's pillar of glory,' says the German edition of a Budapest newspaper, commenting on his death.[1] 'Born in 1826, in his youth he was like a young Adonis, tall, thin and strong, with a nicely formed nose and a small mouth that showed even teeth like pearls when he smiled. His eyes always seemed to be laughing, but radiated unbridled bravery,' comments another article. He was brilliant at riding and fencing. In the space of five years he was successively promoted from cadet to captain of cavalry first class, an unusually fast advancement in peacetime.

He distinguished himself repeatedly in military campaigns and became a lieutenant general in the cavalry and a privy councillor. He was made a field marshal and, in 1869, became inspector general of the cavalry. As such, he won great renown for his training and reorganisation of the Austro-Hungarian cavalry. He reformed everything from the saddling and bridling of the horses to the dressage and riding instruction. He introduced the English trot to the army's cavalry regiments, thereby greatly sparing both horses and riders. The cavalry rules and regulations that he drew up were so successful that the leading armies in the rest of Europe adopted them.

In 1874 he was made commandant-general of Hungary, and Budapest Corps commander. Thanks to his adoption and his inheritance of the Gyulai estates – but much more so to his great sympathy for the Hungarian nation, to whose sons, the Hussars, he owed his military victories – he felt totally Hungarian, and demonstrated it on many occasions. He was well known for leading humanitarian campaigns and helping with disaster relief. This earned him the affection of the Hungarian public, but the leading military circles were not of the same opinion – it was thought that he had become too good a Hungarian to be a totally impartial commander. He was obliged to take a hint from 'above' and request retirement, which was immediately and honourably granted; he was awarded the Grand Cross of the Order of Leopold.

The Baron became a very popular figure in Budapest society. The cover page of another newspaper, dated 1888,[2] shows him in a top hat throwing himself in front of a carriage with two rearing horses. The inscription reads: 'Baron Edelsheim Gyulai, the life-saver'. Thanks to his presence of mind and quick reflexes he had saved a young man from the wheels of a runaway carriage and pair.

Beside his military profession – to which he had dedicated all his energy – my great-grandfather had only one other passion: the theatre. His criticisms and reviews of plays were always popular. He had been passionately devoted to the theatre since he had been a cavalry colonel. If you go to the Karl Theatre in Vienna today you will be shown the seat where he sat every night to admire his fiancée, Miss Friderika Kronau, a celebrated and beautiful actress.

My father told me that when his grandfather married Friderika, people thought that they would never be accepted at Court because she was an actress. The first time Great-Grandfather took his wife to a reception at Court, everybody formed a big circle awaiting the entrance of Emperor Franz Joseph. When the Emperor arrived, he looked around and without greeting anybody else, went straight up to my great-grandparents and extended his hand to Friderika, whose theatre performances he had himself seen and admired. She was totally accepted at Court after that.

There was a beautiful portrait of her in the living room of our home in Elefánt, painted by Winterhalter, who was the leading court painter of the time. She was so lovely that I sometimes sat looking at the picture for a long time. I often wonder what happened to it, as I cannot imagine anyone destroying it.

My father used to tell us many stories about my great-grandfather's legendary fearlessness – and maybe it is from him that I inherited this lack of fear I was born with. Apparently, when he heard of haunted houses he always made a point of going there and finding out the reason for their reputation. It seems that he always managed to prove that there was some natural explanation. I remember my father telling us about how Great-Grandfather went with a friend to an old house in which people complained of hearing someone go downstairs every night at around midnight, but no one could ever see anything. They stood at the bottom of the large wooden staircase and patiently waited until they heard footsteps coming down. They lit a candle and the steps stopped, but there was nothing to be seen. They put out the candle and waited, and after a while the sound of the steps coming down started again. So they stood on either side of the stairs, held hands and waited again as the steps came closer and closer and then passed under their joined hands. They quickly lit the candle and found a big toad, which lived somewhere upstairs. When the house was quiet at night it came down to find food. Every time a light was lit, it withdrew under the protruding wooden edge of the stair and waited until it was dark and quiet again before continuing its descent. There were many such stories!

The general's son – my grandfather – was also named Leopold; he was born in Salzburg in the Austro-Hungarian Empire in 1863. His main interest was charitable work. He was the founder of the National Child Protection League. For a while he was chairman of that association, vice-chairman of the National White Cross Association for Foundlings and co-chairman of the National Home for Disabled Children.

I found a newspaper cutting (unfortunately the date and name of the paper is missing) praising an article that Grandfather wrote:

> The prominent nobleman, Baron Leopold Edelsheim Gyulai, son of the deceased corps commander, who has inherited his father's outstanding qualities in every way, wrote an article in a leading newspaper a short time ago, in which he speaks with real feeling about the interests of the poor. He says that everybody should give to the poor according to their income.
>
> May the harvest of this noble thought be as abundant as the writer's heartfelt intention and show the narrow-minded the way to happiness, as nothing gives such happiness as doing good deeds.

My grandmother, born Princess Irma Odescalchi, was a lady-in-waiting at the imperial court. Her family was from the Hungarian branch of the Italian Odescalchi family. One of her ancestors, a great, great grand-uncle, was Pope Innocent XI. I am glad that he was one of the good popes. People said that my grandmother was a very good woman, like a saint. She had a heart condition and I remember her being in a wheelchair, very thin and hardly eating anything. She was very affectionate and never complained. When she died, my grandfather moved from his large home on the Elefánt estate to Budapest, to the house in which I had been born. We then moved from the so-called 'little castle' in Elefánt village to the 'big castle' of the estate, Szent János.

There are two legends about the origin of the name Elefánt. The first says that someone captured an elephant during a battle against the Turks, and when he presented it to King Zsigmond, the King rewarded him by adding *Elefánthy* (Elephantine) to his name as a noble title. The second says that he was given an elephant after distinguishing himself in battle, and then took on the name.

Szent János, a large country house, was named after Saint John the Baptist. From 1369 to 1786 it had been the largest monastery of the Paulist Order, a Hungarian religious order – the only order unique to the country – but was abandoned when the Paulists were expelled from the country at the end of the eighteenth century by the Austrian Emperor Joseph II. He dissolved all religious orders and took over their estates. The Paulist Order was reinstated in Hungary after the First World War, when Admiral Horthy was Regent.

Once the Paulists had left, the monastery was abandoned and fell into decay. Owls and bats lived in the church, and wind and rain blew through the broken windows, until in 1894 my grandfather, 'the noble art expert Baron Leopold Edelsheim Gyulai, whose soul was captivated by the tempest-beaten monastic ruin, put an end to the desecration and ruin and created a paradise on earth for his family.'[3]

Situated in the middle of a half circle of mountains – the foothills of the Carpathians – the former monastery was surrounded by pine and beech woods and looked down on an entirely open area of extensive grassland in front. When I was a child, red deer grazed in front of the house and the grass looked like a huge, well-kept lawn. In the winter the deer were fed with beets and hay, and ran off only a little distance when a carriage drove up the drive. They gradually even got used to cars.

The house was an upside-down T in plan. The church was in the middle and had been made into a huge, beautifully furnished hall. When the ceilings of the church were cleaned, five lovely frescoes were found, in perfect condition. They were painted by the outstanding church painter Bergl in the second half of the eighteenth century, and portrayed five episodes from the life of John the Baptist.

The church had been divided up, and the first two frescoes formed the ceiling of a large, light cream-coloured dining room. The other three formed the ceiling of the big hall with its huge wooden staircase and gallery. The monks' cells that had run all along the front of the monastery had been made into rooms by joining two or three cells together. Because they were all vaulted, they made lovely rooms, which looked out onto a woodland setting where deer could be seen wandering about at any time of the day. All the rooms opened onto a long corridor that ran the whole length of the house. It was decorated with the antlers, pelts and heads of moufflons (wild sheep), polar bears and so on – trophies from my grandfather's and my father's several expeditions to the North Sea off Spitzbergen.

After the First World War it was of course impossible to keep such a large house open all the year round. From as far back as I can remember, we lived in the right wing of the house all year round, while the rest of the house was only used in the summer months, when we had family or friends to stay.

No one could have enjoyed living in such a fabulous place and being so close to nature and wildlife more than I did. It was a wonderful time, riding the carriage horses and driving the special 'long carriage' made for the woods, on which you sat astride as if on a horse. You kept your balance with your knees and could drive very fast. There were delicious wild strawberries growing all over the woods, and lilies of the valley grew in abundance in one area, filling the air with their wonderful scent.

My father was trying to restore the stock of both the red deer and the moufflons to their former levels, because they had suffered a lot from indiscriminate killing during the First World War, and within a few years he had developed the most beautiful herds of red, fallow and roe deer, as well as moufflons and wild boar. I spent a lot of my time taming and looking after animals, particularly the deer. And photographing them became one of my passions.

Abandoned or wounded animals were usually brought to me, and I fed the small deer or nursed them until they were well again, before letting them loose in the woods. My first experience of this kind was with a small deer that I tried to bottle-feed. When it died I was heartbroken. I put it in a tin cake-box and went off to bury it with tears running down my cheeks, much to my sisters' amusement. The next time I got the milk mix correct, and succeeded in saving several deer over the years.

Two of my favourite roes I named Bambi and Faline, after the Walt Disney film. Bambi was found abandoned and brought to me, and Faline was badly cut and lost one eye to a scythe cutting wheat during the harvest. They became inseparable, and would always come when I called them by imitating the call of the mother roe, which I had often heard.

Although I usually released the animals in my care into the woods when they were grown up or healed, Bambi had to be kept in an enclosure because he became too tame and unafraid of humans. He thought it was fun to attack people from behind, and was a real danger because of his small but sharp antlers. So every year when his antlers were full-grown and hard, I caught him and sawed them off at the roots. Faline I eventually took deep into the woods, left her grazing and hid – watching with a sad heart as she disappeared into a thicket. I met her two years later, in dense woods far from the house. I heard her calling, and when I answered she emerged from the shrubbery. There was no mistaking her, with her single eye. She let me stroke her and then disappeared again, this time for good.

One long, snowy winter I decided to try and tame a young stag, taking food to the same spot every day. I was attracted to him because his first small antlers already had ten points, which is rare. I started by putting down food and hiding, then gradually started staying nearby so he would see me. And so we went on, step by step – it took a lot of patience – until he got so used to me that I could walk with my arms around his neck, even when he had grown an enormous twenty-two-point set of antlers. He was the living proof to me that not all male stags become dangerous when they lose their fear of people. He even took great care not to touch me with his antlers, bending his head to one side as he approached me.

He always remained completely free in the open woods, and I would go looking for him and calling him. One day an amazing thing happened. It was autumn, the mating season, and being a big stag he already had a large herd of hinds. I wish I could describe the setting – the colour of the woods all around, with a large meadow in front of me. As I walked out into the meadow I saw a dead stag lying in the middle of it, obviously having just been killed by one bigger and stronger than himself. As I was examining him, my stag came out from the woods with his antlers covered in blood. When he saw me he galloped straight at me, and instinctively I looked around for a tree to hide behind or a stick to ward him off, but there was nothing close. To my utter surprise, he slowed down on approaching me and, bending his head to the side so that his antlers should not touch me, put his nose on my shoulder and clearly forgot about his dead foe. If anyone had told me this story I simply would not have believed it.

As the herds grew, my father began selling deer to other estates for breeding. Some even went to the famous Hagenbeck Zoo in Germany. He worked out good systems to catch the deer and the moufflons, and I always helped him. I found everything to do with running the estate very interesting, and regularly accompanied my father in his work in the woods and on the farm, on horseback, on foot, or by carriage. As my father had no son I had sort of become the boy in this family of girls.

2

Family Life

The thing that most affected our lives was my parents' separation. Of course, I can only tell you about it from my own observations, and hope that they can convey the truth of the situation.

My father – whom we called Papi – was an extraordinary person. To me he seemed to be thoroughly good, decent, loyal and truthful. He never put himself forward or tried to draw attention to himself – although he had a talent for telling stories and very funny jokes and anecdotes. His integrity and honesty were widely appreciated by those who knew him, and he was often asked to arbitrate in difficult family situations. As far as I know, the decisions he made were never contested. He seldom reprimanded us but when he did, we never dared disobey. He never hit us, because a stern word was enough when it was said with truth and love. It was only when I grew up that I realized what a terrible blow it must have been to him when he found out that my mother was regularly meeting the man she loved, who lived in the nearby village where everyone already knew. When she eventually went to live with him she left my father with three young daughters: Éva aged six, Maritta (usually called Myro) aged four, and myself – Ilona (usually called Ily) who was one year old. I feel that deep in his heart he never forgave her.

My mother had met the love of her life, and she stayed with him until the end of his days. Although I do not understand what she did, I do not want to blame her. Joseph Kochanovszky, the man who so completely dominated her, whom she loved so dearly, and with whom she completely identified herself, had a remarkably imposing appearance. He was tall and dark, and wore a black band that covered one blind eye. He was an atheist and, as my mother followed him in everything, she became one too. They were truly happy together and this is why I cannot blame her for what she did. It seems that she had found her real partner.

We three girls remained with our father, and soon afterwards he married my stepmother, Ella Rothkugel Rollershausen, who had been left by her husband and who had one daughter Alexia (usually called Sya). That is how we became four sisters: Éva, Myro, Sya and Ily, collectively known as EMSI. My stepsister Sya was the nearest to me in age as there were only ten months between us. She was the one I grew up with, sharing a room and all our studies. We got on very well and never quarrelled. All four of us had a happy carefree childhood together, which was only disturbed a few years later when my mother suddenly wanted to see the three daughters she had left. My good-hearted father gave in and said she could have us for six weeks each year until we reached the age of sixteen, when we could decide for ourselves.

This meant that every year the family was disrupted, as three of us went to stay with our mother while our stepsister naturally stayed behind. When the time came for this visit we cried and did not want to go. I found it quite disturbing psychologically. People do not always realize the strength of the bonds between children and what a blow it is to be parted for what, when you are young, seems to be such a long time.

Later on, my two elder sisters had a serious quarrel with my mother because she said something about Father that they disapproved of, and they refused to go to see her after that. I was not present at the time and somehow I did not want to hurt her. We all agreed that at least one of us ought to go on visiting her, so, very reluctantly, I continued to go by myself.

My mother used to talk to us about the divorce, but luckily I was not a gossiping or curious child and never listened much when she did so. She probably had a subconscious feeling of guilt or a need for self-justification. One day I decided to ask my father to tell me once and for all how it had all come about, so that I would know the facts and never again have to listen to stories about which I could not be certain. I was about ten years old at the time, perhaps even younger. My father told me his view of what had happened and from then onwards when it was discussed by my mother, I blocked it out and just shut my ears. I have been very close to my father all my life and always felt that what he said was true.

In the years when I went to visit my mother by myself, she and her husband twice took me on a journey to Italy. I will never forget some of the special moments, like our trip to see Vesuvius. The volcano erupted regularly at the time and it was possible to go into the crater, in the middle of which was a deep hole. We could go to the very edge and see glowing lava like a vision of hell. We were allowed to look for four minutes and then had to run back to the outer edge of the crater because a short eruption occurred punctually every five minutes. This was preceded by a great rumbling noise from the depths of the mountain – which was a good reminder for everyone to start running. Then out shot glowing stones and fire, flying high up into the sky and reaching a radius of about 100 metres. That strong rumbling noise deep inside the earth was very overpowering. I can vividly recall the feeling of being a tiny helpless speck beside the power of nature, of being absolutely nothing, liable to disappear without trace like a little ant. Later in life I would sometimes get the same feeling in huge crowds or when I looked at big apartment blocks in the suburbs, where behind every window there were presumably people who were happy or sad, loved or hated, and I would ask myself what it all amounted to. At such moments nothing seemed worthwhile, and I would wonder whether I would ever find out why it had to be so. Were human beings and their feelings of no value? Were we dispensable?

The time came when I also stopped seeing my mother. I was about sixteen. One evening, during one of my yearly visits to her in Budapest, my mother, her husband and I were having a late supper after having been to the opera. They started talking about my father in a rude, unpleasant way. I just got up from the dining table, took my coat and, although my mother tried to stop me, walked out.

We did not see our mother again until we were grown up and married. We then invited her to our homes but refused to go to her husband's house. Happily all these differences disappeared later on, after the Second World War, when her husband was getting old and blind. They were given permission to leave Communist-controlled Hungary because of their old age and ill health, and went to live near their only daughter, my half sister Harry, in Switzerland. After her husband died in Lausanne in July 1961, my mother visited all her daughters, but lived by herself in the south of Switzerland most of the time. She taught languages, wrote articles, looked after sick people and went to visit hippies to talk to them about God. Strangely, on her husband's death her religious feelings had come back more strongly than ever. In fact, faith and prayer dominated her life.

My stepmother was very beautiful, with a lot of lovely golden-blond hair. Although she was very strict we all loved her, and we called her Ellamami. Actually, I think we would not have dared not to love her. She was an active, forceful person, and very efficient. She was brilliant at organizing the household and making our home beautiful. Papi left practically all decisions to her and perhaps gave in too much. Only when a matter was truly important did he sometimes put his foot down. I think this was a result of the failure of his first marriage. He could just shut himself off and leave the everyday organisation to her.

I know she loved us in her own way and surely thought she was doing what was best for us, but boy, did she organize us. We had to be dressed alike all the time (in order to know whose clothes were whose, we had crosses sewn into them. I was number four, so I had four crosses). She told us that this was the only way we would make an impression – all dressed alike – as individually we would not be noticed.

Although we had maids, we had to do our own beds; we also had to clear the road of weeds around the house. During meals we were allowed to speak only when spoken to, had to eat everything we put on our plate and were not allowed to look at the dishes as the butler brought them in. It was no use arguing with her because she always won! She was no more lenient with Sya, her own daughter, and treated her in exactly the same way. I can still see Sya sitting on the toilet, where she was ordered to sit until she had eaten the food she had vomited on her plate in the dining room. This upset me very much, as there was no way I could help her.

It seems quite strange today to think of the way we were educated. We never went to school at all, mainly because we lived in Czechoslovakia and my father did not want us to go to a Czech school, where we would not be taught Hungarian. Being Hungarians, my parents wanted us to learn Hungarian, and my two elder sisters followed the school curriculum with a Hungarian governess and then travelled to Budapest for exams.

Sya and I, the two younger ones, did not even go for exams. We always had four governesses in the house – Hungarian, English, French and German. It must have been a great sacrifice for my parents to have all these strangers permanently in their home. A Hungarian teacher taught us the normal school subjects, and the others gave us lessons in languages, history and art. Papi taught us geography himself and I loved those lessons. He made us play games. We had to point at random to a letter in a book and then had five minutes to write down countries, cities, rivers or mountains beginning with that letter. When we read out the results, we had to show where they were on the map in order to win a point.

I am most grateful to Papi for awakening my interest in the whole world – little did I then imagine that one day I would travel all over five continents and think of him in the places he taught us about. When I saw the Cimborazo Mountain in South America from the plane for the first time, with its lovely, snow-covered shape, it brought back the memory of my father so vividly that I started to cry.

Our English nanny, or governess, stayed with us for many years, in fact until her death. Her name was Kate Masterton. She was very small, thin and full of wrinkles, with her white hair tied up in a bun on top of her head. We loved her and called her 'Missy'. Fortunately for us she spoke only English and not a word of any other language. She was already with us when it became law that everyone must possess a passport or identity papers. As nobody had ever mentioned any such thing to her before, she was very upset and told us that we Hungarians were the most impossible people she had ever come across. She did not even know her own age, so we tried to help her reconstruct her life. She was born on a merchant ship of which her father was the captain, and she remembered that she had gone to China as a nanny when she was sixteen. We tried to work out how long she had stayed with each family from then onwards. We finally concluded that she had probably been born in 1876 and wrote to England to get her papers. When the answer came we were afraid to tell her what the UK authorities said. Registration had started in 1870 and, as she could not be traced, they suggested that she might have been born in 1867 instead of 1876. Understandably, she strongly resented ageing nine years from one day to the next.

She had very fixed habits and was convinced that the English way was the only right way in everything. In the 1920s skirts started to become very short for the first time. Missy thought this was a perverse Hungarian invention. She continually argued with us, saying that nobody in England would wear such clothes. Then one day she found a photograph of Queen Mary in a magazine. The Queen always wore clothes like those from the nineteenth century, including skirts right down to the ground. Missy brought the magazine to us in triumph, saying, 'You see, in England one wears long dresses. Queen Mary is the proof.'

We learnt English with Missy without even noticing it. And at this early age, besides our native Hungarian language, we also picked up German and French without any difficulty.

My parents thought that we actually did not need to learn anything other than what was necessary to make us fit for marriage and to lead the same sort of life as they themselves did. This seemed obvious to them. Of course nowadays nobody would teach children that way, and in fact the time soon came when we had to find out what we could do to earn our living.

However, at the time we took it for granted, and learned history, literature, art, geography and languages but very little mathematics or science. Looking back – and with due respect to my parents – although everything we did learn was actually very useful to us later in life, I feel that they made one very big mistake: we were never taught how to cook. In fact we were not even allowed to go into the kitchen. I suppose it must have seemed impossible to them that we would ever have to cook for ourselves, because we would always have someone to cook for us. As a result, later on we knew more or less what to tell a cook but could do nothing for ourselves; we had to learn the hard way. Today I love to cook, and I am fully aware of how useful it would have been to have learned at an early age.

When we were very young our parents wanted us to learn to play the piano. A little old lady came to teach us, but her teaching style managed to put us off piano playing very rapidly. After a short time all four of us stood up to our parents and said that since we had the gramophone and the radio we did not want to play the piano. They accepted our decision but warned us never to blame them for not having tried to teach us.

Some years later I really wanted to play the piano. There was a grand piano in the billiard room, a room that was hardly ever used. Every time the family was away I went in there to play. My shyness and secrecy was due to the fact that I knew that my real mother had played very well, and I was afraid that people might say that I was like her, so I did not want anyone to know that I was playing.

I played by ear and liked to improvise melodies. My sisters found out and secretly came to listen. Once, I composed a fox-trot and an English waltz and my sisters arranged for a cousin of ours who could write music to listen in the next room and write down the tunes, which they then handed over to the jazz orchestra that was to perform at my eldest sister's 'coming out' ball in my father's house in Budapest.

When the day of the 'coming out' party arrived we three younger sisters were not allowed to attend, but were having great fun watching the guests from an interior balcony on the top floor. Suddenly we heard a fanfare played to draw attention to an announcement, and someone said on the loudspeaker: 'Now we will play a composition by the family's youngest daughter.'

I was stunned when I heard my song being played by the jazz band, and when people came running upstairs calling my name I ran into my room and locked the door. But our nanny had another key and they picked me up and carried me on their shoulders around the ballroom with everybody clapping. I was told later that I was very pale and looked terrified. After that I never composed again.

Let me tell you a little more about how we lived in our forest estate of Felső Elefánt. Later, I was aware of the rumours which enemy propaganda spread about a 'terrible feudal Hungary'. It was on the whole – and certainly in our case, as Hungarians living in Czechoslovakia – an unjust statement.

Working on an estate was surely not a terrible way of living by the standards of the time, for the people who worked on these private estates were mostly better looked after than the ones who did not, and were helped by the landowners whenever they needed it. At the time it seemed to be a normal way of life, and I remember them as smiling, happy people. There may well have been estates where this was not so, and I entirely agree that there must be a social security system run by the state, so that everyone is looked after. However, in the 1920s the governments of the neighbouring countries all suffered from social problems, and they tried to cover it up by criticising Hungary while keeping very quiet about what happened within their own borders.

The people my parents employed were truly like a family to us, and when someone was in need or in trouble we tried to help them. I remember when our driver's wife had her first baby. It came so suddenly that she could not get help. I was still very young but was made to hold the lamp while Mami assisted the birth. I still remember how my arms hurt and how I had to make a great effort not to drop it, but I was very proud to have been given the job.

We had a number of permanent servants including two butlers, a cook, two maids and a coachman. We called the head butler Uncle Fritz, the cook Aunt Balika and the coachman Uncle Jóska. Uncle Fritz treated us almost like his own children. He would certainly tell me not to do this or that if he thought I was doing wrong.

Our driver, Béla Táncos, whom we called Tánci, taught us to drive; we were very fond of him too. Tánci was incredibly loyal after the Second World War, when Communism started and the house and estate were confiscated. He took all the silver he could and buried it. He and his family lived in absolute poverty for years but it never occurred to him to sell any of it. When the opportunity arose he sent the silver to us abroad, little by little. I wish I could have seen him before he died and thanked him for his deeds, which were of the kind that restore one's faith in human beings. It is wonderful and very touching how the good in people survives and comes shining through, and it is also the proof that my parents treated their employees in the right way.

Indeed, even when my parents had moved to France after the tribulations they suffered following the war, they still tried to find ways to help the families on our former estate. They corresponded with some of them and gave them what assistance they could, despite the fact that they themselves had difficulties.

The neighbouring forest-estates to ours were Gymes and Appony. We saw our neighbours quite often and regularly went over to visit Appony. Count Magi Apponyi was a passionate hunter and had travelled widely, especially throughout India, and had also organized an expedition to the Himalayas. He lived with his sister Adél, and later on they were joined by their two nieces, Geraldine and Virginia, who were our age and with whom we became friends for life.

One of my most vivid recollections of Appony is the visit of the Maharaja of Patiala, as the guest of 'Uncle Magi'. He came with his latest beautiful Indian wife who was twenty-one years old, and his eldest son who was nineteen. The Maharani and her stepson were not allowed to speak to each other – which I think was wise of the Maharaja. Geraldine and Virginia were given saris to wear and looked enchanting. After the big luncheon party the six of us girls sat around the very good-looking young Sikh prince in his turban, and as he seemed very friendly we asked him many questions about life in India. He told us about the Sikh religion and said that men were never allowed to cut their hair. Confronted by our disbelieving glances he boldly unwound his turban and showed us the cap he had underneath, which held his hair in place. It was a fascinating and unforgettable visit.

When she left school Geraldine got a job in the Museum of Fine Arts in Budapest, selling catalogues and cards. It was at that time that sisters of King Zog of Albania came to Budapest in search of a suitable bride for the King. He wanted to create a dynasty for his kingdom – which was only a few years old – and felt an affinity for the Austro-Hungarian Monarchy, in whose army he had served. He wanted to marry an Austrian or Hungarian aristocrat. Eventually he was shown a photograph of Geraldine and something about it touched him deeply. He sent her a message via her cousin Countess Kati Teleki, saying that he would pay for her, with no strings attached, to go to Albania accompanied by her cousin; and that she could decide for herself whether or not to accept his offer of marriage. He guaranteed that she would be free to go home if she declined.

I remember the evening when Geraldine and Kati came to our house in Budapest and told us this amazing story. Kati said that she had found the King to be charming, and Geraldine asked us what we thought of the proposal. We all were of the same opinion: that she should go and enjoy a trip to Albania with her cousin and then come back – we never thought that she would stay there. But when she met King Zog it was a true case of mutual love at first sight, and she never did return. Her meteoric journey from the foyer of the Museum of Fine Arts on the banks of the Danube in Budapest to the Albanian throne made her a world celebrity.

Geraldine was very beautiful, and one thing is sure – the King could not have chosen better. Although she was twenty years younger than he was, Geraldine was the perfect Queen for both him and his country. She had a radiant smile and became the sunshine of his life. Everybody who met her loved her. Even in everyday life it is rare to encounter your true partner, but with royal marriages it is rarer still – truly a gift from God.

Their reign did not last long. In April 1939, one year after the royal wedding and one day after Geraldine's son Leka – the heir to the throne – was born, Mussolini's army invaded Albania and the Royal family had to flee. Geraldine refused to accept the protection of the American Embassy, but with enormous courage chose to follow her husband's instructions, escaping in a car across the Albanian mountains, crossing steep precipices and travelling over bad roads, feverish and lying on a mattress, with her son Leka in the arms of an Albanian nanny, all the way to Greece. Her husband followed shortly afterwards, and they went on to make their home in Egypt for several years.

My sisters and I always remained in touch with Geraldine and I have many letters from her, written from Alexandria, Paris and Cannes. When the King fell ill she nursed him with loving devotion, and after his death in 1961 she lived for a long time in Spain. She sometimes came to Portugal to stay with her friend Queen Giovanna of Bulgaria, who lived in exile there, and we met together and shared happy childhood memories. As I write these lines she is living in South Africa, where her son Leka bought a farm some years ago.

Our parents also took us travelling abroad. When we were younger they took all four of us, but later it was two at a time. We could choose whether we wanted to go in the winter or in the summer. I mostly chose the winter, because I loved the snow.

The first journey I remember vividly was in the summer of 1930, when I was twelve. Our parents took all four of us in our large, fawn-coloured open-top Steyr car, which Papi drove. Mami sat beside him in the front, we four girls sat in a row in the back seat and our driver Tánci sat on the folding seat in front of us. All of us, Tánci included, wore identical fawn-coloured trench coats. We must have been quite a sight and created a sensation in some of the towns and villages we drove through. We drove south across Austria to Italy to spend two weeks at the Lido, the famous beach in Venice. We stayed in the Hotel des Bains, a lovely big hotel, and had a wonderful holiday. We four sisters had identical red bathing suits and on the beach we were called 'the four red devils'. In the evenings, when we were supposed to be asleep, we were actually very naughty and went tiptoeing along the balcony onto which many of the hotel bedrooms opened. We were fascinated by the dressing tables in the guests' rooms and inspected all the lipsticks and beautycreams. We never took anything but thought it was great fun. It is strange that nobody ever saw us – we got away with it every time.

In the winter of 1935 our parents took my sister Sya and I to Saint Moritz in Switzerland. We stayed in the house of Fritz von Opel, the son of the Opel car factory owner, Wilhelm von Opel, who was a friend of my parents. The young Opel couple were first class skiers, and the day after our arrival they took us two sisters to the training field, put skis on us and told us to go down a small slope. Sya was terrified, but I went down without hesitation, and from then onwards they took me out every day, going down steep slopes and just telling me to follow them. I am sure they must have gone a bit slower than usual, but I had the feeling they never looked back. I stumbled – at times falling head first – all over the place, but was delighted to be able to follow as best I could. After a week Ellamami saw me in the bath and called a doctor. My whole body was blue and red and she thought that I had a strange disease. The doctor came and laughed, he said it was all bruises and told me to be a bit more careful. I did it the hard way but I really learned to ski. At the end of our stay, which lasted about ten days, Fritz and Margot von Opel took me to a 'no-fall' race and put a number on me. They told me to go slowly and whatever else I did, not to fall. I did as they said and won the race. I was very proud when I received my prize at the nearby hotel that evening.

During a Mediterranean journey the following year we met a very friendly English girl, Sheilagh Potter, whom we invited to Hungary. She came, and in her turn invited my sister Myro and me to go to England for the coronation of King George VI. I was nineteen, and it was a truly wonderful first visit to England. We watched the coronation coaches from a balcony on Pall Mall and then went inside, where for the first time we saw a television transmission, showing the procession arriving at Buckingham Palace. We went for a walk in London on this crazy day when everybody was celebrating and having fun; the whole of London was in a joyful frenzy. We made our way to the front of Buckingham Palace to see the Royal family appear on the balcony. The crowd was so big that we could hardly see anything so, to my sister's horror, I copied two other people and climbed up onto the big iron gate and had a wonderful view. It was not for nothing that I had climbed so many trees in Elefánt. We all shouted, 'We want the King!' until they all appeared.

Sheilagh took us to the races at Newmarket and Myro urged me to make a bet. I suggested that we put our money on the jockey with the light blue cap. Myro said that this was stupid and wouldn't allow me to bet on him. But the jockey with the light blue cap came in first! After that Myro said she would now do whatever I suggested. I looked at the programme and saw that one of the horses was called 'Tipsy Pudding'. I decided to put all the money I had (it was not very much) on to win. Believe it or not, Tipsy Pudding came in first. We did not win very much as it turned out that she was the favourite – nevertheless it made us happy.

Some years later, when I was married, I went to the stables of my husband's uncle, Eugene Horthy. Looking at the mares I suddenly saw the name Tipsy Pudding. I rushed to see Uncle to ask him where he had got the name. He said that he had bought the mare in Newmarket! It was my Tipsy Pudding – the one that won for me! I often took her carrots and gave her kisses.

Budapest, the capital of Hungary, was actually only 160 kilometres away from our home and we went there several times a year, having to cross the Czechoslovak-Hungarian border every time. Until his death in 1928 my grandfather still had his house there – the one where I was born – and we stayed in part of this beautiful spacious family home whenever we visited the capital.

We usually stayed in Budapest for 'the season', which was in the winter at 'carnival' time. Before the war this was when young girls aged eighteen 'came out' as it was called. My sister Éva was said to be the loveliest girl in Budapest when she 'came out' and all my other sisters were regarded as the beauties of the season. Nobody talked about me until I married the Regent's son, when they suddenly 'discovered' how beautiful I was! This was good for me, as I knew where I stood and it helped me not to get bigheaded.

Naturally it was quite different from the cocktail-party season one might find nowadays. We went skiing on the hills around Budapest and skating too, and there were a number of private balls. We were never allowed to go to nightclubs or go out without being chaperoned. People gave balls at home or else in the Park Club, which was the centre of social life. As a rule I did not like going to balls. I only enjoyed them when there were Viennese waltz competitions. If I remember rightly my waltzing partner László Satzger and I won two. The last ball of the season was always held at the Park Club on Shrove Tuesday, after which Lent started and there was no more dancing. I liked the 'end of season' ball because as midnight approached there was the farewell to all the dances. This meant that the jazz band played a tango, a fox trot and whatever other dances were in fashion. Then the gypsy band took over and played the farewell csárdás, ending up with the Viennese Waltz, which, as the Hungarian saying goes, the gypsies can play to 'under your feet'. People usually reserved their best waltzing partner of the season for the dance. Exactly at midnight the gypsy band began to play more and more softly until we could not hear the music any more and just floated around the dance floor, not even conscious of our feet moving. This is one of the loveliest memories of my youth, and I still delight at the memory of the feeling and wonder if anyone feels such a sense of romantic delight when they do today's dances.

Events in Europe were becoming tense. In 1938 negotiations followed negotiations in rapid succession and finally resulted in the dismemberment of 'Czecho-Slovakia' – the artificially constructed product of the Treaty of Trianon at the end of the First World War. The negotiations ended in the so-called 'First Vienna Arbitration', the aim of which was to return the purely Hungarian-inhabited parts of Slovakia to Hungary.

Hungary asked for a plebiscite but the Slovaks refused. The Germans, who wanted to dominate Slovakia so as to have direct access to and communication with Russia, backed them up. For this reason they were opposed to the Hungarian occupation of Lower Carpathia, but – urged on by Poland – the Hungarians carried it out anyway. If they had not done so there would have been no common Hungarian-Polish border for more than a hundred thousand Polish soldiers later to flee over to Hungary and thence join the Allied armies. If, for example, we had not re-annexed the town of Kassa, the German army would have been able to attack the Poles from the rear. As it was they wanted to advance through Hungary but the Regent refused them permission. The Germans then made their attack – without any hindrance – via Czechoslovakia.

All these events are well-known historical facts, which I only mention because they affected us very deeply. It is easy to imagine how exciting it was for us to follow these developments, when parts of Slovakia were ceded back to Hungary by arbitration and not by war. The Regent made a moving speech to the people – to all the national groups now returning to our common homeland. We were glued to the radio and listened with tears to his proclamation.

The first town to be 'set free' was Komárom, which the Regent entered riding a white horse, just as he had done when he entered Budapest in 1919, when Hungary was liberated from Communist rule. Understandably it was a great disappointment to us when we heard that although part of the Province of Nyitra had been returned to Hungary, the town of Nyitra itself – and us in Elefánt along with it – was still in Slovakia! The territory that was returned to Hungary was mainly inhabited by Hungarians, whereas our area was mostly populated by Slovaks, although they themselves had often said that they were not happy under Czech rule.

In the winter of 1938, when I was twenty, my parents went on a cruise to South America and gave me permission to go skiing in the Black Forest in Germany for two weeks, with a German couple to look after me. While I was there I was visited by the nephew of one of my parents' friends, let's call him 'Rob'. I hardly knew him, and I was surprised when he gave me a portable radio as a present. This was something new at the time and I was delighted with it. Rob could not stay long and did not say much, but I understood that he was very seriously interested in me. He told me that he would come to Hungary very soon. After he left, my friend and 'waltzing partner' László Satzger arrived from Hungary and it became obvious that he too was very fond of me. Although I liked him, and had the loveliest memories of waltzing with him, I was not in love with him. I was grateful that he respected this.

One day when I was alone, I went for a walk in the snow and discovered a church. I went in, remembering that I had once been told that on entering a church for the first time you can make a wish and your prayer will be answered. I knelt down and prayed with all my heart that God would show me and lead me to the right man, and please, please, not let me make a mistake and get involved with someone who was not the right person for me – I was wondering in particular whether Rob might be my right partner.

When I got home to Hungary I received a letter from Rob saying that he would come to see me soon. This made me happy and I was looking forward to his visit. Shortly afterwards a thick envelope arrived. It was also from Rob. He wrote kindly and at great length, telling me the story of his life. He explained how he wanted to marry me; but, he said, he had lived for some years with a close relation of his, and when he had told her about his intention to ask me to marry him she was terribly upset and told him that she would kill herself if he left. He realized that he was morally obliged to marry her and try to make her happy. He hoped that I would have more luck in my life and would find real happiness.

I was devastated. It seemed such an awful tragedy – but then I remembered my prayer in the church in the Black Forest, and felt that for some reason God had prevented this from happening. Little did I guess that about a year later I would meet the man who was to be my real partner. God is great.

3

Meeting Pista

The winter of 1939/1940 turned out to be the most exciting winter of my life. It was a bitterly cold time; temperatures reached 36 degrees below zero and there were snowstorms – unusual weather for Hungary.

Six years earlier my sister Sya had married Count Kálmán Tisza, the grandson of one of our most famous politicians, Count István Tisza; but unfortunately their marriage was not a happy one. I often stayed with her and so it came about that, that winter, when her marriage was already breaking up, we decided to avoid the 'season' in Budapest and go skiing in the north of the country.

On arriving in the town of Munkács we travelled on a one-track mountain train to Uzsok, the northernmost settlement in the Carpathian Mountains, which was on the newly established border with Russia. It was already dark when we arrived at the last station on the line and we immediately realized that we could not possibly stay there – it looked like the end of the world. But we had hardly got off when the train started up again and was gone. The only building was a dilapidated-looking wooden house with a sign saying 'Hotel'. Inside, three men sat around a petrol lamp drinking heavily. They showed us our room, which had no lock. What else could we do but pile up all the movable furniture against the door and spend a miserable night lying fully dressed in the freezing cold room. The next morning we soon discovered that the only train expected that day was a goods train without a single closed wagon, but by then we were so desperate to leave that when it arrived we clambered up onto it. We covered ourselves up as best we could and the train started off on the way to Munkács. The journey seemed endless, and I think it was probably only due to Sya suddenly producing a flask of cognac she had brought with her in case of cold weather that we were saved from becoming frozen stiff by the time we got there. In Munkács we heard that the snow was so heavy that most of the trains were not running. We spent the night in the hotel, where they installed two beds for us in the heated ballroom because all the rooms were full; and the next day, with great difficulty, we returned to Budapest.

So it was that, instead of being away from Budapest that winter, I returned a few days before the major social event of the season: the 'Living-Art Exhibition' and Charity Opera Ball.

The purpose of the evening was to raise as much money as possible for a charitable campaign to help destitute artists, which had been started by the Hungarian First Lady, Mrs Miklós Horthy. The Living-Art Exhibition could not have been better fitted to the purpose. Some of the most beautiful women and girls in Budapest portrayed fifty superb works of art – as if calling the immortals of the history of art to the aid of living Hungarian artists.

Under the personal guidance of the Regent's wife, the Art Council planned the event and the Opera House's famous stage manager, Gusztáv Oláh, gave instructions to the stage and costume designer. The people chosen to represent each work of art were selected for their resemblance to the figures in the paintings – leading figures in Budapest society, members of the diplomatic corps, and others all took part. I learnt later that Madame Horthy had sat through the whole nine-hour dress rehearsal, actively contributing to all the final details. The results were astounding; even the artists were amazed at the unexpected effects that were conjured onto the stage. The leading Hungarian actress of the day Gizi Bajor, and the actor Tivadar Uray, introduced each 'tableau vivant' one by one, as if in a museum. The whole thing was remarkably well organized and unbelievably beautiful.

The public was able to enjoy the Living-Art Exhibition on two nights, and the long-awaited Opera Ball also took place on the first evening. The *Képes Vasárnap* (Sunday Pictorial) magazine wrote:

> Thursday's Living-Art Exhibition at the Opera House was without doubt the most glittering social and artistic event. ... In the Regent's box, His Serene Highness was accompanied by his wife, whom we can truly thank for this brilliant evening, and his two sons Stephen and Nicholas junior. His Royal Highness Archduke Jósef and members of his family were present, and practically the whole of Hungarian society was represented in the other rows of boxes and on the ground floor. Prime Minister Count Pál Teleki and his family headed a distinguished gathering that included members of the aristocracy and the diplomatic corps.

As my sister and I arrived back too late to be in a 'tableau vivant', I was asked to be one of the sixteen girls who, wearing full-length white evening dresses, were to welcome the Regent and his wife. We were each to hand Madame Horthy a red rose, one on each of the sixteen steps of the Opera House, and then escort the couple to the Royal Box. We were mainly chosen as being among the best dancers of the Viennese waltz, because we were also to open the ball after the performance by dancing one of my favourite waltzes – 'Tales of the Vienna Woods' – on stage. I was very much looking forward to this and I had an excellent dancer, Count Gábor Szécsényi, as my partner.

It so happened that I was placed on the last step but one on the Opera House staircase and therefore walked to the main box side by side with the Regent's two sons, who came up the stairs behind their parents. Little did I guess that this was to decide the course of the rest of my life.

We all knew the younger son Nicky, as he sometimes came to my parents' house and liked to teach us to dance – preferably cheek-to-cheek. But I had never spoken to his brother Stephen, whom everyone called Pista (a diminutive of István, the Hungarian equivalent of Stephen). He seemed to know who I was – perhaps Nicky had told him – and asked if I were the one among my sisters who was a good skier. When I admitted this, he asked how he could get in touch with me. I was so surprised that I do not even remember what I said. Unlike his brother he was seldom seen in the company of girls of my age. He was then thirty-five years old, unmarried and had travelled abroad a great deal.

When the performance was over, we sixteen girls in white opened the Opera Ball with our partners. After that everybody came down from their boxes, and the ladies who had taken part in the 'tableaux' changed into evening dresses. There was a huge buffet, which had been donated by the ladies of Budapest society so that the evening's income would remain intact for charity. While everybody was eating, the ground floor was transformed into a scintillating ballroom.

At the very beginning of the ball I could see Pista going around the huge hall looking for someone. To my amazement, he was looking for me, and we spent the rest of the evening together.

A few days later, he came to my sister's house outside the city and took me skiing in the Budapest hills. I told my sister that I thought his invitation could not mean much because I had heard that there was a lady in France whom he loved and was the reason why he never showed any sign of being interested in us girls in Hungary. I was determined to be very much on my guard and certainly not fall in love with him.

We went skiing together a few times and he telephoned regularly. We enjoyed each other's company but nothing more; not even a furtive kiss was exchanged. This continued for about two weeks. Then one day he said that he would drop me at the ski run but could not join me as he had an important appointment. I got out of the car, and just before he drove off he asked, 'Will you marry me? Don't say anything now, but please think about it.'

I was utterly taken aback and did not quite know how to react. It was so unexpected and unbelievable that I could not even decide what I felt for him. The deep attraction had still to penetrate the barriers I had built up in the past weeks, and I could not believe that this could be true.

We were to meet that evening at a party at the house of a Countess Cziráky, who had two attractive daughters. Pista arrived late; he went straight to the room where the prettiest daughter was putting records on for us, and did not come out again. I happened to be sitting next to her brother, who told me that Pista and his sister were very well suited to one another and that they had been waiting for this opportunity to spend the evening together.

I felt angrier and angrier as the evening went on. When the party was breaking up, Pista appeared and offered to give me a lift home. I thought to myself that this would be the last time, but that I would go with him just to be able to tell him what I thought of him. So all the way home I let off steam, telling him that I had known all along that this was the sort of man he was, asking me to marry him in the morning and then spending the entire evening with someone else.

When we arrived at our destination he just said, 'Thank God! This is just what I wanted to hear. I really doubted whether you loved me, because you haven't shown any sign of affection at all over the last two weeks. I did it on purpose, thinking that if you didn't react, then it would be because you really don't feel anything for me at all.' Amazing! – and it worked! It made me reveal my feelings, just as he had planned. We kissed for the first time, and the mutual feeling was so strong that I did not need to say the word 'yes'.

Next day, 28 February, we told our families of our engagement. Some people said later that our marriage was planned and arranged by my stepmother, but this is quite untrue; she did not even know about our acquaintance until I telephoned with the news. I first rang my father's house and Ellamami answered. I asked her to call my father to the other phone so that he could also listen to what I had to say. When I told her that I was engaged to Pista Horthy, who would like to come in person and ask for my hand, Mami was thrilled and asked, 'How did you do it?' I did not answer her, but said that I would like to hear what Papi had to say. My father just said very quietly, 'In five years I will tell you whether I am happy or not.' I was deeply touched by his answer. It meant that what was most important to him was my happiness, and that he did not know Pista well enough to know whether he would make me happy.

*   *   *   *   *

Let me now take a moment to tell you more about this amazing young man called Stephen Horthy – although I am sure you will think I am biased. For a long time I was unable to talk about him because I felt that people would put it down as the opinion of a doting wife. My attitude only changed when, in 1943, Olaf Wulff and Jenő Maléter published a book about him entitled *The Life of Stephen Horthy and Transport in Hungary*[4] in which fifty prominent and extremely competent people, experts in the various fields Pista worked in, each contributed a chapter describing their experiences of working with him.

Led by Prime Minister Miklós Kállay, plus several cabinet ministers and experts on communications, engineering, aeronautics and other subjects, the authors describe the Pista they knew, and they make his personality emerge as it really was. All these opinions mean a great deal to me, and in the appendices there is an extract of the tribute from Jenő Markotay-Velsz, the managing director of the State Iron, Steel and Machine Works (MÁVAG), with whom Pista worked closely for seven years.[i] The book has to be read, as it cannot easily be explained in a few words. As one reads the one hundred and fifty pages it becomes clear what an exceptionally hard-working, knowledgeable, straightforward and quite unusual person Pista was. He was meticulous in his love of the truth; he loved to work, but also loved to have fun. These characteristics were allied with remarkable good looks, of which he seemed quite oblivious.

I was often amazed how all these qualities could really be found in one person. The authors of the book said much more about him than I found out first-hand. This irrefutable proof of his qualities helped me to stop being shy about talking about him. But let me start from the beginning.

About Stephen Horthy

Pista was born on 9 December 1904. As a boy he hoped to follow his father's example and pursue a career in the Austro-Hungarian navy, but the outcome of the First World War, and the disintegration of the

[i] Appendix 1.

Austro-Hungarian Empire and with it their navy, made it impossible for him to do so. This was a very heavy blow for a boy of fourteen. His mother told me that he used to sit quietly in a corner reading about the navy, and that a big tear would occasionally roll down his cheek.

As a child at school he always came first in geometry and mathematics. He knew what he wanted and engines were his hobby. He studied engineering at the Technical Academy and following his military training he was commissioned as a first lieutenant in the Air Force Reserve in 1929.

After obtaining his diploma as an engineer he went to work in the Csepel motor-factory because it was the only place in Hungary that built aeroplane engines. He did assembly-work with the other workmen and refused to accept any exceptional treatment.

After gaining experience at Csepel, and at the age of twenty-five, Pista felt that there was still a lot for him to learn. It was his own idea to go to the United States, where he succeeded in getting a job as a labourer in the Ford Factory's Dearborn Plant in Detroit. He worked his way up through all the categories to the position of engineer, and was able to see how one of the most efficient factories in the world operated. He declined any advantages that he could have obtained as the son of the Hungarian head of state. He eventually got a job in the 'experimental design division', which suited his engineering qualifications. The great Henry Ford obviously kept in touch with his experimental engineers, and he soon noticed the talented and diligent Stephen Horthy. He invited him to his home several times and they held long discussions there. He adopted one of Pista's patented designs for part of a car suspension – and as far as I know it has been manufactured ever since.

The eighteen months he spent at Ford made a big difference to his way of thinking and working, and to his future life. When he left Detroit he bought a small Ford car and drove across practically all the United States. He found it fascinating. He returned from America as a qualified specialized engineer and joined MÁVAG, which was a state-subsidised concern.

MÁVAG managing director Jenő Markotay-Velsz soon noticed his abilities and made him his deputy. He went on working as he had done in the States and introduced many of the things he had learnt there. He learnt that one could work hard and also have fun. In those days very few people in Hungary understood this; there were two kinds of people in his social 'milieu' – those who worked and did nothing else and never had fun, and those who mostly had fun and spent money without earning it.

He was usually the first to arrive at the factory and left late. I sometimes went to pick him up and would find him still at his desk when everybody else had gone. I think very few people knew this side of him, as he was the type of person who would observe but say little. In the evening he would go out to dinner parties or to a nightclub to dance. People who met him there said that he never worked, while those who knew him at his work said that he was very serious and never stopped working. It was not customary to rest at the weekends as it is now, but he always did. I think that this was another habit he had acquired in America and kept up when he returned to Hungary, just as he continued to smoke Chesterfield cigarettes and read *Esquire* magazine.

In Hungary it has often been said that Pista was the personification of the modern engineer. He specialized in exports; and he visited a number of countries, taking advantage of his knowledge of languages. It was well known that it was largely due to his efforts that the factory was able to increase its staff from five thousand to twenty-two thousand; and before long it became a paying concern. He promoted the manufacture of cars, locomotives and aeroplanes.

This was also how he came to make a 4,000-mile trip to try to sell locomotives to the Indian government. He found out that another factory had made an offer, which was likely to be accepted, and when he tried to go out there to make a competitive bid he found that all the commercial airline seats to India had been booked up. So without hesitation he took off in his own small plane, without radio or blind-flying instruments, and flew to Bombay. His valet, who took part in all the preparations, recorded his account of these events in his diary.[ii]

I was married to Pista for two years and four months, and I never heard him say anything to promote himself. I found out about all the outstanding work that he did, before I knew him and during our time together, from others or by accident. If no one asked him to comment, he was capable of listening to a conversation about something with which he was perfectly familiar, without interrupting or showing that he knew better in any way. He would only step in when it was really important and necessary, and then he would go right to the heart of the matter, whereupon his opinion would normally be readily accepted. My first Christmas present to him was two enormous volumes of the Larousse Universelle, because he was constantly looking things up in dictionaries or reference books. He seemed to pick up the Larousse every day after that – I was amused to see him take it with him to the bathroom. He used it to look up things he really wanted information about, but never to show off his knowledge.

ii Appendix 2: György Farkas, 'By sports plane to India'.

Pista worked in the steel factory for ten years, from 1930 to 1940, and was deputy managing director for seven of them. During his last three years he was the managing director. Soon after we got married, he was chosen to be director of the State Railways (MÁV).

In a chapter entitled 'My master – as I saw him' in *Horthy Istvan Repülő Főhadnagy Tragikus Halálá* (The Tragic Death of Stephen Horthy),[5] his valet György (Gyuri) Farkas wrote about the personal, human contacts between the factory workers and the former deputy managing director, and about his relationship with the workforce when he became president of MÁV:

> Let me recount just one of many stories which show how the president, Stephen Horthy, acted when a man who had got into trouble needed his help.
>
> There may be some people who still remember the case of the coupler Elek Pál. It was a hot summer's day in August. The Palace was very quiet: only Stephen Horthy and his wife were in residence; the Regent and his family were staying in Gödöllő. It was lunchtime, and the two of them were sitting at the table. Suddenly the telephone rang: it was the porter.
>
> 'There's a man here who wants to speak to you. He mentioned Mr Stephen. Shall I ask someone to bring him up?' (Between ourselves we called the Regent's family by their first names.)
>
> 'Yes. I don't know who he is, but if he's asking for me by name then he must know me, or maybe I know him.'
>
> The guard on duty brought up a man who was wearing a raincoat even in the August midday heat, and worn-out shoes from which his toes stuck out. He greeted me politely and introduced himself: 'I'm Elek Pál, a coupler at MÁV. We shunt trucks, crawl under carriages, and so on.'
>
> I looked at his ragged clothes. 'Wait,' I told him. I sent the guard away. I was just serving lunch, the door was open and our talk could be heard in the room.
>
> 'Who is it?' asked my master
>
> 'Elek Pál, sir. I don't know him. He says he's a railwayman. He would like to speak to you.'
>
> 'Tell him everything's all right, he doesn't need to thank me for anything.' Turning to his wife he said, 'I'm very sorry for the unfortunate man. He was convicted of embezzlement and fraud. MÁV dismissed

him and he served his sentence. Then there was a retrial and this time the Court's verdict was different. His innocence was established: he hadn't committed any fraud or embezzlement. The real culprit received the punishment he deserved and the Court reinstated Elek Pál in his job. I ordered that he should immediately be re-employed in the place where he had worked before and that his pay should be backdated. It's the least I could do. I'm very sorry for the poor man. But there's no need for him to come here and thank me.'

'Sir, this man says he knows about the director's instruction, but that was two months ago and he hasn't been taken back,' I said to my master as he sat at the table, eating his lunch.

Stephen Horthy practically leapt from his chair. He hurried out and came face to face with Elek Pál, whom he had never seen in his life.

'What do you look like, you unfortunate man?' he said.

'Sir, my working clothes were taken away, and I haven't got any ordinary clothes. I was only given these rags out of charity.'

'Wait,' said my master. Striding over to his wardrobe, he took out a dark suit, gave it to him and said, 'Report to me in the office tomorrow morning at eight o'clock.'

'They won't even let me in as far as the gate, sir,' he answered.

'See to it that he gets in,' the president of MÁV said to me. I took Elek Pál out to the gate with his package, and said I'd see him the next morning at eight o'clock at the office.

The next morning we were at the president's office at a few minutes before eight o'clock. Stephen Horthy didn't allow himself to be late for work. He was very strict with himself; he was more tolerant with others. So anyway, Elek Pál was standing there in front of the gate, at a discreet distance. The president strode in, up the steps two at a time, and was up in his office in half a minute. Elek Pál was dressed as he had been the previous day. He couldn't put on the suit he'd been given: after all, a suit made for a man 197 cm tall won't alter itself just like that in half a day to fit a man

160–170 cm tall. The porter was watching the people going in, but before he could say a word I loudly told him that this man was with me. He stared, but by the time he opened his mouth we were inside. The president's secretary stared as well, wondering who was with me. We went straight into the president's office unannounced. The president of MÁV told his secretary to send for the manager whom he had told two months ago to deal with the matter.

'This is Elek Pál. See to it that he starts work today, and that he reports to me tomorrow in uniform to tell me that he has taken up his duties and has received all his back pay.'

This is typical of the way Stephen Horthy acted. I have recounted it in detail as an example. There may still be some retired railwaymen from the Rákos shunting yard who remember the incident.

I don't want to glorify him. I've just described one case out of many to illustrate how my master valued ordinary workers; and especially those who – in whatever position – were 'colleagues' of his. They all were railwaymen. (Even the president was considered a railwayman.)

Two years later, in February 1942, Parliament elected him vice-regent of Hungary.

At this point it is important to clarify something. It was perfectly clear to everyone who really knew Pista that his election to the vice-regency was not an attempt to found a dynasty. It was simply due to his own personality, his knowledge, his ability to inspire confidence, his honesty and his dynamism, and last but not least to his outspoken anti-Nazi feelings. The fact that he was the Regent's son was just another advantage – a vice-regent could only be of real help to the Regent if the latter had complete trust in him. Being able to count on the son he loved and trusted was a big help in the difficult circumstances of the day.

I can well understand if this seems almost impossible to believe for those who did not know Pista. It would be natural to think that he was only made vice-regent because he was Admiral Horthy's son. But if the Regent had planned and intended to form a dynasty, he'd had many opportunities to do so. On the contrary, he flatly rejected any idea that he was reaching out for the Crown for himself or for any member of his family.

As I witnessed most of these events first-hand I feel that it is my duty to state this authoritatively. I have seen the opposite view expressed by people who do not know the truth, who did not know the admiral or his son, and whose political views have made them all too ready to embrace an anti-Horthy argument. How often have I heard or read: 'the Regent felt ...' 'the Regent thought ...' or 'the Regent knew ...' I do not know what the Regent felt or thought or knew. I only know what I saw and what he said to me.

* * * * *

To return to my story: Of course it was big news that the Regent's elder son was getting married. The engagement had taken everyone by surprise because nobody except for my sister Sya had any idea of our meetings. From now on events followed rapidly, one after the other. Pista brought a selection of rings from one of the best jewellers and told me to choose my engagement ring. I knew at first glance which one I wanted, but did not want to tell him as it had the biggest stones in it. It was a conventional engagement ring with one sapphire between two diamonds, but with an especially attractive setting. Pista told me not to be shy but to choose the one I really liked, as I would be wearing it all my life. So I finally told him which one I liked most – and I am still wearing it now, fifty-five years later.

Ellamami was approached by photographers who wanted to take engagement pictures of Pista and me together. Pista opposed this, saying that it was a pilots' tradition not to pose for photographs 'before the start'. There was a need for convincing arguments, and Ellamami was just the great master the situation required. She told Pista that this big occasion had to be recorded and that it had nothing to do with flying. Reluctantly, Pista finally gave in. My position was an awkward one, but Pista understood that my relationship with Ellamami was not always easy.

On 10 March the magazine *Képes Vasárnap* appeared with a full spread of photographs of us, and of me, together with a long article on our engagement entitled 'Countess Ily Edelsheim Gyulai, the country's happiest bride-elect'. Our picture appeared in many shop windows. This meant that from then on I was recognized wherever I went. It made me feel uncomfortable – I was not sure what was expected of me.

One morning my sister Sya and I decided to go shopping. We went into a department store and walked onto the escalator. By the time we got to the top the manager, his assistant and several others were already waiting for us, and the manager asked me whether he could help in any way. I whispered to my sister, 'I've forgotten what I wanted to buy, let's get out of here,' and replied aloud, 'How kind of you, we just want to look around.' We quickly left and I told Sya that I would never go shopping again.

We had a short two-month engagement and our wedding was set for 27 April. This meant there was much to do in the little time available. An important decision had to be made – whether the marriage was to be a Catholic one or not. This presented Pista and me with a problem we had never anticipated.

In 1921 the Catholic Church had issued a new rule decreeing that if a marriage were 'mixed' all children had to become Catholics in order for the marriage itself to be acknowledged by the Church. There had to be an agreement, signed by the Protestant partner, in which he or she promised to educate all their children in the Catholic faith.

At that time, 64 per cent of the Hungarian population were Catholics and most of the rest were Protestants, with small numbers of people of other denominations. Strangely enough, most of the young men I knew were Protestants, whereas most of my girl friends were Catholics. Before this regulation appeared in the early twenties things were easy, as boys followed their father's religion and girls that of the mother. There were never any problems. But now for most of us young people it made life very difficult. Understandably, Protestant fathers did not want their sons to become Catholics, but if they did not conform their Catholic wives were excommunicated, which meant that they could no longer receive the sacraments of their church or go to communion.

In both our families – Horthy and Edelsheim Gyulai – all the women were Catholics. My father was a Lutheran, a Protestant, and we never had any differences or arguments at home about religion. We sisters all went to our church with Mami, while Father went to his church, and everybody was very tolerant of each other. In Hungary it had even happened that people found out a lifelong friend did not belong to the same religion only at his funeral. I know this would be difficult to imagine in some countries. It was one of the shocks of my life when I first went to Ireland and saw the problem there. I had never heard of Catholic and Protestant football teams before.

The Horthy family was similar to mine. The Regent was a Calvinist and so were his sons, but his mother, wife and two daughters were Catholics. To the annoyance of the Calvinist Bishop László Ravasz, when Pista told my father-in-law-to-be that he wanted to get married, the Regent said that he hoped that whoever she was, she was a Catholic – all the women in his family were Catholics.

By the time I got engaged, two of my sisters were already married – both to Protestants. They were married to men from old aristocratic families where religion was very much a matter of tradition. They had found a way to solve this difficult problem. If you got married in our village in Czechoslovakia, no written contract about the future religion of the children was required. On returning to live in Hungary, the children could then be baptized in either the father's or the mother's religion. So they could take sons to the Protestant church to be baptized and daughters to the Catholic one. It then remained for the Catholic mother to tell this to her confessor or do whatever her conscience bid her to do.

Although going to Slovakia for the church ceremony seemed a good enough way out of the difficulty, it was not for me. I did not contemplate such a solution for a moment. I knew that my future husband would not and could not consent to a son of his becoming a Catholic. He was an active member of his Calvinist church, and any solution of the kind my sisters had adopted was unthinkable for someone who was in the public eye. I also felt that for myself I could not live in doubt as to whether I could go to communion or not and be dependent for that on the decision of a priest: one might give me communion while another might refuse me.

I alone could decide what to do, and it caused me profound concern. I made up my mind that I must be the one to give in, but I was surprised at how difficult it was for me to take this step. My church meant a great deal to me and taking communion was an act of real significance. I went to several priests for advice and also to the Calvinist bishop, who, to my astonishment and shock, was very cold and distant. I tried to tell myself that this was what Calvinist priests were like, but it did not help. I was very inexperienced in dealing with problems of this kind entirely on my own, and as I had come to him for help and advice his attitude was almost too much to bear. When I left our meeting I started sobbing bitterly.

However, I kept all this very much to myself. I could not talk to Pista about it because I did not want him to see how difficult things were for me, so I fretted in secret, while at the same time being amazed at the depth of my own feelings. I had not been able to shed a tear for the deaths of my godmother or my grandmother, although I mourned them deeply.

The present problem seemed to me to be senseless, foolish and unnecessary, and there seemed to be no possible solution to it, so my feelings were also those of frustration and helplessness. I suppose what helped me through was having a great number of other things to think about.

It was also at this time that I learnt to fly. What a joyful relaxation! My future husband was a very good pilot and had his own single-engine Arado aeroplane. He gave aerobatics displays at the annual Air Force

Day display. We often went on short flights within Hungary in Pista's little plane. He sometimes did aerobatics with me and I took to it all like a duck to water. The only thing I did not enjoy was flying upside down, because the dirt from the floor of the plane kept falling in my face.

Learning to fly was wonderful. At Pista's suggestion I first learnt to glide. He said that he himself would teach me to fly an aircraft after that. Pista was not sure what the powered-flight teachers were like, and since it was a dangerous sport he wanted to make sure that I learned the right way. I went for gliding lessons on a mountain near Budapest called the Hármashatár-hegy (Three-frontiers Mountain). I found it very easy and enjoyed every minute. I could not go for gliding lessons very often, but I eventually got my A, B and C grades.

This was definitely the fun side of my life and I enjoyed it much more than the social or official part. To be suddenly cast into the public eye at the very 'top of the tree' was not easy, to say the least.

I can clearly recall my first public appearance. It was a charity performance at the Opera House in aid of flood victims. Pista and I accompanied the Regent and his wife. I remember it so vividly, as if it happened yesterday. When we entered the Opera House's main box we stood between the Regent and Madame Horthy, and the orchestra started to play the national anthem. All the people stood up and turned towards the main box; and of course they were looking at the newcomer – me.

We who lived in the former Hungarian territories always felt very emotional when we heard the national anthem, often much more so than the people who lived in the 'mother country'. At that moment – standing beside the Regent and his family, listening to the anthem and facing the whole opera audience – I almost burst out crying. But I felt that it would not be right to show my emotion, so to help myself I pressed my nails into the palm of my hand till it hurt ... and thought that the national anthem would never end.

One evening during our engagement everybody from a dinner party went to the Arizona nightclub. My father did not allow us girls to go to nightclubs and so I had never been to one before. This time, with my fiancé present and everybody from the party going together, I honestly felt that it was all right to go. It was great fun dancing on the revolving floor and sitting around in boxes like those in the theatre. There were also telephones from one box to another.

But next morning, when I told my father that I had spent the evening at the Arizona, he was very angry and told me that until I was married I must obey him – engagements could always be broken off. After my marriage I could do whatever my husband agreed to. I was taken aback to see my father so angry, but I knew that he meant well.

I did not have long to wait. The day of our wedding was rapidly approaching. Presents were being delivered every day and we had to clear a room especially for them. I had a lovely, purpose-made white suit for my civil wedding, an evening dress for the big reception-party given at home the night before, and my wedding dress. I had to try them all on and allow myself to be studied by Mami and my sisters. I wondered whether it was all really happening to me or if I would suddenly wake up. Thinking back to my meeting with Pista, which had come about as if by seemingly 'planned coincidences', more than ever I now had the feeling that it had been inevitable.

4

Our Wedding

Before I go on with my story, I think I should warn readers that the next part of my life seems too good to be true. It may sound as if I am giving everything a gold lining, but it is the truth as I experienced it, even though at the time it seemed – and still seems – like a fairy story. You may feel that real life is not like this, but the fact is that I married into a family who were honest, just and loving, and who did not make a fuss or exaggerate. Maybe I was loved because I myself loved them. Whatever the reason, it is a true story.

Our civil wedding took place on 26 April, and that evening a big reception, with music provided by my favourite gypsy band, was held at my father's house. The church wedding took place the following day, 27 April 1940. It was held in the Calvinist church on Szilágyi Dezső Square in Budapest, by the Danube. My wedding dress had been made by one of the best dressmakers in Budapest, Klára Rotschild, who copied my grandmother's traditional Hungarian family *díszmagyar* costume in white. It was decorated with hand-embroidered pearls – not real ones, of course. The American ambassador's wife, Mrs Olive Pell, was a painter. She painted the two of us in our wedding outfits and called the picture 'Cinderella and the Prince'.

Before we went to the church we stopped to visit and embrace Pista's sister, Paulette, who was very ill. She had suffered from tuberculosis for years, and it seemed that there was no possibility of a cure. She was no longer able to get up, and an oxygen cylinder had recently been placed beside her bed for the first time. It was the only dark cloud on that otherwise beautiful day. So many wonderful things were happening to me that it was almost too much for me to fully appreciate, but standing beside her bed in my wedding-gown I somehow realized that we need to be reminded of suffering and death even at the height of happiness, so that we can maintain a balance. I kept thinking of what she must have felt, seeing me in my lovely wedding dress going to my wedding, when she herself was so near to death's door. At least she was with her loving husband Gyula, who dedicated his life to making hers bearable.

I cannot remember much about the wedding ceremony, except that we were all standing in a circle around the altar, which I found strange. We were married by the Calvinist Bishop, László Ravasz.

As we came out of the church, young pilots stood on both sides of the steps and held up an arch of propellers. It was a perfect spring day as we drove in a long cavalcade of cars alongside the Danube and then up the hill to the Royal Palace. I can still clearly see the most fascinating and unforgettable sight: there was the Danube with its lovely bridges and with the most beautiful Parliament building in the world on its far side and, circling above it all, were what seemed at least a hundred white pigeons. We found out later that the pigeons had been an inspired idea on the part of the owner of the Arizona night club, who had them released when we were leaving the church; I wondered if they would bring us peace.

A big wedding luncheon was held in the Palace for all the members of the two families. The huge official dining hall was a beautiful sight with its fabulous flower arrangements. We were surrounded by our loving relations, all in their traditional *díszmagyar* costumes. Each family wore its own traditional colours, but the styles of the costumes were similar. The women wore real lace aprons over full skirts, and tight blouses with puffed sleeves, with bonnets if they were married, while the men sported narrow trousers and boots. Both men and women draped fur-edged capes called 'mente' over one shoulder. It was a truly memorable sight – the photographs I have, even though they are just in black and white, give some idea of what it was like.

At the end of the reception we hurriedly changed into our travelling clothes and were escorted to the airport by all the guests, some still in their traditional clothes. We found our little Arado plane ready to take us on our 8,000-kilometre honeymoon journey. Goodbyes were said and, climbing into the plane where we sat side by side, we took off, waving vigorously. I can still see the heart-warming picture the guests made, waving back at us.

This little red Arado 79 sports plane had one engine and no radio or blind-flying instruments. The cockpit was enclosed but visibility from it was excellent. Both seats were equipped for piloting and my flying lessons now began in earnest as we flew to Venice, Naples, Catania, Tunis, Tripoli, Benghazi, Cairo, Tel Aviv, Damascus, Adana, Ankara, Istanbul, Sofia and back to Budapest.

We had the most wonderful aerial send-off anyone could dream of. Two fighter planes escorted us. Of course they were much faster than us, so the pilots shot off, circled and came back again, flying in graceful circles around our plane. It gave us a marvellous feeling of speed and comradeship as we set off into the distance with our whole future before us. The world, the modern world, was all ours to live in. It was still 1940, when despite the many worrying signs it was still possible to hope that things might settle down. Diplomatic relations with the Soviet Union had been severed in February of the previous year, but they were re-established in September and there was still a vague hope that German expansion would not go any further.

The fighter planes signalled goodbye and left us at the Hungarian border, and we flew on to Venice. The beautiful, poetic Italian city was to be our first stop. I remembered my visits to Venice with my parents when we were children. Little had I imagined then that one day I would fly back there with my husband in our own plane and stay in the Hotel Danieli on the first day of our married life. It seemed to me that nobody could possibly imagine how happy I was.

From Venice we flew on to Naples and went over to the island of Capri by boat. Here nobody official, no ambassadors or anyone else came to greet us, and we had the most blissfully informal two days. We visited the Blue Grotto and toured the island. Looking back they were the best two days of our trip.

After that we were supposed to fly on to Tripoli, but a big gale blew up and our small plane was tossed about. Our heads were banged against the fuselage as the wind blew us up and down. It was quite an experience. Pista decided that we could not continue, and landed at Catania in Sicily. I was interested to find that I did not feel sick or even frightened. I felt so safe and calm with Pista beside me that I never gave a thought to any danger. I instinctively felt that I would always be safe with him and was overwhelmingly glad that my life was in his hands. Later on, I found that others had experienced the same sense of safety when they were with him, the same feeling that he would always find a way and that problems would just disappear.

We spent the night in a hotel there and finally reached Tripoli the next day. We were the guests of the Italian governor of Libya, General Italo Balbo, for one night. The governor's White Palace was fabulous with its palm trees and Arab servants. It was like a dream-oasis. Balbo, our host, was by far the most pleasant of the top Fascists. A general in the Fascist Militia and a champion pilot, he was good mannered and received us very kindly. We spent some time talking with him at dinner, and he made a good impression on us. By all accounts he seemed to have worked wonders in Libya and to have proved that the Italians could be good colonialists. The Arabs also seemed to like Balbo, who had given them roads, drinking water, schools, housing and plantations, but we both got the definite feeling that he himself was not happy about everything that was going on in Italy under Mussolini.

After a good night's sleep we went to the airport. The only request the authorities made was that we should not take any aerial pictures or films on the way to Cairo, because at that time most of the coast of Africa was a military zone. We agreed and our cameras were put on board without even being sealed. We continued our flight, navigating with the help of specially prepared strips of maps, with one strip leading on to the next. As we did not fly very high I found it quite easy to follow them and we had no need of navigational aids.

It was a spectacular flight, which I will always remember. I was tempted to break our promise not to film or take photographs whilst we were over any potential war zone. It was the yellow of the sand, the deep blue of the sea and the sky, the vivid white of the clouds, and our small red plane alone in that heaven that tempted me so much. Surely none of them could possibly cause any military problems. As our cameras had been left unsealed I begged Pista to let me take just a few shots of the sand, the sea, the sky and the red wings, but he reminded me of our promise and said I should not do it – and of course he was quite right.

We landed in Alexandria on 6 May 1940, from where we continued our flight to Cairo's Almazan Airport, where we were met by the Hungarian Chargé and driven to the Continental Savoy Hotel.

Cairo was fascinating and I wished our stay could have been longer. The first thing we did was go to the Abdin Royal Palace to sign the visitor's book, because there was a long-standing friendship between members of the Horthy family and the Egyptian Royal Family. Queen Nazli the queen mother, who we visited two days later, had spent a long time in Hungary and loved Budapest.

We had been asked to visit Abdin Palace the next day, to call on King Farouk and his lovely Queen Farida. On arriving at the Palace I was surprised to find that I was taken one way and Pista another. I realized that even in this modern world Moslem etiquette demanded that men and women's visits should be separate, and that in some ways the rules of the harem still held. I was taken to a large reception room where Queen Farida was sitting at the far end waiting to receive me. I had been told to make three curtseys, one on entering, one in the middle of the room and the third when I arrived before Farida. I managed all this, and I was chatting comfortably to the Queen, who was very kind and charming, when without ceremony the door opened and King Farouk came in. He came over and threw himself on a sofa, sitting half slumped against one arm of it. He then eyed me up and down in a most impertinent way and I felt uncomfortable. I heard later that he had a bad reputation, but at the time I was unaware of it. He asked whether our plane's seats were located one beside the other and, smiling sarcastically, asked whether it was safe to go on a honeymoon in a small plane.

I was amazed at King Farouk's behaviour and was glad when his curiosity was satisfied and he left to join my husband again. Once we were alone, Queen Farida said that she expected I would soon have children and that I surely hoped for a son. She looked so sad as she explained that she only had daughters herself. As I had only been married for a few days I was rather amused, and told her that I had not really thought about it yet.

I remembered this conversation the next day when, on the recommendation of King Farouk, we visited the Industrial Fair. It was the first one in Egypt to show goods made entirely in that country. It was of some interest to my engineer husband, but what I remember most clearly was that as we entered the Fair a man selling all kinds of goods at a stand called us over – it was rather obvious that we were a young honeymoon couple – and told me to take one of the sweets he had for sale, as it would ensure that I had a boy child! We both laughed, but I took one. When my son was born nine months later, I reminded Pista of the sweet and said how sad it was that Queen Farida had so long wanted a son when the remedy was right there to hand, had she only known about it.

During our stay we of course visited the Pyramids, the famous Egyptian Museum, tried to ride camels, and saw the colourful crowds in the streets and markets. We also drove down to Suez and bathed in the Red Sea. But it was while we were in Cairo that the war in Western Europe began in earnest. Our original plan had been to fly south to Luxor, but to our dismay our stay in Egypt came to an abrupt end. We received an urgent telegram from Budapest asking us to return immediately as German troops had invaded Belgium and Holland and the war was escalating inexorably.

We got the strip maps out at once and planned our route until we were able to tell my father-in-law that we would be back in Budapest at seven thirty in the evening three days later. Next morning we climbed into our little plane once more and began our flight to Palestine. We landed at Tel Aviv to refuel and have lunch. The waiters at the restaurant we chose were all Hungarians and we got a great welcome, which was a delightful surprise.

We flew on, following our strip maps to Damascus. I was navigating all the way and felt very proud of my work. Pista had said that he would not interfere and left it to me. As we entered Syrian airspace and turned inland from the Mediterranean to approach Damascus, I suddenly got confused. So far the maps had proved their worth and I felt secretly pleased that I had mastered them and succeeded in picking out the right course, but now I was in trouble. Right in front of us there appeared a huge blue lake, which I could not find on the map. I thought that I had lost the way and turned to Pista in my predicament. I had to confess that I was lost and could not understand how I could have gone so wrong. The lake I could clearly see in front of us was not on the map. Pista had obviously anticipated my problem and laughed as he explained that there was rich agricultural land around Damascus, and the constant watering gave the area a greenish-blue tinge. Surrounded by the yellow of the desert, from a distance it looked like a lake.

We spent the night in Damascus, fuelled the aircraft again and flew off intending to be in Istanbul that evening. We planned to refuel in Adana in southern Turkey, but this was where we met our first setback. As we had not been able to signal our arrival in advance there was no fuel available. The Turkish authorities were very apologetic but said they had no petrol that day. We would have to wait – maybe three hours or more. We sat at the airport and thought. We could not wait three hours, as it would then be dark before we got to Istanbul and we were not equipped to fly at night. If we stayed another day and were not able to notify our families, they would be worried. Pista made a quick calculation and told me that we could just get to Ankara with the fuel we still had in the plane. Although it was a detour, it was still a better bet to spend the night there and get petrol. He was confident that we could then fly from Ankara to Budapest in one day. To the astonishment of the authorities, we jumped into our plane without delay and flew off.

As we had not planned to go to Ankara, our strip-maps did not cover the route and we had only a small-scale general map to go by. It turned out to be very inadequate and we lost our way. We experienced our first anxious moments over the Turkish mountains. All we could see were very bleak rocks, and every mountain seemed to be so very like the others – they were just barren expanses of stone; and if we ran out of fuel there was no way we could find a place to land. We flew on for some time, just looking for a landmark of some sort. Suddenly we saw a railway line. 'Thank God!' said Pista, 'But the question is, which way to follow it?' By then we had lost all idea of where we were. Pista made an instinctive decision and turned to follow the track, which took us to … Ankara. Luckily his intuition had proved right and we eventually came in sight of the Turkish Capital.

The fuel situation was a severe worry by now. We saw an airfield and descended towards it, only to receive signals from the ground that we were not to land. Obviously this was a military airfield. As we had no radio or communication system on board we had no other choice but to hold our breath and fly on over Ankara. It was getting dark by now and Pista's face was stern, but he flew on until we came in sight of the international airport. With only a few drops of petrol left in our tank we landed safely in Ankara and heaved a sigh of relief. To my surprise, I had not felt at all scared and had remained calm all along. I had been busy watching the scenery to look for landmarks, and I relied on Pista's judgement. When one is young, with no children to worry about ... live together and die together.

We saw nothing of Ankara, but after a good night's sleep started off early, fully fuelled, on our way to Istanbul. The clouds were lying low over the mountains and as we had no blind-flying instruments we climbed higher and higher, working our way around them and trying to get over the top. Suddenly the plane started to shudder. It was freezing up, so we had to descend again and play hide and seek with the clouds to find our way out. We finally got out of that situation but found ourselves above a dense, unbroken carpet of clouds, unable to see anything below, with a strong crosswind from the south. It was not easy to tell how much it had pushed us off our route. Pista told me to look out for a hole in the clouds below and to tell him immediately if I saw water underneath. He was watching on his side and I on mine. I suddenly spotted a gap and there was water below. I hastily pointed it out to Pista, who instantly dropped the plane into the opening, diving nose-down. I was caught totally unawares, and for the first time in the whole trip I felt we might have reached the end of the road. But Pista skilfully pulled the plane's nose up until we were flying between the clouds and the sea. I told him that I had been sure that we were heading for a crash, but he only laughed and apologised. He explained that there is always a gap between the sea and the clouds and enough space to pull up – unless there is thick ground fog. There had been no time for him to tell me, as he'd had to take advantage of the gap; he was very sorry that I had been scared.

Luck had been on our side. A crosswind had driven us off towards the Black Sea, and we found ourselves at the entrance to the Bosporus. Shortly Istanbul appeared in the distance, a beautiful sight. We landed, refuelled and flew on to Sofia, the capital of Bulgaria, where we had a meal. We filled up the plane again and on we went. Full of expectation as the evening drew on, we finally saw Budapest airport ahead of us.

The cable we had sent from Egypt said we would arrive on 10 May at seven thirty in the evening – and at seven thirty precisely we sighted Budaörs airport, where the Regent and many others were waiting for us. As the time we had indicated in our message from Cairo grew near, my father-in-law had gone outside, looked at his watch and said, 'They ought to be arriving now.' At that very moment a small red speck appeared on the horizon. It turned out to be our little red Arado on course towards them. His son and new daughter-in-law made a perfect landing right on time. Little did they know what difficulties we had encountered. I myself could hardly believe that we had made it, but Pista seemed to find it quite natural.

*My paternal great-grandmother, Countess
Friderika Edelsheim Gyulai (née Kronau)*

*My paternal great-grandfather,
Baron Leopold Edelsheim Gyulai*

*My paternal grandmother, Countess Irma
Edelsheim Gyulai, born Princess Odescalchi*

*My paternal grandfather,
Count Leopold Edelsheim Gyulai*

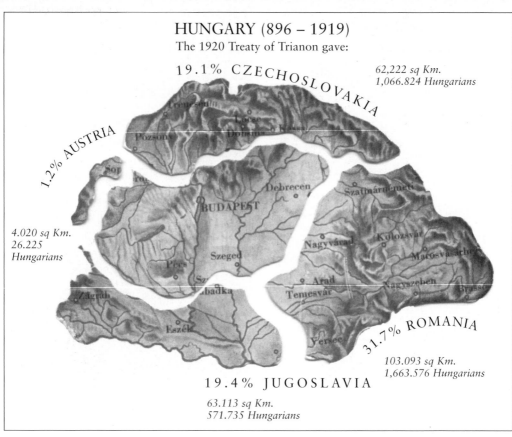

HUNGARY (896 – 1919)
The 1920 Treaty of Trianon gave:

19.1% CZECHOSLOVAKIA

62,222 sq Km.
1,066.824 Hungarians

1.2% AUSTRIA

4.020 sq Km.
26.225
Hungarians

31.7% ROMANIA

103.093 sq Km.
1,663.576 Hungarians

19.4% JUGOSLAVIA

63.113 sq Km.
571.735 Hungarians

My maternal grandmother, Countess Lilla
Pejacsevich, born Baroness Vay.

My maternal grandparents in the 1930s

Grandmother Lilla with her
3 Maltese terriers

My mother,
Countess Gabriella Edelsheim Gyulai

My father,
Count Leopold Edelsheim Gyulai

My step-mother with 'EMSI'
(L to R: Myro, Sya, Ily, Ellamami, Éva)

With my father, aged two

*Our family home, the castle Szent János on
the estate in upper Elefánt*

The family dining room

*Reception hall (formerly the nave of
the church)*

With the roes Bambi and Faline

With my tame stag

EMSI with their motorbikes

The royal box at the 'Living Art' performance:
the Regent, his wife and their two sons

Our official engagement photograph

In my evening dress, especially made for the
pre-wedding reception

Leaving the church between the honour guard of pilots

With my father-in-law, after the wedding

After the wedding lunch, the newly-weds with their relatives

Leaving for our honeymoon in Pista's Arado plane

Our families wave us farewell

Part Two

5

My New Family
Life in the Royal Palace

When we came back from our honeymoon in May 1940 a whole new life began for me in which everything was unfamiliar. From living in the country – or more accurately in the middle of a forest – a life I had enjoyed, I now had to get used to life in the capital of Hungary, living in the Royal Palace. Here I was expected to attend official dinners and luncheons at which I had to sit next to ministers, diplomats and other important people, and know how to behave and carry on intelligent conversations. I would have done anything for Pista, but despite all the happiness, as a country girl I did not find this new life easy, especially at the beginning.

I hope that as I describe the events of the following four and a half years I shall be able to portray accurately the personalities of the various people involved, but it will not be easy. You must remember that I was inexperienced, and overwhelmed by so many new impressions and events that now I have to search for the detail because I could not take everything in. The events are all clear in my mind, but I have somehow lost many interesting and possibly important personal experiences.

So, how did my new family appear to me? From the start they accepted me as part of the family with genuine, not feigned, love. Everything seemed so simple; nobody tried to push themselves forward. Everything was based on punctuality and fulfilment of obligations, and this came naturally.

Of course, I already knew a lot about the public side of the Regent, Admiral Miklós Horthy, whom I knew from then on as Miklóspapa. Now I came to know him as someone who was always warm-hearted and considerate towards me. Many people have asked me about the Regent's day-to-day habits and characteristics, so here are a few details about his everyday life, as I knew it in the Palace.

The Regent got up regularly at seven o'clock and had breakfast with his wife at eight o'clock. After breakfast he went across to his office, where he dealt with current business on the basis of his colleagues' reports.

He always had meals with his wife, and often with his sons and me, although we had separate apartments and catering. Before the war there were often guests for lunch or dinner. Later, and particularly after Pista's death, this effectively came to an end, except for close friends or family members. Miklóspapa was not a gourmet; he liked any good food, and would sometimes fondly remember something he had enjoyed, like Peischl mit Knödl (tripe with dumplings) when he was in Vienna, or a particularly good goulash someone had made, or a Szeged fish soup. Black coffee was an important part of his menu, and he drank a good few cups of it every day. I asked him once whether he could sleep after four or five cups of coffee in the evening, to which he replied with a laugh that he could only sleep after drinking coffee. He liked smoking, and particularly liked Turkish cigarettes. Both he and Magdamama smoked, but not to excess: they smoked their first cigarette after lunch.

Miklóspapa was very keen on sport: he swam, rode, hunted and played tennis. He often rode along the Vérmező behind the Palace. Of course he was always escorted, whether on horseback or on foot, but it was done unobtrusively because he did not like it. Sometimes he walked down to the Danube from Castle Hill and thought he was alone, but even then someone would follow discreetly. This was unavoidable, though the other members of the family – and particularly Pista – did not like it either.

In his younger days he liked painting, playing the piano and singing. In his later days – when I knew him – I never heard him playing the piano or singing, and only saw him painting once, at Kenderes, the Horthy family home. He wrote about that late artistic experiment to Olive Pell, the wife of the American ambassador, in 1949 saying, 'Later I made an atelier in Kenderes and was looking forward to painting quietly during the two months that we used to spend there in the summer. But when it came to that, to my great disappointment I found that I had forgotten it all – and then I never tried again.'

Miklóspapa's life was full of success and enjoyment, even if we leave out the achievements that were well known. He spoke several languages well, enjoyed running the estate, and could speak to everyone easily. Only the illness and death of his beloved children caused him deep sorrow; and the 'royal coup' remained a constantly painful memory.

My mother-in-law, Magdamama, with her lovely white hair and big dark eyes, was beautiful both on the outside and within. She had a deep and firm faith, and her high position did not influence her in the slightest. She lived for her family and her duty. It was she who made me feel, for the first time in my life, the meaning of the word 'mother'. These were my first impressions. Later – during the course of almost twenty years living together – these impressions gained in breadth and depth. And it would be wrong if I were not to make use of this opportunity to say more about her, something I have wanted to do for a long time, as Magdamama's achievements have gone for the most part unrecorded. If the Horthy family is mentioned nowadays very little is said about her, though her exemplary modesty and capacity for work deserve to be remembered.

Magdamama occupied herself with charitable work on a very large scale, directing everything personally with a calm decisiveness that was quite unique. She made decisions, she acted, and her forceful persistence ensured that the work was done. She worked mostly without secretarial help, thereby reducing administrative costs.

Her campaign to ease poverty was very dear to her heart, and every year before winter set in she broadcast an appeal on the radio to help the destitute and those who were hungry. These broadcasts drew society's attention to the problems that needed to be addressed, and her appeals always elicited a generous response. Her campaign, carried out with a feeling of warmth that was to become familiar, extended over the whole country, and always began with donations from leading figures.

In the early days the Regent's wife helped the families of disabled soldiers returning from the First World War, and widows and orphans. Her campaign broadened its scope and started growing between 1930 and 1933, when unemployment hit broad sections of the population and the number of people relying on charitable assistance increased markedly. Covering more than a decade, her work had become so much part of Hungarian national consciousness that there was a constant increase not only in applications for help but also in donors. A document giving data from 1937/38 shows that during that time the campaign received thirty-six thousand applications for help.

She wanted to create institutions based on solid foundations. The first of these were day-care centres for children, which she set up and also provided with food until the Budapest city council took over control. There were a hundred of these by the end of the 1930s, providing education and social care for eight thousand children under school age. Outside Budapest she delegated this task to the lord lieutenant of each county, giving them full powers and allowing them to organize collections on her behalf; from time to time she would check upon their work.

Another example was the setting up of 'little homes' for older people who were no longer able to work. There were eighty-three such institutions providing homes for the elderly. There must be people who still remember the two identical houses that constituted the Magdolna Home in Tas Vezér Street. These provided homes for the widows and families of officers who had died for their country, and also for ninety-three elderly ladies. Magdamama made personal visits to make sure they received adequate care.

My mother-in-law knitted amazingly quickly, and was able to provide these old people with warm, soft wool shawls, which they were pleased and proud to wear.

It was as a result of her campaigning that charitable homes were set up in factories left idle in the dark times of unemployment; they provided clean beds and care in warm well-lit rooms. One of the best examples of the success achieved by her efforts was a refuge that – with the help of the Defence Ministry – she equipped with thirteen hundred beds and bedding for homeless people.

I was there in 1940 and 1941 when she gave out five hundred parcels to families in need, in and around Budapest. The distribution was carried out by the Child Protection League within the framework of her national campaign against poverty. The work of this campaign was carried out in three large rooms in the Palace and involved various organizations. It was here that applications were opened, and recommendations for assistance were made. These were made on the basis of a study of individual circumstances. But every single application was passed to the Regent's wife, who wrote on each one the recommended amount to be given to the applicant. In the winter months sometimes fifteen to eighteen thousand applications were received.

In this way an unemployed man received tools, a woman who had to work at home received a sewing machine, a large family who could not pay the rent was saved from eviction. Just to give those who have never heard about all this some idea of the scale of the operation: between 1930 and 1940, 107,000 families received cash and 1,263,583 families received assistance in kind.

She launched a campaign for Hungarian artists – and no significant artistic event took place without her presence. Sometimes she attended rehearsals at the Opera House. As I mentioned earlier she took a great personal interest in the very successful 'Living-Art Exhibition' at the Opera House, the aim of which was to raise a large sum for the campaign she had launched to help destitute artists.

When the war started and our soldiers enlisted, in view of the approaching winter the Regent's wife issued an appeal for Hungarian women to knit for the soldiers. Even her first appeal drew an incredible response: women set to work, and those who had no wool unpicked their sweaters and scarves at her request.

Magdamama did not talk about herself. She got up early, she came and went and conducted her affairs quietly and calmly. I remember when we unpacked the many thousands of wrist-warmers, scarves and sweaters that we then sent to the soldiers through the Defence Ministry: in exemplary fashion she worked alongside her colleagues, spending days on her feet, apparently tireless.

When a heavy snowfall was followed by a hard frost in Budapest, she launched a campaign for those who were working eight hours a day clearing the snow. She telephoned people on Saturday afternoon to launch the campaign, and on Monday, half way through their day's work, the snow clearers received their first bowl of hot soup, distributed through the snow-covered streets by eighteen mobile kitchens.

Rank and standing had no effect on her; her social position did not change her in the slightest. First and foremost she was a wife – few people know what enormous support she gave to her husband – and a constantly concerned mother. She lost three of her beloved children in her lifetime. I know what this meant to a mother who loved her children passionately, but she never complained.

Miklós Horthy and his wife were really wonderful parents. They had four children, two sons and two daughters: Magda, Paulette, Stephen (Pista), and Miklós (Nicky). My father-in-law had served in the Austro-Hungarian navy in Pola and all four of his children were born there. He never wanted to be away from them, so he took his family with him wherever he was serving: to Constantinople when he was appointed commander of the *Taurus*; to Vienna when he served as aide-de-camp to the Emperor Francis Joseph; and to Ischl when he was in the emperor's service there.

Of their four children, they lost Magda first when she fell victim to scarlet fever at the age of sixteen. This was a terrible blow for the whole family. Paulette, their second daughter, was already seriously ill with tuberculosis when I came into the family. Paulette's illness had been a painful ordeal for the family over a number of years, and now the end was drawing inexorably nearer. My Pista was the only one of their children who so far had caused them no anxiety. Nicky, the youngest, had suffered two serious accidents. The first was at a motorcycle race, when a deaf man walked across the track and Nicky swerved to avoid him and overturned. The second was also a sporting accident: his horse fell with him at a polo match, and the horse stood on Nicky's head as it was getting up. His skull was indented and he was unconscious for days. He had double vision for the rest of his life and this often made him nauseous.

I was always moved by the relationship the two sons had with their parents. For their mother they felt devotion, an affection that is difficult to put into words but was obvious from the way they looked at her and spoke to her. Their feelings towards their father are perhaps best summed up by the respectful but affectionate way in which they greeted him, and consisted of an all-pervading respect and love that was unshaken even when they disagreed on something.

Before our marriage, Pista had a bed-sitting room above his parents' apartment, which was at the back of the Palace, overlooking the Tabán district. Out of the 814 rooms of the Palace, the Regent occupied only nine – 1 per cent of the Palace's floor space. The Horthy family never showed off. Even György Barcza, a Hungarian diplomat who later made critical remarks about Horthy based on misunderstood and incorrect information, wrote about this in the following terms:

> When he was elected Regent they tried to find a suitable house or palace for him, but then for reasons of security and location they settled on the enormous and uninhabited Royal Palace. The first floor of the side of the Palace, which overlooks the Krisztinaváros district, was furnished for him. His reception and living rooms were here, and the Regent's Cabinet Office was located on the ground floor below. The sum of 10,000 pengős per month was earmarked for the Regent's honorarium. His household was what his position merited, but not excessively extravagant; it was as simple as possible, and comparable to that of an ambassador. His staff were his excellent chef Marek, his butler Mr Szauter, a few footmen, a chauffeur, a suitable number of house staff, and two guards outside the doors: that was all. Many people criticized Horthy at the time for going to live in the Palace, but in the given circumstances this was the best possible solution, and the fact that the Regent and his family only occupied the guest apartment, leaving all the royal apartments overlooking the Danube empty, shows that Horthy was not trying to usurp the dignity which befitted a king, but occupied the apartment simply because he was the country's leading dignitary.[6]

Three rooms were now added to Pista's bachelor flat: a bedroom, a dining room, and a living room. Our living room was in the corner of the Palace, with two windows looking out onto the Gellért hill, the other two onto the Tabán district. We had our own kitchen adjacent to our flat. This was our apartment, and we furnished it with our own furniture. The only things we could not replace were the curtains and the big chandeliers, which belonged to the Palace.

So this was where we started our married life. It was our intention to find a house somewhere in the vicinity of Budapest so that we could have a home of our own, but because of the seriousness of Paulette's condition it would not have been right to move away at that time. In many ways it was wonderful to live in the Palace, but the only place we could be sure of not being disturbed was our flat. Guards with halberds stood motionless in their decorative uniforms in all the corridors. There was something unreal about all this, and it was hard for me to get over the feeling that I had to be careful because they were watching me. But I soon got used to my surroundings and knew they were not watching, just looking.

Since only a spiral staircase separated our apartments, we went down to my parents-in-law almost every evening to play bridge and chat. At these times they told us many interesting stories. I would never have believed, for example, that I would be able to hear their own personal account of their meeting with Hitler.

My father-in-law said that when he first saw Hitler in 1936, Hitler made a relatively good impression. At that time Hitler still asked questions and sought opinions, and what he said still made sense. Their second meeting took place two years later, and the Regent said that by that time Hitler had changed a great deal and considered himself master of Europe after the successes he had achieved. This was the first official visit to Germany by the Regent and his wife, and it left a deep uneasy impression on both of them.

They had been invited to the launching of the German cruiser *Prinz Eugen* in Kiel in the summer of 1938, and my mother-in-law was asked to perform the launching ceremony. They travelled through Germany to Kiel in a special train and with a large German escort, and my mother-in-law was surrounded by the wives of prominent Germans. Magdamama had always had a real talent for acting and mimicry, and she made us laugh with her excellent imitation and description of the behaviour of the ladies assigned to her. They spoke in rapturous terms about the Führer, telling her that when she looked into his eyes for the first time she would understand who Hitler really was. So she looked forward with interest to meeting him. But when she finally looked into Hitler's eyes in Kiel she could not understand what these ladies had been talking about; she was surprised to find that he had eyes that were expressionless and like fish eyes.

My parents-in-law did not know beforehand the real reason for their invitation, but it soon became clear when, in a private conversation, Hitler told my father-in-law in detail about his plan to 'trample the Czechs', and if necessary destroy Prague. He expected to receive an assurance from the Regent that Hungary would simultaneously attack Slovakia from the south. The friendly atmosphere very quickly disappeared when my father-in-law stated categorically that there was no question of Hungary getting involved, because even though we did have revisionist claims against Slovakia we wanted to achieve these by peaceful means.

What seemed particularly worrying was that, when my father-in-law later mentioned this matter in the course of a detailed conversation he had with Field Marshal Brauchitsch, commander-in-chief of the German land forces, Hitler then reproached him for talking to Brauchitsch about the planned action against Czechoslovakia. The Regent answered that he alone would decide to whom he would talk and about what, and that he assumed Hitler's generals knew about his plans. Hitler replied that he was the only one who made decisions, and that the generals had no say in the matter. Naturally, the Regent did not know that at the time, the leading military were preparing the arrest of Hitler and his closest collaborators in case an attack on the Sudetenland would lead to war.

My father-in-law gives a detailed account of all this in his memoirs, which were published after the war.[7]

Among other things, my father-in-law entertained us with his account of the visit they paid to Reich Marshal Göring in Karinhall. He said that when they arrived, Göring was standing in front of the entrance to receive them and told them that he would like to emphasize that everything they were about to see was his property. A very interesting statement considering that it was well known that he had collected the valuable paintings and other treasures in his huge and incredibly lavishly furnished home from museums. That large, fat man changed his clothes and even his rings and jewellery two or three times during the one short day they spent there. My mother-in-law was very funny as she demonstrated how Göring wore his puff-sleeved modern version of the old Germanic hunting costume.

In Nürnberg they were shown the huge Parteitag building, which was just being built. Himmler, the interior minister, who was showing them around, said proudly that this huge building would use more stone than the Pyramids. My mother-in-law, who liked to follow everything up, asked what this building was for, what would happen in it? Himmler replied that this would be where the party members, Gauleiters and the like, would gather once a year. My mother-in-law asked whether there would be statements and reports, as in a parliament, at which Himmler looked at her as if she were completely stupid and said, 'No, there will only be one speaker, the Führer. Nothing else will happen here.'

'Isn't it rather extravagant?' my mother-in-law asked. But all she got in reply was a contemptuous look.

After these experiences they returned home full of anxiety about where all this would lead, because their impression was that neither Hitler nor anyone in his entourage was a rational, normal person.

Miklóspapa also told us about his visit to Poland, where he warned the Polish leadership, headed by President Moscicki, of the German threat. All the leading politicians unrealistically believed that they could win a war against Germany, when in fact this was clearly impossible. Poland was not well enough armed, whereas Germany was very strong.

On our return from our honeymoon we had been shocked and horrified to hear the details of the invasion by German forces of Belgium and Holland. Holland had been caught unprepared by the German attack. After four days, with Rotterdam lost and The Hague about to fall, further resistance was hopeless. The royal families of both countries fled to London, except for King Baudoin of the Belgians, who did not want to leave his country.

The invasion of Norway and France followed soon after that. Pista was greatly concerned by these events, and kept voicing his conviction that Germany could not win such a war, even if it did make a pact with the Soviets. He knew England and the United States well, and already his thinking was that England would not give in and that sooner or later the Americans would step in on their side. His intuitive feelings were subsequently confirmed.

Despite this he had no political role or ambition. He pursued his career as a mechanical engineer wholeheartedly. When Pista's good friend Jenő Markotay-Velsz left the post of director general of MÁVAG, Pista was appointed in his place. For a time all the company's problems fell on his shoulders.

On 1 June 1940 Pista was appointed president of the Hungarian State Railways (MÁV), and vacated the post of director general of MÁVAG. He now threw himself into leading the State Railways with all the dedication and enthusiasm he had put into leading the factory.

On 18 June the whole country celebrated the Regent's birthday with enthusiasm, as they did every year. For the first time I took part in this family celebration, and was not surprised that the family spent the day in rather low spirits because of Paulette's condition. My father-in-law did not even take part in the festivities in Budapest; we went to their home in Kenderes for a quiet celebration. On 26 June, eight days after my father-in-law's birthday, Paulette closed her beautiful eyes for the last time. We buried her in the family crypt at Kenderes.

After Paulette's death I was often aware of her mother's deep, inconsolable pain. For instance, one evening we were invited to a gala performance at the Opera House, but she stayed at home. The performance was of Puccini's *La Bohème*, in which Mimi dies of consumption, and she could not bear to watch it.

This tragic event was followed by a joyful and happy one: my sister Myro's marriage to György Darányi. They were married, as I had been, by Bishop Ravasz in the church on Szilágyi Dezső Square. I wore my wedding dress, but of course with a married woman's bonnet instead of a veil.

Before Myro's wedding I found out that I was pregnant. This knowledge gave me a happy and warm feeling, like an unbelievable blessing – but at the same time it was a little frightening. I was afraid I would not be able to share everything with Pista as much as I would like. What about all the riding and flying? After all, we had only just started our life together. This apprehension very soon proved to be unfounded. The doctor advised me not to stop doing anything as long as I felt well; and in the summer months, despite Pista having a lot of important business, whenever he had time we made short flying trips. These provided a good opportunity for him to carry on teaching me to fly.

Pista taught me to land in his own small Arado plane, although it would have been better to use one without a retractable undercarriage. We practised taking off and landing several times, then Pista said it was time for me to do a landing on my own. He would pretend he was not there, he would not even look, and I was to land by myself. Everything went well until we were on the final approach. I noticed that several people on the airfield were waving, and I thought they were waving because I was approaching so well. As it turned out, they were signalling to me that I should drop the undercarriage. I, however, landed the plane as if it were a glider, as I had been gliding a lot recently. Fortunately it was a smooth landing, so only the propeller broke as I touched down, and they quickly lifted the plane up and managed to release the undercarriage.

Naturally, everyone was greatly concerned about events in Europe, but we were particularly interested in the demands of the Hungarian minority in Transylvania, which was now part of Romania, and the negotiations in connection with this.

In August 1940 the second 'Vienna Award' restored part of Transylvania to Hungary. A decision had been requested, not by us but by Romania; the Hungarian prime minister, Pál Teleki, had not even wanted to go to Vienna. The Germans and the Italians were the arbiters. The Italians tried to help us, but the Germans simply pushed through what was in their own interests, which essentially involved ensuring that neither side was satisfied. It was obvious that Hitler did not want either country to be strong in its independence. Pál Teleki pointed out that nobody could really be satisfied with the new frontiers because they would cause dissatisfaction and conflict between Hungary and Romania.

My father-in-law had always wanted the Hungarian-inhabited areas that were lost through the Treaty of Trianon to be returned to Hungary not by force of arms but by peaceful means – and frequently said so in my presence – but he had similar concerns, and was also dissatisfied with the outcome of the negotiations. The general public did not appreciate all this. The whole country was understandably ecstatic, as people felt that something had been done to redress the wrong done by Trianon.

Many people have written about the Hungarian army's entry into Transylvania, but anyone who did not experience the joy manifested by the Hungarians there will find it difficult to appreciate its true significance. I spent my whole childhood in an 'occupied' area, and perhaps that was why it moved me so much and made such an unforgettably deep impression on me. But Europe's future was full of uncertainty, and this joy was not without anxiety.

The restoration of part of Transylvania gave Pista, as president of the Hungarian State Railways, an enormous amount of work. With the re-establishment of these areas the network of lines increased by 2,300 kilometres. Completely new railway lines had to be built, particularly to the Székler region, which was returned to Hungary without road or railway links and was in difficult, mountainous terrain. Fortunately the prime minister gave Pista's plans his full backing, and the line to the Székler region was built in record time. However, this involved a huge amount of work, and Pista turned his attention to every detail: in particular he made sure the workers had the best possible accommodation and catering.

He spoke to me about this only because, as the MÁV women's president, I had to know the circumstances of the families. The only other way I found out about his enormous achievements was from the people who worked with him and from the wives of employees. It was only afterwards that I could fully comprehend how much he had done and how hard he had worked.

The question that springs to mind is how could one man do so much in such a short time? It was as if he suspected that he did not have long.

One of the secrets behind this tireless activity – as I discovered after our wedding – was that every day after lunch he lay down and slept deeply, if only for twenty minutes. The Regent also had this habit, and told us that in the navy they could even sleep standing up. I also adopted the custom of resting after lunch, and soon discovered how much more energy I had in the afternoon and evening after a short siesta.

As the wife of the chairman of the Hungarian State Railways I took part in a number of charitable activities. There were various sections in the National Association of Hungarian Women, and because of my husband's job I became president of the railway workers' section, the principal function of which was to provide for the welfare of railway workers' families. I had to attend meetings where the women who headed the other sections were much older than me. There was a great deal of talk at these meetings and I could not make head or tail of it. I asked my mother-in-law for advice about what to do because I could not make speeches like that, and most of the time I could not even work out what the ladies were getting at. My mother-in-law reassured me and told me not to worry. She told me to say only what I really knew and what I wanted to achieve, and to do so as briefly as possible. This made my job much easier because it was simpler to decide what to say than how to say it. At first the others were surprised that I spoke so briefly, but I noticed that a few of them began to follow my example.

On 13 October we flew south in our dear little Arado plane to Nasice in Croatia, for my grandmother Lilla Pejacsevich's eightieth birthday celebrations. In this way Pista did not lose a lot of time, and my grandmother could meet my husband.

Grandmother looked very beautiful, surrounded by her grand-children in a moving and loving celebration. She even danced a Viennese waltz and played the piano for us. That was the last time I saw her; she died three months later on 14 January 1941, on my birthday, just three days before the birth of my son.

Grandmother Lilla left us a poem:

To my Grandchildren now that I am Old
Don't think, you young people,
That in old age everything is in the past,
That everything beautiful is long buried,
That every picture is hopelessly grey.

It's not true!
In a bent body, under the wrinkles,
The heart can beat warmly,

The sun can shine;
Your laughter finds an echo,
I look with pleasure at your radiant faces.

I too can daydream in flowery meadows.
I don't imagine death as a skeleton,
After all, our soul flies away
To be glorified through God's mercy,
And if it puts on a body in heaven
That body won't be old,
But young and radiant,
Surrounded by light.

So don't you lose heart,
Go bravely into old age.
I can tell you it's not so terrible,
Even if it's not dazzlingly brilliant.

I'm dozing now, waiting
For eternal rest to come to my body.
Don't cry too much for me,
But scatter lots of flowers on my grave.
I will bless you,
Who have lit up the end of my life.

In November 1940 Hungary joined the Tripartite Pact; and in December Hungary and Yugoslavia signed an Eternal Friendship Treaty in Belgrade. If Germany's actions had not interfered, and we had gone on along this road, how different Hungary's destiny would have been.

On 2 November, the twentieth anniversary of the defeat of Béla Kún's Communist regime, I was deeply impressed by – and remember to this day – the sight of a large crowd flowing up to the Palace to express their gratitude to the Regent. My parents-in-law, Pista and I received the procession on the balcony above the main entrance. It was evening, and the Palace yard was filled with people singing the national anthem. Prolonged cheering from the crowd followed speeches expressing gratitude to the Regent. Then Miklóspapa said a few words of thanks. I do not remember his exact words, but I liked his brief and simple response, and the fact that he did not take the opportunity to make a rousing patriotic speech, as most people would have done; he was not a politician and did not try to appear to be one. He concluded by saying that everyone should now go home to sleep. Immediately there was silence and everyone left.

As the year ended and Christmas time approached, Magdamama made her radio appeal to the country on behalf of her charitable work. She personally attended the Child Protection League's Christmas party, the bodyguards' Christmas party, and many others, and I greatly admired the way she wasted neither time nor words. I tried to learn from her and help as much as I could; fortunately I was able to cope well with everything even though I was in the final month of my pregnancy.

6

The Birth of my Son István
January 1941

The greatest blessing of my life was approaching, a gift of the Almighty: the birth of my son.

On the night of 16 January, Miklóspapa and Pista attended a showing of *Dankó Pista* – the two-hundredth talking film made in Hungary – at the Forum Cinema. Magdamama and I stayed at home; we had not gone out for the last few evenings. It must have been after eight o'clock when my waters broke and we called Béla Csaba, my mother-in-law's driver, to take us to the Siesta sanatorium, sending Gyuri the valet to tell Pista that the baby was on the way.

Everyone was in a state of great excitement, as there were no male descendants in the latest generation of the Horthy family. Miklóspapa was the only one among seven brothers who had two sons, Pista and Nicky. And Nicky – who had been married to Countess Consuelo Károlyi but was now divorced – had two daughters, Zsófi and Nicolette, so there were no other boys in the family. Of course they kept saying it did not matter whether it was a boy or a girl – after all, there might be more – but naturally everyone was secretly hoping for a boy. I personally did not mind and would have liked to have at least three more children after this one, but for the sake of the family I was hoping for a boy too.

Only a mother knows the blessed, happy feeling that overwhelms her after the moment of birth, the great gift of the Creator. It showed me clearly that we have to suffer for everything good, for every blessing, for every progress; and that without suffering we cannot achieve anything durable or worthwhile. I felt I had suffered a good deal for my son, but that it was certainly all worth it, because on 17 January at seven in the morning I gave birth to a healthy child, who weighed 8 lbs [3.6 kg]. He brought an incalculable blessing to my life, inasmuch as now – more than fifty years later – I can say that I have always enjoyed a good understanding with my son. He has not only been a companion with whom I could share everything but also, thanks to his own search, in 1958 he put me in touch with a 'higher way of life' that makes sense of everything and has had an increasingly profound influence on my being.

I received masses of flowers, most of which I distributed among the other patients. Journalists and reporters flooded in, all wanting to take photographs. I was surprised when I discovered that Pista, who never liked having his picture taken and always avoided photographers, had lifted the hours-old baby out of his crib and posed with him for them in the corridor.

We did not have to think about a name for our son because the question never arose. It had been a tradition in the Horthy family for the last nine generations to call every firstborn son István (Stephen) as a mark of respect for Hungary's first apostolic king, Saint Stephen, who had laid the foundations of Christianity in Hungary. So my son was baptized István Miklós Lipót Gyula – the traditional István being followed by the names of his grandfathers and godfather. My brother-in-law Gyula Károlyi was his godfather, and my sister Sya his godmother.

István was baptized into my husband's Calvinist faith in our flat in the Palace. There was never any argument or disagreement in the family about this. The men were all Calvinist and the women were all Catholic. My mother-in-law was very supportive of me in this matter whenever any friction arose, even if it was only in fun. For instance, I hung a small picture of the Virgin Mary in my son's room, and when Pista came in and saw it, half jokingly and pretending to be angry he asked why there was a Madonna in his Calvinist son's room. My mother-in-law happened to be there and said, 'I don't want any comments from you about that, because when you were a little boy you said the Hail Mary with me and it didn't do you any harm.' Pista laughed heartily and did not concern himself with the matter again.

People have vivid imaginations, and over the years I have been asked questions like: 'Is it true that the Regent converted to Catholicism?' or 'Didn't the Regent's wife promise the bishop that she would convert her grandson to Catholicism?' People who ask such questions obviously did not know my father-in-law or my mother-in-law. The possibility of my father-in-law converting was never mentioned, and he had very firm ideas on the subject. Although he was a very liberal Calvinist, and got on well with Catholic priests and bishops and with the Primate himself, he considered that it was almost inconceivable that someone should convert to a faith other than the one into which he had been baptized and in which he had grown up.

Nor is it true that my mother-in-law made any promise in connection with István's upbringing. They never interfered in my religious problem. I was the only person in a position to make any kind of promise because I was the only one who discussed the matter with priests when – due to my Calvinist wedding and later the Calvinist baptism of my son – I was no longer allowed to practise my faith. Not one of the priests with whom I talked ever questioned István's future, and there was never any suggestion that I should convert him or influence him in any way. The only request or advice I received – which could not be described as a condition – was that I should live a pure life and set a good example to my son. I was told this when I received permission to practise my faith once again, following my husband's death.

On Ellamami's recommendation we offered the position of nanny to Ilona Sajni (Nanny Ila) a highly qualified children's nurse. She had spent many years with the family of Count János (Bibi) Esterházy, who lived near Elefánt. When the two Esterházy children, János and Alice, outgrew the need for her services she returned to the Heim clinic, where she had originally been trained. Ilona had not wanted to go back to private employment, preferring to work in the clinic, but when she heard I wanted to employ her, she immediately decided to accept.

We could not have chosen a better person. Nanny Ila was tall, with an erect posture and a cheerful nature. She was such a perfect child nurse that I practically never had to call out a doctor to see my son. We all became fond of her, and she enjoyed our complete confidence and became a member of our family. Later on she came with us into captivity and exile.

Despite the fact that I was very busy with my little István, political events now began to impinge on my life, which was not surprising as important decisions affecting the country were being made in my father-in-law's office and reception room below our flat. There were few days when the family did not get together, and naturally we discussed many things on those occasions.

At the end of March there was a military coup in Yugoslavia. As I have already mentioned, Hungary and Yugoslavia had signed an Eternal Friendship Treaty in December. Prime Minister Pál Teleki's government had worked to keep Hungary out of any military conflict, and my father-in-law also thought that Hungary should hold all its forces in reserve until the end of the war and should pursue its revisionist claims only by peaceful means.

General Lajos Dálnoki Veress has given an account of these events, which coincide with what I know of the period:

> We did not have to wait long to discover the

Germans' plans, because the day after the coup Hitler sent a confidential message to the Regent informing him that he would attack Yugoslavia at the earliest possible time. He stated that he fully acknowledged Hungary's revisionist claims up to the frontier specified by the Regent, mentioning the Bácska and Bánát regions by name, and holding out the prospect of establishing a Hungarian naval base on the Adriatic. He requested the Regent's permission for German forces to advance through Hungarian territory. Finally, he hinted in an unambiguous manner for Hungary's cooperation.

General Henrik Werth, the [Hungarian] army chief of staff, constantly pressed for orders to be given for the mobilisation of certain divisions and formations. In addition, he held talks within his own sphere of competence with representatives of the German military command who had been sent to Budapest, and only informed the government of these talks after they had taken place. For this reason there was some tension between Prime Minister Teleki and the military leadership. The government did not permit the mobilisation of the Second Army Corps on 1 April.[8]

The historian Péter Gosztonyi points out a consideration that was important at the time:

The Germans might not have needed the Hungarian army but they certainly needed Hungary itself as a transit route for the Wehrmacht. If they did not receive permission to pass through Hungary, Hitler might use force to advance to the northern frontier of Yugoslavia. Should the army resist such an advance? Should Hungary sacrifice itself for Belgrade? Not to mention the fact that a war between Hungary and Germany in 1941 would have been a lost cause right from the start! The Royal Hungarian Army did not have the spirit or the equipment for a war against Germany.[9]

This situation and Hitler's proposal confronted the Hungarian government with a difficult decision, because it was not just a question of allowing the German forces to pass through, but of participating in the action. The atmosphere in the Palace was tense: pro-German generals, including some who were of German origin, tried hard to influence the Regent. One of the many arguments they used was that the eternal friendship and non-aggression treaty had not been signed by the new government, so we were not bound by it. Looking back now, it is difficult to decide what information and what criteria had a bearing on the final decision. For instance, there was also the news that the Germans were planning to create a 'Prinz Eugen Gau', an independent administrative territory that would incorporate many Hungarian-inhabited areas.

Was there any way out of this dilemma? Pista tried to draw his father's attention to a number of things and to certain individuals' attitudes. He thought it was important not only to emphasize the advantages, but also to point out the things that were wrong and to put them right. Pista believed that the activities of the pro-German generals had brought this situation about: they had reported their own ideas to Hitler, not saying the same things as they were saying in Hungary. He was worried by the growing Nazi influence, believing that some of the generals were in Hitler's pocket, and thought Henrik Werth and the other similarly pro-German generals should be replaced immediately.

He complained to me disconsolately that his father thought he did not know anything about the issue, and that he had no say in matters concerning the army. I was aware of the difficult position Pista was in, given that his opinion differed from that of the people whose official duty it was to counsel the Regent. He had already asked me on one occasion to tell his father something instead of saying it himself, because it was different coming from me. With me, his father could just chat about it; coming from Pista, his son, it might have looked like criticism. Very important decisions were at stake here. I was able to talk to Miklóspapa about the situation, and could see that he was convinced that if he said no to Hitler it would result in the invasion of Hungary. Prime Minister Teleki knew that too.

Who can tell what would have happened if we had resisted the German ultimatum. As so often in the course of our history, it had once again become clear that the Hungarian people had settled in a difficult part of Europe. Would it be possible for Hungary somehow to survive with honour between Nazism and Communism?

The next day an answer was sent to Hitler granting permission for the Germans to pass through Hungary. The advance began on 4 April, before the Regent's response had even reached Hitler.

The Hungarian ambassador in London, György Barcza, reported that, although the British government was aware of Hungary's particularly difficult position, we could expect Britain to break off diplomatic relations. Pista was very depressed. I knew what this meant to him as someone who had close contacts with England and many friends there. His best friends included Lord Mountbatten of Burma and his wife Edwina. He had a photo of them, signed 'Dickie and Edwina,' in his room.

Everything Pál Teleki had been working for collapsed with the German advance through Hungary; at the same time his beloved wife was gravely ill. He discovered that the chief of staff had already agreed on the technical details of the German advance with the Nazi general staff behind the government's back; on top of this, he was informed that same evening of the threat by London to declare war against us.

The next day, 3 April 1941, Pál Teleki committed suicide. Being aware of the serious consequences of the events, he wanted to draw the West's attention to the fact that we were acting under duress, and Hungary's attention to the fact that a policy of peace was no longer tenable. As he put it, we had been swept into the war against our will 'on the side of the villains'.

My parents-in-law were long-standing and good friends of Pál Teleki, or 'Bóli', as they called him. You can imagine the effect the loss of this friend and colleague in such tragic circumstances had on them. We were all deeply shocked.

Churchill hailed Teleki in a radio speech a few days later, saying that what he had done must be remembered at the coming peace negotiations and that a seat must be kept there for Count Paul Teleki. The thought was there, but no seat was kept at the peace table; by the time it was constituted nobody acknowledged the duress to which Hungary had been subjected, or remembered Teleki's act of self-sacrifice. Yet after his death even the British press paid generous tribute to him as a great patriot, 'Hungary's first gentleman', who had given his life to protest against the Germans' use of force.

Later on all sorts of rumours began to circulate that Prime Minister Pál Teleki had been murdered, but they were completely without foundation, as was proved by the farewell letter he wrote to the Regent before his suicide.

Miklóspapa indignantly told us that Pál Teleki's son had come to see him and, in an unpleasant and insolent manner, had demanded to be given that letter. My father-in-law said that he would willingly have shown him the letter but could not understand why he was behaving in such a hostile manner, and had refused his request because of it. This was unfortunate, because it seems that Géza Teleki thought Miklóspapa wanted to conceal the letter's contents from him.

The country could not remain without a prime minister in this critical situation, so on 4 April the Regent appointed Foreign Minister László Bárdossy to the post. He was widely popular and was said to be independent in all respects.

After the German forces entered Zagreb – where the population received them enthusiastically – Croatia proclaimed its independence on 10 April, thus breaking free from Serbian oppression. The next day, seven days after the Germans initiated their action, Hungarian forces crossed the Yugoslav border and advanced to Hungary's pre-Trianon frontier.

On 24 April my father-in-law paid a one-day visit to Hitler. He told us afterwards that when he asked Hitler about the tension between Germany and the Soviet Union, Hitler assured him that Germany had no intention of attacking the Soviets. (Operation Barbarossa – the plan to attack the Soviet Union – had been finalized in December 1940, four months earlier.)

On 22 June Germany attacked the Soviet Union without declaring war, advancing quickly and victoriously.

The Regent was undoubtedly against becoming involved in the war; I clearly remember that when, on 20 March and amid much pomp and ceremony, the Soviet Union returned to Hungary fifty-six flags captured in the 1848 war of independence, Miklóspapa had taken it as a good sign and had remarked, 'We don't want to get mixed up in a war with the Soviets, it's not in our interests.' In fact I heard him say that more than once. But he hoped that the German action might possibly help liberate Russia from Bolshevism. On the other hand, both Pista and I thought that a Nazi victory would have been no better than Communism.

My father-in-law wrote in his memoirs:

> At the next cabinet meeting in which this was discussed, Prime Minister Bárdossy would not even agree to the breaking off of diplomatic relations with Moscow, putting forward the argument that we could justify this attitude in German eyes by pointing out that our Moscow Legation would provide us with an excellent source of information. When this came to the knowledge of the German minister via the Press Service of the Ministry of Foreign Affairs, he at once called on Bárdossy and told him that breaking off diplomatic relations was the least that Berlin expected of the Hungarian government. On 23 June, another Cabinet meeting was held to consider a letter from Werth, the chief of general staff, to the prime minister, in which an immediate declaration of war was demanded. Romania had already entered the war, so that Hungary risked being left behind should she hesitate any longer, and instead of securing the whole of Transylvania, would

perhaps lose even those parts that had been returned to her by the Vienna Award. Bárdossy refused to be moved by this argument; he voted against a declaration of war and was supported by the other members of the Cabinet. It was decided that we should break off diplomatic relations with the Soviet Union, but we would not go beyond that. [p. 250]

Then completely out of the blue came the shocking news of a bombardment by unknown planes on the towns of Kassa and Munkács.

General Lajos Dálnoki Veress wrote:

> On 26 June at 12 noon, a time of peak traffic, four biplanes of unknown type, presumed to be Russian bombers, carried out a raid on the centre of Kassa and hit the main post office. 30 people were killed and about 500 injured. The Cyrillic script on the bomb fragments and on one bomb which failed to explode and was dug out intact, indicated that this was a Russian bomb of the most recent type, manufactured in the Putylov Works in Krivoy-Rog on the river Dnieper.[10]

The Regent and Bárdossy were informed that there was no doubt that the bombers were of Soviet origin. The cabinet was convened immediately and, acting on its decision, Prime Minister László Bárdossy announced on the following day, 28 June 1941, that Hungary was at war with the Soviet Union.

It was only three years later that my father-in-law found out that Bárdossy, who by that time had given in more and more to German pressure, had kept from him and his fellow ministers the contents of a telegram sent by Kristóffy, our ambassador in Moscow. The text of Kristóffy's coded telegram, which arrived in Budapest via Ankara on 24 June 1941, was as follows:

> Molotov asked to see me this afternoon and asked me about the position Hungary would adopt with regard to the German-Russian conflict. He informed me that the Soviet government had, as he had already stated several times, no demands or aggressive intentions against Hungary. He had no comment on Hungarian demands being met at Romania's expense, and would have no comment on that in the future. However, due to the rapid course of events, the Soviet

government had to know as soon as possible whether Hungary intended to take part in the war or maintain a neutral position. I informed him that I have no instructions with regard to the government's position and so could not give him clarification on that point. … Since Molotov asked for an answer as soon as possible, I request instructions as a matter of urgency.

Kristóffy.[11]

When the Regent found out about this in 1944, he summoned Bárdossy and asked him whether it was true that he had received this telegram. Bárdossy admitted that it was. I remember that day and my father-in-law's anger. How easy it is for people to stray from the straight, correct path; how easy to choose, perhaps with the best of intentions, sly scheming instead of honesty. The impact of all these different influences is terrible because so many lives can depend on them. Poor Bárdossy paid heavily for his mistakes. He was very brave in November 1945 when he was condemned to death and executed by the Communist 'People's Court' – something he certainly did not deserve.

At the time, Moscow denied that Soviet planes had carried out the bombing raids against Hungarian towns. Although that does not prove anything, and any denial could be designed to mislead, one thing is certain: it could not have been in the interests of the Soviet Union to provoke us.

In July 1941 Pista was appointed Secretary of State. Soon afterwards we took little István to Kenderes, the family's country estate, for the first time. For this occasion Miklóspapa had the flag of the Austro-Hungarian navy raised. It was so big that it nearly took the roof off. We unveiled a war memorial and Miklóspapa made a speech. There were many guests, and the ceremony was followed by luncheon. Everyone admired István, who behaved impeccably for a baby of six months: he did not cry, and put up with everyone patting and stroking him much better than I did.

Kenderes was where we really felt at home. I rode out on the estate with Miklóspapa and Pista. Miklóspapa was a completely different person there and I could see how much he enjoyed being at home. He spoke to everyone, and I was amazed at how much he knew about managing the estate. There was a swimming pool in the garden and a clay pigeon shooting area. Gyuszi Tost, his aide-de-camp, went shooting there with Pista, while I was an enthusiastic spectator.

The war felt so far away. It was difficult to imagine that while we were enjoying this wonderful home, somewhere else soldiers were fighting, suffering and dying.

On 22 July we celebrated Miklóspapa and Magdamama's fortieth wedding anniversary, which coincided with Magdamama's name-day, the feast of Saint Magdalene. Soon afterwards the two of them went to Szabadka – the capital of the Bácska region, which had 'returned' to Hungary – to attend a beautiful ceremony in which the first bread from the harvest was presented to the Regent. They were welcomed with enormous enthusiasm: there were triumphal arches, the streets were strewn with roses, the houses were all decorated in red, white and green, all the windows and balconies were crowded. They brought the harvest wreath and placed it at my mother-in-law's feet. Endless lines of young men and women paraded in beautiful folk costumes, carrying wheat wreaths; there were sacks of the new flour, and bakers with the bread. Every nationality was represented, including delegations from the northern region and Transylvania; Slovaks, Csángós (Hungarians from Moldavia), Catholic Serbs, all bearing many flags that had been hidden from the occupiers for twenty-two years. There were displays, dances and games. What a shame we could not live and build in peace in such a rich, enthusiastic country.

At the beginning of September Miklóspapa went with the prime minister and the army chief of staff to visit Hitler for three days, to discuss what would happen to the Hungarian troops at the front. As a result of the discussions it was agreed that some of the troops were to return home in the following months; and best of all was the news that from now on our men would serve only as occupying forces. This again proved to be a lie, and events unfortunately took a different course.

The trainee pilots of the Miklós Horthy National Flying Foundation took their examination at Budaörs, and Pista, as president of the Foundation, made a speech about its work. At the same time he addressed the young people of Hungary in the flying journal *Magyar Szárnyak* (Hungarian Wings):

> I call on the youth of Hungary to conquer the
> country's vast airspace, I call on them to protect the
> frontiers of the holy Hungarian homeland, and I invite
> them to share the glory of our pilots. With confidence
> and faith I call on fathers, mothers, young people and
> the old, I call on all members of Hungarian society, but
> first and foremost on young Hungarians who long to
> fly: I call on them to serve the cause of flying in
> Hungary. One of the most important guarantees of
> Hungary's future is strength in the air, and the number
> and excellence of Hungarian pilots will be one of the

most important factors in determining our position in Europe, our security, and the weight of what we have to say.

Anyone who is a good Hungarian and has the future of Hungary at heart must concern themselves with developing flying in Hungary and with the methodical training of young people. If the future belongs to our young people and we want to build the future of the Hungarian homeland on them, we must train these young people, make them strong, and give them a steely determination to break through all obstacles and overcome all difficulties to serve and work for Hungary's future.

For this reason I call on Hungary's youth to fulfil great and holy duties; I call them to the uplifting service of flying for Hungary, in the hope that they will be good pilots, just as our ancestors were good warriors and chivalrous horsemen.

Signed: István Horthy, secretary of state, president of the Miklós Horthy National Flying Foundation.

On 14 November there was a ceremonial reception for the returning mountain brigade. How I wished everyone would come back home. Magdamama and I made up parcels for the soldiers fighting on the eastern front, and many kind ladies helped us. Two large rooms were available in the Palace for such projects, and that was where we worked, sitting or standing at long tables. Magdamama organized everything wonderfully, almost unnoticed.

Despite the severance of diplomatic relations with Britain, Pista and I remained friendly with some of the British diplomats, particularly Ambassador O'Malley and his wife, until they left the country. Unfortunately, O'Malley and some members of the embassy staff had been to Romania quite often recently and had a rather hostile attitude towards Hungary. It seemed that they appreciated the pressure Germany had applied to the Romanians more than they did the pressure that had been applied to us. I know this was just politics, but it made me sad.

Once diplomatic relations with Britain had been broken off, the United States ambassador in Budapest, Herbert Pell, represented British interests in Hungary. We were also friendly with him and his wife Olive. As I have already mentioned, after our wedding she had painted a picture of Pista and me in all our finery. She also painted portraits of the Regent and his wife.

We had other friends among the American diplomats, in particular Bill Schott, a counsellor at the American legation, and his wife Janet, whom we often met. So it was doubly awkward when the British government sent Hungary an ultimatum at the end of November, stating that if Hungary did not withdraw its troops from the Soviet Union by 5 December, Britain would declare war. Despite the fact that some troops had returned home, in the circumstances a complete withdrawal would have been impossible.

On 7 December 1941 Great Britain declared war on Hungary. This meant that the staff of the British Embassy had to leave the country. Pista – as president of the State Railways – made all the arrangements to ensure that their departure went smoothly, and accompanied the Minister and his wife to the station.

On the same day, the Japanese attacked and destroyed the American fleet at Pearl Harbour. The Regent writes about the subsequent Hungarian declaration of war on America in his memoirs:

> Bárdossy thought he had to pre-empt the demands we expected Germany to make. So, without discussing the matter with me – I happened to be in hospital for a few days at the time with food poisoning – or asking for Parliament's approval, he broke off diplomatic relations with the United States. This satisfied neither Berlin nor Rome; so then Bárdossy did what they demanded. On 12 December he summoned Mr Pell, the American minister, and informed him that Hungary regarded itself as being at war with the United States. He also told Mr Pell – who during the course of their conversation had given him a golden opportunity in this regard – that the Hungarian government was acting of its own free will. This was a blunder. If Hungary was under duress, it would have been wiser to say so openly. [p. 255]

We organized a real demonstration when Herbert and Olive Pell left the country. We were not only seeing off friends but also wanted to make clear our opinion that it was madness for Hungary to declare war on the United States. Large numbers of people turned up at the railway station, and we gave the departing American minister and his wife flowers and gifts. This made the real mood of leading Hungarian circles perfectly clear to everyone – and of course could not have escaped the attention of the Germans either.

After the war I corresponded with Ambassador Pell and his wife – they had made considerable efforts to find out where we were living – right up until their deaths. Olive Pell gave her paintings of my parents-in-law and of Pista and myself to my grandchildren.

Bill and Janet Schott stayed in Budapest a little longer to see to outstanding business; they lived in my father's house on Dísz Square. We carried on seeing them just as frequently, but at their request kept our meetings secret. They were good friends and remained so after the war.

Christmas of 1941 was approaching and gave us plenty to do, helping the various charitable organisations with their events. As part of her charitable work, Magdamama organized the giving out of Christmas presents in the Vigadó concert hall, and I naturally took part too, distributing Christmas presents of donated clothes to railway workers' children. On 19 December there was a beautiful and moving reception on Heroes' Square for the returning Budapest Rapid Advance Corps. Along with the Red Cross ladies I distributed cigarettes to the River Forces.

Despite all the worries, despite the war, that Christmas was a wonderful one for me, the first Christmas with my little son. He brightened up the season for the whole family, and it is impossible to put a value on the support his presence gave to his grandparents.

7

Pista Elected Vice-Regent
1942

From now on I can base my memoirs on my diary. This five-year diary went everywhere with me from 1942 to 1946. Without it I would not have found it easy to describe the years that followed.

On New Year's Day Magdamama and I attended mass in the Palace chapel. Afterwards Pista and I allowed ourselves the rare pleasure of going skiing on the Sváb-hegy, just the two of us. This brought back memories of when we had first met two years before, and we both enjoyed it very much.

News came of the terrible raids in the southern region, which had been made part of Yugoslavia after Trianon, but returned to Hungary in 1941; what is more, the news was very late in reaching the Regent. We could not be sure it was all true, but there were reports that a great many people had been killed in Újvidék. It was inexplicable, and we waited anxiously for more news.

Miklóspapa received another letter from Hitler urging Hungary to participate more vigorously in the war. In his reply, my father-in-law listed the limitations that prevented the Hungarian army from taking a more active part in the war; to sweeten the pill he also emphasized his readiness to cooperate.

Five days later, on 6 January, German Foreign Minister Ribbentrop arrived in Hungary on an official visit. That evening Pista and I went to the Engineers' Ball – where we made our entrance accompanied by a fanfare! But we could not stay long, because Pista was going to the hunt organized for Ribbentrop at Mezőhegyes. I accompanied Pista to the railway station and got on the train with him just for a few minutes, but I was so interested in what he was saying that I nearly ended up travelling with him. I went back to the Palace alone.

Magdamama and I had made a request to the government to help the needy; and after talking everything through with her I went to Györffy-Bengyel, the minister for food and agriculture, to request his help for our charitable work. The minister very kindly agreed to give us everything we wanted.

17 January was István's first birthday. He got a big teddy bear and a rocking horse, and so many presents arrived that we did not add any of our own. He had a birthday cake with one candle, and everyone took photos.

Over the next couple of weeks both Pista and I were very busy with official functions, including those in honour of the Italian foreign minister, Galeazzo Ciano, but we managed to arrange a short break to go to Tátrafüred in Czechoslovakia to spend the weekend together, skiing. What a blessing that I could safely leave István at home with Nanny Ila.

We drove through beautiful snow-covered mountains and arrived at the Grand Hotel in Tátrafüred at midnight. The next morning we drove across to Tátralomnic, where we spent the whole day skiing with friends in wonderful weather. In the evening all our friends came over from Lomnic and we danced in the hotel. I am grateful for having such a delightful day.

The next day was Sunday and I went to mass, and then we drove over to Lomnic again, through strong winds and heavy snow, for some more skiing. The plan was for Pista to go back to work and return the following weekend. He wanted me to stay, as he knew how much I was enjoying the skiing, and I could not resist this offer. But on the following Saturday, instead of Pista's expected return we received a telegram saying that he had flu and could not travel, which was a great disappointment. It also meant that I would have to go home by train on Monday.

But events took a different turn. Later that day I went over to Lomnic to ski with some friends, and during my fourth descent I suffered a bad fall. They had to take me down the slope on a sleigh, which was a very painful experience. An X-ray showed that my leg was fractured, and it was put in plaster. I consoled myself with the thought that I had enjoyed the skiing so much that it was worth it.

The next morning I was very happy when our good friend János Esterházy, whom we called Bibi, arrived. As the representative of the Hungarians in Slovakia he was able to obtain permission for me to telephone Budapest, to find out how István was and talk to Pista about what I should do next. He suggested that I should stay where I was and he would come and fetch me by car the following weekend. Everyone in the hotel was very kind. I was moved to a room on the ground floor and given a radio, and everyone brought flowers. I had a lot of visitors.

On Monday Bibi Esterházy came again and told me about the situation in Slovakia. Although during the previous year a law had been passed enforcing the deportation of the Jewish population, it had not yet been implemented. However, the situation was very tense, and he was doing everything he could to help the Jews escape to Hungary. He asked me to pass on his thanks to Pista, the Interior Minister and the Regent for their help in this matter. Bibi's courageous stand was admirable, but unfortunately it was also unique. After the war his sister Lujza Esterházy wrote:

In May 1941 Hitler instructed President Tiso to have all Jews deported from Slovakia to concentration camps in Germany. 'Slovakia must rid itself of Jews completely,' Hitler said; adding, 'If Slovakia refuses to do this, it can expect the worst from me.' The intimidated Slovak government immediately worked out a draft law ordering the deportation of Jews to labour camps in the Reich. The next day this draft was submitted to the Slovak national assembly for a vote. János, as the only Hungarian Party deputy, was present when the draft was read out. The day after the vote, Professor Sumbal and his first assistant came to me brandishing a newspaper and congratulated me on János's bravery. The report in the paper said: 'The Slovak national assembly voted unanimously to pass the law on the deportation of Jews with one exception: only the Hungarian Party deputy, János Esterházy, did not vote in favour.'

The Nazi press ranted and raved about him. The banner headline in the *Völkischer Beobachter* read: 'Only the Count didn't vote in favour.' During the day I found out that János, having announced that his Christian and democratic conscience categorically opposed the deportation of Jews, had walked out of the assembly chamber in protest.

The Hungarian population of the town was proud of its leader. One of them told me that Wehrmacht officers revolted by the Nazis' inhuman measures had expressed their deep admiration saying, 'János Esterházy is the bravest man in central Europe!'

The next day in Újlak, János told our mother and me about the events of the previous day. 'It was sickening,' he said, 'And the most dreadful thing about it was that the chamber was full of men in black cassocks, as most of the Slovak People's Party deputies are priests. They all voted in favour of this terrible law too, fearing Hitler's anger. This is how low Hitler's reign of terror could make those responsible for small nations sink, even priests – fearing that Slovakia might suffer the same fate as Poland.'

'Can't anything be done to save the Jews from deportation?' asked my mother.

'Of course it can,' said János, 'I want to help them escape to Hungary.'

'But how do you think that will work?' I asked, 'Now that the German army has passed through Hungary to attack Yugoslavia the Jews won't be safe from deportation there.'

'Yes they will,' he replied, 'Although the Germans have passed through Hungary, the Regent and the Hungarian government are protecting the Jews, just as they are protecting Polish refugees. Despite Hitler's fury Polish refugees and Hungarian Jews now live freely in Hungary.'[12]

To my delight Alice Cziráky arrived from Budapest bringing letters from Pista and Magdamama. In the evening my father, Papi, arrived from Elefánt, which made me very happy. He was extremely kind; I loved him so much.

The following days were easier because my leg gave me hardly any pain. I enjoyed being with Papi and we listened to the radio together and read. Lots of acquaintances came to visit, as well as diplomats from Budapest, and of course the doctors. It was strange being so far away from all the bad news. High up in the Tátra Mountains it was as if we were in a completely different world. But I was counting the days till Pista's arrival; I felt as if I had been away from home for too long.

Pista arrived from Budapest, and the next day he drove us home. I was afraid István would not recognize me, but the next morning he greeted me with great delight. Here again many people came to visit me because they had heard I'd broken my leg, but now I found it rather tiring. The names are written down in my diary and it makes me feel quite dizzy to read them. I was grateful for their sympathy, I liked them, but sometimes I wondered how many of them would have come if I had not been Mrs Horthy, here in the Palace. It was important for me to spend every free moment with István; we both needed it.

News of the events in Újvidék, which I mentioned earlier, worried and angered us a great deal. Those involved seemed to be trying to hush everything up, and had completely misled both the prime minister and the Regent. But these events were too dreadful and too shameful to cover up. Terrible atrocities had been carried out by the army and the police, originally against Yugoslav partisans, but then it had developed into a massacre. The officers in charge were all pro-Nazi sympathizers. The story of the inquiry is very complicated and I cannot go into all the details here, but the suspicion was that the action in Újvidék was intended to turn an anti-German atmosphere into ill feeling between Serbs and Hungarians.

When the Regent was informed at last, he ordered an immediate court martial. Later (by this time Kállay was prime minister), everything was brought out into the open and the trial eventually took place. In 1943 the judgment was shown to the Regent, as supreme commander of the armed forces, before being made public. Four men were sentenced to death and about twenty to several years' imprisonment. But then came the most contemptible thing: the Germans helped those under sentence of death to escape – the ringleaders were all officers of German origin who had carefully planned and then carried out the massacres. They fled in German military cars, and the German authorities were waiting for them at the border. When the Arrow Cross Party (the pro-German anti-Semitic fascist party led by Ferenc Szálasi) came to power in 1944, these men were given important positions.

The Election of the Vice-Regent

I have often read in newspapers and books that the Regent was 'ill' or 'seriously ill' at the time and that was why a deputy had to be chosen. This is pure fiction. The Regent was fit and well, and his decision to appoint a deputy was not the result of ill health. He had begun to feel the weight of the increasingly troubled times and was concerned about what might happen if he were to fall ill or be unable to continue working for any other reason. Since this eventuality was not covered by any existing regulations he proposed new legislation, sanctioning the election of a vice-regent; but, and this is important, he waived his right to submit nominations for the post.

The government submitted the proposed law to Parliament at the beginning of February, and it was accepted by the lower house on 10 February and by the upper house on 14 February, by a large majority in both cases. This legislation gave the Regent the power to nominate three candidates but, as I said, he did not exercise it. Section 11 stated explicitly that the existing regulations with regard to the election of a successor to the Regent would remain in force, so that the office of vice-regent would cease to exist as soon as a new regent took the oath of office.

Three possible candidates emerged, but two of these – Count István Bethlen and Count Gyula Károlyi – were the same age as the Regent. There is no doubt that the third, the Regent's son Stephen Horthy, was the most suitable person for the job: firstly because of his age, but also because of his character, his sensible political outlook, his qualifications, and the fact that he had the Regent's complete confidence. But as he was the Regent's son, it is very important to add that under the new law the vice-regent had no right of succession. For it may appear to those who do not know this that the Regent wanted to nominate his son to succeed him, despite the fact that he did not exercise his rights in this matter.

Miklós Kállay later wrote to me:

> The post of vice-regent had to be created and Stephen Horthy had to be the man to fill it, because he was the only person we could trust; and this was why the country was behind him. With his well-known anti-German opinions he would stand his ground in carrying out Hungary's foreign and domestic policies. He was the one who had to be elected because he was not committed to any particular path: whilst the Regent was bound by past events, even though they had been forced on him, the vice-regent as an individual could ignore them at any time. This was demonstrated by the fact that only Imrédy [the right-wing ex-prime minister] and the Arrow Cross people didn't attend the session of Parliament at which he was elected; and the German protests against him appeared in the Hungarian Arrow Cross papers, which they financed.

The joint session of the upper and lower houses of Parliament opened on 19 February, with 203 members of the upper house and 280 members of the lower house present – well in excess of the quorum.

Magdamama and I went to the Parliament building at 10.30 a.m. – I using two sticks because of my broken leg. The domed hall was packed when we arrived: ministers and diplomats with their wives, all the country's leading figures, Church dignitaries, nobles, deputies, etc. The session was opened at 11 a.m. by Count Bertalan Szécsényi, the president of the upper house, who announced that the only item on the agenda was the election of a vice-regent in accordance with law II of 1941; and since the Regent did not wish to exercise his right to make a recommendation, nominations could be made from the floor. He then called for nominations. Someone cried out, 'Long live Stephen Horthy!'

This was greeted by a huge storm of applause and cheering, which someone later described in these terms: 'There followed a roar of applause and cheering the like of which I have never heard. From the intensity of the applause and the voices leaping up like the flames of a fire I felt that what had occurred was almost an explosion of souls.' So Pista was elected vice-regent by acclamation. And the opposition? Those who stayed away in protest were the Habsburg archdukes, Béla Imrédy and his party, and the Arrow Cross party members.

A delegation then went to bring the Regent and Stephen Horthy, who came in his air force officer's uniform to take the oath. This event, which took place in perhaps the world's most beautiful Parliament Building, remains a very moving and unforgettable picture in my mind; and, if I might be permitted a personal comment, in my opinion the scene was centred on perhaps the world's most handsome and outstandingly remarkable man. As his wife I may be assumed to be subjective, but my opinion was shared by many others, and for this reason I would like to quote here an extract from an article written at the time by a well-known personality Sándor Márai, which was published in the *Képes Vasárnap*:

> The four-man delegation that is to summon Hungary's chosen vice-regent before the Parliament leaves the assembled members of the upper and lower houses and sets off on its official mission along the corridors of the Parliament Building. There is now a pause of a few minutes in the official proceedings. The members of the Parliament stay in the domed hall, and some of the spectators start walking around on the landing of the large staircase. The light sparkles on the marble walls of the red velvet-carpeted staircase, on every tenth step a guard stands in decorative uniform, holding a halberd; everyone waits. I go out of the journalists' area and stand next to one of the marble columns at the top of the stairs. Suddenly I catch sight of vitéz Stephen Horthy, who has just arrived from one of the rooms in the upper house with the delegation of four dark-suited gentlemen and is waiting here in the entrance hall for the moment of legal ceremony when he will step up in front of the members of Parliament and take his oath. A few minutes separate him from this moment. The prime minister has left the Parliament Building to bring the Regent, who will sign the law on the election of the vice-regent after the oath has been taken. ...

In these few minutes before he steps into the domed hall to take the oath before the Regent and before Parliament, the thirty-eight year old man is pale. This pallor endears him to us. Even at this moment his legendary politeness prompts him to chat willingly with his companions and answer their questions, but again and again his eyes seek out the entrance hall, where the Regent and the prime minister will soon arrive, passing between the lines of halberdiers. He also looks towards the domed hall, where a soft murmur, the quiet conversation of several hundred people gathered in the large hall, indicates that they are waiting and watching. This is the greatest moment of his life. ...

The smile flashing onto and quickly disappearing from his face is familiar to everyone in the country: it is his mother's smile. ...

He radiates the politeness, modesty and quiet confidence of the Hungarian nobility. But there is more in the flash of his eyes than modesty: his is the glance of personal courage, of self-awareness and readiness to act. ... He is one of the new generation: he is an engineer, a specialist, a pilot; he has spent years in factories in Hungary and overseas as an ordinary worker; as an engineer he knows the life, the worries, and the desires of the working classes in a way that few of his class do ...

To lead a community is always to be lonely. Everything which, and everyone who is still of primary importance in his life will step back a shade and become paler for him in a few minutes, when he has taken the oath. ... He will now have to leave an intimate personal and friendly familiarity and step into the particular solitude of his new role, which even the greatest can only endure with great strength of character. It is apparent from his behaviour that he knows this. ... He looks around, searching for one face he really knows among the many he half knows. He examines the hundreds of faces with narrowed eyes, and when he catches sight of his mother, the seriousness and tension in the young man's face eases for a moment and becomes softer and more boyish. Now an officer of the Regent, wearing a morning coat, steps up to him, bows deeply and tells him something. Pista Horthy

> draws a gloved hand across his forehead, before drawing himself up to his full height, and the next moment His Highness vitéz Stephen Horthy, vice-regent of Hungary, steps into the room, where he is met by the acclaim of the nation. At this moment a happy, colourful, hard-working, interesting, and varied youth has come to an end; only the shadow of his work follows him into the bright room where he takes the oath, swearing to devote his life and all his abilities to the service of his country.

After the vote in Parliament we had lunch with my parents-in-law, and discussed the event. They also invited us to dinner and to play bridge in the evening, as there were many things that needed to be discussed.

When we got back to our apartment, Pista stood in the middle of the room, staring straight ahead with such an infinitely sad expression that my heart sank. What a responsibility he had taken on, and how dark the future seemed. I knew what it meant to him to be unable to continue his work as an engineer. What could I do to reassure him and cheer him up? Straight away I – who never drank alcohol of any kind – poured a drink into two small glasses and told Pista that from now on I would address him informally.[13] This was something he had always wanted me to do: he had always addressed me informally, but I was more used to the formal address and had carried on using it to him. I gave him his drink and told him that the toast was 'to brotherhood'. He smiled. I could see he was pleased that I had shared his feelings and had let him know that I would be with him whatever happened. But I also realized that he was completely alone with this enormous responsibility, and any part I could play would be extremely small. All I could do to help him was never to hold him back or restrain him in any way, but to be with him and give him my full support.

Miklóspapa wrote in his memoirs:

> Numerous congratulatory messages arrived from Hungary and from our allies, and above all from Italy. Only Germany sent no official message. Goebbels had already written in his diary on 4 February that my son becoming vice-regent was 'very unfortunate' because the boy was 'even more pro-Jew than his father.' He made an even nastier entry on the same subject on 20 February, adding, 'but we won't take a stand on this. Now is not the time to deal with such 'delicate' matters. We have to leave some things to be dealt with after the war.' The implication is perfectly clear. My

son had from the start of the war indeed considered the Allies' superiority in both men and equipment to be so great that Germany had no chance of winning, and those who elected him were well aware of his opinion. One of our friends happened to have an opportunity to look into the files of the Reichssicherheitshauptamt [the security service headquarters], and told me that very copious notes on my son had been collected there.
[pp. 261–62]

The foreign press also mentioned the election. The Swiss paper *Baseler Nachrichten* pointed out that 'considering that the Regent has served in this onerous position for a long time, during which he has barely allowed himself any rest, and considering the particular demands of these times, it appeared necessary to free the Regent of at least some of the burdens of his office.' The *Neue Züricher Zeitung* highlighted the fact that both traditions and the existing laws had been respected, which accorded completely with the Hungarians' sense of justice and with the nation's sense of historic tradition. The papers in Pozsony carried detailed accounts of the election, with photos and biographical details of Stephen Horthy; and in Britain the *Times* even carried the text of the oath sworn by the vice-regent.

Pista was given a very warm send-off when he left MÁV and moved to the vice-regent's office in the Palace. At the same time, everyone was surprised when Pista proposed Kálmán Imrédy as his successor at the State Railways. The reason for their surprise was that Kálmán Imrédy's younger brother Béla, who after serving as prime minister had set up the extreme right-wing opposition Hungarian Renewal Party, was very hostile to Pista and had openly opposed his election as vice-regent.

I too received a very moving send-off from the National Association of Hungarian Women when I stepped down as the president of the Railway Section, and not just from those ladies but from the many others who came too. I carried on going every week to their meetings to do sewing and other jobs. Margit Imrédy took over from me as president. We got on very well and I was happy to be able to help her.

Pista occupied his new office in the Palace on 3 March, with a completely different range of duties. In the following weeks he deputized for the Regent on several occasions. He paid official visits to the prime minister, to the primate of Hungary in Esztergom, and attended the papal coronation mass in the Matthias Church. He also received diplomats and politicians and carried out inspections and other representative duties, freeing his father from a great deal of work.

I was with him at the 15 March celebration, (commemorating the start of the 1848 War of Independence) when he handed over his gift of a flag to a delegation from the Levente organisation. Similar to the Scouts, the Levente was a movement directed by the state for the girls and boys of Hungary. He also inspected troops, visiting each unit of the army in turn. Deputizing for the Regent he flew to Kassa to dedicate the standard presented to the units stationed there, and was greeted with great enthusiasm by the population of the city. He inspected the guard of honour and laid a wreath on the tomb of Prince Ferenc Rákóczi in the cathedral. (Rákóczi had led an unsuccessful Hungarian revolt against the Habsburg supremacy in 1703.)

At Easter he made an appeal to the Hungarian youth with the following slogan: 'We were a nation of horsemen – we will be a nation of aviators!'

Prime Minister Kállay described this period in a letter he wrote in 1947: 'From his election until he went into battle, Stephen served as deputy head of state in such a way as to demonstrate how well suited he was to the task, justifying the nation's confidence in him.'

Most importantly, from then on it was Pista's reports that carried the greatest weight with the Regent – and there was no more need for my diplomacy. This was now his official duty, and I hoped that whenever necessary he would be able to convince his father of the true facts. Because Pista lived 'outside' and was in contact with all kinds of people as well as with the technical world, his views were certain to differ at times from his father's, who for many years had been surrounded by people who 'reported' to him and whose reports were often 'conditioned'. Luckily there were also those like Bethlen, and formerly Teleki, who honestly pointed out the true situation to him.

On 7 March the Regent recommended that Prime Minister Bárdossy should resign, because he was very disappointed with his performance. I know that many people have subsequently implied that the reason for Bárdossy's departure was my father-in-law's dissatisfaction with his behaviour in connection with the election of the vice-regent. This assessment is wrong; during our family conversations no objections to Bárdossy were raised. Miklós Kállay also said nothing of this in his memoirs, though he gave a very detailed and precise account of the reasons for Bárdossy's departure.

Bárdossy had been pro-British and anti-Nazi when he took office, but his position seemed to have gone to his head, because as time went on his political ambitions led him increasingly towards a pro-German attitude. In my opinion his greatest mistake was to declare war on Russia, having allowed himself to be influenced by the army chief of staff and by civil servants who wanted us at all costs to fight alongside the Germans.

It was clear it was the Bárdossy government that had swept us into the war: the declaration of war on Russia and on America, the deployment of forces to the Russian front, and our commitment to the anti-Comintern alliance had all been the result of Bárdossy's policies. In addition, on each occasion he had presented the Regent and Parliament with a *fait accompli*. By dismissing him the Regent prevented Hungary from advancing in this dangerous direction; but another important reason for Bárdossy's dismissal was that he wanted to go even further with regard to anti-Jewish laws.

On 9 March the Regent asked Miklós Kállay to form a government. Both Miklóspapa and Pista thought that not only was Kállay the most suitable person for the job, but that there was nobody they could trust more. They were both very pleased when he accepted the post.

In his memoirs Kállay gives a detailed account of his conversations with Miklóspapa, and the following extracts will shed some light on the situation:

> ... after our meeting, the Regent summoned me almost daily and tried to convince me that it was my duty to take on the job. ... finally I gave in. When I told him my decision he was moved almost to tears and hugged me; this showed just how worried he was about the situation we were in ...
>
> After this I worked out my programme. In essence, this consisted of protecting, maintaining and, where it has been lost, regaining the country's internal and external autonomy and independence. This was how I outlined my plan to the Regent: with the Germans we would conduct a cautious but consistently Hungarian policy, exercising the utmost intellectual and moral resistance; economically we would make only such concessions as were absolutely necessary. Nevertheless we would be careful not to provoke an invasion of Hungary by the Germans, because that might mean the end for us, whether we resisted or not ... On the other hand, if the Allies won – which could be taken for granted – then a country and a government which had attempted to conduct a relatively autonomous foreign policy at least with the neutral countries, and had not carried out crimes against the world moral order and against humanity as all the east European countries – with the exception of Finland – had, such a country and such a government – or rather such a nation – would certainly emerge from the war with the sympathy, the

respect, perhaps even the gratitude of the world's peoples ...

After the war we, together with Poland, Finland and Serbia, had to be one of those countries which had stood up to the aggressive conqueror and fought for their autonomy and independence. However, the way to achieve this was not, as the example of Poland and Serbia had shown, by armed resistance, which resulted in rapid defeat and complete subjugation, but rather by firm, persistent and consistent opposition. The effectiveness of this passive but unyielding resistance would be proved – I hoped – by the fact that we would be the only country in central Europe and the Balkans that had been able to maintain the values of its European culture, its civilisation and its humanity, even during the war ...

One of our most important national aims was to get out of the war as soon as possible. Unfortunately we had already promised the Germans that we would send an army to the Russian front and it was not possible for us to withdraw this promise, but I was determined that after this we would not provide a single soldier. I wanted to equip a new army here in Hungary, so that it would be available when we needed it.

We could only preserve the nation's honour and the traditional humanitarian values it espoused by revoking the regulations brought against the Jews and by conducting an entirely new policy towards the other ethnic minorities.[14]

A few months after Pista took up his post, his work was interrupted by his decision to volunteer as a fighter pilot on the front line. He wanted to see the situation there for himself. This was a fundamental turning point in our lives, which now took a completely different direction.

Pista took his duties as vice-regent very seriously, and decided as early as February that he would go to the front. He wanted to experience for himself the battles in Russia, the conditions in which the army was fighting, and the extent of Nazi influence. In this way he felt he would be able to take a more effective stand against the generals who were under German influence, because until then he'd had no experience of active service.

'In order to do my job well, I have to go out to the front and get to know the army. When I have been in active service for two months, then I can review the situation,' he said. This was the main reason for his decision and not – as some people said – that he was not able to ignore the defamatory propaganda leaflets distributed by the Arrow Cross party, according to which he had not fought in the war because he was a coward. He was understandably outraged by the Arrow Cross party's libel, and did not want people to be able to accuse him of now using his position as vice-regent to escape from military service, but it was not the determining reason.

Of course many people opposed his resolve to join up, saying that the vice-regent had been elected to help the Regent and not to risk his life at the front. Pista's response to that was that there had not been a vice-regent before, and now there just would not be one for two months while he gained experience at the front. The government did not approve of this decision either, but were unable to take any action because the Regent had not opposed it. Miklóspapa told me that he himself would have done the same in Pista's place, and so he could not dissuade him.

8

Nursing
Pista on Active Service

At the end of February the plaster came off my leg at last. It was a great relief and also important for me to be fully active again, because I had applied to join a voluntary nursing course which was due to start shortly. So it was that at the beginning of March 1942, my friend Ilona Andrássy and I went for the first time to the Red Cross to start our community nursing training. I was pleased that Ilona and I could be together. Later on, four of us, Alice Cziráky, Mady Waldbott, Ilona Andrássy and I, were almost always together and became very good friends.

Many people attended this first meeting, and the national head nurse, Baroness Gizella Apor, gave that first lecture. She was very strict with us. She needed to be, because some people might have thought they were there to enjoy themselves. Aunt Gizi (as I called her in deference to her age) said that anyone who did not like it had better leave straight away, because discipline was of fundamental importance in nursing. She called some students out and told them to wipe off their lipstick, because nurses were not allowed to wear make-up or perfume. Some removed their lipstick without a word and returned to their seats, but others protested and walked out indignantly – and better so.

I was in a difficult situation because I had never attended school, and had never had to sit at a desk and stand up to answer questions. At first I panicked, as I did not find it easy, but I soon got the hang of things. It was a three-month course; I got through the first exam successfully, and then we started a more advanced work in the military hospital.

Although all four of us were Countesses by birth, and as wife of the vice-regent I now had the title of Serene Highness, I was happy that we were not given any privileges: fortunately right from the first day everyone called me 'Sister Ily'. (A friend asked me what it felt like to have the title 'Her Serene Highness'. At first I just stared at her, baffled, not knowing what to say. To me these titles were just words. Looking back, I can see what a good thing it was that the title and compliments I received at this time in my life did not affect me, either when I received them or when they came to an end. I realized this three years later, when we had lost everything and nobody paid any attention to us on the street: it did not change either me or my mother-in-law – on the contrary, we felt relaxed, somehow even liberated.)

Like all the other student nurses we began by mopping up the wards and corridors. I think I was promoted sooner than was customary, but would like to think that I earned it because of the standard of my work.

Before going in to the first operation we were to watch, we were warned to go out if we felt ill. After a while I started to feel sick and hurried out to find Ilona already there breathing deeply. We had a good laugh. Interestingly, after that I never felt ill again: it did not happen while I was working because I was so absorbed with the job in hand that I could not pay attention to anything else. Surgery was definitely what interested me most. I was not drawn to general medicine and felt that I would not be very good at it.

We started work early. On weekdays I worked at the Jurányi Street military hospital from 6.45 a.m. until 2 p.m. and at first had the afternoons off, so there was time to do things at home. I sometimes even had time to go gliding. I could never spend enough time with István, but the times I was together with him and the family in the evenings were the best of all.

We were called upon to do more and more work. There were days when we had four hours of theory in the morning and again in the afternoon, followed by lectures until 9 p.m. From there we went straight on to night duty at the hospital. There were usually three of us on night duty. We got together twice during the night, at 10 p.m. and again at 1 a.m. for some refreshments. I could cope quite well with staying awake, but the difficult period was always around four o'clock, when time suddenly seemed to drag terribly for the three hours until our shift ended at 7 a.m.

On 3 April 1942 Pista again spoke on the radio to the young people of Hungary, calling on Hungarian youth to serve Hungarian aviation. As István Jánosy wrote later: 'This appeal received a huge response. Young people besieged the aviation authorities, and queued up outside the vice-regent's secretariat, all wanting to speak to him.'[15]

On 27 April, our second wedding anniversary, Pista gave me a small diamond heart for my bracelet with a picture of István inside. I managed to keep it safe and still have it now, fifty years later. The same day, Prime Minister Miklós Kállay and his wife Helen came to introduce their son Kristóf's fiancée, Vera Vásárhelyi. I immediately took a liking to her – no wonder, as she was a close relative of Magdamama. The engagement was officially announced at a dinner at the prime minister's residence. It was a lovely party – the kind of party I was not destined to have again, because the following morning, 1 May, Pista joined the air force as a reserve flight lieutenant, based at Szolnok, from where he would later go out to the Russian front.

I do not know who suggested that he should go to the front as a general to visit all the units – but understandably Pista was not prepared to do that, because how could he, as a flight lieutenant promoted to the rank of general, stand face to face with a general who had won his promotion step by step? So he wanted to go out to a posting appropriate to his rank of flight lieutenant, which also suited his modest personality and unwillingness to tolerate any special favours. Just as in the Ford factory he had started on the factory floor and worked his way up to being an engineer, so now he wanted to start experiencing life at the front serving as an ordinary soldier.

However, someone should have been in charge of the vice-regent's security. Who should have been responsible for that? The government or the army? Or both? I thought this role would be taken on by Major General László Szabó, who had been appointed to serve as the vice-regent's 'military and political advisor.' When Pista was told of this appointment he told me – in our apartment in the Palace – that he was not at all pleased with their choice of an officer who was a great fan of Mussolini, and with whom he did not sympathize. I said he should tell his father about this and ask him to arrange for someone else to be chosen, but Pista was unwilling to do so because László Szabó had already been appointed. To my knowledge Pista never showed his dislike of him, and never mentioned it to anyone else.

We now know that László Szabó was not the right person for the job. He took very little trouble over Pista's security, and on 9 August even left his designated post – and his wooden hut, which was much more comfortable than the vice-regent's tent – to take over command of the Seventh Light Division, which was better for his army career. Nobody was appointed in his place.

Much later I read an article in the *Keresztény Élet* (Christian Life) weekly entitled 'How did István Horthy crash?' written by Gy. F. Simon. The writer of the article says he spoke to eyewitnesses, who wrote down what they had to say, endorsed by their signature. The article contained nothing new to me, but I read and re-read several times with amazement the last paragraph on Major General Szabó:

I found this news in the *Képes Vasárnap* 1944, July 11, written at the time of the German occupation: 'Major General vitéz László Szabó was nominated by the Regent as head of the Hungarian Legation to the Socialist Republic of Italy.'

Two weeks later, on 25 July 1944, Ferenc Szálasi (leader of the Hungarian National Socialist Party and later head of state under the German Occupation) already wrote in his diary that he went to see Edmund Veesenmayer, German ambassador in Budapest, and made suggestions for a government: Minister of Foreign Affaires: László Szabó, our present minister in Italy.

How justified were Pista's premonitions and his distrust of the man.

My own inner presentiments and fears about Pista's going to the front were a little confused at first, and I just put my trust in the luck Pista had enjoyed in his hazardous life so far. It was only later, when I too was on my way to Russia, that this confused feeling left me completely. I know that at the time I could not believe anything would happen to Pista. The feeling of security I had always had when I was with him meant I did not even consider that possibility seriously.

While he was in Szolnok preparing for his service at the front, I went to meet Pista for an official engagement in Nagyvárad, travelling from Budapest by train with his personal staff and advisers. At Szolnok Pista joined us, and we arrived at Nagyvárad the following morning. Our first stop was at the Artillery Cadet School. There was a flag dedication ceremony followed by a banquet. Then while Pista inspected the cadets I was given a tour of the city, which was very enjoyable. We had tea with Lord Lieutenant Hlatky, and after a festive general meeting we boarded the train, I to return home, and Pista to return to the quarters he and his valet Gyuri had in Szolnok.

Back in Budapest there was much to keep me occupied. On 9 May the usual Children's Day collection organized by the Child Protection League took place. Not many people knew that it was my grandfather, Leopold Edelsheim Gyulai, who had founded this excellent institution. Magdamama and I spent the morning helping at the Red Cross table and collection box, and I also visited the MÁV collecting centre.

15 May was the twenty-fifth anniversary of the battle of Otranto. I watched the parade, patrol-boats and so on, from the deck of the *Zsófia* with my parents-in-law, before returning for an official luncheon at the Palace.

This celebration had particular significance. During the First World

War, Miklós Horthy, at that time the imperial chamberlain and navy captain, was in command of the battle cruiser *S.M.S. Novara*. It was on this ship that he fought several victorious actions against the combined British, French and Italian fleet. His heroic feats in these battles elevated him to the position of one of history's world-renowned heroes. He also earned the respect of enemy forces for his determination to save sailors whose vessels had been sunk. On one occasion, although aware of the approach of an overwhelmingly large hostile fleet, the captain spent several hours organizing the rescue of eighty-two seamen from enemy ships that had been destroyed in battle. Admiral Kerr, the commander of the British fleet, reported his behaviour as being 'exceptionally polite and fully in keeping with the respected traditions of chivalry at sea'.

On 14 and 15 May 1917, the then Captain Horthy spearheaded the attack to break through the extensive Allied blockade of the straits of Otranto, a defence put up to stop the passage of the German submarines. He used various tactics, including – for the first time in the history of naval warfare – creating a smokescreen in order to help him come within range to fire on the enemy. The outcome, which on paper should have been a clear-cut Allied victory, was that the Otranto blockade was destroyed and the straits freed for the passage of submarines for months afterwards. During the battle the *Novara* sustained heavy damage, and Miklós Horthy was gravely wounded. He refused morphine, because despite being in severe pain he wanted to continue in command of the battle from his stretcher, and the stokers came up on deck to bring cigarettes to their semi-conscious commander, stroking his face with their sooty hands.

For this achievement Miklós Horthy received the monarchy's highest honour, the Knight Cross of the Order of Maria Theresa; and in March 1918, at the end of the war, he was appointed commander of the Austro-Hungarian navy.

Pista came back from Szolnok whenever he could, so we were able to spend time together: he played polo, and we watched the King's Cup horse race with my parents-in-law. Once he flew back just for a Sunday and we were able to watch an international match between Hungary and Germany – which ended in a 3–3 draw.

I was also progressing well with my gliding lessons with Tibor Szilas on the Cimbora glider. I really enjoyed gliding; by then I could even do a corkscrew, which was quite easy: after banking, one just had to straighten the hand and foot controls and then pull the plane back up into a straight line.

On 28 May I took my final examination in military hospital no. 205. The examining committee consisted of three doctors, a general, the president of the Red Cross, and of course head nurse Gizella Apor. I was very relieved because the examination went well. Magdamama came to the swearing-in ceremony that followed, and pinned on our medals. In the evening there was a dinner at the Gellért Hotel for both the students and the examiners.

Two days later, Magdamama and I had to get up before six o'clock because I was picking up three patients to take them to the pilgrimage site of Mária Remete, and Magdamama was coming too. There was a beautiful outdoor mass. It was very moving and sad to see all the sick people. A conversation I had with an eighteen-year-old young man lying on a stretcher made a deep impression on me. He was completely paralysed by polio; he had been an energetic sportsman, and now he could only move his head. Despite this, he told me, his face radiant with joy, that he felt privileged to have been chosen to suffer for others. He dedicated all his suffering to the Virgin Mary for those who were suffering even more than him. What faith and strength of character he radiated. I think only those who know what suffering is are able to accept the will of the Almighty to such a degree. Why is it mostly when we suffer or when we want something that we turn to God? We ought to be able to achieve such acceptance and deep love without illness or suffering. But how useful illness can be if it brings us closer to God.

My duties in the hospital were varied. I carried on nursing, but increasingly I was assigned to the operating theatre, especially after the exam. By May I was already working in the operating theatre as instrumentalist, anaesthetist or assistant to the surgeon. I eventually reached the stage of assisting in a major operation – a resection of the stomach, which took three hours. Anaesthetizing patients was something I really did not like to do. Whenever I had been anaesthetized I'd had a concern that I would not come out of it, so when I was giving anaesthetic I had an uncomfortable feeling that the patient might possibly die on me. But of course I did not have a choice and could not even mention it; I just had to try not to think about it. I found that what helped me most was saying a prayer.

One day, after spending the morning working in the hospital, I put on a proper nurse's uniform for the first time – until then we had worn white overalls and nurses veils – and with Aunt Gizi Apor went to officiate at the voluntary nurses' examination. Luckily the nurses who were being examined by me could not hear my heart beating. It was due to nervousness of course, because I was worried about conducting the examination well. But my guardian angel must have been there behind me because everything went very smoothly.

I was photographed in my nurse's uniform: the photo was to be put on a postage stamp. I could not believe it and wondered what they would think of next. The other nurses were not put on stamps, though most of them worked harder than me.

At the beginning of June we took the train with my parents-in-law to Kenderes, where they were going to stay for about three weeks, and where I hoped to spend as much time with them as I could. As soon as we arrived we took István for a walk around the garden. Pista also arrived from Szolnok, but he had to go back the same evening. István really enjoyed his new surroundings – perhaps he could sense that here we all felt at home.

We lived a completely different life in Kenderes: playing tennis, riding, doing embroidery with Magdamama. We also saw much more of Pista. Because Szolnok was less than 40 kilometres away he could spend all his free time with us. We mostly played tennis with Miklóspapa and Gerlóczy, his aide-de-camp on duty here, while Magdamama and István enjoyed watching us. I was a very mediocre player without much talent for ball games, but I thoroughly enjoyed our rides with Miklóspapa, Gerlóczy accompanying us – or rather accompanying the Regent.

The previous year my sister Sya had married Józsi (Count József Esterházy), whom we all liked very much. I was very pleased that after her unhappy first marriage and divorce, Sya had found a wonderful person she could spend her life with. This marriage resulted in the birth of my godson Pál, on 7 June. I went every day to admire the baby and have long chats with Sya. Pista came in one day, straight from Szolnok, and we had a very pleasant dinner with Sya and Józsi. I wished I could have another baby – I wanted a girl who would be like Magdamama.

The next day Pista had a lot to do in Budapest. I went off to take my grade B test in gliding. I had not mentioned this to Pista because I wanted to surprise him. I did the test from Hármashatár Mountain, flying down from the top of the hill. My teacher Tibor Szilas allowed me to take the grade C test straight afterwards: this involved gliding alone for fifteen minutes. I cannot describe the pleasure it gave me to be gliding in figures of eight on my own for the first time. Unbeknown to me, Pista was involved in some inspection at the bottom of the hill and noticed the glider overhead. When he asked who was gliding so well, they made enquiries and discovered that it was none other than his wife. When I landed he was there, waiting for me, and hugged and congratulated me. That was a happy moment I will treasure forever.

News came of the war in North Africa, and of the Germans' victorious advances, but we did not know what to believe, as all we ever heard about were victorious advances.

Another year had passed and once again it was 18 June, Miklóspapa's seventy-fourth birthday. In accordance with his wishes, the day was once again spent at Kenderes. We went to mass in the morning, which Pista also attended, and the people of Kenderes turned out to greet their landlord.

Jagow, the German ambassador, came to visit with his wife. Frau Jagow astonished us with her statement that she would like to have at least six children 'because that's what the Führer wants.' Was that a reason to have children? On the other hand, if every German woman thought similarly, then there would be plenty of Germans, or rather Nazis. Pista came over from Szolnok to join us for dinner, and only then did the guests leave. We'd had enough of them, but it seemed that Hitler wanted lots of Jagows.

The following weekend, with the wives of the MÁV officials, we took a special train to Szabadka to attend the ceremonial opening of a new railway establishment. We were moved by the welcome we received in Transylvania: a carriage drawn by five horses, and masses of flowers. The ceremony took place, followed by a gala performance. I stayed with Lord Lieutenant Reök and his wife, who looked after me with touching kindness. In the evening a torch-lit procession came and serenaded us. It made me think that with such enthusiastic people great successes could be achieved, as long as the war did not ruin everything. The next day was Sunday and I went to the convent for mass. Afterwards we attended meetings, had a tour of the city, then a trip to Palics spa for tea and a walk. We enjoyed the journey back to Budapest on the special train, discussing events and playing bridge. The whole trip was a memorable experience.

The next morning of course I was back in at work at the hospital.

On the anniversary of Paulette's death, her husband Gyula and I flew down to Kenderes. When we landed at the small airfield I was delighted to see my parents-in-law and István waiting for us. Pista came over from Szolnok for the memorial mass and stayed with us all day. And as it was Friday, he came back the next day to spend the weekend with us. We discovered two carp in the swimming pool, and had a great carp hunt equipped with the sub-aqua gear we had bought in Italy. Afterwards we had a doubles tennis tournament in which Pista and I played together – and won! That night Pista and I had a long walk and talked in beautiful moonlight.

It's only now that I can really appreciate that weekend we spent together at Kenderes, because on the Monday we had to say goodbye. There was a last singles tennis tournament in the morning and then I helped Pista pack. We said goodbye to him, and he left for Szolnok and then the Russian front.

Later that day I flew back to Budapest, because the following day I was leaving early with the Women's Railway Section on a special train for Keszthely, to open a boarding school for railway workers' children. I stayed on in Keszthely for a day in the beautiful Festetich castle with Mia Festetich, whose little son György was born in the Siesta sanatorium at the same time as my István. The weather was so good that we bathed in the lake.

But that was not why I particularly remember that 1 July. It was because that was the day Pista left for Russia. In my thoughts I accompanied him, wondering what kind of scenery he was flying over and what was awaiting him at the front.

I went to Kenderes for the weekend to be with István. We bathed and played, and after dinner I was driven to Szolnok, where I boarded a train and arrived in Budapest at midnight. The apartment was deserted: I had rarely felt so lonely in the middle of the Royal Palace as I did then.

A train carrying wounded men arrived and I went as a Red Cross nurse to meet it. It moved me deeply, how happy these soldiers were to have come home, wounded though they were. They would need a lot of help to pick up the pieces of their lives.

The examination sessions for volunteer nurses continued; the only unpleasant thing about it being that László Endre, the deputy lord lieutenant, always accompanied me. He gave me an unpleasant feeling even though he always behaved correctly, and later I heard from others that he hated Jews. Of course he could accompany me officially by reason of his post, so I did not know how I could dissuade him. He made a speech every time, and although he did not speak for long and did not say anything objectionable, it did not have a lot to do with the nursing examinations. At least if he had said something to which I could object I would have had a reason to ask that only members of the Red Cross attend the examinations. I found his presence disagreeable.

Pista sent a much welcomed letter from Russia, letting me know what he needed there. Gyuszi Tost was to go out to the front to see him soon, and I managed to get everything he required in good time.

I spent four days, including Magdamama's name-day, at Kenderes, which was very refreshing. I liked nothing better after all the work in the city than to be with István and ride out on the estate with Miklóspapa to look at the threshing or the stud farm. I remember these rides with great pleasure; after all, I grew up in the country and felt at home going around the estate on horseback, looking at the crops and talking to the people. The force of life comes from the arable soil, and what wonderful fields those were!

Gyuszi Tost arrived back from the Russian front. He brought a letter and told me in detail about Pista. I was interested to hear how he and

Gyuri were getting on there. In general Pista was enjoying the flying, but he had a very pessimistic view of the situation. He had flown several sorties, and Tost thought he should not stay there any longer because he was exposed to too much danger.

A situation arose where there were not enough professional nurses out at the front but volunteer nurses were not allowed to go. Gizi Apor thought the solution would be for me, as a volunteer nurse, to ask permission to go to the front. They would not be able to refuse me, and then they would have to allow other volunteer nurses to serve at the front too. We tried it, and I had no trouble obtaining permission to go out to the front with a hospital train, on condition that I wore the blue uniform of a professional nurse so that my different uniform would not be conspicuous. I was told that Aunt Gizi and I might leave soon.

The days before I left went by much too fast. There was a lot of work in the hospital, and I should have rested when I got home but did not always manage it. For instance, one afternoon I had to be at the station to meet over two hundred wounded men arriving from the front.

On 1 August Magdamama and Miklóspapa took István by train to Gödöllő, which had been the summer residence of the Hungarian Royal family since 1867. The Regent spent a month each year in the palace in order to maintain it. I joined them for the weekend, in order to spend as much time with István as I could.

The news from all sides was very worrying. We listened to a radio broadcast by Pista, transmitted directly from the front. In my opinion the interview was not conducted very well. Suddenly it was somehow difficult for me to understand what was happening to us: destiny had brought us together and now we could not live a normal life. I knew that all the members of the family did what was expected of them according to their best judgment and I knew that this was our duty, but so many things were happening to me that I found it difficult to understand the reasons.

Here we were in this wonderfully beautiful palace at Gödöllő. Surrounded by so much beauty I found it hard to comprehend that we had been forced into a dreadful war; that Pista was speaking from the front, where soldiers were facing each other with the intention of killing one another; and that soon I'd be there too. I wondered if we would wake up from all this one day and be able to live like normal people.

All this made me look deep inside myself and prepare for every eventuality, so that I would not be caught off guard. During those few days Miklóspapa and Magdamama were so kind to me that I did not know how I had deserved such kindness and love, and wondered whether I would ever be able to repay them – yet they said they were grateful to me … .

Two days later I went to Slovakia, to see my parents in Elefánt; Papi wanted to see me before I went to the front. They had asked Filippo Anfuso, the Italian ambassador, to drive me there, and he was kind enough to oblige. I hoped they were not thinking they might be seeing me for the last time because I would be working in a hospital at the front. To the best of my knowledge I was not going to be in any danger.

What joy it was to be back in Elefánt. I was very happy to see our old butler Uncle Fritz, and Uncle Jóska the coachman, and I hugged everyone. My sister Éva and her children Mária and Péter were there too. We went out into the forest on the 'long carriage'. I drove the horses like in the old days and we went like the wind, sometimes going off the tracks, and we felt as if we were children again. In the evening we played poker and had fun with Anfuso – I had not realized he was so amusing and such good company, a typical Italian. We all laughed a lot, but Papi was the best, he told jokes so well; it was a wonderful evening. When we finally went to bed I could not stop thinking: this was another world again. The next day was Sunday and we went to mass, then celebrated Ellamami's birthday and bathed in the small swimming pool. Such vivid and moving memories.

We drove back to Budapest and then straight to Gödöllő, where I spent my last morning with István before I had to leave. That evening I started packing. There was a lot to organize before such a big journey; I did not even know how long I was going to be away – were we really leaving the next day?

9

At the Russian Front
Pista's Death

On the morning of 11 August, Magdamama and I went to the Western Railway Station to see the hospital train on which I was going to travel to Russia. Miklóspapa and Magdamama had lunch with me before they left for a tour of Western Hungary, and several people flocked into the palace to say goodbye. At 5.45 p.m. I left in the train with Gizi Apor and several other professional nurses. Many people came to the station to see us off; I even received a farewell telegram at the border station Galánta.

We awoke the next morning at the Slovak-Polish border, and spent most of the day making bandages. It kept us busy; and as we had to make lots of them, we set to work with a will. The train passed through Oderberg and Auschwitz; we admired the scenery. We had no idea that we were passing the place where the most monstrous genocide planned and carried out by man in the history of the world was taking place.

After supper some of us played bridge before retiring to bed; the train continued on its way. The second day passed much like the first: we made bandages and rested, and in the evening we played bridge and talked. As we passed through Jaros³aw and Przemys³ we saw the first signs of bombing raids that had taken place.

We were awakened at 6.30 a.m. on the third day, when the train made a stop for a few hours in Lemberg. We all drove into the town. What I saw there had a terrible impact on me. German soldiers were taking the Jews – including women and children – out of the town, and each group was led by a Jew wearing a yellow star. When I asked about the leader I was told that, in return for revealing where Jews were living or hiding, those people were not going to be deported. I found it hard to believe, even though I saw it with my own eyes.

Deputy Kunder and two others deputies, Erős and Pászthói, were with us on the train. All three seemed to be right-wingers. They returned to the train very downcast – I think their eyes had been opened. They commented that they did not know this was going on. There were many elegant mansions in Lemberg in which well-to-do families must have lived, but now they seemed abandoned, as if nobody lived in them any more. The train set off again at 1 p.m. The atmosphere was one of extreme depression, and nobody asked to play bridge; everyone went to bed early. On the fourth day a train carrying Ukrainian prisoners stopped next to ours, and everyone took photos of it. We made bandages.

At 10 p.m. on 15 August we arrived in Kiev. Getting off the train in the darkened station, I suddenly found myself face to face with Pista. It was wonderful to meet again, and I was welcomed with a bouquet. The war correspondents were filming and taking photos, their cameras kept flashing in the darkness, which disturbed me a little. On the other hand it is thanks to them that I have a photo of our reunion. Pista had been given three days' leave, and to our surprise we were accommodated in Kiev in the elegant villa of General Kitzinger, the German military commander of Ukraine, who was away at the time and had apparently left his house at our disposal. Apart from the staff, we – and Gyuri Farkas, who was acting as Pista's batman – were the only people staying there. The two of them had flown from the front; a Storch plane had been made available and Pista had flown it to Kiev.

The villa was very well furnished, and Pista and I had long conversations in the comfortable sitting room during our three days together. After being apart for so long we naturally had a lot to talk about. Despite his pleasure at seeing me again, Pista was in a very sombre, almost desperate mood. His experiences at the front had merely served to reinforce his conviction that the war was a lost cause. He had pondered a lot on how Hungary could be saved from 'its predicament between two enemies,' as he put it. He planned to discuss the matter in detail with his father on his return home.

I passed on his father's messages, including the one that he should return to Hungary as soon as possible. The government also asked him not to stay any longer at the front: as vice-regent he should first visit one or two units on the Russian front, but only briefly. Pista accepted that and asked that if I returned home before he did, I should tell his father that the Germans had irretrievably lost the war; that it was intolerable how without any consultation they took our soldiers wherever they wanted; and so on. He himself could no longer see any way to do anything at the front or at home to extricate us from this predicament.

How desperate the situation was at the front in terms of supplies and training I only read in detail years after the war, but I did know that requests were continually being made to the Germans for suitable equipment. The German leadership promised and promised to transport more arms – but their promises remained just that. Pista knew that, of course, and I could feel his despondency and hopelessness when he said that there was nothing more that could be done at home. During those three days Pista told me everything he wanted his father to know, and in addition he told me his secret plan. He had decided that as soon as possible after returning home he would fly out to England or the United States, where he felt it was vital that someone with authority should provide the Allies with the full information about what was happening, and try to do something for his country from there. But, he said, we – the family – must not know about this. He had planned everything, but would not tell us the details in order to prevent his father's position from becoming even more difficult. We should even officially denounce him as a traitor if necessary. He again stated categorically that it was no longer possible to help Hungary from within, particularly as there were still large numbers of people, especially among the military leadership, who believed in a German victory.

We had a lot of other important things to say, and although we were so pleased to see each other again we were careful not to speak loudly. But I still cannot understand how we could have been so careless, or perhaps just forgetful, that we did not count on the possibility of alien 'ears' being present. Even in the Palace in Budapest we were mindful of that possibility and had the phones, etc., tested. I subsequently found out from a German officer that the house had been equipped with hidden microphones.

How could it not have occurred to us – the outstanding engineer and the careful nurse – that our conversations would be bugged? Looking back now, it appears to me perhaps to be something that was destined to happen, something we could not avoid. I say this because I believe that sometimes our choices and actions depend on us, that we have free will, but there are also times when it seems as if we are being directed.

Our three days together in Kiev were very happy, despite the fact that the future looked terrible, indeed frightening. I tried to imagine it: what would happen to me and to István if Pista went out to England or America? Sooner or later the Germans would lose the war, which would send shock waves through the country; we might even be captured ... But I could not allow myself to think about that: we would escape somehow and order would be maintained in the country ... the British would land in Dalmatia and Pista would come back with them to save us ...

The first day was a Sunday and we did not get up early. We were enjoying being together, and Gyuri brought us a big breakfast. Later we toured the city by car and saw churches and a beautiful monastery, where an elderly, shabbily dressed woman took us round and told us in perfect English about the frescoes and icons. It was obvious that this poor woman had seen better times – she might even have been beautiful once; perhaps she came from some well-known aristocratic family. We asked her name, but she was unwilling to engage in conversation. I told Pista that if we too were overwhelmed by Communism perhaps I would one day take tourists around the Royal Palace ...

In the afternoon the two of us went for a walk along the bank of the river Dnieper in the sunshine – Gyuri following us at a discreet distance. I took a lot of photos, but they were all lost later and only a few shots taken by the Hungarian Press Agency remain. We went into a shop and were puzzled to find it empty. We could not see any goods, but when we asked, lots of things emerged from under the counter. The owner told us that they hid everything because they were afraid that Germans would take goods without paying. We were glad to hear that they were not afraid or mistrustful of Hungarians. After supper we had another long talk. It had been a beautiful day.

On Monday morning Pista dropped me off at the Hungarian hospital to which I was assigned. On this first morning I assisted in a blood transfusion and an appendectomy. Afterwards I gave out cigarettes and chatted to the wounded. I had lunch with Pista and then we rested. At five o'clock we went back to the hospital, where a performance had been organized and I was fêted for my name-day. We had not even remembered that the next day was Saint Ilona's. Pista said a few words of thanks afterwards, saying, 'You're spoiling my wife!'

On Tuesday, our last day, I went in to the hospital alone for my shift. I was removing a shell fragment on my own when I suddenly realized that I was being photographed. I was too preoccupied with the job in hand to let it worry me. Aunt Gizi and I went out to the station to meet a train carrying wounded, but it did not arrive so I hurried back to the villa, where Pista was writing letters.[iii] He and Gyuri were going back to the front, to Nikolayevka, that day.

We were perhaps never so close and so undisturbed as in Kiev. We had lunch together, and I remember clearly Pista mentioning that fortunately he had not so far received any decoration from the Germans and that it would be the worst day of his life if he did. 'Don't worry, they wouldn't give me one anyway,' he said.

I had been interested in everything to do with flying ever since Pista

---

[iii] Appendix 3: Pista's letter to his father from the front.

first introduced me to gliding and later had taught me to fly, which was why he always told me about his flights. By then he had won his first dogfight, but when I asked him about that he was as modest as ever, giving me the briefest details and then immediately changing the subject. Among other things, he described the unfortunate tendency of the Falco plane he was flying to slip when making a sharp turn. He told me that this had happened to him at a height of 4,000 metres. He had made a sharp turn and the plane had slipped and fallen into a spin. He said how lucky he was, not only that it had happened at that height so that he had time to pull the plane out of its slide, but also because he now knew to be particularly careful in that situation not to make sharp turns.

Looking back, in light of what happened two days later, and of the official explanation that was given out, I find it interesting that Pista told me about this in such detail, especially when, as I discovered from the memoirs of pilot Mátyás Pirithy, the incident Pista referred to took place before he had left for the front. I cannot help feeling that something must subconsciously have prompted him to tell me about it in detail so I could bear witness to it later.

Along with Gizi Apor and Gyuri, we were driven out to the airfield in a large, comfortable car, where we said goodbye to each other. It was not my imagination that at the moment of farewell Pista looked at me with such love as perhaps never before. He took hold of my arms, squeezed them, and gazed deep into my eyes with a look of encouragement and support, and then gave me a farewell kiss such as I had never before received from him in the presence of others.

The moment was recorded by photographers: it is unfortunately reflected only by my expression as Pista had his back to the camera, but it is still a good record of this unforgettable moment ... a souvenir of our last three very happy days. I had no idea that that would be the last time I would look into his eyes, but somehow the moment has remained with me as vividly as if it had only happened yesterday.

Pista got into the pilot's seat, Gyuri got into the seat behind him, and the plane took off. I watched it go, I could not take my eyes off it. Then there was just a tiny dot in the sky. I was still looking when there was nothing more to be seen ... I had a strange feeling in my heart that I cannot easily describe. I have never been able to forget that moment. The memory of it has remained so strong and painful that since then I have never been able to watch a plane flying away.

Aunt Gizi and I went back into the city and I moved my things from the villa to the hospital, where I was given a small room. After assisting in an operation I went to another hospital to distribute cigarettes and chat to the patients. I had supper with the nurses, and though I was very tired I wrote a letter to Pista – which he never received.

On Thursday 20 August, the feast of Saint Stephen, I spent the morning working in the ward, and then went with Zsófia Marschalko, the hospital matron, to the inauguration of the Hungarian Soldiers' Home. There was an outdoor mass in front of the building; a prayer stool was placed at the front for me. We had no idea that by then Pista was no longer among the living.

We returned to the hospital, and I was resting on the bed when the matron came into the room and over to me. She said, 'You won't be angry with me, will you?' 'Why should I be angry with you?' I replied. Then, with some difficulty, she managed to blurt out that Pista had crashed with his plane. 'But he is alive, isn't he?' I asked, but she just shook her head. I asked her to leave me alone.

I felt paralyzed by the news. The one thing I had not prepared myself for was that something might happen to Pista. I went over to the window. The sun was shining outside, but I just kept telling myself that if this was true the sun could not shine … it could not be true because the sun was shining.

After a while the matron came back and I asked her to make arrangements for me to go back to Hungary immediately because I had to go to Pista's parents. She said she would make arrangements, but those in charge did not want me to fly, because of the accident. I could not understand the logic but did not protest, just told her to ask Aunt Gizi to release me from my duties and let me leave for home at once. As though in a trance I packed my few things, and late in the afternoon we left by car, along with an armed military escort. When I queried this I was told that it was necessary because of the danger of a partisan attack. If the partisans were a threat, why did they not let me fly?

The journey seemed endless. I was told that we were going through Zhitomier to Vinnitsa, where we would be able to stay overnight. I felt as if I was being tortured. Finally we arrived at Vinnitsa at 4 a.m. and stopped in front of a brand new building. I was taken into a very pleasant guest room, but I asked not to stay long. Suddenly a German officer came in, greeted me with a 'Heil Hitler', and said that the Führer would like to extend his condolences in person. I gaped in astonishment, and only then realized that this must be Hitler's General Headquarters. I can remember exactly what I said: 'You can tell your Führer that the only thing I want is to go back to Hungary as soon as possible.' There was a moment of silence as we stared at each other, and then the officer said he would report this to the Führer.

A short while later he came back and said that the Führer would refrain from giving his condolences in person, and would make his private plane available to me early the next morning. With that he thrust out his arm saying, 'Heil Hitler,' turned on his heel and left. This would have been my only opportunity to meet the Führer, but it was the last thing I wanted.

What could I have done? I did not want to arrive in Hungary in Hitler's private plane, but I was still too dazed, I did not know whether I was dreaming or whether all this was true. It was only later that the feeling of outrage came, that none of the Hungarians had told me where I was being taken; this must have been planned behind my back. Did they suspect that I would not have agreed under any circumstances to go there if they had asked me? Perhaps they knew I would not. Zsófia Marschalko should have told me and asked for my opinion. What is certain is that the Germans had a hand in it: I would not have been taken there without Hitler's knowledge; now that the vice-regent they hated was dead they were treating me like a friend.

Early in the morning I boarded the plane. I was left alone; nobody talked to me, for which I was grateful. We flew straight to Budapest, where Prime Minister Kállay and several members of my family were waiting for me. Miklós Kállay was always very good at finding the right words; he was an exceptionally good friend. I was taken straight to Gödöllő. I ran into the sitting room, where I found Miklóspapa, Magdamama, and Gyula. We fell into each other's arms and wept, there was no need for words. We were all shocked and stunned by this tragedy. None of us could believe that Pista was no longer alive. I felt deeply sorry for my parents-in-law.

That day Prime Minister Miklós Kállay spoke on the radio:

> On the feast of King Stephen, a feast that celebrates one thousand glorious years of Hungary's history, fate has dealt our nation a terrible blow. Flight Lieutenant Stephen Horthy, son of our Regent, and vice-regent of Hungary, died a hero's death on the front line. On this glorious and historic day, the one in whom Hungary's future hopes lay sacrificed his life on the field of glory. The whole country, his young widow and his small son are in deep mourning. Many mothers tremble with anxiety about their sons at this time, but we are suffering the greatest loss any Hungarian mother, any Hungarian, can suffer.

> King Stephen, the Saint, the founder and builder of our country, lifted his right hand as a warning towards us all. He too lost his son, but his nation survived and became great. We must see the day of this disaster as a symbolic one, and with our faith we must rise to the

occasion so that we here at home can fulfil our duty to the nation, to the future and to our comrades fighting out at the front, while those at the front fulfil their duty to the country and to their own honour. We must all strive harder, as every son of this nation must: a nation deep in contemplation but unbroken, undaunted, destined for eternal life, gaining strength once again after adversity and misfortune. We have an example to follow.

And on this day of mourning the nation turns its tearful eyes with even more devotion and love to the Regent and his wife. Let them feel that millions share their grief and bow in respect before the sacrifice that the Father and Mother have given to their nation. Let us all, together and individually, go to our Regent and beg him to be like Saint Stephen who made our country great, to remain strong and lead us because he is the nation's faith, confidence, security, and strength. Providence gave us Miklós Horthy in difficult times, and ever since then the nation has stood by him as one, and more so today than ever. And because such are the fathers and such are the sons, the Hungarian is eternal.

I cannot remember the following days: they passed in a daze. It was only from photos I saw later that I knew of the crowds in Budapest, apparently hundreds of thousands, who came to pay their respects. People were crying in the streets. All I know is that we were all in Gödöllő, and when Pista's coffin arrived in the domed hall of the Parliament Building on 25 August, we went there to pray by the coffin. The domed hall was cleared for the time we were there.

I subsequently learned that a beautiful ceremony had been organized in Kassa when the train carrying the coffin had arrived there. The same red, white and green shroud was laid over the coffin that had once covered the coffin of the great Prince of Transylvania Ferenc Rákóczi II on his return from exile. A huge crowd came to file past the coffin during the hour the train spent in the station, and the same happened in Miskolc.

Wounded soldiers sent flowers from the hospitals for the bier of their heroic comrade. There were so many wreaths and flowers that they could not all be put on the train.

The train pulled into the South station, a huge bronze wreath under the funnel, draped in black crepe, with the Hungarian coat of arms in the middle. Psalms were sung, followed by the national anthem, during which time the coffin was placed on a gun carriage. The vice-regent's air force officer's hat and sword were placed on top of the oak coffin. The cortege – a long line of carriages carrying wreaths – made its way through Buda and across the Chain Bridge to the Parliament Building, watched by enormous crowds all along the route.

The *Army Gazette* published a special edition on 20 August, containing this black-edged Notice of Mourning:

> Our armed forces have suffered a terrible blow. This morning at five o'clock His Highness the Vice-Regent, vitéz Stephen Horthy de Nagybánya died a hero's death in action while serving as a flight lieutenant.
>
> By his own decision he entered the theatre of war on 1 July, where he served as a squad commander. His behaviour both in and out of action was exemplary. In addition he was an outstanding comrade and warm-hearted leader who shared both the troubles and the happiness of his subordinates.
>
> With his noble, simple and modest personality, his outstanding expertise, and his individual capacity for work, he stood head and shoulders above us all.
>
> Let us take strength and faith from his exemplary life and heroic death, so that we may fulfil our duty in a manner worthy of him and his heroic memory. The armed forces will preserve his memory forever.
>
> Long live the Supreme Commander, Regent of Hungary, and long live the eternal Hungarian homeland.
>
> Signed: vitéz Bartha
> General vitéz Szombathelyi

The Funeral Service

The funeral service took place on 27 August in the domed hall of the Parliament Building, the very place where the vice-regent had taken the oath of office six months earlier. We only found out after the funeral that, before the procession arrived, the huge central chandelier in the room immediately beyond the main entrance had crashed to the floor. They managed to clear it away immediately so that the mourners attending the funeral could pass through unimpeded.

Magdamama and I accompanied Miklóspapa, both of us in black, with veils completely covering our faces. Miklóspapa walked resolutely and stiffly beside us. The hall was packed. There was an enormous bier covered with flowers, and when I was able to have a better look at it I gasped, because there among Pista's decorations, in fact right at the front, were two high German decorations placed on a cushion. It was only then that I looked around and saw Ribbentrop, the German foreign minister, quite close to us. He must have brought these decorations with him: 'for the hero who fell in our common cause,' as I subsequently heard. I could still hear Pista's words ringing in my ears as he told me that the day he received a German decoration would be the worst of his life: '... but don't worry, they wouldn't give me one anyway!' I wanted to get up, go over to the bier, pick up the two decorations and throw them in Ribbentrop's face. This impulse was so strong that I had to hold one hand with the other to stop myself. I wondered what the reaction would be. Perhaps I would only cause trouble for Miklóspapa. It would cause a big scandal, but I knew it would give great satisfaction to Pista. I hesitated for a few minutes, struggling with myself, taking deep breaths in order to be able to think clearly ... then I was overcome by a feeling that it did not matter any more; nothing really mattered any more.

The Calvinist bishop László Ravasz gave the eulogy, which was followed by the singing of the *Szózat* (a poem about loyalty to the homeland written by Mihály Vörösmarty in 1840 and regarded as being almost as significant as the national anthem). Then we set off slowly: first the coffin, then Miklóspapa, Magdamama and I, followed by the rest of the family. Behind us came the foreign dignitaries: Foreign Minister Ciano representing Italy; Foreign Minister Ribbentrop, Field Marshal Keitel and a whole delegation representing Germany; representatives of the Emperor of Japan and the King of Bulgaria; plus representatives from several other states. They were followed by Cardinal Jusztinián Serédi, Primate of Hungry; Archduke József Habsburg and Prime Minister Miklós Kállay; the leaders of the upper and lower houses of Parliament; members of the government; the bishops, the generals, and all those who had attended the service. We all followed the coffin to the Nyugati station. The streets were lined with people displaying their shock and sympathy with loud audible sobs.

As the procession moved on, the air raid warning sirens sounded, but nobody in the crowd moved, nobody hurried to the shelters: everybody stayed devotedly where they were. Those in the procession also ignored the air raid warning. Turán, the Regent's train, was waiting for us at the station, and on the next platform there was another long train to take those invited to the funeral at Kenderes.

The walls of the rooms in the station were covered in black drapery from floor to ceiling. A band struck up the national anthem as the gun carriage carrying the coffin turned to enter the station. Air force servicemen lifted the coffin from the gun carriage in front of the royal

My father-in-law, Admiral Miklós Horthy

My mother-in-law, Magda Horthy

The Royal Palace as it was before the war

Ready to play polo (Pista, far right)

About to take my level C gliding exam

Skiing in the hills near Budapest

The birth of my son István

Pista with his newborn son

*My son's first visit to the Horthy family home
in Kenderes*

In my Levente uniform

Inaugurating a flag at the Educational Institute of the Hungarian Railways, September 1941

The voluntary nurse postage stamps

EMSI in 1942 (in the correct order this time)

My husband being sworn in as Vice-Regent

The Vice-Regent of Hungary

I arrive in Miskolc as a voluntary nurse

Pista in his Heja plane at the front

My arrival at Kiev, August 1942

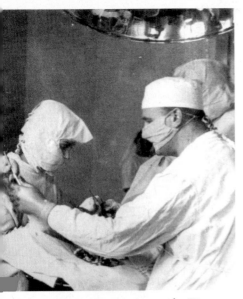

*Assisting at an operation at the Kiev
military hospital*

*Saying goodbye at the airport in Kiev,
18 August 1942*

The remains of Pista's plane, 20 August 1942

The funeral procession

People mourning in the streets

Stephen Horthy's catafalque in the parliament building

waiting room and carried it on their shoulders into the glass hall. A large Hungarian coat of arms draped in black crepe had been placed on the front of the engine, and small black flags had been put on each carriage. A long line of white gloved, black arm-banded railway workers formed a guard of honour, each holding a conductor's lamp covered in black crepe; they lit their lamps as the train moved out of the station. I was told later that these workers should have had a day off that day, having been on duty the previous day, but they had all volunteered to attend.

The train pulled out to the sound of gunfire and the strains of the national anthem, past the guard of honour formed by the railway workers. On every station the train passed through, a line of railway workers stood with lamps covered in black crepe in honour of their former president. From Kenderes station, which was also draped in black, the cortege went to the family house. As the church bell rang, the catafalque was set up in front of the house. Bishop Imre Révész said a prayer, and then the procession went to the Horthy family crypt, where Stephen Horthy was laid to rest. From that day on, 'pilgrims' started arriving to visit his tomb.

Lots of telegrams, letters and poems arrived, but the most moving one was from the diary of a nineteen-year-old young man, of which I enclose an extract:

> Let us stand for a moment by the coffin and reflect. On the morning of 20 August 1942 the golden rays of the sun shone over Budapest in all its festive finery as the procession carrying the holy relic, the preserved right hand of Saint Stephen, left the chapel of the Royal Palace. Who could have guessed that this golden sunshine was signalling the tragic end of a young life? Who could have thought then that Flight Lieutenant Stephen was already standing by the heavenly throne of King Stephen, fulfilling the promise he made in his last telegram to attend the procession in spirit?
>
> The procession must have reached the Matthias Church when once again – and perhaps more so than at any time since the death of István Széchenyi – the words of the poet János Arany were suddenly appropriate:
>
> A word shot through the country,
> So much pain in a fleeting word,
> We felt the earth's heart quake,
> And plains, valleys and hills quiver.
> The first news, on saying the word,

Startled back at the sound of its own voice.
The first dismay wondered:
Has God abandoned the Hungarians?

And then the word really did shoot through the country
and through people's souls, and we felt the earth's heart
quake and the plains of Hungary quiver. We stood and
felt as if absolutely everything in which we had placed
our trust and hopes was about to collapse.

A whole country was dressed in mourning. Music fell
silent, cheerfulness melted away, and Saint Stephen's
day, usually one of the glittering highlights of the year,
was transformed into a day of mourning. This was
more than just a death; the pain was doubled because,
as János Arany said, 'How painful it is if flowers wither
when they are still in bud, if a new spring's hope dies as
soon as it is born.'

This was what we felt too, and our pain was bitter
because we also were bidding farewell to the hope of a
new Hungarian spring.

His words are still alive, we can still hear him saying,
'I call on the young people of Hungary to take up a
career in flying.'

But we search for him in vain; he is no longer with
us. He has gone to be an eternal example to young
people, though our fallible eyes could not – and would
not – see him as anything but an earthly leader. And
then we thought of his father. At that time the whole
nation's thoughts were together with those in the Royal
Palace. A father had lost his most beloved son ... we
mourned our brother and wanted to be together as a
big 'family' in the first moments of grief.

10

The Circumstances of Pista's Accident

On the fiftieth anniversary of Pista's death I published a book entitled *The Tragic Death of Flight Lieutenant Stephen Horthy,*[16] to which I contributed only the foreword. What prompted me to publish this book was the wish to give coherence to the continual stream of magazine articles, reminiscences and arguments about the fatal flying accident, all of which gave various detailed accounts of the tragic event.

Other witnesses, people whose statements at the time had not been passed on to us, had also contacted me. Fortunately we were able to track down the official record of their statements and photocopy them for the book.

But the most important factor was that after many years I met our dear valet György (Gyuri) Farkas again. He had served Pista for eight years, and when he got married his wife Szidi joined my staff. Gyuri and I had a long chat, during which I discovered that he had kept a diary throughout the time Pista and he had been at the front. He offered to send it to me, telling me to do whatever I wished with it.

You can imagine the excitement with which I opened the handwritten diary of Gyuri Farkas, in which he noted day by day everything that had happened at the front. From his tone and his descriptions, from the style of his narrative, I am completely convinced that every word is true. He records the events of the time with such accuracy, and brings my husband to life within them so faithfully, that I can almost see with my own eyes the things he describes. He portrays my husband exactly as I knew him. My family and I owe him a debt of gratitude for this rare gift, the existence of which we had never even suspected.

Gyuri's diary was a major contribution to the book, and can be read there in full. Here I would like to quote only the most important details from his writing, and from the witness statements. But first I would like just to refer briefly to one or two connections that may be worth taking into account when considering the possible reasons for the accident.

Not only had the Third Reich been notably absent from the stream of well-wishers when Pista had been elected vice-regent, but an eloquent testimony to the opinion held by leading Nazis about him is given in a long report written on 23 February 1942 by Dietrich von Jagow, the German ambassador in Budapest. Drawing mainly on extreme right wing and Arrow Cross party sources, it describes my husband as a most evil person, emphasizing that he was pro-British and anti-Nazi, and particularly that he was not above being friendly with Jews. One of the accusations made against him was that, when he was deputy director general of MÁVAG, he prevented the implementation of certain German business plans; so Germany could expect nothing but trouble from him in the future.

If our conversations in Kiev were indeed bugged, and the German leadership thus came to know Pista's secret plans, then – knowing their methods – it is not difficult to imagine that they would have tried to take action, to get someone they considered so inconvenient out of the way as soon as possible.

When I think back now, the other thing that strikes me is the strange lack of common sense in the implementation of security for Pista's safety, considering that he would be surrounded by so many enemies. It should have been obvious that a more effective system of guarding him would be necessary, rather than just leaving it to Major General László Szabó – whose sympathies were clearly not in tune with the vice-regent's.

Taking these things into consideration, I cannot help feeling that some inescapable factor, some force of destiny, must have come into play here. The fact that the accident happened on Saint Stephen's day, and the Horthy's family tradition of naming every firstborn son Stephen after Hungary's first king, reinforces this feeling. Could it simply be coincidence? I believe that nothing happens by chance, and if his death had a deeper significance I would not have missed him any less, it would just have been easier to accept. I would also like to draw attention to the last paragraph of Jenő Markotay-Velsz's tribute to Pista, in which he muses on God's secrets.[iv]

Returning to the possible cause of the accident, I have always had the feeling that the circumstances were not investigated as thoroughly as they should have been. Reading Gyuri's diary totally reinforces this feeling. The wreckage of the plane was hurriedly packed up and taken away, but there was no supervision and many pieces had been removed

[iv] See appendix 1

earlier. All this is not just conjecture on my part: as well as Gyuri's reliable account, I received proof of this years later in the form of letters saying that the writers still had the pieces of wreckage they had taken away as souvenirs. An article appeared recently in which the mother of a pilot who died in action said that she had two bits of the plane. Her son had removed them from the wreckage – although he knew it was strictly forbidden, his love and respect had proved stronger. She handed them over to an air force officer, who told me that they had been deposited in the museum in Szolnok.

The most despicable of the false rumours spread at the time was the accusation that Stephen Horthy was drunk when he took off, as he had been celebrating his name-day the evening before with his fellow officers. This rumour was spread mainly by the Nazis and the Arrow Cross party. Gyuri Farkas' diary refutes this allegation quite clearly; and, quite apart from that, three factors also prove that it was untrue: Firstly, the pilot Mátyás Pirithy was present on the evening before the accident and gives a detailed description of it in his memoirs,[17] which confirm Gyuri's statement. Secondly, Stephen was a Calvinist and celebrated his name-day on 26 December, not 20 August, which is a Catholic holiday. And finally, I myself can state that I never once saw my husband drunk in all the time I knew him. He was very abstemious in both eating and drinking, as others have also noted.

Gyuri's diary begins on 5 June 1942, the day he left Szolnok for the front, and has entries for every day up to 21 August, the day after the accident. Here are some brief extracts just to give an impression of the circumstances at the front:

2 July. Thursday. ... The engineers have built the wooden hut, which consists of a single room. My tent is opposite the hut, 5 or 6 metres from the entrance; I've got hold of a lamp too, and everything's in perfect order ... The front must be quite far away from here, but it's strange that we can hear gunfire all day. Last night Kursk had a major visit: by morning there were about a hundred wounded and a few dead; quite a lot of both German and Hungarian casualties. The hospital is full to bursting; it was hit in the night. Every day there are lots of mass burials, because large numbers of defenceless Russian civilians die in each attack ... At night we were on alert: until midnight we listened, fully dressed, to the Russians droning over our heads.

3 July. Friday. The planes have arrived! ... Harmath and the others have brought lots of nice things to eat and drink: we needed it too, because the food's very meagre here, and there's no water for drinking or washing. For breakfast and supper we get coffee or tea instead of water,

but it's unbelievably bad. Photographers and the MFI [Hungarian Film Agency] are here, and journalists too. The arrival is expected at 3.00 today. The room looks nice, there's even a vase of flowers in it ... The planes arrived at 2 p.m., with much rumbling and droning, but two of them were left behind at bad airfields on the way. Here too, one overturned while landing; luckily the pilot wasn't injured. There were lots of photographers here too, and journalists as well. Everyone was very pleased; my master embraced me – he seemed pleased to see me again ... In the afternoon we went in to the Hungarian Headquarters in Kursk. Lodgings had been reserved for us here too, in a solitary house that even had a bathroom. Half the baggage was already in the house, and it was getting dark. We were standing there in front of the house with the car, when a sudden decision was made: my master decided that we wouldn't stay here but on the airfield in the little hut ... We talked a little in the evening; I found out that everyone at home is well. Then, just as we were going to bed, red flares started flying around, indicating that the bombers had arrived. Soon there were fire beacons near the airfield too ... A unit went out and was able to put out the smaller fire, but then a stack of straw was set alight and they couldn't put that out. Fortunately the Russians left us to sleep in peace, they just carried on bombing Kursk relentlessly. In that night's raid the house in Kursk which had been repaired for His Highness received a direct hit. Even the communication trench in the small yard was hit. It's lucky we hadn't occupied it, we'd have been killed on the very first night!

7 July. Tuesday. This morning was the first time His Highness took part in a sortie. They were escorting bombers, and the raid was successful, but they didn't encounter any enemy aircraft that they could engage in battle. The Russians only come at night, like owls. In the afternoon His Highness and I went down to the nearby lake to wash ourselves down a little. The water's terribly dirty but not very smelly. It's swarming with frogs and leeches. First His Highness went in and I stood guard in case someone surprised us. It was as much as he could do to throw off all the leeches. Then I went in, though I didn't fancy it much. They attacked me too; I could hardly wash myself. We walked home, somewhat refreshed.

9 July. Thursday. ... we received orders that we will have to move to a new airfield near Tim, where the land section has been for a few days already ...

10 July. Friday. ... we left for the new airfield at 9.30 a.m. ... and arrived at 6.30 p.m. The airfield is very bad: it's full of potholes and it

slopes. As the plane runs along the ground the engine drops and the tail is thrown forward. Even His Highness overturned on landing. He was lucky this time, he had a near-miraculous escape. When a plane overturns, either it catches fire and burns out, or the pilot is crushed between the armour plate and the fuselage. The plane broke up. There was a full complement of service personnel at the airfield, who reached the overturned plane in their truck within minutes and lifted the tail enough for the pilot, [the vice-regent] who was hanging upside down strapped into his seat, to open the canopy and crawl out of the plane. There have hardly been any sorties so far and already four planes are wrecked. The airfield is completely unsuitable for planes like this, though the forced labour company here has cut the grass and flattened the hummocks ... We don't even have a tent; the vice-regent will spend the night in a shared tent ...

11 July. Saturday. ... No flying, so we go to bathe in a lake 7 km away, where there's a water mill. ...We took a machine gun with us, and I sat with it on the shore while the vice-regent bathed: I was bodyguard and sentry all in one; then we changed over while I bathed. Such was the security for vice-regent Stephen Horthy at the front, where partisans sprouted like weeds in the fields. Walking back, we see a man suspended from a tree at the edge of the camp: an aircraftman, who had been disciplined in this way by a second lieutenant. This second lieutenant was a reserve officer; in civilian life he was a teacher. And the reason for the punishment? The aircraftman had been squatting in the grass, fiddling around with something. The second lieutenant saw him in this position and shouted at him, 'What do you think you're doing there? Are you s- - - - - -g or what?' The aircraftman stood up and responded properly, but with a touch of humour, to the strange question: 'Things are very lean here, sir, there's nothing to s- -t.' The second lieutenant flew into a rage at this response, as if stung by a wasp. 'Two hours suspension!' He immediately arranged for the punishment to be carried out, and the aircraftman was suspended from a tree by his wrists, which had been tied behind his back. Luckily the man hanging in a strange position didn't escape Flight Lieutenant Horthy's notice. He got his knife out of his pocket and cut the rope, muttering 'Unfortunate man' – that was all. The news spread like wildfire around the camp. This happened immediately before lunch; soon we were on our way to the table. The mess area was in the open, in the shade of some trees. When the officers were all there and had sat down, Flight Lieutenant Horthy got up and said, 'Gentlemen, on my way back to the camp I saw a soldier suspended from a tree. I cut the unfortunate man's rope. Gentlemen, I would prefer not to see this or

similar disciplinary measures here at the front, please.'

The officers knew about the affair already, and were casting sidelong glances at the second lieutenant, who was also sitting at the table, eyes downcast. That was the end of the matter; it was edifying and extremely effective. ... His Highness is very upset that he won't have a plane for some time ...

12 July. Sunday. It's very hot; there are no flights because the overturned plane is waiting to be repaired. But there's another lake where bathing is possible; Major General Szabó and Flight Lieutenant Horthy drove there to bathe. They got back towards lunchtime and Flight Lieutenant Horthy sat reading in a folding chair outside his tent. At lunchtime I always have to organize the officers' meal. ...The service unit always ate first, and so I usually had my lunch before His Highness. Today they made a meat hash with the fresh mutton and rice ... My tent was opposite His Highness's tent, I was sitting outside my tent eating my lunch. He saw that I was eating with enjoyment, and asked me what there was for lunch and whether it was good. I replied that it was a rice and meat hash and that it tasted very good. 'Could I have a taste of the men's lunch?' The kitchen was nearby; within five minutes I was back with the rice and meat hash ... Flight Lieutenant Horthy ate with relish ... Then he went to the officers' table and said, 'Gentlemen, enjoy your meal, and thank you for lunch – I ate the same as the men, it was excellent, and there was plenty of it.' With that he sat down at the table and chatted with the officers as if nothing had happened. But in fact something very important had happened: it wasn't difficult for the officers to realize that they didn't need to have separate catering from the men. So everyone benefited: there was no need to cook two lots of meals, and the general quality improved, because Flight Lieutenant Horthy was satisfied with what was provided for the men. ...

13 July. Monday. ...We're moving to Stary Oskol tomorrow. There's a proper, good airfield there, and a good forest as well. The river Oskol is nearby too, we'll be able to bathe there ...

17 July. Friday. The people live better and are a lot cleaner here. Their favourite flower here is the geranium, just as it is in Hungary. These are the Don Cossacks who sing so nicely, though the poor souls are pretty unhappy now. Around their houses the gardens and fields are cultivated just like ours at home. They keep horses and cattle, and also pigs and sheep. If they spoke Hungarian they would be just like us; their customs and temperament are like ours. Poor Acting Pilot Officer Romer was unlucky again today. He was bringing the squadron leader's plane from

the workshop where the bullet-holes had been repaired, but overturned badly on landing. The plane was completely wrecked. This is the third time this has happened to him. He got away with it again.

18 July. Saturday. ... Major Tost (the Regent's ADC) arrived today. Major Tost and Stephen Horthy are close friends and it was no accident that it was Major Tost who came to the front to give him a personal briefing.

20 July. Monday. Today again there were a few missions to secure air-space, and some bombing raids. The weather is beautiful. Major Tost went out again to look at the battlefield, where there are enormous numbers of Russian dead, with the dreadful summer stench which usually accompanies such events. ... It's the period of calm which follows a big battle. They've reconnoitred the new airfield; we're waiting to move there.

21 July. Tuesday. Major Tost left today. ... I sent home all the sugar and chocolate I'd collected up to now. I wrote a separate letter describing our situation here. In my opinion the vice-regent is in great danger here. This letter is for Her Highness, I promised to keep her informed.

5 August. Wednesday. Set off at 8 a.m. to advance 186 km to Nikolayevka ... We left this nice place which we'd got so used to, and it was just as well, because as we got down to the road, it must have been 8 a.m., three bombs hit the site of our camp about 500 m away. The Russians have only just started bombing, though they knew we were there... We got to the new airfield at 7.30 p.m. ... The nearest town is Nikolayevka, about 5 km away ... His Highness was accommodated temporarily in one of the tents, while I lay down under an apple tree next to the tent – the whole camp is in a big orchard.

6 August. Thursday. Had to get up at 2.30 a.m., because His Highness was going on a sortie. There's more chance of encountering the enemy here, because today two of them have already had to face thirty-six enemy aircraft. They were greatly outnumbered and his escort – Sergeant Zoltán Nemeslaki – had fallen behind, so he was alone. The Ratas pounced on him, but he shot at them and made off. He would certainly have been shot down if he hadn't escaped by going into a dive. He pulled the plane out of the dive close to the ground and set off back to the camp. By 5 a.m. he'd got back safely. His plane had been hit twice. Nemeslaki landed safely too. He saw one of the attacking aircraft catching fire. Later they found the wreckage of the Rata that had been

shot down. The outcome could have been different. ... His Highness's first kill.

8 August. Saturday. The Russians are throwing everything they've got into a strong land attack, with vastly superior numbers: they have three or four times more men than us. The land forces stand their ground well and repulse all local breakthroughs during the day. Our bombers help them, but the Russians are bombing heavily as well. The fighters take off too, towards noon. They return with two kills, though they only have four working planes, the rest all need minor or major repairs. So Flight Lieutenant Horthy's plane, being one of the four, takes off daily. In the afternoon a good bath in an oil drum that has been cut in half: a stylish bathtub here. During the night the Russians did manage to cross the Don with significant forces, mainly tanks. They broke through by the Seventh Division, which was the weakest point. We must have suffered heavy losses, as ambulance cars pass continuously, day and night.

Major General Szabó will take over command of this [Seventh] division, leaving the vice-regent, whose military and political adviser he's been until now.

9 August. Sunday. General Szabó left to take up his new duties. We move into the house that he'd occupied up to now, a comfortable wooden hut, much better than the tent. ... His Highness went up with the second group; Nemeslaki, his escort, fell behind again and disappeared. The Russians are bombing heavily and attacking strongly everywhere. At night they set every village and town alight. We can't put the fires out, and there's nobody to put them out for anyway ...

11 August. Tuesday. His Highness goes in the second sortie at 7 a.m. In the first we lost Sergeant Gémes, one of our best non-commissioned pilots. He was shot down by the Russian anti-aircraft artillery over enemy territory. We found out later what had happened to him. Those who were with him saw the plane going down in flames, but Gémes ejected, his parachute opened properly, and he came down on the Russian side. They'll probably capture him, and then he won't have an easy time ... At 5.30 p.m. a football match between the Szolnok and Kolozsvár companies. His Highness played too. Lots of laughter ...

14 August. Friday. ... Get a message that Her Highness will arrive in Kiev today on the Red Cross train. Pack quickly ... Leave-pass; military passport. A Storch plane is made available; we leave ... Get to Kiev by 5.30 pm; it's raining ... We are accommodated in a large villa ... The

rooms are nicely furnished, but the black marble bathroom with white bath and washbasin is peculiar. Hot water! ... There's a woman of around thirty here; she hands the place over to me. I don't know who she is and what her job is; I don't ask whether she's Russian or German ... I'm sure she's not Russian ...

15 August. Saturday. The train will arrive at 10 tonight. A big bunch of flowers is brought to welcome Her Highness. War correspondents film and take photos ... Though it was quite late and Her Highness has just arrived after a tiring journey, Their Highnesses talk for a long time in the lounge.

16 August. Sunday. Get up late. A large breakfast is brought, which I serve. At 11 a.m. they go to visit a hospital. They talk to the patients. The doctors tell them about the hospital and how the patients are looked after. I can tell from the conversations that Her Highness is very well informed, she mentions several patients by name. In the afternoon the two of them walk along the bank of the Dnieper and in the town. I follow at a discreet distance. Had the afternoon off: went out to the stadium and watched a football match between Hungarian and German teams – the result was 4–0. We're back at the house by 10 p.m.

18 August. Tuesday. Pack again, a quick lunch. Said our goodbyes and Her Highness came out to the airport with us. We said goodbye to Her Highness, and at 2 p.m. we were airborne and on our way back. Got to our airfield in Nikolayevka at 5.30 p.m. ... There are Germans in the tent next to ours: five or six of them, they came here a few days ago. 'What are they doing here?' I ask Sándor Horváth, who's sharing my tent. 'They've been here one or two days. They're signalmen,' he says. Staff Sergeant Harmath of the Guards doesn't know any more either, just that they're Germans and they've just arrived. General Szabó isn't here any more, and Second Lieutenant Ortutay doesn't know anything about them either.

19 August. Wednesday. His Highness tells me that tomorrow he will start a tour of inspection of the Hungarian forces. We'll leave at 10 a.m. in the plane we had yesterday, and first of all we'll visit the Szombathely armoured division, which is now under the command of General Szabó ... Then at the beginning of September we're going home. We've been left very much on our own. In the afternoon His Highness goes out to see his plane, which has been undergoing minor repairs while we were away. He found it in good order. Towards evening he asks for a bottle of brandy and takes it with him when he goes to play cards with

Squadron Leader Csukás. He comes back around 10 p.m. and tells me
to wake him at 4.30 a.m., because he's going on one last sortie. He
brought the brandy back unopened because nobody had wanted any.
He's asked the sentry to wake me at 4.00.

20 August. Thursday. Woken at 4.00; get dressed quickly. Bring a
thermos of coffee from the cooks. Wake His Highness at 4.30 a.m.; he
gets dressed quickly. The car turns up. Nemeslaki's here, and somebody
else; he offers them coffee but they don't want any. He tells me that the
plan for today hasn't changed. I understand; there's still plenty of time
to pack. The planes drone off and circle over the camp as usual. He
waves from the plane. The sun's already up. I'm sitting on the bench
under the pear tree when Second Lieutenant Fehér comes running up,
looking for me. He can hardly speak, but tells me that the vice-regent's
plane has crashed and he's dead. The bombers have just telephoned; the
ambulance people are already by the plane and are burying it so it
doesn't burn out. I run to the squadron leader, who's standing outside
his tent in his boots, his coat over his pyjamas, his hat on his head.
'István, start the car so it warms up,' I say to the driver. Quickly we get
into the Horch jeep and drive straight to the scene through a field of
sunflowers. We find the plane already buried. Nobody's allowed near it
because there's a danger it might explode. I have my camera with me
and take photos undisturbed. Later we return to the scene, by then
many high-ranking German and Hungarian officers are there. I easily
recognize the body. I identify the objects and verify that they belong to
him. A coffin is made from the door of the hospital in Nikolayevka.

21 August. Friday. Leave for home on road no. 21, in ambulance car
no. 21, on the 21st of the month. I don't see the Germans around, but
I'm not interested in them any more.

Later, Gyuri wrote an addition to his diary, in which he recalled the
events that took place in 1942 and from which these extracts have been
taken:

I can well understand how Squadron Leader Kálmán Csukás, the
commander of the flying division, felt. He practically broke down when
he received the terrible news at dawn on 20 August, there in front of his
tent, half dressed. Perhaps this outstanding pilot and humane
commander, whom everybody respected and liked, felt that he too was
responsible for what had happened. After all it was he who had given
the order for the sortie the previous evening. If only he had known that
General Gusztáv Jány, commander of the Hungarian Second Army, had

told the vice-regent the same day that he had completed his flying service at the front!

He and I went out together to the scene of the accident ... the plane – the heap of wreckage – was lying belly down, its undercarriage raised and locked. The heated and deformed mass of metal had not yet cooled down. They buried it, not to be opened up until the afternoon. Until then it ought to be guarded. But by whom? And from whom? Officials and onlookers came and went, Hungarians and Germans. In the afternoon: opening up, examination, identification, official record. Everyone saw something different; everyone saw it differently and gave a different account. For instance, corporal Rafael Mészáros from the Huszt battalion saw that the plane was on fire as it fell – but he wasn't even questioned. ...

But what could have caused the accident? What made the plane crash? Nobody examined the wreckage for clues. The remains of the plane were dispersed; they were not kept for a technical committee to examine later in detail, component by component, in order to try and determine the cause.

... There were also rumours of a deliberate attempt on his life, saying that the Germans had had a hand in the affair. It was well known that Hitler disliked Stephen Horthy because he was pro-British. ... It's also true that the Germans were constantly there with us in the area, on the airfield and everywhere. There had even been an incident when German planes fired at Stephen Horthy's plane 'by mistake'. And they could also gain access to the Hungarian planes on our airfield. Nobody can prove anything now, but the suspicion cannot be dispelled.

A few days after the burial the Regent summoned me to his office. To my surprise the prime minister, Mr Miklós Kállay, and the defence minister, Mr Károly Bartha, were there too. They wanted to know my opinion. The Regent knew me well; I met him and was able to talk to him every day, since as a bachelor I'd been the only member of the staff who could live in the Regent's apartment. Most of the times we met, he would stop me and say a few words beyond simply acknowledging my greeting. In any case, he knew all his employees by name, not only in the Castle but also at Gödöllő and Kenderes. So I felt free to tell him what I thought about his son's death. Of course I didn't say how much Hitler infuriated him: the Regent clearly knew that without me having to tell him. But I gave a detailed account of the last days, and the visit to Kiev. ... The Regent ordered the most rigorous investigation, but whatever the investigation could subsequently uncover, it couldn't bring Stephen Horthy back to life. [pp 84–89]

* * * * *

This is an extract from the eye-witness account of Rafael Mészáros, who was on observation duty at dawn on 20 August 1942:

> It was exactly 5 a.m. when the planes started up on the neighbouring airfield. I watched them taking off through my binoculars. I knew they were Hungarian planes from the direction of the sound, but I also definitely recognized their markings through my binoculars. A Hungarian fighter was coming towards the airfield, flying east to west. I recognized it easily with binoculars and also with the naked eye. It was three minutes past five, I looked at my watch. I couldn't believe my eyes – the plane was on fire! I saw a yellow flame on its side, but no shot anywhere. Why was the side of the plane on fire, where was that flaming yellow trail coming from? Then the dull, distant sound of an impact, and then silence. I immediately reported what I'd seen to Captain Fraknói, my commanding officer. Captain Miklós Fraknói acknowledged my report. Lieutenants Endre Antóny and László Palotai were present too. ...
>
> It was nearby; we arrived quickly at the scene. Soldiers were already there who must have been even closer to the scene; they were already burying the plane so it wouldn't burn out. That was when I found out that it was the vice-regent's plane. I had thought he would make it to the airfield in the burning plane, but there was a low hill there, and the plane had crashed nose first into it.
>
> I'm sure the plane wasn't shot down, because I was so close that I would have heard the shot. I saw the yellow flame on the side of the plane with the naked eye too. [18]

In the early morning of 20 August 1942 Acting Pilot Officer Wágner was piloting the reconnaissance plane that was to be escorted by Stephen Horthy and Zoltán Nemeslaki in their fighters. Behind him in the plane was the observer, Captain Elek Baranyi. Both fighter planes were airborne when he took off, and as he banked steeply he saw them below him. This was how he described what he saw on that morning, in a letter written to me:

> While still climbing steeply, I caught sight of two fighters slightly below and about 300 metres behind me. In the same moment the leading plane of the pair banked to the left and went into an increasingly sharp,

over-banked turn, then its nose dropped and it fell into a near-vertical spin.

Shocked, I watched it and started counting the turns, which I could see very clearly. One, two – at this point I sensed that he wouldn't be able to pull that heavy plane out of the dive – three, four, five. A little after the fifth turn it hit the ground. Immediately a flame several metres high exploded upwards and a thick black column of smoke was formed; it rose in the gentle breeze, clearly visible against the background of the forest, which was still in shadow.

... In my opinion the most significant part of this tragic event was something which no other air crews and nobody else apart from us mentioned when they were questioned, but which I saw perfectly clearly: *Flight Lieutenant Stephen Horthy fired his flares before crashing.*

The fact that the flares exploded into reddish stars by the *second* turn proves that they had been fired by the pilot, using the flare gun which was in its holder ready to fire. These small luminous bodies, four or five of them, then fell – from my angle – parallel to the falling plane, as if escorting it.

...This is the decisive fact. The plane must have gone into this low-speed over-banked turn and stalled *of its own accord,* despite the actions of Flight Lieutenant Horthy, and in this awful predicament – in the last phase – all he could do was *fire his flare to let us know that he was in deep trouble.*

This fatal situation is also confirmed by the statement of Acting Pilot Officer Gyula Szabó, who as the reconnaissance squadron's duty officer that day watched the plane's flight from the ground. He states: '... the other [plane] was to the right of it, and flying roughly along the river, it made an over-banked and increasingly tight side-slipping turn and headed towards the forest north of the airfield. As the plane got near the forest, still in a banked position, its nose dropped.' So this was a fairly long period of flight. My own observation joins on to this one, as if continuing on from it.

These two observations were made completely independently of each other – one from the ground, the other from the air. *Both suggest that the plane was out of control.*

I feel that it is important also to mention here the meticulous research and conclusions made by Lieutenant Sándor Horváth, former dive bomber, fighter pilot and unit leader, which for me represents the final truth of what really happened in connection with the tragic death of my husband.[v]

* * * * *

After Pista's death some people came up with the preposterous idea that my son István, then aged two, should be crowned king! It was Béla Lukács – state secretary and national president of the Hungarian Life Party, the ruling party from 1940 to May 1944, and son-in-law of my mother-in-law's brother – who came to the Regent at the head of a delegation with this hair-raising proposal. I was present at the time and can confirm that my father-in-law, outraged, rejected it categorically. It was not just a stupid idea, it was madness.

You can imagine that I was also incensed by the suggestion: how else would a mother feel when people want to single out her two-year-old child in this way? To choose an adult for some office on the basis of his abilities and his achievements would be understandable, but to choose a small child who is not even a member of a dynasty is preposterous. I was reminded of the German saying: 'Lord, I can defend myself against my enemies, but protect me from my friends.'

Looking back, however, this preposterous act of his did have one positive outcome. It was the instigation of a renewed, clearly clarified, expression of my father-in-law's views on the foundation of a dynasty. It would not otherwise have occurred to me to ask the Regent to tell me his honest opinion of that idea, and I would not have been able to quote here his own words and give a reliable and authentic answer to that question. For that I am grateful to Béla Lukács. Miklóspapa told me that it would never even occur to him to reach for the crown, either for his own sake or for the sake of his family. Indeed, he said, if he ever did so, his own brother ought not to consider him worthy of a handshake. That is what he said, and that is what he believed; though if he had ever wanted to become king, he'd had more than one opportunity to achieve it. As he describes in his memoirs, he had been offered and had refused the crown as early as 1922.

[v] Appendix 4: Sándor Horváth's account of the death of Flight Lieutenant Stephen Horthy.

Barely six days had passed after the funeral when, on 2 September, my brother-in-law Gyula Károlyi and his flying instructor crashed into the Danube in their plane and were killed. Gyula was swept away and his body could not be found.

It's difficult to explain the degree of indifference I felt. There was hardly anyone who was closer to us than Gyula: he and Pista agreed on almost everything; over the last two years we had seen him almost every day, and yet I felt nothing when I was told that his plane had crashed. My thoughts were almost along the lines of 'oh well, so he's gone too.' The only thing that hurt unbearably was the realization that, through my fault, a meeting he had requested had not taken place.

A day before Gyula's death I had received the following short letter from him:

> Dear Ily,
>
> Could you please arrange for us to have an hour together in the near future when we can talk undisturbed? There are so many things I want to tell you which I can't bring up in the usual evening conversations in the drawing room in Gödöllő, if only because then I would be talking all the time. You can reach me on the phone any time: at my flat in the evening or in the morning, and through my secretary during the day.
>
> Kindest regards,
> Gyula.

I did not think at the time that this was particularly urgent, and rang him only the following day, when he had already left on his fatal flight. I will never find out what he wanted to tell me – and if we had arranged the meeting for the next day, perhaps he would not have gone flying ... .

Gyula was a deeply sensitive man, and I know that he was extremely distressed by Pista's death. I remembered the strange thing he had said to me barely a month earlier when he came to see me off on the Red Cross train: he said he wanted me to know that if anything happened to me out there, then I would not be alone because he would go with me. I had pondered about this at the time, but now I felt that he must have been talking not just about me but about Pista too, because after Paulette's death we were his real family.

The cause of the accident was never established. Other people also saw how devastated he was by Pista's death and they wondered whether his death might have been suicide – though until now I have never told anyone what he'd said to me as I was leaving for the front. I do not think it could have been suicide, because he was flying with his instructor, but I cannot rule out the possibility that he was thinking about death.

On 4 September, thirty or forty Soviet planes bombed Budapest. We only found out the details later, because we were in Gödöllő. But a few days later at 10 p.m. there was an air raid warning in Gödöllő and we all went down to the shelter. This was our first experience of going to the shelter; later our trips there became almost habitual. My sister Sya was with us and, as normally she was easily frightened, I was surprised at how calm she was. When we went back to our room I found a half-empty bottle of sedative – she had drunk the remainder before going down to the shelter. It made me smile. At that time I would never have believed Sya could be as incredibly brave as she was later, when she suffered so terribly in the worst Communist prisons, with no sedative to help her.

There was a requiem mass for Gyula at Gödöllő and another the following day in Budapest. The same day – nine days after his death, and following extensive searches – Gyula's barely recognizable body was found in the Danube at Ráckeve, near Szigetujfalu.

I was the only member of the family who attended his funeral at the Károlyi estate in Mágocs. Later, however, in accordance with Gyula's wishes, his remains were taken to Kenderes and placed in the Horthy family crypt next to his beloved wife Paulette.

During September Miklóspapa went hunting in Szin for a few days, and he asked me to go with him. I found some consolation from being in the forest and in that beautiful area; but when we saw a magnificent bear approaching and Miklóspapa shot it, my heart ached.

At home Magdamama and I knitted lots of socks and gloves for soldiers. I was beginning to get the hang of it but was always amazed at how fast Magdamama could knit. It was a good way of keeping busy, it held our attention and soothed us: just what I needed in my state of mind at that time.

On 13 October 1942 a bill was put before Parliament entitled *Expression of the Nation's Gratitude*. The following extract is from István Jánosy's book *Vitéz Stephen Horthy the Pilot*:

> The president, András Tasnádi Nagy, opened the session of the house, and Kálmán Petró introduced a bill to preserve the memory of the vice-regent and express the nation's gratitude, which among other things also stated that the office of vice-regent was in harmony with Hungary's constitution and had brought reassurance to the nation.
>
> 'Six months ago the nation, full of great hopes, saw

the aims of the law setting up the office of vice-regent realized. The vice-regent fully lived up to the hopes placed in him and selflessly fulfilled all his duties. Having died a hero's death, the vice-regent became an example of a devotion to duty which is strong enough to sacrifice itself on the altar of the homeland. As the country's vice-regent it was not his job to serve in the front line as a flying officer. He chose to do so in order to share in the common destiny of the nation's many thousand heroic sons. By passing this law in memory of vitéz Stephen Horthy, the nation pays its respects not only to his memory but to the memory of all heroic Hungarian soldiers. In the war we are now fighting destiny makes no exceptions. Vitéz Stephen Horthy's death still rises above the others because in him death snatched away one of the best pledges against the nation's future, and at the same time the country's second-ranking constitutional dignitary. The vice-regent is *primus inter pares* among the heroic dead. The Horthy family has, in the person of the Regent, given strength and reassurance to the nation in one of the darkest periods in the history of the Hungarian state.

'The first aim of this bill is to give constitutional weight to the memory of the vice-regent, as is customary. The second aim is to provide for his widow and son in a manner appropriate to the office of vice-regent, and to grant the title His Highness to male descendants of Stephen Horthy. The third is to give greater expression to the nation's gratitude and its solidarity with his widow and son by ordering that increased support should be provided to the widows and children of the heroes who have fallen in this war through the setting up of charitable institutions.' [p. 147]

He and Prime Minister Miklós Kállay asked that Parliament should pass the bill. Great applause followed, and the members gave the Regent a prolonged standing ovation. Both the upper and lower houses accepted the bill without debate, and so it was enforced.

In October my brother-in-law Nicky arrived from Brazil, where he had held the position of Hungarian ambassador. Although it was of course a comfort for his parents to have their one remaining son home again, it was also a painful time, as telling him all that had happened renewed our feelings of grief.

He told us many interesting things about Brazil, where the atmosphere was full of anti-German feeling. Since Hungary had been categorized as pro-German, Nicky's position – although himself anti-Nazi – had become increasingly difficult. He had done his best to protect the interests of the many Hungarian citizens who had emigrated to Brazil, when the authorities wanted to limit their rights using the Hungarian-German alliance as an excuse. But eventually, under German pressure, Hungary was forced to break off diplomatic relations with Brazil and Nicky had to leave.

At home the German ambassador presented his government's pressing demands with regard to a radical resolution of the Jewish question, but these were rejected by the Hungarian government. In the meantime Allied forces landed in Morocco, and people in Hungary were hoping that the Allies would invade the Balkans, and then liberate us.

I fell ill with scarlet fever. I was immediately placed in isolation in our apartment on the upper floor, and István and Nanny Ila moved down to stay with my parents-in-law.

That was something I could really have done without: I was in bed on my own and was not even allowed to read. My only link with the outside world was the telephone. Magdamama's maid, Margit Csécs, stayed in isolation with me; she was the only person I was allowed to see apart from the doctor. I was touched by her dedication and how well she looked after me.

I was in this horrible isolation from 7 December to 21 January, and could find nothing to cheer me up. Life had given me more than I could ever have dreamed of and then, only two years later, everything had collapsed. Pista was dead, and we were involved in a terrible war. I was overwhelmed by deep depression and sadness. What would happen to my lovely little son? Perhaps we would all be killed …

I tried to be cheerful when I talked to my parents-in-law on the phone, but it was very difficult. If only I could escape from this inactivity – I knew that nursing, or indeed any productive activity, would help me through this difficult time. Maybe I had to accept God's will and not lose heart. But no amount of reasoning or brooding could really improve my state of mind at that time.

How different this Christmas time was from last year's! I heard that the Leventes had come to play a traditional nativity scene for István and give him a present. I was told that István had behaved impeccably: he had watched the performance earnestly and then thanked them for the present. Magdamama and Nanny Ila were with him – I wished I could have been there. My parents-in-law spent a long time talking to me on the phone, and refused to put up a Christmas tree or celebrate until I was better. I was touched by this and tried to dissuade them, but without success. I knew that they were very worried about me – after all, their daughter Magda had died of scarlet fever. Margit the maid was an angel and stayed with me, and many others rang: István, who was very sweet and sensible, my parents, my sisters, and several friends. I gave thanks to God that I had such a loving family and so many good friends.

11

Unwilling Ally
of Germany, 1943

Another year began – without Pista. It was hard to bear the thought that this was how it would always be ... .

I had spent four weeks in bed with scarlet fever. On New Year's Day Ellamami came to see me and read to me from the papers and from one of the books I had been given, as I was still not allowed to read. This restriction I found particularly hard, because during my illness I had received many interesting new books and they were all piled up next to my bed. I really appreciated Ellamami's kindness in coming to visit me, because she had to be disinfected, which was not pleasant.

On 14 January, my twenty-fifth birthday, I received many phone calls and loads of flowers. István rang too: he was a few days short of his second birthday but could make himself understood very well and had got used to talking to me on the phone every day. He let slip that I would get a birthday cake, saying, 'Mama, cake, candle!' Nanny Ila took over and told me that it was supposed to be a surprise. That was my best birthday treat. The next day for the first time my doctor, Dr Nagy, gave me permission to read a little.

A week later Dr Nagy and Professor Stühmer decided that finally, after more than six weeks, I could be released. I had a bath and washed my hair, as did Margit the maid, who was also released at last. For the time being I was moved into a room on the ground floor as my apartment was being disinfected. I could read again; and I could walk with Sya and enjoy long conversations with her; and once again I could have dinner with Miklóspapa and Magdamama. After such a long period of deprivation I enjoyed all this very much. I was still very depressed inside, but knew this was a symptom of my illness and would pass.

Finally the great day arrived when I was allowed to go out with

István – although I was not allowed to kiss him for another week, which was very hard – and we could visit my parents-in-law together. István was very sweet; he was so pleased to see me that he got quite over-excited.

Exactly a month after Christmas, on 24 January, we celebrated Christmas Eve for István in the big Mátyás room. I stayed in bed in the morning and then went to help decorate the Christmas tree. I was very touched by the fact that my parents-in-law had not celebrated Christmas in December but had waited until I could celebrate with them. They were so considerate – and such things can only be motivated by love. Papi, Ellamami, Myro with her husband Gyuri and Sya all came too. At six in the evening the lights on the tree were lit. István was radiant with delight, and seeing him made me feel much better.

It was only after I had recovered that I began to find out what a terrible tragedy was unfolding on the Russian front, along the river Don. The fate of the Hungarian Second Army on that front is now well known, but at the time the full extent of the disaster was still not clear. The heavy losses suffered by the Hungarians were caused not just by the cold and by Russian weaponry but chiefly by the way Hitler and the German leadership treated them, and by the brutality of our German 'comrades'. At the time we could only guess at the terrible suffering they endured.

I had lunch with my parents-in-law every day, and Miklóspapa talked about many things during that time. He was devastated by the loss of the Second Army and talked about Prime Minister Miklós Kállay's attempts to investigate the possibility of a ceasefire.

Gyuszi Tost, the aide-de-camp, came to see me and we had a long talk. He said that Pista had foreseen all this – he'd known that the Soviets would only get stronger and the Germans would inevitably be defeated. Gyuszi hated the Nazis, and his thoughts agreed with Pista's in every respect. I valued our talk, and was deeply moved when he said I should never forget that he was not only the Regent's aide-de-camp but mine too.

It was at this time that István Jánosy brought me his beautiful book about Pista's life as a pilot, which contained sixty-six lovely photographs, most of which I had not seen before.[19] I lost this book along with everything else in 1944, but I received an original edition quite unexpectedly forty-three years later, in 1987, which was sent secretly from Hungary. Pál Törzsök, a very kind well-wisher whom we did not even know, went to enormous lengths to succeed in this. He wrote to me about one of the many problems he had to overcome:

Unfortunately my cunning way of sending you a book that I thought would please you has failed. Yesterday I was called in to the post office at the Keleti station, where the parcel was given back to me. It had been opened, and they had written on it: 'Only books published in Hungary after 1 January 1957 may be sent abroad.' In the end we were just pleased they didn't confiscate it or threaten any kind of punishment. They gave it back.

I heard nothing more, but when I finally received the book I saw that it had been posted in Singapore. That book is a great treasure to me, and I will be eternally grateful to our friend Pál Törzsök.

For the first time in my life I received a decoration: the official citation read: 'Mrs Stephen Horthy, 'Sister Ily', received the Hungarian Cross of Merit on a military ribbon for her dedicated service at the front.' I could not decide whether I had merited it or not – after all I had spent only a very short time at the front, although I had volunteered to go. The fact was that I did not understand the whys and wherefores of such honours.

I was deeply upset by the news that Pista's commanding officer at the front and good friend, Squadron Leader Kálmán Csukás, had died a hero's death on the eastern front. I was later told that since Pista's death he had always volunteered for the most dangerous missions, as if looking for death himself.

Miklóspapa still carried out all his official duties – I mention this because later on it was said that he did not show himself much in public, thereby distancing himself from the people. In March of that year, for instance: on the fifteenth he attended the Scout Association festival at the Opera House as chief patron of the scout movement; on the sixteenth he spoke to the young people of Hungary; and on the twenty-third he inaugurated a bridge at Medve. And so it went on.

A painting of Pista by István Boldizsár was unveiled at the county hall in Szolnok: it was a fine painting and a very good likeness. I sat between Miklóspapa and Prime Minister Kállay during the ceremony, which was both moving and sad; I felt as if it all was unreal, perhaps I was just dreaming ...

In Parliament's Foreign Affairs Committee, Kállay put forward his proposal that, in view of a possible Allied landing in the Balkans, we should continue fighting only against the Soviets. He secretly sent Aladár Szegedy-Maszák, the head of the Foreign Ministry's political department, to Stockholm to discuss with Allied negotiators the possibility of our surrender. The Hungarian government also rejected

Germany's request that it should send Hungarian forces to Serbia.

Miklóspapa visited Hitler at Klessheim on 16 and 17 April. He returned in a state of outrage, and told us about the strained and bad atmosphere that had pervaded the visit. He had found out that immediately before his visit Mussolini and the Romanian marshal Antonescu had visited Hitler, and had both stressed the need to establish peace in Europe. (By then Mussolini had lost North Africa.) As a result, Hitler was in a state of great agitation and almost attacked the Regent, giving him a whole list of the Kállay government's 'crimes'. Hitler knew that Kállay did not believe in a German victory, and told the Regent that Kállay should leave office in the interests of German-Hungarian friendship. Miklóspapa rejected this, and protested strongly at such interference in Hungary's affairs. Foreign Minister Ribbentrop said that Kállay was only paying lip service to the resolution of the Jewish question, while at the same time protecting and pampering more than seventy thousand Jewish refugees in Hungary. Miklóspapa stood alone against Hitler and his entourage. According to the official notes taken at the time, Miklóspapa defended Prime Minister Kállay, forcefully rejected all these allegations, and refused to set up concentration camps for the Jews. He told us about all this at length, saying that the only important thing was to devote all our attention to protecting our own borders. In his opinion Trianon was the main reason for our being unable to build friendly relations with our neighbours, and had resulted in our being surrounded by enemies because they were afraid that we would want to regain the territories that had been taken from us.

On 7 May Miklóspapa wrote a letter to Hitler refuting every single accusation he had made. I did not read the letter, he just told us about it. It was only when we were in exile – after my father-in-law's death – that I read the purported text of these letters in a book entitled *Horthy Miklós titkos iratai* (The secret writings of Miklós Horthy), published by the Communist government. In my view this cannot be regarded as an reliable historical document, and I wonder what the Communist government's hidden aim was in publishing this book in 1962. It was supposed to provide evidence against the Regent, but when I read some of the letters I could sense clearly which parts my father-in-law could have said, or rather written, and those in which the tone was completely alien to me. It is important to point out that after the war I filed and copied every letter Miklóspapa wrote for twelve years, so I know better than anyone else the way he thought and his style of writing.

On 13 May the Germans and the Italians surrendered in North Africa – that must have been the result of all those 'victorious' advances!

The Martfü coach works sent István a beautiful carriage as a present. We harnessed up Bogár, the little pony, and István was able to drive well by himself. This was a happy moment of which we have a photographic record, as we do of his first visit to a Zoo and of the Easter egg hunt held that year in the palace gardens.

But feelings cannot be photographed. If you go to the statue of Eugene of Savoy, in front of the Palace – which survived the siege intact – and look down at the Danube, perhaps you will get a sensation of what I felt every time I went there. The beautiful architecture of the riverside buildings on the Pest side: Parliament, the Basilica, the bridges, Margaret Island ... at times like that I wished I had the talent to express my feelings poetically. But it was not only uplifting thoughts that the impressive view inspired; the Danube could conjure up all kinds of feelings, because the 'blue Danube' was very often not blue! Sometimes it was brown and dirty, almost ominous as it flowed past, warning us not to be over-confident, and to be on our guard because there are more brown days than blue ones.

Prime Minister Miklós Kállay came to see me, and I had a long conversation with him about all sorts of things. What he said was very interesting; he was a wise, warm-hearted, humane person. Having him as prime minister made me happy and hopeful for the future, knowing we were in good hands.

To my great regret I was not allowed to go back to hospital nursing for a long time because of my illness, and it was only in May 1943 that I again began examining trainee community nurses and large numbers of volunteer nurses. I soon got the hang of it again, and it went quite smoothly. In the military hospital the candidates were outstanding. Next day their answers were broadcast on the radio together with my speech to them, which to my relief turned out very well.

Later that month Aunt Gizi Apor, Lieutenant General Marschalko, Elemér Simon and Gyula Vállay from the Red Cross and I left for Újvidék for the inauguration and tour of the beautiful military hospital there. We also visited the headquarters of the Red Cross, where they held a banquet in our honour. We were driven around Újvidék and had tea with Lord-Lieutenant Reök, and then rejoined the train.

After Pista's death I had once again been allowed to receive the sacraments. Bishop Folba had given me permission to do so and had attached no conditions. (The fact that my son was still Calvinist had not been mentioned.) So now I had my confirmation, in the Capuchin Church. My sponsor was my aunt, Countess Klára Keglevich. The Reverend Lajos Harza was waiting for us and the primate, Cardinal Serédi, confirmed me. I was besieged by many thoughts and feelings, which I found confusing. I had been disowned by the Church because

my husband had not agreed to our sons being brought up as Catholics ...
I had a Calvinist son, but as my husband was dead I could not have any
more Calvinist children, so the Prince Primate was confirming me ... I
would have given up the confirmation without a murmur if Pista had
still been alive – how big a sin was that? I tried to pray with complete
devotion and not think about it any more.

I went with my parents-in-law to see the Army Orthopaedic Hospital
on Margaret Island, where useful rehabilitation work was being done:
we saw soldiers who were amputees, swimming, cycling, and so on. I
met Captain János Iványi there: I had assisted in the operation on his
foot, and he was there for rehabilitation. Iványi and I were to meet up
again after the war, when he was one of the officers who helped us so
much in exile in Bavaria, and he and the other officers became our
friends for life.

Miklóspapa, Magdamama, Nanny Ila, István and I went with
aide-de-camp Gerlóczy for our annual visit to Kenderes. A year earlier
Pista and Gyula had been there too; now the house seemed empty – I
could not comprehend why they were no longer with us.

It is interesting to note how differently I perceive all this now, fifty
years later, not even trying to understand what the mind cannot
comprehend. But now I know that everyone has a destiny in life that
must be accepted. Once we understand that life is hard and suffering is
necessary, then life is no longer so hard and we can even endure the
suffering, because we can only grow through suffering, and that can be
valuable. So, we must learn to be glad to suffer.

Every morning at seven o'clock, Miklóspapa and I went riding, with
Gerlóczy in attendance. Shagya XXIII, an Arab horse, had been
brought from Budapest for me, which was a lovely surprise; and
István's little pony, Bogár, had also been brought to Kenderes, which
delighted him. We were able to spend time looking at Miklóspapa's
projects, swimming in the pool and playing bridge in the evenings. I
walked out to the crypt every day to pray and arrange the ribbons on
the wreaths, which was somehow comforting.

On 18 June Nicky and Uncle Jenő arrived for Miklóspapa's seventy-
fifth birthday. The day began with mass; then a local delegation arrived
to pay their respects. Many relatives and neighbours came for tea, and
later we played tennis. I could not help thinking about the previous
year, when we had played tennis with Pista and Gyula. Pista had come
over from Szolnok in his khaki uniform, and he'd looked so handsome
in it that I could not take my eyes off him. Then a few days later we'd
said goodbye, and I still remember vividly how I'd helped him to pack.

At the beginning of July I went to visit my sisters, Myro at Őrs and
Sya at Réde, and then to spend time with Papi at Szent János. The main

reason for the trip was Papi's fifty-fifth birthday on 6 July. How I enjoyed riding with him in the mornings on Rigó and Panny! In the afternoon we played tennis, and then of course we drove out into the woods: I drove the famous 'long carriage'. In the evening we talked until late or played bridge, and listened to the news. We visited old friends, and I went to Nyitra to see our dear old cook, Aunt Balika. The visit to the village brought back many memories, although everything seemed so much smaller than I remembered.

After a very happy week, Papi, Ellamami, Sya, Józsi and I all went back to Budapest together. Sya and Józsi got out at Örs, and I took my parents to Dísz Square in Budapest, where a lovely lunch was waiting for us. Then I carried on to Kenderes. I drove at least 350 kilometres that day. I wonder now where I got all the energy from, but I wanted to arrive in time for Magdamama's birthday, which we celebrated the next day.

Day after day we listened to the news in a state of tension, and on 26 July it was reported that Mussolini had resigned; that is to say, the King had relieved him of his duties and he had been arrested. Well, he had certainly got things wrong. If he had not allied himself to Hitler he could have been useful to his country. István Bethlen came to Kenderes that day and we had a long talk together. It was always good to listen to him and I wished he would come more often.

On Sunday after mass I spent the whole morning arranging the crypt. Gyula's coffin, which had rested in his family crypt for several months, was now coming to rest beside his beloved wife Paulette at Kenderes, as had been his wish. The Reverend Harza and Gyula's friend István Boldizsár the painter came before lunch; Gyula's coffin arrived from Mágocs at three o'clock accompanied by his sister and brothers. Reverend Harza received the body into the crypt. Everyone had tea in the house, and after they had gone I went back to the crypt. I was happy that Gyula was at last resting where I was sure he wanted to be – suddenly the crypt was so full! It was as if Pista was in good company there with his sisters and Gyula. I know that sounds stupid, because they were not really there, but that feeling stayed with me.

On 2 August we all moved to Gödöllő for two months. It was very hot and we enjoyed bathing in the pool. I felt sorry for my sister Myro, who was heavily pregnant with her second child and must have found it difficult in that heat. In Gödöllő there was time for everything. I was there on holiday for a month, and really made the most of my time with István. I cycled around the garden with him sitting on a seat fixed to the front of my bicycle; he thoroughly enjoyed it, sometimes shrieking with delight. He was presented with two goats, which we harnessed to a little carriage. I also rode every day; and, being given the role of Master, rode

Shagya XXIII for the first series of drag hunts to be held in the area.

I went riding at six thirty every morning with László Hanthy, commander of the horse guards. He said I should go on ahead and they would follow. At first I could not understand who 'they' were until, looking round, to my astonishment I saw all the horse guards were following me! I felt embarrassed and did not know where to go, but I tried to pretend that I was alone and after that it was easier. In the beautiful woods there were lots of spacious clearings with jumps made out of tree trunks. Every time I looked back, there they all were behind me: all the horse guards in uniform on grey Arab horses – an unforgettable sight. I kept thinking of the Empress Elizabeth, who rode many times in these woods; I could understand why she had so loved Gödöllő.

It was when we were at Gödöllő that my father-in-law and I met Olaf Wulff and Jenő Maléter, who came to show us their book about Pista, which I have already mentioned.[20] The book, with its fifty tributes to Pista and with his biography, I considered a very valuable gift, which I wanted to keep for my son. But when the Germans took us away it was of course – like everything else – left behind in the Palace. And despite all my efforts after the war I could not find a copy. In Communist Hungary all books about the Horthy family were banned except the ones published by the government.

Whenever anyone asked what I wanted them to bring me from Hungary, I always asked them just to try to find that book. Then, in 1974, quite miraculously the book was sent to me from two different sources. First the historian Péter Gosztonyi, who was living in Bern, let me know of the whereabouts of a copy. As far as he knew there was only one copy in Hungary, kept under lock and key in the Széchenyi National Library's 'poison cabinet'. Nobody was allowed to remove it. For me the important thing was that now we knew there was a copy in existence. Gosztonyi had a friend in the library, and in order not to cause him difficulties, said that he needed just the photographs. His friend sent him the book on loan to Switzerland by official post, and Gosztonyi photocopied the whole book and sent it to me. My heart almost stopped when I opened the package. How can you ever repay something like that? At the same time we came across an original copy in South America. A woman responded to an advertisement I put in the paper *Kanadai Magyarság* (Canadian Hungarians), asking who wanted the book. When she discovered that it was for me, she sent me her copy, saying that she would not have given it to anyone else because it was one of her most treasured possessions. Unfortunately, out of tact or modesty, she did not give her name, so I could not thank her personally and tell her how much it meant to me.

Using the original book, dear István Vörösváry, the editor of the weekly *Kanadai Magyarság*, republished it in a beautiful new edition with the original text and photographs. This was perhaps what gave me most happiness in these years of exile.

An outstanding event took place on 13 August. During lunch there was an air raid warning, and it was reported to Miklóspapa that American planes were approaching. But immediately it was also reported that they had been diverted and were bombing Wiener Neustadt. This sounded to us like a miracle, despite the fact that we knew about a secret attempt to come to an agreement, and that until then Hungary had not been bombed by the Americans or the British.

After dinner we had the usual bridge party and conversation, the main topic of which was, as usual, how Hungary could make peace with the Western Powers and how it could get out of the war – this had been Miklóspapa's firm intention since 1941, and he had talked about it a lot with Pista.

The next evening a film was shown in the palace cinema at Gödöllő, but I crept out right at the beginning as I was in no mood to watch a film on that day, which was the anniversary of the day I had met Pista in Kiev, and I'd been reliving it all that day. I wondered whether I would always feel like that on these anniversaries. I can now say that these feelings weakened a great deal over the years, which is fortunate as well as natural. But in that first year all those days had a profound effect on me.

Early on Saint Stephen's Day Magdamama and I went to Kenderes, and I arranged the crypt. Many people came and brought lots of wreaths: a very moving tribute on that first anniversary of Pista's death. Naturally Miklóspapa did not attend the usual Saint Stephen's day procession in Budapest. He was represented by the Prime Minister, Miklós Kállay, who I imagined was himself reliving the previous year's event, when he had been told about Pista's death as he walked behind the Regent, and had to carry on with the procession ...

That very painful day was very hot, and we went straight back to Gödöllő from the crypt. Anti Szapáry came to visit. He and his sister Erzsi were very active in the work of Hungarian-Polish societies which were helping Polish refugees. As their mother was Polish, the refugees included relatives of theirs. Anti had been very fond of Pista, who since the German invasion of Poland in September 1939 had done a great deal to help Polish refugees. I remained in close contact with Anti after Pista's death, and he visited me several times.

Jagow, the German ambassador, came to tea and brought with him General Kitzinger, the Commandant of Ukraine. It was at Kitzinger's villa in Kiev that Pista and I had stayed in the previous year. I was petrified, but have to admit that Kitzinger seemed to be quite a likeable person. Was it possible that he had received orders to give us his villa and it was not his fault that our conversations there were monitored? I would have loved to question him about it, but unfortunately that was impossible, if only because Jagow was more than 100 per cent behind Hitler, and we could not have spoken openly about that in his presence.

I wonder whether we will ever find out the true story. There is no doubt that our conversations in the Kiev villa were monitored – as I mentioned in chapter nine – a German officer told me he knew that the house was equipped with hidden microphones. Unfortunately I did not make a note of the officer's name at the time and was never able to trace it. But the offer of the villa and the Germans' hatred of Pista make it much more than likely that the Nazi leadership, far from ignoring such an opportunity, had actually planned it.

On the morning of 27 August, the first anniversary of Pista's funeral, there was a requiem mass in the Palace chapel. In the afternoon the defence minister Lajos Csatay broadcast such a moving and beautiful tribute to Pista that none of us, Miklóspapa, Magdamama or I, could bear to listen to the end.

In the first week of September Magdamama and I went on a three-day retreat to Pécel, spending the whole of each day there. It was held by Father Belányi, at the retreat house of the Girls of the Heart of Jesus. We started each day with mass and communion, then four meditations, rosary, adoration of the Blessed Sacrament, and litany. It was very beautiful and uplifting, but the day was long and Magdamama and I both became very tired. The next day we took Nanny Ila and István to Pécel to show them everything, and I took some toys for the children of the level crossing keeper at one of the level crossings on our way. I had noticed them each time we went past. They were surprised and overjoyed. The same afternoon – 8 September – Western news bulletins disclosed that Italy and Britain had agreed a ceasefire from that afternoon. I wished it would extend to all of Europe.

Seen from outside and through official channels, it may have seemed that the relationship between Hungary and Germany was perfectly in order, but in fact there was always considerable friction for one reason or another. To superficial observers the Hungarian government may have appeared to be a faithful ally of Germany, but if they looked more closely they would have seen that during the war the Hungarian government did everything it could to frustrate German demands. The Germans had to exert continuous pressure on us until at last we provided them with a Division for the front, and there were some demands that were rejected outright. For instance, the interior minister refused to allow the German anti-Semitic propaganda film *Jud Süss* to be shown in Hungary (although in spite of this it was eventually shown); and the Hungarian government refused a request from the commander of the German air force for two airfields in Hungary to be placed at their disposal. And of course the Germans were very displeased about the privileged position enjoyed by refugees and prisoners of war who escaped to Hungary, and Hungary's postponement of the 'final solution' of the Jewish question.

This 'question' first arose to a significant degree when Slovakia became an independent state and decided to eliminate all its Jews. Then thousands of Jews flooded across the border to Hungary. Miklós Kállay wrote about this in his memoirs:

> Early on, the border guards let everyone across the border, and some twenty-four thousand came across in this way. However, soon the Slovak government – under pressure from Germany – of course protested. At first we didn't pay too much attention to this, but the increasingly forceful interventions and threats by the German ambassador to Budapest posed a greater danger. The German standpoint was that if we didn't want to proceed against Jews in Hungary in the same way as the other allies of the Axis, then that might be a regrettable divergence. It might be the short-sighted policy of a Hungarian leadership degenerated by the infiltration and influence of Jews. But the Hungarian government did not have the right to impede the unified action of the whole block and frustrate the complete solution of the Jewish question; that would be a rejection of their obligations as allies, a breach of faith, and could not be tolerated. [vol. II p. 325]

Plainly there would have been no point listing the counter-arguments to the Germans, as it's useless to argue with lunatics. The interior minister had to instruct the border guards to make it more difficult to cross the border, and only to admit those who had permits to cross into Hungary; whilst the authorities entitled to give out such permits were instructed to adhere strictly to the legal provisions. In this way the number of people crossing the border legally was significantly reduced. On the other hand, the border guards were also instructed not to expel those who crossed the border illegally but to hand them over to the local police for transfer to reception camps. Thus even though the number of people crossing the border illegally was reduced, Jews continued secretly to cross the sparsely guarded border in their thousands, helped by their co-religionists. According to the Interior Ministry's data, in the end more than forty thousand Jews came to Hungary from Slovakia.

Although some four thousand of those trickling illegally through the border ended up in concentration camps, most of the rest found shelter with relatives, friends or co-religionists, without appearing on any official records.

The Polish issue started in 1939: we opened our borders to members of the Polish army and to civilian refugees, and they flooded across in large numbers after the invasion of their country in that year by Germany and the Soviet Union. Everyone was happy to receive them. Hungary had the only Polish grammar school in Europe, and there were Polish courses at universities. They were politically active and even had a radio station. Many secretly crossed into Yugoslavia to continue fighting on the Allied side with General Anders. These secret border crossings were assisted by Hungary. With the knowledge of Interior Minister Ferenc Keresztes-Fischer, a regular courier contact was established between Poland and the Polish government in exile in London. I had been well informed about all this through my brother-in-law Gyula Károlyi, who did a lot for the Polish refugees and worked closely with Anti and Erzsébet Szapáry.

Compared with the other countries, Hungarian Jews and the Jews who fled to Hungary lived in peace, despite the anti-Jewish laws. Of course they were afraid of the Nazi threat. We hoped that when the Western Allies won, everyone would be able to return to their homeland. It would be a great moment if the British forces arrived – I longed for them to land on the Balkan coast. We discussed these possibilities many times in the evenings, but after a time I did not comment, as a favourable outcome seemed so uncertain.

In a surprise raid on 12 September the Germans freed Mussolini, and he formed a Social Republic in northern Italy. The Germans pressed us to establish diplomatic links with the Republic immediately, as Romania, Slovakia and Croatia had already done so. In Hungary the accredited ambassador for Italy represented the royal government. At first the ambassador was Anfuso, and he remained ambassador when Mussolini was dismissed; but as soon as Mussolini was freed and summoned him, he went straight back. So then the royal ambassador was General Emilio Voli; we just 'acknowledged' the existence of the new republic. Despite this, Mussolini sent an ambassador, so a situation arose where for a time there were two Italian legations in Budapest, one *de facto*, the other *de jure*. Of course, we continued to deal with Voli. Unfortunately, in this affair Sztójay, our ambassador in Berlin, represented not our viewpoint but that of the Germans.

Miklóspapa was called to Budapest to discuss the issue of

recognizing Mussolini's government. As a result, the next day, 29 September, we recognized the new government, and at the same time granted political asylum to the representatives of the Italian government led by Badoglio.

Our own work continued: Magdamama and I knitted a lot for various charitable causes. We were almost in competition with each other. She taught me to crochet, at which she also excelled. I went to Budapest to the State Railway's main northern workshop to distribute parcels to the families of the men who had gone to the front. I was very touched by their fortitude.

Our good friend István Eszláry, who had headed Pista's vice-regent's secretariat, still helped me with everything. He came to discuss the content of letters that needed to be written for the upcoming Red Cross collection day. The next day I went to Budapest to sign 320 letters that Eszláry had prepared; and on 1 October in my Red Cross uniform I stood at the Vörösmarty Square collection table with Aunt Gizi Apor. We collected for the Red Cross for two days: there were lots of people and we raised a great deal of money.

We said goodbye to Gödöllő on 14 October. Two days later there was an 'obligatory' luncheon in the Palace, because Hitler had sent Miklóspapa a belated and unwanted seventy-fifth birthday present: a yacht. Admiral Raeder and his wife, with State-Secretary Meissner and others, came to hand over the gift officially. I was not the only one who wondered what this was for. The yacht was beautiful. It was called *Hungaria* and there was a separate cabin for Magdamama with a prayer stool in it.

Miklóspapa accepted the gift and never set foot on board again. It was something he would really have enjoyed in peacetime, but now Hitler's present was a positive embarrassment. Who would have thought that, after the war, the *Hungaria* would turn out to be the only potentially claimable item out of all our former possessions!

Miklóspapa and I went on the Turán train to Szolnok to ride our horses as part of a greyhound racing event. I had a long talk with him about the family, the war, and Hungary's hopeless situation. I admired the way he could see great dangers but, in spite of them, still believed that somehow Hungary's fate would be resolved. That viewpoint had advantages and disadvantages. He believed that some miracle would happen – or perhaps he just hoped it would. But I had to admit that at that time his confidence was not entirely misplaced. Although, as Pista had seen, the situation was such that there was nothing that could be done within Hungary, and the final catastrophe could not be averted, at that time there was still a hope that Germany would collapse before Hungary also became a battlefield. This was based on the proximity of the Allies in Italy and the possibility of a landing in the Balkans. That was what gave my father-in-law energy for the fight, and he simply did not believe that the British and the Americans would hand over any part of Europe to the Soviet Union. If only he had been right!

We arrived in Szolnok on the morning of the twenty-second, and took part in the race. I was riding side-saddle on Shagya XXIII and Miklóspapa was on Csodás. I was very frightened at one point when Miklóspapa almost fell with his horse. He always rode audaciously, and a fall would have been dangerous at his age. It was very hot. We had lunch in the stables and then rode again in the afternoon. We got back on the Turán at five o'clock. Somewhere on the way home a stone was thrown at the train – just one, but we wondered who had thrown it and why. I was very happy playing with István in the evening and naturally we did not tell Magdamama about the near fall or the stone-throwing incident.

Magdamama and I carried on knitting. We listened to *Carmen* on the radio, with Svanholm Set – magnificent! Miklóspapa had gone to hear him in the opera that evening. My father-in-law loved opera. He had been to many enjoyable musical events while serving as the Emperor's aide-de-camp in Vienna, the 'city of songs'. He told us about several beautiful opera performances, and was still visibly moved when telling us about Caruso's 'Rose aria' in *Carmen*, which, he said, 'made you want to kneel down'.

Two days after All Souls' Day, which we spent at Kenderes arranging in the crypt all the bouquets and wreaths that had been sent, we went to Szolnok, where the national greyhound championships were to be held. Prime Minister Kállay had come to see me the morning before to ask me to persuade Miklóspapa not to follow the next day's greyhound race on horseback. I tried, but did not know whether I had succeeded. Miklóspapa arrived – and he was not wearing riding clothes! I took part in the competition, again riding side-saddle on my favourite horse Shagya XXIII, because Pista's greyhound Délibáb was running. I was very depressed, but hoped it did not show. Being here in Szolnok, and taking part all through the event, I missed Pista very much. How could it all take place without him being there?

Miklóspapa and I went to the MFTR works (the Hungarian Royal River and Sea Shipping Company) at Ujpest to open the István Horthy naval barracks. A statue of Pista was also unveiled. It was an excellent likeness, made by the sculptor Erdei. I visited a children's home and then we had lunch on board the ship *Zsófia*, watching a display of various Danube-ships.

On 20 November I had to go to the studios in Sándor Street to broadcast a speech to the Levente girls. It was very difficult, as they had to make three recordings before they were satisfied, and then it was recorded as a film soundtrack as well.

From there I went on to see Anti Szapáry, where I met Mr Jean de Bavier, a Red Cross delegate from Switzerland and some other people. We had a very interesting discussion about the current position of the refugees in Europe, and they convinced me that no other country in Europe was doing as much for refugees as Hungary.[vi] I got back to the Palace in time to hear my radio broadcast, and was reassured to hear that on the whole it sounded all right.

On 25 November Franz von Papen, the German ambassador in Ankara, came to lunch. He was a friend of my father-in-law and particularly of his brother, Uncle Jenő Horthy, from the days when they raced horses together. For me Papen remained an enigma, because when he was with us he always spoke 'our language', sharply criticizing Foreign Minister Ribbentrop and even Hitler himself. He told us how difficult his position was as German ambassador in Ankara, but said he had been able to prevent many Nazi blunders. What I could not understand was that if he could see what National Socialism meant and the methods they used, why did he stay on as its representative? But he explained that if he left he would be replaced by a rabid Nazi, who could cause Germany a great deal of harm. So did he have to support this Germany? Five years later, at the Nürnberg trials, Papen's son, Franz von Papen junior, a lawyer who had never been a party member and had always opposed Nazism, defended his father and managed to secure his acquittal. After that, Papen stayed in touch with my father-in-law for many years.

The Christmas preparations began: charity Christmas fairs and the distribution of parcels. The Bodyguards' Christmas party in the Palace was very moving; the previous year I had been ill and unable to take part. This year I could also attend when the Leventes came to perform the Christmas story for István.

What can I say about that Christmas, when I did not buy a single thing for my son? So many presents came for him from all parts of the country that I wondered whether to give them all to him. We put up a Christmas tree that was as high as the ceiling in the huge Mátyás room next to Miklóspapa and Magdamama's apartment, and placed all the presents underneath. There was an electric Meccano set, suitable for a fifteen-year-old; three stuffed animals on wheels: a lion, a donkey and a horse; a bicycle, and lots more. He received a big chocolate village that took us months to eat, and a Transylvanian guard's uniform in his size, which he put on delightedly.

[vi] Appendix 5: Report by Jean de Bavier.

All this made me think ... we could not carry on like this. Of course we gave lots of toys away to poor children, but what would István be like as an adult if he was so spoilt as a child? Luckily it had not had an adverse effect on him as yet: he naturally and willingly shared his toys with other children. Fortunately he was not at all selfish, but who knew what would happen if things continued like this ... .

Eventually I came to the conclusion that it was a waste of time thinking about it, the future being so uncertain – and the following Christmas in Gestapo captivity in Germany could not have been a bigger contrast to that last Christmas in the Palace.

My mother also came to visit me one afternoon. I was always upset by her visits because, though I am sure she loved us all in her own way, I never felt that she loved me. She always found something to criticize. For instance, the first time she came to see me in the Palace, she looked around and said, 'I don't know how you can live here with all these chandeliers and curtains ...' I explained that we could not change the Palace fixtures and fittings, only the furniture was ours. I was sorry she did not have any other observations to make and that we could not better relate to one another. Fortunately this changed over time, and by the end of her life I finally grew closer to her.

On the last day of the year Papi and Ellamami invited me to a family dinner: 'EMSI' (we four sisters) were all there, and my sisters all brought their husbands: Éva with Adam, Myro with Gyuri, and Sya with Józsi. It was a very happy evening; we talked for a long time. I got back to the Palace at 11 p.m. Miklóspapa and Magdamama were waiting for me with drinks and doughnuts. We went to bed at midnight, but I was besieged by so many thoughts that I read and listened to the radio for a long time. How many people in Europe had been able to celebrate the end of the year as pleasantly as us? How many destroyed homes and broken families there were, how much physical and mental suffering, despair and poverty there was – it was hard to imagine what the new year would bring.

12

Contacts with the West
January 1944

The first day of the new year began quite peacefully and agreeably. Magdamama and I went to mass and then I played with István in the garden. Many people came to wish the family a Happy New Year.

On 7 January my mother invited us to lunch to celebrate her fiftieth birthday: she said that her husband would not be present. After so many years her three daughters – Éva and Myro with their husbands – went to see her at her home. Our half-sister Harry (from my mother's second marriage) was there too, with her husband Viktor. It was a very strange feeling for me because I had not been there since the night – almost ten years earlier – when I had left, saying I would never go back to a house where bad things were said about my father. Even then I had felt no anger or hurt, I simply felt that I had to draw a line. Time dulls many things, but the line was still there somewhere. Everything went relatively well, but the past remained with us … .

Miklóspapa had heard reports that the Germans were concentrating a large military force on the Hungarian border. In response to enquiries from the foreign minister and the chief of general staff, both the German ambassador Jagow and the military attaché denied any knowledge of this but promised to make enquiries. Later they claimed that the concentration of troops was exclusively a German military matter, and they did not know why this should be of any interest to the Hungarians. Indeed, Kállay told us that they added insolently that 'perhaps Hungary had a guilty conscience'. The chief of general staff was informed that the reason for the concentration of forces in the region of Vienna was that it was a significant transport and railway junction and therefore the best place from which reserves could be sent in various directions, particularly to the Balkans. As so often before, they once again lied to us and tried to mislead us.

Perhaps understandably, many people thought it unlikely that Germany would invade Hungary. After all, Germany's position had become increasingly difficult, particularly on the Russian front. An armed invasion of their last 'ally' would have involved an enormous loss of prestige, particularly at a time when German forces were so urgently needed elsewhere. Prime Minister Kállay said as much in his memoirs: 'I myself thought it was entirely possible that the troop concentrations were merely for the purpose of threatening us, and I shared Szombathelyi's view that Germany's invasion of Hungary would be politically a strategic error and militarily a tactical one.' [vol.II, p.166]

Miklóspapa told us in a state of outrage that the officers responsible for the bloody raid in Újvidék had escaped to Germany with German help before the Court could pass sentence on them. They were later to return – with the German invaders. The first defendant, Lieutenant General Feketehalmi-Czeydner, and the second principal defendant, Major General József Grassy, were enlisted by Himmler into the armed SS; later, Czeydner became a general and deputy to Defence Minister Beregfy in the Szálasi government, and Szálasi promoted Grassy to the rank of lieutenant general.

We had several air raid warnings, but no bombs.

One evening the news bulletin carried a report that Ciano, the Italian foreign minister, had been executed. This had a profound effect on me; not so long ago Ciano had been hunting in Hungary – and now such dreadful things were happening in Italy, not far away from us.

My days were filled with official business: in one morning, first Elemér Simon, president of the Red Cross, came to see me with László Lelle, deputy head of the delegation; then István Eszláry came to help me with my correspondence and paper work. The Levente girls put on a puppet show, which I went to see; and then I went to the Palace first-aid post for a civil defence lecture in the afternoon.

In the evenings I played bridge with my parents-in-law and we discussed the latest news. I accompanied Miklóspapa to the opera one night. The performance was beautiful, but I still found it painful to sit in the royal box, where I could almost feel Pista's presence. I was pleased when, later that month, Magdamama finally decided to go to the theatre again, which she had always enjoyed so much before.

I was given a new car, a Wanderer, as a present by a friend of my parents. This was very well timed because I'd had a few bad experiences with my previous car, a Tátra, which was getting on a bit. I tried the new car out straight away and drove to Nagykáta to examine some nursing students. There were fifty-seven candidates and the examination went very well. The only problem was that Deputy Lord Lieutenant László Endre turned up again.

A ten-man delegation of pilots from Szolnok came to see me. Apart from the commander they had all been with Pista at the front. I was deeply moved by their visit; it is very heart-warming when people remember and make the effort to show it. All this in Pista's honour, and I too felt honoured to be regarded as his representative.

One afternoon I attended a lovely presentation given by Aunt Gizi Apor and a Jesuit Father at the home of Edina Zichy. It was about Fatima – the pilgrimage place in Portugal. I would have found it hard to believe if told that seven years later I would be working in Fatima as a volunteer servita. After the presentation I visited my cousin Elly Blanckenstein and her three-day-old son Péter. Here again was something I would have found hard to believe: that within a year Elly and her husband would be shot dead – presumably by a Russian soldier – for no apparent reason. Two such contrasting future events: one beautiful and peaceful, the other almost unimaginably terrible … .

On 1 February 1944 my friend Ily Erdődy and I started a theatre-nursing course at the military hospital where I had done my nursing course in 1942. As theatre work had suited me best when I was doing the volunteer nursing course, I wanted to study it in depth. On my first day Captain Iványi came in for an operation. I had been present at the first operation on his leg the previous year. We were pleased to meet again – never suspecting that eighteen months later we would meet again for a long period of exile in Bavaria.

By the end of the first week of the theatre-nursing course I had assisted in three operations, first as second instrumentalist, then as first instrumentalist, and in the third – for the first time in my life – as assistant. I was touched by the doctors' confidence in me.

Some very interesting operations were carried out in the military hospital. I assisted the surgeon, Captain Somogyi, who very successfully used new methods involving bone transplants in re-amputation of limbs that had previously been amputated under combat conditions. I was also sole instrumentalist for Professor Ertl in several brain operations.

The Szikla (Rock) hospital was inaugurated on 20 February. I worked there later, during the bombing raids. Some people called it the first-aid hospital, others the air raid hospital. The caves under Castle Hill had been there since the Turkish occupation and had originally been intended as shelters. The dangers of the Second World War prompted the idea that a centre should be built where injured people could undergo surgery undisturbed even during bombing raids. After many months of work a hospital had been built deep into the rock of Castle

Hill that could accommodate a hundred patients in bunk beds, in several wards. It had its own generator to provide electricity, and a supply of fresh air was also provided in a very ingenious manner: enormous air turbines drew in fresh air, which was warmed before being passed into the operating theatre, the wide corridors and the other rooms, and stale air was removed. There were three air changes each hour, and four in the operating theatre. The wells dug in the caves by the Turks were enlarged, and the water from them purified and piped into an enormous water tank. This automatically came into use when the external water supply failed. The hospital was supposed to be completely bombproof, even in the event of a direct hit by the most powerful bombs. At the end of an air raid, patients could then be transferred to other hospitals.

Around that time there were several reports of aerial incursions and alerts, but until then there had been no serious threat. This was due to Kállay's secret contacts. Under an agreement made covertly with the British and the Americans in the autumn of 1943, we would not impede the activities of Allied aircraft – which since 1943 had flown over Hungary almost daily – and they for their part would not bomb Hungary. Until the German invasion this agreement was kept by both sides, and benefited them as much as it did us. It also applied to Soviet aircraft. The Allied aircraft grouped over Hungary every day in preparation for attacks on Austria. They did not harm us and we did not shoot at them. But they did carry out bombing raids against Romania and Bulgaria.

As early as September 1943 the Hungarian government, through Turkey, told the Allies that if Allied forces reached the Hungarian border, Hungary would not resist. The British acknowledged this and agreed not to publicize it until the Allies did so. In preparation for this, at a suitable time they would send a delegation to Hungary by air. They would set up regular radio contacts between the Allies and the Hungarian government. A Hungarian was entrusted with a radio transmitter and code to bring in to Hungary, which as far as I know worked successfully until the German invasion.

There were also negotiations with the Americans through the Hungarian ambassador in Bern, György Bakách-Bessenyey, and the outcome was that an American delegation parachuted into Hungary. Unfortunately they landed a few days before the German invasion. It was a pity that these contacts and negotiations always took so long – but of course great care needed to be taken. Somehow things were always too late, and slowly the Germans found out about everything. It is undeniable that they had good reason to be mistrustful, as we were not very comfortable 'friends'. On the other hand, they were also clever, and all their tricks succeeded. Even the plots against Hitler failed. They succeeded with everything until their final collapse – when they dragged us down with them.

In my opinion Kállay's attempts to make contact with the Allies – and indeed to make secret agreements with them – were acts of great courage. I think he also chose his emissaries well, which was especially important. Could it be that all his efforts were in vain? Is it only in the afterlife that we will be given the recognition we deserve for our good deeds? It is not difficult to imagine how much Pista's presence in England or America at that time would have meant. Was his sacrifice on Saint Stephen's Day more important than that? I would have liked to understand how it all linked together, but I was just feeling around in ignorance. It looked to me as if everything that was honest, honourable and noble was being trampled underfoot, while hatred, criticism and greed were coming to the fore and indeed were victorious.

The situation became increasingly critical for Germany. By now they were suffering setbacks on every front. In March 1944 the vital question was whether we could gain enough time until they were finally defeated ...

We were also concerned about the many prisoners of war – Polish, French, British, etc. – who had fled to Hungary. So far we had achieved something little short of miraculous, and this should not be underestimated, in that so many refugees were living in peace in our country. At that time there was still some hope that the British and Americans would not hand us over to the Soviet Union; that, at worst, they would jointly invade us. Kállay received a telegram from the Hungarian ambassador in Lisbon just before the German invasion, which he published in his memoirs:

> Letters from American air force prisoners of war made a very good impression at the American Embassy here. Some high-ranking American air force officers happened to be there when the letters were handed over. The ambassador listed the names in a telegram to Washington, adding that a nation who treated its prisoners of war in this way deserved every consideration. [vol. II, p. 325]

We also knew what the Nazi leadership felt about our treatment of the prisoners of war, and we were aware of the Arrow Cross party and Nazi elements in Hungary, who would have preferred to bring in the Germans to take over power. We did not like to think about what would then happen to those people who had fled here from the Germans and were opposed to them – or in fact, what would happen to ourselves, who also would officially be considered enemies.

In the city, the news of the reverses suffered by Germany led to a general feeling of relief and people being less afraid of an imminent invasion. In Budapest society and in diplomatic circles there was a definite festive atmosphere in the carnival period leading up to Lent. I could not share this optimism and took no part in it, even though I received as many invitations to cocktail parties and dinners as in peacetime. Little did we think that this temporary 'peace' would last only another few days.

On 15 March, the day called 'Hungarian Freedom Holiday', on which the 1848 War of Independence was traditionally celebrated, I went to the County Hall to watch 430 Levente girls make their promise. Two years earlier on this day Pista had given the Leventes a flag on Heroes' Square and had made a speech, and I had stood by his side … . After 1944, Hungary was not to be free again for forty-six years. It's almost beyond comprehension why the world always has to destroy what it has painstakingly built up. Will this earth always be a scene of trials and temptations? Is this what our religion calls purgatory?

Later the same day there was a gala performance by the scouts in the Opera House. The celebration was organized by university students, and was attended by the Regent, members of the government, diplomats and other notables. During the interval the counsellor at the German Embassy gave the duty aide-de-camp a message that Jagow, the German ambassador, requested an urgent audience after the festivities in order to hand over a letter written personally by Hitler. Miklóspapa agreed, telling us that he expected no good to come out of the audience. He immediately asked Prime Minister Kállay to join him in his box and told him what had happened. We returned to the Palace in downcast mood, and Ambassador Jagow arrived during dinner and handed over Hitler's letter. It contained an invitation from the Führer for the Regent to go to Klessheim to discuss the matters raised in the Regent's letter to him, to which Hitler had been unable to reply before, due to illness. Hitler wrote that he now had to return to his General Headquarters urgently, and requested that the Regent visit him within two days, together with the war minister and the chief of general staff, as military decisions would be discussed.

My father-in-law held a series of discussions with Prime Minister Kállay, Foreign Minister Ghyczy, General Szombathelyi the chief of general staff, Defence Minister Csatay and others, asking each of them in turn for their opinion. A detailed account of these discussions can be found in both Prime Minister Kállay's and my father-in-law's memoirs. For myself, all I can say is that my mother-in-law and I were in a state of near desperation as we waited for their decision. We both thought that under no circumstances should Miklóspapa go to Hitler: some excuse should be found to postpone the visit.

As we subsequently found out, the best proposal came from Kállay: that Szombathelyi should go on behalf of my father-in-law, and Miklóspapa approved of this. However, Szombathelyi himself disagreed, and emphasized that the Regent was the only person who might possibly succeed in having our forces returned home.

When my father-in-law returned from these discussions he said that he had decided to go to Hitler himself and told us why: the withdrawal of the Hungarian troops from the Russian front, something we had been demanding constantly for a year, might be decided at that meeting, and our troops would never return home if he did not accept the invitation. He had to try personally to secure the return of the Hungarian soldiers. We played bridge after dinner in a very sombre mood, knowing that the next day Miklóspapa was going to see Hitler.

On 17 March the Regent left for Klessheim, escorted by Foreign Minister Ghyczy, Defence Minister Csatay, and General Szombathelyi.

I was in despair: I could not understand how Miklóspapa could be put in such danger. How could anyone believe that the German leaders were telling the truth? They would not allow the Hungarian troops to come home anyway, so what was behind all this? Everything was full of doubt and uncertainty.

The next day, 18 March, I had to go to Szolnok for the flag dedication ceremony and the unveiling of a statue of Pista, which were planned for the following day. I drove there, and in the evening attended an official dinner with Corps Commander Ferenc Farkas, Air Force Commander Csathó and others. My thoughts were always in Klessheim. After dinner I rang Magdamama to find out the news, but nobody knew anything; there was not even a phone link to Vienna, and even Kállay knew nothing. I could not get to sleep for a long time, I was so preoccupied with what was happening. What would we wake up to the next day? What was the worst that might happen: that Miklóspapa would not be allowed home, everything would collapse, the Germans would invade, and the Russians would fight them in Hungary? I hoped this was just my fears working on my imagination, that it was just a nightmare ... .

The reality turned out to be worse than anything I could have imagined.

13

The Germans Invade, 19 March 1944

19 March 1944: one of the worst days of my life. In Szolnok that morning we heard that large numbers of German troops had crossed our border in several places. Of course resistance was impossible, because in the absence of the Regent and the defence minister nobody could give the order to resist. What would have happened had the vice-regent been here?

On the other hand, the Nazis thought that the country would welcome them with jubilation. But in that they were disappointed, because people did not wave and did not cheer them; on the contrary, several people told me that the population displayed only indignation.

The Germans had planned the invasion very cleverly, with great attention to detail. 19 March was a Sunday, so all offices were empty. It was impossible to assess what the consequences of the invasion would be. I felt as if I had been hit over the head.

In Szolnok, Ferenc Farkas the Debrecen Corps commander came to me in a state of indignation to tell me the news, and from the way he spoke that morning I was convinced that he thought the way I did. I would never have believed that after 15 October – when Szálasi was in power – Farkas would join him and sit with the Arrow Cross Court that passed judgment on his fellow generals. General Lajos Dálnoki Veress told me personally after the war that at his trial he had been shocked to see Ferenc Farkas sitting there, and that during the trial Farkas had not looked at him once.

But to return to Szolnok: I went to mass in the morning and to communion, and asked the Almighty to have mercy on us. The flag dedication ceremony was of course cancelled, and perhaps it was just as well that Pista's statue was not unveiled, because either the Nazis or the Communists would have removed it anyway. (Years later it was found and replaced.) I was in constant touch with Budapest by phone. I found out that Miklóspapa was returning home, but that his train was progressing very slowly because it was being held up at every station; he finally arrived at eleven o'clock that morning. I could imagine his state of mind.

A car was sent straight away to take me back to the Palace with Lieutenant General Miklós Kóos and – horror of horrors – a German second lieutenant. I protested that I did not need a German escort, but I was warned that if the German officer was not with us we might be held up on the way and it was by no means certain that we would get to Budapest. Had we reached the point where I could travel safely in Hungary only with a German escort? The officer sat in front next to the driver and did not speak to us. We were indeed stopped twice on the way, and were allowed to continue only when the German officer confirmed who we were. Anyone who has not experienced this will find it hard to imagine what a dreadful feeling it was. Something was boiling up inside me and I thought I would explode. Unfortunately many people in Europe came to know this feeling.

We got back to Budapest at four in the afternoon, and then the real shock hit me: I saw two armed German guards standing, feet apart, on either side of the Lion Gate leading to the Palace courtyard. I could not believe my eyes; this was very hard to bear. I did not even wait for the lift, but just ran straight upstairs to find my parents-in-law. Miklóspapa was in a meeting of the Council of State and I had to wait until that was over before I could see him. Magdamama was in despair too, and we just looked at each other without speaking: we were thinking the same thing and did not need to put it into words.

The German guards were removed from the Lion Gate after about ten days, due to protests from my father-in-law; but during that time I drove in and out several times, and each time I drove past the guards I got in such a rage that I had to fight to control myself in order not to drive into them. But even though the guards were taken away, there were always some Nazi observers on Szent György Square, through which one entered the Palace grounds.

Jean de Bavier, the Red Cross High Commissioner, came to see me the same afternoon for urgent discussions and with all sorts of questions in connection with the current situation. He had often been to see me in the preceding months, when we had mainly discussed the situation of the Poles in Hungary. He was followed by Anti Szapáry, who was very downcast about the situation.

The family was finally together again in the evening. During and after dinner my father-in-law recounted to us the events of the previous days. He was pale and exhausted; he had not had a proper rest in days. He described this dramatic encounter with Hitler in detail in his memoirs. Others too have described it, including Prime Minister Kállay, whose account in his memoirs is based on what he heard from my father-in-law that day. I will just give a brief outline of the events as Miklóspapa related them to us.

He and Hitler met alone for their discussions. Hitler spoke of the Italians' shocking act of betrayal. He did not even mention the return of our forces from the Russian front, launching straight into an allegation that Hungary wanted to go over to the side of the enemy, of which he had proof. He listed the evidence and said that he had to take certain precautionary measures in order to avoid being betrayed again. When it became clear that he was talking about invading Hungary, my father-in-law got up and walked out. He went up to his apartment to tell the other members of the party what had happened, and demanded to return home immediately. What the Regent did not realize at the time was that Hitler's 'precautionary measures' had already begun. An attempt was then made to prevent their departure. He was told that the train had been shunted to Salzburg and that there was an air raid alert. The castle was put under a smoke screen, and it was reported that telephone links had been broken.

At the same time, Hitler sent a message requesting the Regent to continue their discussions and to accept his invitation to lunch. My father-in-law went to lunch in the hope that he might be able to do something to improve the situation. The atmosphere was tense, nobody spoke; Hitler picked irritably at his vegetarian dish. After lunch Hitler pretended that he had regretted his former decision, and in Miklóspapa's presence asked Keitel whether the invasion of Hungary could be stopped. (Pure theatre!) Keitel reported that the troops were already marching. Then Hitler started pleading with Miklóspapa and insisted that he had always liked Hungary and would not dream of encroaching on its independence.

Miklóspapa continues in his memoirs:

> [Hitler stated,] 'I give you my word that the German troops shall be withdrawn as soon as a new Hungarian government that has my confidence has been formed.' I replied that I had to reserve judgement on that point, and withdrew once more to my apartments.
>
> What was I to do? It was plain that my resignation would not prevent the military occupation, would indeed merely give Hitler an opportunity to introduce a hundred per cent Nazi-Arrow-Cross regime. The precedent of the Italian débâcle with its horrible attendant circumstances constituted a timely warning. So long as I continued as head of state the Germans would have to show a certain circumspection. They

would have to leave the Hungarian army under my orders, and would therefore be unable to incorporate it into the German army. While I was in charge, they could not attempt putting the Arrow Cross party into office to do their deadly work of murdering Hungarian patriots, of exterminating the eight hundred thousand Hungarian Jews and tens of thousands of refugees who had sought sanctuary in Hungary. It would have been easier for me to make the grand gesture of abdication, and I should have been spared many a denunciation; but to leave a sinking ship, especially one that needed her captain more than ever, was a step I could not bring myself to take. More important to me then was that Hitler had promised to withdraw his troops from Hungary as soon as an acceptable government had been appointed.

One thing was clear to me: whatever 'proofs' Hitler may have had of our negotiations with the enemy, his treachery in overrunning our country after having lured me and my ministers away from Budapest was so iniquitous that henceforward we should be entirely released from any obligations to Nazi Germany. [pp. 284–85]

As there was still no report that the train was ready for departure, my father-in-law asked whether he was to consider himself a prisoner. As a result the air raid alert was cancelled and the train turned up. But it was then that their most despicable act came: Foreign Minister Ribbentrop arrived just before they were due to depart and showed them the text of the report which was to be published about the 'visit.' This stated that German troops had entered Hungary by 'mutual consent'. Of course the Regent was outraged, and asked Ribbentrop why he did not improve on the story by adding that the Regent had begged Hitler to invade Hungary with Slovak and Romanian forces, which was another of the threats Hitler had actually made. Ribbentrop wriggled desperately, putting forward the plea that in life minor untruths were often necessary, and that phrased as it was the communiqué made the occupation appear less hostile. The Regent demanded that the reference to a joint agreement be deleted, and Ribbentrop agreed. Despite this, the original text appeared unaltered in the German press.

My father-in-law was then left weighing up the consequences if he resigned or if, as he felt he must, he stayed in office. If he resigned, his position would be taken by an Imrédy or Arrow Cross government, one that would be completely at the service of the Nazis. On the other hand, he knew that in holding on, from now on he would be alone; anyone who could help him would be removed. But he had to stay whatever happened and save what he could; being still in command of the army he might be able to defend those who had placed their trust in him. He tried to look at it from every point of view – it is only now that it occurs to me that the only viewpoint he did not consider was that of his family and himself.

So the situation was that a new government, acceptable to Hitler, had to be formed as a matter of urgency. The Germans allowed three days for this, otherwise they would proceed with a full invasion.

As I later found out, all these events were being recounted in the Council of State meeting while Magdamama and I were sitting together in her apartment. Kállay refused to take any further part in the government, and also called on the Regent to resign or at least step back from the day-to-day running of affairs. He recalls in his memoirs the clarity of the Regent's response in giving the reasons why he could not do so. Kállay concludes:

> Unfortunately his calculations and his ideas proved incorrect. It's true that he helped many people, he saved almost half of Hungary's Jews, but he couldn't help the country as a whole. And he could help himself least of all, although I can confirm that this factor affected him least of all. He was right in suggesting that any resistance could only develop around him: if he hadn't stayed in post, then Sztójay wouldn't have been followed by Lakatos, which meant reversal and brought about an incredibly big change ... And without Horthy the proclamation of 15 October also couldn't have happened. And even though it failed – because it couldn't have succeeded – in that proclamation Horthy was able to speak for the Hungarian people's soul and express their true desire. [vol. II, p. 190]

Much to my indignation the new German ambassador, Edmund Veesenmayer – whose official title was now plenipotentiary of the German Reich – did not even give my father-in-law a chance to rest but came for an audience that same evening.

It was not long after this that, early one morning, the prime minister's residence was surrounded and an SS officer came beating on the door. Lieutenant László Zólyomi of the guards managed to delay the SS troops, who were armed with hand grenades and held machine guns at the ready, while the Kállay family escaped through an underground passage to the Palace.

You need to know that there is an elaborate but linked system of tunnels between Bécsi-kapu Square and the Palace. These underground passages linked the Interior, Finance, Foreign and War Ministries, the prime minister's office and the Regent's residence, and also the army Chaplain General's residence and the Archduke's palace – or rather, the bomb shelters for all these places. These had been extended to provide the maximum possible accommodation and furnishings for the Regent's family and staff, and also for officials. There were several exits: to the tunnel, to Szent György Square, plus two others.

This happened at six in the morning. My parents-in-law were woken up, and Miklóspapa immediately arranged for the Kállays to stay in the Palace under his protection. He rang Commissioner Veesenmayer to protest. Veesenmayer replied that he did indeed want to meet Kállay, but there was no question of arresting him. Later events proved this too to be a lie.

On the previous day the Turkish ambassador, Sevket Fuat Kececi, had offered Helen Kállay refuge in the Turkish Embassy for her husband. The ambassador now repeated his offer, and sent his car to the back gate of the Palace gardens.

Miklós Kállay said an emotional goodbye to his family, and was taken safely to the Turkish residence. Ambassador Kececi and his wife welcomed Kállay and received permission from their government to give him asylum. From that time the Turkish Embassy was under constant German guard, surrounded by four armoured cars and lit up by searchlights at night. Helen Kállay and her children were accommodated on the ground floor of the Palace, and we saw a lot of each other over the following months.

Miklóspapa spent the whole day involved in difficult negotiations on forming the new government. Those whom the Germans wanted were rejected by the Regent, and those whom he wanted to appoint were either not acceptable to the Germans or were already in hiding or under arrest. As Hitler had given his word that he would withdraw his troops as soon as an acceptable government was formed, it was important for the Regent to form such a one as soon as possible, and clearly it was also important for the Germans. On this subject the historian Péter Gosztonyi writes:

> In the following days Gyula Kádár, who was soon
> arrested by the Gestapo because of his British links, was
> still looking for a way of meeting Nicholas Horthy

junior, the head of the 'Escape Office'. [More about the 'Escape Office' later in this chapter.]

On 21 March, in pouring rain, he knocked on one of the side doors of the Palace. He wrote: 'In the Palace yard German soldiers in camouflage raincoats and armed with machine guns stood close to the wall. The gates of the building were locked. Inside the gates, bodyguards stood next to machine guns. Horthy junior told me that the Germans had given his father an ultimatum that if the new government wasn't formed by 6 p.m. they would occupy the Palace and take over complete control. Then he said that they were prepared to defend themselves.[21]

We found out later that when the Sztójay government was formed and the Regent rejected certain nominations such as Béla Imrédy, Jenő Ruszkay, etc., the plan to occupy the Palace and take control was already in place. Péter Gosztonyi quotes from the diary of Baron Maximilian Weichs, the German general charged by Hitler with implementing the invasion of Hungary:

'In the days following 19 March the situation became strained. Horthy dug his heels in and kept rejecting the nominations for ministerial posts and for prime minister, which Veesenmayer was trying to push through with the interests of the Reich in mind.' Weichs grew restless. The German High Command wanted him to prepare for 'repressive acts to be implemented as soon as possible.' These were the military occupation of the Palace and the disarming of the Hungarian army. Weichs' diary entry for 22 March reads: 'If we did all this it would be a despicable policy, the consequences of which cannot be calculated. If we took such a step, then the various groups in the Hungarian opposition who are still on our side and who are dissatisfied with the current situation would immediately line up against us. The newly formed government would resign, together with the Regent. There would be a general uprising in Hungary. So in the end we ourselves would produce partisans to fight against us, and to combat those we would be forced to keep a strong contingent of troops in the country. In other words we would achieve exactly the opposite of what we wanted! Instead of gaining new troops for the

> eastern front we would have to withdraw some from
> there to keep order. Yes, there would be strikes and an
> uprising ...[22]

It is interesting to realize that on the one hand we were able to do only
a little here and there, very carefully, as we were afraid that the Germans
might seize total control, but on the other hand the Germans did not
dare do away with us completely for fear of provoking a total rebellion,
and in order to maintain the appearance of cooperation.

I have read in Péter Gosztonyi's account that it was chiefly Foreign
Minister Ribbentrop's idea that the Regent should be removed and the
army disarmed. So Weichs requested an audience with Hitler in which
his idea was accepted, and he made the following entry in his diary on
28 March:

> The Führer is extremely mistrustful of the
> Hungarians. He particularly hates Horthy, whom he
> accuses of standing completely against Germany. He
> still has contacts with the enemy powers. Therefore we
> can count on his continuing treachery, which may even
> endanger the eastern front, so we won't request too
> many corps. But it's not a good idea to disarm the army.
> We will use the excuse that we have no equipment for
> them ...[23]

I felt terribly sorry for my father-in-law during those days. He had to
fight for our freedom; he lost reliable colleagues, who were either under
arrest or in hiding; he received reports that drove him to despair; and
day after day he had to weigh up vital questions and make decisions.
This continued for many months, until finally he was left completely on
his own.

There were people who later said and wrote that the Regent became
apathetic and withdrawn after the German invasion. This is not true at
all: I did not see it, and I was with him every day. The one thing that
kept his hopes alive was Hitler's promise that, if a government which
suited him were formed, he would withdraw the occupation forces. This
was what Miklóspapa wanted to achieve, and he hoped that Hitler
would keep his word. If a head of state – in this case Hitler – gave his
word about something, it was unthinkable to the Regent that he would
break it. We, who belonged to a different generation, had no such
convictions. If Hitler gave his word about something then I immediately
wondered what was behind it, what he was trying to achieve; and in this
instance I did not believe for a moment that he would keep his word. It
is true that when the government was formed Hitler took part of his

army out to the south, but they were replaced by more Gestapo and SS units coming in from the west.

Now I would like to give some more details about the 'Escape Office' mentioned earlier. In order to be better informed about the situation in the country and about the people's mood, in the autumn of 1943 the Regent had – in agreement with Prime Minister Kállay – set up a special office. Situated on the ground floor of the Palace, this was headed by my brother-in-law Nicky Horthy, working with his secretary, Dezső Ónódy. Nicky – like Pista – was known to be anti-Nazi. Their official brief was 'to manage the affairs of Hungarians living outside Hungary', but its main aim was to obtain information about the meetings and activities of anti-Nazi and opposition parties inside Hungary. Thus it strove to strengthen the anti-Nazi parties. In addition, in order to keep the Regent better informed, it allowed people – mainly Jews – who would not otherwise have had the opportunity to approach him. It formed a link between the Regent and the illegal organisations. It also maintained constant contact with the Council of Jews, and after the German occupation it served mainly to give exemption certificates and help to those who were being persecuted. For instance, it managed to help some British, American and Polish former prisoners of war who had fled to Hungary, making their stay there more tolerable.

This office did not really have a name, but public opinion later called it – appropriately enough – the 'Escape Office'. The other members of staff were Domokos Szent-Iványi and Géza Sóos. Another office was set up in Tárnok street, and I heard that there, Miklós Mester, the state secretary for religious and education affairs, did outstanding work in granting exemption certificates on the Regent's behalf, in cooperation with Nicky and with Ambrózy, the head of the Regent's Cabinet Office.

As the Regent was entitled to grant exemption certificates, one of the jobs of this office was to make out 'letters of protection' on behalf of the Regent for persecuted Jews. In this way, for some given reason – such as 'activities in the service of the homeland' – several thousand Jews were able to avoid being moved into a ghetto. The office received instructions 'from the top' that no applicant should be rejected. There was also no need to track down any given information by those who applied. I heard from Nicky how depressing it was to see the former leading figures of the country's economy coming to the office for help, wearing the yellow star of David. Despite many difficulties, the office worked very well and helped innumerable Jews to escape.

I had lunch with Nicky and my parents-in-law on the twenty-first, and we had a very long talk afterwards. Miklóspapa said among other things that he would never sign any anti-Jewish decree or law, nor would he countersign any such measure issued by any ministry.

After dinner we had a long family discussion in a sombre mood. We were worried about our friend and former prime minister, István Bethlen; although he had managed to escape and was in hiding somewhere, we did not know how long he would be able to avoid capture. Many people had not been so lucky, such as Lipót Baranyi, Ferenc and Lajos Keresztes-Fischer, Baron Dániel Bánffy and Count György Apponyi, as well as leading Jewish figures and others, who had immediately been taken away by the Germans. Numerous others were in hiding. Several leading aristocrats had also been arrested. The feeling of dread was terrible – one tried to avoid thinking, because it would just make one despair.

Ferenc Chorin and Baron Manfred Weiss – both members of the upper house – had also been arrested. The Weiss Manfred factory in Csepel was the country's biggest heavy industrial works, employing forty thousand workers. We were later told that a high ranking SS officer went to see them on behalf of Himmler with the proposal that if they 'agreed' to sign over all the profits from the factory to the SS for twenty-five years, then the forty-two members of the families would not be harmed but would be allowed to leave Hungary and go to a neutral country. The 'agreement' was made, and at the end of June members of the Chorin, Weiss, Kornfeld and Mauthner families reached Portugal. Most of them later went on to the United States, and Ferenc Chorin was one of the people who later supported the Regent financially when he was in exile.

In the afternoon of 22 March the government was finally formed: Döme Sztójay was prime minister, and foreign minister; and unfortunately László Baky and László Endre, known to be anti-Jewish, were appointed state secretaries in the Interior Ministry.

My diary says: 'This was a dreadful day!' It was almost physically painful because I felt that the Nazi gang was achieving everything they wanted. The only hope was that it would not last long.

Miklóspapa told us, 'Poor Sztójay didn't want to take it on,' and added that as Sztójay was a lieutenant general, he hoped he could count on him doing what he, the Regent, wanted when the situation became critical.

I now started working regularly as a theatre nurse in the military hospital, starting at seven each morning, which kept my mind off other things. On the first day there was a very serious cranial operation. I assisted Dr Somogyi, and I found the shell fragment in the brain. During cranial operations our faces were very close to the ether used to anaesthetize the patient, which gave me a bad cold, but I got used to that. This was followed by work on a variety of plastic surgery techniques.

We had to do a lot of reconstructive surgery on the chins, mouths, eyes and noses of men who had been wounded at the front. We even constructed a new jawbone for a soldier, using bone taken from his leg.

At that time in the Szikla hospital we had a young patient whom I will never forget. She was a gypsy girl, about six years old, who had been brought in to us with severe leg wounds. Changing the dressings was very painful and she bore it with amazing courage. In order to distract her, we suggested that while we change her dressings she should sing the gypsy song we had heard her singing in the ward. After that she dutifully started singing every time her dressings were changed. Her little mouth twisted with pain and she was on the verge of tears, but she carried on singing, 'Iste chale, iste chale ...' We sang with her. This little gypsy song – of which we did not understand a single word – became our hospital song; whenever one of us was in trouble or upset, we sang. I can even sing it now, so many years later.

In April – with the help of the Interior Ministry – the Germans started the secret deportation of the Jews. What now followed was a different kind of story. Over fifty years have passed, and thinking back – reading my diary – memories come to life again of happenings which of course everyone experienced from their own point of view. But when I think back I can still feel that strange feeling in the solar plexus, what causes it I do not know: helplessness, desperation or disgust?

The Regent's Responsibility and the Jewish Question

Before I continue describing these events we should pause a little, while I try to cast some light on two important topics: the question of the Regent's responsibility, and the Jewish question – in relation to and independently of the Regent's responsibility.

Hungary's constitution is about as old as the British one, and the two are very similar. Among the states of the Danube valley and the Balkans, Hungary was the only strictly parliamentary country. During the period leading up to the German invasion the Regent cannot be called to account for the government's actions: under constitutional law it is the government which is responsible. Those he appointed as head of government all started out as anti-Nazis. But beginning with Gömbös, the Regent gradually lost his confidence in any government, or rather prime minister, because their policies began to be directly influenced by Nazi Germany. The most obvious examples of this were the declarations of war against Britain, Russia and the US, when the prime minister in effect presented the Regent with a *fait accompli*.

The issue of the Regent's responsibility after 19 March may be disputed, but then he had no freedom to act, in a country occupied by a foreign power. All he could do was act as a restraining force and prepare for resistance, which he undertook to do and carried through. Not one of his actions in that period was in favour of the Germans, and there is clear proof that he prevented German interference whenever he saw an opportunity to do so.

It could be said that the Regent perhaps could have acted earlier and done more, but we must not forget that any step too far could have provoked a reaction from the Germans and resulted in their seizing total control. Hitler did indeed threaten these things. The Regent would not have been able to prevent this except by waiting for opportunities to arise. Who can decide, who can judge what might have happened if he had intervened more forcefully and at an earlier stage ... . It happened that, due to the position in which he found himself and with his advanced age, sometimes he could not command an overview of the situation. He could not trust the government at the time, and he could be influenced by the reports of high-ranking army officers he assumed were reliable. There were always those who deliberately tried to mislead him, concealing the real situation and only reporting what they thought he would like to hear. But it is undeniable that the Regent always tried to resist Nazi pressure as far as he was able.

You must remember how many upsetting events the 76-year-old Regent had lived through in the preceding years. Just in the four years since I had joined the family he had lost his beloved daughter Paulette, his good and valued friend Pál Teleki, his 38-year-old son Stephen who, with his firm and strong determination would have been an inestimable support to him; and I could say that through the German occupation he had now even lost his country.

I know that after 19 March many people said that, in audiences, the Regent sometimes did not give his visitors an opportunity to say what they wanted to say. I had experienced this sometimes at family gatherings too, when some problem cropped up and he changed the subject. At such times I had the feeling that he did not want to hear any more requests or arguments because he knew he could not satisfy or change them; and when he could not see a way out, he sometimes symbolically blocked his ears.

To give a wider view than that of my own, I will quote the opinions of two well-known personalities who were in positions of responsibility at that time. First some extracts from the introduction written by Nicholas Roosevelt (US ambassador in Hungary from 1930 to 1933) for the American edition of Miklós Horthy's memoirs. While he was serving as ambassador he frequently visited the Regent, and he renewed his contact with us after the war:

Throughout most of the two decades that followed the armistice of 1918 [Admiral Horthy] was a symbol of sanity, order and stability in an unstable, disordered and sick Europe. ... As Regent his policy was to try to restore to Hungary the boundaries it had had before the Habsburg empire broke up – a policy which, however commendable to Magyars, ran counter to the nationalist aspirations and fears of non-Magyars and was doomed to failure. ... Royalists never forgave him for having twice thwarted ex-King Charles's attempts to regain the throne of Hungary – attempts which, if successful, would surely have brought about the invasion and occupation of Hungary by the neighbour states. The words put into the mouth of Brutus at Caesar's funeral by Shakespeare could well be paraphrased: 'Not that Horthy loved Charles less, but Hungary more.' When, twenty years later, Regent Horthy appeared to go along with Hitler, it was because he was faced with force which neither resistance nor appeasement could curb. What the outside world did not realize was that Hitler's hatred of Horthy's independence and fearlessness was one of the reasons why the Führer took over control of Hungary and virtually made the Regent his prisoner. ...

Fearless, incorruptible, steadfast, his influence, like that of George Washington, stemmed from strength of character rather than brilliance of intellect. Men might disagree with him, but even his enemies respected him. They might question his judgement, but none questioned his integrity and uprightness.[24]

Prime Minister Kállay wrote about the 'Horthy regime' in the following terms in his memoirs:

The Horthy regime! How it has been abused and attacked! What a campaign of slander is directed against it even now in the countries calling themselves People's Republics! He has been called a dictator, a bloodthirsty sadist, an antisocial autocrat and oppressor. None of these charges are true. Horthy was no dictator, only a restorer of order and authority. It was he who gave back liberty to our people after the Communist terror of 1918 and the ensuing Romanian occupation. Neither before and certainly not since,

under the present regime, have so many social and
welfare institutions been created as were during that
quarter of a century. After the defeat of Communist
rule there came, certainly, the judgement of the people
– the vengeance of the incensed masses is not always
just or equitable – and the procedure taken against the
criminals was very mild indeed. But what happened
then was not a thousandth part of what is being done
today: a few hundred victims, compared with hundreds
of thousands. ...

Tragic as was the close of Miklós Horthy's rule, in
the eyes of the Hungarian people he will always remain
one of the country's great sons. His personal qualities,
his high character and chivalrous disposition, the purity
of his motives, his unquestionable good will and
complete devotion to Hungary and its people, will
decide his place in our history. ... I for my part will
remain faithful to him, in love and loyalty, as long as I
live. [pp. 466–48]

I think sufficient proof of the Horthy regime's attitude was
demonstrated by the situation of Jews and refugees in Hungary up until
the time of the German occupation. And what could have been done
during the occupation? When the German position became increasingly
critical and the first opportunity arose, the deportations were stopped
and the government imposed by the Germans was replaced.
Unfortunately there were groups who helped the occupiers with
enthusiasm; such distasteful behaviour could be seen in every country,
and cannot be defended.

Some people have asked why my father-in-law stayed in post after 19
March 1944. As I heard him say many times, he did so because he
wanted at all costs to give Hungary back its lost freedom; he wanted to
regain his own ability to act. Slowly but surely he succeeded in the
latter: in July he was able to save the Jews of Budapest; in August he was
able to dismiss the government approved by the Germans and send a
delegation to Moscow to propose an armistice agreement; and in
October, after his radio proclamation when he told the world about
Hungary's desperate plight, the Germans arrested him. There is no
doubt that he did what he could.

Another important thing we must not forget is that because the
Regent stayed in post the Germans were unable to achieve their aims in
full. His presence and his resistance made it impossible to go over
completely to a German or Arrow Cross system. Hungary provided

only 2 per cent of Germany's war effort, whereas Czech industry contributed 40 per cent. By leaving and allowing Hacha to take over power, Benes left the whole of Czech industrial production at the disposal of Germany. This is not intended as criticism; it is just a statement of the facts.

People have also argued that by withdrawing and resigning, the Regent could have obtained lasting approval for Hungary when it came to signing the peace treaties. We now know that this is incorrect, because it had already been decided in Teheran, well before the end of the war, that the Soviets would be allowed to occupy Hungary. Even Count Pál Teleki was not mentioned in the peace negotiations – Churchill's promise to keep a seat for him at the negotiating table had been forgotten.

In fact, the Regent staying in post definitely served the interests of the Allies too. After 19 March, having lost Kállay – who had begun to seek contacts with the Western Allies in 1942 – he himself took up contact with them. Hungary always took the initiative in seeking contacts; and although the Allies made no promises as to the advantages we would gain by resisting, there is no doubt that the Regent did not give up trying. It was his firm intention to free the country from the occupiers. He persisted in the hope that the Allies would not hand these countries over to the Soviet Union, and his fear of Soviet occupation proved to be completely justified.

As Nicholas Roosevelt also wrote:

> The last time I saw this staunch old admiral was when I paid my farewell visit to him before returning to the United States in 1933. He spoke with passionate earnestness about his conviction that Russia was the greatest threat not only to Hungary but to the Western world. For years this subject had been an obsession of his – so much so, in fact, that the members of the diplomatic corps in Budapest in the '30s discounted it as a phobia.
>
> Events have proved that his fears were justified. True, it was the Nazis who started Hungary down the path of destruction. But it was the Russians who crushed the spirit of the Hungarian nation and reduced the economic level of the Magyars to pre-feudal poverty. The Hungarian Regent in this case had foreseen correctly, but he was unable to convince either British or American leaders that Communist Russia was even more rapacious and greedy than Czarist Russia, that it was folly to believe that if Russia was

treated as a friendly ally that country would respond in
kind. [p. 9]

As for the persecution of the Jews, this incomprehensible, abominably
evil act and dreadful tragedy in the life of the country: an account of the
degradation and hellish suffering these people endured would take
several chapters, and these are now well known and documented.
However, we should not make judgments on the situation at that time
from the benefit of hindsight, from what we now know happened in
Hungary and in the extermination camps outside Hungary.

Though outraged by Hitler's words 'ich werde sie zerschmettern,
ausrotten,' (I will crush them and exterminate them) I myself
understood them to mean that he would destroy the Jews' influence in
society and in the economy. A rational mind could never have imagined
the reality, the brutal genocide. I would like to know who could have
imagined that millions of people could be exterminated in gas chambers,
in concentration camps, or that a civilized, cultured people like the
Germans could produce such monsters.

Nobody actually knew exactly what was going on. The newspapers
did not report events, news just spread by word of mouth. It must also
be remembered that many reports were circulating at the time which,
like those about a 'miracle weapon', were spread deliberately both by
the Communists and the Nazis. It was difficult to judge what was true,
and people began to distrust such rumours. I did not hear about
exterminations in gas chambers – but I do not think I would have
believed it if I had – until I read the Auschwitz Records (see chapter 13).
And we only discovered the full truth many years after the war about
the number of trains on which the four hundred and thirty-seven
thousand Jews were transported out of the country, and the brutality
with which this often was done.

At the time this was all very skilfully hidden from the Regent. He was
told, 'They aren't being deported, they're just being taken away to
work,' and so on. The deceptions were limitless. A shocking example of
this is the agreement the German Reich made with the Sztójay
government specifying the amount of food Hungary should transport to
Germany to feed the Hungarian Jewish workers who had been taken
there.

Some people portray my father-in-law as being responsible for the
deportations; on the other hand others are grateful to him for managing
to save so many Jews. I do not find it difficult to assess my father-in-
law's role: whatever anyone may say or write about it, his attitude was
perfectly clear to me.

There is no question that my father-in-law did condemn the Jewish leaders who were part of the Communist regime that committed horrible atrocities after the First World War. But he made it clear, when in the aftermath of the counter-revolutionary victory of 1919 there was an increased atmosphere of anti-Jewish feeling and the Jews of Budapest feared a pogrom, that he was most determined that no such reprisals should occur. Everywhere he emphasized collaboration and reconciliation.

Between 1920 and 1938 the only discriminatory act passed by Parliament was the *numerus clausus* bill of 1920, which limited the proportion of students to enter higher education according to the proportion of 'various races or nationalities' within the nation as a whole. This resulted in only 5 per cent of Jews being allowed into universities. And when Bethlen became prime minister in 1921, the Regent fully agreed with and supported his reforms, which over the next ten years included amending the *numerus clausus* bill, granting the Jews the same rights of representation in the upper house of Parliament as other religious communities, and in 1927 authorizing the activities of the Zionist organization.

It was only with the rise to power of right-wing elements within the government and the growing pressure from Nazi Germany in the late thirties that Parliament passed further anti-Jewish legislation. Bound by the constitution, the Regent was unable to prevent its implementation.

It is important to mention that whenever Hitler wrote or spoke about resolving the issue of the Jews in Hungary, our understanding was that this would mean stricter economic and cultural laws, and more Jewish workers being taken to work in German munitions factories. There were already many Hungarian workers in Germany – though they had not been forced to go – and as they were also being expected to contribute in full strength to the war effort we understood that there was no way out of this predicament: we had to tolerate this solution which had been imposed on us, and send out a larger contingent of workers – mainly as a way of gaining time. We had no way of knowing that they were going to be exterminated.

Another accusation frequently made against my father-in-law is that he sought to save only the rich Jews. This is an ill-intentioned interpretation of something he said in front of me more than once: that he would not send to work elsewhere Jews (or any one) whose skills were needed in our own country. When he found out at the beginning of July 1944 that the Jews were being taken not to factories but to extermination camps there was no question of who could be taken and who could not: he was not selective but saved the entire Jewish population of Budapest. It is undeniable that nobody else would have been able to do this. The tragedy was that the German collapse was delayed, so by the time he was able to act it was too late to save the Jews who lived outside Budapest.

After the war my brother-in-law Nicky, through his secretary Dr Dezső Ónódy, asked the leaders of the Council of Hungarian Jews at the time of the German occupation for a declaration about his father's behaviour, which they wrote and sent to us.[vii] I later received a letter, written in Brazil on 22 March 1956 by Dr Ernő Pető – one of the signatories to the declaration – addressed to Dr Lajos Marton in Jerusalem. This letter was published in issue 1989/4 of the cultural magazine *Tekintet*, and the following extract complements the declaration:

> Dr László Sándor told me that the Horthys had, through Dr Ónódy, asked for a declaration on their behaviour during the German occupation from the leaders of the Jewish community in Budapest at that time. I told Samu Stern and Károly Wilhelm about this. We felt that we couldn't refuse ... The declaration confirms things which actually happened ... On page 272 of his book, Horthy discusses events which took place under the German occupation from the beginning of July to about the end of August. As I have said before, his analysis is based on true facts and his assessment is not exaggerated.

On one occasion during the German occupation Miklóspapa asked the leaders of the Jewish community to come up to the Palace for discussions about their situation. He sent his son Nicky to fetch them in his own official car, on which the Regent's pennant ensured that they would be allowed through all checkpoints. I do not know that anyone has ever mentioned this.

From as early as 1939 there had been attempts to organize an emigration route for Jews from Czechoslovakia and Hungary along the Danube and into Palestine, but only small successes had been achieved. In 1943 there was another attempt to make this happen, and the Regent again gave this his full support. Unfortunately it could not be implemented, though it would have been an excellent solution in that critical situation.

After the war, when we had been freed from German captivity, Dr Ruben Hecht, an avowed Zionist who later served for years as an advisor to the Israeli prime minister Menachem Begin, came to Germany to recruit Jews for Israel, and used the opportunity to visit us.

[vii] Appendix 6: Text of declaration signed by Dr Ernő Pető, Samu Stern, Dr Károly Wilhelm.

He had come to thank the Regent for what he had done for the Jews because, he said, he knew that my father-in-law had supported the plan and been involved in negotiations concerning the emigration of Hungarian Jews to Israel. He also knew that it was not the Regent's fault that this plan had failed.

I regret now not having asked him to record his opinion in writing, but at the time I never imagined that I would need it; I thought my father-in-law's attitude was sufficiently well known. If all this had not been so, then my parents-in-law would never have received the financial support from Hungarian Jews that they did during their years of exile.

We should also remember how many Jewish contacts the family had: not just their friends, the Chorin, Weiss, Páthy families and others; the family's doctor, Dr Lajos Ádám; my mother-in-law's milliner Vilma Gergely; her dressmaker Klára Rotschild; and her shoemaker, the outstanding Bertalan Kovács – who on his deathbed after the war asked, in the presence of one of our friends, for the last letter my mother-in-law had written him to be taken out of his pocket because he wanted to die with it in his hand – they were all Jews.

I feel it shameful that I should have to talk about these things. In our families there was never any question about whether anyone was a Jew or a Christian – this was how we all lived together. These are the real facts, which refute all the distortions that have been made, mostly quite intentionally, since then.

*   *   *   *   *

But now let us return to the events of 1944.

Unfortunately I never recorded in my diary – I hope a historian will find out sometime – exactly when we received a secret report that the Germans sent to Hitler about Hungary. We passed it to each other within the family in a state of shock. This secret report outlined their plans for the future of the country following a German victory. It stated that Hungary would become a German 'Gau' or administrative district, but as the Hungarian race was unworthy of acceptance into the great German Aryan community, it was to be eliminated in due course. So this was what was in store for us if the Nazis won the war – and what if they did not? But the West had many problems of its own and did not care about Hungary's fate … .

On 30 March I passed my theatre nursing examination with distinction, and received many congratulations; but the reassuring feeling resulting from this recognition of my work did not last long: when I got back to the Palace I found out that Anti Szapáry had been arrested by the Germans. I spent the rest of the day trying to help Anti, with the help of aide-de-camp Debreceni and Bavier, the Swiss High Commissioner, but it was futile. I got as far as Veesenmayer making an appointment to see me at five o'clock, but then at three o'clock he cancelled it. I felt I could not help Anti, but also did not want to do him any harm – perhaps it would have been better not to get personally involved. The worst thing was the feeling of helplessness. No one knew when their turn might come.

The first heavy American bombing raid took place in the morning of 3 April. They hit Horthy Liget and the Ferencváros station. Afterwards I went to the Szikla hospital and visited first-aid points. In the afternoon Gizi Apor and I went to Ferencváros to take nurses away from the damaged military hospital. There was another air raid warning after dinner: this time British planes bombed the Weiss Manfred factory. We got to bed at about 2.30 a.m. It was dreadful to think that such bombing raids could now be a daily occurrence.

There were many critical operations. I tried to rest, but I was continually exhausted. Dr Andor Nagy came regularly to give me iron injections, and on 5 April he told me to have a complete day's rest. I made use of this to visit the first-aid points in the Palace. Bridge with my parents-in-law was a suitable ending to a rare restful day... .

It was from that day that it was compulsory for every Jew to wear a yellow Star of David. I wondered how much more humiliation they would have to endure. But the Jewish Council was full of hope that there would be no deportations, because the Germans – including Eichmann in person – had assured them of this several times. But it was in April that the Germans, with the help of the Interior Ministry, secretly began deporting Jews.

During a heavy bombing raid I assisted in several operations and re-amputations in the military hospital. From there I went straight to the Szikla hospital, where many people, wounded by bombs, had been taken with severe injuries. I felt very sad.

At the Ferencváros station 280 bombs had been dropped, causing terrible devastation; and many of the railway workers' homes had been destroyed. I collected up some of Pista's clothes for distribution to victims of the bombing. I wondered why it hurt so much to let them go. It was as if they were a part of Pista, his clothes still contained the essence of his personality. I knew I was helping others by giving them away, but whether I wanted to or not, I found it difficult.

Distributing items to bomb victims at the railway workers' branch of MANSZ (the National Association of Hungarian Women) was very upsetting. I could not stop thinking how many people all over Europe had lost everything through these bombing raids – what needless waste. The bombs and planes cost so much and they were being used to destroy families and homes ... why did a Hitler have to come into the world to drive people mad, cause terrible suffering, and take millions to their deaths?

After mass on Easter Sunday we hid eggs in the Palace gardens for István, but he did not want to look for them – the previous night's bombing raid had disturbed him. There was an air raid warning every day, so trips to the shelter were a regular occurrence. We tried to make it as welcoming as possible, and took some of István's toys down there. He had grown to like going down to the shelter because he had a seat on my bicycle and that was how we got around the long corridors. So he was not afraid of air raid warnings, in fact he was pleased when he heard the sirens because he knew that meant he would be able to ride on my bicycle. Sometimes I played the mouth organ for him in the shelter. But if we had to go down at night it disrupted his routine.

Miklóspapa asked that if there was an air raid warning all members of the family – wherever they might be – should go at once to the Palace shelter. Of course I could understand Miklóspapa's anxiety, if contact was lost after a bombing raid they would be very worried if they did not know where we were; but for me it was a problem. It was hard to rush away from the hospital just as we were taking patients down to the shelter and my help was needed there. In one raid, because I left only when the patients were all safely in the shelter, as I was on my way to the Palace the bombs were already dropping – not close to me but on the Pest side. I could see the planes and the falling bombs, and hear the loud explosions. I was surprised not to find it at all frightening; in fact I had to admit that it was a fascinating sight. I hoped that everyone was safely in their cellars and that there would be no casualties. I drove home calmly, and did not tell anyone about my experience.

In the shelter we always met the Kállay family, and sometimes I carried little András down. In their apartment on the ground floor there was a table-football game, and we sometimes played it to take our minds off things. It was on these occasions that I heard news of Prime Minister Kállay, who was still in the Turkish Embassy. An armed German car still stood at each corner of the four streets surrounding the embassy, and the building was lit up with searchlights at night. Anyone entering the embassy was checked and everyone leaving was searched for letters. Mica could go only as far as the embassy garden for a little fresh air.

An interesting situation arose one day in the Szikla hospital. Eight young doctors assigned there happened to be Jewish. Most of the injured brought in during bombing raids were also Jewish. This was because the bombers were targeting factories in which the workers were Jewish labour groups. I was informed that the air raid shelters provided for these workers consisted of ditches dug beside the factories. These gave insufficient protection and many workers became injured. Some were brought in with horrific burns. The Red Cross published an appeal for blood donors for the Szikla hospital, and the wife of Andor Jaross – the interior minister appointed under German pressure – came to give blood. Naturally she had no idea that the patients and the doctors were Jewish. There was a degree of black humour in the situation, and we nurses and doctors privately wondered what effect Mrs Jaross' blood would have on our poor patients. The minister's wife was proud to give her blood and we thanked her for it.

After dinner one evening as we played bridge with my parents-in-law as usual, I heard some distressing news. Many hundreds of Hungarians had been arrested, mainly in Budapest. Miklóspapa said that he had tried to intervene in several cases with the intention of persuading the Germans to transfer the 'prisoners' to Hungarian prisons. He was very downcast and said that in the Subcarpathian region people were being brutally rounded up and taken to concentration camps.

We were informed that the rounding up of Jews into ghettos had begun, and it seemed that outside Budapest they were being taken by train in terrible conditions to work in Germany. Miklóspapa gave instructions that enquiries should be made as to when and where such a train was due to leave so that he could prevent it. Unfortunately this was very difficult because these deportations were organized in secret. Nobody knew in advance when and where such trains were going to depart. We from the Hungarian Red Cross asked why old people and children were being taken as well, if the Jews were being taken away to work. The official response was that the workers would work better if their families were with them, as it was well known that Jewish families were very close. They had an answer for everything.

After the war there were accounts written about how the population appropriated the belongings left behind by Jews and how brutally the police rounded up these unfortunate people. These were shameful and terrible manifestations of the depths to which people can sink. But very little was heard about how many people gave them refuge: convents, church institutions and individuals hid Jews, placing their own lives and safety at risk. In many cases Jews were helped across the border with the cooperation of the border guards. Many people came to see me and brought me mixed news, but I also heard many moving stories of people's courage and willingness to help.

I was very concerned about all this and tried to think of some way in which I could help to prevent these deportations. On one occasion when Miklóspapa received information on when the next Jewish transport train was due to depart, I remember standing for a long time by the living room window, looking out at the Tabán district and trying to plan in detail how I would board one of these trains in my Red Cross uniform to find out how much of what was being said about them was true. I thought it would lead to a big scandal, and perhaps that would achieve something ... . That evening I told Miklóspapa my plan but he said he did not think it was possible because they would simply take me away too and then who knows when I would come back. He asked me not to do such a senseless thing, as he did not think it would help anyone.

In any event we submitted a request to Prime Minister Sztójay, asking permission on behalf of the Red Cross to provide refreshments on the train carrying deportees. We had to try everything, though it was hard to imagine that we would receive permission, and indeed we did not – we did not even receive a reply.

Many new decrees were issued to the effect that in addition to having to wear a yellow star of David, Jews were only allowed to marry Jews, could only teach Jews, and so on. However, as there was a shortage of doctors in the country, these regulations had so far not been extended to the medical profession.

Then one day I was called out urgently from an operation in the military hospital, and there I found 'Aunt' Erzsi, the wife of Professor Lajos Ádám. He was the doctor and surgeon our family had always consulted, and was the Horthy family surgeon too. He was Jewish, but his work had so far not been impeded at all by the anti-Jewish laws. Aunt Erzsi told me in tears that her husband had received notification that he had to stop working as a surgeon and was no longer allowed to treat Christians. She said all her husband wanted to do was to treat anyone who was sick and needed treatment, and that if he could not do that then he did not want to live any more. She begged me to help. I tried to reassure her and told her to ask 'Uncle' Lajos to come to the Palace the same day. When he came Miklóspapa took him into his study, where they had a long conversation. Uncle Lajos received a 'letter of protection', which gave him exemption from the regulations so he could continue working. It was effective help for him, but what humiliating circumstances; I was deeply upset by the incident. Dr Ádám was not the only one to receive help: other doctors, active and retired university lecturers and many others, all received similar exemptions from the Regent.

Unfortunately many people remained insensitive towards these problems, but one must not forget that in all layers of the population there were those who helped these unfortunate people wherever they could, be it demonstrably or in secret.

Two days later we all went out to Gödöllő. István and I walked around the garden and picked flowers in the woods. Nanny Ila knew a lot about flowers and plants, and István showed great interest in her explanations. I wondered whether all children were as attentive. I was moved because he reminded me so much of Pista. In the evening the radio announced that British troops were on the outskirts of Rome. We wished they would hurry and come here.

We were very excited to hear about the Allied landing in Normandy on 6 June. Now British forces were on the continent, which meant that the war was getting closer to Germany. On the other hand, the German news broadcasts found some twisted way of announcing even this as a success.

Miklóspapa wrote to Hitler asking for the German occupation forces to be withdrawn from Hungary. He had to try everything. I said nothing, but was sure that Hitler would not accede to his request – in fact it might just make him angry ... .

Nicky joined the army, because until then he had done no military service. He had quick and concentrated training from Colonel Gyula Kádár of the general staff. He chose to join the infantry, and received practical training as a reserve second lieutenant in the Szeged infantry regiment. Later on, they drove around the liberated areas of Transylvania, visiting the military formations there. He was happy to report that the units were in high spirits and that he had not encountered much Nazi or Arrow Cross influence, so he could speak openly with his comrades.

On 18 June we celebrated Miklóspapa's seventy-sixth birthday after ten o'clock mass, and then we all went down with István to the Palace gardens. My father-in-law's brother Uncle Jenő came to lunch; his dry humour always created a happy atmosphere. I wondered what this birthday would be like the following year.

Listening to the BBC on 26 June, we heard that the Germans had suffered heavy losses on the Russian front – but this could not be made out from German news broadcasts.

Miklóspapa spoke animatedly about the Council of State meeting that day. He said he could not tolerate any longer the sadistic anti-Jewish activities implemented by the two state secretaries dealing with Jewish matters, László Baky and László Endre, and wanted to put an end to it and get them removed. Although the position was that the nearly quarter of a million Jews living in Budapest were not yet under threat of deportation, they had been forced to move to 'Jewish houses' and their situation was desperate. I wondered when he would succeed and who would help him to do it. From that time the issue of removing the Sztójay government came up often in our talks. Sztójay was in poor health and had many problems with members of his government. His deputy, Jenő Rácz, and one of his ministers, Béla Imrédy, had left the government.

Miklóspapa was also very anxious because there were still Hungarian troops outside our borders. General Beregfy, who was pro-German, was recalled and replaced by General Béla Miklós, which was very good news.

Dr Somogyi, the surgeon at the military hospital, returned from Germany where he had been on a study tour. In a pause between two operations he told me that he had not learned much: he had been surprised to discover that war surgery was far more advanced in Hungary. He said all he ever heard was how much better the Germans were than the Hungarians, not just in surgery but in everything, but in his opinion this was just propaganda. During the operation there was an air raid warning and Pest was bombed. I obediently went to the Palace shelter and when the raid was over I hurried back to the hospital.

On 2 July, while I was at the Szikla hospital dressing wounds, there was a major air raid on Budapest. American bombers came and dropped their bombs, seemingly at random. Many seriously wounded people were brought in: what terrible injuries, and how much tragedy. We worked without stopping until 7.30 p.m. It was only when I got home that I realized we had not eaten all day.

14

Save What Can Be Saved
July – October 1944

After the German invasion, when the deportations began at the end of April or the beginning of May, a small group of news-carrying 'conspirators' was formed, including myself. We met in various places: sometimes at the Papal Nuncio's residence or at Aunt Gizi Apor's, but mostly in my apartment in the Palace. Our aim was to pass on and use information we acquired to help people where we could, and to make sure the Regent was kept appraised of things about which he might otherwise have been left unaware. Through caution I did not record the time and place of every meeting in case it fell into the wrong hands, so I will only mention those which I definitely remember and which I recorded in code in my diary.

The regular members of this group were Baroness Gizella Apor; Angelo Rotta, the Papal Nuncio; Gyula Vállay, the quite outstanding vice-president of the Hungarian Red Cross; Jean de Bavier, the Swiss International Red Cross High Commissioner; József Cavallier and the Jesuit Father Jánosy, lay and religious leaders respectively of the Holy Cross Society. Occasional contributors included Countess Gabrielle Hunyady and Countess Edina Zichy.

It was Aunt Gizi Apor who first brought the writer Sándor Török up to the Palace to see me. He was vice-president of the Society of Christian Jews in Hungary. By that time it was compulsory for Jews to wear a yellow star of David, but Sándor Török always took his off when he came to the Palace in order not to attract attention; that was strictly forbidden, and if he had been stopped and checked in the street, he would have got into serious trouble. I showed Aunt Gizi a side entrance to the Palace, which Sándor Török used later when he came to see me alone. For the purpose of these visits we decided that he would be Bardócz the bookbinder, and from then on he phoned me practically every day to ask if I had any books for him. If I said I had, he would come up to see me; on the other hand, if he said the job was finished and asked when he could bring it up, then I knew he had something important to tell me. In the same way as Sándor Török was my informant, so Dr Ernő Pető, one of the leaders of the Hungarian Council of Jews, went regularly to exchange news with Nicky.

The information Sándor Török gave me I passed on to the Regent, telling him where and how he could try to improve the situation of the Jews in general, or of individual Jews. Török told me about the constant flow of new regulations; it was not easy for the Regent to obtain information about them in good time. Sometimes I was able to tell him something valuable, but I felt constantly helpless in the face of so many problems. When necessary, I naturally contacted Nicky's 'Escape Office', which also aimed to help the Jews and victims of Nazi persecution in general.

I was always careful to make sure that we did not talk where there was a telephone because we suspected that they were bugged. My father-in-law was also careful about this and only held important discussions in rooms where there wasn't one. From time to time engineers would come to check the phones, but we did not trust them. As we later discovered, our feelings were not misplaced: the head of security in the Palace, Major Vámos, who was in charge of all this, later became Szálasi's aide-de-camp!

In 1986 I was very surprised to receive from the journalist Sándor Szenes a copy of his book *Befejezetlen Mult* (Unfinished Past), which told the story of Jews in Hungary and those who helped them, and which contained the following dedication:

> To Mrs Ilona Bowden, the former 'little Mrs Regent' of Hungary, whose compassion is remembered with the utmost appreciation by those looking back on their lives in this book, and has commanded the author's sincere respect.

Sándor Szenes, Budapest, 30 September 1986.[25]

I was deeply moved by this warm commendation, though I deserve no praise for my actions. I only did what came naturally in the given circumstances, and I still wonder whether I could have done more. I have always felt that everyone has a duty or an obligation, and if in a given circumstance they do not carry it out, then that is a mistake. Life shows us and presents us with duties; we do not have to look for them. It is not my merit – and perhaps I was lucky – that I was not tempted by fear or anxiety to turn away from what I considered my duty, or rather from what I simply had to do. I only saw one way to act, and I certainly hope I have not missed any opportunities.

In his book there is a long interview with Sándor Török, which moved me very much because he gave such a vivid and accurate account of the events we experienced. That was how I found out that between themselves they called me 'little Mrs Regent'. Török also describes things I had forgotten, like a 'trickery' – as he called it. He wrote letters addressed to the Regent that were ostensibly from aristocrats living in the country and who wished to remain anonymous. In these letters they described how they saw the country's situation and asked him to accept their suggestions. He and Aunt Gizi brought me the first of these letters and I liked it so much that I promised to pass it on. I was amused by reading Török's comment that 'the "little Mrs Regent" – I have to say – used a certain noble astuteness with the Regent and was able to impress him'.

According to my diary, Sándor Török first came alone to see me on 1 July, and during the next three months he paid frequent visits. His second visit on 3 July is underlined; that was the memorable day on which he brought me the 'Auschwitz Record'.

In his interview with Sándor Szenes, Török states that he first took a copy to a state secretary in the Foreign Ministry: 'I thought the Record would carry more weight with Horthy if it was sent to him from the Foreign Ministry.' He asked the state secretary to pass it on to the Regent, but when the state secretary declared that this was just Jewish hysteria and that the Jews exaggerated everything, Török understood that the Record would get no further. Then he discussed the matter with Gizi Apor and with Vállay, and they agreed that he should send a copy to the Regent via me.

Historians have tried to determine when this record was distributed, and to find out the exact date on which the Hungarian translation of the record reached the Regent. As far as I can make out from what I have read so far, I am the only person able to specify the date without having to rely on memory.

I remember little of what else occurred during that day, because what happened at the end of it overshadowed everything. All I know – from my diary – is that at five in the afternoon I went to see the bomb-damaged Keleti Station and Ferencváros, and it was when I returned to the Palace that Sándor Török came to see me. That was when he handed me the 'Auschwitz Record'; and, in his presence, I read the harrowing account of the extermination camp and gas chambers, written by two Slovakian Jews who had miraculously escaped. A German version of this record had secretly been translated into Hungarian in Budapest. It was illustrated with diagrams, and its content is difficult to put into words. Somehow I sensed straight away that every word of this account was true, that it was not written for propaganda purposes but was a matter-of-fact account of the horrors they had experienced, and which the human mind could barely comprehend.

We had to wake up to the truth, that the reality was more dreadful than anything anyone could have imagined. Sándor Török and I just looked at each other: neither of us could speak because we would have ended up sobbing.

As soon as Török left I went down the spiral staircase to my parents-in-law's apartment. Only my mother-in-law was there because Miklóspapa was in a meeting in his study. I handed her the record without comment, asking only that she should read it straight away. Magdamama was moved to tears, and she promised to give it to Miklóspapa as soon as he returned from his study.

In connection with this I would like to clarify something my father-in-law wrote in his memoirs, published in 1953. He wrote: 'It was only in August that I discovered the dreadful truth about the extermination camps, from a secret informant.' My father-in-law wrote this from memory at the age of eighty-five, and clearly he was mistaken. But the fault is mine, not his, because I typed the manuscript of his memoirs and helped to research dates where I could. However, I did not check that date in my diary because I did not notice it. I had no idea that it was so important and would become so controversial.

I was not there when my father-in-law read the record: Magdamama told me afterwards that he was deeply shocked and initially thought that this monstrous story could not be true. He said something to the effect that he had never heard of such unspeakable things, and reiterated that whatever happened the deportations must be stopped.

Three days later, on 6 July, the Hungarian government halted the deportation of Jews. Prime Minister Sztójay informed the German Plenipotentiary that on the Regent's instructions the government would not allow any more Jews to be deported. It was only due to their own worrying situation that the Germans swallowed this. But – as we found out much later – by then four hundred thousand unfortunates had been deported from various parts of the country. It really is difficult for me to write down this figure, because it is just a number – whereas each one of those were individual, feeling, suffering human beings. At the time we had no idea of the scale of this tragedy; it was only after the war that I discovered these details, when the Germans' secret calculations came to light.

Some people allege that the Regent knew much earlier about the Auschwitz extermination camp. In my judgment this is impossible, because when we discussed the Auschwitz records in the evening after reading it, he would certainly have told us if he had known about it already or if someone had told him such things. He would have had no reason to hide it from me. I remember that when we met that evening he asked me what I thought about the authenticity of the papers I had passed on to him. I told him I was convinced it was authentic because to me every word rang true; it was not the sort of thing people could just make up. He agreed with me completely.

I have also been told several times that the Regent only took action against the deportations when – and because – the Pope, the King of Sweden and President Roosevelt intervened by letter. At the time I was not aware of any such letters; after the war, through the Papal Nuncio's office in Switzerland, I was able to read the letter Pope Pius XII wrote to the Regent on 25 June 1944, asking him to do everything in his power to ensure that those unfortunates who had suffered because of their nationality or race should be spared any further suffering. I was also shown the Regent's reply, which was dated 1 July – two days before he found out about Auschwitz – where he asked the Pope to rest assured that he was doing everything he could. I do not know about the others, because my father-in-law never mentioned any such letters to me. It is perfectly clear to me that it was the Auschwitz Record that made him take the decisive step to stop all deportations.

The next meeting was at my cousin Marie Pejacsevich's house with Edina Zichy and the Jesuit Father Jánosy. My cousin Marie was a quite outstanding character; she too did a great deal for Hungarian Jews. At that time she was working for the Caritas, the Catholic Church's charitable organization. She also hid people with the nuns in the Sophianum Convent.

In the evening of 5 July we faced an alarming situation because Baky had unexpectedly ordered some police battalions to come to Budapest on the pretext of attending a flag dedication ceremony, but actually to deport the two hundred and thirty thousand Jews still living in Budapest and also those who, under the Nürnberg laws, were considered Jews. They had prepared this move thoroughly together with the Germans. And then came the Regent's forceful intervention, as described by the historian Péter Gosztonyi:

> The arrival of the police battalions in Budapest prompted an immediate reaction from Horthy ... Through the commanding officer of the Guards Károly Lázár (and bypassing Chief of Staff János Vörös) he ordered the mobilisation of units of the First Armoured Division from Esztergom and other camps in the vicinity of Budapest. Horthy himself briefed the acting commanding officer of the division, Colonel Ferenc

Koszorús of the general staff, in the Palace on the evening of 5 July. 'He informed me,' Koszorús wrote, 'that according to reports received, Baky and his cronies were planning the coup (that is to say the armed action organized to thwart the Regent's order to stop the deportation – P. Gosztonyi.) for 6 July. He gave me spoken orders to have sections of the armoured division standing by and use them to prevent the coup. I was to remove Baky's battalions from Budapest by force, if necessary.' Koszorús went into action on 6 July at 6 a.m. With his forces he cut off the western exit routes from Budapest level with Óbuda, and then sent an officer patrol to László Baky to inform him of the Regent's order that he should remove his forces from Budapest within 24 hours.[26]

One other incident worth mentioning – a completely different one – occurred that same day. After Prime Minister Miklós Kállay sought refuge in the Turkish Embassy, a journalist wrote a defamatory article about him in an Arrow Cross paper, saying that he was a paid agent of the Jews, that he had stolen money, and so on. Kállay's youngest son András was serving as a guardsman in the Palace, and asked the Regent's permission to challenge the journalist to a duel. The Regent replied, 'All right, make mincemeat of him!' so András got two 'seconds' and the duel took place in the waiting room above what was then the Forum cinema in Kossuth Lajos Street. András attacked at once and cut his opponent's arm, so the arbiter stopped the duel as the first blood had been drawn. András's brother Miklós was sitting in his car outside the building with a machine gun, because they were afraid that the journalist's Arrow Cross friends would attack them, but fortunately this did not happen. Anyway, that was the last duel fought in the Kingdom of Hungary.

My diary also says that Magdamama and I went down to the ground floor to see Helen Kállay, who told us happily about András' success in the duel. 'He took care of his opponent all right!' she said proudly. In the evening I went to see them to celebrate with a little champagne, but not a great deal of merriment.

On 7 July, watched by the armoured division, the police battalions left Budapest! The Jews of Budapest had been saved – because the Regent resisted any further attempt to deport them.

It was so good to see that the moment had arrived for Miklóspapa to step into action, it was as if a great weight had fallen from his shoulders: I could see this from the way he behaved. Of course this also raised his hopes ... perhaps he never suspected how many people would sabotage his subsequent actions. He decided that day that the time had come for the present government to be removed, and chose General Lakatos to be the next prime minister.

But I had a strange feeling in the evening of the very next day, when Miklóspapa told us that he had summoned Lakatos to discuss the forced resignation of the Sztójay government, which he was planning with Count István Bethlen (who was risking coming from his place of hiding to meet with the Regent). Lakatos had asked for a delay, or for time to think about it, because he was afraid that the Germans might boost their occupying forces. All the airports were in German hands and there were still more German than Hungarian soldiers in Hungary. Apparently István Bethlen also eventually accepted this delay, so for the time being only the Interior Ministry, which was responsible for the excesses against the Jews, had a change of staff: Baky and Endre were sacked, and Miklós Bonczos appointed Interior Minister.

If Pista had been there, would he have accepted a delay? And what would have happened if Lakatos had undertaken to form a new government right then? It still seems now as if that would have been the best time ... .

Péter Gosztonyi writes about how the Regent asked János Vörös, the chief of general staff, if there were enough forces available to take military action against the Gestapo and the SS forces in the country if necessary:

> Vörös stated in his diary: 'I reported that our forces were insufficient for military action against the Germans. ... I told His Highness emphatically that he should not think about such military solutions in the current circumstances ...'
>
> Thus, far from giving support the chief of general staff was dissuading him from evolving a military resistance. And if the Regent had taken that step he would – probably – have received solid support in the summer of 1944 from the civic and social democratic leaders of the Hungarian Front.[27]

Protests and threats came via Veesenmayer, but the Regent flatly refused to reinstate Baky and Endre; Sztójay remained for the time being.

We have to acknowledge that Miklóspapa had listened to many people, and cautiously but persistently took preparatory steps towards leading the country out of the war. There is no doubt that every step was dangerous.

Magdamama and I went to eight o'clock mass every morning and received communion. It seemed somehow natural that we should do something not just through our actions but also on a spiritual level, and at that level nobody tried to prevent us. There was not a lot of time to ponder, there was so much to do. I attended the general meeting of the office for the welfare of disabled ex-servicemen and their relatives; a meeting of first-aid-point nurses; and first aid lectures. I spent a lot of time dressing wounds in the Szikla hospital.

The after-dinner bridge games carried on, while we listened to broadcasts from London. We listened to the news from Britain, to Aylmer Macartney's broadcast in Hungarian. His Hungarian was very good, though he spoke with a strong English accent. I never suspected that I would meet him several times after the war ... .

The excitements continued: we heard that Eichmann was preparing to deport fifteen hundred Jews from Kistarcsa, just outside Budapest, using his own men rather than the Hungarian gendarmes. Dr Ernő Pető, in his letter to Dr Lajos Marton that I mentioned earlier, recalls the events as follows:

> The SS Einsatzkommando which remained in Budapest under Eichmann's command did not want to allow the Jews of Budapest, whose numbers had been swelled by Jews fleeing there from other parts of the country, to slip through their fingers. The Regent's order to stop deportations was already public knowledge when, after a few days, we heard that the Germans were putting 1,700 unfortunates from the Budapest and Kistarcsa internment camps into railway trucks in Budapest. By that time Prime Minister Sztójay had written to the Primate informing him that the deportations would end. Through Dr Cavallier, a representative of the Catholic bishops who always helped us, we raised the alarm in the Catholic Church, and through Sándor Török we did the same in the Calvinist Church, in order to prevent this deportation.
>
> As the preparations were well advanced and had reached the stage where the trucks were being sealed, I only had time to ring Nicholas Horthy junior on his secret number and tell him that those 1,700 people were in mortal danger because the Germans were disregarding the Regent's wishes and preparing to deport them. He undertook to inform the Regent immediately and ask him to take steps as a matter of urgency. In the meantime the train left. We later found

out that the Regent, acting on the request we had passed to him, had ordered the Interior Minister to have the train turned back. Police Captain Lallay, adjutant to László Ferenczy, who had been charged with bringing the train back, caught up with it at Gödöllő, and it was turned back to Kistarcsa.

We heard that everyone had come back, and thought we had achieved a great success.

On 19 July the Germans, who must have suspected that we had a hand in preventing this train from leaving the country, ordered all the members of the council to go to their headquarters on the Svábhegy in the early hours of the morning. We were all held there without food or drink and asked trivial questions about our organization. We suspected the worst. We subsequently found out that on that day Gestapo men had stormed the Kistarcsa internment camp, disarmed the Hungarian guards, cut off the phone, and taken the approximately fifteen hundred people interned there out of the country.[28]

On 20 July, during our evening bridge game, we heard that an attempt had been made to assassinate Hitler – a momentary ray of hope! But the reality, that Hitler had survived, was terrible. There would be horrible reprisals, and the hellish war would continue. Why did such an obsessed madman who had caused millions to suffer terribly have to escape? It was not even possible to think about it, one just had to live for the present. The past and the future were not my problem, they just confused the issue.

I continued to assist in several operations at the Jurányi military hospital and work with those wounded in the bombing raids, often not returning to the Palace until after ten at night.

On 2 August there was a lot of excitement in store for us. I had heard there was a plan to remove the eight Jewish doctors on labour service at the Szikla hospital, so I went there to find out more. At my request General Gusztáv Jány, the corps commander, came to see me, and I protested against this proposed action.

Later that day we received news that Turkey and Germany had broken off diplomatic relations. The Turkish Embassy in Budapest was surrounded by armed German soldiers, and we in the Palace were very concerned about what would happen to Miklós Kállay.

On the third, Sándor Török came with Gyula Vállay. For once they had good news: the Red Cross was now allowed to visit and help the

Jews, and their situation had eased somewhat. Those who had Christian spouses could return home. A few thousand Jewish children emigrated to several European countries and to Palestine. Sándor Török was able to help many Christian Jews. They mentioned that Raoul Wallenberg, a Swedish diplomat who had recently arrived in Budapest, was doing a lot to help the Jews. (Wallenberg later became a legendary figure: many people owed their lives to him even under the Szálasi government. The Russians took him away early in 1945 and he was never seen again.)

After Török and Vállay left, Defence Minister Csatay came to see me about the Jewish doctors in the Szikla hospital. He was very understanding; and one morning soon after, while we were in the shelter because of an air raid alert, his secretary István Oláh came to see me with the news that the eight doctors could stay at the hospital. When the alert was over I went straight to the hospital with the good news.

But the next day I had a disagreeable experience: Incze, the government commissioner in charge of medical matters, made an appointment to see me and tried to convince me of the pressing need for the eight Jewish doctors to be at the front. He asked me to agree to their transfer from the Szikla hospital. I explained to him very patiently that they were very much needed in the Szikla hospital to care for those injured in the bombing raids on Budapest. Then the commissioner asked me what I would think if I were a bomb victim and realized that the doctor treating me was Jewish. Somewhat surprised, I told him that I would be pleased, because Jewish doctors were usually very good. Then I asked him a question: if these doctors were moved to the front and if he were a wounded soldier, would he not be surprised to find a Jewish doctor treating him? At this he turned crimson. I did not give him a chance to reply but told him that if he tried once more to remove those eight doctors I would go straight to the Regent, and then it would not be the eight doctors who were removed! He jumped up and without another word stormed out, slamming the door behind him. It was not the way government commissioners usually behaved in the Royal Palace. That was when I realized what unbridgeable chasms can exist between two people.

However, for as long as we were in the Palace our doctors were left alone, and I was relieved to hear that they also escaped from harm after we had left.

On the sixteenth, Sándor Török came to see me for a long discussion. There was much disquiet because the Germans were once more apparently preparing to deport the Jews from Budapest, this time on 26 August. There were more policemen to be seen in Budapest again, which understandably filled the Jews with fear. Dr Ernő Pető, who with his family had been taken for questioning by the Gestapo on the seventeenth and only released three days later because of intervention by the Regent, wrote about that attempt:

> Police Lieutenant Colonel Ferenczy showed me the plan prepared by Eichmann, according to which the deportation would be carried out from the Csillaghegy brick factory between 26 August and 18 September. Members and officers of the Council and their families were to be included in the first transport. He informed me that the unreliable police officers had been replaced and that the Esztergom rapid deployment force was already in Budapest. As far as I remember, he told Eichmann on 23 August that he had orders from the Regent to refuse to allow the deportation, and that if Eichmann forced the issue he had orders to resist by force of arms. We heard that Eichmann was beside himself with fury and flew to Berlin to seek further instructions from Hitler's deputy, Himmler. ...
>
> In the Interior Ministry, Zsigmond Székely-Molnár told me that we would be able to find out what decision had been made in Berlin from Ministerial Advisor Mór in the Foreign Ministry. Károly Wilhelm and I waited anxiously there for news from Berlin, and were greatly relieved when Mór told us that Himmler had agreed that the deportations should be postponed.
>
> The police were withdrawn too; after a few days they weren't visible on the streets, and the Jews of Budapest breathed a sigh of relief. ...
>
> The three of us who had taken part in this plot – the success of which had been guaranteed by the Regent circumventing the government and directly ordering Ferenczy to prevent the deportation planned by the Gestapo for 26 August by force of arms if necessary, and by his orders for the Esztergom armoured division to come to Budapest – were convinced that the deportation of Jews from Budapest had in this way been prevented for good.[29]

After that, Eichmann made one more attempt to remove Hungarian political prisoners from the Fő street prison one night, but fortunately this too was prevented with the help of the gendarmerie and the police.

On the morning of the eighteenth, István pushed a table into my room with some flowers for my name-day. He was very sweet: I thought there could hardly be happier moments in my life. I had forgotten, but Nanny Ila – who is also Ilona – had remembered. Levente girls also came to wish me a happy name-day, and I received many letters and flowers.

Ellamami was in bed with erysipelas, so I went over to Dísz Square to see her. I was pleased to see Professor Lajos Ádám there, who was giving her an injection. It was good to talk to him. I did not know how this noble, kind man could bear this dreadful situation. Although he had an exemption certificate, his position as a Jewish doctor was very difficult ... it was hard to believe that such a situation could exist in the twentieth century. Was it only technology that was progressing? And was that to our benefit or our detriment?

Helen Kállay, Magdamama and I started a novena in honour of Saint Stephen. We prayed at six every evening in the Palace chapel.[30]

That year there was no Saint Stephen's day procession in our occupied country. Everyone celebrated the greatest Hungarian holiday quietly at home and in their souls. That 20 August – which was a tragic date for us anyway, a day when I was always besieged by 'why's about Pista's death – began with an air raid warning: Szolnok and Szeged were bombed. Miklóspapa went to the Hávösvölgy military academy to make a speech at the joint swearing in ceremony of the three officer training academies. We listened to the speech, which was broadcast on the radio.

On that day Romania stepped out of the war. They managed to take the big step, and we wondered what consequences it would have – after all, that was what we wanted, what we were waiting for, and what we were afraid of. Paris fell to the Allies. Miklóspapa was up late in a conference, and Magdamama and I stayed up until 2.30 a.m. waiting for him. His thinking was still that, until help arrived from the Allies, we should continue to resist the Soviet forces. Veesenmayer told him that Hitler opposed and would not tolerate any change of government. But Miklóspapa had decided once and for all to do just that. The next day he summoned General Lakatos again in order to ask him finally to form a new government.

When I returned from the Palace chapel after our novena, I was met by a startling, incomprehensible, but joyful event: Anti Szapáry had returned after spending five months imprisoned in Mauthausen extermination camp. We could hardly believe it, because we did not know of anyone who had been set free from there. Anti told us that he had been given a relatively easy job right from the start in the camp kitchens, and that he had probably been released because so many requests had been made on his behalf – even by the King of Sweden. He'd had to promise and sign a document saying that he would not say anything about the camp – but despite that he asked for an audience with the Regent straight away and told him everything he knew about the Mauthausen camp and the gas chambers. He found his flat ransacked, and from that time he remained in hiding, never staying long in one place. When he came to see me, I took him into our storeroom and gave him a full set of clothes: as he and Pista were the same size he could choose what he wanted from Pista's things. I knew Pista would have done the same. Then the next day I packed everything up for him and took it to the address he gave me. There was an air raid warning, and when I got home István and I played the mouth organ in the shelter. It was a funny feeling to be crying inside and laughing on the outside, but I was getting quite good at it.

We reached the end of the Saint Stephen novena and Father Witz gave a very moving talk in the Palace chapel, a balm to my heart as it groped its way around this incomprehensible situation.

29 August was a memorable day. Despite the fact that only a few days earlier a letter had come from Hitler in which he demanded that we continue to meet our obligations and said that he would under no circumstances tolerate a change of government, the Regent took the Germans by surprise and dismissed the Sztójay government, appointing General Géza Lakatos as the new prime minister. It was incredible that the Germans agreed to all this. It was only the situation which had arisen as a result of the Romanians stepping out of the war that made it possible: it seemed that the Germans wanted somehow to maintain for the outside world the illusion that Hungary was still a good ally, so they did not want to take any action against my father-in-law openly. Miklóspapa's declaration that we would continue fighting against the Soviets seemed to reassure them for the time being. It was on knife-edges such as this that events then depended.

General Géza Lakatos appointed his ministers the same day. The composition of this government was very important, because the Regent saw their task as being to prepare for Hungary to join the Allied side – so these were all to be men the Regent could rely on.

Unfortunately, as Miklóspapa later told us, his original plan had not been kept to. His list of ministers had included, among others, Lieutenant Generals Szilárd Bakay, Kálmán Hardy and Ferenc Farkas, all men the Regent could rely on; and he had wanted simply to inform Veesenmayer, rather than ask for his approval. But these men were left out of the government, and at first I could not understand what had caused this change. I did not want to ask many questions, and only found out later that it was Defence Minister Csatay who, fearing German resistance, insisted that the list should be shown to

Veesenmayer beforehand. He himself gave the list to Veesenmayer as a 'proposed' government, which of course Veesenmayer did not accept. The wrangling ended when Reményi-Schneller and Jurcsek were included, and our suspicions were soon confirmed that they were acting as informants for Veesenmayer. Veesenmayer had other demands, like including Bárdossy and Ruszkay, but Miklóspapa rejected all other suggestions.

It's difficult to judge what the German reaction would have been if Csatay had not interfered. I think Csatay was wrong to do what he did, because if the Regent wanted simply to inform Veesenmayer of the government he had formed, Veesenmayer's approval should not have been sought. Veesenmayer would have tried to suggest others even without being asked, but our bargaining position would have been completely different if we were informing and not asking – and the fact that the decision was the Regent's and not theirs would have protected the ministers.

Miklóspapa's success in stopping the deportations and changing the government showed that his decision to stay in post might still enable Hungary to step out of the war, and then the sacrifice would have been worthwhile. In any event, the new government's policy was little short of miraculous: to stop the persecution of the Jews and to limit the activities of the Gestapo.

As he now did not have complete confidence in the government, Miklóspapa could not let them know about any further attempts or preparations to ask for an armistice. This was a definite disadvantage and made his plans less likely to succeed.

During our usual evening bridge games we listened with excitement to the radio – the latest news was that the Germans had occupied Slovakia and the Slovaks were resisting. The Russians declared war on Bulgaria. The war was spreading – would there ever be peace? Every evening Magdamama, Nicky and I discussed events at length with Miklóspapa.

On 7 September there was a Council of State meeting chaired by the Regent. The whole government attended, as did the chief of general staff and the heads of the Military and Cabinet Offices. Afterwards Miklóspapa told us how it had gone, and the following is based on what he told me and on the account written by Vattay, the head of the Military Office.

First the Regent informed them of the situation that had arisen: through Bakách-Bessenyey, the Hungarian ambassador in Switzerland, he had been informed that it was now clear that we could not count on an Allied invasion. The requirement was nothing less than unconditional surrender, and we were to make contact not with them but with the Soviet Union. The Russians had broken through the Carpathians, and the Germans were unable to hold them back. For that reason he had finally decided that we had to act: we had to put our desire to stop fighting into effect. Prime Minister Lakatos immediately asked to speak and announced that the matter had to be put before Parliament. An argument developed, but the Regent stated that Parliament no longer represented the people's wishes, because some of its members were under arrest, others were in hiding, and those who were still free had been intimidated, therefore he would not agree to the prime minister's request. He concluded, 'I assume responsibility before the nation and before history.' Acting on Defence Minister Csatay's proposal, the Germans were informed that if they did not send four divisions and more armoured units Hungary would be forced to ask for a ceasefire. The Regent also informed Hitler of this in writing.

I always had misgivings about these disclosures to the Germans. Did we have to inform them of our intentions when they had never been honest with us? Of course there were many details I did not know about, so it may have been simply my prejudice that gave rise to these misgivings. People made judgments subsequently, but they had no idea of all the factors that came into play.

It was now that the Hungarian Embassy in Finland reported how well the Russians were treating the Finnish leader Marshal Mannerheim, and that they had not occupied Finland. But at the same time we heard reports of the atrocities perpetrated by the Russian occupation forces in Romania. Naturally these reports struck fear into everyone.

Many people have described in detail the events and negotiations that followed. All I would like to add here is what I experienced, together with some explanations I obtained later. I hope you will be able to sense the uncertain, desperate atmosphere in which we lived: in a country occupied by a ruthless power with a hostile ideology, having to await liberation by the army of a country which was equally ruthless and whose ideology was equally hostile. Even Hitchcock could not have made up a more dreadful horror story.

But we had to come to terms with this. And, as there was no landing by the British in the Balkans as we had all hoped, the Regent decided to send a delegation to Moscow. This was perhaps the hardest sacrifice he ever had to make for his country.

On 10 September, Miklóspapa summoned his reliable advisors to ask them for their opinion. The only members of the government who were there were Prime Minister Lakatos, Foreign Minister Hennyey, Defence Minister Csatay and Vörös, chief of general staff. The others at the meeting were Count István Bethlen (who had again been smuggled into the Palace), Count Móricz Esterházy, Count Gyula Károlyi, Kálmán

Kánya, Baron Zsigmond Perényi, three generals (one of whom was General István Náday, who later flew to the Allied Headquarters in Italy on a secret mission) and Count Béla Teleki, the president of the Transylvanian Party.

First János Vörös informed them all of the military situation, which essentially was that, since the end of August, Russian forces had been advancing through the Székler region in Transylvania. Then Miklóspapa told them that it was necessary to end the war immediately. István Bethlen agreed with the Regent's decision in every respect, and said there was no sense in continuing the bloodshed – we had to step out of the war. It was decided that we had to do what the Finns had done: stop fighting but not lay down our arms. Everyone at the meeting was in agreement, and it became clear that the Soviet Union was the only power to whom we could – and indeed had to – turn.

After this meeting, the problem arose of how István Bethlen could be smuggled back out of the Palace. We were afraid that news of his presence might have leaked out. I do not know whose idea it was that his distinctive moustache should be shaved off. The deed was done, but then he looked even more suspicious because the skin that had now become exposed was white and contrasted sharply with his suntanned face. Then I remembered Pista's ultra-violet lamp, which was still in our bathroom. So they all came up with 'Uncle' István to my apartment on the first floor. I covered his face with towels, leaving only the white skin exposed, and carefully shone the ultra-violet light on it until the white patch disappeared completely. It was a great success: Uncle István, wearing a soldier's uniform, was unrecognisable, and he got back safely to his hiding place in the country.

Count Ladomér Zichy, whose estate in Slovakia was next to the Hungarian border, was chosen on the recommendation of his brother-in-law, Baron Dániel Bánffy, a former agricultural minister, to make contact with the Soviet Lieutenant Colonel Makarov – who was cooperating with the Slovak partisans – in order to pass on a ceasefire request. I was there when he came up to the Palace to discuss the details and accept the task. The following day, the eleventh, he left for Slovakia.

At the same time another opportunity to make contact with the Soviets arose. Baron Ede Aczél, a Transylvanian landowner, offered through my brother-in-law Nicky to travel to Moscow accompanied by two Communists. Miklóspapa agreed, and they set off.

On 11 September there was a meeting of the Council of Ministers in the Regent's study. According to the official notes made by State Secretary István Bárczy, who took the minutes, Prime Minister Géza Lakatos opened the meeting by first explaining the final and irrevocable decision the Regent had come to concerning asking for a ceasefire, and all the steps that had led to that decision: 'The prime minister stressed again that His Highness the Regent's decision was final and irrevocable. ... He therefore requested ministers observations, wanting to know who would accept political responsibility for this decision made by the Regent and who would not.'[31]

The ministers then spoke in turn, making uncertain statements such as: 'I can understand the Regent but it is difficult to accept this ...' 'If the Regent orders me to accept it I will, but ...' 'The Germans will exact dreadful retribution ...' 'It is too early to ask for a ceasefire ...' 'I cannot accept stepping out of the war this very day ...' etc. And Lakatos shared these views! So, the twenty-fourth hour was 'too early' for them

I will again draw on Vattay's recollections to illustrate Miklóspapa's situation:

> It's only now, twenty-one years later, that I have seen what looks like an authentic record of that Council of Ministers meeting on 11 September. On studying it I formed the impression that Bonczos, the Interior Minister (who had right-wing tendencies and later left the government) had snatched the initiative in a spirited speech, saying that they couldn't accept responsibility for the Regent's wishes and decisions ... Bonczos was immediately supported by Reményi-Schneller and Jurcsek, the two pro-German ministers. Slowly, one after the other, those ministers who were still wavering joined them; and finally Lakatos came to share the ministers' view and joined them in the decision that the government couldn't accept responsibility and would tender its resignation.
>
> Even now, twenty-one years on, I can't understand that government's behaviour. When it was formed, the most important and primary task it undertook was to achieve a ceasefire, and when the opportunity to do so arose, the government simply announced that it wasn't prepared to go through with it. The ministers must have known how difficult it was to form a government and what obstacles had to be surmounted. In that critical situation they abandoned the head of state – they didn't care what he did, but they wouldn't accept responsibility. Even the military members of the government voted with the rest.[32]

In the evening a small 'inner' circle met in the Regent's study:

Miklóspapa, Magdamama and Nicky; General Szilárd Bakay, the commander of the First Army Corps, with responsibility for the security of Budapest; Lieutenant General Károly Lázár, commander of the Bodyguards; Lieutenant Colonel Gyuszi Tost, aide-de-camp; Gyula Ambrózy, head of the Cabinet Office; Antal Vattay, head of the Military Office; and myself.

Miklóspapa told us what had happened in the Council of Ministers, and we could tell from his voice how much their decision had upset him. It was hard to believe that the whole government had deserted him. He told us what a struggle it had been to appoint this government, and that now there was not time for another conflict with the Germans over this. He had been abandoned, but wanted to implement his decision, and so he would act without involving the government.

All of us who were there undertook to support the Regent in every way. General Bakay, whom Miklóspapa praised as being the best man for the job, said that he could defend Castle Hill against the Germans successfully if he received reinforcements – if he could be given a division, then he would be able to defend both the Palace and the city.

Vattay adds the following observation to his memories of that day:

> How different the situation would have been, how much more forceful and unified the preparations – both political and military – would have been if the government had carried out its duty with complete dedication. The Regent was seventy-six years old, but despite his age he was prepared to take that difficult step even in the face of opposition from the government ... His willpower and vitality were not what they had been, he was showing signs of his age, but despite his advanced years he persisted in his intention, surmounted the obstacles, and stuck to his decision.[33]

Even now, many years later, people wonder whose responsibility it was that Hungary did not manage to go over to the other side. Perhaps they have lost sight of the real problem, that we were being worn away between two hells, between two cunning, lying, murderous great powers, and whatever we did, the final result would have been the same. Our fate was decided in Teheran in November 1943, when the Heads of State of the Western Allies met and decided the fate of Europe; that was the only place anything could have been done to help. If we go back to the distant past when our ancestors settled in the Carpathian basin, they should have gone on further – they would not have found a lovelier place, but maybe a safer one!

During the following weeks the country was bombed heavily, both by American and Russian planes. I went to the Jurányi military hospital every day, and then to the Szikla hospital; in the evenings we listened to the radio and played bridge in the shelter.

Ladomér Zichy came back from Slovakia on the eighteenth. His negotiations with Lieutenant Colonel Makarov had been successful. He brought a message that Makarov could get a properly authorized emissary to Moscow by plane immediately. In the event of a ceasefire being agreed, Makarov – apparently on behalf of Stalin – gave written conditions that were very favourable and lenient towards Hungary.

Vattay summarized the contents of this letter in his memoirs:

> Makarov ... stated that he was writing his letter on the instructions of Marshal Stalin. ... The delegation would enjoy complete diplomatic immunity and be able to move and travel freely. It was allowed to use Schiffer code and a radio. ...When the delegation arrived, both they and the British and Americans would stop bombing Hungary.
>
> They would guarantee complete independence and freedom for Hungary, and would not interfere in its internal affairs. The army and the police would remain, nobody would be disarmed. Where there were no Germans, and the Hungarians were not cooperating with the Germans, the current public administration – both military and civil – would stay unchanged. The Hungarians would choose their own government. The Russians would exert no pressure on the country in this matter, not even in a form of an underground movement. The Romanian army would stop outside Transylvania and only the Russian army would advance. A referendum then would be held to decide which country Transylvania should belong to. This would be Marshal Stalin's standpoint at the peace conference. The Russians didn't want anything in central Europe, as it was decided in Teheran. In Moscow the Hungarian delegation would negotiate with British, American and Soviet representatives; that is to say, the three powers would come to a joint decision.[34]

Vattay added: 'We didn't doubt the seriousness of the letter, and Police Colonel Kudar was ordered to find out the practicability of the route to take.' A few days later Ede Aczél returned from Moscow outlining similar conditions.

These unexpectedly favourable prospects prompted Miklóspapa to act immediately, and he started to make up the delegation he would send to Moscow. Nevertheless, he also made one more attempt in the following days to seek contacts with the Western Allies, saying, ' we can only solve our problems together with the Anglo-Saxons.'

On the evening of 20 September there was a short air raid alert, but Nicky and I did not go down to the shelter: instead, we talked in Gyuszi Tost's apartment with Colonel Charles Howie, which was most enjoyable; he seemed a decent and trustworthy man.

Colonel Charles Telfer Howie was a South African-born officer serving in the British army, who had been captured by the Germans and had escaped to Hungary from a prisoner-of-war camp in Silesia at the end of 1943. Sándor Szent-Iványi, a Unitarian deputy bishop, who had been asked by the British and the Americans to look after their prisoners of war and refugees, managed to get Colonel Howie released immediately, and invited him to stay with him. He introduced him to Ferenc Szombathelyi, the chief of general staff, who then put him in touch with Nicky and István Bethlen. He also met Kállay and had an audience with the Regent. Colonel Howie worked out a plan whereby the British forces would gain occupation of Hungary from the air, and he was given a radio transmitter to contact them. It was in this way that Kállay had been able to negotiate with the British about an airborne mission. But there were a number of delays, and nothing was achieved following the German invasion. When the Germans came, Colonel Howie went into hiding and his radio set was secreted in a safe place; this of course was not without its dangers. I did not know many details at the time because Nicky was dealing with it.

As I have mentioned, while preparations were being made for the delegation to travel to Russia, Miklóspapa wanted to make one more attempt to make contact with the British, and wanted to propose once more that if British forces came to Hungary – whether on the ground or by air – we would help them and join forces with them. He entrusted this mission to General István Náday and Colonel Howie, intending to send them by air to the Allied General Headquarters in Caserta, near Naples. It was not an easy task, as all airfields were in German hands. But Gyuszi Tost found a reliable air force officer called Majoros, who succeeded in doing what seemed to be impossible: he found an aeroplane which had not been used for a long time, moved it to a disused airfield near Pest, and fuelled it. When all the preparations were complete, Colonel Howie was called for a final meeting. So, on that evening of 20 September, he was smuggled into the Palace.

ADC Tost took part in all these preparations, and Colonel Howie was hidden for two days in his apartment, which was on the same floor as mine. As even the staff were not supposed to find out about his presence, I offered to provide him with food. When I had lunch or dinner – usually alone – Gyuri the valet brought in the food, put it on the table, and went out. I had a mahogany food carrier in which two or three plates could be put on top of each other – it was in the dining room as a decorative object. I put most of my meal in this food carrier, and when the table had been cleared and everyone had gone out, I took it across to Tost's flat. I think Gyuri must have found it odd that I had such a good appetite for two days, but nobody said anything.

On the second day there was an air raid warning. As usual everyone went down to the shelter, but Howie had to stay in his hiding place. Before going down to the shelter I thought I would call in to Tost's flat, as it could not have been a pleasant feeling for Colonel Howie to have his own bombers flying overhead. When I got to Tost's apartment I could hear Colonel Howie singing in the bathroom! There's real English *sang-froid*, I thought; he does not need my words of sympathy.

On the same day we received the news that my brother-in-law Józsi had been wounded at Kolozsvár. He was being brought to Budapest by car. We were very worried, as we did not know how serious his injuries were. I rang Sya, and the next day she arrived from the country and I took her with me to the Szikla hospital, where I would be told when and where Józsi would be taken. As soon as we heard, Sya and I went to hospital no.11, where we found Józsi relatively well in spite of three wounds caused by bomb fragments. One of the wounds was on his neck, right above the artery, and his knee and arm were shot through; but the important thing was that he was back.

General István Náday and Colonel Howie left on 22 September for the British General Headquarters. When Nicky and I said goodbye to Howie I gave him a small, blessed Saint Kaszap medal to help him on his dangerous journey.

Tost took them to the secret airfield; we found out later that pilot Majoros' wife went with them, having been told only ten minutes earlier that she was going 'somewhere' with her husband. They arrived safely in Caserta. Náday had only one written document – a note written by the Regent himself.[35] They could not take any other written document with them in case the Germans arrested them.

Unfortunately this mission ended in complete failure. First of all we heard that they had arrived safely, then for a long time we heard nothing. The next message could not be decoded. Apparently their code key had been lost or left at home. We subsequently found out that the British had been suspicious of the mission and had taken exception to the fact that Náday did not have a letter of authorisation; and in any event we had been told to talk to the Soviet Union. Náday and Howie were separated and could not communicate after that.

I do not know what the Allies could have done to prevent the occupation of Hungary by the Soviets, but it is unforgivable that they did not take our proposals seriously, and that it was with their consent that Hungary and its neighbours suffered fifty years of human, material and moral devastation as a result of Communism.

Soon after the war ended we received several letters from Howie in South Africa, much to our delight. In these he expressed his concern that Miklóspapa might be regarded as a war criminal, and if that were to happen he was prepared to send statements in Miklóspapa's defence. He thanked me for the whisky and cakes I had provided in the Palace, and for the medal – he called it a talisman – which he still carried in his wallet. He asked in every letter how he could help us. He even wanted to send us food parcels. He wrote very appreciatively of Nicky and Gyuszi Tost, and regretted that Gyuszi had not flown out to Italy with them. I continued corresponding with him until his death.

There were many air raids, mainly aimed at military targets. The looting perpetrated by retreating German forces caused outrage – but we also heard descriptions of brutal behaviour and mass rapes by Soviet forces from witnesses in places the Soviets had captured but could not hold, and which were later recaptured by the Germans. As was to be expected, the German and Arrow Cross press made good use of these reports.

A flood of refugees began to arrive from the east. After the bombing raids traffic in Budapest sometimes came to a virtual standstill, and we began to suffer food shortages.

How could people destroy the Almighty's wonderful world with all its beauty and goodness? And what effect would all this suffering have on the next generation? Though I too belonged to a post-war generation and knew that things could return to normality, still we were not able to prevent repeated and increasingly serious conflicts.

In the meantime Miklóspapa was making up the Moscow delegation. Lieutenant General Gábor Faraghó, supervisor of the gendarmerie and Hungary's former military attaché in Moscow, was to head the delegation; the other members were Domokos Szent-Iványi – a ministerial adviser and head of Nicky's Escape Office – and Count Géza Teleki, a university lecturer and the son of former Prime Minister Pál Teleki. Ladomér Zichy was sent back to Slovakia to report that the delegation was on its way, and to make sure that the offer still stood.

Then the Regent composed the letter he would send to Stalin with his delegation. He wrote it in English and read it to us:

Field Marshal,

In the name of and for the sake of my people in their extreme danger, I address myself to you – doing so in the name of the Hungarian people, who have no responsibility for this war. For a thousand years and particularly during this last decade, the fate of our people has been influenced by the neighbouring German Colossus.

It was again under this influence that we were carried into this unfortunate war with the Soviet Union.

I have to lay a particular stress on the fact that my poor country has been practically filled with the German 'Fifth Column'. This penetration began on a large scale at the same moment when German forces marched into Romania and Bulgaria. As a result, every movement and every step in Hungary have been closely watched by German agents, and the most important news and reports have never reached me. I have now come to know that, after the air attack upon Kassa and Munkács, Foreign Minister Molotov – during a conversation with the Hungarian Minister – emphasized the peaceful aims of the Soviet Union towards Hungary. If this was really so, then it is fatal, for it did not reach me at the time.

For the sake of justice, I would like to inform you that we have never ever wanted to take a single inch from anybody that was not ours by right. On the contrary, the Romanians took Bessarabia from their own Russian ally after the First World War and wished to take an important part of South Russia during the Second World War, with German help. Furthermore, when in 1940 we intended to make an end to the monstrous treatment of the Hungarian people in Transylvania, it was again the Romanians who requested help from Germany, asking Hitler to help them to retain at least a part of this land through the Vienna Award.

When sending with full authorisation my delegates to the negotiations for armistice I beg you to spare this unfortunate country, which has its own historic merits, and the people of which have so many affinities with the Russian people. Kindly exercise your great influence upon your allies, that you may make conditions compatible with our people's interests and honour, who really deserve a peaceful life and a safe future. I avail myself of this opportunity to express to you, Field Marshal Stalin, my highest consideration.

Yours truly,

Horthy

P.S. As our troops are still on the borders and we are being invaded by strong German units, I am asking you to treat my letter with discretion, until we are able to master the situation.[36]

It is difficult to put that unforgettable, truly dramatic moment into words. Though he did not say or show anything, one could sense how difficult it had been for Miklóspapa to write that letter. As he read it out to us – asking us to give him our comments – I was filled with an indescribable sadness. That moment somehow contained all the pain and despair that had descended on us. At that time I did not even know that the favourable conditions sent by Makarov – apparently with Stalin's approval – were only bait. The Soviet government later declared them to be invalid.

The atmosphere was one of excitement and tension on the day Gábor Faraghó, Domokos Szent-Iványi and Géza Teleki – disguised as a shooting party – set off for Moscow by way of Slovakia. They had passports provided by the Cabinet Office, and took with them the Regent's handwritten letter to Stalin. They split up while they were in German-occupied Hungary. They crossed the Slovak border illegally, on foot and across a river and there, in partisan territory, Stalin's plane came to pick them up. It was a very important, difficult, risky and exciting journey. Their instructions were that the delegation should refer to Makarov's letter, set up a coded link to the Royal Palace with a short wave transmitter, and that once the negotiations began, the allied air raids would stop.

A special code was compiled for this mission, and there were only two copies of the key-book: one was taken by the delegation, the other remained with us in the Palace. The 'black book' containing the key to the code was being used by three of us: Gyuszi Tost, Nicky and myself. For security reasons we did not want to involve anyone else.

The Interior Ministry had a short wave radio transmitting and receiving station on the floor above Tost's apartment in the Palace, which since 1939 had served as the Regent's link to the Palace if he was away, and now served as his link to the armed forces as commander-in-chief. Four police telegraph operators from the Interior Ministry were permanently on duty. The link between the radio station and the Regent was Gyuszi Tost. It was he who discussed with the telegraph operators the possibility of setting up a secret link between the Palace and Moscow – without any information leaking out. The police telegraph operators undertook to do this without the knowledge of the Interior Ministry.

Helen Kállay decided to move in with her husband at the Turkish Embassy. We saw her off on 1 October and were sorry to see her go. We did not suspect that we would never see her again. When the Germans took us away, Kállay was forced by German ultimatum to leave the Turkish Embassy – and that was when his tribulations really began. He was taken to the Margit körút prison, then to Sopronkőhida, and finally to the Mauthausen extermination camp. Here, as my brother-in-law Nicky would be, he was held in solitary confinement. Helen stayed in the Turkish Embassy, and it was there, in front of the embassy's shelter, that she was killed by a German grenade in February 1945.

In the Palace we waited anxiously for news from Moscow, and in the meantime Miklóspapa tried to mobilize the military forces he had available – which unfortunately seemed to be very limited. Clearly this was important for the success of his attempt to achieve a ceasefire. But of course the need for strict secrecy, and the fact that he had to leave the government and the chief of general staff out of the ceasefire negotiations was a disadvantage as far as the success of his plan was concerned. Often we could not inform people whose help we really needed.

In August the Regent had appointed Lieutenant General Szilárd Bakay as commander of the First Army Corps in Budapest. In the face of the greatest difficulties, this outstanding, loyal and anti-Nazi soldier organized the military security of Budapest with the limited forces at his disposal. He constantly visited the troops in Budapest, and was in agreement with the Regent over the absolute necessity for Hungary to leave the war. On 6 October, in a misty autumn dawn, when Bakay was returning to his quarters, he was caught up in a staged traffic jam, snatched from his car and taken away. This abduction was a dreadful blow to us in every respect, and made us realize how defenceless we were against the reign of terror of the occupying forces.

We later found out that Bakay had been taken to the Mauthausen extermination camp, from which he returned only in 1945. He retired to the country, and despite everyone's advice he refused to leave Hungary. The Russians arrested him and sentenced him to death in Russia; he was shot by the Soviets in Sopron in 1947. That is the sort of thing to which one can never reconcile oneself ... .

A suitable replacement commander had to be found immediately, and

Miklóspapa quickly found one in the person of Lieutenant General Béla Aggteleky, who – it was hoped – would be able to take care of his own security.

A series of telegrams were now sent between Budapest and Moscow, between 5–16 October. The Hungarian text of the telegrams sent is not available to me, but Aylmer Macartney has published the official text of these in German and I have retranslated them.[37] The wording may not be perfect, but as far as I remember, it is reliable.

Whenever the secret radio started operating in the Palace, German planes appeared overhead. They must have been trying to break the code. Tost said they would not be able to do it – and he proved to be right.

The first telegram from Moscow arrived on 5 October. It was a great relief that the delegation had arrived there safely, but we were puzzled that they asked us to send a pair of size 43 black shoes for Faraghó. We thought it must be important … .

A second telegram arrived, in which they urgently requested full written authorisation to sign the ceasefire and other agreements; without this the Russians would not talk to them. Faraghó even named Major Nemes as the person who could take the written authorisation to them.

It was difficult to decode the telegrams, so in our first telegram to them we asked for a repeat of their first two telegrams. This they did, plus in a new telegram they said:

> … the letter has been handed over to Stalin, but as it does not say who has full authorisation to sign, they ask for this to be rectified. Atmosphere not bad, they want to reach agreement with us quickly … they are mainly interested in military cooperation.

Their next telegram reported mainly what our delegation told the Russians, including:

> … the Regent wrote his letter to Stalin after receiving the promises made by Makarov. Makarov's promises were put on record. Since the new government has been in office at home our increased freedom of movement has made it possible to make contact …

Naturally Miklóspapa requested that the precise conditions be made known, because without knowing them he could not give an authorisation to sign. Therefore in reply to their second telegram, we sent:

Ceasefire agreement desirable. ... Willingness exists
for the cooperation they want. Major Nemes en route
via Kőrösmező with written authorisation. Ladomér
route being watched. Urgently request disclosure of
conditions before signature.

Their next telegram was sent at 3 a.m. on 9 October:
Foreign Minister Molotov last night gave the
Hungarian delegation the 'preliminary' ceasefire
conditions. If Hungary accepts these, the committee
will meet in Moscow and discuss the final conditions. If
Hungary does not accept them, they will not talk to us
any more. The conditions are identical to Romania's.
Makarov and his activities are not recognized. The
Russian government asks for a speedy response.

The preliminary conditions are as follows: Czech,
Slovak and Romanian territories that have been
occupied beyond the 1937 borders must be vacated. All
troops and government employees must be withdrawn.
This process must begin immediately and be completed
within ten days. The starting date is the date on which
the Hungarian government receives this note. The three
governments will send an Allied committee under
Soviet control to Hungary to supervise this process. The
Hungarian state must end all contacts with the
Germans and must immediately declare war on
Germany. The Russian government is prepared to help
Hungary with its own troops.

This telegram disappointed and shocked us all deeply; in particular, the
withdrawal of the Makarov promises.
As Ayler Macartney later wrote:
It seems that Faraghó did everything he could to
make the Soviets give credence to the Makarov
promises, but a three-hour argument essentially boiled
down to the fact that the Western Allies simply had no
knowledge of these promises. Faraghó's insistence –
that these had been given to the Regent in writing and
that it was on this basis that the delegation had been
sent, and that their flight had been arranged by
Makarov so it was clear that he had authorisation –
was futile. The final response was that the only basis
they would recognize was that of an unconditional

surrender, and they asked him to inform the Regent that the Soviet government regarded the Makarov promises as null and void.[38]

This was also the day when General Béla Miklós, commander of the First Army, had an audience with Miklóspapa. It was decided that the Regent and all his family would travel north to Huszt, to have the protection of the First Army. Miklóspapa told Magdamama and me that we should make preparations. We started packing and discussed what we needed to take. About three days later Miklóspapa told us that the trip had been cancelled because János Vörös, the chief of general staff, thought it was too risky in terms of security. (Years later I was surprised to read in Vörös' memoirs that, according to him, it was the Regent who had cancelled the trip!)

10 October. From this day onward Miklóspapa would not allow Nicky or me to leave the Palace in case the Germans captured us, so I was no longer able to do my hospital work, or take the nursing examinations. This gave me time to make preparations in case we needed to flee. I packed all sorts of vitamins etc. for István into an old fashioned doctor's bag. I also made a belt in which I could hide some items of jewellery under my clothes – in this way they remained in my possession all through the war.

I had more time now to encode and decode telegrams. While Nicky was working in his office and Tost was on duty, I had time to work on my own, decoding the telegrams we received and encoding the telegrams to be sent. That day the reply arrived, saying the delegates had received our last telegram and had taken the steps specified. It went on:

> Informed the foreign minister orally and in writing of the points contained in the Makarov letter, and asked him to bring these to the attention of the Allies. It seems we will only be able to negotiate military cooperation. In order to save Budapest we will suggest that they break through at Vác and Párkány ...

We sent the following reply:

> Hungary accepts the preliminary ceasefire conditions. We ask to be informed of the detailed ceasefire negotiations as soon as possible, and for these to be kept completely secret until we can bring troops from the front to combat the Germans – who greatly outnumber us in Budapest – in order to prevent a coup

and the associated bloodshed and persecution of the
Jews. For this to be implemented, and for the ceasefire
conditions to be met, we ask for the Russian forces
advancing towards Budapest to be halted.

On the same day as he accepted the ceasefire conditions, the Regent
ordered the First and Second Armies to be withdrawn to a position
behind the river Tisza – that is, well within the Trianon borders –
according to the requirements outlined in the conditions. By
withdrawing the two armies despite German protests, he 'effectively
began his active military campaign on 10 October.'[39]

A letter was then sent to Lieutenant Colonel Geréb in reply to
concerns expressed by Lajos Dálnoki Veress, the commander of the First
Army. Vattay dictated this on behalf of the Regent:

We too are aware of the critical situation. The
ceasefire negotiations are in progress. As a
consequence, our troops have to withdraw to the
Trianon borders. Hungary will be occupied by the
Russians for an extended period. The Supreme
Commander gave the chief of general staff orders for
the First and Second Hungarian Armies to be
withdrawn and the chief of general staff will take the
necessary steps today.

We will fight on the side of the Russians against the
Germans. Our change of side can be expected within
one or two days of the ceasefire agreement being made
public, and must be implemented when the army
command receives a telegram as follows: 'Order of 1
March 1920 to be carried out.' This must be carried out
even if the chief of general staff or anybody else acts to
the contrary.[40]

11 October. After morning mass I worked with Tost on the telegrams.
Another one arrived from Moscow:

This morning at 4 a. m. we informed the foreign
minister that Hungary accepts the interim ceasefire
conditions. The atmosphere became friendly and warm.
The British prime minister and foreign minister are
here, which will certainly speed things up...

They assured us that a reply to the contents of our telegram would be
sent that day. In the afternoon another telegram arrived. It was full of
questions such as: how much time will Hungarian units need to arrive

in Budapest? What is their strength? Gendarmerie? What is the German strength in the capital? In the surroundings? What is the Jewish Peoples' attitude? Is the Hungarian government in Budapest? And so on. And it emphasized the importance of the matter:

> ... They are discussing military cooperation today and after that there will probably be a 1–2 day delay in the advance.

The next telegram was very short, and asked: 'how are our families?' The twelfth telegram arrived at 10 p.m.:

> Today at 20.00 hrs we signed the preliminary conditions. They have acceded to the Regent's request, and tonight the advance of the Russian troops was halted for 1–2 days. They agree to Hungarian troops being sent to Budapest. They will inform us which Hungarian commander should go over to which Russian commander to discuss the details. They want to send the Allied delegation as soon as possible. Nemes has not yet crossed the border, though we urgently need full authorisation in writing. We also ask for this to be sent by telegram. They asked whether the forces would remain loyal to the Regent. We confirmed that we were convinced they would. They ask whether the government and the Regent are still in Budapest. It is important that contact is not broken.

Before and after dinner Nicky, Gyuszi Tost and I worked on the telegrams, occasionally snatching something to eat. We sent the next telegram, in which we repeated:

> Permission granted to sign ceasefire. Major Nemes set off with full written authorisation in the morning of the 12th.

At their request we also repeated the conditions sent in their sixth telegram and which we had accepted, the last of which was that 'Hungary had to end all contacts with the Germans and declare war on Germany immediately'. Finally we said that the Regent was staying in Budapest, and again emphasized the great importance of keeping this matter secret until the forces withdrawn from the front were available, particularly because the Germans had a high concentration of armoured forces.

I would now like to refer to something that has frequently been disputed: that the Regent accepted the ceasefire conditions – and therefore the declaration of war on the Germans – but was not prepared to attack the Germans. The explanation is very simple. As one can see from the telegram, the conditions stated that Hungary had to declare war on Germany immediately – there was no mention of attack, just a declaration of war.

Before he knew about the ceasefire conditions, the Regent did indeed say to some people that he did not want to stab the Germans in the back; that he wanted to avoid this at all costs. But he accepted that he had to declare war, and informed Veesenmayer on the morning of the fifteenth that he had asked the Russians for a ceasefire. If as a result of this the Germans had attacked us, he would have defended himself with all the forces at his disposal. As he said in another telegram: 'If the Germans find out about the ceasefire or it becomes public knowledge, we can count on a German attack, against which we will certainly defend ourselves.'

My father-in-law just would not have been prepared to attack the Germans without warning them beforehand. This was his position, and this was why he told Veesenmayer about the ceasefire and stated clearly in his proclamation that Hungary was at war with Germany. He did all this with the intention of fulfilling the ceasefire conditions.

I would add that I did not share his opinion: I thought we had every reason to attack the Nazis as soon as possible before they took over control. On the other hand I can imagine that it would have been difficult to give the army an order to attack without German provocation and without sufficient reason.

I have to mention here something I suppose is generally known: that in 1954 Miklóspapa wrote a letter to German Chancellor Adenauer. Many people point to this as evidence that the Regent did not comply with the ceasefire agreement and that in addition he lied to Adenauer.

Among other things, he wrote in that letter: 'As Regent of Hungary I would like to assure you that all the rumours spread by certain parties that Hungary would have been prepared to stab Germany in the back in 1944 in connection with the ceasefire are complete fabrications.' He then explains the critical situation Hungary was in at the time, adding: 'Nobody in Hungary thought of declaring war on Germany on Russian orders or Soviet dictates; that would have been unthinkable.'

It's possible that Miklóspapa wrote this because he would only have attacked if provoked by the Germans, not on Soviet dictates. But this sentence is misleading, and could only have got into the letter by mistake – my father-in-law was eighty-six at the time. I was not in Portugal then: if I had been, I would have pointed out that he had written 'declaring war on Germany' instead of 'attacking Germany'. At that time I copied and filed every letter my father-in-law wrote, so I would have been able to warn him about this mistake. I asked my mother-in-law to copy his letters while I was away, and the copy of this letter in her handwriting is in my possession.

Representatives of the resistance movement had previously sought contact with the Regent through Nicky, and the Regent was pleased to acknowledge them and give his support. On the evening of 11 October Árpád Szakasits, leader of the Social Democratic Party, and Zoltán Tildy, leader of the Independent Smallholders' Party, came to the Palace for discussions. The talks took place in a friendly atmosphere, but did not produce any serious results. Everyone agreed that the war had to be brought to an end. They discussed arming the workers, and the Regent told them about his plan to 'get out of the war', and even told them he was going to announce the ceasefire by proclamation. He promised to free all political prisoners.

The next day the principal political prisoners were indeed transferred to a transit prison on the outskirts of Budapest. The idea was that when the reinforcements diverted to Budapest arrived, the resistance movement would call on workers to go on a general strike.

The plans were ready, but as a result of a betrayal by the office of the chief of general staff, events took a completely different turn. The reinforcements the Regent had ordered never arrived, there were bombing raids, a railway bridge was blown up and the ceasefire had to be announced earlier than was originally intended.

By 12 October there were reports that the Russians had already crossed the river Tisza in the south and had occupied Szeged. Several secret telegrams were sent in both directions, asking for certain illegible sections to be repeated. The main points of the telegrams were:

> The Russians are not attacking along the Tisza south of Szolnok, so Hungarian forces can immediately be ordered back to Budapest from this front. They ask for an immediate answer on whether this will be done. The Russians do not understand why it has not been done already. They suggest that armoured forces should be withdrawn too.

And in answer to our request for clarification of incomplete communications:

> We asked the Russian government to stop the bombing raids on Budapest and to inform the British and American air forces too. There is some hope that they will agree because we gave the Jews and the bridges as arguments in favour. Russian advance and

details have to be discussed in Hungary. Russian troops there have excellent contacts with their capital, and suggested that Romanian troops should advance only on Hungary's southern borders in order not to become mixed up with Hungarian troops. Thus they will have contact mainly with Yugoslav troops and this would be very good ...

Veesenmayer had requested an audience for 13 October, but Miklóspapa sent him a message that he was unable to see him; he did not wish to have a meeting with the German plenipotentiary until he had made a final decision about announcing the ceasefire agreement.

That day, although an air raid warning was sounded, Nicky, Tost and I did not go down to the shelter, because there was a lot of work to be done on a telegram. We explained that two divisions of Hungarian troops would gradually reach Budapest in 8–10 days, mainly from the First and Second Army Corps. And we gave detailed information about the positions of the German forces: SS, Gestapo and armoured units. We assured the delegation that their families were safe. We told them that the Jews waiting to be saved were grateful for the Regent's support and looked to him to free them from German rule. It was a very long telegram, and it was late at night by the time we finished working on it.

I spent most of the next day, partly with Nicky and Tost but mainly on my own, receiving and sending telegrams. Rumours were circulating of preparations for an Arrow Cross coup and of more German forces arriving around Budapest – but our reinforcements had not arrived yet. Veesenmayer again requested an audience with the Regent, and again was refused. He was finally informed that the Regent would receive him the next day, the fifteenth.

That afternoon, nearly three days after the preliminary ceasefire agreement had been signed in Moscow, Miklóspapa called a meeting of a select committee: Károly Lázár, commander of the Guards; Gyula Ambrózy, head of the Cabinet Office; Antal Vattay, Gyuszi Tost and the family – Magdamama, Nicky and myself.

At this meeting Miklóspapa announced that he had decided not to wait any longer but to bring matters to a head the next day and announce the ceasefire in a radio broadcast. As Aggteleky observed, 'He was probably forced to act more quickly by the rapidly deteriorating military situation, particularly as the railway bridge at Csap had been blown up, making it impossible for the Tenth Division to be withdrawn as he had ordered.'[41]

But first the Regent wanted to bring his decision to the attention of the Germans. He repeated his belief that no Hungarian soldier should stab an ally in the back, even if that ally had betrayed him, so if he was going to ask for a ceasefire he would personally inform the Germans of that fact. For that reason, he said, he had arranged for the German plenipotentiary commissioner to come to the Palace the next day so he could tell him. But it was important that the proclamation should be broadcast the moment he had informed Veesenmayer, and before Veesenmayer left the Palace, so he would not be able to prevent it being repeatedly broadcast. He asked me to be in the next room and listen to the conversation; as soon as he told Veesenmayer that he had asked for a ceasefire, I should quietly leave the room and tell Ambrózy, who was to be in telephone contact with Endre Hlatky, the director of Hungarian Radio, at the studios. He made it clear that the proclamation should be broadcast at that moment, before Veesenmayer left the Palace.

On Miklóspapa's instructions, Károly Lázár had to organize the defence of the Palace; and that same night he made arrangements with the forces at his disposal. The roads up to Castle Hill were mined and barricades were placed across them. It was strictly forbidden to let anyone in or out.

Thus the statement in the memoirs of Gusztáv Hennyey, the then foreign minister, that Károly Lázár 'acted arbitrarily and on his own initiative in sealing off the roads to Castle Hill' is completely without foundation.[42]

From Lieutenant General Aggteleky's description of his experiences we can discover what was done to prepare for the defence of Budapest and for a successful ceasefire:

> As Commander of the First Budapest Army Corps I was in a leading position when the attempt was made to implement the ceasefire ... I reported to the Regent on 6 October.
>
> In an audience lasting an hour and a quarter, the Regent gave me general information on the situation and the spirit and extent of the proclamation he was to make on 15 October. But he told me in addition that negotiations for a ceasefire were in progress ... He stated categorically that if there was a German (Arrow Cross) coup or the Germans tried to prevent the ceasefire coming into effect by force, he would resist by force of arms. He ordered me to organize the defence of the capital for either eventuality, with the constraint that I was not responsible for the defence of the Palace because he had ordered Lieutenant General Lázár, the commander of the Bodyguards, to organize that. He told me this so resolutely and so forcefully that I was

convinced that he wanted to defend the Palace to the end. He told me that my general duties were to ensure the government's freedom to act and to maintain order in Budapest. He spoke out repeatedly and furiously against the unspeakable villainy of Hitler and the German leadership, and expressed his firm intention and desire to do everything he could to preserve the country from the destruction of this war, which had become pointless.

I found it striking that the defence minister and the chief of general staff didn't mention a word of this when I reported to them, and it was unusual that I received these orders directly from the Regent himself, bypassing these two men. At the time I was at a loss to explain this.

In the afternoon of 10 October I went to the Regent again to give him information. As we learned years later, that morning he had received Molotov's ceasefire conditions, accepted them, and ordered that they be signed. He had also ordered the First Army to withdraw from the frontier ridge in Subcarpathia and the Second Army to withdraw from the region of Kolozsvár and go up from Tokaj to the line of the Tisza and Bodrog rivers. Most importantly, he had given direct and confidential orders that the commanders of the First and Second Armies should, with their armies, go over to the Russians on receipt of a special signal.

The Regent didn't say a word about all this. He repeated the orders he had given me on the sixth, with similar decisiveness; and he was extremely pleased when I told him that I had posted army guards to the bridges across the Danube in the capital in order to prevent the Germans blowing them up. With regard to the future, he simply expressed his conviction that the ceasefire would come about without significant upheaval in the country. My audience lasted about three-quarters of an hour. ...

In the meantime I had obtained information on the strength of the First Army Corps and found that for the execution of the duties I had received I had no mobile detachments or troops available for use in combat ... So as a last resort I used the civil defence technical battalions stationed on the outskirts of the capital – the latter were ill-equipped and their duties consisted only of clearing rubble. I placed the necessary mobile detachments – equivalent to about six battalions – on standby, and at the same time ordered them to be combined in the centre of the city. On 15 October, early in the morning, one regiment rested at Pilisvörösvár on its way to Budapest, while the civil defence technical battalions gradually arrived during the course of the same day ...

When I was also informed that the Germans had deployed a significant number of the troops they had had stationed around the capital to the battle at Debrecen, I saw that our relative strengths were not quite so uneven. I also knew that the Hussar Division was in the area of Örkény, and counted on other reinforcements arriving from the front line in the region of Szolnok. But once again fate took a hand – to our disadvantage. ...

The Regent decided, in connection with the ceasefire campaign, to set up a bridgehead in Budapest, and appointed Lieutenant General Farkas to command it. Farkas arrived in the capital in the early hours of 14 October... My information is that for this task the Tenth Division, which had until then also been fighting on the Carpathian front, was made available to him, and the withdrawal had only just begun.'[43]

So it is clear that the Regent took steps to withdraw troops, Aggteleky took steps to reinforce the capital, and Károly Lázár provided effectively for the security of Castle Hill. Some other reinforcements would certainly have arrived by the original date, 20 October. But we now know that this would have been thwarted by the strengthening of German forces around Budapest and by the coup they had planned.

My father-in-law himself wrote the proclamation he was to broadcast the following morning, with Ambrózy's help. His intention was to bring to the attention of the country and of the outside world many things about which they had no idea.

Just before midnight we received a telegram from Moscow, which told us very sternly that:

The Soviets have stopped their advance but the Hungarians have not withdrawn their troops towards Budapest; indeed they have been very active near Szolnok. From this it appears that the Hungarian government is probably not prepared to comply with the ceasefire conditions. Therefore we have been given 48 hours to comply with the conditions we have accepted:

1. End all contacts with Germany and begin active fighting against them.

2. Start withdrawing troops from Romanian, Yugoslav and Czechoslovak territories.

3. Send full details of the positions of Hungarian and German troops, and a precise account of how the ceasefire conditions have been complied with to date, to the Soviet Headquarters in Szeged at 8 a. m. on the 18th.

Signed: General Antonov

Please comply with these to the letter and send me detailed information. A first class general and Colonel Nádas should travel to Szeged.

We were able to send a reply at 3.30 a.m. on the fifteenth:

Our emissary has returned from Szeged. The commander there demands immediate fighting activity. We cannot do this at our current strength until supplies arrive in Budapest. These are unfortunately making very slow progress due to the bombing of trains ... The Germans already have suspicions, which are fuelled by foreign radio reports. If they find out about the ceasefire or it becomes public knowledge, we can be certain that the Germans will attack, in which case we will certainly defend ourselves. If this happens, the main task of Russian and Hungarian troops will be to liberate Budapest. Until then we will certainly hold the Palace as the seat of government. Our emissary will hand over this request in Szeged on Monday.

This was the only response made to their final telegram, so there is no truth in Gusztáv Hennyey's assertion that the Regent, in agreement with the government (i.e. Lakatos, Hennyey and Csatay), rejected the Russian conditions for a ceasefire around midnight on 15 October as a result of these demands. This is a baseless statement made after the war, and there is no evidence for it.

15

---

15 October 1944

Ye worked very hard at encoding and decoding until four thirty in the morning – unfortunately on account of delays and misunderstandings things did not progress as quickly as they should have done.

Before we retired to get a little sleep, Nicky told me that later that morning he would go down to Eskü Square to meet an emissary from Tito. I reminded him indignantly that Miklóspapa had forbidden us to leave the Palace, but he answered that, 'Papa has agreed,' to which I could say no more.

Reconstructing the events later with Miklóspapa, we found that Nicky had asked permission to talk to Tito's emissary, to which his father had agreed, assuming that Nicky would meet him in the Palace. He had not asked where they would meet; on the other hand, Nicky had not told him that he was going to leave the Palace.

After a few short hours of sleep I decided to go down to the Palace chapel for mass at nine o'clock, because this was an important day and I thought it would be helpful to face the unknown and unforeseeable future with a prayer. Before I left my apartment I heard the sound of explosions. As I looked out of the window overlooking Gellért Hill, it was clear that there was shooting in the city centre, on the other side of the Danube; I wondered who could be shooting on such a beautiful sunny morning. I went to ask what was going on in the city but nobody knew. Soon afterwards, I was called down to the ground floor to see one of the guards who had accompanied Nicky to Eskü Square. It was dreadful to hear then that our fears for the safety of the family had been realized: Nicky had been captured by the Germans.

When we were together again after the war, Nicky told us what had happened. The meeting with Tito's emissary was arranged for 9.30 a.m. in the office of Félix Bornemissza, the director of the Hungarian Danube Free Port Company, in Eskü Square. Nicky had asked three guards to accompany him on this trip. They drove to the square, and he told the guards to wait while he went up to the fourth floor, and that if he did not return within ten minutes they should come in after him. Félix was waiting alone in the office. He said he'd had a terrible nightmare that he had fallen into a well. Then there was a ring at the door and Félix went to open it. He came back with a Yugoslav, who greeted Nicky very cordially: 'Good morning, sir, I have Marshal Tito's message here.' Félix translated all this into Hungarian. The man was short and dark, and had a pleasant and open face. He seemed calm and honest, but somehow Nicky was not convinced. He watched the man slit his trouser turn-up and take out the letter. All this increased Nicky's suspicions; the whole thing seemed too much like a film plot. When he saw that the letter was written in Croatian he knew for certain that it was a hoax. A letter of such importance would not be written in a language the recipient could not understand.

Félix did not have time to read it. Shots could be heard from the street. There was another ring at the door and Félix went to open it. A rough voice shouted in German, 'Hands up!' Tito's emissary ran the length of the long hall and out of the front door, through about half a dozen men in leather jackets. Nicky thoughts were racing: how awful it would be for his parents if he died – all four of their children would be dead ... and what an awful position his father would be in if he were captured .... He went into the hall and took his revolver out of his pocket, but he did not dare shoot because Félix was standing among the leather-jacketed men. Then he was hit on the back of the head: someone had managed to sneak up behind him.

He was hit on the head several times. By now there were several men surrounding him, shouting crude expressions to which he responded in kind. Meanwhile he was thinking calmly – he thought it was hatred that cleared his mind – 'I wonder what they're hitting me with?' He managed to catch sight of a hard rubber stick with a rounded metal end. He kicked and struggled, and felt handcuffs on his wrists. 'Cowards!' he shouted, still kicking, but they hit him until blood streamed down his face and obscured his vision. He fell onto a sofa and the blows ceased. They left him lying there until the bleeding stopped and then they pulled a sack over his head. He realized they were taking him down the stairs. They got outside and whatever was covering his head slipped off. He saw a big crowd.

'Help! These rotten Germans are taking me away!' he shouted in Hungarian, but nobody moved; they seemed not to understand him. He discovered later that apparently about two hundred Germans had been hired by the Nazis to surround the block. Nicky thought Hungarians would definitely have recognized him and come to his assistance. A small closed van was waiting for them, Félix was also brought out in handcuffs, but he was not being beaten.

They were put into the van and five SS soldiers got in with them. The van set off and he knew they were heading for the airport. Soon they were aboard a plane, which landed two hours later; he thought it must be in Vienna. They were put into another closed van and travelled a short distance. An SS officer got in, and after calling him 'Horthy *Schwein*' he left, seemingly satisfied. They spent two hours in Vienna and then took the road for Linz and Salzburg. After a sharp right turn he knew where he was being taken: to the Mauthausen concentration and extermination camp. (A year earlier, when Count Antal Szapáry had been released from Mauthausen, he had told Nicky the way to the camp from Vienna.) When the van stopped, the Gestapo guards jumped out and laughingly told them, 'Here we are in Mauthausen sanatorium!'

But now to return to the Palace on 15 October, when we discovered that Nicky had been captured.

I listened to the bodyguard's story and discovered that when he and another bodyguard tried to get into the building to find Nicky they were prevented from doing so. Hand grenades were then thrown at their car, which wounded the other guard and killed the driver. This guard managed to flee to a nearby phone box, from which he tried to summon help. A man in plain clothes yanked open the door of the phone box, but the guard knocked him down and ran around the corner, where luckily he managed to stop a taxi. He forced the driver at gunpoint to drive to the Palace. It was a miracle he managed to get there.

I went immediately to inform Miklóspapa that Nicky had been abducted. The Council of State meeting was due to start within minutes. Miklóspapa was already in a meeting with someone and I asked for him to be called out urgently. I told him that Nicky had been captured and hurriedly added that we had to make up a story so Magdamama would not discover the truth. I thought it would also help Miklóspapa if we could not talk about it. My plan was formed immediately: I suggested that we should tell Magdamama that Nicky had travelled south to make contact with Tito's emissary. Miklóspapa thought it was a good idea; and, although he grew pale, he controlled himself admirably. After asking about the details the guardsman had given and being told that a detachment had gone to the scene immediately, he went into the Mátyás room, where the Council of State meeting began, half an hour late.

Meanwhile, I ran up to the first floor to Nicky's room and packed a few items of clothing that he might have taken with him in a suitcase, which I hid. Then I had a short rest to calm down, and carefully thought through what else I should do. I knew I had to spare Magdamama from finding out the truth; after all, Nicky was the only one of her four children who was still alive – if indeed he was still alive. I went in to see her and told her that Nicky had travelled south early in the morning. She immediately asked whether he had taken warm things with him and hurried up to Nicky's room to find out. I have to say even I was surprised at my intuitive foresight and the extent to which I knew my beloved mother-in-law. Love can do many things.

There were several occasions later when I lied to Magdamama, when I thought the truth would be too hard for her to bear, and she always thanked me for it afterwards. This time I told her the truth about Nicky only when we too were in Nazi captivity and on the way to Germany. When I told her the truth on the train she thanked me for keeping it from her; she said she would not have been able to bear it.

I had to keep an eye on the time because Veesenmayer was due to come at noon and I would be on duty as eavesdropper. So I went down to the first floor and settled myself in the room next to the Regent's study. While I was waiting, doubts began to weigh on me. What was the point of this audience? No good could come of it. If we were already burning our bridges by making the proclamation, why did we have to tell him about it? Correct procedures are all very well, but they do not work with villains.

When Veesenmayer arrived, I took off my shoes and quietly went over to the door so I could listen clearly to what they were talking about next door. It was not difficult to hear: everyone involved in this truly dramatic scene spoke quite loudly. Prime Minister Lakatos and Foreign Minister Hennyey were also present. My father-in-law reproached Veesenmayer and protested against the abduction of his son. Veesenmayer at first denied any knowledge of this, but when Miklóspapa furiously threw down in front of him the German cartridge container found at the scene (I heard the impact clearly), saying there was the evidence found at the scene of the gun battle, then – without any transition – Veesenmayer said that Nicky had been arrested legally because he had colluded with the enemy. Then Miklóspapa told him that he had made his decision and had asked the Russians for a ceasefire.

There was a momentary silence – as my father-in-law told us later, his announcement had taken Veesenmayer by surprise and he had paled.

This was the moment I was waiting for: quietly I went to the next room, picking up my shoes on the way, to tell Ambrózy that the proclamation could be broadcast immediately. But Ambrózy – the old lawyer – replied that we first had to ask the Regent whether he wanted to make any changes to the text after his conversation with

Veesenmayer. I could not believe my ears! Why was he quibbling? But before I could contradict him I caught sight of Endre Hlatky, the director of the Radio, in the background. According to what had been agreed, he should have been waiting by the phone at the Radio Headquarters. I asked what he was doing there, and why he was not where he was supposed to be. I could see that Ambrózy would not give way, but as I had been put in charge of this I said, 'All right, we'll wait for Veesenmayer to go, and then get the Regent's agreement; but I demand that in the meantime Hlatky should go at once to Radio Headquarters and wait for the final decision there.'

I had to point out – though I thought this would have been obvious to everyone – that if Hlatky only left the Palace when Veesenmayer did, then the Germans could occupy Radio Headquarters before he got there, or block his way, because Veesenmayer would immediately take steps to ensure this.

Hlatky left hurriedly, but I stayed where I was because I now wanted to make sure there would not be any more obstacles. When Veesenmayer left the Regent's study, I waited to see what would happen, but nobody moved. Then I followed aide-de-camp Tost into the study, where Lakatos and Hennyey were standing in the middle of the room talking and Miklóspapa was tidying papers on his desk. Tost asked whether the proclamation could be broadcast. Miklóspapa clearly did not hear the question, but Lakatos answered, 'Under no circumstances! We have to wait for Ambassador Rahn to come, because that could result in changes being made.'

Then I went straight over to Miklóspapa and told him that the proclamation had not yet been broadcast because Ambrózy wanted to know whether there were any changes. Miklóspapa was very surprised and said he could not understand why it had not been broadcast, and we should immediately arrange for this to take place. By then Ambrózy was standing in the doorway, and when he heard this he hurried out to the phone.

I found out that, before leaving, Veesenmayer had asked the Regent to postpone his decision until he heard what Ambassador Rahn, Hitler's special emissary, had to say. Rahn had just arrived in Budapest with the mission of resolving the disagreements that had arisen recently. He had brought a special message from Hitler. The Regent stated that he would receive Rahn, but would not change his decision.

I went back to my apartment and waited by the radio. After a short time – which to me seemed like an eternity – the Regent's statement was read three times, and then the orders for the armed forces were read twice.

The Proclamation of 15 October

Ever since the will of the nation put me at the country's helm, the most important aim of Hungarian foreign policy has been, through peaceful revision, to repair, at least partly, the injustices of the Peace Treaty of Trianon. Our hopes in the League of Nations in this regard have remained unfulfilled.

At the time of the beginning of a new world crisis, Hungary was not led by any desire to acquire new territories. We had no aggressive intention against the Republic of Czechoslovakia, and Hungary did not wish to regain by war territories taken from her. We entered the Bácska only after the collapse of Yugoslavia and in order to defend our blood brethren. We accepted a peaceful arbitration of the Axis powers regarding the Eastern Territories taken from us in 1918 by Romania.

Owing to our geographic situation, Hungary has been forced into this world war against the Allies by German pressure, but we did not seek power, we did not want to take even a square metre of territory from anyone.

It is now clear to anyone with any common sense that Germany has lost the war. Any government that is responsible for the destiny of its country must draw the appropriate conclusions. As the great German statesman Bismarck said: 'No nation is obliged to sacrifice itself on the altar of its ally.'

Conscious of my historic responsibility, I am duty bound to take any step which will avoid further unnecessary bloodshed. A nation which turns the land inherited from its forbears into the scene of rearguard action in a war which is already lost, led by a slave mentality and defending foreign values, will lose the respect of public opinion around the world.

Filled with anxiety, I am forced to state that Germany has long since broke the faith to which its alliance with us obliged it. For some time it has sent increasing numbers of Hungarian troops to fight outside our borders, against my wishes and without my knowledge.

This March the head of the German Reich called me to Klessheim for negotiations after I had asked for

Hungarian troops to be allowed home as a matter of urgency. There, Hitler announced that Hungary would be occupied by German forces, and this was carried out despite my protests, while I was outside the country. At the same time the German political police inundated Hungary, arresting many Hungarian citizens, including many members of Parliament and the interior minister. The prime minister only avoided a similar fate by fleeing in good time to a neutral embassy. When Hitler made a firm promise to end this occupation which violated Hungarian sovereignty if I were to appoint a government in which he had confidence, I appointed the Sztójay government, which did indeed enjoy the confidence of the Germans.

But again the Germans did not keep their promise. Under the protection of the German occupation forces the Gestapo tackled the Jewish question in a manner incompatible with the dictates of humanity, applying methods it had already employed elsewhere. When the war drew near our frontiers and even crossed them, the Germans repeatedly promised assistance, yet again they failed to honour their promise.

During the course of their retreat they looted and destroyed on this country's sovereign territory. These actions, contrary to an ally's loyalty, were compounded by acts of open provocation. Corps Commander Field Marshal Lieutenant Szilárd Bakay, commander of the Budapest Army Corps, was treacherously attacked and abducted by Gestapo agents in the middle of Budapest on a foggy October morning as he was getting out of his car in front of his house.

At the same time German planes dropped leaflets over towns inciting the population to take action against the government. I received reliable information that troops of pro-German tendency intended to raise their own men to power by using force to effect a political upheaval and the overthrow of the legal Hungarian government, which I had appointed. The aim of these people was to turn the country into the scene of rearguard action in the defence of German interests.

I have decided to protect Hungary's honour in relation to our former ally, although this ally, instead of providing the military help it promised, ultimately deprived the Hungarian nation of its greatest treasure: its freedom and independence: I have informed the representative of the German Reich that *we are asking our enemies for a ceasefire and will cease hostilities against them.* [my italics]

I trust in the love of justice, and hope together with you to preserve our continued existence as a nation in the future, and to be able to implement our peaceful intentions.

I have given appropriate instructions to the commanders of the Hungarian army. Bound by their oath, the troops are still obliged to obey their commanding officers, whom I appointed. I ask every honourable Hungarian to follow me on this path, beset by sacrifices, which will lead to Hungary's salvation.

Originally, the sentence I have emphasized above was followed by: 'From today Hungary regards itself as being at war with Germany.' Prime Minister Lakatos also quotes this sentence in his memoirs *Ahogy Én Láttam* (As I saw it)[44] and writes that he told Ambrózy that he thought this was completely erroneous and impossible to implement.

In his memoirs, Foreign Minister Hennyey quotes from a letter Lakatos wrote to him from Australia on 14 April 1966: 'When Ambrózy came to me at the prime minister's residence at noon on 14 October to show me the text of the proclamation, I deleted the sentence "From today Hungary regards itself as being at war with Germany." My opinion was that only the stronger party could use such a tone ...'[45]

It was preposterous and completely unacceptable for Lakatos to delete this from the text of the proclamation the Regent had approved, without his agreement. The whole point of the proclamation was that the population, the armed forces, and the outside world, should know that from that moment we were at war with Germany. But this was not the only alteration he made to the text: the phrase 'we are asking for a ceasefire' must without doubt originally have been 'we have asked' or 'we have concluded'. It is hard to imagine that Lakatos could have made these alterations with my father-in-law's approval, when I clearly heard the Regent telling Veesenmayer that he had asked for a ceasefire ('Ich habe um Waffenstillstand gebeten'), and that nothing would change his decision. *This* was fully in the spirit of the ceasefire agreement.

Thus the prime minister, instead of countersigning the proclamation, deleted the most important part of it. Knowing these facts I believe his action to have been inexcusable, despite one mitigating circumstance: he did not know that the preliminary ceasefire agreement had been signed three days earlier. But the fact that he was capable of doing this without asking the Regent's permission proves that the Regent had good reasons for not telling him about the signing of the ceasefire agreement, and also that Lakatos' outlook was different from the Regent's.

After the third reading of the proclamation, there came two readings of the orders for the armed forces:

General Order

Soldiers! In this destructive war raging in the heart of our beloved country, taking account of the strength of the combatants, I can no longer expect a decisive turn of events in Hungary's favour. For this reason I have decided to ask for a ceasefire. As commander-in-chief of the armed forces I call on you to remain true to the oath you swore and to obey with loyalty and unquestioning obedience the orders I give you through your commanding officers. Our continued existence depends on every single soldier showing responsibility and the utmost discipline in this critical situation. Horthy.

At the time I did not know that the text had been altered, because I had not read it before it was broadcast, and I did not notice that vital omission. It is hard after all these years to describe my exact feelings, but I know that when I finally heard the proclamation on the radio I felt relieved, as if a great heaviness had been lifted from me. It was good to know that at last something had been done to tell the country and the outside world the truth. It was good to hear the Nazis' despicable acts listed openly. On the way to my parents-in-law's apartment, I met Károly Lázár on the stairs and said, 'Kari, I'm so relieved we've managed to make the true situation known. Pista would have been so pleased to hear the proclamation!' I can still see how Kari's face brightened up as he replied, 'Thank you, it's good to hear such a positive opinion; it's a great help to me.'

I know it did not have this effect on everyone: perhaps they somehow could not grasp its significance. We were certainly in great danger, but somehow I felt better that at least the truth had been told, come what may.

Unfortunately, many things came which should not have come. Who would have thought that the prime minister himself would delete the most important sentence – in fact the key sentence – of the proclamation; or that the office of the chief of general staff would suppress the coded order to the commanders of the First and Second Armies to go over to the Russian side? Even if everything had failed in Budapest, the ceasefire could still have succeeded if the First and Second Armies had gone over to the Russians. The commanders should have known what they had to do without a coded message. And who would have thought that, through betrayal, the Germans would have military control of the city even before the proclamation was broadcast.

Before that morning's Council of State meeting – and before the Regent's proclamation – the Germans had been busy making preparations. We only discovered the details much later. Lieutenant General Aggteleky, who had taken over command of the Budapest Army Corps after Bakay's abduction, sent me a detailed account of his experiences that day, and this is important for a full understanding of the situation. Aggteleky wrote:

> On 15 October it wasn't just the Regent who wanted to take the struggle with the Germans to breaking point: it's very likely that the Germans wanted to do so too. On the fifteenth at about eight o'clock in the morning ... a very agitated voice told me on the phone from the Regent's residence that the Germans had captured the Regent's son after a gun battle, and had taken him away wrapped in a blanket. As I couldn't make contact either with the Regent's residence or with the chief of general staff or with the defence minister, once I was convinced of the truth of the report, on my own responsibility I ordered the Budapest garrison to be placed on full battle alert.
>
> I was sure that I was faced with a German coup against the Horthy regime, and this soon proved to be the case. Soon an armed German detachment occupied the further peak of Sas-hegy, threatening the Army Corps' Headquarters. I took counter-measures to defend the Headquarters. Around ten o'clock I received a report that a large German detachment had occupied Gellért Hill – barely 1 kilometre away from the Royal Palace, where I knew that a Council of State meeting was due to start at 10.30 a.m. As I couldn't make telephone contact, taking full responsibility I ordered the mobile squads that had arrived to reoccupy Gellért Hill by force of arms. My order was never carried out. An informer told the Germans, and they incited Iván Hindy – a general posted to the Army Corps Headquarters – to break into my office with two

companions armed with machine guns and arrest me. When German troops occupied the northern peak of Sas-hegy, I ordered a special company of soldiers based at the Headquarters to occupy a defensive position on the southern peak. In order to be sure, I placed my orderly officer Lieutenant General Somos in command of this company ... Thus the orderly's office was empty, and I was working completely alone in my office that morning. My belt, with a loaded pistol, was hanging on the coat-rack next to the door. I usually put it on when the orderly officer reported that someone had arrived to see me.

It was in these circumstances that Hindy burst in with two armed soldiers, one of whom aimed a machine gun at me while the other held a bayoneted gun to my chest. Meanwhile another soldier armed with a bayoneted gun appeared through the side door. Hindy called on me to hand over the Headquarters. I refused and reached for the phone ... but one of the soldiers pulled the lead out of the wall socket. Then the raiders took my belt and pistol from the coat-rack and left, locking me in.

Hindy kept all this secret from the outside, and not only countermanded my order to attack but also gave orders in my name countermanding all my anti-German measures. He cancelled the state of alert I had ordered, withdrew all the guards, including those guarding the radio studios, and confined the troops to barracks. The troops thought all these orders were indeed mine and carried them out faithfully, suspecting nothing.

Thus the Germans seized military control of Budapest without a shot being fired on 15 October, before the Council of State meeting had even begun. The government and the Hungarian military leadership had no idea that this had happened, even hours after the proclamation had been broadcast.

Hindy's act of betrayal was fatal and seems almost incredible. The Council of State meeting went ahead, Veesenmayer was received at the Palace and the Regent's proclamation was broadcast, without either the government or the military leadership suspecting that they had lost control of their troops in the garrison and that, apart from the guards on Castle Hill, Budapest was completely defenceless against the German Forces. The government and the duped garrison troops only realized this gradually, several hours later. ... Hindy was sentenced to death in 1946 and executed.[46]

Aggteleky then goes on to explain in detail why, despite this, in his view the ceasefire would not have failed if the contact with the Russians and the change of sides by the First and Second Armies had been implemented successfully.[viii]

Meanwhile, in the Palace, Hitler's emissary Ambassador Rahn came to see the Regent and tried in vain to make him change his decision. However, the Regent asked him to try to have German troops withdrawn to the Austrian border. Rahn said he would ask the Führer and report back to the Regent (he was playacting). Miklóspapa asked Lakatos to receive Rahn when he came back, as he had nothing more to say to him.

Magdamama and I were still listening to the radio broadcasts when suddenly they were interrupted and military marches were played instead. Then came Szálasi's first speech!

Miklóspapa told me later what had happened at the Council of State meeting. It had been extremely disappointing. Despite the fact that the Council of Ministers meeting held the previous day – without the two 'informant' ministers – had decided on the proceedings for this Council of State, on both occasions those who attended expressed anxiety instead of making positive comments.

But all this is well known and there is an official record of the Council of State meeting, so I will only give the main points here: After the Regent told the meeting that his son and Lieutenant General Bakay had been captured, and had listed the Germans' broken promises, etc., he announced that he was making a ceasefire agreement. János Vörös, the chief of general staff, gave a detailed report on the military situation and read out the German ultimatum, received at ten o'clock that day, which stated: 'the whole territory of Hungary is a German military operations area. Only the German high command is authorized to give orders. The order for the withdrawal of the First and Second Hungarian Armies must be withdrawn immediately, and the previous situation must be restored within twelve hours.'

[viii] Appendix 7: Observations of Lieutenant General Béla Aggteleky on failure to implement ceasefire.

According to Vattay, 'the tone of the ultimatum was insulting and degrading'. Such a tone, he suggested, 'could only be used with subjugated peoples'.[47]

Then those present gave their comments; and instead of giving their full support to the Regent's decision they expressed their doubts. Prime Minister Lakatos referred to the promise he had given to Parliament that he would not ask for a ceasefire without consulting them, and asked that this be done. The Regent stated that he was not prepared to do this, because legally he had the right to ask for a ceasefire and because in its current form Parliament did not represent the people's will. A long argument followed, mainly between the justice minister and Ambrózy. The Regent put an end to it by saying that he alone carried responsibility for the ceasefire and that he was not prepared to change his decision. At this, Lakatos announced that the government would resign. The Regent asked Lakatos to form a new government and said that any of the ministers who did not agree could leave.

This had been prearranged, because they hoped that at this point the two ministers who were German informants, not wishing to be part of the new government, would leave. Then they would be able to give the newly formed government full information about the ceasefire negotiations. But this manoeuvre was futile because Reményi-Schneller and Jurcsek – probably on German instructions – did not leave, much to everyone's surprise.

The Council of State meeting was interrupted by Veesenmayer's arrival for his meeting with the Regent, and continued after he left, when the new government swore loyalty to the Hungarian constitution and to the Regent. The new government included Jurcsek and Reményi-Schneller, who, it subsequently became clear, had already been nominated for posts in the planned Szálasi government, and actually joined Szálasi as soon as he took over the next day.

According to State Secretary István Bárczy, who took the minutes of the meeting, the Regent closed the meeting with the following words: 'We are facing difficult times and a great deal of suffering, but this step had to be taken. The Germans have flouted our sovereignty and behaved like scoundrels. A German politician once said that it was lucky for Germany that there are only fifteen million Hungarians in the world. We were always in the way of their eastward expansion, and we still are. For my part I have burnt all my bridges, and I regret the bitter hours and all the suffering I have caused members of the government with this decision.' Then he shook hands with everyone and left.

That was when the Regent's coded order 'Order of 1 March 1920 to be carried out' should have gone out to the commanders of the First and Second Armies; meaning that they were to make contact with the

Russians. But this order was suppressed at the transmission station at the General Staff Headquarters: Colonel Lajos Nádas gave instructions that it was forbidden to transmit any orders coming from the Royal Palace.

It's interesting to read the account written by Vattay's deputy, Colonel Imre Pogány, who had been given the job of sending out the orders to the armed forces:

> When the Council of State meeting ended, János Vörös came out and wanted to give me a sealed envelope to be passed on to his aide-de-camp Major Kapitánffy. Vattay was just giving me the orders for the armed forces, and when he saw that I was busy János Vörös gave the envelope to Lakatos' secretary, Lieutenant General Szentpáli. As I discovered later, this was the 'preliminary step' for the army commanders, the coded message 'Order of 1 March 1920 to be carried out' which was the signal for them to implement our exit from the war. Major Kapitánffy received the envelope but did not have the message transmitted on the telex: instead he and Colonel Lajos Nádas between them destroyed it.[48]

When Vörös returned to his office, he found himself face to face with his pro-German colleagues. Several people have written about what happened then – the fact is that a notice was broadcast on the radio ostensibly from Vörös as the chief of general staff, which in essence stated that nobody should interpret the Regent's proclamation as meaning they should lay down their arms. What the Regent had referred to were just negotiations about a ceasefire, which might or might not be implemented. So all Hungarian soldiers and units were obliged to carry on fighting as they had done up to now, with all their might, from whatever side they might be attacked. We listened outraged to this broadcast.

During the afternoon we had sent a telegram to Moscow:

> The Regent's son was captured this morning by Germans and Arrow Cross men. Shots were fired at the building in which he was present, we have no further news. The city is surrounded by strong German forces. We have received an ultimatum from the Germans.

Now we sent another telegram:

> The German ultimatum expires tonight (15th) at 22.00 hours, then we can expect a German attack. We

ask for urgent assistance and a rapid advance to
Budapest. The Radio is in German hands.

Tost was on duty, Nicky was no longer with us, so I encoded the last
telegrams alone.

> Our contacts have been cut off, it is doubtful that
> the emissary will arrive tomorrow. Please make contact
> through the front with the commanders of the First and
> Second Armies if we should lose contact with them.
> Tell them that negotiations must be carried on with
> Lajos Veress – the prime minister appointed him for
> this eventuality, and he is authorized to take further
> steps. The radio was taken over before the broadcast
> from the chief of general staff.

Soon after that, János Vörös turned up at the Palace and claimed that
the notice had been broadcast without his knowledge. I thought I
should inform the Moscow delegation about this, whether it was true
or not, in case they thought that the broadcast had come from us. For
this reason I composed a short telegram and took it in to Miklóspapa
for him to approve:

> The notice from the chief of general staff was
> falsified and broadcast on the radio, which was by then
> in German hands.

I encoded it and passed it on to the radio operators. This was our final
telegram. I passed these on between ten and eleven o'clock that night,
so it remains a mystery why, as stated in the official notes, the last
telegrams were sent from the Palace only at five the next morning.

János Vörös should be grateful to me for this last telegram, because
it probably contributed to his being appointed defence minister in the
first Communist government. I found it extremely interesting, sixteen
years later, to read the despicable account in his 'war diary' which
proves that he lied to the Regent when he said that the notice had been
broadcast without his knowledge; he wrote: 'I learned about His
Highness' proclamation telling the people about the ceasefire, a few
minutes after 13.00 hours. In order for us to be able to maintain the
striking power of the Hungarian army, I had to issue an order at 14.30
in which I explained the proclamation broadcast on the radio, because
its text was not quite clear and might lead the troops to the conclusion
that they were to lay down their arms, which was to be avoided at all
costs ...'[49]

His double-dealing is astounding: the Nazis trusted him and

recommended him for his post, then the Russians trusted him and gave him a post in the government ... .

By then the success of the change of sides – or at least part of it – depended on whether the First and Second Armies would succeed in making contact with the Russians. We know from Vattay's deputy at the Military Office, Colonel Imre Pogány, that during that afternoon and evening he had been in contact with Béla Miklós and Lajos Dálnoki Veress, the commanding officers of the two armies:

> Early in the afternoon of 15 October 1944 the phone rang in Vattay's office. Vattay was with the Regent, so I answered it. It was Béla Miklós, who asked me: 'Pogány, what's going on in Budapest? The radio is broadcasting instructions in János Vörös' name which completely contradict the Regent's proclamation.' I reported that the radio was in German hands and that the operational staff who were supporting them were transmitting misleading orders and news reports. Then Vattay returned and took over the conversation.
>
> Around 8 p.m. Csontos, a senior civil servant at the news centre of the General Staff Headquarters at 7 Szinház Street, telephoned to say that General Lajos Veress, the commander of the Second Army, requested Vattay or one of his officers who knew the situation to go to the telex so that they could communicate in confidence. As Vattay had to stay with the Regent he asked me to go, but I had to be very careful as it was already in Arrow Cross hands. Two guards with Arrow Cross armbands, armed with machine guns, stood outside ... when they saw that I was an officer of the general staff, they let me in.
>
> I ran up to the news centre, and as soon as I entered, Csontos locked the door. Then I was able to spend at least twenty minutes on the telex with the commander of the Second Army. I gave him detailed information on the situation, telling him about the Regent, the abduction of Nicholas Horthy junior, the misleading news given out by the Germans, and the operational staff going over to support the Germans. I emphasized that the Regent's decision hadn't changed, and that every word of his proclamation was still valid ... I reported that we reckoned on a German attack that night. In the meantime Csontos stuck the tapes onto

telegram forms. I hid these, then crept out. Luckily the corridor was deserted and I managed to leave the building unnoticed ... the two guards saluted, and I got back safely to the Palace, where Vattay and Lázár were waiting anxiously. ...

Vattay was most pleased to see me back safely, and was even more pleased when I dug out the text of my telex conversation. He ran straight down to the Regent and read it out to him. When he returned, he said that the Regent was in full agreement with the text. On 16 October, when the German SS occupied the Palace and collected all the keys to the office safes, I flushed the text of the conversation down the toilet so it wouldn't fall into their hands.[50]

We subsequently discovered that the attempt to have the two armies join the Russians had also ended in failure. This is how commander of the Second Army, General Dálnoki Veress, looked back on those events:

On 16 October at five o'clock I set off to check that my order to withdraw was being carried out ... a mixed detachment of cars and tanks blocked my way. The commander of the detachment opened the door of my car and told me that on the orders of General Wöhler he was arresting me for breach of orders. 'Look around,' he said, pointing at the weapons trained on me, ready to fire. 'There's no point resisting, follow me to the German Army Headquarters.' He took me to Nyíregyháza and handed me over to General Reinhardt, who told me to withdraw the order I had given. This I summarily refused to do.[51]

The reason for his arrest was his refusal to make a statement of allegiance to the Germans. This was why he was imprisoned by the Gestapo. Altogether he spent twelve years in captivity, died in exile, and was rehabilitated only posthumously.

The commander of the First Army, Béla Miklós, with his chief of general staff Colonel Kálmán Kéri, went over to the Russians but without his troops:

Kálmán Kéri's thinking was this: if he was no longer prepared to take orders from the Germans, and his superiors in Budapest couldn't be contacted, then – if the ceasefire was to take place as the Regent's proclamation stated – he had to go over to the Russians to discuss with them what the First Army should now do ... 'That was when I decided to go over. Mentally I was ready, I didn't care what happened to me there,' he said later.

After midnight Kéri told Béla Miklós, who had just arrived back from Beregszász, what he had decided ... Early the next morning a polite but firm request arrived from the German General Heinrich: Miklós and Kéri should go and see him as soon as possible to discuss the political situation ... Colonel Röder of the general staff would accompany the gentlemen. Neither Miklós nor Kéri had the least intention of complying with this request. That was when a phone call came from the Hungarian chief of general staff: János Vörös wanted to speak to Béla Miklós. Kéri heard the conversation and this is his account of it: Béla Miklós asked, 'What is the army to do?' János Vörös replied that the army was to cover the right wing of the neighbouring German army so the Russians couldn't outflank them ...

'What?!' Béla Miklós yelled. János Vörös briefly repeated the instructions, then added: 'Please, this is what it has to do. Anyway, German gentlemen are sitting in the corridor ...' At that, Béla Miklós hurled the receiver down onto the table. I don't think anyone could use that again ...

In the light of what happened subsequently, we can even consider it a success that Miklós and Kéri, with their escorts, were able to go over to the Russian side in the early afternoon of 16 October unharmed, and were at a Soviet Divisional Headquarters by evening ... Around 3 p.m. on 16 October a Hungarian colonel of the general staff, accompanied by a suitable number of armed soldiers, was looking for Béla Miklós on the front line in order to arrest him. He was too late: by then the commander of the First Army was in the military operations area of the Fourth Ukrainian Front.[52]

Meanwhile in Budapest, on the other hand, Lakatos and Hennyey tried repeatedly to restore contacts with the Germans and to comply with their requests. The most amazing example was the way in which they reacted to the German demand that the mines securing Palace Hill should be removed. First of all I cannot understand why they had to go to the German Embassy and talk to Ambassador Rahn. After all, an ambassador or his representative should go to the prime minister, not vice versa. As I have already mentioned, the Regent did not want to see Rahn again because he could not see any point in doing so, and had asked Lakatos or Hennyey to talk to him instead. I think it is perfectly clear that this should just have been to reinforce the Regent's view that the situation could not be changed; the die had been cast. But Hennyey writes in his memoirs: 'First of all we decided to discuss the situation with the German ambassador and special emissary Rahn.' [p. 130] The Regent had not asked them to 'discuss the situation' with the Germans, nor had he instructed either of them to instigate further negotiations. After all, they had heard from the Regent's own mouth that he had burnt his bridges – and Lakatos himself had told the September meeting of the Council of Ministers that the Regent's decision was irrevocable.

In his memoirs Lakatos gives a more understandable, though naive, reason for starting negotiations: 'My idea was to bring about an agreement which would make it possible on the one hand for the two countries to separate amicably and on the other hand to avoid internal conflict ... I rang the Regent to ask for his agreement, which I received.' [p. 171] (Miklóspapa had no memory of this at all!) And then Lakatos notified the German Embassy that he and Hennyey would go there. The two men's accounts of their negotiations with Veesenmayer and Rahn do not agree, but the essence is that because in the meantime the Germans had found out that the roads leading up to Castle Hill were mined, Veesenmayer announced that in those circumstances they were not prepared to negotiate.

What if Lakatos had taken advantage of Lázár's excellent measures to secure Castle Hill and announced that we would not remove the mines until the Germans withdrew their forces from Budapest? The entire German Embassy and all the leading Arrow Cross people were there – what a load of hostages! But this never occurred to him: 'I rang Lieutenant General Vattay and asked him to arrange for ways to be opened through the mine blockades immediately.' [p. 171] And neither Lakatos nor Vattay asked the Regent for his opinion on this extremely important decision: they let Rahn out with a special escort, and so made it possible for Szálasi to be smuggled out from Castle Hill.

I no longer dared let the black codebook out of my sight, and took it with me everywhere until finally I was able to give it to Tost for him to destroy. He did so early on 16 October; and after the last telegram had been sent he thanked the telegraph operators for sticking to their post through difficult circumstances.

We were prepared for a siege; we could even hear shooting here and there. The whole family moved down to two rooms in the basement.

These rooms were connected. My parents-in-law occupied the inner room, which could be entered only through our room, where Nanny Ila, István and I were settled down for a short and restless night. Thus my parents-in-law could only leave their room through ours. We all lay down fully clothed, and I was pleased to see that István fell asleep straight away. Suddenly there was a knock at the door. I went to open it: it was ADC Tost, asking me to call Miklóspapa because Vattay and Ambrózy requested an audience as they had something important to tell him. I called Miklóspapa; he went out, and returned after a few minutes, closing the door firmly behind him as though annoyed.

Presently there was another knock at the door: it was Gyuszi Tost again; this time he asked me to go and talk to Ambrózy and Vattay as a matter of urgency. I found them in an outer room, and the four of us sat down around a small table. It was after midnight; a small lamp in the opposite corner lit the room dimly. It was a bit like conspirators gathering for a secret meeting.

Vattay said they had tried to persuade the Regent to accept an offer of asylum from the Germans, for himself and his family, if he resigned and handed over power. The government could see no other way in which we, the family, could escape from this situation alive. But the Regent had categorically rejected this and had left saying, 'Don't bother me with this again!' Now they turned to me for help and asked me to persuade the Regent to accept this plan, because otherwise the whole family's lives would be at risk during the imminent German attack. (I found out later that this offer had not come from the Germans, but was Vattay's own idea.)

I remember every word of this conversation clearly because the scene was dramatic and charged with responsibility. I looked at Tost incredulously – he had been such a good friend of Pista's and hated the Nazis – and said, 'Tost, are you also trying to persuade me to do this?'

He replied with an expression of despair: 'Please remember that your lives are at stake, your son's life!'

'I'm sorry,' I said, 'but I agree with my father-in-law. And you can't count on me because nothing will make me persuade him otherwise.'

I went back to my room, knowing I could have done nothing else. I could not imagine the ceasefire ending with us travelling peacefully to Germany – where I was convinced nothing good was awaiting us – while in Hungary everyone would be fighting on to the bitter end.

Three years later we discovered, from a letter written by Lakatos in 1947, that Vattay returned alone to the prime minister's residence after the conversation with me. The ministers were still assembled there, and Vattay told Lakatos, not that the Regent had refused to accept the offer but exactly the opposite.

Lakatos said Vattay had told him that 'His Highness had completely accepted the solution proposed on one condition, that he could take his closest colleagues with him in order not to leave them exposed to the vengeance of the Arrow Cross people.' These colleagues were Ambrózy, Lázár and, of course, Vattay. Lakatos added: 'At the time I never suspected or even presumed that the adjutant general's account was so terribly at variance with the truth that I later discovered from the witness statements of Ambrózy and Lázár, which was that Your Highness did not want to hear of it.' [ix]

If this is true, we will never know what could have led Vattay to take this step. We must acknowledge the fact that it is very difficult for people who were not there to imagine the atmosphere at that time: the state of siege, the country's hopeless situation between the threats of the Germans and the Russians, and people's anxiety for their families. So it could even be possible that Vattay became worried and confused, and wanted so much to carry his idea through that by the time he got to the prime minister's residence he felt he had no other choice. I found it very interesting to read his memoirs, where even the order of events is confused, and not a word is said about his request to me to persuade the Regent to place himself and his family under the protection of the German Reich. Whom can we believe? Lakatos or Vattay?

If there had been another exit from the Regent's room then I would not be able to prove whether or not my father-in-law had changed his mind during the course of the night, and there would always remain the possibility that he could have spoken to Vattay again. But the incontrovertible fact is that, during the time between my leaving Vattay, Ambrózy and Tost, right up until we went to wait for the car to take us to the Papal Nuncio's residence, Miklóspapa did not once leave his room, and nobody came there to talk to him. Indeed nobody could have talked to him without my knowing about it.

Nuncio Monsignor Rotta had earlier made an offer to the Regent that, if the need arose, he would offer the family refuge. So at four o'clock in the morning we all went over to the main entrance and sat on the large, wide staircase leading to the statue of Justice, to wait for the car which would take Magdamama, Nanny Ila, István and myself to the Papal residence. Miklóspapa spoke with Károly Lázár, the commander of the Guards who was there with us, saying if the Germans did attack, to resist them with all our strength on Castle Hill.

According to the official shorthand record of Ferenc Szálasi's trial in the People's Court in 1945, Károly Lázár's witness statement included the following:

[ix] Appendix 8: Letter of General Géza Lakatos.

Lázár: '... the Germans had been carrying out reconnaissance throughout the previous night. ... At four in the morning I received a reliable report that they were grouping for an attack and it looked as if they were going to attack. I immediately reported this to the Regent ...'

Foreman of the jury: '... didn't he say anything about Lieutenant General Vattay having seen him during the night, possibly with Ambrózy, the head of the Cabinet Office?'

Lázár: 'Not a word.'

Foreman of the jury: 'And did the possibility of the Regent placing himself under German protection come up then?'

Lázár: 'Not at all, in fact he said, "Whatever happens, we will resist here." He said this at five or six minutes past five o'clock in the morning.'

Sitting on the stairs, Miklóspapa was not excited or nervous, we talked together quite calmly. Then I noticed that Gyuszi Tost was sitting directly behind me on the steps. I can still see his despairing expression and the beads of perspiration on his face, which seemed to indicate: 'It's all over ...' I wanted to do something to ease his despair and tried to say a few encouraging words. I asked him to trust in the future, something would turn up – but I could see that he did not even hear what I was saying. Then I was distracted by Magdamama's announcement that she was not going to the Nuncio's residence because she wanted to stay with Miklóspapa. In the meantime the car turned up, and Miklóspapa and I managed to persuade her to go after all.

It was just starting to get light as we drove out of the Palace courtyard through the Lion Gate, Nanny Ila sitting in front and Magdamama and I in the back with István between us. I leaned over my son so that if anyone shot at us then he would not be hit. As we crossed Szent György Square I saw a small armoured car, and wondered how long we would be able to hold out with this against the big German tiger tanks. It's a very short distance from the Palace courtyard to the Nuncio's residence on Dísz Square, but it seemed endless then ... I never suspected that I would not see the Palace – the way I had known it – again.

We went into the Nuncio's residence, where we were received by nuns who told us that the Nuncio was away on a trip to the country. Monsignor Verolino, the Nuncio's deputy, soon arrived and welcomed us very kindly. He arranged for us to be taken into a large room where there were two beds and a divan. The nuns said they would bring a third bed from the convent next door straight away.

From this room on the first floor, Magdamama and I looked out from behind the curtain at the window onto Dísz Square. Opposite was number 12, my father's house, where I was born. It was dawn, and a column of tanks rumbled past. We could hear gunfire. No more than half an hour later German soldiers beat on the gate of the Nuncio's residence. The nuns quickly took us down to their cellar shelter and said we should stay quietly there. Through a small crack we could see that as one nun opened the gate the others walked up and down the yard praying. (Many years later I saw the film *The Sound of Music* in which a very similar scene occurs in Austria.) What a pity the Nuncio was not there, I thought, he could have prevented them entering, because the Nuncio's residence was 'foreign territory' in the same way as an embassy was. Of course it may be that that would not have helped either.

After looking over the whole house they came down to the cellar and demanded that the nuns open the door. Three German soldiers came in, had a good look at us and then left, leaving two armed guards at the entrance of the building.

Presently Veesenmayer and Lakatos came to the Nuncio's residence and found us, still in the cellar. Magdamama and I received them very coldly. As if by prior arrangement neither of us shook hands with Veesenmayer, we did not even look at him, and Lakatos had to translate every question and answer into German because we spoke only in Hungarian. Veesenmayer, who looked very tired and kept mopping the perspiration from his brow, told us very briefly that Miklóspapa was well, and in the Hatvany Palace – which was the Gestapo headquarters – and that we could visit him that afternoon. He also told us that the next day, the seventeenth, we would all travel to Germany by train, so we would be allowed to go to the Palace with a German escort to pack. At the time we found Lakatos' role as intermediary incomprehensible and infuriating, because we did not know the background to it – that he believed the Regent had accepted going to Germany.

When they left we went up to our room, and Magdamama and I discussed what would happen if we simply announced our refusal to leave the Nuncio's residence. It was true that Veesenmayer had not asked us; he had simply stated that we were all travelling the next day. We discussed every possibility, and Magdamama decided that she wanted to go with Miklóspapa, no matter what. What would happen to us, István, Ila and me, if we stayed? After much debate we realized that we had little choice, and decided that the family definitely had to stay together because we could not bear it if we did not hear news of each other. Then I had a long discussion with Nanny Ila, and I told her that she should just leave the Nuncio's residence after we were taken away, because nobody would look for her. But our Ila stood her ground; she said that whatever happened she definitely wanted to stay with us.

We went to the window again and looked down onto Dísz Square, where Arrow Cross officers were gathering by the memorial to the defenders of the homeland. They all wore Arrow Cross armbands and were smiling proudly. Was this possible? Had they no idea what was coming? I could see Kelemen, the porter at our house on the Square, who had gone upstairs from his flat on the ground floor to watch the events from an open window. He was not smiling, just staring fixedly down at the square. Of course he had no idea that we were behind the curtains of the house opposite, also watching what was going on.

At midday Archbishop Angelo Rotta, the Papal Nuncio, arrived. I had often been in contact with him. He was very sorry he had not been at home that morning, and regretted that the Germans had so quickly discovered that we were staying there.

If we were being taken away to Germany the next day, we had to sort out what we could take with us. The Nuncio strongly advised Magdamama and myself not to go over to the Palace to pack, because he had heard that everything had been ransacked and the Palace was full of SS men. He suggested that Monsignor Verolino should go with Nanny Ila, who, together with the staff at the Palace, could pack the essential items. I would have liked to go myself, but in the end we accepted the Nuncio's proposal, and they set off with a German military escort for the Palace.

When they returned with a couple of suitcases they told us some dreadful things. Poor Ila had been able to collect only a few things, because everywhere was occupied by SS men under the command of a man we only found out much later to be the notorious commander, Skorzeny. They filled every room and were even lying on my father-in-law's bed. She said that two German soldiers were lying in my bed. She opened a few drawers, and on finding them empty, remarked that there was nothing there. She was taken straight to the commanding officer, who was sitting at my father-in-law's desk, wearing my father-in-law's leather jacket. He shouted at her, 'German soldiers don't steal!' Ila was very brave and replied calmly that she had not accused anyone of stealing, she had simply stated that the things which had been there were not there any more. After that she was not allowed to pack anything else and was brought back to the Nuncio's residence with Monsignor Verolino, who had accompanied her faithfully throughout.

I know that some people thought that my father-in-law had changed his mind and accepted German protective custody, because they had heard eye-witnesses saying that when Veesenmayer and Lakatos drove into the Palace courtyard early that morning, immediately before the expected attack, my father-in-law was in the entrance hall with his coat on, and he shook hands with Veesenmayer and got into the car without any resistance. From this they concluded that somebody had told him to expect Veesenmayer. Of course they did not know that the Regent had been sitting there since four o'clock that morning, but not because he was expecting Veesenmayer.

As we heard from Miklóspapa when we saw him that night at Gestapo Headquarters, just before six o'clock he had changed his mind about defending the Palace, because he had been told that there were now several hundred German tanks in Budapest; he had therefore decided that it would not be right to sacrifice the guardsmen who were ready to take up the fight and defend the Palace to the last man. The defence of Budapest had been thwarted by the capture of the Army Corps commander Lieutenant General Szilárd Bakay by the Germans and the arrest of his successor by Arrow Cross men. So the ceasefire order was given out. But it did not reach the guardsmen led by András Kállay at the bottom of the Palace gardens. Six German soldiers fell there, and András was captured and taken to Mauthausen concentration camp.

A few minutes before six o'clock, Veesenmayer drove into the Palace courtyard. Miklóspapa had no idea that he was coming, but when he came up to the main entrance with Lakatos, he offered my father-in-law his hand and asked him to go with them in order to be spared the unpleasant sight of the Palace occupation. Miklóspapa said, 'I interpreted this as my arrest wrapped in polite formality.'

I am convinced that Vattay changed the Regent's refusal into acceptance in order to save us. Despite the fact that his action was comprehensible, it does not justify it. However, when I look back at what happened and think about our chances, I realize that by doing this he may have contributed to our survival. For if we had stayed, even if we had survived a siege of the Palace we would have fallen into German hands in a different way. And I certainly do not know what would have happened to us under Arrow Cross and Communist rule.

When we discovered all this later, another thing my father-in-law told us that day became clear. When he and Veesenmayer arrived at the Hatvany Palace, Veesenmayer said to him, 'Your Highness, here you are under the Führer's protection.' To which my father-in-law replied, 'Who does Hitler want to protect me from? I never asked him to protect me.' My father-in-law said that at this Veesenmayer looked at him with some surprise, as if not understanding what he had said. It is quite clear now that Veesenmayer thought the offer of protective custody had been accepted, because that was what Lakatos had told him the previous night.

By eight o'clock in the morning Skorzeny's SS troops had occupied the prime minister's residence and arrested all the ministers who were there – but Prime Minister Lakatos had been held at the German Embassy since the early hours.

Between nine and ten o'clock that night Magdamama and I were taken with a German escort to see Miklóspapa at the Hatvany palace – to this day I do not know what the point of this was, if not for them to monitor our conversation. Lakatos and Vattay were there with Miklóspapa, occupying two rooms. The house was full of guards; they even lined the corridors. There was a guard in Miklóspapa's room too. We spent half an hour there, and Miklóspapa told us what happened to him after our departure early that morning.

I have rarely heard so many dreadful things in the space of half an hour. To our absolute shock we were told that Gyuszi Tost had committed suicide. A few hours earlier, when they had left Miklóspapa to rest and gone into the other room, he went into one of the window recesses and shot himself in the head with his pistol. It was shattering news.

We also heard that Szálasi had been there twice. The first time Miklóspapa had been told that the prime minister requested an audience with the Regent – while Prime Minister Lakatos was sitting next to him. When Miklóspapa went into the next room, he found Szálasi, who gave him a Nazi salute and asked to be appointed prime minister. Miklóspapa suggested that he ask the Germans to appoint him, adding that he could see they had already done so. He said that he was a prisoner and so unable to perform any official function, and anyway Szálasi would be the last person he would appoint. Despite this, Szálasi came back later with the same request, and received an even more curt rejection.

During the afternoon, Feine, the embassy counsellor, accompanied Miklóspapa to the Palace so that he could pack for the journey. What my father-in-law told us about that is in his memoirs:

> I was prepared to see the signs of a thorough search, but what I saw surpassed anything I could have imagined. Skorzeny's men were lounging about on the silk damask furniture. Every cupboard and drawer had been forced open. Everything that was movable and looked valuable had been taken, from my wife's jewellery to the money the staff had saved. There was even a moment of comedy in this repulsive scene: as I went into my bathroom to collect my toiletries I met a

soldier coming out, dressed in my bathrobe ...

I was still in the bathroom – three guards armed with machine guns had accompanied me there – when Prime Minister Lakatos suddenly turned up with Veesenmayer. Lakatos handed me a piece of paper containing a statement in German to the effect that I was resigning and that I appointed Szálasi prime minister.

I scanned the typed sheet, and under the German text it said, 'Signed Horthy.' I handed it back and asked, 'What is this supposed to mean? Am I to sign this?' Lakatos gave an affirmative reply, at which I reminded him with some surprise that Szálasi had already asked me to appoint him twice that day and that Lakatos had witnessed my rejection of his request each time.

I regarded the matter as closed, and carried on packing. But Lakatos stayed, hesitant. I noticed him hesitating, as if he didn't understand my behaviour, so I asked why he wanted my signature when as prime minister he should be advising me to refuse it. Then he hinted that the life of my son Nicholas was at stake. I asked for Veesenmayer, who was standing outside the bathroom, to be called in, and he immediately confirmed that my son's life and freedom did indeed depend on my signature. I had to assume that, whether or not I signed the paper, they would publish a statement that I had resigned and appointed Szálasi. This intention was given away and confirmed by the words 'Signed Horthy', which were already typed in under the text. I could see that I wouldn't achieve anything by refusing to sign; on the other hand, if I did sign, I could perhaps save the life of my son Nicholas, my only remaining child. So I said to Veesenmayer, 'I can see that you are trying to give this coup the appearance of legality. Can you give me your word of honour that my son will be freed and will be able to join us if I sign this paper?' 'Yes Your Highness, I give you my word.' So I told him that I was neither resigning nor appointing Szálasi prime minister: the only reason I was signing was to save my son's life. A signature forced out of me through blackmail and at gunpoint cannot have and does not have constitutional validity. [pp. 313–15]

In the appendices there is a legal opinion on this signature obtained through blackmail: it was sent to us in Portugal in 1953 by Dr Géza Töreky, former president of the High Court of Justice.[x]

Miklóspapa was tired: it was not surprising that the effects of the day's events were beginning to show. But he told us everything in detail, as if it helped him to be able to pour out his distress to his family – or as if he wanted to recall the events in order to be able to judge them more clearly. I very much regretted that there had been nobody there to support him, but I particularly felt sorry for him because I did not trust the Nazis' word of honour.

We spent about half an hour with Miklóspapa and then we were taken back to the Nuncio's residence. It was late and we needed rest. I did not know if any of the family had slept the previous night, but I certainly had not. But now I had an unexpectedly bad night. The bed, which had been brought over from the convent for me, was full of bed bugs! After I had been bitten a few times I shone a small torch on the sheet and was horrified to see that there were two long and closely packed lines of bed-bugs coming out of the mattress. If I moved around and shone the torch on them, they quickly retreated to their hiding place. If I had not been in the same room as Magdamama, Ila and István, I would have lain down on the floor to sleep, but I did not want to wake them. So I spent the whole night moving and shining the torch on the bugs under my blanket. I have hardly ever spent a worse night, and the ridiculous thing was that I would happily have exchanged the bed-bug attack for another night of waiting for a German attack.

In the morning we decided that it was really necessary for Ila to go over to the Palace again to pick up some vital things. We made a list of what we needed, and poor Ila went over again with Monsignor Verolino. With the help of our excellent staff, who where still there, they managed to pack a few useful things that they had been able to rescue from the rooms.

The Germans said that three members of the staff could come with us because there would be nobody to serve us in Germany. Miklóspapa's valet Miklós Kerencsi, Magdamama's maid Margit Csécs and my maid Gizi Gaál immediately offered to come. The situation in the Palace was frightening: nobody knew whom the Arrow Cross people would arrest or when, and the Russian troops were approaching rapidly ... . In the meantime there was another air raid warning. After lunch we took our leave of the Nuncio and Verolino, and at four o'clock German soldiers came to escort us by car to Kelenföld station.

It was a grey day when we were taken away from the Nuncio's residence

[x] Appendix 9

and from Castle Hill to an unknown future. My heart sank; but just when I reached the point where I felt I could not take any more, something came along and helped me through. Suddenly I realized that 'it does not matter where I am: I am a little nothing, but I exist! And wherever I am, that's where I have to be! I must not look back or forward, it is the present that matters.'

We arrived at Kelenföld. I wondered who all those people were, standing expressionless on either side. As far as I remember, one or two coaches from the Regent's train had been coupled onto a train in which there were German soldiers in front of and behind us. Soon Miklóspapa arrived, wearing civilian clothes, and the train left.

So, who was in our sad little group? The family: Miklóspapa, Magdamama, István and myself, together with Nanny Ila Sajni; Lieutenant General Antal Vattay and Lieutenant General György Brunszwik; and the three members of our staff: Miklós Kerencsi, Margit Csécs, and Gizi Gaál. Vattay said that Ambrózy did not want to come because of his wife, although the Germans would have brought him and Karoly Lázár. Instead they brought Brunszwik – or did he offer to come? We never found out for certain. We discovered that our German escorts were the embassy counsellor Feine (Veesenmayer's deputy), and a certain Oberst Wolff.

The train did not stop at all in Hungary, it just sped through the stations, which were all deserted because air raid warnings were sounded in every place the train passed through. We could hear the sirens on the train. We wondered what they were afraid of. Nobody knew who was on the train anyway – perhaps they were afraid that someone might wave to us.

The train stopped for about ten minutes in Vienna and again in Linz. When we stopped in Vienna at 11 p.m., in the dark, Miklóspapa ran along the train shouting, 'Wo ist mein Sohn? Wo ist mein Sohn?' (Where is my son?) It was dreadful to see his suffering, because it must have been then that he realized they were not going to keep their word. But how could he have believed that they would? Miklóspapa could always be won over with a promise on someone's honour. He could never imagine that someone might not keep an 'official' promise. He himself had only given Hitler an oral promise to notify him if Hungary left the war, and he could not bring himself to break his word … .

This scene was repeated in Linz, but there was no sign of Nicky. We spent a hard night on the train: I could hardly remember when I had last slept. This was my fourth night without sleep, and now on the train I was not even tired and could not have slept. I wondered what was keeping me going.

I tried to think through the events of the previous days and work out the reason for the complete failure of our plans, and why we had been left completely alone with just the guardsmen in the Palace. I certainly did not know about everything, but the planning and preparation of the ceasefire, the sending of the delegation to Moscow, the orders given to the First and Second Armies, and the move of the Mountain Brigade and the Mounted Division to Budapest – most of which were Miklóspapa's ideas – were well thought out.

Our leaving the war was not prepared half-heartedly or amateurishly. It was just the execution that was doomed to failure, because we did not take enough care of those key and reliable people who could perhaps have acted decisively and carried it all through. We exposed them to attempts on their lives and to capture: Nicky, Bakay, Aggteleky. We were not careful or suspicious enough – Pista was a victim of this too. Added to all this there was of course fear of the German invaders and of the Russians, as a result of which many people acted in a confused, half-hearted and uncertain manner; and, unfortunately, many went over to the German side.

Dawn broke and we looked out of the window. Ila, István and I were sitting side by side in the compartment when suddenly the door was thrown open and a uniformed SS officer looked in. He was so huge that he had to bend down in order to look through the door. There was a long scar from a cut on the left side of his face. He didn't say a word, just looked at us, and I wondered why this man hated us. It was only after the war that I discovered who this officer called Oberst Wolff really was, when I heard him described in a radio news item, and later saw a photo of Otto Skorzeny in a newspaper.

Before we arrived, we were told that we were going to somewhere called Waldbichl, near Weilheim. Waldbichl was a code name for Schloss Hirschberg, but we only discovered that months later. The train did not go into Weilheim station but stopped outside the town, where some cars were waiting for us, together with Baron Alexander von Dörnberg, the giant, handsome, red-haired German chief of protocol.

I had seen that there was a Hungarian railway worker on the train, and this gave me the idea of sending my sisters a sign of life. I wrote on a slip of paper: 'Long live Szálasi' in order not to arouse suspicion, and then: 'Please deliver to 12 Dísz Square. Stand firm, sister! (A Szálasi greeting!) We are well, in Waldbichl, near Weilheim. Lots of love.' I folded the slip of paper up very small and, when we got off, I asked the MÁV employee to give me a hand to help me down and passed him the note. I was very pleased when he pretended not to notice, and found out later that he had gone to Dísz Square and delivered it. I never knew his name and very much regret not ever having been able to thank him for doing it.

Dörnberg welcomed us on behalf of the German foreign office. He got into the first car with Miklóspapa and Magdamama. Nanny Ila, István and I sat in the back of the second car and Oberst Wolff sat in front next to the driver. When we set off the driver was a little clumsy changing gear, and Oberst Wolff said something to him that I did not hear, but I could see the driver's neck turn crimson and he was trembling as he drove on. 'Well!' I thought, 'We're in good hands!'

Part Three

16

Imprisoned by the Gestapo
Somewhere in Bavaria
October 1944

We drove through richly forested hills, and a barrier was opened for us to drive up to Schloss Waldbichl.[53] The area was beautiful and the air healthy, as we were at 700 metres above sea level and in the middle of a pine and beech forest. Our destination, a comfortable and tastefully furnished country mansion, had superb views of the Alps, which were about 40 kilometres away, now covered with snow.

A small part of the parkland surrounding the Schloss was fenced with barbed wire. This was the only place where we were allowed to walk, and then only with an escort of armed Gestapo guards. One hundred SS men were accommodated in barracks inside the fence, and there were nine Gestapo guards with two dogs in the house. With all of us on the first floor, the Gestapo above and below us, we were very well guarded – but from whom or from what? Where could we have fled? And who would come to liberate us?

They called us all together and told us that in the hall on the ground floor a radio would be installed, on which we could listen to German and Hungarian news broadcasts. Listening to any other foreign station was strictly forbidden, and anyone caught doing so – no matter whom – would immediately be executed. They showed us a room they said was for Nicky. I had a brief talk with Baron von Dörnberg about why Nicky has not joined us yet. I sensed that it was all in vain, but still they carried on playacting; I wondered why.

We unpacked, and then went for a walk with an armed Gestapo escort. After four sleepless nights I was completely exhausted and slept soundly all night. The next morning we, the family, had breakfast together, then Dörnberg came to say goodbye before leaving for Budapest.

That day we walked and rested, and after dinner we played bridge, as Vattay had brought a pack of cards. Legationsrat Leite-Jasper, a German diplomat posted there from the foreign office, and whom I did not like very much, said he would join us for a game; Hueber, the Gestapo commander, came to introduce himself.

Three days later we received the radio we had been promised. Being allowed to listen to Hungarian radio was no great delight. We listened to the broadcast of Szálasi's investiture, and to my surprise the elder Archduke József spoke out in favour of continuing the war. Miklóspapa was not surprised, however; he said that during the first Communist period twenty-five years earlier, Archduke József had adapted to communist customs and had taken on the name of József Alcsúti. (Alcsút was his estate.)

A few days after our arrival I started writing a detailed diary in a simple school exercise book, which I wrote as though writing a letter to my sisters. Magdamama also kept a diary, which I still have and will also quote from at times.

Waldbichl Diary

28 October. I will probably have a lot of time on my hands here, so I have decided, despite my lack of talent as a writer, to describe the more interesting events of our monotonous, bitter exile. Of course you mustn't forget that my pen is constrained: I don't dare to write with complete freedom here in captivity – you must take that into account.

It's ten days since we arrived here, and already it seems as if we have been here forever. Having read a lot about captivity and exile, it's extraordinary to realize that we ourselves are now in that situation. All possibility of taking any action or making any decisions has been removed, we don't know where we are, what's happening around us, what they are planning to do with us … .

Of course we don't show all this to each other. I feel that I must continue to do as much as is humanly possible to make this hard time easier for my poor tormented parents-in-law. This seems harder here than ever before. Poor Miklóspapa is taking it particularly badly, which of course isn't surprising. After being fully occupied in a position of responsibility, now that he has nothing to do all the problems of the recent past are weighing heavily on him. I too agonize about how this or that could have been done differently, so I can imagine how the same thoughts must be tormenting him. Nicky's absence is a terrible worry and another source of pain for his parents – they guess what he might be going through.

We can't get enough of the beautiful view, which is a balm for our souls. You can see the high peak of the Zugspitze with the naked eye. The forests around the house are particularly magnificent now, resplendent in a thousand October colours that seem to glitter, and there are different shades of red, which aren't so predominant at home. But however beautiful this is, I'd rather see Hungarian forests!

My feelings soon dull my vision and I can't appreciate the beauty for long. In short, our mood isn't right for this otherwise lovely place, because we are locked in, and you could cut the hostile atmosphere with a knife. The important thing is that the mountain air is good for István, as is the catering, which is what we had been worried about. There's lots of good bread, which is a pleasant surprise; there's also plenty of butter, and for the moment we are being given sugar too.

We are very strictly guarded: there are a hundred SS guards on constant duty in the garden surrounding the house. At night they patrol around the building with dogs, and they often shine lights on our windows despite the fact that in the house there are Gestapo men both above and below us. It's quite unpleasant, because if you open the window before going to bed or if they hear the slightest noise, they immediately shine a light there.

If we want to go out for a walk we have to report to the Gestapo on the ground floor, and then they unlock the front door, which is otherwise permanently locked. (Between ourselves we call the Gestapo *fogdmegs*, which means 'grabbers'.) During our walks we are each followed wherever we go by an armed Gestapo guard, despite the presence of the SS guards. Though we always walk the same route, there and back, at least we are making the most of the clear, sharp air.

We are pleased that Antal Vattay is here with us; he is a likable, natural, kind person. He left his wife, son and daughter in Budapest and of course he is very worried about them.

We don't really know why György Brunszwik is here, why the Germans brought him as the second escort. He is taking it badly so far. I think he didn't imagine it would be quite like this, and now his discomfort is compounded by a pain like sciatica in his lower back, which makes him even more downcast. The presence of Papa's butler Miklós, and of Margit and Gizi, is very comforting for us because, apart from the fact that it's good to see faces from home, we certainly wouldn't get any help here. Miklós in particular – of whom I have always been very fond – has shown in this difficult situation what an outstanding person he is.

I think of you, Éva, Myro and Sya – will we sisters ever see each other again in this life? How will we find each other again when this war is over? And how will we get away from here? But I mustn't worry about that, or lose faith in God.

29 October, Sunday. At Miklóspapa's request I spoke yesterday afternoon to Legationsrat Leite-Jasper about the whole Nicky affair, because apparently he had said he didn't have any information about it … Well, let him find out how we view it! Though he tried to reassure me, our discussion only served to reinforce my conviction that we won't see Nicky again. I can only describe as medieval the way in which a head of state and a father was blackmailed with his son's life in exchange for a signature; an ambassador and a plenipotentiary emissary gave their word of honour that his son would be restored to him on the train in Vienna; and when he signed, they had not the least intention of keeping their word. Anyway, it said in the paper today that 'Veesenmayer, the German plenipotentiary in Hungary, received a high honour for his outstanding services …' It seems you are honoured for breaking your word!

Poor Nicky must be enduring the most dreadful conditions; it's hard to imagine how he might be suffering. I can see that his parents still hope that he will be brought here, and I have to keep this hope alive for as long as I can.

1 November, All Saints' Day. Our thoughts go to the crypts at home, where perhaps no candles have been lit and nobody has taken any flowers. On this day every year we always went down to Kenderes, sadly taking more and more flowers as the inhabitants of the pretty little crypt multiplied.

Today we have been here for two whole weeks, and I will tell you about our daily routine. We have breakfast in our little drawing room at eight o'clock: Mama, Miklóspapa, Ila, István and I. Then everyone has a bath and spends the morning in their room doing whatever they can to pass the time – reading or writing. Then we all go for a walk – István goes out much earlier with Ila to enjoy the fresh air – naturally with a Gestapo escort. Lunch is at one o'clock, and Miklós brings the food in from the kitchen. After lunch we sit by the fire in the hall, drinking black *Ersatzkaffee*, which is just about tolerable; luckily Miklóspapa quite likes it.

Miklós the butler told us that when the SS troops overran the Palace and their commander settled into the Regent's room and study, he summoned Miklós and instructed him to bring him coffee exactly as he would for the Regent. When Miklós brought the coffee, the man swore at him and demanded that he bring the same coffee as the Regent drank. He didn't believe it when Miklós told him the Regent always drank second-rate coffee and not the best. Miklós nearly got into serious trouble over that.

One of our afternoon pastimes is rolling pieces of paper into spills, which we use instead of matches to light cigarettes from the fire. Matches and cigarettes have to be used sparingly, so those who do are trying to smoke less. Vattay is the heaviest smoker, and apart from him only my parents-in-law smoke. It is very touching the way they share one cigarette between them in order to be economical, taking turns to smoke it. At two o'clock we listen to the German news and try to extract some sense from the reports. Then everyone retires to their room until four, when we have another hour-long walk, up and down the same short path. We could go for some wonderful walks around here if we could only go beyond the barbed wire fence.

At five o'clock we have tea, the same people together as in the morning, and at six o'clock Vattay and Brunszwik arrive with the cards for a game of rummy, with which we entertain ourselves until seven thirty. Then we get changed and at eight o'clock we have dinner. We listen to the news from Hungary (generally bad news) by the fire, and then we play bridge. We go to bed between ten thirty and eleven – or rather the others do; I spend time talking to Ila, knitting and so on.

We fixed this daily routine precisely, thinking the days would be more tolerable if we followed some kind of routine. Changing for dinner is also compulsory. In this way the day passes relatively well – if only we weren't tormented by anxiety. We can't complain about the catering, but somehow we never eat well, we're used to different food. István picks at his food, he doesn't like it after the home cooking he's used to, and he craves sweet things, which we rarely get here. I hope he will get used to it in time. The doctor's bag I packed full of vitamins is coming in very useful now.

5 November, Sunday. Yesterday we had a lovely surprise: two parcels arrived from Budapest! They contained lots of wool – who sent it and how it got here we don't know. Of course the smokers were very disappointed because they hoped to find some cigarettes in the parcels. Magdamama and I are very pleased to have all the wool because it will give us plenty to do, and we can even give some away, because wool seems very hard to get hold of here. Frau Hergenhahn, who is the housekeeper, told us that they got their last pair of stockings before Christmas last year.

We started knitting straight away – it is an excellent way of passing the time. Magdamama is knitting a pullover for valet Miklós, and I'm knitting warm socks for Vattay. The wool gives out a little of the home atmosphere.

I have never dreamed so much or had so many nightmares as I've had here, but it's happening to all of us. I almost always dream about Budapest: often I'm in the hospital, which is one of the better dreams, because I liked working there very much. I often think about the patients too: I wonder how pretty little Mártika, four years old, whose left leg was severed by a train in a milling crowd, will manage.

I know I will always miss my apartment in the Palace because that was where I felt Pista's presence most. I could almost hear his footsteps, hear him closing the door, hear his voice. His pipes were left behind on the little table with the picture of me that he put there – I can see his hand picking up a pipe. I can't bear to think who is smoking those pipes now.

I'm surprised at what I've just written as it clearly shows a captive mentality. Our destiny is in the hands of others, we can't plan, we have nothing to decide, and our minds occupy themselves with anxious questions. Today is a particularly sad, misty, rainy day, which kills almost every ray of hope and the will to live. What will we live for in future? If Pista was alive I know everything would interest me, but without him I feel I have nothing to do on this earth. I know I have to live, and it's worth living for István, little Pista. It's a major task to bring him up to be worthy of his father. I wish I could guide him as Pista would have wanted ... but enough of this.

Magdamama wrote on this day: 'I'm sorry I didn't keep a diary from the very first day, but I was incapable of calm thought. We have lived through such dreadful times, gone through so much anxiety, had so many bitter disappointments that I needed a little time to calm down and restore my spiritual balance. Now I have found the way to my God again and once more, as so often in my life, I have reconciled myself to His holy will.' How I admire her!

8 November. Last night the first snow fell. It snowed all night and a huge amount fell on the forest. The poor trees are groaning under the weight, and lots of branches have snapped off because most of the trees still have all their foliage. István was delighted and could hardly contain himself all morning. Sometimes he climbed up on the windowsill to admire the snow, and demanded more and more impatiently to be allowed out. The Legationsrat brought him a little sledge, which made him even happier, but gave me pangs of conscience for having disliked the man until now.

In the lounge in the middle of the house there are books, and in a cupboard we found a chess set, much to Miklóspapa's delight. Now after meals he plays chess with Brunszwik and Vattay in turn, and always wins. Today I finished Vattay's socks, and in return he promised to deal me good hands when we play rummy! Apparently the Russians have reached Vecsés and Csepel – poor Budapest!

9 November. Brunszwik received two letters from home – we haven't received anything so far. He heard that on the twenty-fourth there had been a major bombing raid. If only I knew how you all are! If I don't hear anything soon it will be much more difficult: if Budapest is under serious threat the German Embassy is bound to leave.

All that's happened here is that it snowed, then it thawed, then it snowed again. I went for a walk on my own because my parents-in-law didn't leave the house today. When I'm on my own I walk quickly, and today my escort lost sight of me. As I went around the house the other way as usual, I found myself face to face with one of the armed SS guards, who asked me for identification; when I told him I didn't have any, he asked me why not. Thinking it would take too long to explain, I just walked on without a word; and, as he saw the Gestapo man hurrying after me, he left it at that. We usually walk the same short route several times in each direction. When I got to the house, Cernota – one of the three Gestapo officers – was standing there and asked if he could walk with me. 'If you don't mind a fast pace,' I said. But I was annoyed, thinking he would spoil my walk. Much to my surprise he was very pleasant, and told me that he had been in the navy in Pola and had seen Miklóspapa there several times. It's interesting how you can see the old school in him – he's different from the rest. I asked him what I should say if a guard asked me for identification again. He replied that I should just say I'm one of the guests. So now we know what we are!

12 November, Sunday. Legationsrat Leite-Jasper said goodbye because he was leaving, and Generalkonsul Hellenthal, who introduced himself yesterday and seems a more agreeable person, will be staying here in his place. He's about fifty, and has just come from Monaco, where it was as peaceful as Paradise; but before that he served in the Polish, French and Russian campaigns. He lost an eye as a result of an infection he picked up in the tropics. It was replaced with an artificial eye, in such a way that it moves together with his other eye, so that even if you know, you can't work out which is the real eye.

We wrote letters today. It may be that the letters will not be sent, but we have to try because I imagine you are just as worried about me as I am about you. What a great force love is: whatever happens, what we feel for each other can't just disappear, nobody can ever take away from us all the childhood memories that bind us together. Sya knows I have never feared death, but I can say without feeling sorry for myself that it's only for István's sake that I must cling to life – even if future happiness were in store for me, I'm not interested. I have had so many wonderful experiences in a very short time, and if Pista were here I would long for many more, but without him I'm not interested. We wrote a few lines to Nicky too, so that we might perhaps get a sign of life. Although Hungarian political prisoners who were taken away after the German occupation on 19 March were allowed to write to their families, I doubt that we will be allowed this privilege, although we are supposed to be guests!

13 November. Today was a very bad day. After lunch the generalkonsul called Vattay and told him that he would be leaving tonight to spend two days in Vienna. This news was a bombshell in our uneventful life. I don't believe for a moment that he will be away for only two days. We really hadn't expected this. We have enjoyed having Vattay with us very much. His natural behaviour and dry humour brought some vitality into this monotonous life. He had dinner in his room and Brunszwik and I sat with him. In the middle of his meal he suddenly turned to me, looked very gravely into my eyes and said, 'I won't be coming back here again.' I couldn't reply – I was so surprised that he, who at home had put so much hope in our coming here and had tried in the Palace to convince me, was now so well aware of how things stood. It was almost as if he was saying, 'You were right.' As I was convinced of this too, I couldn't find anything reassuring to say, and the silence that followed his words was very painful.

He packed for only two days, though I begged him to pack warmer shoes, socks, and so on. He said he couldn't take a bigger bag as they had told him he was just going for two days. I couldn't convince him that it didn't matter what they said ... He left by car before seven o'clock, in the cold winter night, with a stranger who had come for him and with one of the officers from here, Cernota. I wonder what is waiting for him in the merciless, bleak darkness into which he has gone. One more victim of this dreadful war and of Hungary's bitter destiny. His poor family doesn't even know he's been taken away from us.

It was difficult saying goodbye; and once again we all feel as if we've been hit on the head just when we were starting to get used to this life, keeping our anxious thoughts and misgivings from each other. It was Vattay who started our afternoon rummy battles; he always turned up at exactly six o'clock with the cards, and carried us all along with his enthusiasm, while continually teasing Brunszwik. We laughed a lot, Brunszwik included. Vattay was also the best bridge player of us all.

We will get away from here too sometime, but it's hard to imagine how. As much as István's presence gives us joy and brings sunshine into our lives, it frightens me that he is here with us. We can only entreat and have faith in Divine Providence that this ordeal will not be too much for us. Tonight we listened to Hungarian radio again – I can't say Hungarian news, because all they broadcast is German war reports and news. They said that János Vörös, the former chief of general staff, broadcast a radio proclamation from Moscow, urging that among other things the persecution of the Jews should end. We were stunned by this, and now I really can't understand Vörös' role in this whole affair. No further details were given.

15 November, Papi's name-day. I wonder whether he can sense the love with which I'm thinking of him? I am worried about him. I tried to prepare him at home for the catastrophe we were facing, but I always had the feeling that he didn't believe it, or didn't want to believe it. Today I made a little memorial card for Tost, to go in my prayer book, so he can be there along with the others when I pray for those who have gone. Today is exactly one month since that dreadful day which started with Nicky's abduction. I have confidence in the strength of prayer, as nothing gets lost.

16 November. Beautiful sunny weather, but we can't enjoy it because the commander ordered us to go down to the bunker, the Schloss shelter, which is said to be 100 per cent bombproof and is extremely well constructed. It's quite cramped, and with a lot of us in there the air quickly goes stale. We get locked in behind an iron door like a safe door. We sat there until eleven thirty. There's an air raid warning almost every day. Magdamama, who can't stand being in a confined space, is suffering terribly in the shelter here; it makes her very nervous.

Towards evening Dr Hueber, the Gestapo commander, came with the generalkonsul to say goodbye, as he was leaving; his replacement, Oberführer Klein, then came to introduce himself. We found out that the Gestapo officer Cernota, who had gone with Vattay, isn't coming back because he's been transferred. I'm sorry that the only seemingly decent Gestapo officer has gone; I hope he's not in trouble ... .

22 November. Yesterday we received Hungarian newspapers for the first time: they were dated 14 November and had got here quite quickly, but we didn't get much pleasure from them. They had a one-sided, primitive attitude and were full of annoyingly stupid, ill-intentioned articles, distortions and lies, all sprinkled with Arrow Cross slogans, like: 'Stand firm! Courage, brothers and sisters!' They weren't just primitive they were a betrayal: they dig a grave for the Hungarian people.

Tonight I spoke to Generalkonsul Hellenthal and gave him a letter for his superior, Foreign Minister Ribbentrop, because after we arrived here Ribbentrop had sent me a message that I was not to worry, he would do everything he could for Nicky, he would take the matter in hand; and he asked me to reassure Nicky's parents! In the letter I said that I couldn't reassure them any longer, and asked him not to forget his promise. I thought Ribbentrop had come to me because my parents were good friends of his wife's family – the Henkells – who were not at all pro-Nazi, and had visited us several times at Elefánt.

26 November. Yesterday and today there was nothing on the radio from Budapest: we heard it for the last time the day before yesterday, very faint and not in its usual place. The fighting in Csepel must have reached the Lakihegy transmitter. I wonder when it will broadcast again and what it will say. I will go on trying.

I wrote this in my diary in code, but now I can amplify it. I knew from when we listened at home that next to the Munich radio station there was a British station broadcasting news bulletins in German. It was called 'Sender West', and its newsreader spoke German exactly the same way as the newsreader at the Munich station. It was a brilliant idea! As we were allowed to listen to German radio stations, about every other day I tried to move across from the Munich station to the British station during the bulletin. I had only to move the dial slightly, but at the same time I had to watch the seven doors leading out of the hall, through which Gestapo men sometimes entered. From behind a closed door it wasn't possible to distinguish between the two broadcasts. While watching the doors I also had to pay attention to the news to hear which towns the Allies had occupied. If one of the doors opened I quickly had to turn the dial back to the Munich station. With one hand on the dial I wrote the names of the towns in pencil on a piece of toilet paper, and took it upstairs to my parents-in-law, who by then were in bed. I told them the news in a whisper and then rubbed the paper to pieces over the toilet with some water. As we had been told when we arrived that listening to foreign radio stations was punishable by death, I had to be extremely careful; and my heart often beat very fast when a door opened two or three times during a broadcast!

28 November. There was great excitement all day because we discovered that Margit the maid had been sent a letter from her ex-bodyguard fiancé by post, addressed to her here! Towards evening the new commander, Oberführer Klein, summoned her, and once he was convinced that she really couldn't speak German he summoned Miklós to act as interpreter. He just showed her the envelope from a distance, but didn't give her the letter, because he didn't like the fact that the sender knew our precise address. (Of course in this way I found out that the kind MÁV employee had passed on my message to my sisters, in which I had given our address!) Poor Margit was so happy, and now she

isn't even allowed to read the letter – though that can't change the fact that our address is known. What mean annoyances these are!

30 November. Today there was a dark, oppressive fog, which made me very depressed, and everyone walked about in silence. As after the cloud the sun comes out, tonight I was amazed to receive a letter from Count János Esterházy, our remarkable and dear friend Bibi. He had somehow got it to us by way of the German Embassy in Pozsony. The first news from home in more than six weeks! He was kind enough to write about everyone.

3 December. As it is the first Sunday of Advent, the housekeeper has made little Advent wreaths according to the local custom, decorated with paper angels dressed in glittering silver and gold robes; István could hardly contain himself when he saw them. Delighted, he ran to fetch Miklóspapa, calling, 'Come on, Grandfather, I'll take you to fairyland.' Later he added, 'It's lucky an angel like those didn't come into my bedroom, because I'd just look at it all the time and wouldn't sleep.' He was never so delighted at home: he had been spoilt by people constantly giving him presents. Through the cruelty of fate he has learned the meaning of happiness, which is very beneficial and healthy.

6 December, Saint Nicholas' day. How different this name-day is from previous ones! I wonder how many Hungarians are thinking of us today, amid all their problems? As there was nothing I could give Miklóspapa as a name-day present, I wrapped three sweets as if they were pills and wrote a regular prescription as 'Dr Habenichts' (Dr Have-Nothing) with instructions on the dosage of the pills. I sent that into their room on a tray with a glass of water, and managed to make them laugh.

Today I walked with Generalkonsul Hellenthal, back and forth on the short path. Although I was with him, a 'grabber' still followed me. When I asked why this was necessary, he said that he didn't count here.

We also congratulated valet Miklós, as it was his name-day too, and he got a letter from his family! Like Margit's letter, this also came by post and fell into the commander's clutches. It must have been here for some time, because it had been posted in Budapest in October. The Oberführer summoned Miklós to his room and there gave him the letter so he could read and translate it, and then he had to give it back, he couldn't even keep it! We can't understand this, unless it was just to annoy him. Even so, Miklós was very happy, because he had been in despair at not having heard any news about his family.

But all this happiness would be too much for a name-day, and it was tarnished by an announcement on the German radio that the Soviets had launched a major attack against Budapest. They also had a different Saint Nicholas' day – the roar of cannons, hunger and suffering, instead of a gala performance at the Opera House. All this is the sad destiny of a small country caught up in the struggle between larger powers.

Very early the next morning they chased us down to the shelter. They didn't take it so seriously before, but the new commander has a habit of ordering everyone to go down to the shelter as soon as an enemy plane appears anywhere, and 'forgets' to let us out for hours, while the Gestapo men go for lunch.

10 December. Yesterday was Pista's fortieth birthday – I can imagine his family's joy forty years ago. I seem to miss him more and more. The extent to which someone is forgotten depends on how much he was loved and what kind of person he was. Pista's personality is unforgettable, and anyone who was close to him will miss him forever.

Up to now we have been given enough food. But they say that from tomorrow 'diplomatic rations' will end throughout the country, and they painted a very bleak picture of the rations we would receive. I talked to Hellenthal about this problem and said that if the food wasn't enough for István, couldn't they let me take him to Switzerland? He said that was completely impossible, because once you're in a situation such as we are in here, you can't get out of it easily. I also asked him to try to arrange for a few lines to arrive from Nicky to his parents for Christmas, because that would be the only and the best Christmas present they could get. I warned him that they might become ill with worry. He promised to try.

We heard that there is an administrative director in the house who is a good chess player, and Miklóspapa sent him a message inviting him to play. He came with pleasure, and Miklóspapa beat him as he has beaten everyone so far. We only found out afterwards that, apart from Hellenthal, the household weren't allowed any contact with us, and that the director had got into trouble because of this game of chess. We don't mind, we're just as happy if we don't have to see any Nazis.

Generalkonsul Hellenthal should deal with any post that comes, but he is not very successful. He has a lot of goodwill but no power – what the Gestapo says goes here. Budapest radio has been silenced for good, so even this contact with our homeland has been lost. There has been no reply to the letter his parents sent to Nicky, no reply to Miklóspapa's letter to Hitler, and no reply to my letter to Ribbentrop – and we sit here, paralysed, almost hopeless as we await the final outcome.

13 December, Wednesday. On Monday, what was rather flatteringly

called 'diplomatic rations' came to an end, and it looks as if hunger has begun in earnest. They say we're getting what everyone in Germany is entitled to, be he prince, worker or pauper, and it's very little. They give us *Eintopfgericht*, all-in-one meals, never with pasta and rarely with meat, and we get one apple a day. Nobody says anything; however, I will record here that I'm always hungry, although it's tolerable because we're so inactive. Rumbling stomachs are in fashion, there's always someone whose stomach is demanding food.

Ila and I often spend half the night working on Christmas surprises for István. We pick up the anti-radar foil strips dropped in the garden by British planes, and use them to make chains, silver threads, etc. After a British raid the forest is full of such strips. The Gestapo wanted to stop us picking them up, but I explained that we wanted to use them to give my son some kind of Christmas surprise – after all there was nothing else we could give him here. So they asked the commander's permission and he very generously agreed. Between ourselves we now call the commander *kapus* (which means 'doorman').

Up until recently I've tried to listen to the British news bulletins on 'Sender West' regularly every other day, but now I listen only rarely because it's too exciting. Yesterday, when I went upstairs after listening, I fainted. Luckily nobody saw me and I slowly came round. I seem to have become very weak; I must try to spend more time lying down.

17 December. The second air raid warning was before dinner and the third was after dinner – this last was a major attack on Munich. We could see the fires from here. Munich was bombed to bits, as were other large Bavarian towns like Augsburg and Regensburg, and Innsbruck and Salzburg in Austria.

The last few days have been lovely. The lakes are frozen over, the mornings are misty and the trees are full of frost – like a beautiful dream world. The cold is easy to take because fortunately so far the rooms are well heated – I just hope we'll have enough coal for the winter! The railways have been so badly hit by the bombing that we can count on having some problems with the transportation of coal. That would be harder to become accustomed to than the poor food, to which we're gradually and quietly resigning ourselves.

19 December. As far as we can gather from news bulletins, dreadful fighting is going on in Hungary; they're completely destroying our lovely country, and the Russians are continuing to advance. How we tried to prevent Budapest from being destroyed! Now it's almost surrounded, but still they carry on fighting … . We came to the conclusion that thinking about that made the hunger much easier to

bear: what must the population of Budapest be going through now, quite apart from being hungry!

20 December. I was furious for the rest of the day after Hellenthal went to see Miklóspapa this morning with an official statement that, in view of the political situation, neither he nor Magdamama would be allowed to correspond with anyone. As they haven't received a word since we've been here, and as far as I know my letters haven't got home either, we really can't understand why they didn't just say this right at the start – what is it that's different now?

German attacks are continuing on the western front ... or so they say.

24 December, Sunday. A sad Christmas morning dawned on the whole of Europe today. Families split up, hunger, cold rooms ... and how much love is left for our fellow men? Reverend Mayer is here, so there was mass at ten o'clock. Then we started making a Christmas tree for István out of virtually nothing. We chopped down a tree in the garden – our walking route is full of young pine trees, as though sent to us by baby Jesus – and Ila and I decorated it in the afternoon. I made a little open house out of moss to go in front of it, and put in it a picture from my prayer book showing baby Jesus lying in the manger. We made snow out of cotton wool and crushed glass, and hung lots of silver threads cut from foil strips on the tree. We had just three tiny candles.

Baby Jesus came at six in the evening, upstairs in our drawing room. (In Hungary this happens on Christmas Eve, and the ringing of a bell is the signal that baby Jesus has been, and the children can go to see the tree and find their presents.)

When the bell rang, István went in first and then the eight of us – Miklóspapa, Magdamama, Brunszwik, Ila, Miklós, Margit, Gizi and I – followed. The little tree looked beautiful, and the best present for Ila and me was when István stopped in the doorway and just looked, then said, 'Mama, I've never seen such a lovely tree!' What a good thing he's forgotten last year's tree, which reached up to the ceiling. But one thing's for certain: this little tree was prepared with more loving care than that big tree in the Mátyás room in the Palace. He was also very pleased with the simple wooden toys I'd asked Stoll, one of the German administrators, to get for him.

Meanwhile I know we were all thinking of Nicky. Wherever he is, I hope he can sense all the loving thoughts surrounding him in his bleak captivity – we don't even know how badly he was injured when he was captured – we hope he will get through the ordeal ... .

As we stood around the tree Brunszwik read the little poem I composed so that everyone – including Miklós and the girls – should feel that we belong together far more than ever before, here in this foreign land.

Christmas Eve in Waldbichl
The Christmas tree is German, the decorations are foreign.
The only reason it doesn't stand coldly herein
Is Hungarian hands that made it all bright
So that István can find in it delight.

Nine Hungarian hearts are in this room,
In a faraway country, cut off from home.
Letters can't get here and parcels are lost,
But the heart can still find its way to most.

And suddenly I see ... just please look around,
Here around the tree many hearts can be found.
Sister, spouse, child, fiancé and parents abound
With anxiety and loving hearts they all us surround.

Nine Hungarian hearts far away and lonely,
But still beating together with many closely.
While love lives among us, that is what matters,
Let's not mind even if we don't get any letters.

United in one desire, we ask all together
That the lot of all Hungarians, God may make better.

There wasn't a dry eye in the gathering, but I had expected that the atmosphere would become gloomy, so I had prepared a little entertainment in advance. I'd written a short scene in the style of two Hungarian comedians of that period, Hacsek and Sajó. So I put on Brunszwik's coat and hat and sat down with him at a little table, just like Hacsek and Sajó on the stage. We were a great success and made everyone laugh.

We all sang Hungarian Christmas carols and enjoyed seeing István's delight. After dinner we didn't stay downstairs, because all the rooms were being used for a *Jul-Fest* – the ancient Germanic feast of light that celebrates the lengthening of the days. (Far be it from them to remember the birth of Jesus!)

31 December. We have had to spend every morning in the cellar, in this cold, cramped bunker. I find it particularly hard because of Mama.

The sensational event of the holiday period was that on Christmas

Day Brunszwik received written notification from the German Foreign Ministry and was informed personally on the phone by von Dörnberg that he is a free man and can go home! He was in such raptures of delight that we couldn't even talk to him. We found it sickening that it seemed not to have occurred to him that the rest of us were staying here. But he didn't receive the documents he needed from the police to travel, and yesterday he heard that he cannot leave for the time being. This news made him terribly depressed.

The other sensational event was the arrival on the twenty-seventh of a case of food from home, which delighted us all: sugar, rice from Kenderes, Miklóspapa's and Magdamama's favourite cigarettes, etc. Unfortunately there was no letter in the case, but perhaps it has been removed here ... .

The only thing which overshadowed our happiness was that at the same time I received a letter from the German Foreign Minister Ribbentrop, saying that no correspondence or any other form of contact between us and Nicky will be allowed until his case has been cleared up completely. I quote:

Foreign Ministry, Berlin, 19 December 1944.

Dear Madam,

Thank you for your letter of the 21 November. I must however reply that at the moment it is not possible for me to comply with the wishes of your parents-in-law. Your brother-in-law engaged in contacts with the enemy that are detrimental to German and Hungarian interests, and so he was arrested. His release is not possible for reasons of state. The question of correspondence cannot be considered until the connections of these regrettable events are clarified.

Mr Horthy junior is currently being held in appropriate custody. I regret this turn of events as much as you do, but the responsibility for it lies exclusively with your brother-in-law himself. The events of recent months bear witness to the devastating consequences for Hungary of the political activity that your brother-in-law also pursued. I regret that I am unable to give you any other information and remain,

Yours faithfully,
Jh. Ribbentrop.

Not a bad interpretation! So in the end it's because of Nicky that they're destroying Budapest! I wonder what we have to thank Ribbentrop's policies for? I really didn't expect any other response, but it was very depressing for my parents-in-law.

That was the day I played my first game of chess with Miklóspapa, and it went quite well. I could get to like this game.

Budapest is surrounded and a great struggle is going on: such a dreadful thought, which hasn't left me all day. What is the point of it all? This is the last day of a dreadful year, and who knows what the next one will be like? I try not to think of you all because then I just have to fight back the tears; and I can imagine that you will be caught by sadness too, especially at midnight. I remember all the happy New Year's Eves we spent together, when we jumped off chairs into the new year. I find that each new year we enter has been worse than the last. I cannot sleep, I have a headache and there is a lot of noise downstairs. A bad end to a bad year!

1 January 1945. In God's name we start a new year. The end of the war cannot be far off now – what will that be like? And what will this long-awaited peace be like?

There's lots of snow, the whole area is under at least half a metre of it; the forest is beautiful. The big advantage of this is that no planes come over and we don't have to go into the bunker.

Brunszwik has suffered a huge disappointment, as his permission to leave was withdrawn without reason. The poor man is in despair that he has to stay here.

3 January. A big surprise: yesterday Hellenthal told Miklóspapa that his younger brother Eugene (Jenő) was coming here today, in his own car, driven by his driver! They didn't say whether he was just visiting or staying for an extended period. He arrived at five o'clock this afternoon, with his valet/driver Józsi Buderer, accompanied by a Gestapo man in plain clothes. The car was filled to bursting with flour, lard, sausages and bacon! Just now, when we were in great need of some decent food. They spent a long time searching Uncle Eugene's luggage, but miraculously left him the food! We heard a lot of sad news from him, and unfortunately he knew nothing about my parents or the rest of my family as he had spent the last two months in the west of Hungary. Many decent people had been executed or taken away – good friends and relatives like Kállay, Hardy, Lázár, the ADCs, former politicians ... . Only those who had somehow managed to flee have avoided being imprisoned.

We can't understand why Uncle Eugene has been allowed to come here when we're not allowed any letters, for of course now he can tell us whatever he likes as they can't padlock his mouth. Uncle Eugene was intending to go to Germany in search of his horses, which had been transported there, but he was lured into a trap on the border between Hungary and Austria. A Gestapo man in plain clothes had asked him where he was going and then got into the car, suggesting he should go to visit his brother. Uncle Eugene said that as far as he knew his brother was in captivity, but the Gestapo man said that wasn't true, he was the Führer's guest, staying in a very pleasant palace. Uncle Eugene was surprised therefore when his bags were searched here, and asked when he would be able to go after his horses. We tried to explain the situation and told him we couldn't leave the place.

It's interesting that neither the Gestapo chief nor Hellenthal can get over their surprise and shock that Uncle Eugene has been allowed into this secret prison-palace which is guarded and secured with seven padlocks. Now the 'doorman' is avenging himself by taking Uncle's car with another driver and zooming around in it without so much as a word to us.

4 January. Today Uncle Eugene realized what the true situation was, because they took his car key from him and immediately drove the car to Weilheim without asking his permission. Then the 'doorman' set off in it for Munich, but it soon broke down and they sent for Józsi the driver to repair it. Miklóspapa summoned Hellenthal and objected. Now the car is in the garage for the time being, jacked up and unusable because the generalkonsul saw to it that it was immobilized.

Despite all this, the atmosphere in our little prison camp has definitely improved since Uncle arrived. His dry sense of humour often makes us laugh, and his presence is a blessing for Miklóspapa. Not to mention the lovely Hungarian food he brought with him, enabling us to organize decent breakfasts.

Just one thing has escaped the Gestapo's attention: a small portable radio, which – whether by accident or design – had been packed with the food! Uncle Eugene gave it straight to me, saying he was too deaf to listen to it. This radio is a wonderful gift for us. We manage to keep it hidden, so now I don't have to listen to 'Sender West' with my heart pounding. My room is the only one on the first floor which doesn't have direct access to the open balcony-corridor around the hall, so that's where I hide the radio, under the medicines in my little doctor's bag. The bag has a lock and I hide the key in a separate place.

I added later: From that day onward, every night at ten o'clock, sometimes earlier, I came upstairs, locked the doors, got out the key and the bag from their hiding places, got in under the blanket and listened to the radio with the volume very low, noting down the news. I listened to the English, German and Hungarian broadcasts from London, and the Hungarian broadcasts from America, Bari and Moscow, making brief notes. After making sure there was nobody in the corridor I went to give my parents-in-law a whispered report.

One night when I was concentrating on the foreign news bulletins I heard a loud noise coming closer and closer. When the door of the next room was noisily opened I quickly put the radio under the mattress. My blood froze – had they heard the radio crackling? Three Gestapo men burst into my room and ran to the window, saying I must be giving out signals because the curtains weren't completely closed. They closed them and gave me a lecture on how the blackout was to be observed strictly and that if this happened again I would get into serious trouble. I apologized and said I would make sure it didn't happen again. By the time they left, my heart was pounding so hard I found it difficult to calm down.

8 January. The 'doorman' has gone away for a few days and Hueber, the previous commander, has come back to stand in for him. It's only now that we realize how good he was. For instance, if there's an air raid warning then he allows us back upstairs with all the others as soon as the preliminary 'all clear' is given. Today there was a major attack on Munich. Huge fires were reported.

I've made the most of the favourable 'doorman' situation and asked my Gestapo escort to ask the commander if I could put on skis for my walk. There's a load of white-painted army skis in the corridor leading to the shelter, and every time I pass them I think it would be easier to use them than to walk in this snow, even if there isn't a slope to go down. One of our escorts, Gandorfer, always talks very politely to us, and once even brought us a packet of butter, 'secretly', he said. Of course we don't talk to him much – we don't trust anyone here and he might be an informer – but I asked him to do me this one favour. I have now received permission from the commander, on condition that my Gestapo escort also wears skis. Straight away I tried putting a pair of skis onto my shoes and the walk went really well. Unfortunately there was no slope, but it was a nice change and good exercise.

10 January. At my parents-in-law's request a doctor from Weilheim, Dr Goltermann, came to examine me yesterday to find out why I've lost so much weight and, if possible, to prescribe some extra food rations for me. Of course he couldn't find anything wrong, but he wants to give me a more thorough examination with X-rays and ECG in Weilheim on Monday. He seems to be a pleasant and conscientious doctor, but either he's pretending or he really has no idea of our circumstances here. He

suggested a bit of variety and asked whether I go hunting here! I was at a loss for words when he asked whether the cuisine here was Viennese, Berlin or Hungarian style. I didn't dare give an honest answer in case it was reported back, but said that the poor cook can't follow any style but has to improvise with what is provided.

14 January, Sunday. István greeted me with a little poem on my birthday, and a lovely beauty box was waiting for me on the breakfast table, a present from my parents-in-law. It had belonged to Paulette and they had brought it with them as a souvenir. I was very touched.

(I was very moved to find, years later, the entry for this day in Magdamama's diary: 'The Lord God has given this lovely person so many outstanding qualities and so much talent, and at the same time He has inflicted such sadness and suffering on her and placed a heavy cross on her shoulders. The question comes spontaneously: why? If anyone, she would have deserved a better, happier life. If only God might compensate her for all the suffering she has borne with patience and resignation, and bless her future life with good things, inner peace, happiness and lots of pleasure in her precious little son, and reward her for the kind and warm love she has given us. These are my wishes for her today, and this is what I will ask the Lord for in my fervent prayers today.'

Thank you, Magdamama, God heard your prayer: I have everything I could wish for and inner peace in my old age, and I couldn't derive any more happiness and pleasure from my precious big son! But I don't know what I have done to deserve all these blessings.)

15 January, Monday. This morning, for the first time in three months, I left Waldbichl! They took me to Weilheim by car. Kölbl the director (whom we never meet otherwise) was driving and I was in the back, squashed in between a nurse and a 'grabber' so I couldn't escape. It was a beautiful sunny, frosty morning, and it took twelve minutes to drive to the hospital in Weilheim. There Dr Goltermann took X-rays, tested my blood, and did an ECG. Apart from being generally run down and weak, the only problem he found was in the last test, which showed a weakness in the heart muscle. He said I wasn't to do any more skiing for two or three weeks, during which time I have to put on weight.

17 January. István is four years old today. We all recall this day four years ago ... and Magdamama tells us, 'I can still see my Pista moved to tears as he saw his son – and how proudly he told his father when he got home that he had a son.' Last night Ila and I managed to make a

cake and put candles on it, and we wished István a happy birthday with it first thing in the morning. The little one couldn't have been more pleased. We toasted bread and lard by the fire, which delighted him. I played chess with Miklóspapa. The evening news bulletin spoke of serious offensives. The news from Budapest is terrible.

19 January. It snowed all day, but István and I spent a lot of time walking. In the afternoon Brunszwik, Magdamama and I were playing rummy when Korinth, the Gestapo butler, came in and said that Brunszwik was to go and see the Generalkonsul about a pressing matter. When Brunszwik left I tried to reassure Mama that it couldn't be anything much, but she got into a state because she thought they were telling him that Nicky was dead. I could do nothing to reassure her until Brunszwik returned. When he came back at last, he said he had heard that his son is in Saxony, but he hadn't been told why he is there or what he is doing.

German radio says that the Russians have launched a strong offensive on the borders of East Prussia, at Warsaw and at Krakow – i.e. all along the current German-Russian border – and have been very successful. They have entered East Prussia and Silesia and are approaching Breslau. The mood of the Germans has been very depressed since the Russian advance was announced. It's not surprising, after all not long ago they were loudly proclaiming that soon the Germans' great offensive against the Russians would begin, and this would soon lead to a German victory and the end of the war. Have they no scruples, misleading their people like this and telling them such rubbish?

26 January. Yesterday Mama fell during her morning walk and hit her hand badly. She wasn't well for the rest of the day, and in the evening she went up to her room while we were still sitting in the lounge. On the way she fainted and fell on her face and suffered a heavy nosebleed. We were all very frightened. We took her into her room and laid her on her bed, and I gave her a cold drink while Nanny Ila put a cold compress on the nape of her neck. Fortunately she soon regained a healthy colour.

Of course this caused great excitement in the house. The Oberführer objected to us not having told him about it last night – saying he would have called a doctor at once, as he's responsible for our lives, and so on. They say they are concerned, but they make us sit for hours in the cellar and it doesn't occur to them that poor Mama is going to pieces because she doesn't know whether Nicky is alive or dead.

29 January, Monday. Yesterday Dr Goltermann came at last. He examined Magdamama and luckily didn't find anything to worry about. He recommended that she stay in bed for three weeks. He was very pleased with me, and allowed me to ski 'in moderation'. I would like to know how I could overdo the skiing here!

I started skiing right away. Gandorfer, the friendly Gestapo man, was given the job of escorting me; and in the morning everything went well. But in the afternoon things took a bad turn. On the way we met Stoll, who wanted to see what we could do. There was just one short but steep slope beside the house – which I had avoided so far as there is a barbed wire fence at the bottom. I went down it fast and turned sharply just before the fence. I think Stoll must have egged the Gestapo man on because he hurried down behind me, but he couldn't turn quickly enough. He fell heavily, skidded into the fence and twisted his foot. There was much shouting; all the Gestapo guards rushed out of the house and surrounded our 'friend'. I didn't know whether to laugh or cry – I hadn't thought such a thing could happen in this small patch of a garden. A few days later he was taken in to Weilheim to be X-rayed (I don't know why they didn't take him sooner) and it turned out that he had fractured his ankle. Gandorfer never came back to Waldbichl. The 'doorman' didn't allow me to ski any more, and one of the guards told me that he'd said this was how I was trying to get rid of the Gestapo guards, one by one. What I learned from the incident was not to try anything, just keep my head down.

4 February, Sunday. The days are quite monotonous; there is no mass on Sundays, and we have hot water only at the weekend. We spend a lot of time sitting in the cellar, even when there is lovely sunshine outside. Magdamama and I knit, I play chess with Miklóspapa, and I listen to the news secretly every night. I write less now because I would only repeat myself. Magdamama still spends her days alternating between bed and sofa. Uncle Eugene continues to greet the arrival of the pigswill with loud chomping noises, like pigs do when they are being fed.

7 February, Wednesday. A big event in our lives at Waldbichl: for the first time in my life I beat Miklóspapa and the generalkonsul at chess! Everyone said what a big achievement it was and how talented I am. I was rather amused at having beaten the two best chess players when I only learned how to play at the beginning of January.

11 February. We're very worried about the heating, because if they don't get some fuel within a few days the coke will be exhausted, and there are wood-burning stoves in only three small rooms. They're making

efforts to obtain some fuel because it affects them too – luckily the other people in the house don't like being cold either!

During our walks I speak German to István, though I find it hard. It might be important for him to learn.

15 February. Today the German radio announced that Budapest had been abandoned because the west wing of the Palace was on fire, which had forced them to leave. It is hard to imagine what conditions must be like there. Who escaped? Who died? Almost all my possessions are – that is to say, were – there in the Palace. Everything must be ruined. But the main thing is that the fighting has ended.

16 February, Friday. This morning we spent a long time in the cellar and it affected Magdamama badly. When the alert was cancelled the guards all went up for lunch, leaving just one 'grabber' standing by the iron door, which was slightly ajar. Suddenly Miklóspapa announced that he had had enough and got up to leave, telling us to follow him. He pushed the door open and the Gestapo man was so surprised that he just stared at us without a word.

What happened next I only dared write down three months later. We went upstairs and Miklóspapa told Miklós to serve lunch. Just as we had sat down to eat, the door was flung open and there stood the Oberführer, seething with rage. He demanded to know how we had dared come up without his permission and told us to go back to the shelter straight away. Miklóspapa jumped up, went up to him, and shouted, 'And how dare you talk to me like that?' There was a minute's tense silence – my blood ran cold, I thought the commander would draw his pistol; but he turned and left, closing the door quietly behind him. It was an interesting incident, which changed the Oberführer's attitude towards us. It seems that Miklóspapa had impressed him. After that, the door to the shelter was always left open. God be praised!

18 February, Sunday. This morning Hellenthal came to see Miklóspapa, at Foreign Minister Ribbentrop's request, about a Swedish newspaper article that claimed that the preliminary ceasefire had been signed in Constantinople in 1943. If that were true, he said, they wouldn't treat us as guests any longer because this act of betrayal would absolve them of any obligation in that regard. The whole thing was really ridiculous, because the treatment we have received so far seems to us a very strange way to treat 'guests', and anyway who are they to talk about obligations? Naturally the information in the Swedish newspaper was inaccurate, and after Miklóspapa explained this to them, we heard no more about it.

20 February. Today Brunszwik had a letter from Vattay! He asked him to send him some of the things he had left here. His letter is in German, and came from the Sopronkőhida jail – so that's where our poor friend ended up! He says that he is weak but healthy. And, he sends greetings from my sister Éva and her husband Ádám Kendeffy, Pista and Ágnes Inkey, and Nándi Zichy. It's dreadful that they're all there in the prison too! But maybe it helps that they're together. He also sends greetings from Kari Lázár, so at least we know he is alive.

26 February, Monday. Brunszwik was allowed to go by car to visit his wife and son by the Tegernsee; Hellenthal went with him. When he came back he told us that they looked very ill and his son was in hospital.

We weighed my parents-in-law: Miklóspapa has lost 7 kilos and Magdamama has lost 6 kilos. They declared that they were pleased, because although they had become older and more wrinkled, at least they were slimmer. I beat Miklóspapa at chess again today! I was very surprised, but Miklóspapa was pleased with his pupil's success.

2 March. Today Hellenthal officially told Miklóspapa that Brunszwik was being released because there was no incriminating evidence against him, and on Sunday morning he could leave and join his family, who are staying by the Tegernsee. Again he's making no effort to conceal his delight, which is rather repulsive. I know he doesn't like it here and longs to leave. Of course we'll miss him in the rummy and bridge games, and we'll miss his news service. It's from him that we found out everything that goes on in the house; he told us all the gossip, romantic intrigues, etc. He got on with everyone and poked his nose into all their business. Despite the fact that when he leaves we will be even more isolated from events, and he was Miklóspapa's last escort to remain with us, the fact is that we too are pleased that he's going. We will probably never find out why he was allowed to receive letters and go away visiting, and why he was allowed to leave here ... but there are bound to be reasons that are hidden from us.

4 March. This morning Brunszwik left, accompanied by Generalkonsul Hellenthal. There are just the four of us now at meals, and Uncle Jenő is forced to play bridge with us in the evenings to make up the foursome.

Magdamama and I are frequently shocked to find how we have declined intellectually: with just each other for company and no outside stimulus, we can't find any new topics for conversation. The only news we hear are reports of the war that reach us through the secret radio, and these, together with our anxiety for our loved ones, our country and our future, occupy our thoughts to such an extent that we can no longer talk about anything else. It's a good thing that there are books here, and we devour Goethe, Balzac and others, which we might not have the time or patience to read otherwise. In this way we try to keep ourselves occupied, and we're lucky to have this opportunity.

Though it seems strange in our current situation – in the middle of a war, in German captivity – we still change every evening; the gentlemen put on a dinner jacket and we put on an evening dress. The clothes are here, we have nothing else to do, we have the time and it's another way of keeping ourselves occupied; it gives the evenings a certain form and helps us to make an effort to keep our spirits up.

8 March. The food rations are being reduced again. This is understandable because food is becoming scarcer, and all the refugees are being squeezed into a smaller and smaller space. I'm worried about István – this is what I think about if I wake up in the night – I'm worried about what will happen to him in the difficult times to come. I will try more forcefully to get them to let him and me go to Switzerland. I asked Hellenthal to submit a request to Berlin, but I want to try the 'doorman' too, because the other day he sounded more understanding than Hellenthal, and if he intervenes he might be more successful.

Uncle Eugene has, up to now, taken the situation with an imperturbability worthy of an Englishman: sitting in the dark, cold hall all day reading, paying no attention to what was going on around him, he gave the impression of not being interested in anything other than his book. He took it amiss when his cigars and cigarettes ran out, but said no more about it and seemed to have resigned himself to that too. But today he told me he cannot stand this much longer and will either commit suicide or escape, because there's no point in living like this. It wasn't a dramatic announcement; he spoke in a matter-of-fact way, as you would about the weather. Of course I listed all the counter-arguments and told him what dreadful consequences either of his solutions would have for us. I hope it was just a sudden bitterness and not a serious intention. It's amazing how much strength and new energy an appreciative or kind word can create. We really need the understanding of others. You can also draw a lot of strength from good memories. But more important than anything else is trust and belief in a Higher Power, although I don't know why we receive it ... maybe it's possible to become worthy of it.

12 March. So much snow fell last week that the 'doorman' gave me permission – without my asking – to walk on skis for a few more days.

István stood on the back of my skis and he didn't fall off once.

Food is discussed at every meal and if anything is a little better than usual it's praised to the heavens – though if we were given something like that at home we wouldn't think of eating it.

16 March. At last some warm sunshine. In the afternoon I opened the door to the small balcony on the first floor, put down some cushions and lay down to sunbathe. I lay in the sun with my eyes closed, listening to the birds twittering. A bumblebee buzzed around me and suddenly I felt as if I was lying on the terrace at Elefánt. I could picture everything around me there and it was so good – I half expected to hear the carriage coming along the 'big road' or the familiar sound of the deer grazing. The images that the simple buzzing of a bumblebee can conjure up! The carefree peace of Elefánt swept over me and I fell asleep with good feelings I hadn't had experienced for a long time.

The other day when we were sitting by the fire, *Traumerei* was on the radio, and as I looked into the fire I was suddenly in Sya's house in Nagykovácsi, looking into the fire as Pista asked me to marry him, while from the next room, where Sya was listening to the radio, the sound of *Traumerei* came through. This impression was so strong that my current surroundings melted away and I relived that wonderful afternoon: I could hear Pista saying, 'I've never been so happy in my life.'

19 March. The Oberführer said as regards my travelling to Switzerland it was out of the question, as the reply he had received from Berlin was 'Mensch, seid ihr verrückt?' (Man, are you crazy?) – that was how impossible they considered it to be. Why it should be so impossible they didn't say. The only argument he gave was that the 'Secret Service' might capture me. So what? I can't wait! But we can sense that the attitude of the people in the house is changing markedly.

25 March. This is my dear and only Sya's birthday. I hope you can feel the love with which I think of you. We are in a state of feverish excitement – the Allies are advancing at enormous speed on the western front, and German resistance seems to have been broken down everywhere. We know now that within a matter of days we can anticipate events of such magnitude that they will change our whole situation here. I wonder what we can expect?

29 March. The Allied troops are advancing rapidly, gaining victory after victory; they have already reached the north west of Bavaria, which is quite close. In Hungary the Russians have taken the offensive and are

approaching the Austrian border. It's an odd feeling to have no idea
what will happen to us. Will they leave us here? Will they take us away?
I think of those days in October last year and know we must trust in
the help of the Almighty.

1 April, Easter Sunday. We were given four eggs per person and a little
edible dye, so we were able to hide some red Easter eggs for István.
Yesterday they told us our rations will be increased. And Uncle Jenő
can go to Donauwörth to see to his horses. What can all these
concessions mean?

5 April. Uncle Eugene, accompanied by a 'grabber', left early this
morning in the wood-fired car for Kaisheim, near Donauwörth, where
the Hungarian state studs were evacuated to save them from the
Russians, and where his thoroughbred mares are being kept. He came
back at nine o'clock at night and had lots to tell us. He had met Pettko-
Sandtner and other Hungarians, and they were very happy to see each
other again. He said they knew we were here and had told him both sad
and good news, including that the mood in Hungary had again become
one full of support for the Regent, whose decisions were now approved
and acknowledged because events had proved him right. We were
touched by the loyalty and love shown by the Hungarians in
Donauwörth, which they expressed by loading Uncle Eugene's car with
food – everyone brought something: sweets for István, salami, tins,
champagne, preserves, cigarettes, etc. László Hanthy, who had stayed in
Hungary, had sent bacon and cheese for us, which had been on its way
for two months. Hanthy's kindness touched me deeply, to think of us in
these difficult times! In the end Uncle Jenő had to intervene forcefully
to prevent them giving him all they had; after all, they weren't exactly
in the lap of luxury themselves.

The love of this small group of Hungarians gave us enormous
pleasure in our exile. They also brought news that when Sopron was
captured the prisoners in the Sopronkőhida prison had managed to
escape – if only that were true! Unfortunately nobody there knew
anything about my family.

It's almost incredible that just as the stock of food Uncle Jenő had
brought was nearly exhausted, all this other food arrived. Magdamama
and I see God's blessing and help in this, and have decided that from
now we will try not to worry but to place our trust completely in Divine
Providence.

11 April. There's an air raid warning every day. In the afternoon István
and I went down to the lake to catch small fish; I caught seven and he

caught one by the shore – with his hands! All at once Oberführer Klein came over and asked me some brief but interesting questions, which I answered by expressing my opinions very honestly; I hope he won't hang me for it. He asked me whether we want to flee if the Americans come, because he will do what we want. That's little short of miraculous! Of course I told him that we wouldn't leave for anything, in fact the only thing we've been afraid of recently is that they, the Germans, would take us away from here. I asked him what he would do if he received instructions to take us away. He said that communications were bad and messages couldn't always be clearly understood. I was very reassured by this because somehow I feel that he's telling the truth, and I'm grateful that he has freed us from this great fear and anxiety. Who would have believed that I would be the intermediary whom the Germans would ask about what we wanted. This shows that links with the centre really have loosened. Of course I didn't say that I could hardly wait for the Americans to arrive.

I made the most of the opportunity and asked him not to be so heartless and to tell us where Nicky is so we would know where to look for him after the war. All he said was 'bei Linz,' (near Linz) but that was enough for me to know that he's in Mauthausen! A German report says Hanover has fallen – the Allies are advancing everywhere.

13 April. The radio announced that F. D. Roosevelt, the president of the United States, died yesterday of a stroke. This won't have any effect on the continuation of the war, but my parents-in-law were shocked. I had always heard from Miklóspapa that President Roosevelt had shown definite goodwill towards Hungary and towards him personally, and had indicated this on several occasions. He thought that the president might possibly have helped us when the peace treaties were formulated after the war. Roosevelt has died, but the one whose death would save millions is still here ...

Hellenthal said today that Nicky had been allowed to write to Magdamama. I wonder when we will see his handwriting? The Russian troops have virtually bypassed Vienna – it was luckier than Budapest!

15 April. Today it is six months since that dreadful Sunday in October. Six months of mental torture and tension. Six months of inactive observation of events each more horrible than the last, and, last but not least, six months with no news of any of you, my sisters.

Despite continuous air raid warnings the 'doorman' only rarely sends us down to the shelter now, which is a relief. He has become very considerate and polite. Nürnberg is now occupied by the Americans, the British are approaching Berlin, and the Russians are only 25 kilometres east of Berlin; but here the propaganda still trumpets the message that though the situation is grave at the moment, all is not yet lost and the Führer is confident of final victory. Germans should stand firm and resist to the last man because there are only two alternatives: victory or death. Such lack of scruples! Berlin must be absolute hell now, because Allied planes are bombing it day and night, the Russians are shelling it, and there's no water or electricity.

It's little short of miraculous that I'm able to listen to our little radio every day and so we know exactly what has happened and don't have to rely on what others tell us. Otherwise the uncertainty would be dreadful. The mood around us is desperate. These people who have been misled and duped by propaganda, trusted until only a few days ago in a German victory, because the Führer had said that the great turning point would come now, in Berlin: they would defeat the Russians, take the offensive and drive them out of the country. People are now waking up to reality, shattered and disappointed; they don't know what to do. I think Hellenthal and Stoll were the two exceptions who saw the situation clearly long ago. I write more boldly in my diary now because I have a feeling that they have much bigger things to worry about than searching through my writings.

22 April. It has snowed and it's very cold. There's been no heating at all for two weeks and we have to wrap up more warmly indoors than outside. The rooms are only bearable if the sun shines in during the day. We can hear planes overhead constantly; they look beautiful in the sunshine, and though we ought to be afraid of them I greet them with delight.

There are lots of surprises. Yesterday evening Dörnberg, the head of protocol, arrived on his way to Austria. Today he saw Miklóspapa and spoke openly and sympathetically; he had lost all hope and had nothing good to say about his superiors. A bit late! Before we knew why he had come, we feared that we were to be taken away somewhere, but we soon realized that the leadership isn't too bothered about us any more. However, we're still guarded here as before.

A few days ago, while I was walking, the 'doorman', Oberführer Klein, came over and said he would come into the hall one evening and play chess with me. Before I could say a word he had gone. They say that he is the best chess player here. I went to Miklóspapa in desperation to say I didn't want to play against him, but Miklóspapa said that now he was behaving so much more decently I had to play him if he came. He and Mama would be sitting with me anyway, and after all, our lives might depend on him.

That same evening, when we were sitting in the lounge after dinner,

Klein came in and sat down by the chessboard opposite me, without a word. He won the first game and said we had to play another. I managed to play more calmly this time, but it was a long and difficult struggle and I had to be very careful. Suddenly I saw that I could checkmate him. I wondered what to do – should I let him win or should I beat him? But straight away I realized I mustn't let him win. Yes, I would beat the great Gestapo player! 'Checkmate!' I said. He seemed not to have been expecting that, because he was obviously furious – perhaps not just because it was a beginner but also because it was a prisoner, and a woman at that, who had beaten him. He got up without a word and went out. I said to my parents-in-law, 'You see, it was a pity to sit down with him.' But on the other hand, I was pleased with the victory I had won on behalf of this small Hungarian prisoners' colony. Miklóspapa was proud of his pupil and very pleased with my victory too.

26 April. The whole household has been packing for two days. They are in a state of feverish excitement because the front is so close. The Gestapo people in the house are behaving properly towards us so far, but Sturmbannführer Lange, the commander of the SS guards outside, is apparently a man to be feared because he hates us very much. However, it's also true that everyone hates him too, his own men most of all.

Planes pass overhead in their hundreds, they turn the sky black – Magdamama says it's like summer at Kenderes when the crows fly towards the forest in the evening. (We discovered later that they were going to Berchtesgaden to drop thousands of heavy bombs on the Führer's home; the famous 'Adlerhorst' was bombed to bits.)

The situation is becoming critical now – the SS guard company are packed and awaiting the order to move on, as are the Gestapo men with the Oberführer. Everyone is going to clear off before the liberation army arrives. The guards, housekeeper, and director: they are all going. Only Generalkonsul Hellenthal and his family are staying – he has lived abroad a lot and took no part in party politics – and apparently Paringer the cook and Korinth the butler are staying too. Of course we don't know what sort of reception and treatment we will be given by the Americans. In fact it's not even certain who will be here first, because it seems the Americans have been delayed by significant resistance before Augsburg, and the French have pressed forward from the south-west, so they are both the same distance from us.

We continually think about Nicky: he must be in a dreadful state. I just hope they don't kill him now.

Yesterday the Oberführer talked to me about the cruelty of fate, at which I gave him a piece of my mind, saying that people who have committed so many inhuman acts shouldn't be surprised when they are punished. I couldn't keep quiet, and listed in detail how the Poles and Jews had been persecuted and how dreadfully they had suffered. He left very frostily and I admit that I was frightened by my outburst, because I could be executed for such things. But today I was reassured because, when Ila, István and I were sitting outside the shelter he came over again, asked if he could sit down by us and asked me to listen to him. He said that it was only now, after I told him about the dreadful atrocities they had committed, that he understood the true situation: until now he had seen it all quite differently. Now everything in him had collapsed. It's hard to believe that this is true, that they allowed themselves to be misled to this extent – but if so, it's a very rude awakening now! It's as if these Nazis have two souls. Oberführer Klein has a grown up son and daughter and he seems to love his family very much, and in addition he's a well-read, educated man – mind you, he is also an alcoholic. But that's just one side of him. The other is an artificially nurtured Nazi soul. I don't want to be unfair, and I try to understand this man; it seems to me that he takes on a role and identifies with it completely.

27 April. We could hear gunfire all night, but nobody knows where exactly the front is. Soldiers arrive constantly wanting quarters here, but the generalkonsul let in three Wehrmacht officers and this enabled him to turn everyone else away. Apparently these three officers are very decent men. In the afternoon there was a rumour that the Americans are in Landsberg. This provoked feverish excitement in the house. Many left in laden cars – the 'doorman' left at ten o'clock with four 'grabbers'. These men are going to their deaths if they continue fighting. The Oberführer must have a lot on his conscience; they say he was the right hand of Heidrich, and Himmler's confidant, so he can't expect to get off lightly. But before he went he came to see us, and behaved very properly. We could hardly believe our eyes when he came in bringing a tray of drinks in small glasses to say goodbye. He seemed to be a broken man, tortured by pangs of conscience. He said he was going to the front to die, and if he wasn't killed he would shoot himself, because he couldn't let himself be captured by the enemy alive ... . We actually felt sorry for him then, because we could see how he was suffering. The Gestapo men who had accompanied us on our walk and seemed to be fairly decent Bavarian men were almost friendly as they too came to say goodbye. Who would have thought that this was how we would part.

Suddenly we have begun to feel more free: I'm starting to write lots of things in my diary which I haven't dared write till now, while they are still fresh in my memory. Today is my fifth wedding anniversary – that's another thing that's fresh in my memory ... .

28 April. The SS company left at nine this morning. It's unusually quiet inside and outside the house. I went out for a walk – through the open gate, where the barrier has been removed! It's a funny feeling to have nobody following me; I keep turning round to make sure. I'm starting to feel as if I'm really free, an almost inexplicably good feeling after six months of confinement. I wish I could just go and fetch Nicky and bring him back to his parents. It's quiet in the distance now, after all the noise of tanks and gunfire yesterday. It seems the retreating German troops have passed through. There are now only three policemen in the house with dogs: they are Sicherheitspolizei (security police), and are staying.

Generalkonsul Hellenthal, who remains in charge of the domestic staff, drove down to see his wife and daughter today, and took me with him. They are living in the village of Marnbach, 4 kilometres from here. When we got to the main road a sorry sight greeted us. Useless vehicles lay in and alongside the ditches everywhere, and tired soldiers were trudging along apparently aimlessly, asking to be picked up. They said they were looking for the rest of their company, they didn't know where it was. Why are they bothering? One of them still had a sense of humour, he said, 'Wir sind motorisierte Einheiten' (we're motorised units). They were walking in the rain with heavy packs, not knowing where they were heading. Hellenthal's wife and daughter are staying in a tiny room in a small farmhouse. Hellenthal said an emotional goodbye to them, because of course he doesn't know what will happen to him either. On the way back I was afraid the car might be commandeered, but fortunately we arrived safely. We stayed up late because we didn't know whether the Americans were about to arrive, but it seems they haven't even got as far as Weilheim, so they cannot arrive before tomorrow.

29 April, Sunday. I spent the whole day running up into the tower – which was forbidden before. From there I could see the whole area with the binoculars Hellenthal had given me. I could see the white flags fluttering in Weilheim, and the American tanks advancing along the road between Weilheim and Murnau, sometimes firing to the left or the right. They continue to advance south along the main road about 4 or 5 kilometres from us. Waldbichl – which from now on I will call by its right name, Hirschberg – is in such a secluded spot in the forest that the war doesn't reach us, even though we are right in the middle of it. The Munich radio station is dead and the phone doesn't work ... .

At midday two German soldiers came up here, and when Hellenthal asked what they were doing they said they had set up two guns not far from the house to attack the Americans from the side and to blow to bits any house on which they see a white flag! They are completely mad. Anyway they will have a lot to do if they intend to shoot at every house displaying a white flag – they can't have enough ammunition to shoot them all. Hellenthal told them quite forcefully that it was madness and they should get out of here. He told them that the house they were shooting at in the next village was where his wife and daughter were. They promised to go away, but didn't; and when we heard gunfire in the afternoon, Hellenthal and I ran up to the tower. I asked him to show me the house where his wife and daughter were. As he was showing me the house he thought was the one, at that very moment an American shell hit it and it started to burn. The poor man ran out of the house, white as a sheet, to go there, though there was quite a battle going on. By now we were worried about him too, but when he returned he told us that it was the house next door which had burned down, not the one where his wife was. A group of low-flying planes then appeared and shot at the two German guns. The noise was so terrible that I took István down to the shelter, but after half an hour everything went quiet.

Hellenthal told us many interesting things about the past few days: Himmler had given orders that if the enemy approached, all political prisoners were to be executed. This order went out to every place where political prisoners were being held, and Sturmbandführer Lange – the SS commander – had wanted to carry it out and execute us all. But Oberführer Klein told him that inside the house he was in charge, and what went on in the house was his affair and nothing to do with the SS commander. Apparently they had a long argument about this. Then Klein went to see Hellenthal and asked what he should do, should he commit suicide? The generalkonsul replied that if he had committed no crime he had nothing to be afraid of, but if he had, then he should admit it honestly and stand up in front of the court. Then Klein said he couldn't tell the German people what National Socialism had been built on, because he knew ... . Somehow I liked this honest statement, at least this man had a conscience. As far as I know, none of the accused in the Nürnberg trials said anything like that. Hellenthal also told us that one of the Gestapo guards had come back and told him that they had been carrying weapons to a designated hiding place in the forest for days on Oberführer Klein's orders, so that if the enemy arrived they would fight on as *Wehrwolf* partisans. When they all met up there, the guards all said to Klein that they weren't prepared to fight on, they had all decided to go home. The last they had seen of their commander was when he set off into the forest with backpack and weapon ... .

Before going to bed we listened to the news – all of us together now, openly and loudly! Mussolini has been captured and executed in Como by Italian partisans. He had been friendly towards Hungary and had defended our interests against Hitler, so my parents-in-law's opinion of him was different from their opinion of Hitler. The German and Italian troops in Italy signed an unconditional surrender today – if only it would happen here too!

17

The Americans Arrive, 1945

30 April. Uncle Eugene had gone for a walk, and I was standing on the road leading to the house, when an American jeep – with Uncle Eugene in it! – drove up to the house. Major Puck was the first American officer to arrive, led here by Uncle Eugene. He was looking for accommodation for the headquarters of the Seventh Army, Thirty-sixth US Division. I was so pleased to see him I could have hugged him. But he was very grave, and began by saying that we would all have to leave the house. I asked him to sit down and listen to me; I explained our situation and showed him the SS barracks, etc. He soon agreed that we could stay while he went to report on everything I had told him.

Soon afterwards, General Dahlquist arrived with his staff. You can't tell who's an officer and who's a private; they all look and behave alike. We had to hand over four of our rooms and also accommodate Hellenthal with us, which we were happy to do as he had always behaved decently, and had helped us a lot.

The house was soon swarming with 'GI's (that's what the American soldiers call themselves), and before we realized what was happening, some of our valuables had become 'souvenirs'. My camera disappeared within moments, although up to now I had managed to keep it safe from the Gestapo. We obviously were a little dazed at being liberated and weren't careful enough when moving our things from one room to another. We should have known that such things are inevitable with occupying troops. One soldier was proudly wearing four wristwatches!

Miklóspapa went to see General Dahlquist, the officer in charge, who came to visit us with his chief of staff and another general. They were friendly; and later, at General Dahlquist's invitation, I went to see him to give him detailed information about Nicky. I said I knew he had been taken to the Mauthausen concentration camp, and if possible I would like to go as a Red Cross nurse and bring him back. General

287

Dahlquist is very kind but there are some who don't know what to make of us, they aren't sure that the name Horthy doesn't indicate an enemy. There are many friendly soldiers – István has already been given lots of chocolate – but the kindest of them all is Lieutenant Colonel Reese.

1 May. We had excellent coffee with cream for breakfast, and lovely American pancakes with maple syrup. It was like a dream! They got hold of some coke from somewhere and now we have heating and hot water! I was loaned a typewriter, and have typed a memorandum about important events and things that Miklóspapa might have to remember, which Uncle Eugene and I translated into English. Before lunch we received news that Miklóspapa had to leave at two thirty for the American General Headquarters, as General Patch, commander of the Seventh Army, wanted to meet him. I was typing from his notes right up to the moment he left, with Uncle Eugene dictating to speed things up. It was a relief that they allowed our butler, Miklós, to go with his master.

This parting was very sudden; we weren't prepared for it, and poor Mama was very upset. It had occurred to me long ago that if the Americans came, Miklóspapa would be interviewed or held in custody pending an investigation, but I didn't think that after having been imprisoned by the Gestapo he would be taken away from his family.

2 May, Wednesday. In the morning three Hungarian officers came to visit us, including Colonel Godányi. They are serving with the Americans and are gathering together Hungarian soldiers. It was good to see how well they look, and to see American heads turning as they walked through the room. Several journalists came, as well as someone from American radio. In a quarter of an hour I told them everything I could; after all, very few people could be aware of what had really happened to us.

In the evening we received the news that Miklóspapa was now considered to be a prisoner of war and wouldn't be coming back for the time being. Mama was desperately upset, despite my efforts to reassure her that this was only to be expected and they must be treating him well. It's terrible to see how much she is suffering: she keeps repeating that her son has been imprisoned by the Germans and her husband by the Allies – the whole thing is truly like a tragicomedy! I wasn't expecting them to be separated from each other for an extended period.

Apparently Hitler is dead, but his body hasn't been found yet.

3 May, Thursday. This morning they took Hellenthal away. He took with him a case and a letter for Miklóspapa, but these were brought back by car after lunch and left here without any explanation.

In the afternoon the Thirty-sixth US Division Headquarters moved away and not a single American is left here. Before they left, Colonel Reese, who had been particularly kind to us, came to say goodbye. He told us that for the time being some French prisoners of war would be here to ensure our safety, and he recommended that we didn't leave the garden as there were many refugees and escaped prisoners in the area. He said if we needed anything we should see Captain Wills, who was the commander of the military government in Weilheim.

The house is empty again, and the good coffee, cream and cigarettes have gone with them. In the afternoon Ila, István and I were just going out of the main door for a little walk in the garden when a terrible-looking French soldier shouted at us and pointed his gun at István who had run out ahead of us, saying that if we took another step he would shoot. I went up to him to try to clarify the position, but he hardly wanted to speak to me; all he said was that they had strict orders not to let anyone out of the house.

At first I thought it was a nightmare: these wild French soldiers, who have spent five or six years in German captivity, now think we're their prisoners – this was no laughing matter. It's impossible that Colonel Reese would have lied to me; he seemed to be such an honest and sincere man. I realized that this must be a mistake, which needed to be cleared up as soon as possible. It's lucky that I can speak French! So I spoke to their commander, a simple man like the rest, but basically a kind and pleasant Frenchman. When I told him our story he explained that their English wasn't very good and there must be some misunderstanding, but we should wait until tomorrow afternoon, when someone would come from Weilheim. Until then we should stay in the house because he was bound to carry out the orders he had been given. We went back to the house feeling very bad because now we're more shut in than ever – at least the Gestapo had let us out for a walk.

4 May, Friday. We waited all day for someone to come from Weilheim, but nobody came. In the meantime we have made friends with the French guards, who are all good men who have suffered a great deal and can't wait to get home. 'Vous savez, ça m'embête de garder des femmes!' (You know, it annoys me to guard women!) said one. I, on the other hand, enjoyed speaking French.

I wrote a letter to Captain Wills and we decided that Korinth the butler should take it into Weilheim with two guards, because this situation is untenable. In the meantime I've noticed that the French are asking everyone questions, particularly the Dutch gardener, and now they are convinced that we are telling them the truth they are even more determined to have our position clarified.

In the evening Captain Wills suddenly arrived! He had business in the area and was just looking in to see if everything was all right. He couldn't have come at a better time. We explained everything to him and it turned out that the whole thing had indeed been a misunderstanding. The French soldiers are here purely for our safety, and if we want to we can even leave the garden, although it's advisable to take a guard with us. We were enormously relieved – we are free after all!

Today the Germans laid down their arms in Holland, Denmark and northwest Germany.

6 May. Mauthausen is in American hands! I wonder when we will hear about Nicky. I hope it will be good news, because poor Mama couldn't bear it if it wasn't.

7 May. In the early hours of the morning the Germans signed the unconditional surrender in Reims. At the moment when we heard this on the radio a swallow flew in through the window – they say that's lucky! For days we have listened to every news bulletin hoping that we might find out something about Nicky, and today the Hungarian-language broadcast from London said that Schuschnigg, Léon Blum, Miklós Kállay and Nicky had been found in a little village near Toblach! When we heard this, Mama and I fell into each other's arms, crying with joy. We were pleased he is with Kállay – will they be coming here? And when? Tomorrow is V.E. Day – Victory Europe Day! If only this victory would bring a just peace to Hungary too. For now it's good to know that Nicky has survived. It was the swallow that brought the news!

8 May. Victory Europe Day! At eight in the morning I listened to the news and they said again that the Fifth Army had found Nicky. Ila, István and I went down to the lake in beautiful sunshine. The soldiers were already enjoying themselves rowing, and István and I went into the boathouse to sort out a boat for ourselves.

Baroness Hirschberg came to visit us and told us how this house had been taken away from her, not bought, and so it will be given back. She's a kind and cultured lady and we're pleased that she will get her home back. We were just about to sit down to have lunch when Miklóspapa arrived! But straight away he said he had only come to pack, and was going back to Augsburg. He had lunch with us but hardly managed to eat anything because of all he had to tell us.

I was very pleased that he had been told he wasn't a prisoner of war but under protective custody. He said he hadn't met General Patch. He was staying with the German generals Rudstedt, Weichs, List and Leeb, and had a small room, which was very cold: they were being held in a worker's house with very basic facilities. The person who had driven him here and had been assigned to look after him was a very obliging Jewish man, who spoke fluent Hungarian, and whom Miklóspapa praised very highly. They had to hurry back to Augsburg because they were expecting to be told at any time that they would be flown to Spa in Belgium, where apparently conferences and discussions would be held. Fortunately Miklóspapa looked very well; he was so alert and sprightly that his escort – who didn't tell us his name – told me he was astonished at how young and lively he was. Butler Miklós was here with them; apparently he cooks and does the washing for Miklóspapa and is wonderfully helpful. We will never be able to repay him for his loyalty and kindness. They were supposed to leave at four o'clock, but the escort allowed him another hour because he could see how much we were enjoying each other's company. Now they've left, and I am afraid we won't hear from Miklóspapa for a long time.

We listened to Churchill's speech and later we heard the King of England, George VI, speaking. They broadcast the crowd outside Buckingham Palace shouting 'We want the King!' and I was reminded of the day of his coronation, when Myro and I were also in the crowd outside the Palace. The whole broadcast from London was simple and moving, nobody praised themselves or abused the enemy. The behaviour of the British was very decent in every respect. Hitler wouldn't have celebrated a German victory in this way – something from which fortunately the Almighty has preserved us.

9 May. Freedom! We can go in and out of the fence and don't always have to be careful what we say. Yesterday the French guards left and there are now fifteen Americans here instead. They are good-humoured lads, their radio is on all day (playing excellent music); they row, swim, and practise shooting at targets. But this afternoon they already received orders to move because a security police office is moving in here. They were sad to leave because they liked the place with its lake and lovely scenery.

11 May. We patched together swimming costumes out of scarves so we could swim in the lake, because it is so hot. Suddenly, Éva arrived! We were so overwhelmed to see each other that we cried in each other's arms without a word for a long time. Éva, her husband Ádám and Antal Vattay came together, through the good offices of an American officer, Captain Grant, who was extremely kind in bringing them so far in order that we could at least spend a day together after such a long time apart. They had suffered the most dreadful tribulations before the American Third Army liberated them. The Arrow Cross had arrested

Éva and Ádám in Hungary, one night in January. They had to dress there and then in the presence of the soldiers and, leaving their children behind, spend thirty-six hours on a train before being locked up in the Sopronkőhida jail. Éva had not yet recovered from diphtheria and was put on the train feverish and shivering, amid much abuse – they were called 'treacherous dogs of the Horthy clique'. They suffered terribly from cold and hunger. When the Russian troops were approaching, they were moved to Austria, walking 32 kilometres in one day, and then lived in a cattle truck for three weeks, sixty of them having to take turns to lie down because that was the only way they could fit in. Often they received no food, and they had to beg for every morsel of bread. Vattay, who was with them, had an attack of pleurisy during that time which nearly killed him. Poor Éva still has arthritis: all her joints are swollen, she has difficulty walking and can hardly turn a door handle. If she doesn't get treatment soon she could be permanently disabled. They spent the whole day telling us their story and we couldn't understand how they could have survived such horrors. They knew nothing about their children, and the last they heard was that the rest of you had all moved to Budapest, which is very worrying.

Éva and the others have to go back to Triftern tomorrow. Captain Grant has arranged for Vattay to go to Augsburg to join Miklóspapa as part of his entourage. We spent half the night talking and Éva told me many dreadful things. While they were at Kőhida, Nicky Odescalchi and Endre Bajcsy-Zsilinszky suffered terrible torture and were then hanged. Lieutenant General Kálmán Hardy, a relative of ours, had been sentenced to death, and every day for six weeks they threatened to carry out the sentence; they don't know what happened to him in the end. Lajos Dálnoki Veress fortunately managed to escape and wasn't recaptured. Many of our friends were with them and were waiting in Triftern to be taken back home.

13 May, Sunday. Mama and I walked the 4 kilometres to Marnbach to attend mass. A GI followed at a distance to safeguard us. We enjoyed the walk and enjoyed being in a church again even more. Tonight we listened to Churchill's speech, which as usual was excellent. He said it was no use destroying Nazism if another totalitarian police state were to take its place in Europe. Will the Soviets understand?

15 May. Unfortunately the security police people are leaving. They were a quiet and decent group. A larger company, the Thirty-sixth Artillery, is replacing them: more than a hundred men, who are carrying out security policing duties here. Their commander is Captain Fitz. They arrived amid much noise, their radios blare all over the house; luckily

it's good jazz. It's not pleasant around the lake now, Frenchmen, Russians and Germans come from all around to swim and row, and some of them don't inspire confidence.

17 May. I'm worried about Miklóspapa. The radio said Tito had asked the Allies to hand him over as a war criminal. There's nobody with him who could help him. He's alone and sometimes he doesn't remember certain things, when a lot could depend on what he might say at a hearing.

Today we heard on the radio that Oberst Skorzeny had been captured: the man who had freed Mussolini, lured Nicky into a trap and brought us here! So this is who our escort Oberst Wolff really was! We recognized him immediately from the description. Apparently he had organized an assassination attempt on Eisenhower, working with German soldiers wearing American GI uniforms. It's a good thing this huge, evil-looking man has been captured – I can't forget the contempt and hatred with which he looked me up and down on the train before we got to Weilheim.

20 May, Sunday. Mama and I walked to Eberfing, a nearby village, for nine o'clock mass. Uncle Eugene heard that the horses at Donauwörth had been distributed among the peasants to be looked after. He was terribly upset at the news, because those horses are his life's work and all he owns. He immediately asked to be allowed to go to Captain Wills in Weilheim to ask if he could go to see about them. When he was about to set off it emerged that we aren't allowed to leave here, even to go to Weilheim, unless there's a special reason. Civilians are only allowed to travel 6 kilometres, and this applies to us too. Uncle Eugene said if his horses were lost he would kill himself. We persuaded him to write to Wills explaining the situation, and this calmed him down a little. I feel very sorry for him because there's really no reason for him to be here.

21 May. This morning Mama asked me to see Captain Fitz and tell him she wanted to speak to him – she cannot stand not hearing about Nicky any longer. The Captain promised to go down to Weilheim to see Wills and press for a Red Cross person to come out. He came back with the news that there was nobody there from the American Red Cross, but said that I could go to the International Red Cross at Uffing tomorrow. He would be happy to take me in his jeep! At last we can start tracking Nicky down; and what's more, going anywhere by car is the best entertainment we can imagine here. The Captain seems pleased to be able to do something for us.

22 May. I was playing with István by the lake when Captain Fitz sent a message that he wanted to speak to me. Suspecting the worst I went to his office, and he indeed greeted me with the news that we couldn't go. In Weilheim yesterday they hadn't been aware of the situation when giving permission for me to go to Uffing. Today when they requested the pass for me, Wills said I wasn't allowed to leave here, but that he would send someone. Captain Fitz was very sorry – and I was very disappointed that the trip had been cancelled. Who knows when someone from the Red Cross will come here? But never mind; 'chin up' as Pista would say.

25 May. Today a depression came over me, a feeling of hopelessness, surely the consequence of recent events. But then I went to the garden and found István in the middle of playing with an American corporal called Seymour Salem, who has very kindly spent a lot of time with him these last few days. It's as if the Almighty has sent an angel to be with us and to cheer us up. Unfortunately, during a pleasant talk with Captain Fitz later in the afternoon, he told me that they are all leaving tomorrow and another group is coming in, which I very much regret. We all will miss Seymour and his sense of humour – particularly István. He sent a farewell present of a pile of books and some cigarettes, with a kind letter inviting us to stay with his sister in America if we had nowhere to go after the war. I was very touched.

26 May. This afternoon the new group of Americans arrived, with two majors and their commander, Captain Price. They announced that we would probably have to leave! I asked them to let us stay in one or two rooms as General Dahlquist had done, but they didn't seem very understanding. Captain Wills – who in the meantime has been promoted to Major – will surely deal with us, so we have to ask him about this.

30 May. We've heard nothing from Major Wills for two days. If they move us out of here I can't imagine where we will end up and what sort of accommodation we will get. But if I think of you, my sisters, I imagine all sorts of terrible things and think your situation must be far worse. I think a lot about my friends at home, and about our Jewish doctors, Mester, Szántó, Auer, Ladányi, Somogyi, Rojkó, Hauer ... did they survive the Szálasi government? I wouldn't have missed for anything the feeling I had when I saw those doctors for the first time without yellow armbands, after they obtained their exemptions. I hope this didn't do them any harm after we left.

4 June, Monday. Some Hungarians came today to ask Miklóspapa to use his influence to help them – two women who came out with Szálasi's Agriculture Ministry, and then two men. Magdamama called me because she didn't want to see them alone; we gave them very short shrift. In the evening, Prince Albrecht of Bavaria arrived with my cousin Jenke Keglevich. We were delighted to see each other, and they had dinner with us. Albrecht has a long beard, which he grew in the concentration camp. He has now been given permission by the American authorities to drive throughout Bavaria with one member of his family, and not far from Munich he found the Keglevich family, so he brought Jenke with him. It was good to talk to this cheerful, genial man. When the Americans liberated him from the German camp, he immediately bought himself a gun and went up into the mountains to shoot a chamois for his family to eat. It was also fun to exchange a bit of banter with Jenke; they've cheered us up enormously.

This ends the detailed diary I wrote like a letter to my sisters. As we now move away from Hirschberg to the town of Weilheim, where a different life is awaiting us, I shall go back to my small five-year diaries and my memory.

18

Weilheim, 1945 – 1948

Our move to Weilheim happened in the following way. One day I got a message that an American captain wanted to talk to us. I went downstairs to the office and found him sitting at the desk – actually, he had his feet on the desk and was lying rather than sitting, with his back to me. Captain Price was present and I heard him say, 'Captain Holmes, this is young Mrs Horthy.' Upon this, without even looking up, Captain Holmes said, 'You have to move away from here and you can choose the place you want to go to, in the Weilheim area.' Having said this, without looking round he threw me a map, which fell on the floor.

Controlling my reaction I picked up the map and said that I would have to study this with my mother-in-law, and if he would be good enough to come with me, we could discuss the matter with her. He reluctantly got to his feet and followed me upstairs. When we entered our little living room, Mama put out her hand to greet him. But Captain Holmes put both his hands in his pockets and shook his head. There was a moment of icy silence, after which Mama sat down and offered him a seat. Again he shook his head in answer. I was beginning to lose my temper and said to Mama in Hungarian that we had better ignore him and get down to the business of looking at the map. After a short discussion we chose Seeshaupt, as it was the nearest place. This was very important, as the Hirschberg's butler, Korinth, had offered to go on looking after our supplies, provided we were not too far away.

After informing us that he was in charge of finding a lodging for us, Captain Holmes – an endearing personality – walked out without another word. Allowing us to choose the location of our house demonstrated the clear intention of the American occupying forces to treat us with kindness; however, it was bad luck that the person in charge had such bad manners and obviously profoundly disliked what he had to do.

Captain Holmes reappeared two days later and asked for someone to go with him to look at a house he had found for us in Seeshaupt. On the way there he asked a few questions, and after my answers I noted a definite change in his manner. He picked up the Mayor's interpreter on the way and drove to a small villa, and he and the interpreter went inside. While I was waiting outside a little boy passed by, and I asked him who was living in the house. He told me that it was a woman known to be a staunch Nazi, and that everybody hated her. This woman then came out of the villa, and by the looks she gave me I could believe everything the little boy had told me.

We looked around the house, which was quite pleasant but obviously much too small for us. The owner never took her piercing eyes off me, and I felt that requisitioning houses was not something I wanted to do. I told Captain Holmes that the house was not big enough and could we please look at another one, but he insisted that all the others were full or unavailable, and that this woman was a Nazi. On the way back to Hirschberg I told him a few things about us. He said that he'd had no idea about all of this, and confessed that Major Wills had already told him to be nice to us, as we were decent people, but this had simply provoked him into being the opposite.

Back in Hirschberg I talked it all over with Mama and, convinced that we could not fit into that house, we realized that we must find something else that same day, as we were due to move the next morning. I then asked Captain Price to take me down to Captain Holmes in Weilheim, which he kindly agreed to do. We arrived at his house, where we found him in a surprisingly jovial mood, asking me to take a seat and pulling off his tie and throwing it into a corner of the room saying, 'No tie after six o'clock!'

The captain then took me to see a villa in Weilheim, no. 25 Pollingerstrasse, which he thought would be big enough for us. Apparently it belonged to someone who also owned another larger house, so this one could be requisitioned. But once again I felt awful looking around it and seeing the fear in the faces of the people who were being forced to move. (The owner of the house was a master-baker called Ohnesorg, and his name means 'without cares'. In the years we were there we sometimes received letters addressed to 'Villa Ohne Sorge' (Villa Without Cares), which under the circumstances was ironic.)

Captain Holmes was rather comic. Obviously anxious to finish this job of looking for a house for us, he tried to persuade me to like it and therefore praised everything about it: the space, the colour of the walls, the tiny garden. Listening to him one would have thought it was a palace, with a huge park.

I made the decision to accept the house, and was concerned only that I had not been able to show the house to Mama first. But, 'beggars can't be choosers,' I told myself, and I did not dislike this little villa with its tiny rooms – and it was big enough to accommodate all of us. At that time we were seven adults, and only the two girls Margit and Gizi could share a room – Mama, Uncle Eugene, his valet Józsi, Ila (with István) and myself, all needed separate rooms. We also had to reckon on Papa and his butler Miklós – and hopefully, Nicky – joining us at any time. It would be a new experience for me to have a room in which I could reach everything from the centre, but I did not need anything bigger.

Next morning we went to the house, hoping to clean it; but we could not do anything because the people who had lived there had not yet taken away their belongings. So we were granted another day. Mama was appalled when she saw how dirty the house was, but I felt that when it had been cleaned we could make it quite comfortable – and I was proved right.

In the afternoon we started cleaning. We then had a big surprise. The commander of the Hungarians in Weilheim, Colonel Godányi, whom we already knew, helped us in every possible way. The ladies from the nearby Hungarian refugee camp in Polling came to help, washing the floors and looking after everything. We were allowed to bring furniture, including beds, from Schloss Hirschberg, which I collected in a truck, driving back and forth three times between Hirschberg and Weilheim.

Next day we took a last look around Hirschberg and said goodbye to the people in the house. I was not sorry to leave this lovely place in exchange for a little suburban house in Weilheim, where we would not have the lovely view, the lake and the woods. No, I was delighted to leave this place, where we had spent so many unhappy hours and endless days of uncertainty and worry.

Some of the American soldiers bid us a touching farewell; every one of them gave something to István, and one of them put a big parcel on top of our luggage, in which we found chocolate, cigarettes and soap.

Finally, on 15 June, an American escort drove us up to the house in Weilheim. And a look of amazement came over their faces at the sight of a line of Hungarian officers standing in front of the house waiting for us, looking very smart in spite of their worn-out uniforms. They saluted and, as they came up to greet us, one by one they kissed Mama's and my hand.

On the first Sunday in Weilheim, it was wonderful to walk with Mama to the local church, accompanied by Colonel Godányi and First Lieutenant Póka. We were free people and we had Hungarian company.

On 18 June, Miklóspapa's birthday, Herr Schuster the drugstore owner drove us to the Hungarian refugee camp, where a Hungarian priest celebrated mass, accompanied by music and Hungarian singing. It was very moving, and people were crying when they sang the hymn to our heavenly Mother Patron: 'Do not forget the poor Hungarians.'

The camp held 250 Hungarians, and we walked through it, talking to many of the people there. This was the best camp in the region and the Americans were very good to the Hungarians. An American officer made a speech, which was translated by a Hungarian officer. He praised the Hungarians, saying that they were the best behaved and most disciplined amongst the many nationalities they had to deal with. This was a big compliment, and it was very kind of him to say so – I was only sorry that Miklóspapa could not be present to hear it, as this would have been the best possible present for his birthday.

Prelate Neuhauser, a German priest who had opposed the Nazis, came to visit us from Munich, bringing wonderful news. He had been interned in Dachau concentration camp for five years, and told us that Nicky had been brought there at the end of the war. Then, because the Americans were approaching, they were all taken – Neuhauser, Nicky and others – over the mountains to Toblach, where the American Third Army finally found them. From then on they were well looked after and supplied with everything, before being taken to Italy, to the Isle of Capri. Nicky had been absolutely famished, but now he was getting double portions and was eating well. He'd had no news of us, but Prelate Neuhauser would send him a message through the Vatican.

We now had a lot of visitors – what a change from the previous eight months. Prince Albrecht of Bavaria came again, with his wife Maritta and my cousin Jenke Keglevich. They brought us letters and told us many stories, while sharing a simple dinner with us. Only a year earlier it would have been a very different kind of dinner we would have offered them in the Royal Palace. So much had changed, but we were happy to be alive and to be together.

Then something happened that excited me: I was approached by one of the young women from the Hungarian camp, Mrs Ilona Binder – nicknamed Cuci – who at home had worked as a parliamentarian shorthand-typist. She asked me to teach her English, as she could earn her living more easily if she could only adapt her knowledge to the English language. She had no money, but would pay me back later. I was thrilled, and suggested offering her English lessons in exchange for lessons in shorthand typing. I was aware of the potential in this opportunity, considering all the languages I knew – it could be a way to earn my living and help the family. So Cuci and I agreed to exchange our knowledge, and we started lessons the next day. I went to the military government and plucked up courage to ask them to lend me a typewriter. They said they had one that was not in use and I could take it with me. It was a very old German machine, but it meant I could just about start to practise, learning to touch type.

From my first lesson with Cuci we began speaking in English. It was not as easy as it sounds. Cuci was an intelligent girl and asked questions about English grammar. I could read and write well in English, thanks to dear Missy, our English nanny. I also had a talent for spelling; but if you asked me why things were spelled or said as they were – well, I neither knew nor had thought about it. English grammar is absurd anyway, how could anyone explain why you say 'koff' and write 'cough', or 'bow' and write 'bough'? I just knew it, without any explanation. However, over the weeks that followed we came together regularly for lessons, and her English and my shorthand and touch-typing made steady progress. After our lessons Cuci and I would sometimes go swimming. To get there we both sat on one bike, changing round every now and then from sitting very uncomfortably on the front of the bike to doing the pedalling, which was tiring. But the swimming was great.

Wishing to alleviate Mama's anxiety about Papa, I went to the military government to ask Major Wills how we might get news of him. Their answer was that they could not do anything and I should inquire at the International Red Cross (IRC). So the next day I travelled with the Hungarian doctor, Dr Hanvai, to Castle Rieden near Uffing, where Mr Galopin of the Swiss International Red Cross very kindly received me. He told me that they obviously could not achieve anything without American help ... another stalemate.

After our liberation I had heard that someone from the IRC had come to 'Waldbichl' with some letters addressed to me, so I mentioned this to Mr Galopin. He immediately called over a Swiss lady, Elsbeth Mayer, who handed me two letters – one from Ellamami and one from Sya! Noting my expression as I looked at Sya's writing on the envelope and clutched the letters to my heart, she kindly ushered me to another room, where I was left alone to read them.

It was just as well, as I cried so much while reading Sya's and my parents' angelic letters that I was quite overcome. Both were writing from Budapest, in our house on Dísz Square, on 19 December 1944. The letters were written in German. They were expecting to spend Christmas there together. Sya wrote about the children, and that 'I am sure that our prayers and thoughts meet – I miss you. Tell me if you need something warm'. My parents wrote that Elefánt and Sajóvámos were plundered; they longed for news ... . I knew that not long after they wrote this, hell had broken loose on Buda Hill; I'd heard not a house was left undamaged, there was no food and no water – and Sya was there with her small children. When would I ever know if they survived?

After I had read the letters, Elsbeth Mayer, whose husband Eric was the delegate of the IRC and with whom we later became very good friends, proceeded to tell me the following story:

When they received the two letters, addressed to 'Waldbichl, near Weilheim', they decided to deliver them personally. She and her husband drove around looking for the address, but no one seemed to have heard of a place called Waldbichl. They finally found someone who told them it might be Schloss Hirschberg. It so happened that their DKV car was similar to the one the Gestapo used, so when they arrived at the entrance of Hirschberg the barrier was lifted and they drove to the front door of the house. They were immediately surrounded by Gestapo guards. She remained in the car, while her husband got out and asked to speak to the commander. He was led into the office of Oberführer Klein, to whom he handed one of the letters addressed to Ilona Horthy, and asked him to give it to the addressee. Klein looked at the letter and said, 'Horthy – who is that?' Eric Mayer replied that he must have heard the name before, as Horthy was the Regent of Hungary. When he heard this, Klein became very angry and handed the letter back, saying that he could not help him. In the meantime Elsbeth, sitting in the car, saw a woman with a little boy walking on the other side of the house with an armed Gestapo guard following them. She felt sure that the family was there.

She finished by saying, 'We were happy to get out of the place; it was frightening, and the Gestapo Oberführer seemed to be a terrible man.' I could just imagine how angry Klein must have been to be handed a letter by the International Red Cross, addressed to me at Waldbichl – when he thought that nobody knew the false address, or that we were there!

Prince Albrecht with his wife Maritta and my cousin Jenke came to pick me up one morning. They drove me to their home in Leutstetten, and then on to Munich, which was a terrible sight. I knew then what a town destroyed by bombs was like and I guessed what Budapest must look like.

A happy surprise was meeting Captain János Iványi, at whose operation I had assisted in Budapest in 1943, and whom we had nursed for a long time in the military hospital there. His presence evoked in me many memories of the operating theatre and the sick-ward. He did not look well and had lost a lot of weight. He, Captains Jenő Halmai and Kálmán Lukács became true friends; one could call them our three devoted knights, as they helped us in many ways during the four years we spent in Weilheim. István became very fond of Iványi and they had lots of fun together, like putting coins on the railway line and waiting for the train to pass and flatten them. Later on, when I got work, I suspected our 'knights' of devising some sort of plot, because every time I travelled to Munich to my job with the International Red Cross, one of them would be on the train. They never mentioned anything about it but I had an idea that they were acting as a sort of bodyguard. They always had 'something to do in Munich' which sounded totally plausible.

One day a friend came to visit us on a bicycle, having ridden 75 kilometres. Such things seemed quite normal at the time, because one tried to avoid going by train. A train journey was always a risky adventure. Trains were few, so they were always packed full – and when I say full, I mean that you rarely got a seat and were lucky to get standing space. One often had to stand on the outside steps, clinging on to the rail. This was bearable in the summer, but in the winter it was agony. I put it down to a post-war phenomenon, that people in Germany did not help each other in any way; they were mostly disgruntled and morose. I was once on the last step of a train from Weilheim to Starenberg, my hands getting so cold that I was afraid of losing my grip, but none of the men standing on the steps above me offered help; they would not even look at me – and I was too proud to ask for a favour.

Once I witnessed a touching scene, when an American soldier went through a whole train making all the men get up and give their seats to elderly women. At the same time he was telling them that it could be their mother or grandmother who needed a seat, and the men just got up without a word.

The military commander in Weilheim, Colonel McCabe, sent me a written invitation to a garden-party. The party consisted mainly of American officers, and also people from the Hungarian camp. One captain, who arrived late, sat down next to me and started talking about Hungary, where he claimed he had been. Then he asked whether I was related to the Regent and whether I knew where he was. When I answered in the negative he made a movement by his throat with his hand, showing that he would be hanged, and then laughed heartily at his own joke, which I felt to be in extraordinary bad taste. I simply got up and walked away, but I saw that Colonel McCabe was shocked – and he later kindly told me not to imagine that this man was in any way informed, it was just his insensitive behaviour and I should rest assured that he would put him in his place.

Next morning when I got home from my lesson with Cuci, I found a present from Colonel McCabe. A typewriter! I was deeply touched and very happy. I now had my own typewriter and could go ahead seriously with my work. I also started giving German lessons to an American officer called Captain Corkran. He came every day and was doing very well, and I was happy to be earning some money.

In the meantime, Uncle Eugene had gone to Bergstetten in a military government jeep to see about his horses. He came back in a rage, as he had had a big clash with the commander, a Major Owens, who had been rude and insulting. This officer seemed to have taken over all the horses and did not consider any former ownership as valid. This was astonishing, as these thoroughbred mares were registered.

Elsewhere, important events were taking place. On 26 July the English election results were announced: Attlee and the Labour Party had won. It was hard to imagine that Churchill had been defeated. The first atom bomb had been dropped. Russia had declared war on Japan. It all seemed a bit remote and I tried not to think about it. But then, on 15 August, the Japanese surrendered – it was a momentous day.

Over the next days letters began to arrive from Papi, Ellamami, Myro and Sya. The first came from Sya, written on 3 August 1945. She had received my note – which I'd written after receiving her letter from the IRC, and which had been my first attempt at sending something by post – and seeing my writing had so overwhelmed her with joy that she'd gone into shock. She went on to say that she had written to me so often in thought, that now she could put it on paper she did not know what to say or what to ask.

She described how, having come to Budapest to be with our parents for Christmas, on 26 December they had been cut off as the encircling Russian army closed in on the capital. On 28 December, Papi, Ellamami, Sya, Józsi with her two children, my nanny Suci and three other relations with another two children, went down to the cellar of our house on Dísz Square, which had several store-rooms, and did not get out of there again for two months, except to obtain essentials. The worst problem had been the lack of water, which they could only fetch in buckets at night, from some distance away. The worst affected by cellar-life were Papi and my nanny Suci, who had become terribly thin. But the most important thing was that they had all survived.

Now, with most houses in ruins, everybody was looking for somewhere to stay – which was no small task. People lived by picking up and collecting rags from the ruins. Sya and her family were now in their country house in Réde, as Budapest was very unhealthy and dusty. But there in Réde nothing belonged to them any more. They were allowed only a few rooms in the house, which was inhabited by 'guests'. Everything they possessed belonged to the past, but she and Józsi looked into the future with good spirit: 'as you cannot imagine what it means after two months of atrocious cellar life to see the sun, green grass, and to breathe the air! What matters is that the children are healthy and we are together.' József had a truck and was transporting milk to the capital – they hoped that would last.

The Germans had blown up all the bridges. There were some small motorboats crossing the Danube, but long queues of people waiting for them. In town there was no transport and no telephone, and all that walking was very tiring and left no time for anything else. Altogether she had written six pages of news.

Papi and Mami were now living in one room in a friend's house. They wrote that whatever horrors I might have heard about the siege of Budapest did not begin to approach the truth of it. They no longer went to Dísz Square as it was too sad – not one house had remained undamaged.

From fairly reliable sources we also heard that the estate in Kenderes had been confiscated and split up; the house was still standing but had been entirely plundered by Germans, Russians and presumably by the local population. I was sure that the same went for my father's home in Elefánt, and all the rest. So, we had no country, no home, no money – we might as well forget it all! I hoped to be able to live for the present and not think of past possessions ... .

A lawyer called Müller, who had been taken to Capri with Nicky, sent a message to Mama telling her that he had just met someone who was in detention in Wiesbaden and had talked to Miklóspapa only a few days before. Müller invited Mama to go to Munich to meet this man. One of our friends lent us a car and a driver, and accompanied by Captain Lukács, Mama and I left full of hopes that we might obtain some news. The man in question did not turn up, but we met an American there who promised to make inquiries and took a letter that Mama had written to General Eisenhower. In this letter Mama asked to be allowed to visit Miklóspapa, or at least to have some news of him. She tried everything she could, and also went to see Cardinal Faulhaber and left a letter to be forwarded to the Holy Father, requesting his intervention in Papa's and Nicky's cases.

László Taubinger – who was the head of the Committee for Hungarian Refugees, which he had created and which was recognized by the American military authorities – took me to Munich so that I could become acquainted with the work he was doing. The next day we went together from there to Triftern, to meet my sister Éva. It was a great joy to spend the day with her. She told me that when they were being herded out of Hungary and had to share any kind of small pieces of food they could get between sixty people, it happened several times that complete strangers gave her food because they took her for me. (We do have a strong family likeness.) She described one particular event in some detail: they had been allowed to rest, sitting together on the ground, quite close to where some Hungarian soldiers were cooking lunch in a big cauldron. A young soldier got up and filled a large mess-tin full of food, and gave it to her saying that this was for her, as he knew who she was. Éva told him that she was not the person he thought she was – upon which he leant close to her and said, 'I understand you don't want to say who you are, but you cannot fool me; although I was very young, I clearly remember meeting you in Kiev. You must accept this food.' She gratefully took it and divided it up between the sixty of them!

On 18 September I received news that Éva had left to go back to Hungary. Would we ever meet again?

The weather turned nasty, a lot of heavy rain and strong winds. It was very cold – the mountains in the distance were covered with snow. This was only the end of September and we were actually shivering in our rooms. We did not talk about it, but obviously everybody was thinking of what lay ahead of us that winter. There was no coal, and it was only with some difficulty that we managed to obtain some wood; not enough, but at least we would be able to cook for a while. The Mayers came quite regularly with parcels – they were very generous and kind. I felt that in the future I would never again take for granted a scented soap or a Kleenex tissue.

A letter came from Nicky from Rome to let us know he was all right! The first direct sign of life for exactly one year since the Gestapo had abducted him. I was especially happy for Mama – she had been very depressed.

I will give a small extract of Magdamama's diary – which she wrote to her husband while he was absent. It shows the deep bond that existed between them. I hope that she would not have minded me quoting her:

> Even poorly and humbly, if only our mutilated little family could again live together! It is now more than five months since mercilessly fate has torn you away from me – deep inside I go on living so closely linked to you that this time does not even seem so very long. What a shame for every day, every hour that we cannot spend together, and nobody can ever make good this wasted time. It is an unbearable and disheartening thought that I cannot be with you in these difficult days – when through all my life I only lived for you. You were the aim and meaning of my existence, and now I cannot share with you these very hard times. I sit here

idle and helpless, all my efforts fail. Eisenhower has not
even answered my letter. My only faith is now in the
help of the Holy Father.

Soon after she wrote this – after almost six months – we received the
first official news of Miklóspapa! A young American naval officer,
Lieutenant Steers, came on 22 October with instructions to tell us that
a few days earlier Papa had been taken from Frankfurt to Nürnberg, to
stand as a witness. He reassured us that Papa was in good health, and
that although the accommodation was not too good, provisions were
excellent. Later we might be able to visit him, now we could write to
him – which we did, and he took the letter with him. What happiness!
But not free from worry … .

One day the doorbell rang and I opened the door to find a familiar-
looking man in civilian clothes standing there. He introduced himself as
Josef Gandorfer, and said that he was the guard at Hirschberg who had
broken his leg following me on skis! He had come to thank me for the
accident, as because of this he was in hospital at the end of the war and
nobody seemed to have inquired as to where he had served before. He
told me that he had been in the SS and never did any Gestapo work, but
when they were short of personnel they pulled in some of the SS men to
serve as Gestapo guards. I was a bit taken aback by all this, but told him
that now I knew he was not an informer I had to thank him for helping
us out with butter, ski-clothes, etc. (It seems that he eventually did have
to clear his name, as in August 1947 I was summoned to the Court in
Weilheim as a witness in his case. I naturally told the truth of how he
had helped us several times.)

I was getting some translation work from the relief organisation run
by United Nations Relief and Rehabilitation Administration (UNRRA),
which always had to be done by a deadline. I had to write at night to
get it all done. These translations were passed on to me by our
wonderful friend Dr Ervin Póka, a Hungarian officer who was
employed by the American military government as public prosecutor,
and heaven only knows what else. There seemed to be nothing that he
could not do. He played the organ on Sundays at church, and we once
attended a concert in the Weilheim theatre where he played Schubert's
Forellen Quintet very beautifully on the piano.

György Jendrassik, an old friend of Pista's, came to see us on his way
from Budapest to Switzerland. It was enlightening to be able to listen to
his views of the situation at home. From what he told us, the policy of
this new democracy seemed to be 'take away what belongs to others'.

At last I was getting Hungary on our little radio, and we listened to
the trial of former Prime Minister Bárdossy, which gave us a taste of the

horrible atmosphere of these trials. Why did some have to pay a much bigger price for their mistakes than others?

Saint Nicholas' Day, 6 December, was the Regent and Nicky's name-day. We had heard only the day before that Nicky had been taken to Nürnberg to be with his father, a very kind gesture by the Americans. It was a wonderful thought that after this long and painful separation they were together on their name-day. And Mama's joy was beyond all bounds.

A few days later the post brought a 'prisoner-of-war postcard' from Miklóspapa, telling us that Nicky was there with him and quite free to come and go. Then two Hungarians arrived from Nürnberg, bringing a letter from Nicky in which he said that he was coming to Weilheim. He arrived on 14 December! There was so much we wanted to hear, that during the days that followed we could hardly stop talking.

Nicky's Story

In Chapter 14 I told the story of Nicky's arrest on 15 October 1944. He now went on to tell us about his detention in Mauthausen concentration camp, where on arrival he first underwent a forty-eight hour interrogation by Otto Skorzeny. He said maybe he should feel flattered that the 'famous' Mussolini abductor Skorzeny was chosen to kidnap him. Nicky later wrote about his experiences for a friend:

I was furious, but tried hard to keep my temper under control. I sweated in my efforts not to give answers that would incriminate others, and I think I was successful, with one exception. When Skorzeny asked whether my father knew about his ADC Tost's activities I said, 'Of course not.' I realized that Skorzeny must know that Tost had worked with Ilona and me in the Underground. After the War I heard that Tost had already been captured before my interrogation, and had shot himself before the Germans could torture him. I was glad that I had not hurt my good friend.

When Skorzeny was angry – and I often succeeded in provoking him – he stood up and glared down at me. He was at least 6 foot 3 inches, good looking, with a long scar down one cheek. My personal correspondence from the time when I was Minister in Brazil had obviously come into his possession – most of which was unfavourable to the Nazis. He seemed already to know the answers to his unexpected questions.

'Why are you anti-German?' he asked.

'Because I am pro-Hungarian,' I replied.

'Why have you helped Jews?'

'Because I am a just man,' I said.

He shouted, 'Horthy *Schwein*, you will be hanged!'

I don't know how he put up with me for forty-eight hours, but he did. From the way he dealt with me, I could see even then what a clever man he was: how else could he have escaped his well-deserved fate and get acquitted at the Nürnberg Trials? Finally I was allowed to return to my cell, and that was the last I saw of him.

I was alone in cell 18 of no.1 prison, which was above the gas chambers. I had no running water, and slept on several slats mounted on four wooden feet. The only other furniture was a small, backless stool. High in the wall was a tiny window, through which I could see by moving the 'bed', putting the stool on the slats, and standing on it. I knew the prison floor plan and routine from Anti Szapáry. Had I been caught spying I would have been severely punished, but curiosity got the better of me at least four times. The first time was when I heard a sound in the courtyard outside, which sounded like cocktails being shaken. I saw tin canisters – just as Anti had described them – filled, I knew, with human ashes from the crematorium. They were being shaken into a cart for use as fertilizer. The second time I looked was at night, when I heard a strange thumping noise. I watched for the guard to pass my door, then stood up on my 'watch-tower' and saw a lot of people running in place to keep warm in the snow. There, in the bitter cold, they were stark naked. Then they were ushered into the chambers below ... from where nobody ever came out.

The third time I peeped, I saw a group of distinguished-looking older men, some with grey hair and moustaches, being harangued by the commander of the camp, a very good-looking but unpleasant man of about forty. The old men stood at attention and wore striped prison garments similar to pyjamas. I climbed down from my perch and soon heard nothing more. My last view was of the pyjamas in heaps where the prisoners had dropped them before being marched naked into the gas chambers. The pyjamas were washed and given to other prisoners in the camp. We, in the solitary prison cells, wore our own clothes, and they became pretty shabby, but we were given changes of socks, underwear and shirts, which often bore a dead man's monogram.

People who are locked up acquire a sixth sense – hearing and other sensations are heightened. One day I was sure that we had an important new addition, as someone was allowed to pace the corridor for exercise. I heard the man telling a story to the guard about having been an amateur boxer in his younger days, and recounting one of his big fights. I knew the story – and realized that I also knew the voice! The narrator could only be Prime Minister Miklós Kállay!

Next time I heard his footsteps approaching and heard the guard go away, as he was passing my door I said, 'Mica!' (Miklós Kállay's nickname) in a stage whisper. He walked the other way, returned and asked, 'Who is that?' I whispered, 'Nicky'. He again walked to the other end of the short corridor and came back. 'Horthy?' he asked. I said, 'Yes.' When he came back again he said, 'Your parents are well.' He walked again, then: 'In Weilheim, German custody.' That was all.

Shortly after this, one of Kállay's sons, András, was brought there too, and was put in barracks on the other side of the camp. Father and son were able to meet once a week and young Kállay brought his father all the latest news. Thousands of prisoners were confined in these barracks, not all for political reasons. Newly captured thieves reported what was going on outside and smuggled in radios so as to keep informed. Short, whispered conversations with Mica kept me informed of the war's progress.

Not long after Mica's arrival we were both taken in a curtained car to Dachau with a fellow prisoner, young Badoglio, son of the Italian ex-Premier. We reached Dachau as the sun was setting. Prisoners were usually executed at twilight, and Kállay said he thought we would be hanged – so did I! The place was grim. We discovered that the reason for our move was greater security against our rescue by the ever-advancing Allies. All the important prisoners were brought there for the same reason.

Nicky thought Dachau was a holiday after Mauthausen, as only the outside of the prison was locked and inside the prisoners could communicate. He said it was like a country club with old friends. They were all introducing each other in English, French and German: Léon Blum, the first socialist premier of France; Russian Minister Molotov's son; Hjalmar Schacht, once Hitler's finance minister; Kurt von Schuschnigg the Austrian chancellor, with his wife and little daughter; the celebrated Lutheran pastor Martin Niemöller (a vocal anti-Nazi); the Catholic bishop Neuhauser; and many others.

He had a toilet in his cell, and the food was better and more plentiful than at Mauthausen. But he was only there a few days before they all were ordered to get into big buses. 'Please, let me stay in Dachau!' he pleaded; but by Himmler's order they were taken to the village of Niederdorf in the Italian Tyrol. Here, to their delight, they were given feather beds to sleep on. The Italian partisans sent word to the German guards that they would all be executed if the prisoners were harmed. The guards then disappeared and they were free! They later heard – just as we did in Hirschberg – that the orders had been to keep them from the enemy as long as they could and then execute them. All this only makes sense if one knows that almost until the end the Germans thought that they still had a chance of winning the war.

The freed prisoners were all so weak that they could hardly walk; but supporting each other they climbed a nearby hill to a small church, where they gave thanks to God that they were alive. The weather was clear, the mountains beautiful, and it was a moving experience to hear an ecumenical mass and sermon by the Lutheran pastor and the Catholic bishop, who had been co-prisoners. The Dachau group was made up of twenty-two nationalities; Nicky sat next to Molotov's son – and thought this was a sign that there would be real peace amongst all nations!

It was a bitter awakening when, after the Americans took over and they were taken to Naples, the Hungarians, Germans, Austrians and Scandinavians were separated from the rest and taken to Capri, to a charming but guarded hotel, and were actually prisoners.

The commander of the area was the English Lieutenant General William Duthie Morgan, who had replaced General Alexander as head of Allied Operations in the Mediterranean. He had been the British military attaché in Budapest between 1929 and 1931, and was very good to the Hungarians. He arranged for them to be able to leave Capri, and told Nicky that he could go to Rome if he liked. So Nicky and Dezső Ónódy, his former secretary, moved into the bombed-out Hungarian Legation in Rome, and were soon joined by his former valet Imre and his wife – who had moved to Brazil and were now travelling with Brazilian papers.

When Nicky was in his teens he'd had a tutor, Father Luttor, who was now attached to the Vatican, and through him the Pope sent word that he wanted to see Nicky. Nicky was received and granted a long audience alone with His Holiness. The Pope asked about his parents and gave him some money. Nicky was overcome by his kindness.

Later, in August, an American army captain named Donovan was sent from Germany to take Nicky to Nürnberg, to 'help clear up the matters relating to his father'. This was the first news he'd had of his family. Nicky relates:

> A Hungarian-American officer had petitioned the Court at Nürnberg to turn father over to Tito, who had tried to have him extradited to Yugoslavia. But our old friend Alexander Páthy the lawyer – by that time a colonel in the United Sates army – came to Nürnberg to help my father. By this time the whole Páthy family had gone to America and became citizens. Alexander suggested that the Court send for the Regent's son and question him before making a decision.
>
> When I arrived, I was not allowed to see Father for three days, and was questioned by ever-higher American officials until I was finally taken to see the chief prosecutor, US Supreme Court Justice, Robert H. Jackson. He received me very cordially, and asked me about my father and about conditions in my country prior to the Nazi takeover. After this examination, the door opened and in walked Father!
>
> We had not seen each other for a year, and had heard very little news of each other. He was much thinner than he had been, but well. I think it is hardly necessary to say how moved we both were by the meeting.

And now Nicky was here with us in Weilheim – looking well, and telling us his hair-raising story.

* * * * *

More letters arrived from my parents and sisters! Not by post but through people who were travelling. It was wonderful to be in touch. They did not complain, but one could read between the lines that their situation was very difficult. The Royal Palace was burnt out and in ruins, so even the family paintings must have been destroyed –

something one could never replace. But surely it was lives that mattered now. They said that nothing remained of our rooms. It was not even painful, as it was all totally unrecognisable; only the Holy Crown of Saint Stephen still stood upright, atop the ruins of the Royal Palace.

Sya wrote every time someone left Hungary, which was quite often. So much love emanated from these letters, which were very long, telling me news of everyone she thought we would be interested to hear about. They had not seen any meat for about a year – with one exception, during the siege, when they ate the meat from dead horses that had been accidentally shot and left where they lay. Nothing brought the siege home to me more than the story of my nanny Suci going out with a knife to cut bits off a dead horse. Suci, who was a hygiene fanatic!

On 17 December the doorbell rang and Mama went to open it. There stood an American officer by the name of Trager, who said, 'I've brought you a Christmas present.' When he saw Mama's look of astonishment he said, 'It is there is the car.' Mama went out to the car and found Miklóspapa sitting in it! It was a wonderful way of bringing him back to the family. At last we were all together again – but alas, forever without Pista.

Our joy was overwhelming. The whole afternoon, together with Nicky, we listened to Papa's stories about how he was taken from one place to another. Once, they were staying in great comfort in the lovely little Lesbioles castle in Belgium, where he could play the piano and play billiards or chess with the German ambassador Franz von Papen and the former Minister Daré, who had fallen out of favour with Hitler as early as 1942. Papa wrote in his memoirs:

> We had no idea why we had been brought to this place. Three years later the answer was given to us. One of my friends, who now lives in Belgium, wrote to me that he had been invited to Lesbioles. During his visit, the owner of the castle had told him that Lesbioles had been occupied by the Americans as they advanced. After they had moved on eastward he was allowed to return, and found everything in perfect order except that, to his surprise, he found that in every room, on the ceilings above the lamps, plaster rosettes had been placed. He had them removed and in each one they discovered a microphone. It is obvious therefore that it was known to the Americans that I was friendly with von Papen, and that it was hoped that, in discussing various matters openly, they might be able to find out something interesting. To make the presence of von

Papen less obvious, a third person had been included –
quite a clever scheme.

From Lesbioles he was taken to a dirty detention camp, where war
criminals were assembled. Although they reassured him that he was not
a prisoner of war but merely in protective custody, he was treated like
the other prisoners. It was very cold, and his butler Miklós was taken
away from him. Poor Miklós, who had never even been a soldier, was
kept in prison for many months. Papa was then moved to a villa in
Wiesbaden and then to Oberursel, near Frankfurt, where everyone in
the camp was expected to perform menial tasks irrespective of their
rank or age. But, in spite of his protests, a naval officer and later a vice-
admiral kindly insisted on doing Papa's share for him.

In his autobiography, Miklóspapa tells in detail the story of this
eight-month ordeal, at the end of which he arrived in the witness-wing
in Nürnberg. Here the cell-doors were open during the day and they
could go for a two-hour walk every day. And here too fellow detainees
helped him: he did not have to join the long queue for food, as the
German co-witnesses always arranged for him to be served first.

31 December: the last day of this amazing year. Nicky and I were
invited as guests of Major Stone for a New Year's Eve party with the
American officers. The venue was Schloss Hirschberg! Was I dreaming?
I was thinking back to 31 December of last year – being in this same
place, but with the SS barracks outside and the Gestapo inside, Nicky
at Mauthausen, and none of us knowing how it would all end. Now I
was surrounded by American officers and Nicky was here with us. I
could not have imagined this possible. If only next year we could be
together with my family too! Was I asking too much?

1946. Another year began in post-war Germany. I was trying to arrange
for us all to become official refugees, so that we could be eligible for
supplies from UNRRA. Miklóspapa and Nicky were entitled to get
supplies at the American Post-Exchange, but we came into a different
category. We had survived until now, so I was confident that we could
carry on until change could come. But for the sake of Mama's health it
needed to come soon.

I was grateful to be part of such a harmonious family. In spite of
losing all our possessions nobody grumbled, or felt self-pity, and in
spite of the uncertain, bleak future we were happy because we were
together.

It was now that I really grew to know my father-in-law. Mama's
attitude did not surprise me; I knew that she would always adapt

herself. She cooked and stood in line for shopping as if she had always done so. But Papa was a revelation; he never complained, was not sorry for himself and always tried to help – even doing the beds. He refused to be drawn into politics. His concern was only for what was right for his country, and he always urged the Hungarians who wrote to him – mainly the generals whose large correspondence I have kept – to avoid dissention and keep harmoniously united until the time when we could return home. But in spite of that, sadly much of their correspondence contained little but accusations against each other, which I suppose is a post-war, refugee disease.

On 7 January we at last got our first 'displaced persons' (DP) rations – by the grace of God and by the goodwill of the military government! But who were displaced persons if not us? I did not want to be presumptuous, but I thought that we deserved it. We needed more calories for a five-year-old child and three old people – Papa at seventy-eight, Uncle sixty-nine, and Mama sixty-five. And we who worked: Ila, Margit, Gizi and myself, were also in need of it.

When the American army finally moved out of Schloss Hirschberg, and with the permission of the owners, the Hungarian Captain Binder arranged a musical evening there. He found a Hungarian gypsy band from somewhere, and besides our faithful Hungarian officers, many Germans and other guests had also been invited. It was a sad, nostalgic pleasure to listen to gypsy music. A White Russian sat next to me, and seeing my sad expression commented that I was just starting, but he had been feeling this way for thirty years. I was shattered, and told myself that Hungary could not possibly be under Soviet rule for thirty years ... . It was forty-five years before the Russian troops finally left Hungary, leaving behind them a country economically and morally in ruins.

One day I noticed some strange men walking past the front of the house and we later heard that some men from Yugoslavia had appeared in Weilheim, threatening to shoot the Regent. I went to the CIC (a branch of the American Secret Service) who – I was told – were looking after Papa's safety, but found nobody there. I finally got in touch with the man in charge, de Pachter and expressed my concern. The next day four dubious-looking men walked into our garden and said that they wanted to borrow some books from the Regent. This was too much for me, and I shot off again to the CIC, where I found de Pachter. He reassured me that he was already dealing with it. I do not know what he did, but the men disappeared from Weilheim and – thank God – we never saw them again.

I had another long letter from Sya, who was delighted with her new baby. With Józsi working on the milk production and delivery to Budapest with two vans, they had an income and food from the country, but she was afraid it could not last long. She told me not to long for home: 'stay far away and keep your lovely memories'. She was disappointed in people and with everything that was going on. Aunt Gizi Apor and Sarolta Lukács – who were still working at the Red Cross – had received my letters. My sister said that Sarolta Lukács cried when she saw my writing, and I was deeply touched by her answer, so full of love: 'My dear Ily, I cannot say what sincere, great joy the first positive news of you has caused us. I can only say that this big 'work-family' of yours, those who know you, were thinking of you and yours every minute. Soldiers, the disabled, came to ask where and how is Sister Ily – sometimes also asking that when there is an opportunity I should transmit their gratitude for 'her devoted nursing'.

Miklóspapa had finally started to write his memoirs, which I typed out for him. I had asked him many times to start writing, arguing that we would not be able to verify certain events when he was no longer with us. He wrote it all by hand, in Hungarian and in German. I was very pleased, although he was determined not to have them published in his lifetime. I have still got many of the handwritten drafts.

Eric and Elsbeth Mayer asked me to help them at the International Red Cross in Munich, which was my first proper working experience. I went regularly for three days every week. It became a routine that I went to Munich on Monday mornings, stayed at the IRC house, then came back to Weilheim on Thursday evenings. Mostly I travelled by train, which was all right if one was at the station two hours before the train left. Otherwise one stood tightly pressed together with people, which was very unpleasant.

The IRC house in Munich was burgled several times – while all of us were in the building. A lot of cigarettes, etc. were stolen from the big store in the cellar, by someone sawing through the door. I took Eric Mayer to see the chief of the CIC, Captain Dinehart – who had been in Capri with Nicky – to ask for help, but we were told that we had to ask the German authorities to deal with it, as the International Red Cross was not under American jurisdiction.

The Germans arranged for two trained German shepherd dogs to be hired from the Police to guard the house. It was fascinating, when the policemen brought them along and introduced us to them. All six inhabitants of the house had to sit down while the two dogs were brought in and taken round to smell us, one by one. We were told that from then on the dogs would let no one except us come in at the gate. They stayed with us only at night, as that was the time the burglars used to come. The dogs came early in the afternoon – by themselves – walking down the street and waiting to be let in at the gate. Once inside, if anyone approached the gate they would rush at them snarling and barking ferociously. They were very frightening. When I approached from the street for the first time they rushed towards the gate growling, but when they got there and saw me they sat down. I admit that I was terrified to open the gate. What if they did not recognize me? But they looked quietly at me and did not move. In the morning we would open the gate for them and they made their own way home. Quite amazing! This did not deter the thieves, who tried to poison the dogs at night; but eventually we had so much police presence that the thieves stayed away.

12 September was a tragic day for us: our helping hands, Miklós, Józsi, Margit and Gizi, came to tell us of their decision to go back to Hungary as soon as possible. We naturally understood, as they all had families at home. We had expected it and were actually surprised that they had not taken this decision sooner. They lived here like we did; we tried to give them whatever they needed, but we could not pay them salaries. Mama's maid Margit was the only one who could not quite make up her mind, so it was Miklós, Józsi and Gizi who left first, and it was a sad goodbye when I saw them onto a Hungarian hospital-train at the station in Munich. They did not know what awaited them at home, besides the happy reunion with their families.

By November 1946 the 'Family Council' – Papa, Mama, Uncle Eugene and I – had decided to try to leave Germany, which was easier said than done. The main reason for this decision was Magdamama's health, which was deteriorating in the cold climate. We also heard with some dismay that at the end of this year the aid from UNRRA would cease, which would cut off our main food supply. We were now heading for another cold winter in Bavaria, with serious difficulty in acquiring heating material. Where should we try to go? Which country would accept us?

From the money we had received from the Holy Father and from generous friends, we had been able to put aside enough for a journey and an initial stay somewhere. I also had with me a cheque, which I had found at home in the Palace after my husband's death, for ten thousand Swiss Francs. I did not know, but hoped that this cheque, signed by him, was still valid. But the most important factor was news we received from the United States that John Flournoy Montgomery – who had been the American minister in Hungary from 1933 until 1941 – was planning to organize a fund in the United States that would provide for our stay, wherever it might be.

We decided that I should try to go to Switzerland and consult with the various Legations or Embassies. My parents-in-law spoke Italian well, and Italy was where they both would have liked to go, but the

Communist Party in Italy was very strong – the same as in France. And, at the moment, for most of the Allies the Soviet Union was the great friend with whom they had won the war. There would have probably been opposition to the 'Enemy Number One' of Communism – as some referred to Miklóspapa – settling in any of their countries.

Our main adviser and 'guardian angel' in all this was the head of the CIC, our friend Captain Alan Dinehart. He instructed me on every step of the procedure. First he accompanied me to the Swiss Consulate, where I got my visa. He then explained to me the whole journey in detail: 'You cross the border to Austria with just a local border-pass, which only entitles you to go 7 kilometres inside Austria. But you go straight on to Innsbruck, where you go to the French authorities.'

He gave me the names of three people to try to see. 'Don't tell them that you don't live in Austria! Get a permit to go to Switzerland and take the Arlberg Express to Zürich. Do exactly the same on your way back.' He then asked his friend, the racing driver Hans Stuck – who often went to Austria – to drive me to Innsbruck, and told me that in Bern I could stay with his friends the Haseltines, whom I had met.

I did not hesitate for a minute; full of hope, I embarked on my illegal journey as if it were the most natural thing in the world.

On the morning of 25 November, Hans Stuck and his companion Christina came to pick me up and we drove to Garmisch-Partenkirchen to get a border-pass. The three of us then drove to the border at Griesen-Schanz and over to Austria – to Ehrwald, then Innsbruck. They dropped me at the home of the Romeisers, a Hungarian couple with whom I had already corresponded. They were very apologetic, as they could only accommodate me in a space like a cupboard, into which a narrow bed had been pushed, but I thought it was perfect, as long as I could lie down. When I told them that I was now going to the French authorities to request a permit for Switzerland, in order to be able to leave the next day, they laughed and said it would take at least two weeks to get such a permit.

Never mind, off I went! When I got to the right office it was full of people asking for permits. I sat down on a chair behind the crowd, and I heard the officer announce that everybody must leave the room and come in one by one. I sat quietly until everyone left and then slowly got up to follow them. The officer, whose name was Flammand, stopped me and asked what I had come for. I went up to his desk and told him that I wanted to go to Switzerland tomorrow. He gave me a form to fill in, saying that I could come back in two weeks. I looked at him pleadingly and asked whether I could come in tomorrow, 'just to ask about it'. He said I could do that. Women have a definite advantage with Frenchmen!

Next morning I went back to Flammand's office. Without a word he handed me my travel-permit. The Romeisers could not believe it – nor could I. It was now too late for today's train, but the next morning we bought my ticket and at 3.42 p.m. the Arlberg Express left for Zürich with me on it. Everything had happened exactly as Alan Dinehart had told me. It felt quite unreal.

I arrived at Zürich that evening. As I left the station, I saw a shop window full of delicious looking chocolates; I dropped my two bags and gaped at all this wealth. A man beside me did just the same – we looked at each other and laughed!

All the time I was in Switzerland I felt inebriated just looking at shop windows, which I thought were incredibly lovely. I stayed with old friends, who made it possible for me to telephone Budapest and talk to my family. After two years it was just fantastic to speak to Myro, Gyuri and Sya. The next evening we did it again, and also called Slovakia to speak to Papi and Ellamami, who were in Elefánt. It was like heaven.

I went to the bank about Pista's cheque and was very disappointed to hear that it was blocked. (It was released two years later, when we travelled through Switzerland on our way to Portugal.)

On the fourth day I went to Bern, where the first Legation I visited in order to make inquiries was the Portuguese. This was only because the Minister, Sousa Mendes, was a friend of Nicky's from Brazil; we actually did not want to go to Portugal, as we did not speak the language. The minister was very friendly and told me that he would have to ask his government about my request. I told him that we would not live on the State, but would receive subsistence from the United States. He said it would take four days to get a reply, and asked that in the meantime I would not to go to any other legation or embassy. I could easily wait four days in this paradise, and promised to come back for the answer.

When I went back to the Portuguese Legation I thought I was dreaming when the Minister told me that we had been granted diplomatic visas for the whole family – including Nanny Ila – and that we were most welcome to settle there.

Portugal? It was curious how our life was apparently set on a course, almost by itself; all I had to do was to go along and accept without argument whatever came my way. Now we would have to start working on this: How to travel? Through which countries? What was the cost of living in Portugal? So many questions.

On 19 December I returned on the Arlberg Express. In Innsbruck, arriving after midnight – nine hours late – I found Hans Stuck and Christina waiting. We drove straight to the border, where I crossed back to Bavaria on the same 7-kilometre permit. We spent the night at

Grainau, and next morning Alan Dinehart picked me up in a jeep and drove me to Weilheim. I was utterly exhausted, slept all morning and then spent all afternoon and evening telling my story to my parents-in-law. When I told them that we were going to Portugal they were very surprised, and delighted when they saw the diplomatic visas.

1947 saw a bitterly cold January. Alan Dinehart got us coal for our heating. How can one ever thank such kindness? My hands were very sore from handling and shovelling the coal, cleaning the stove and from exposure to the open flames, but I did not mind, as long as we were able to heat the house. Magdamama was in bed on and off, which was worrying. Ila and I spent a lot of time knitting, especially in the evenings when we chatted about the old days when there were no electricity restrictions. We only had one small candle.

One day Mama came to me in despair, as we only had fuel for about another week – what could we do? Without a blink, I told her that I had already ordered some wood, although I was not quite sure when it would arrive (this was a blatant lie). She was so relieved that I felt I had done the right thing, but now I had to seriously start looking for wood.

Two days later a big truck stopped in front of the house and the driver started unloading wood! Mama came running to me: 'Ily, your wood has arrived!' I went outside and, so that she did not hear, I asked the driver why he was unloading wood here. He showed me a piece of paper, on which our name and address were quite clearly written. 'But who sent you?' I asked. He explained that there were some Jesuit priests up in the mountains who thought that we might be in need of wood this cold winter, and they had plenty. I was stunned, and thanked God with all my being for having rewarded my charitable lie.

Not long afterwards this happened again. We had no UNRRA supply now, and things like sugar were difficult to come by. Mama was worried about what we would give Papa with his coffee, and István was growing and he too needed sugar. I told her not to worry as I had already found a place to get hold of some. It was another lie. That same day, a few hours later, the postman brought a big parcel containing a sack of sugar. It had been sent by our friend Inge Hesse, God bless her. I did not tell Mama that this was not my supply, so that she would believe me again next time.

Ilona Andrássy, my former nursing companion, managed to leave Hungary and go to Vaduz in Lichtenstein for three weeks to visit her parents and brother Géza. She used this opportunity to write a very long letter to me about the situation in Hungary. After the siege she and Alice Cziráky had stayed together. They had no furniture but they got two beds from the Red Cross and they still slept on the mattresses I had given them. She was satisfied with what she had got and was already used to this new life, because after two months of siege – compared to which Dante's hell was child's play – one was just glad to be alive. The worst thing was that after the siege, the Russians picked up men in the street at random because they had declared more prisoners of war than there really were, and this was how they filled up the gaps. Those who were lucky escaped after a few days of bridge building without food, but many never came back. In those days, Ilona wrote, only the women dared go out in the streets: 'Thanks to God nothing happened to us, as the Russians liked our uniforms. They said, "Madarska sestra, roboti, roboti"(Hungarian girls, working, working).' So gradually all the women started wearing napkins or towels, and all kinds of funny armbands.

This was only a small part of her letter, which was very descriptive but very depressing for me to read. I was sad that we could not meet – it was actually to be forty years before we met again.

I was invited to stay in Baden-Baden by Christian de Charmasse – a friend from the old days – who was then the Governor of the French Zone of West Germany. I travelled by train and, after a very restful few days, left to return home. I was happily sitting in the train when at Bruchsal station it stopped. We were informed that the train would not go any further; however, we could continue on the train that was stationed next to ours. Everybody hurried onto this train – which was already tightly packed with passengers. I felt that there was no hope and stood quietly wondering what to do next. Then a woman called to me through an open window: 'You, if you can climb in through the window, there is a standing space here!' I rushed to the window, handed her my suitcase and then tried to climb. Have you ever tried to get up through the window of a train? It seemed impossible – people came up to help. They pushed me whilst the woman pulled me, and eventually I reached the standing space. In Heidelberg, friends were waiting for me; and you can imagine their surprise when they saw me climbing out of the train through a window – which incidentally was easier than getting in.

The next morning, back in Weilheim, I saw an article in the paper about a woman who had tried to climb in through a train window. A man had helped her, but when she was half inside he had taken off both her shoes and run away with them! If I had read this before, I would never have dared take the risk.

One day soon after this, Military Governor Paul Paynick asked very seriously if he could have a private conversation with me. He wanted to know whether we trusted Ervin Póka, who had been working for two years for the military government. The reason for his question was that Póka was the prosecutor of all the different nationalities in the region – and that they had had many different nationalities up for trial but never a Hungarian. Póka being a Hungarian, Paul Paynick wanted to know whether I thought that he could have been instrumental in not bringing any Hungarians to trial. I told him that from my knowledge of Póka (and I knew him quite well), I was convinced that he would never do such a thing; on the contrary, he would be more likely to prosecute any guilty Hungarian because he was a Hungarian himself. Paynick then asked me whether it was because Hungarians were so honest or so clever that they were never caught? I said that they were probably both, honest and clever. We laughed, and Paul was happy with my answer.

At the end of August I had to say goodbye to Eric and Elsbeth Mayer, who were leaving Germany for good. I was really sad to say farewell to this couple, who had been such a sustaining part of two years of my life here, and with whom I shared so many memories.

On the morning of 3 September, István went to school for the first time. This was a big turning point in his life. If he was anything like his father's family, then he would surely be good at his studies. Ila and I accompanied him to school; he looked so different with his school bag on his back. Two hours later we picked him up. He was clearly affected and awestruck; he said he had a bad taste in his mouth and asked for water. He did not eat his lunch and could not eat all day, but did not complain. The next day I took him to school and picked him up on my bike. He proudly announced that things were getting serious, as he had to answer a question and was called to go to the blackboard, which he enjoyed.

In Hungary they had just had the general elections and the news was very alarming. By fraudulent means the Communist Party had won the elections. In every future election the Communists won 90 per cent of the votes. Mátyás Rákosi's reign of terror had started.

Most of the Hungarian refugees in the camp wanted to emigrate overseas. The trouble was that Hungarians were classified as 'ex-enemies', and at the moment the only country that would accept them was Argentina. Because of this my friends all wanted to learn Spanish as quickly as possible, and they discovered a Spanish lady in Weilheim, Señora Maria Fritz, who was prepared to give lessons. So I thought, why not? It is always good to know another language, and with my knowledge of French and Italian, another Latin language could not be very difficult. I joined the Spanish lessons once a week, which were hilarious. For some of my compatriots it was not easy to learn a foreign pronunciation, and when they spoke it sounded like Hungarian. We had great fun and laughed a lot.

That year we were sent many parcels by mail, real lifesavers! The largest came from Madeleine Apponyi, an American who had been married Count Antóny Apponyi and whom we had known well in Hungary; she had moved to Cuba at the start of the war. We also received gifts from Mrs Olive Pell, the wife of the former US ambassador in Hungary; but the most frequent parcels came from Consul Lutz in Switzerland. God bless them all.

On 24 December, Consul General Sam Woods, the American Consul in Zürich, arrived straight from Switzerland laden with parcels, just like Father Christmas. John Montgomery had originally introduced him to us, and he had become a good friend who often called on us on his way from Zürich to Starenberg. Our faithful Hungarian officers, Iványi and Halmai, came to help decorate the tree and had fun with István. We even had a turkey that Christmas.

1948. We had a happy celebration for István's seventh birthday on 17 January, with an excellent lunch. He asked for tomato beans, which was very touching for me, as he did not know that it happened to be his father's favourite dish.

One particularly outstanding event that month was the visit of Dr Ruben Hecht, a Swiss Zionist living in Israel. He was in Germany to recruit Jews for Israel, and came to thank the Regent for what he did for the Jewish people in Hungary, especially for supporting the plan of the Jews' emigration from Hungary to Israel. He said that he knew it was not the Regent's fault that the plan did not succeed. After this visit, seeing how we lived, he offered to help me to get our visas to Switzerland. He came back to see us a few times and I also met him later in Switzerland. I found him to be a real friend, with whom I corresponded until his death in 1993. I will always be grateful for his help to us at this time.

I got some surprising news one day from a Hungarian who was working in a garage in Aham: he had found my name inside one of the cars! This turned out to be my Wanderer, which the Germans had taken away from the Palace in Budapest. Not really believing that such a miracle would happen, I immediately made an application to get my car back, and took it personally to the Military Government Headquarters.

After talking it over and getting a lot of help from Paul Paynick, I handed in our exit-permit requests to the military government. Many of our friends were emigrating. It made me feel sad to think that we would all be dispersed over the globe and might never meet again. We could come together again only if one day we returned to Hungary, which at that moment was difficult to imagine. How right I was. Looking at what has happened to those dear friends now, fifty years later: Ervin Póka,

János Iványi and Colonel Godányi – all of them died in faraway countries, and we know nothing about the families they left behind.

Near the end of February, Military Governor Captain Dunn came officially to tell Papa to be at home on 1 March, because someone was coming from Nürnberg to question him. Then we received a telegram saying that Papa should be in Nürnberg on 2 March. I went immediately to Garmisch to talk to Tom Mullen at the CIC and asked him to ring Nürnberg and get us some information about this summons. All I could find out was that Papa would appear as a witness.

Back in Weilheim, Captain Dunn told me that a car would be sent for Papa, and I asked him to enquire whether Papa's nurse, his daughter-in-law, could accompany him to Nürnberg. The answer was positive, which was a great relief for Mama.

19

The Admiral Testifies at Nürnberg
Our Last Year in Germany

On 2 March 1948 a man called Wulf arrived with a car and drove Miklóspapa and me to Nürnberg, where we had dinner with Chief Prosecutor Robert Kempner (Director, Political Ministries Division), and three other gentlemen at the Grand Hotel. They were very forthcoming, and told us that Papa had been asked to come here in order to appear as a witness in two day's time at the trial of Edmund Veesenmayer. A Mr Caming would come and talk things over with us first. We were then taken by car to the home of Count Faber – 15 kilometres from Nürnberg – where we would be staying for a few days. I spent that evening reading through the many papers that I brought with me, and looking up dates, etc.

Next day we made some notes with Papa to refresh his memory. Mr Caming, who would be questioning Papa for the prosecution at the hearing, came with his secretary in the afternoon and stayed until early evening, explaining to Papa what he would be asked at the trial.

It was interesting to read for the first time about Veesenmayer's career. Since 1932 he had been a member of the National Socialist German Workers' Party, and a member of the SS since 1934. From 1938 he was Undersecretary of State for special assignments at the Foreign Office. There were reports of Veesenmayer's key role in the 'take over' of Austria, the Sudetenland, Slovakia and Croatia. His special political assignments were: Italy (1940), Croatia, Serbia (1941), France, Spain, Ireland (1942) Slovakia, and Hungary (1943). He won the lasting confidence of Foreign Minister Ribbentrop, and 'became the spectre of Nazi aggression'. He received continual approbation from Ribbentrop, Keppler, Himmler and Hitler.

In Caming's papers there was also mention of a telegram from Veesenmayer to Ribbentrop, on 20 March 1944, which gave 'ample

evidence of the extreme pressure used on the aged Hungarian leader.'
[Ex. C-438]

At ten o'clock that evening the secretary came back alone, and while
I translated Papa's text into German he wrote it down. We worked on
until four o'clock the next morning, when I finally went to bed very
tired but somewhat reassured.

The next morning we were driven to Nürnberg, where I spent time
with Papa reading through his text and talking about it. I was amazed
at his clarity of mind. At eleven thirty Papa was taken into the
Courtroom, which was completely full. They told me that lately the
Courtroom had been mostly empty, as people had lost interest in the
Nürnberg proceedings, but when it was announced that Admiral
Horthy would appear as a witness the courtroom became filled to
capacity.

There was no place left for me and I was standing outside feeling very
disappointed, when Mr Kempner arrived and said that I had helped so
much that I ought to be present, and would I follow him? I walked
through the packed courtroom behind him, and he led me into the
prosecution box and put a chair for me behind his own. Although I was
happy to be present at the hearing, I felt a little bit awkward sitting in
the prosecution box.

All the accused were present in the courtroom. According to the
protocol of the Military Tribunal (Nr. IV, Fall XI) 4 March 1948, which
is in my possession: 'Three witnesses, who were the most prominent
observers, testified before this Tribunal: The Regent of Hungary,
Admiral Miklós Horthy; the lawyer Dr Dezső Kastner of the Jewish
community; and the higher SS and Police Leader in Hungary, SS
General Otto Winkelmann.'

After Papa was sworn in, he had to state his name, present address
and age – he said he would be eighty in June. He was then asked to
relate the story of the German occupation of Hungary and to state why,
in his view, Veesenmayer was the highest German authority in Hungary.
He told the Court how the pro-German government was formed
because Hitler had promised him the withdrawal of German troops
once there was a government in place that he could trust.

In answer to a further question, he testified to the power of
Veesenmayer as follows:

> Question: 'Admiral Horthy, what according to your
> judgement was the position that Veesenmayer held in
> Hungary?'
> Answer: 'It was the supreme German post in
> Hungary ... this would naturally be an ambassador or
> a minister in any foreign country, but here it was

emphasized by the title of plenipotentiary, which was
added to it.'

Question: 'What reasons did you have to regard
Veesenmayer as the highest German functionary in
Hungary?'

Answer: 'He was actually the only one whom I had
to deal with. If I had anything to discuss or anything to
ask in connection with the Third Reich, of course I had
to ask Veesenmayer to call me.'

Question: 'During the period, Admiral Horthy, that
you knew the two gentlemen in Hungary, General
Winkelmann and the accused Veesenmayer, which one
in your opinion at that time did you consider as the
superior?'

Answer: 'Plenipotentiary Veesenmayer, absolutely.'

He was asked a series of questions to which he gave clear answers. Some
times he asked for the question to be repeated, as he was not used to the
earphones. At 12.15 they had a break for lunch and started again at
1.30.

After the prosecution hearing was finished, Veesenmayer's defence
then began his questioning, somewhat over-politely, constantly
addressing Papa as 'Durchlaucht' (Serene Highness). After the hearing
had been going on for some time I had the feeling that Papa was getting
tired, so I tapped Kempner on the shoulder and asked him to request a
recess. Kempner immediately announced over the loudspeaker that the
nurse and daughter-in-law of the admiral had asked for a recess after
forty-five minutes. Judge Maguire immediately announced an
adjournment, during which he invited us to his room for a drink. He
was very friendly.

Whilst we were there I was called out by the son of Franz von Papen
– one of the accused. He was a lawyer and had taken over his father's
defence. He himself had never been a Party member or a Nazi. He told
me that he was sitting next to Veesenmayer's lawyer and had therefore
been able to read the notes that Veesenmayer sent to his defence, telling
him that he should start by being very polite to the admiral, calling him
Serene Highness; flattering him so that he would become well disposed
towards him. I thanked Franz von Papen Jr for his kindness and warned
Papa not to be misled by such tactics.

When we returned to the courtroom there then followed some rather
strange questions from the defence lawyer Dr Dötzer, who obviously
hoped to confuse the witness. Not only do I have the minutes of the
interrogation, but I also remember quite clearly when he asked, 'Did

Your Serene Highness personally offer Minister Veesenmayer landed property, to keep him in Hungary because of his friendly conduct towards Hungary?'

The Regent's answer to this absurd question was clear-cut and emphatic: 'I? To him? Never! Never! On the contrary!'

There was a lot of laughter in the courtroom. And Papa went on, 'But I know, I think it was Himmler who demanded through intermediaries some land with a Schloss.'[54]

'This is not what I wanted to get at …' Veesenmayer's defence council changed the subject, but he was defeated and obviously angry.

Later, I asked Dr Kempner why the defence had asked such a stupid question, and it seemed apparent that it was another trick to make Papa's relation with Veesenmayer appear friendly. If Papa had answered with just a simple 'no', maybe the likelihood of such an idea would have prevailed, and not seemed impossible.

As the hearing went on, the admiral several times answered that he could not remember certain things, and emphasized that he was under oath and due to his age his memory now was not so good. Many years later, in 1987, Dr Robert Kempner wrote in a letter to the historian Péter Gosztonyi that: 'As a prosecution witness Admiral Horthy made a very good impression on the jury.'

It was a relief when we finally left the courtroom and were driven back to the Faber's home. It had all gone rather well, and we spent the next day relaxing in the sun.

At the end of his trial in Nürnberg, Veesenmayer was sentenced to twenty years imprisonment. I never found out why he was freed soon afterwards.

We continued with our efforts to be allowed to leave Germany. I went to the American and Swiss consulates many times. Madeleine Apponyi wrote a very kind letter inviting us to go and settle in Cuba. (Had we followed this one up, with Fidel Castro's subsequent take-over we would have been in trouble again.) We certainly did not have any shortage of similar touching suggestions. Eventually our persistence paid off, and the whole family travelled in Sam Woods' car to the CIC in Munich to be screened for our visa and exit application. Gusztáv Hennyey and Albert Győri were our witnesses.

I was now regularly receiving letters from my family in Hungary, which was a great joy and at the same time a constant worry, as their situation worsened every day. The takeover by the Communist Party was extremely worrying. In their letters my sisters called me Anna, in case they fell into the wrong hands. Practically all their friends had left the country by then, anybody who had the slightest opportunity went either to Switzerland or further abroad. My parents had gone to Slovakia and were living in two rooms in the 'little castle' in the village of Elefánt. The rest of the house was empty and they were obviously very lonely. They wrote that they were truly touched by the help from their former employees, despite the danger to themselves. They were actually being fed and looked after by our old butler and driver and others, who brought eggs, chicken, flour, etc. They found all kinds of food on their windowsill when they woke up. I was sad to hear that the only former employee who tried to make trouble was our old coachman, of whom I had been very fond. Because of this, my parents eventually left, so as not to create trouble for those who were good to them.

Occasionally Myro sent me letters via the American Minister in Budapest, with whom she was friendly. In these letters she and György wrote quite openly about everything that was happening. They said that although many people were asking for news about us, they were frightened to admit that we were in touch. Magdamama's maid Margit, who had left us not long ago, had now gone to help Myro, as she wanted to remain with the family. She had come originally from Kenderes, the home of the Regent, and had been back there recently. She asked Myro to tell me that the Horthy family crypt was locked up, but on all anniversaries or occasions like Christmas, flowers were placed in front of the crypt. She said that this was truly remarkable, as she had been told that the place was being watched – but the flowers were still put there.

My sisters were worried about their children's schooling. Myro wrote that little Magdi was about to start school now and that she knew it was all right to let her go, as she was an intelligent child who had a degree of understanding about things, but that she had decided to teach her son at home, as he was younger and could therefore be more easily influenced, which would be dangerous for the family. She wrote that what the children were being taught was hair-raising, it had to be experienced to be believed. Religion was no longer a subject at school: parents could officially ask for it in writing, but this would naturally reflect unfavourably on them. In spite of that, so many parents had requested religious instruction that it was almost a form of demonstration against the government.

It seemed that leaving the country clandestinely was becoming too dangerous, and asking for an exit permit was equally hazardous. The request could be refused and then, because you were attempting to leave the country, you could lose your job or your work permit. This also explained why they did not tell the children about my letters, so they could not blurt something out inadvertently.

Through Prelate Neuhauser we received some financial help from Pope Pius XII, accompanied by a very heart-warming letter from Monsignor Montini (later Pope Paul VI). Miklóspapa was deeply touched and wrote to thank the Holy Father. In the name of His Holiness, Monsignor Montini wrote back to thank Papa for his kind words. (Both letters are still in my possession.) At this time we also received a remarkable letter from John Flournoy Montgomery which you can read in the appendices.[xi]

We were delighted to have a visit from Professor Aylmer Macartney, the Oxford historian whose broadcasts from the BBC we had listened to so avidly in those difficult days in Budapest during the war. I greeted him in the style in which he addressed himself in Hungarian: 'Macartney Elemér', imitating his English accent. He was amused, and pleased to hear that in Hungary we had never once missed listening to his transmissions. He wanted to discuss with Papa a number of points for his book *October Fifteenth: A History of Modern Hungary*, which was to become a standard reference work on this subject.

On 12 July, Nicky left via Switzerland for Brazil, a move he had been planning for some time, and where he hoped to find a living through contacts he had from the time he was Hungarian ambassador there. After he left he wrote me a long letter, explaining that he had left his parents and gone as far away as possible because he could not live near me. He was deeply in love with me and, as I did not reciprocate this feeling, he had made this decision and might never come back again.

I felt that this could not be as tragic as it sounded, because we all knew how easily Nicky had fallen in and out of love in the past. I wrote to him and explained that we were a family so reduced in numbers that we had to stick together in the future, and help his parents by being a united family. He never replied to this, but seemed in time to have accepted things, as he later returned to live in Portugal.

Mario Spányi, whose father – like Admiral Horthy – had been ADC to the Emperor Francis Joseph, came to visit us with a proposal for Miklóspapa. He suggested that it would be a most welcome gesture, and an example for the Hungarian emigrants to reconcile differences and show unity, if Papa and Archduke Otto Habsburg were to write to each other and, later on, maybe even meet. Spányi then told Papa that the Archduke would like it if Miklóspapa were to address him as Majesty in his letter; he would then address Papa as Regent. Papa welcomed the suggestion of the letters, but we had quite a discussion about the Archduke's request to be addressed as Majesty. Papa said that

[xi] Appendix 10.

this was not strictly correct, as the Archduke was heir to the throne and not the king, and Papa could not do something that was not correct.

I confess that when we talked about it the next day, I exerted some influence over Miklóspapa's decision to comply with the request. In Hungarian the way to address an Archduke would be 'Fenség' and for Majesty it would be 'Felség'. There is only that one letter which differentiates between the two titles. I told him that this one letter should not prevent a rapprochement or reconciliation, if it would help the rallying together of the emigrants. Papa reluctantly gave in, and wrote a very correct letter assuring the Archduke of having always regarded himself as the procurator of the crown, and of his loyalty to the reigning house.

Mario Spányi also brought an additional letter, in duplicate, for Papa to sign, which stated: 'Regarding the time of publication of this letter exchange, the distinguished partners agree that it can only happen by mutual consent.'

The original and its duplicate would be handed to the Archduke for his signature – he would keep one for himself, and the other would be returned to Miklóspapa.

On 5 August Papa received a letter from György Bakách-Bessenyey in Paris, confirming that he had received the letters from Mario Spányi that day, but could not hand them over to His Majesty, who was then in the United States. He would personally take the letters to America and would also ensure that the reply would be forwarded in the correct manner.

What happened after that was – to say the least – very disappointing. According to diplomatic custom there is a particular significance attached to the length of time taken to respond with a written reply or return visit – any lapse of time being regarded as unfavourable. We heard nothing more about the letter. Only at the end of January 1949, almost six months later, when we had left Germany and arrived in Portugal did the answer come; and not as had been agreed but addressing Papa as, 'Dear Horthy'. The letter was dated 15 January 1949, and in it the Archduke thanked Papa 'for his letter of 5 August 1948'.

I could see what a blow and a disappointment it was for Papa, but he said nothing. We did not discuss it, as he obviously did not want to do so. He was deeply devoted to the monarchy and even when slighted did not want to criticize. Much later, with the planned visits, exactly the same thing happened – but that comes later.

Uncle Eugene left on the Orient Express for Paris, where he hoped to settle for a while. I had obtained all the necessary papers for him in Munich, which was quite a job. I was now quite an expert in getting things done at consulates and hoped that our exit from Germany would be just as successful.

Ruben Hecht came over to tell us about the difficulties with regard to our stay in Switzerland. He sent a car to take me to Munich, where we had lunch while he told me about his endeavours to facilitate our transitional stay in Switzerland. He had asked me to meet him in Munich because he did not want to let Papa know about the disappointing results. This first application was for a transit-stay of six months in the south of the country. He was not happy about their attitude, and left with me copies of all the letters he had written to the various chiefs of departments, and the originals of their answers, which are still in my possession. I was deeply impressed by Ruben Hecht's letters, as nobody could have intervened or argued our case better than he had done. His very first letter was to the Chief of the Police Department in Bern, who replied that the application had been passed on to the Foreign Police Department for examination, and requested information as to what financial means would be at our disposal during our stay in Switzerland.

The last two letters from the two departments constituted an outright refusal. The one from the Police Department being a refusal for the whole family, whereas the Federal Public Ministry said that the entry of Admiral Horthy had been refused but it remained open for the rest of the family to apply if they so wished. They had of course received the doctor's report on Mama's health, outlining the urgent need for a change of climate. Ruben Hecht then let them know that it would be detrimental to Mama's health if she were to be separated from her husband and she would probably refuse to leave without him anyway. He urged me not to give up.

The next morning was spent writing letters to Switzerland and the telephone never stopped ringing. We finally decided to attempt an official application for a week's transit.

Ruben Hecht came to say goodbye, as he was going back to Israel via Switzerland. We would certainly miss this good friend, who had been so solicitous of us and so very helpful in trying to get our permit to travel to Portugal via Switzerland.

Then a minor miracle happened. I had been trying for a long time to get my Wanderer car back, and now at last I had news that I could reclaim it. I was once again a car owner! Together with my Hungarian friends, I made plans to go to pick it up at Aham. It was miles away and we did not know what state the car would be in. Iványi got hold of four car wheels to take with us, just in case. We planned to overhaul the car and then sell it.

On 23 September we finally set off in Dr Hanvai's DKW car, he, his wife, János Iványi and myself. It was three times as far as Munich, about 120 kilometres, and first we had to stop in Vilsbiburg at the military government for our permits. From there we went on to Aham. After some searching we found the car in a garage and it was like meeting an old friend – I had last seen it in the courtyard of the Royal Palace in my parking space. I fought with tears at the sight of it. We towed it to a car workshop, where Iványi and Dr Hanvai worked on it. As it refused to go, Hanvai finally towed it with his DKW; and when lo and behold it suddenly started, there was great rejoicing!

The next morning we again had to start by towing the Wanderer, but finally we went on our way with two cars, and I drove to Weilheim to pick up István from school. You can imagine his amazement at seeing Mama in her own car. We had a lot of fun.

At this time I received a letter from my sister Myro's husband György Darányi, who until recently had been the general manager of a big Steam Mills Company. He said that he had been informed that any company employees who were not 'party members' would face demotion. I then received a second message, via the American Minister in Budapest, that György had lost his job and must leave the country in order to escape serious trouble. The Minister advised him to try to go to the United States with his wife and two children. My brother-in-law being a farmer with a diploma in agriculture, the Minister would help him leave the country legally if he could get a promise from the United States assuring him employment.

I immediately wrote to Mr Montgomery. Although I knew he would understand, I still asked him to forgive my request. I also told him that my brother-in-law wanted to work and did not want any financial support; he could even pay for his journey to the States, but had no other access to funds. I asked him to send an answer to the American Minister in Budapest by courier. I gave him several names and addresses of people in the States who would give him information and vouch for György, and who knew what part he had played in the underground movements during the war.

About a month later, after a lot of correspondence, Mr Montgomery wrote: '... I have sent Mr George Darányi a letter from a farm offering him a position and housing. This is simply a formality and he cannot count upon either, as no one knows what the situation will be by the time he arrives. However, this will be sufficient, or should be, to get him over the first hurdle as per your previous letter.'

Sadly, to cut a long story short, their emigration passport was refused. The reason given was that both their names were being kept in evidence by the 'police for state defence'. This was a terrible blow, as not only had all our efforts been in vain but they were now also in constant danger. There had never been any action against them, so nobody understood what the reason might be. From now on there was absolutely nothing that we could do from the 'outside'; we could only pray that they would find a way of getting out.

It was decided that if we wanted to leave Germany before winter set in, I would have to go to Switzerland personally to arrange our transit permits and our stay there. I got the Swiss visa quite easily, enabling me to go and stay for a few days.

In Zürich I got in touch with our good friend Consul Lutz, then went on to Bern by train. After completing my business in the Bundeshaus assembly building, I went on to see the Portuguese Minister Sousa Mendes. I spent two days in Geneva with Nicky's children, where Uncle Eugene joined us; it was a real joy to see him looking so well and making plans to go to Africa to visit his white-hunter friend. I kept in touch with Bern and finally got the excellent news that our transit had been granted, with one week's stay in Switzerland. At last we seemed to be getting somewhere.

Back in Weilheim I had to go to the Italian Mission in Munich to get our Italian visas. From the Swiss Consulate I received a written promise for our Swiss visas. We needed many certificates and papers for our exit-permit, but at last I got them all together. That evening there was a beautiful full moon, and I wondered if it would be the last one we would see in Germany ... .

Our departure from Germany was announced over the radio! We had no idea who could have communicated this information. We were therefore not surprised when three journalists from Hamburg came to interview us – but we did not talk to them.

In the meantime we had lacquered my car, preparing it for sale, and it looked almost like new. The deal was made with the help of 'salesmen' Halmai, Iványi and Binder, and just three days before our departure we managed to load it into a goods-wagon to send it to its new owner. With the money from the sale I immediately went to pay our outstanding bills and bought myself a present: a new Leica camera, to replace the one the American GIs had taken on their arrival in Hirschberg.

A long series of farewells now needed to be made. To say goodbye to so many good friends was truly painful. I had the feeling that we would never meet again, as everybody was going on their way to a different part of the world. To those who had made no plans to leave Germany because they were hoping to be able to go back home, I said that my sincere feeling was that this was a mistake. I asked them to try to accept the present situation, not just to sit back and wait. They had to imagine and accept that things would always stay as they were, and try to start living accordingly – allowing themselves to be happily surprised if things changed for the better. Even if this was hard to do, it was the only sensible way under the present seemingly hopeless circumstances.

In the new Hungarian weekly paper *Hungaria*, Papa published a message to our compatriots:

> Because of my wife's health I am forced to leave Bavaria. We are in search of a milder climate but we are not leaving Europe. This does not mean that we will lose contact. I shall remain in close touch and always be together with you, with whom I am irrevocably linked by fate. I know this fate is very hard, but that is precisely why I want to share in it with you.
>
> I have seen and experienced with joy and appreciation with what noble determination the Hungarians, having been abandoned here, sometimes do the most arduous work, not only in the interest of their subsistence but also for their country. For those who were forced to leave our homeland could mostly not take anything with them into exile but their honour.
>
> In such nerve-racking, difficult times, differences of opinion are inevitable; but we should avoid dissension, because only unity can produce useful results.
>
> Let everybody be assured that those who work for their country, sometimes despite danger and despair, will never do so in vain and will not be forgotten. That is why I ask every Hungarian to go on working with faith, trust, perseverance and solidarity for a better Hungarian future.
>
> Herewith I say goodbye to my compatriots, asking the Almighty to bless and help them, in the certain hope of meeting again.[55]

The day before our departure we travelled to Munich, and on 18 December 1948 we left for the station. There, to our amazement, we found Mario Spányi, Gusztáv Hennyey, and many other Hungarians from the Hungarian camp, who had come to wave goodbye. The photographers of the United Press were taking pictures.

The train left at seven, stopping in Lindau and in Bregenz, where we were again greeted by groups of Hungarians. At the German-Swiss border my dear friend Consul Lutz met us and there was also someone from the Fremdenpolizei. We had to change trains in Zürich, where my half-sister Harry and a huge group of friends greeted us. They had balloons for István and flowers for Mama and me.

We arrived at last in Vevey at eight thirty in the evening, and went to the little apartment we had booked for our week's stay. We were physically and emotionally exhausted.

A poem to my husband unexpectedly came to me:

Hopeless Dreams
Have you been gone a year, a month, a day?
And still I am here, while you are away.
Waiting for you to suddenly appear
That I may love you for another year –
A year, a month, a day just let it be,
It will be worth eternity to me!

20

Safe Haven Portugal, 1949 – 1953

On that Sunday morning, after a good night's sleep, Mama, Ila, István and I went to mass. We were exhausted, but looking forward to our week's stay in Switzerland.

24 December, which should have been our last day, was very eventful, as during the night Mama tore a muscle in her back. She was in so much pain that she could not move. We called a Swiss doctor and, with his certificate, I immediately tried to contact the authorities in Bern to ask for a three-day extension of our stay, hoping that by then Mama would be able to travel.

The next day the answer to our request arrived from the Fremdenpolizei in Bern: to our shock they had extended our stay by only one more day. It was hard to believe that the Swiss could be so mean, and even Mama decided that she did not want to stay longer than that. She would ask for a strong bandage and we would leave then, and not ask for more humane consideration.

On 27 December we left by the Simplon express for Italy. It was evening when we arrived at the Hotel Minerva in Rapallo, where to our surprise Countess Madeleine Apponyi, the American friend whom we had known in Hungary, and who had arranged to sail with us, was already waiting.

The next morning I went by bus to Genoa to apply for a visa extension, which was no problem, and then to pick up our tickets for the cruiser *Ana C*, on which we were sailing for Portugal in eight days time. Now I understood why Madeleine had arrived before us: she had changed our tickets from second class to first class, and for Papa and Mama she had booked a large suite. This was a wonderful gift.

On the thirty-first, we joyfully welcomed Anci Zalai Scholtz, who had served with Miklóspapa during the big battle of Otranto in the First World War and later had become his ADC. But the best was yet to come: that evening ex-Prime Minister Miklós Kállay – our beloved Mica

– arrived in the company of Bandi Esterházy, my sister Sya's brother-in law. We all had dinner together, and an immensely happy reunion. We spent the next few days enjoying the company of our visitors, especially being able to go sailing with Kállay. What a wonderful way to start the year.

On 8 January 1949 we drove with Madeleine to the port of Genoa, to board the *Ana C* and set sail for Portugal. Four days later, on 12 January, we sailed up the estuary of the Tagus river and into Lisbon harbour. It was an unexpected delight to see Veronica Gracie standing on the quay waiting for us. She was the daughter of the Brazilian ambassador, Sousa Leão Gracie, whose family we knew well from Hungary, where he had been Brazilian Minister for several years. The other person greeting us was Arthur Baján, former Hungarian Consul – who was still the Acting Honorary Consul in Portugal, as the present Hungarian Communist government was not recognized here.

We drove along the coast to the Hotel do Parque in Estoril. To me it all looked rather bleak, with no green trees, just some palm-trees, and the hotel resembled a railway station. I remember my first impression so clearly, which must have been tainted by being so far from home and not wanting to accept that this was where we were going to stay, whether we liked it or not. When we got to our rooms I realized that I was not the only one feeling this way, as Mama said, 'Let's go back to Weilheim!' She went straight to bed with a temperature.

The next morning, the cheerful Professor Doctor Bilkei Pap – another friend from Hungary – came to see Mama. In this lovely weather, with so much sunshine, it did not take long for her to completely recover.

During the next few days many people came to welcome us. Consul Baján and his wife Viola offered to help us in any way they could. King Umberto of Italy, who lived here in exile, came to greet Papa as an old friend. Archduchess Anna Habsburg and Count Endre Csekonics also came, and it was wonderful to meet Kálmán and Margit Imrédy, with whom we had worked in Hungary serving the Hungarian Railways.

That first evening I was invited to dinner at the next door Hotel Palacio by the Austrian Baron Eddie Friesen and his wife Burgl, and whilst we were sitting in the hall afterwards many people came up to us, amongst others the pretender to the Spanish throne, Don Juan, Count of Barcelona, along with his wife.

When I was back in my room everything in me rebelled. We had arrived in a completely different world, where people knew very little of the horrors of war and had never experienced the kind of misfortunes and disasters we had lived through. Indeed for a while we felt like strangers: we missed our Hungarian friends – that feeling of fellowship created by the participation in a similar fate. There we did not have to explain, everybody understood what preoccupations or worries others had. Here, we did not even try to explain, for very few understood or even suspected our situation. Only now did I realize how we had been jolted out of a generally carefree, peaceful life, to which it did not seem possible to return, or get used to, mentally or financially.

However, the kind help we received from the people here soon made us feel more at home in this beautiful and hospitable country. And it did not take us long to discover the loveliness of our surroundings, and to take special delight in the weather.

The fact that it was by a series of 'coincidences' that we came to live in Portugal, I truly consider a gift of God. Not only for the climate and the kindness of the Portuguese people, but we were on the shores of the Atlantic Ocean, which was a real blessing for Miklóspapa. He could observe ships that passed, and in the harbour of Lisbon, the estuary of the Tagus where there were very strong currents, he could watch with admiration the berthing manoeuvres of the Portuguese sailors. It was a pleasure to observe how his expression changed when he was looking at the sea. He himself wrote this about it:

> Here, every day I can see the sea, the so very beloved element of my original calling in life, and I can take delight in the sight of it. But even from the shores of the Atlantic Ocean, I quite often shut my eyes and my thoughts turn eastward to the banks of the Danube and the Tisza; to my beloved fatherland, which no country on earth, however beautiful, can replace. The sea is deep and endless, but the love that binds me to my homeland is deeper, and the longing that draws me to Hungary and her people is even more endless. [p. 339]

I learned to love and appreciate the 'marginal' road along the coast to Lisbon, where the colours of the ocean were always changing; enjoying the sunset and the sunrise, and the clear sight of the moon.

I ought to clarify here that we had not been invited to Portugal by Prime Minister Salazar; this rumour was spread erroneously by someone to whom Papa had mentioned in Weilheim that it was good of Salazar to have given permission for diplomatic visas to be issued to us. This person thought that it meant that Salazar had invited us.

The Portuguese people are on the whole very good hearted. I was struck by the contrast in their disposition to the general attitude in post-war Germany. In Portugal you did not get very far if you were not friendly, but you could easily achieve what you wanted with a smile, talking about the weather and how much you enjoyed being in their lovely country, and then: 'By the way, could you help me with ...' I found great pleasure in this, and after all the rebuffs and struggles of the past years it suited me in every way.

The Spanish I had learnt in Weilheim with Señora Fritz came in very handy, but I realized that sooner or later I would have to learn Portuguese. For Portuguese people it was easy to understand Spanish, it was another matter to understand the Portuguese, because they not only talk quickly but also swallow parts of their words. There was an Englishman sitting in the hall of our hotel most of the time. He asked me one day whether I was going to learn Portuguese. When I said that I was, he gave me the following advice: 'Write down the word you want to learn and put half of it in your pocket!' But he failed to tell me which half it should be, as sometimes it was the first and sometimes the last half of the word that was not pronounced.

Madeleine Apponyi flew back to the United States. Before she left she told me that from now on she would contribute to Mr Montgomery's fund. She emphasized that her contribution was for me, and gave me her contribution for three months in advance. I was deeply touched, as this meant that we would probably have $400 a month to live on. I had been doing a lot of calculations, and was slowly beginning to see what we would need once we had our own household.

The 'Montgomery Fund' now consisted of four subscribers: John Flournoy Montgomery, Francis Chorin, Alexander Páthy and Madeleine, who each contributed $100 a month. It is difficult to express the gratitude we felt towards these friends, without whom we could not have survived. There is no way we could ever thank them enough – and particularly John Montgomery, who got them together and organized the fund.

Archduke Joseph Franz and Archduchess Anna were members of the Habsburg family who had settled in Hungary, and who had then emigrated to Portugal. We went on the local electric train to Carcavelos to have tea with them, and Archduchess Anna went with me to the English Portuguese St Julian's School in Carcavelos, to obtain István's admission.

On 24 January, István went to St Julian's for the first time. Ila and I accompanied him on the local electric train, and went again to pick him up in the afternoon. I accompanied him to school for two more days, and then went with him just to the station, from where I picked him up again in the afternoon. The school was very near the station and he soon got used to coming and going on his own. Luckily there was no fear of Yugoslav terrorists here. István got on well throughout his years at St Julian's, regularly coming first in his class. We were very proud of him.

It was at this time, the end of January, when the letter from Archduke Otto arrived in reply to Miklóspapa's letter written in August. Beginning, 'Dear Horthy,' it went on to thank Papa for his letter, quoting it point by point. It was not what had been agreed, and the letter concerning mutual consent for publication, two of which Papa had signed, was not included. It would have been nice to have had at least some explanation for the delay. Papa asked me to write to Mario Spányi – who was the intermediary in this affair – and tell him that he was sorry that he had entered into this situation at all.

When I wrote to Mario, I told him of our disappointment and that we wanted to believe that it was someone else who caused the misunderstanding. I pointed out that Mario himself knew very well that the whole situation had arisen from a wish to express an equal and mutual recognition, with both sides making a gesture of goodwill, as an example to others. Unfortunately this had not happened, and it was very sad to think that this might have occurred with the full knowledge of one of the participants. Every endeavour had been made from our side, so it was a shame that it was entirely unreciprocated.

An answer came from Mario, saying that he had talked to Archduke Otto and 'was convinced that it was not done on purpose'. He thought it was due to 'the mistakes of the people surrounding the Archduke, and the wrong way to address Papa was due to the forgetfulness of the person who wrote out the letter and handed it over for signature'.

The latter was difficult to accept. But we were happy that Mario felt it was not deliberate, and wanted to believe this. I replied to Mario on Miklóspapa's behalf: 'he is of the opinion that, under the circumstances, it is better not to force things, let us leave things as they are. Because every 'rapprochement' could cause further confusion and would activate those in whose interest it is to work against this. I think you know that from Papa's side there has never been any form of thought or action against the 'high partner', nor will such a thing ever happen.'

For me the arguments were not sufficiently clear. Why were no names mentioned – who was the person who wrote out the letter? I felt that from our side, with such an important issue at stake, such 'forgetfulness' could never have happened, or if it had occurred the mistake would have surely been put right. In June, Mario wrote that he now had in his possession the signed note of the mutual consent for publication, which he would personally hand over to Miklóspapa at the first opportunity. He said that he was delighted by Papa's message about letting things rest for the moment, which corresponded entirely with his and Hennyey's opinion and was renewed proof of Papa's noble attitude that they had recognized during this whole affair. (The originals of all these letters are in my possession.)

All this time we were looking for a flat or house, as it became clear that having our own household would be more economical. Rents were very high in Estoril, and it took me about a month to find what seemed to be the right house, a small villa with a tiny garden. It was cheaper because no linens or refrigerator were included, and it had straw mattresses. It was in Estoril and was called Chalet Ramuntcho. Burgl Friesen and others gave and lent me some sheets and a refrigerator. Veronica and Betty Gracie brought some blankets. Eddie Friesen drove me back and forth by car. It was exhausting but exhilarating – and almost unbelievable.

On 3 March 1949 we moved from the Hotel do Parque to Chalet Ramuntcho. It was a big moment, everybody was happy and our first meal at the house – a Hungarian *pörkölt* – was a great occasion. I hoped that we would get used to the straw mattresses. I was truly worried that it was not good enough for my parents-in-law, but after a few days Mama told me that she had never slept so well as on these mattresses. and Papa had not said anything. I admit truthfully that I did not sleep well during the first week and always woke up with a headache, but after that I got completely used to it.

Domestic staff were not expensive, and we soon found a Portuguese cook. It was not easy at first, as she only spoke Portuguese. We had hilarious scenes in the kitchen as I was translating for both the cook and for Mama, who was speaking to me in Hungarian, and neither would wait for my translations. I would just stand between them and laugh.

I had to go to the Foreign Office for the extension of our diplomatic visas and cards. I was the only one in the family who had managed to save my very large Royal Hungarian diplomatic passport, into which the Portuguese diplomatic visa was stamped and always renewed. This passport naturally was not recognized by the present Hungarian Communist government, but because of the Portuguese diplomatic visa, it was considered valid by other European governments, so I could use it for my travels.

There was now a follow-up in the attempt at the Habsburg-Horthy contacts. On 29 March, Viscount José Saldanha da Gama – with whom Archduke Otto Habsburg usually stayed when he was in Portugal – came to have tea with us. We had a long conversation with him in preparation for an exchange of visits between Papa and Archduke Otto. A few days later he invited me to dinner and we shared a long and, I hoped, fruitful conversation.

A sensational piece of news was the arrival of Papi and Ellamami in Vienna from Slovakia. We had last seen each other five years earlier, and I wanted to go and welcome them as soon as possible. They planned first to go to Switzerland. As I still had money from Pista's Swiss cheque, I used it for this purpose. As soon as I knew they had arrived in Switzerland I organized my visas and flew to Geneva.

Papi and Ellamami were waiting at the airport. How often I had wondered whether we would ever see each other again. I stayed with them for four weeks, and we talked and talked. They told me hair-raising stories about the siege of Budapest. But they were also very good at telling jokes and we managed to laugh a lot too. During this time we met many old friends. I will mention only the one with whom my parent's future was closely connected. Sir Oliver Duncan was an Englishman, a citizen of the Principality of Liechtenstein, and very wealthy. We knew him from before the war, when he had been to our home in Elefánt. We now met him several times and he took us to his beautiful home in Montreux. When he realized that my parents had nothing to live on and had no idea where they were going to live in the future, he invited them to settle in another of his houses, the lovely Villa Beau Desert in Cannes, France. But my parents would only accept this offer if they could be helpful and look after the place for him. Reluctantly he gave in to this arrangement and my parents went to live there for many years.

One of the things I'd looked forward to in coming to Portugal was that I would probably be able to go to Fatima, about which I had heard so much. Fatima is one of the great pilgrimage sites of Europe. Here, in 1917, the Virgin Mary appeared to three little shepherd children six times, on the thirteenth of the month. Ever since, on these dates, many thousands of people assemble there.

In July, Veronica Gracie and her daughter Betty took me there by car. On the night of the twelfth we went to see the candle-procession. This takes place at midnight, when thousands of people gather in the large square in front of the Basilica. Everybody carries a candle and follows the statue of the Virgin, singing hymns. It was an unbelievably moving sight, and to take part in it was a memorable experience. I lit candle offerings and prayed for my sisters. In the morning we returned for the big mass, where I walked amongst the sick people who were brought there on stretchers. At the end of the mass one of them got up and walked away – of course we did not know how sick he had been. What I liked about Fatima was that they were not giving much heed to physical miracles. I was told that the miracles of Fatima are for the soul. This appealed to me.

That summer we met up again with Jean and Stuart Bellingham, who had been to Hungary before the war. They lived with their three sons in

Ireland, where they had a big farm. When they got home they sent me a plane ticket, inviting me to the Horse Show in Dublin and to their farm. I did not really want to go but my parents-in-law said that I ought to accept their kind hospitality, as the change would be beneficial for me.

I spent the most delightful two weeks with these good-hearted and generous friends in Ireland, which was the first of many such wonderful holidays I, István and later my niece Denise, spent in this very special country. Occasionally however I had arguments with Irish people. Every time they mentioned 'our enemies in the North', referring to the British, I could never leave it at that, and explained to them that I would thank God on my knees if Hungary were occupied by their 'enemies in the North'.

An incident that remains vivid in my memory from one of our visits shows the delightfully original attitude the Irish have towards life.

I had gone to Galway to visit Dr Michael Browne, Bishop of Galway, whom I had met in 1938 when he and his party had stayed with Sya whilst they were attending the Thirty-fourth International Eucharistic Congress in Budapest. It was a great pleasure to see this exceptionally warm-hearted man again, who had such good memories of my sister and was interested in her fate. He told me to go and visit Sean T. O'Kelly, who had been with him in Hungary and remembered Sya and me, and would love to see me. Sean T. O'Kelly just happened to be President of Ireland at this time!

Jean Bellingham was delighted at this news, and when we got back to Dublin we telephoned and were promptly invited to tea. As we drove up to the Presidential Palace the large gate was closed, with one policeman standing in front of it. He strolled up to us and, peeping into the car, said to Jean, 'Bad weather we're having these days, are we not?' Jean answered him, and they chatted for a while about the weather. Then he pointed with his thumb at the gate and said, 'By the way, are you going in?'

I do not think this could have happened at the gates of Buckingham Palace.

Returning from my holiday it was wonderful to embrace Miklóspapa, Magdamama and István who were waiting for me at Lisbon airport. We were joined for supper by Madeleine Apponyi. She had recently arrived from the States, and was now looking for a villa for herself in Estoril.

The next day Madeleine fell ill, and while she was unwell I went to her hotel to see her every day. On one occasion when I was there, when she seemed better but still very weak, she gave me the key of her hotel safe, where she had all her jewellery and money. She said that if anything happened to her I should just get everything out of the safe and keep it without telling anyone. She wanted me to go there now, just to open and shut the safe, to see if the hotel clerk would let me do that. I felt a bit embarrassed but was really overwhelmed by her trust in me. She had once told me that everybody was only after her money, and she never trusted anyone. I did exactly as I was told, and two days later when she was feeling much better I gave the key back to her, thanking her for her confidence and friendship.

A few days later Madeleine announced that she wanted me to have a car. She thought that I needed to be able to drive my parents-in-law around, do my shopping in Lisbon, and such like. She wanted me to go and look at cars and tell her what I thought of them. I had actually got quite used to the fast electric train – the station was within walking distance – and I could not quite imagine how it would be to have a car again. Now I went around looking for a villa for Madeleine and looking for a car for myself; it felt like a fairy-tale.

12 September was a memorable day for me: Veronica and Betty Gracie took me once more to Fatima. I had decided by then that I was going to ask to work in Fatima as a nurse, as an offering to our Lady of Fatima for my sisters. So I went to see Dr Gens, the head doctor of the first aid hospital, and asked him whether I would be allowed to work as a servita – a volunteer who worked there on the pilgrimage days. He said that this depended on Don José, the Bishop of Leiria, and he warned me that the bishop had lately forbidden him to take any more servitas. According to the bishop, most of the people who came there just wanted to be servitas but did nothing.

When he came back he was smiling. He said that he had told Don José that there was a Hungarian lady here who had lost her husband and her country and would like to work in Fatima. The bishop's reply was that it was not his fault that I had lost my husband and my country, so why should he do anything about it, and he had repeated that he did not want any more servitas. Dr Gens then got up to go, saying sadly, 'It is a pity, because she is a nurse.' The bishop exclaimed, 'A nurse! But of course we need her to be a servita.' So I was in. This was the beginning of my five years as a servita in Fatima.

But for the moment there was another hurdle to be overcome: the head nurse of the servitas, Marquesa Olga de Cadaval, who seemed a very severe person and was obviously not in favour of another 'aristocratic society lady' joining the servitas. She reminded me of our Hungarian Red Cross Head Nurse, Baroness Gizella Apor, my beloved Aunt Gizi, who was extremely severe when she dealt with the nurses under her care.

With the bishop's permission I started work immediately in the first aid ambulance. All night Olga de Cadaval made me do all the dirtiest work. I took very sick elderly men to the toilet and bandaged terrible wounds – but for me, with my war experience, it was all easy work. I knew why Olga de Cadaval was doing all this: as Aunt Gizi would have said, 'If she does not like it and leaves, it is just as well, as she will never become a good nurse. Good nurses must be able to put up with anything.' I worked until one thirty in the morning – we saw the midnight candle procession from the window – then we were allowed to sleep for half an hour before going to two o'clock mass and communion for the servitas, after which we returned to ambulance duty. In the morning Olga de Cadaval just said to me, 'Yes, you can stay with us.'

A big pilgrimage day of Fatima was 13 October, because in 1917 that was when the last of the six apparitions of the 'lady in white' came to Lucia, Francisco and Jacinta. Dr Gens told me the most fascinating first-hand account of being at that event.

He was a medical student at the time, an atheist, and with a student friend of his had decided to go and see this 'circus' that people were talking about: the apparition of a lady in white who was supposed to be the Virgin Mary. As they were walking up the hill, where many people were supporting the sick and pushing wheel chairs of those who had come in the hope of being cured, it started to rain heavily. By the time they arrived at the spot where the three shepherd children were waiting, there was mud everywhere. He managed to get near to the children, and after a little while saw them all look up at once with a happy expression on their faces. He had heard that Lucia had been told to ask 'the lady' to let everybody see a sign of her presence, not just the three of them. After Lucia had been speaking for a while, he heard her say that the people were asking for a sign. Lucia then asked, 'Where?' then got up and pointed with her outstretched arm towards the sky and said, 'Look there.' At that moment the clouds opened and the sun came spiralling down towards the crowd. This phenomenon was seen as far as 40 kilometres away. Dr Gens thought that the end of the world had come and fell prostrate to the ground. This lasted for about two minutes and then the sun circled back again to its place. What Dr Gens first noticed was that everything was bone dry. He promised himself there and then, that if ever a hospital were to be erected at this place he would do voluntary work there. He had gained an unshakable faith in the Power of God. He kept his promise and was now head doctor at the first aid hospital.

There was another most interesting feature of his account, namely that there were people in the crowd who did not see the 'sun miracle'. Someone standing quite near to him did not see it, only noticed the strange behaviour of the people around him. This proved to me that there is no such a thing as a miracle, but there are happenings which people notice at the level of their 'inner openness'.

I considered myself very lucky to have heard the story from someone who had been there, and to have known Dr Gens, who died a few years later. He was a very sincere, natural person, with great inner – not faith – knowledge, and as is usual with such people, had a wonderful sense of humour.

Once our address in Portugal became known, Miklóspapa received many letters from Hungarians from all over the world. He answered every letter, and I helped him by typing his answers and filing all his correspondence. It was interesting to read the letters from the Hungarian émigrés: they were not satisfied where they were, comparing everything with 'home', and most of them were trying to go somewhere else. From Argentina they were trying to go to the United States, and at the same time in a letter from the States we read that someone hoped to go to Argentina. But most of the letters came from Hungarian generals living in Germany, Austria and Switzerland. This developed into a huge amount of correspondence, a lot of it containing disagreements and accusations. Some nasty articles appeared in the more irresponsible periodicals criticising certain generals. All this was naturally the result of the war: of so many officers having fought by the side of the Germans, convinced that they were defending the country against Communism, others with different opinions being jailed by the Nazis, and so on. Everybody now wanted to prove their story to the Regent, and Papa just tried to appease them and asked them to maintain a quiet unity until we could go home. To put an end to all this, from the three highest-ranking generals he nominated a Military Council, to arbitrate in these disputes and accusations.

Madeleine decided that I should go to London to buy the car. She had originally planned to come with me but she was not well enough. When Madeleine decided something she wanted to see it done quickly. She worked out that the only fast way to get a car was for me to pick it up and bring it with me. Ordering an English car in Portugal took months. The pound sterling had fallen, and I had been promised a diplomatic number plate, so there would be a great advantage in buying the car cheaper in London with no import duty to be paid in Portugal.

I had to have someone to help me in London and wrote to Geoffrey North, a friend of the Bellinghams, asking for his assistance. I got my English visa and on 29 October flew to England. Geoffrey North met me at the airport and, during my ten-day stay, not only helped me to find a car, but took me out several times to dinner and to the theatre.

I finally chose a Humber Hawk as being the most suitable car, and Geoffrey insisted on driving me to Liverpool to get the boat to Portugal. On the way he talked to me about marriage. I was fully aware that Geoffrey and I had a strong physical attraction for each other, but I realized that he would just not fit into my life. I had my parents-in-law to look after and did not want to get involved. Geoffrey fully understood this and said that he, on the other hand, could never share a wife with other members of the family. And so we parted – a bit more than good friends. My heart ached and I knew that Geoffrey must have felt the same. We never met again.

Papa, Mama and Arthur Baján were waiting for me at Lisbon harbour, the car was unloaded, and I drove us all to Estoril! I was suddenly very happy and drove to the station to pick up István from school; he was overjoyed and just loved the new car.

Madeleine, who told me that she did not want me to have any expenses with the car, paid me a monthly upkeep, but never used the car herself, always taking a taxi if she wanted to go somewhere. We were a little bewildered, never having expected to have a car again – but now that it was here we enjoyed it immensely. We felt quite embarrassed thinking of the situation of our family and our compatriots at home.

Madeleine had taken a new villa, Santa Margarida, which was very large, having two separate apartments. She had chosen it because she wanted us to move in with her. This seemed a very good arrangement to me, as I knew Madeleine to be very tactful and discreet. She would not be there much of the time, as she could not sit still for long and was always travelling. We never would have thought of moving if Madeleine had not suggested this; but once we were there everybody was more than satisfied with the change. We enjoyed the comfort and the lovely view, and especially the good beds and the hot baths.

1950 did not begin on a happy note. On 11 January a cable came from my sister-in-law Móci Darányi to say that my sister Myro, with György and the two children, had been arrested at the border, and for ten days nobody knew where they were. The children had eventually been released and brought to my sister Éva. This was a terrible blow; it did not bear thinking about, and one felt so helpless, as nothing could be done from outside. Knowing that in Hungary this was now considered one of the biggest sins against the state, I could only pray that God would protect them and they would be soon set free. Even if they let them go what would they do, having probably sold everything they had in order to attempt an escape? A month later I received the news that they had not been arrested at the border, but before they actually tried to escape. As there was only a supposition of an escape, they were not badly treated and their sentence might not be very severe. They thought that Myro might get six months and György double that. That was bad enough! May God help them.

For some time we had been corresponding with Ambassador Montgomery about the possibility of getting restitution or compensation for the Yacht *Hungaria*, which the Regent had received from Hitler and had never used. It had been confiscated by the American army in Germany. It seemed farcical that this was the only property of value that now belonged to my father-in-law. John Montgomery tried everything he could, forwarding Papa's letter to President Truman through Senator McMahon.

I have a large correspondence about this, the culmination of which was that – after two years – nothing had been achieved. An extract from the last letter about this from John Montgomery to Papa states, 'I am afraid, at the rate they are going, your great-grandchildren will be the only ones to receive any benefit ... You certainly have gotten the worst of it all round, and I wish there was something I could do to get a measure of justice for you. I wait for these lawyers and hope they get somewhere before we are all dead.' Papa had written that he only made this claim so as to no longer be a burden to unselfish, generous and kind friends. Mr Montgomery's answer was, 'I don't think any of your friends are worrying about that, so I wouldn't give the idea any thought.'

In March, Papi and Ellamami sent me a ticket to go and visit them. Cannes was beautiful, with its long beach, the mountains, the charming residences and the delight of the warm Mediterranean Sea. On this occasion Oliver Duncan was also in residence.

While I was there a letter came from Sya, saying that her husband Józsi had been arrested. She did not know why, and now the police, who had come several times to search the flat, were constantly watching her. The poor children must have been terrified. It had become the practice for family and friends to ring the doorbell several times so they would know it was not the police. Luckily Myro was back home now with the children, but György was still in detention. So now my two brothers-in-law were in jail and God only knows what would happen next. One could not concentrate on anything, knowing how they all suffered.

I got back to Estoril just as István's Easter holidays began. His English was very good by now; he read and wrote fluently. My new scheme was to try to speak a different language with him every day of the week – English, French, German, Portuguese and Hungarian. It was not easy to keep this up, but with István's willing cooperation we managed quite well. He was nine years old; I had learned these languages at his age from different governesses, and I knew what a great advantage it had been for me. I could not afford governesses or extra lessons for him, so this seemed the only way to get him used to several languages

On 11 May I went to Fatima in preparation for the big pilgrimage day two days later. At lunchtime Olga de Cadaval asked each of the servitas in turn which of them had already been to Fatima on foot, from Lisbon or wherever they lived. I heard all the others say that they had done that at least once, and when Olga asked me, I felt almost ashamed to tell her the truth.

'Have you been on foot to Fatima, Ilona?' she asked. I said simply that I had not.

'So, when are you going?'

'I don't intend to go.'

'Why?'

'I feel that going on foot all this way would only make me tired and unable to do my work here properly when I arrived; also, my parents-in-law would be worried, as they already worry about me coming here. And to tell you the truth, if I were to do it, it would be purely to enable me to tell you that I had done so, and that doesn't seem to me to be the right reason. I fully appreciate that other people might want to make a promise or want to make such a sacrifice, I admire them for it.'

Olga looked at me with stern disapproval but did not say any more.

When we met in Fatima the following month she had been to see Sister Lucia, the only one remaining of the three children who had seen the miracles, and who now lived in a convent in Coimbra. Olga told me that she asked Lucia what kind of sacrifice Our Lady of Fatima would ask of us servitas? Lucia, in her simple way, told her that she did not really know what The Lady would ask for, but she herself thought that the sacrifice should be the one that seems easy but is the most difficult – that is, that parent and child, husband and wife, should be always loving, helpful and understanding towards each other.

'How did you know?' Olga asked me. I said that it seemed logical to me and I was happy that Sister Lucia was of the same opinion.

In May there was a Foreign Ministers' Conference in London, to which the Regent and the representatives of all the Hungarian Churches – Roman Catholic, Reformed, Lutheran, Unitarian – and the MHBK (Hungarian Combatants Fellowship) sent a telegram, in which they asked the Council to take up the case of the multitude of Hungarian prisoners of war still in the Soviet Union. It was known that three hundred and fifty thousand people were still missing.[xii]

[xii] Appendix 11: Full text of telegram published in *Hungaria*, 19 May 1950.

The meeting between Miklóspapa and Archduke Otto Habsburg, which had been initiated in March 1949, was now finally going to happen in May 1950. The mediator, Tibor Bartheldy, who had settled with his wife in Portugal, had been a career diplomat; he was a correct, straightforward person with a vivid sense of humour. We saw him quite regularly and considered him a friend.

The events that I am going to describe are recalled from my own notes, written down at the time in Hungarian; and it is my own translation that I am quoting:

On 21 May, Sunday, at 7 p.m. Bartheldy came to us; in the presence of Papa, Mama, Nicky and myself, he told us that Archduke Otto had instructed him to arrange a meeting. The Archduke would be leaving tomorrow evening and regarded the Saldanha's house as his own. His host would not be present, only Bartheldy himself, who said, 'Come whenever is suitable to your Serene Highness, but the best would be between four and six o'clock.'

There followed a slight pause, after which Papa said that would be all right. It seemed that Archduke Otto asked Bartheldy whether we had a car, and then asked him to inform Papa that, with the exchange of letters, he considered the past as good as settled and would find it agreeable if the past would not be mentioned. To this Papa answered that one could not prescribe to him what he could or could not say. Bartheldy tried to explain very politely why this would perhaps be better, and that it had been said with the best of intentions.

The decision was made that I would take Papa by car, and Bartheldy got up to leave; the question of whether or not the past could be mentioned during the meeting remained unresolved. When I accompanied Bartheldy to his car he asked me to exert my influence so that Papa should not talk about the past. I told him that I did not think I could do much except repeat that it was probably suggested with good intentions.

When Bartheldy left, Papa told us that at first he had wanted to say that his home was here, and why could not Archduke Otto come here? Why should they meet in a stranger's house? But he did not say so, because he did not want to cause difficulties, just like last year with the exchange of letters. 'One of us has to set a good example and show good intentions, if our aim is that the serious elements within the émigrés should stick together,' he said.

The two of us set off today by car to Alges, 1 Rua Josef Bleck, where Bartheldy was waiting to accompany Papa into the house. I remained sitting in the car. A few minutes later, Bartheldy came out of the house and said the meeting was taking place upstairs and that I should not stay in the car but come into the hall to wait there with him. I told him that I was all right, but he insisted, and I then sat down with him in the entrance hall.

We talked over all that had preceded this meeting, and Bartheldy asked me to tell him what I knew about the chain of events; after I had told him exactly what happened at our end he was entirely in agreement with me, and was particularly amazed at the date of the Archduke's answer.

The meeting lasted fifty minutes and then they came down the stairs, Papa on the right and Otto on the left. When they got to the bottom of the stairs Papa introduced me as 'my daughter-in-law, who came with me as my driver'. After this they said goodbye, and the Archduke went upstairs while we were escorted out by Bartheldy. In the car Papa told me that everything had gone very well, and that Archduke Otto spoke excellent Hungarian. (End of my notes.)

I remember all this very clearly, and that I was happy that things seemed to have gone so smoothly. Papa had obviously received a very good impression; he said that he had told the Archduke that he really would have preferred to have had the meeting at his home, upon which the Archduke said that this time he was in a great hurry, but when he came next – which would be soon – he wanted to see Papa at his home, and also to meet his wife.

The next day I got a phone call from Bartheldy, who told me that he had had a severe reprimand from the Archduke about my presence in the hall, because it had been agreed that nobody else should be there. Bartheldy was just as surprised at this as I was. If Papa had not introduced me as his driver it might have seemed that I had just forced my way there; but what did it matter if the driver waited in the hall? Without question, there was a bias or misinterpretation on the part of the Archduke in whatever we did. The influence against Papa that he had received from an early age never wore off.

In June I was not allowed to go to Fatima by Professor Pap on account of my anaemia, something I had suffered from for a long time. It was not easy to accept this, but I often felt unusually tired. Finally I decided to go to Dr Pedro da Cunha (Marques de Olhão) who was supposed to be the best gynaecologist in Lisbon. After examining me he ordered that I should have an immediate blood transfusion; I then had to go to the Casa de Saude das Amoreiras hospital, where I stayed for twenty days.

I found Dr Cunha to be an exceptionally understanding, serious doctor, who looked after me with great care; he came to see me every day. I had a lot of time to think about my sisters and about the events at home, which were becoming increasingly worrying. Papa and Mama came to visit often, and Nicky, who was now back in Portugal, came several times at midday to help me with my lunch. István liked to do his lessons at my bedside – it was wonderful to receive so much care and love.

István and I had been planning a trip to Ireland, which my hospital visit had postponed. The timing of this had been arranged around the fact that we had to leave the villa Santa Margarida, as the owners wanted it back. Now, on my return from hospital, we had only three days before having to leave the house.

Papa and Mama had a room in the Hotel Atlantico for the summer, Ila had a room in a small guesthouse and now István and I moved into the Hotel do Parque, where we had great fun sharing a room for a few days. I got everything ready, visa, tickets – but the next day Dr Cunha said that he was against us travelling just yet.

He was soon to be proved right, as that night I started bleeding. I did not want to wake up either István or Dr Cunha, and rather foolishly waited until the morning. When Ila arrived I asked her to take István away and then rang the doctor, who got into his car and came immediately. I was terribly weak by then and ashen-white. He asked me if I would give my consent to have an operation, explaining that I would not be able to have any children afterwards. I asked him what would happen if I did not give my consent. He said that in about five hours I would be dead. 'So, what are you waiting for?' I asked him. Two days later, after two blood transfusions, I underwent a hysterectomy.

I was a little weak, but back on my feet again within a month, and István and I set off by plane to Ireland, where the dear Bellinghams made sure I rested a lot.

On our return to Lisbon we were met by my parents-in-law and Arthur Baján and were driven to our new home in Estoril: Casa San José, 19 Rua Melo e Sousa. They had moved into this furnished villa while we were away. I knew that we could make this into a home. We stayed there for nine years, and Mama transformed it into a cosy family abode. In no time the tiny garden was full of flowers and the big hedge along the fence gave us additional security.

The people at the British Embassy at that time were all very friendly, and we were lucky to have Meg and Jock Colville as near neighbours. We became great friends. Jock had been first Secretary to Winston Churchill before he took this post. The Colvilles were a delightful couple, and we saw them often during their time in Lisbon. The British ambassador was Sir Nigel Ronald, an elderly bachelor who seemed to like me, as he asked me twice to be hostess at the Embassy.

Miklóspapa received a lot of information about the Hungarian National Council, which had been officially formed in the United States. These men, who should have been using this good opportunity to express the interests of the Hungarian people, were unfortunately not entirely equal to this task. They had achieved some good results, but there were those who waged war against each other. This was also the case in the army. The post-war atmosphere and the varying political affinities affected people in strange ways. People tried to assert themselves by incriminating others. This was like a disease, from which I feared it would take a long time to recover. Luckily Papa did not let himself get involved.

The year 1951 started quietly. On István's tenth birthday we not only celebrated with him, but also included Ila's tenth anniversary of being with us. An invitation came from my parents for István and me to visit them in the South of France for the Easter holidays. So we had a joyful three weeks in Cannes. We made several excursions between the islands on Sir Oliver's yacht. I felt very close to my father and could see how uprooted he was. He had lost everything he had worked for, though he never spoke of it.

A bolt from the blue came on 28 April, when a letter came from Ellamami saying that Sya's daughter Denise had escaped from Hungary and arrived in Austria, but that Sya with her two boys – nine-year-old Paul (my godson) and five-year-old Szuszu – had disappeared. To be caught at the border, trying to cross the Iron Curtain, was a serious crime in all Communist countries, and this was the worst possible news one could have expected. Ellamami said she would send a cable as soon as she got any more information.

What could I do? I started a novena for Sya and went to mass and communion every day for nine days. Two weeks later Mami wrote that they had had news that Sya had been arrested on the border and the children were in the children's quarters in prison. She later wrote that though there was no news at all of Sya, the children had now been handed over to my sister Éva. What a terrible experience for the children, their father and now their mother in prison; it hardly bore thinking about.

I read and re-read Sya's last, long letter, which she had written about five months previously and in which for the first time she sounded quite desperate. She described her visit to Józsi in jail. 'He looked well and was invariably cheerful, which for me was quite difficult to simulate. He said that he knew that he was in the more enviable position, because he had no worries except thinking of me having all the difficulties to bear, and so he would make arrangements for me to join him, because there one can have a rest.' He went on to say that naturally he was joking but 'I did not feel like laughing, as he did not really know that he would not have to make a lot of arrangements!' Here Sya was referring to the police raids at their flat, and the constant threats of arrest. She then wrote that she'd had her hair cut quite short and straight. This showed me that she was already preparing herself for the possibility of arrest.

István had now started swimming and diving lessons in the pool at the Hotel do Parque. On one occasion Papa came with us, and every time István took a dive his grandfather did the same, then swam under water to the end of the pool before getting out again for the next dive. After the sixth performance I went unobserved to the trainer and asked him to terminate the lesson as the admiral was eighty-three years old and I thought that he had had enough. The trainer would not believe Papa's age, he said that it was impossible.

10 July was a Big Day! It was Mama's birthday, but we also celebrated her and Papa's Golden Wedding anniversary, which was due on the twenty-second. They each wore a golden flower buttonhole. First we went to the Church of the Salesians in Estoril, where our dear Father Francisco Pippan celebrated mass. Papa knelt with Mama at the altar and was blessed too. There were many Hungarians and others there, headed by the King of Italy and the Archdukes. Then we went back to our Casa San José, where we had prepared fifty presents, all wrapped in gold. There was a buffet lunch with a wedding cake, which the 'bride and groom' had to cut! It was altogether a great success and a blessing that we could have this lovely celebration for them.

István and I went to stay with my parents in France again; we were expecting Sya's twelve-year-old daughter Denise to arrive there. I was hoping to hear some details of her escape and what she thought had happened to her mother. When she arrived it was a very emotional meeting. It made me very content to see that she and István took to each other immediately, as if they had always been together. Our stay was very happy – except for the stories that Denise had to tell. She told us about the terror they had lived in since Józsi's arrest: several times without warning the police had searched the flat – the Communists allowed only a kilogram of sugar or flour to be kept at home, if they found any more than that in one's possession it would result in arrest. The children feared each time that their mother would be taken away as their father had been.

I arrived back in Portugal in time for the big Fatima Congress, in which many bishops from all over the world took part. The American bishop Monsignor Fulton Sheen was there, and though he spoke for only five minutes his speech had by far the most content. What impressed me most was his pointing out that there must be a reason why these apparitions happened in a place called Fatima. The woman most revered in Islam is Fatima, the daughter of Prophet Mohammed. Therefore our Lady of Fatima has become the only outward link between Islam and Christianity. Obviously the Almighty wants to unite all religions.

This was an important revelation to me, and later on I had proof of what the bishop had said, when I was in Baghdad. There was a Catholic church there called the Church of Our Lady of Fatima, and Moslem people came to the church with their prayer rugs to say their prayers.

One evening we were invited to go to a reception at the British Embassy to say goodbye to Colonel Tim Consett, the departing military attaché, and to meet the new one, Major Guy Bowden of the King's Own Hussars. As Tim introduced us he said, 'I want you to meet the only two people I will be sorry to leave.' Later, Tim told me that after we had exchanged a few words Guy Bowden said to him, 'If I see more of her, I will marry her,' upon which Tim apparently replied, 'You could do worse.'

A few days later during a lunch party, I had quite a long conversation with Major Bowden. He invited me to Queluz, where we had lunch and talked to each other for a long time. He told me that he had lost his beloved wife only a short time ago in Egypt, and did not quite know how to face life now. I told him that I knew that feeling only too well.

Madeleine Apponyi was staying with us at this time, and the Major invited us both to his house for lunch. Madeleine seemed to like him very much and later I discovered that he reminded her of her first husband, an Irishman by whom she had three children and who had tragically died one Christmas day in Ireland.

As the school year had ended I was wondering why István had had no report from St Julian's School, and finally I asked him about it. He said that he had the report, but did not show it to me 'because I came first again, and I can assure you Mama that the others know just as much as I do'. This attitude of his made me much happier than the good report.

Early in 1952 we heard that some American air force personnel had been forced down and detained in Hungary. The rumour got around that in order to obtain the release of one of the men, Mr Robert Vogeler, the United States were prepared to discuss the Hungarian government's suggestion that the American government return the Holy Crown of Saint Stephen – which was in their safe keeping – in exchange for him. On hearing the news Miklóspapa asked me to drive him to the American Embassy, where he personally delivered a letter of protest. The letter was acknowledged by the ambassador and forwarded to Washington. There was genuine alarm amongst the Hungarian emigrants all over the world. Our dear friend Ambassador Montgomery made inquiries and sent us a letter from Senator McMahon, which quoted a letter from the Department of State:

> Mr Davis, representing our government, informed the Hungarian Foreign Office that: 'The Government of the United States is not prepared to discuss the return of Saint Stephen's Crown as a condition of the release of Mr Robert A. Vogeler. This property was not removed by force from Hungary but was surrendered to the United States authorities for safekeeping and is being held in trust by them. It is therefore outside the scope of restitution and continues to be treated as property with a special status.'

We were naturally wondering why the Communist government wanted the Holy Crown returned, was it perhaps to make this symbol of a thousand-year-old monarchy disappear for good?

The first NATO conference was held in Lisbon that February, which was attended by all heads of governments – except Mr Churchill, who was not well and was replaced by Sir Anthony Eden, the foreign secretary. I knew from the military attaché, Guy Bowden, that they had long working days and the British Embassy had to entertain their guests. 'In trying to keep them amused,' Major Bowden said, 'I thought they would be interested in meeting the ex-Regent of Hungary, Admiral Horthy, who as a captain in the Austro-Hungarian navy had defeated the British at the battle of Otranto.' So Guy Bowden gave a lunch party at his house for head of NATO, Lord Ismay (known as Pug); the first sea lord of the navy, Admiral Lord Fraser; General Sir Alistair McLeod, head of Churchill's military committee; the British consul, Mr Selwyn; Papa, Mama and myself.

The party was a great success. Lord Ismay told us fascinating stories about Churchill, and after we left – Guy Bowden later told me – said, 'Admiral Horthy is a nice chap, but was he with us or agin' us?'

After a moment's silence Admiral Fraser said, 'Come on, Pug!'

To us, our present circumstances seemed a luxury – especially when compared with other Hungarian refugees. My parents-in-law never complained, even in Germany, where we were in a really difficult situation. Now I thanked God every day for what we had. That we lived in Estoril in a villa, that we did not lack food and help, having a maid and a cook, were blessings indeed.

Madeleine insisted that I join her for a few days at the Hotel Alfonso XIII in Seville; and Guy Bowden, who was going by car to England, offered to give me a lift. He was leaving Portugal to spend two years in the Staff College in Quetta, Pakistan. On the way we had another long conversation, during which he told me that his family had been connected with the military for very many years. He had six brothers, all of whom were in uniform at the beginning of World War II. His mother was still alive, his father had died when he was very young and after his death things became very difficult – Guy went out delivering newspapers when he needed new shoes. We talked a lot about the future and then he told me that he wanted to marry me.

My answer was that I did not want to get married. I could not contemplate leaving my parents-in-law and therefore I did not even want to consider it. He replied that if I was still not married when he returned from Pakistan then I would have no option, because he would not take no for an answer.

On 11 May Papa went to visit Prime Minister Oliveiro Salazar. Our consul, Arthur Baján, accompanied him. Papa was very impressed by Salazar, by his simple, courteous manner and the way he talked about his country. He said that this benevolent dictator seemed to be dedicating his life to his country, and nobody could deny that he had done a lot of good.

Miklóspapa had now finished his memoirs and we were in touch with Mr Gerhard von Reutern of Atheneum Verlag, a German publisher. He said that his collaborator, Mr Egon Heyman, was in Portugal to cover the NATO Conference, and he would like us to receive him to discuss the layout of the book. Mr Heyman stayed for three weeks and we worked with him throughout many days, Mama and I doing a lot of translations from the original Hungarian text.

When Mr Heyman stepped in as a 'ghost-writer' for the German edition, I insisted that whatever he corrected had to be vetted by us. There was no doubt that he was a good writer and he did an excellent job in dividing the chapters. He would send us the corrected texts in stages from Germany. This was where my main work began, for I soon realized that I needed to compare the text word for word with Papa's original writings, as Mr Heyman had made a lot of changes that he was not supposed to do. I did not let anything pass and sent it all back to him, pointing out every time that he was not supposed to change the text. He had sometimes even changed things in such a way that they became contrary to Papa's original meaning, and if I had not been vigilant some remarks in the book would have become a plea in defence of Germany. I did point out to him quite clearly that being a good writer and a German did not entitle him to put the German point of view into a Hungarian book. He replied saying that he was sorry, and that he only wanted to argue a point, not change the text ... which did not satisfy me as a reasonable excuse.

Every time we received chapters back for approval I went to work at once and sent them back very quickly, but the publishers often delayed sending us the chapters for revision. Heyman's letters, in which he explained the delays, were proof of this. These delays finally caused the book to come out five months later than stipulated by the contract. They said the delay was our fault and therefore did not pay us anything for the first edition.

When we received the first four copies of *Ein Leben für Ungarn* (A Life for Hungary) in December, we could not complain. The design was excellent and the photographs very good. Atheneum sold the five thousand copies but did not print a second edition, at which point – according to them – we would have been entitled to royalties. As so often in the past, the German connection did not work for us. According to our contract they were entitled to negotiate other publications in Europe, but only with the author's consent. They ignored this, and without our knowledge or consent negotiated an Italian edition with Editore Corso, who ceased trading shortly afterwards. The Italian translation was very unsatisfactory and we never received any payment.

A good friend of Pista's, the Dutchman Wim van Andringa de Kempenaer, was managing director of Enschede en Zonen, one of the largest and oldest printing works in Europe. At this time they were printing the banknotes for Portugal. Consequently he visited Portugal regularly, and kindly offered to advise us on all editions of Papa's memoirs – other than German or Hungarian. He had excellent connections and through him we found Mr Harben, a very good English agent, who organized the publication of the English, French, Spanish, and American editions. We received royalties from these publications; and when István went to Gordonstoun School in Scotland in 1955, where he still had expenses in spite of the scholarship, Miklóspapa made a settlement in his favour of the rights to all royalties from the English edition. We appointed two trustees whose duty it was to pay over the money received to Gordonstoun School, and to claim the income tax rebate.

When the Hungarian text was complete, Count Endre Széchenyi, who had a publishing firm in Argentina, produced a simple but attractive Hungarian edition of the memoirs: *Emlékiritaim*. All this required a lot of correspondence, and it became quite natural for me to look after the 'family archives', keeping all these files, newspaper cuttings, books and documents. So many years later these have proved a great help to me in writing this book, refreshing my memory – but often I wished that I could get rid of all these old letters and documents, as they sometimes weighed on me.

My main concern at that time was the education of my son. Papa and Mama said that they were too old to judge what was needed in this modern world and they would accept anything that I thought was right. I was well aware that it was my responsibility to give my son the best education possible, and I corresponded about this with friends and various schools in Switzerland and England before making a choice.

I found that without consulting me, my Irish friends had put István's name down for Eton. It had naturally been done with the best of intentions and was meant to be a surprise. The next time I was in England I went to Eton to find out more and get a sense of it. Although I was impressed by what I saw, and thought that it must be an excellent school, the people I had met who had been taught there gave me the feeling that there was a sort of Etonian stamp on them – which for an Englishman might be advantageous. But my son was Hungarian, would it be right to make him into an Etonian?

I was helped in my decision when I heard from my sister-in-law Móci Darányi that her son was at Gordonstoun School in Scotland. She thought very highly of it and her son was happy there. I liked the things she told me about this school, which was founded and run by Dr Kurt Hahn. He, being Jewish, had fled Nazi Germany, where he had created the famous school, Schule Schloss Salem.

An aspect we had to consider was that in order for István to go to there he would have to gain a scholarship. And that meant he would have to know Latin. Fortunately, Latin is part of the curriculum in private schools in Portugal; so when, together with István, we made the decision to apply for Gordonstoun, I talked to Mr Traynor who had a private school in Cascais, and of whom I heard very good reports. This proved to be a good choice. When István attended the school the following term, Mr Traynor supervised his scholarship studies with great attention, and István made excellent progress, again coming top in his class.

To our delight, my parents announced their intention to visit us for six days at the end of June. One evening after their arrival, when we were sitting together and the children had gone to bed, to our surprise Ellamami told us that this trip of theirs had been paid for by their host, Sir Oliver Duncan, in order that they could ask Miklóspapa on his behalf for my hand in marriage! Mami then explained how much Oliver wanted to help with István's education, how very rich he was, and that I was at liberty to stay with my parents-in-law as much as I wanted, plus lots of other advantages that I have forgotten.

Miklóspapa's answer was that the question should not have been put to him but to me, as I was an adult and was absolutely free to do whatever I wanted. So Ellamami turned to me, and I had to weigh my words carefully as I did not want to offend Oliver. I asked Ellamami to tell Oliver how touched I was by his offer, but stated quite clearly that it was impossible for me to accept it. My dear Papi said nothing during all this time and sat there with a noncommittal expression, but I knew what he was thinking – he knew very well what my answer would be.

Early in 1953 Madeleine started urging me to go with her to Paris and on to Cortina d'Ampezzo for a little skiing. She had never been so insistent and, as her birthday was coming up, I finally decided to join her. She did not tell me that she had been corresponding with Guy Bowden, and had invited him to join us there. When we arrived he was waiting for us. We were very amused when he told us that he had arrived a few days before us because he had heard that I was a good skier, so he wanted to get in a bit of training beforehand.

I was annoyed when Madeleine tried to talk me into marrying Guy. I did not want to be pushed, and told her that I would make up my own mind, if ever the right time came. I did enjoy his company and we spent a very enjoyable week together. We celebrated my birthday, but Guy went on giving me presents every day, scarves, gloves, boots. He told me that he was well aware of my situation and, having met my parents-in-law, he understood it. He wanted me to know that he was not rich but could give me a good life, and if I were to marry him, as long as they lived my parents-in-law would be number one and he number two: I could stay with them as much as I wished. My answer to this was that a man does not get married to be number two. But he said that this was an exceptional situation, which touched me.

At the end of the week we left, saying goodbye to Guy, who was going back to Pakistan. We stayed in Paris for three days, and while we were there Oliver Duncan rang me and invited me to dinner at Maxim's. When I arrived I was surprised to find that there were just the two of us, and I soon found out why. I had noticed that he was carrying a briefcase, and from it he suddenly produced a blank sheet of paper, which he put in front of me with a pen, saying that he wanted to marry me, and that I should write down a list of my conditions, which he would sign without reading what I had written. Having said this he wanted to withdraw, but I stopped him, saying that firstly my parents must have already told him my answer and secondly, when I was in Cannes I had heard him say that he wanted to have children, therefore he ought to know that I could not have any more since my operation.

Here he interrupted me saying that this was no problem, as he had enough money to have it arranged that I could have children again. I was amazed at this naiveté. He then said that even if I had no other children, István would be the child he would look after, send to the best schools, and so on. I made it quite clear that it was no use going on talking about it, as I just could not marry him. I would always be grateful to him for his great kindness to my parents and to so many Hungarians, and hoped that he understood that I wanted to stay with my parents-in-law and would never marry for money. The dinner was excellent, but the conversation became a bit strained.

Although I felt no sense of urgency, I gave a lot of thought to Guy's proposal. One day Miklóspapa and I were sitting alone in the living room when, without any previous intention, I found myself saying, 'Papa, I am thinking perhaps of getting married.' I stopped and thought, 'Oh, why did I say that?' But Papa put up his hand to prevent me saying any more and said, 'Whomever you marry will be my son.' I was astounded and deeply moved; I could never have imagined this reaction. Papa did not even ask me who the person was. He seemed to indicate that he would surely like anyone whom I chose. At this point Mama entered the room and we did not talk about it any more.

But what amazed me most was that, whereas previously when I was away he had always written things like, 'Don't stay long, come back soon, we need you,' or 'We can hardly wait for you to be back,' from this moment on he never said that, as though he did not want to put pressure on me. This was the man who had commanded a fleet, had been commander-in-chief of the army, head of state for twenty-four years, and who now made no attempt to selfishly keep me back, the one who looked after his finances, his correspondence, his only grandson – because he wanted me to be happy. I never imagined this could happen.

It was with much sadness that we heard from John Flournoy Montgomery the news of his wife's death, as we knew how heavily it would weigh upon our dear friend and benefactor. It was only now, after her death, that he wrote to us about her part in precipitating Miklóspapa's release from Nürnberg. He said that she would never let him mention it. One night they had read in the paper that the Regent of Hungary had been imprisoned in Nürnberg and would be tried there if he was not turned over to Tito, who was demanding that he be sent to Yugoslavia for trial. This got them both very excited and his wife said, 'What can we do? We've got to do something.'

'The only thing is to engage a lawyer for him and send him over to Nürnberg.'

'Let's do it at once,' she said.

'All right,' agreed John, ' I'll call Homer Cummings in the morning.'

'No,' she said, 'Call him now.'

'But it's eleven at night, and he will be in bed.'

She said, 'I don't care. I won't sleep until I know we have engaged somebody.'

Homer Cummings was the former attorney general and one of the most outstanding lawyers in the US. John Montgomery continued:

> At my wife's insistence I called Homer Cummings in Washington, who sure enough was in bed, but agreed to take the case. About a week later the Regent was released and sent back to Weilheim.
>
> My wife, with characteristic modesty, never let me tell this to anyone. But I thought you would be interested to know, and I would like to have it known. She was a great admirer of both Madam Horthy and the Regent, as was I, and she felt that the idea of his being held even for a minute in Nürnberg was revolting, and even more so the idea that he would be tried.

On 15 April 1953 Archduke Otto – after three years – finally returned Papa's visit of 21 May 1950. While he was with Papa in the living room, Mama and I had a chat upstairs with José Saldanha, with whom he had come. We went down later to join them and, thank God, both Papa and Archduke Otto looked contented. When he left we stood outside, and I was really impressed when Papa said how difficult this must have been for him. This to me proved again what an unselfish person Papa was, to be thinking of the Archduke and not of himself.

During the Archduke's stay in Lisbon we were invited to a cocktail party held in his honour by José Saldanha. Although the atmosphere was friendly, Archduke Otto seemed icy towards me, and I realized that he must dislike me profoundly. The reason for that could only be a comment made to his brother – which I was told by a person who overheard it – that I only stayed with my parents-in-law because I still hoped that my son would become king of Hungary.

Do people say these things to ingratiate themselves? When we were told this story, Magdamama said to me that she had been the target before, and now it seemed that I was the one under attack. Nothing could be further from us than royal ambitions.

István had taken his scholarship exam for Gordonstoun, and just as we were about to do our summer move the good news came that out of over twenty applicants he had won the scholarship to go there. We celebrated his success and his grandfather gave him a wristwatch.

Our plans now were to visit Scotland on the way to Ireland, presenting ourselves at Gordonstoun School to meet the teachers and personally take a look at the arrangements. We sailed to London and caught the train to Edinburgh. On the journey I had a chance to have a serious conversation with István. I wanted to find out how he would feel about my getting married again. This was very important to me, as Ila told me a few years ago of a conversation between her and István, when she had said that she hoped that one day his mother would marry again. István was then about eight years old, and his answer was, 'If she gets married I will kill her!' Now he was thirteen. First I asked him whether he remembered Guy Bowden. 'Oh, yes,' he said, 'I do, and I like him very much.' So I ventured to say that Guy had asked me to marry him and I was thinking about it, but wanted to have his opinion on the matter.

After a little pause he said, 'I think that is very good, Mama; for now that I am away from home you will need someone to look after you.' For the moment we left it at that.

We went on to Aberdeen where John Paton, one of the trustees of the school, was waiting for us. We knew that he had spent many years in Hungary, but were amazed how well he spoke Hungarian. It was a great relief for us that he had offered to look after István while he was at Gordonstoun.

Next morning I went for a meeting with the headmaster, Kurt Hahn. When I entered his study he said to me straight away that I did not have to worry, because my son would remain a Hungarian here, nobody would want to change him. What a judge of character! I was relieved and grateful for this reassurance. Things were better than I had hoped, and István seemed happy and interested in everything. We went on to our Irish holiday with light hearts.

On our return from Ireland, John Paton picked us up from Aberdeen and drove us to the school. It was hard for me to leave István there; I knew that I would miss him terribly, and Gordonstoun seemed very far from Estoril. But I also knew that it was the right thing for him to get away from Mum and Ila and the grandparents. I was aware that this first separation was also very hard for him, but we just had to do what made sense and was right. From Aberdeen I sent a big parcel to him with things that might be useful, so that he should feel that he was not left entirely on his own or forgotten.

On account of Papa's memoirs I had to travel to London and Paris. My parents had mentioned my stay to a friend of theirs, Mr Árpád Plesch, who happened to be in London at the time. He was Hungarian, and extremely wealthy. He was very kind and helpful to me while I was in London and, as he was also going to Paris, arranged for us to travel on the same plane.

My parents arrived from Cannes, and after my meeting with the publishers we all met to have dinner at Árpád's flat. After dinner my parents suddenly declared that they were tired and, insisting that I should stay on, left rather hurriedly. It was obviously some kind of a plot, and after putting on some music, Árpád told me that he wanted to talk to me undisturbed, to tell me that he wanted to marry me. He asked me not to interrupt, then told me that he was very attracted to me and how much he could help all my family, particularly my sisters in Hungary. He said that he realized he was much older than me – and I will never forget the sentence with which he ended his arguments: 'To anyone who marries me, I can guarantee twenty-five years of happy widowhood.'

In my answer, I thanked him for his offer and told him that I could not accept it, that I could not leave my parents-in-law while they still needed me, and I could not marry for money. I ended up by saying that I thought I knew the person to whom such an offer would really appeal, and that was Countess Eti Esterházy, who I heard was at the moment in South America. After a long conversation about life and things worth living for, he took me back to our hotel and we parted as friends.

I really do not know why I mentioned Eti to him; but Eti – being a straightforward person – once told me that she would leave any husband if a richer one turned up. She had already been married several times. Imagine my surprise when, after a relatively short time, Árpád and Eti got married! The things he had predicted came true, because he only lived for a few years after that; Eti lived on, breeding racehorses very successfully and winning prizes in France and in England, and enjoying her happy widowhood.

It may sound a bit hasty to refuse two such large fortunes as were offered by Sir Oliver Duncan and Árpád Plesch – particularly when we had lost everything and my family to a certain extent depended on me – but never for a second was there a doubt in my mind that no good could come out of marrying purely for money. I had no problem with this, and I knew that none of my sisters or my parents-in-law would expect this from me.

I thought of what I had felt when I was with Guy Bowden, which was a sense of stability and reassurance in my feelings. In Portugal there were letters from him waiting for me, in which he said that it looked as though he might be staying in Pakistan for another year.

When I got back I found my parents-in-law in good health and looking very well. Estoril was really an ideal place for them. They had much to occupy them: their friends whom they visited, the walks they took every day, and Miklóspapa had his huge correspondence. We all missed István very much. Luckily he wrote quite frequently, and his letters were very cheerful, including drawings and amusing descriptions of all the teachers. He had received some money as a present, and asked me to order two books for him: *The Borderlines of Science* and Einstein's *The World as I See It*, which showed where his interests lay. His fascination with this subject remained strong all through his school years, and in the holidays we would often read these books together. Later, when a generous American friend subscribed to *Nucleonis* and *Scientific American* for him, he would read these periodicals from cover to cover, as other children read comics.

That winter we received the sudden and unexpected news from Switzerland of the death of our dear Uncle Eugene Horthy. Recently we had received a letter from him telling us, in his usual amusing way, about his recovery from bronchitis. He was ten years Papa's junior and the last surviving one out of Papa's six brothers and two sisters. I knew István would be heart-broken, as they had been very close. I broke the news to him on his return for the Christmas holiday.

I had been feeling rather unwell for a few days before Christmas, and on Christmas Day itself my complexion suddenly began turning yellow and we discovered that I had jaundice. Professor Pap, our 'Uncle Doctor' came to work out my diet and medication programme. It seemed that there was an epidemic of infectious jaundice going round that I had somehow picked up. I had to remain in bed, which gave me a lot of time for reading with István. He also brought his chemistry experiments into my bedroom. There were explosions, squirts and spatters and a great deal of laughter.

21

I Marry Again

Magdamama was in bed with bronchitis, and I had an infectious strain of jaundice. What a way to start the new year!

István left to go back to Gordonstoun. We agreed that he should write to me in Hungarian to stay in practice while he was in England. His letters were very entertaining, full of humour, and the way he addressed me changed all the time. He first called me Édesmama, which is often used in Hungary and means 'real mother'. Then came his own inventions of Mimici, Minusz, Muzuk, in all kinds of varieties, until he ended up by calling me 'Dear Muzulmán' and maintained that for a very long time. This is 'Muslim' in Hungarian. There was no understandable reason for this, as we had never talked about Islam or Muslim people.

A long and very moving letter came from Sya's husband Józsi in Hungary. Here are some extracts about his visit to her in jail:

> I hardly know where to begin. The last time I saw my unique darling she was in very low spirits, as she had been in bed with flu for three days, and still had a temperature. On first glance her condition seemed to be good – possibly 65 to 70 kilos! [approximately 140–150 lbs.] (Many inmates had this strange puffed-up appearance; it was the result of being fed on potatoes and bread, and crouching on stools for ten to twelve hours a day.)
>
> Because of her fever, standing up for very long exhausted her, so our meeting was not really a success. Since then I have had news that she has completely recovered and is working again, and have heard lately that at last she has achieved her wish to get an office assignment. ... It is a great relief that she no longer has to bend over on a stool all day, but can move freely around in the workshop. This carries many other

advantages: times of visits, possibility of writing letters, duration of conversation at visits, receiving of food parcels. She can also more easily achieve a reduction in her sentence, on which everything depends. The room she has occupied since January has an iron stove, so after all these years she does not suffer from the cold ...

The Nescafé I sent her for Christmas was such a joy after three years that she said it was worth more than ten honeymoon nights! So I continue to send her some every time. And I will not be modest, but ask you to send me some more, as I have run out of it ... Thanks and thanks again for the IKKA parcels. They made our Christmas. If we are ever able to spend this special time together again, it will bring us almost unbearable happiness. ...

Of her freedom there is still no positive news, although lots of promises; the quarter-time reduction of sentence concession still stands, which is her reward for good conduct and work-percentage. This means that she could be home in July. Any decision on this won't be reached until the end of March, but you can imagine that her spirits are still high ...

It was all such painful news that I was reduced to tears reading about her suffering. One can barely imagine what was involved in reducing her sentence by 'hard work'. Thanks be to God that she survived. On her birthday I went to church to pray for her and lit a candle ... if she were to be let out of jail this year, how would she be, what would she look like? Would she be able to recover?

After the Easter holidays an urgent call came from Madeleine: she would like to take me to Gibraltar to meet Guy, who would be arriving there from Pakistan. I was not quite sure whether it was right to go, but I went nevertheless. When we got to Gibraltar, Guy was waiting for us and drove us to the Hotel in Algeciras. The next day was Sunday and he accompanied me to church, and afterwards we lay in the sun on the beach and talked. We had lunch with Madeleine, and then later, when we went for a rest, she exasperated me by again trying to talk me into making a decision about Guy. But we had been apart too long and I felt that I needed some time.

We spent two days in Gibraltar, going shopping, walking on the golf course, or just lying on the beach and talking. The similarity in our lives was interesting. Guy had been very happily married to his wife Jean, the daughter of the Governor of Burma, Sir John Wise. Jean had died very tragically whilst they were in Egypt. She was expecting their first child and her ectopic pregnancy had not been detected. One afternoon Guy went off to play polo and she stayed at home because she felt unwell. When Guy returned he found that she had been rushed to the hospital with serious haemorrhaging, and by the time Guy got there she was dead. I told Guy that I could not have any more children, but he did not seem to mind, and I felt that after his experience with Jean he would probably have been very worried about a pregnancy.

When we had discussed seemingly everything, we decided to get married. Suddenly all the tension was gone and I felt very happy. Guy gave me a beautiful aquamarine engagement ring, and when we went to dinner Madeleine spotted it immediately. So we told her about our decision and she ordered some champagne to celebrate. It had been a wonderful day, ending in a very happy evening.

From Gibraltar we drove on to Cannes, where Guy met my parents. I had naturally also written to Estoril about my engagement, and both Miklóspapa's and Magdamama's letters were waiting for me. These were full of wonderful expressions of love and affection. Mama said:

> My dear Little One,
>
> We were reassured and happy when we received your letter yesterday. It felt infinitely good that all doubts and uncertainties have been resolved, and that you are happy and contented. One can feel that a clean and deep feeling binds you together, which is the biggest guarantee for lasting happiness. We are only sad that at this decisive and happy moment of your life we cannot hold you to our hearts. But be assured, my dear Ila, that with all the warmth and love of our hearts we share in your happiness and are very satisfied with your decision. At last the uncertainty is at an end. There will be a content and aim in your life, and there will be a truthful heart to share your worries and be a support in the struggles of life. We know Guy very little, but nevertheless somehow have great confidence in him. And it is also a guarantee for us that you have chosen him ...

Miklóspapa just wrote a short letter saying:

> Mama expressed so nicely our feelings on hearing of your big decision that I just want to say that she spoke from my soul! Although it will be difficult to get used to you being absent more often – not entirely from

With István (aged three)

István with his grandfather in the grounds at Gödöllo

István with his many presents, Christmas 1943

Our arrival at the railway station of Kelenföld, with Gestapo escort

The SS barracks at Waldbichl (the Hirschberg mansion)

'Waldbichl' as it looks today

*ván's Christmas tree with our handmade
decorations, 1944*

Admiral Horthy with the American General Dahlquist

The 'without cares' villa in Weilheim

Family togetherness; Uncle Eugene still with us

My small room in 25 Pollingerstrasse, Weilheim

My mother-in-law cooking

István's first day at school

The Admiral, István, Nicky and Dr Reuben Hecht

Leaving Switzerland, December 1948

Admiral Horthy testifying at Nürnberg,
March 1948

My father-in-law sailing with István and Miklós Kállay. Rapallo, 1949

On our way to Portugal: my father-in-law on the deck of the Ana C

The family in front of the Hotel do Parque

The Admiral watching the ocean at Esto

I meet István with the Humber Hawk car

sentimental but also from selfish motives – I am happy about your decision. I think I know Guy well enough to feel that he is worthy of your decision. Until we meet, I send him my hearty greetings as the new member of our family.
Miklóspapa.

In Paris, to my tremendous joy, for the first time in many years I met Lujza Esterházy, the sister of our dear friend Bibi, (Count János Esterházy) who had fought so hard against the anti-Jewish laws, and saved so many Jews in Slovakia. She told me in detail about what had happened to him.

His ordeal started in 1945, when it was proclaimed in Slovakia that all minorities were to be expelled because Czechoslovakia had to become a 'national state'. Bibi was arrested and deported to Russia without a trial. He was condemned to death in absentia – just because he was a Hungarian politician. There was no news of him for four years. When, in 1949, Bibi was sent back to Czechoslovakia from a concentration camp in northern Russia, he was already very sick with tuberculosis. On his arrival in Slovakia the family managed to have his death sentence transmuted to one of life imprisonment, with the hope of an eventual amnesty. He was so ill that he needed hospital treatment, but then he was suddenly taken to another jail. Thereafter he was transferred from one jail to another, eight times, while they tried unsuccessfully to 're-educate' him. He wasn't included in the general amnesty, because amnesty 'was not an act of mercy'; it was given only to those whom they considered to have received the 'requisite punishment'.

After twelve years in prison, on 8 March 1957 at the age of fifty-five, Bibi died in jail. The authorities even refused to hand over his body to the family for burial.

Lulu Esterházy later wrote a book, which Bibi's daughter Alice published in 1966. *Szivek az ár Ellen* (Hearts against the Tide)[56] is a book I would highly recommend to everyone, outlining as it does the only possible path to reconciliation – through tolerance. Lulu was Hungarian but loved the Slovak people, just as I do. We have both lived among them and therefore know that the dissentions are only the result of political manoeuvrings.

Guy had to get back to London, and I returned to Estoril after my eventful month. I was back in time to do my service in Fatima for the June pilgrimages. I had to tell them that I would no longer be able to continue regular work as a servita, because I was getting married and did not know when I would be available.

The latest news from Hungary was wonderful: Sya had been released from jail after three years and three months of hell. The family were together again at last. I prayed that God would protect them, and that my sisters and I might also be reunited one day.

On Papa's eighty-sixth birthday there was a big Hungarian gathering at Casa San José, with champagne-cocktails. Miklóspapa made a point of announcing my engagement to everyone present, a surprise that was greeted with touching enthusiasm. I paid a special visit to the British ambassador, Sir Nigel Ronald, to tell him the good news, as I particularly wanted Guy's friends at the Embassy to hear it from me.

Guy felt that the plans for our wedding now depended on where he was going to be stationed by the War Office, as life would be difficult if he had to go very far away. A week after my return he telephoned to say that we could now get married, as he had been transferred to his regiment in Germany. I then went to the Cardinal Patriarch's office to enquire about the possibility of a quiet wedding in Portugal. This seemed almost impossible, because the preparation of the necessary documents would apparently take at least two months, and possibly up to six. This was because we were both foreigners and of different religions and who knows what else. But I was told that it could take just as long for Portuguese nationals. Seemingly it was easier to get a divorce in Portugal than to get married! We realized that a wedding in London would be much easier.

At this stage our dear Brazilian friends the Gracies stepped in; their daughter Betty, who had recently been with me in Fatima, had put them in the picture. Samuel de Souza Leão Gracie was now the Brazilian ambassador in London, and they invited me to stay with them at the Brazilian Embassy, from where they would be pleased to 'give me away'.

We worked out our plans in detail. We offered a slightly higher annual rent to the owner of Casa San José, in order to keep it all the year round in the future; so from now on my parents-in-law would not have to move somewhere else in the summer, which was a great relief. Guy had to be in Germany on 1 September. Therefore, as soon as the papers were in order, we would get married in London; and after a two-week honeymoon in England we would go on to Scotland to collect István at the beginning of his holidays. We would all then be together in Portugal until Guy was due to join his regiment. I would remain in Portugal until the end of István's holidays, and then join Guy.

The wedding was fixed for 8 July, and I flew to London three days before. We had dinner at the Gracies. I will never forget the touching way in which they received me. I felt very much at home.

On the day of the wedding I went to mass in the church along the street from the Brazilian Embassy. Guy chose to come with me, which as he was an Anglican I found very touching.

For the wedding I wore a light silver-grey suit with a white toque, white gloves and a bunch of my favourite flowers, lilies of the valley, pinned to my shoulder. At eleven thirty we arrived at Westminster Cathedral. Guy's witness was Keith Matthews (our friend from the British Embassy in Lisbon) and mine was my cousin Count Marc Pejacsevich. Marc brought with him his adorable little daughter Mausi, who held the ring. It was sad for me that my family was absent, and I thought it strange and sad that none of Guy's family were present. I had not yet met his mother or any of his six brothers, but Guy said they were all away. After saying goodbye to everyone at the Cathedral we left for the Goring Hotel, where we were staying before driving to Wales.

Before leaving the hotel I received a letter from Magdamama. The letter was hand written and sent on my wedding day, and I have kept and cherished it as the most precious wedding gift of all:

Our dear, beloved Little Girl,

On this day, which is a big turning point in your life, our hearts are so full of love and warmth towards you that we don't want to send a trivial short cable, and have chosen this way of expressing our feelings. With a grateful heart we thank providence, which guided you into our family as a substitute for our many painful losses. And gratefully we thank you for the attachment, devotion and warm-hearted solicitude with which you brightened up our difficult years. You sacrificed the young years of your life for us, helped wherever you could, with your heart, your love, good advice and work – the good Lord should bless you for it with undisturbed, clean, everlasting happiness in your future life.

One thing we ask from you in the future, don't drift away from us, remain our daughter for ever – with whom we can share our joys and worries. Tell Guy that we welcome him into our family with sincere sympathy and confidence; and if he will make you happy and take István into his care with love and understanding, then he can count on our love.

We are with you in our thoughts today and pray for you, for if anyone deserves to be happy, then it is you, our dear, good, sweet little daughter. Accept our blessing, and with the protection of the Holy Virgin begin your new life.

We love you very much and embrace you together with Guy,

Your Mother

Miklóspapa had added to the letter: 'Again she spoke from my soul! And I can only add that we will miss you terribly in every way. With true love, your Father.'

I was speechless; tears were running down my face. I had not sacrificed anything; I just did what I felt was right, and was just responding to the love that they had always given me. This love and harmony we had for each other was indeed a great blessing.

From Wales we drove north to Gordonstoun to pick up István. And from there we all went on to Lincoln to visit Guy's brother Desmond, who had a big farm nearby at Ranby Hall. Desmond was a very good-looking, friendly person, but a heavy drinker. His wife Pat was charming and they had three lovely children. When we got back to London we discovered that Guy would not be able to come back with us to Portugal, because he had to leave early for Iserlohn in Germany. This was a great disappointment; István and I only stayed in London for two days before going home to Portugal.

As Guy's wife, I was now entitled to a British passport. I went to the Consulate to take the Oath of Allegiance. Afterwards we went to watch the cinemascope film of the Royal Tour, which I found very affecting, having just sworn allegiance to the Queen.

I received my British passport and made preparations for my journey to Germany. Ila was coming with me, which she seemed pleased about. There was not much for her to do in Estoril; Papa and Mama were well cared for by our dear cook Maria and their very special maid Guilhermina.

In September Guy wrote a very gloomy letter from Iserlohn. After serving two years in Pakistan as an instructor and chief of staff coordinator at Quetta Staff College, Guy was told by the Ministry of Defence that he must return to regimental duty, it being normal army procedure to do tours with the staff before returning to the troops. Now, his commanding officer, Colonel N. Wall, had told him that he did not want him to come back to the regiment. Having such a bad relationship with his commander was very depressing. The colonel in chief of the regiment had told Guy that all the squadron leaders had asked to be transferred because they would not continue to serve under Colonel Wall. 'Go and be firm with him,' he added.

Old friends who had served with him in Palestine and Germany had welcomed Guy, but Colonel Wall was rude and went out of his way to make Guy's life unpleasant. The colonel in chief had told Wall of the squadron leaders' complaints against him, and he obviously thought that Guy had been sent there to replace him.

When Ila and I arrived at Iserlohn I found myself in a rather embarrassing situation, as Colonel Wall ignored me for two days; and when eventually we met by chance, he greeted me very coldly. I pretended not to notice so as to avoid any further embarrassment. The other officers were friendly, but they did not seem to like their commander.

Then Guy was sent for by Colonel Wall, who asked him why he had disobeyed certain orders the colonel had given. Guy was astonished, and replied that the colonel's orders had been carried out to the full. The next day Guy was sent for and formally charged with insubordination and failing to carry out orders. This meant a court martial.

The day of the court martial was a terrible one. Naturally I was not present, but could sense the tension and was afraid of what might happen. There had been no witnesses at the crucial conversations, and this meant it was the commander's word against Guy's. If five officers of the King's Own Hussars had not volunteered to give evidence, goodness only knows what injustice might have been done. They gave evidence in support of Guy and stated quite openly what they thought of their commanding officer: that he had an ungovernable temper, during which it was impossible to reason with him; and that he made false accusations, which he later regretted.

Colonel Wall had also seemingly made comments about me. During his cross examination, he denied that he had called me a 'Nazi'; but Captain Peter Clark stated that he had received instructions to find out if it were possible to stop Guy being posted to the regiment, 'because of his marriage to a Hungarian Nazi'.

The Brigadier General, who said later that it had been a 'frame up', dismissed the charge. So Guy was acquitted. Found not guilty! As he was coming out of the building people rushed up to congratulate him. That evening almost all the officers came with their wives to our house to celebrate.

What nonsense it all was. The story was featured on the radio, and there were articles about us in the *Daily Telegraph* and other papers, with photographs of us coming out of church after our wedding, and headlines such as: 'Major's wife checked up on by colonel'; 'Major was not insubordinate'; 'Our colonel had a bad temper'. Luckily they were stating the truth.

Guy went to London to discuss his future. Hope was running high among our friends that he would replace Colonel Wall. But eventually we heard that the colonel would remain for the time being and that Guy has been posted back to England. He was going to Catterick – which was a training centre for Armoured Corps conscripts. While Guy was making the move to Yorkshire I went back to Portugal, to tell our strange story of being the losing winners.

The year 1955 began with beautiful weather. Having spent a wonderful Christmas with the family in Portugal, my thoughts were straying homeward to Hungary all the time. My family there were all free now; they could at last be together. And although their lives must be full of problems and fears, that at least was a wonderful blessing.

I left for England having prepared myself to expect the worst, but the Catterick camp was in fact a pleasant surprise. Our first house was quite adequate, and we soon moved to an even better one. People were very friendly. Yorkshire was very cold at that time of year, with lots of snow and strong winds. Coming downstairs on the day after my arrival, I saw a strange sight. Inside the front door a small carpet was vibrating a few inches above the ground! I had heard a lot about ghosts in Scotland, and thought that perhaps one had come down south to Yorkshire. When I investigated, I found there was a large gap under the front door and the strong wind from outside was lifting up the carpet. Why was there no double-glazing, as we had in Hungary? And why have gaps under the doors?

István wrote to me:

> This evening I am going to a 'Gordonstoun Society' debate; the motion is: 'This house deplores all American influence on world affairs'. I am sure that everyone will be for the motion, so I am preparing a violently pro-American speech. It is frightfully cold here, the snow is quite deep, and this morning going over to classes my legs were just about to drop off – it must have been at least 201 below zero. I am convinced that the day of judgement has come ...
>
> I am sorry I have still not sent off the letter but I can only write about half a dozen words at a time and then I have to thaw out my fingers above the radiator to be able to continue – no exaggeration. Room temperature could be about -20° C ... Thermometer falling. Power running out. Frostbite. Barometer falling. Below survival level. Blizzard getting worse. Ink running out – sorry, freezing solid, have to thaw it out. Sun obscured. Not a chance. Feet frozen. Fifteen pullovers beginning to let through the cold. Must last out – only five weeks more ... must thaw out.
>
> Lots of love,
> István
> P.S. My speech was a great success!

I sent him a pair of warm gloves, hoping he would survive!

My life settled into a routine. When Guy was at work I did all the domestic things. I had no help for the first few weeks because Ila was not able to come until she had the appropriate papers. So for the first time in my life I started to cook all the meals on my own. I read recipes and enjoyed following them, and luckily Guy was full of praise. I was also given the use of a horse called 'Lady' and rode every day; a much-needed form of exercise and one that I fully enjoyed.

Our commander, Colonel Dodkins, together with his wife Lorna and their children, were very friendly. Through them I met all the 'C' Squadron families, whom I visited regularly. Together with Colonel Dodkins we were often invited to social events such as cocktail parties, which I found rather difficult as so much drinking went on. At one such event I had a strange conversation with one of the officer's wives who had several children: she told me that all her children were a result of cocktail parties. I could hardly believe what I was hearing – if children were conceived in this way what effect would this have on them?

I also became aware for the first time of how much Guy drank and how it affected him. He was by nature considerate and thoughtful, but when he had a drink he was a different person altogether, impatient and rude, blaming me for everything. It was not his fault – I discovered later that there had been a drinking problem in his family – but it was something I could never have imagined and was completely unprepared for. This continued for many years, and at times made life very difficult for me.

István arrived for his Easter holidays. At school and amongst his English friends he was now known as Stephen, and Guy had also started calling him by that name. So from now on I too will refer to him as Stephen. We took him out riding and Guy gave him squash lessons. And on Easter Sunday I hid presents for them both and made a roast beef lunch – for which Stephen gave me a written diploma!

At this time the Austrian Peace Treaty was due to be signed, and Miklóspapa wrote letters to the foreign secretaries of the three great Western Powers: John Foster Dulles of the United States, Harold Macmillan of the United Kingdom and Antoine Pinay of France. My brother-in-law Nicky in Estoril and I in Yorkshire helped with the translations of these letters:

> In all likelihood the Austrian Peace Treaty shall be signed in the near future. The significance this will have in shaping the fate of Hungary prompted me to address myself to the foreign secretaries of the three great Western Powers.
>
> According to the dispositions of the peace treaty of

1946, concluded in Paris between the victorious Allied Powers and Hungary, the Soviet Union guaranteed the withdrawal of occupation troops from Hungary within ninety days dated from the conclusion of the Treaty of Peace with the State of Austria.

In view of tactics adopted hitherto by the Soviet Union it is to be foreseen that she will attempt to avoid fulfilment of the above commitment. In concordance and agreement with the Communist government of Hungary, the Soviet Union is able to furnish the legal pretext necessary for maintaining occupying troops in Hungary.

If the Western Powers, signatories of the Paris Peace Treaty, accept the violation of a guarantee undersigned by the Soviet Union within the framework of the same treaty, Moscow gains another victory over the oppressed nations behind the Iron Curtain. These nations would feel completely abandoned by the West. Not only their faith in a future liberation would be tragically shaken, but their heroic – open or passive – resistance against Communism would be fatally broken. In the problem of the defence of Europe and the Western world the complete cessation of the resistance of these subjugated millions would mean a grave loss. The situation would be quite to the contrary should the Western Powers oblige the Soviet Union to withdraw all occupation troops from Hungary and Romania in accordance with the pledge signed at Paris.

I am convinced Communism will never renounce the aim of global domination of the world. The period of so-called peaceful co-existence is employed to increase military preparedness, with a view to striking at a chosen moment at the freedom of the world ...[57]

If only the Western Powers had heeded this warning, and been firm and decisive in carrying out the terms of the peace treaty, then much bloodshed, suffering and immeasurable damage would have been avoided in my devastated country.

This year was the first time that I was not with Miklóspapa on his birthday; and early in the morning I sent him a long telegram. I got a lovely, hand-written reply, telling me that words could not express the joy they felt about coming to see us that summer, and that from my letters he could feel the harmony in which we lived. He told me about his birthday, when he had received from one of the guests some old photographs of himself starting the Saint Stephen's Day procession in Budapest. He said he looked like a fully decorated Christmas tree in that photo.

The admiral's upcoming visit created quite a wave of excitement in the regiment. Colonel Dodkins invited me to a secret meeting, where the Regimental Band was being taught to play the Hungarian national anthem. He wanted me to hear whether it was being played correctly. The way they played it was quite wrong; they made it into a march, whereas our anthem is a prayer. So they practised it with me until they got it right.

I was very touched by the efforts of the colonel, who was also organizing a special dinner at the Officer's Mess, with all the officers of the regiment, and planning to serve Tokay wine to toast Papa.

I went to London to meet my parents-in-law. This was a very happy moment. We went by train to Darlington, where Guy and Stephen were waiting for us with Robert Bidolf, assigned as ADC to Papa, and a detachment of soldiers, all arranged by our Colonel Dodkins. The whole visit was a great success, the highlight being the 'guest night' at the Officers' Mess, in honour of Miklóspapa, to which he and Guy went together. Mama and I heard the details afterwards: the fanfares, the beautifully played Hungarian Anthem, the Tokay wine and the toast to the Queen and to my father-in-law, as guest of honour. It was a wonderful thing to have done and I am forever grateful to Colonel Dodkins.

One evening during their stay we received a surprise visit from a young guards officer, bringing to the admiral the compliments of Field Marshal Lord Ironside, who was in the nearby military hospital having had an accident. The local general had mentioned to him that he had a VIP, Admiral Horthy, staying in the area, and the field marshal would be delighted if he could visit him in hospital: he had met the admiral in 1919 in Hungary.

The next day we all went to meet the field marshal, who was laid out on two beds put together, he being over 6 ft tall. As we entered he said 'Jó estét kivánok Miklós.' (I wish you a good evening, Nicholas) and turning to Guy said with a smile, 'As you know, the best families in Britain have Hungarian blood; the Queen of course, and my family – who fled to Hungary during the religious troubles in the past.' Nodding towards Miklóspapa he continued, 'You know, he is just like a British admiral. I was in Budapest after the end of the First World War, in November 1919, as head of the British Military Mission. The streets were crowded with excited screaming jubilant people. The admiral got off his horse, handed it over to someone, saw the British Mission and walked up to me smiling, saying, 'They all get so excited' – just like a British admiral.' After this visit, Field Marshal Ironside and Miklóspapa often corresponded.[xiii]

We all went by car to Gordonstoun for the school's twenty-first anniversary celebrations. What a young school it seemed compared to the other centuries-old schools in the British Isles. But a strong youngster nevertheless! The Duke of Edinburgh attended the celebration and we all had the pleasure of meeting him. Miklóspapa was invited to attend the lunch given in honour of Prince Philip by the headmaster.

At the end of their visit we drove Papa and Mama to London, where they met the many Hungarians who flocked there with their families to see them. Then, at Southampton, we put them on the boat home. Miklóspapa wrote later that they 'very much enjoyed and liked Ily's new home'.

Later in the year I went to spend some time with them in Portugal. On the way back, I met Guy in Paris and we spent a wonderful few days exploring that beautiful city. We visited the cathedral of Notre Dame, which was a great experience, including one amusing moment when I went up to the wall where the names and pictures of all the Popes were listed, looking for my ancestor Pope Innocence XI. I had forgotten to mention him to Guy, who came up and asked what I was doing. So I told him that I was looking for my great-uncle. Guy thought that I was joking, until I showed him the Pope's name, Prince Odescalchi, which was also the name of my grandmother. We had a good laugh about it.

In November I went with Guy to my first English foxhunt. In ideal weather, the lovely countryside covered in splendour of autumn colours, we lost the first fox and then had a long exciting run with plenty of jumps; lost the second fox, and ended the hunt near Catterick. I was always on the side of the fox, so this was the perfect hunt for me.

I had asked Stephen what he wanted for Christmas and he answered that he did not expect anything, because our biggest present to him this year was that we were all going to be spending Christmas together in Portugal.

It was delightful to be back again with Papa, Mama, our maid Guilhermina, our cook Maria, and my dear dog Ramuntcho, who went berserk with joy. It was also wonderful that, for the first time, Guy too could be with us for this special time of year.

[xiii] Appendix 12: A letter by Field-Marshall Lord Ironside to Admiral Horthy.

22

End of an Epoch

For the coming term Stephen had been transferred from Gordonstoun to the Schule Schloss Salem in Germany, the former school of Dr Kurt Hahn. He left Portugal on 8 January 1956, and a few days later Guy embarked on the *Argentina Star* to London. I missed them both. The next morning I found presents on my breakfast table – I had forgotten that it was my thirty-eighth birthday.

Six weeks later I rejoined Guy in Catterick. It was good to be back, and I realized how lucky I was, because I felt very happy when I was in Estoril and also very happy when I was back with Guy.

Stephen wrote a long letter from Salem to say that, compared to Gordonstoun, he was living like a king – some of the rooms in the building were heated and they were altogether much more pleasant. He also liked the food, but they gave them very little to drink and they were never given tea.

In his own words (which revealed how much his English had improved):

> It is terribly slack here compared with Gordonstoun, the constitution is far more elastic, the big shots are far less pedantic, which is a tremendous improvement. ... It is even more slack for me as it seems to be an established fact that all foreigners are either dumb or *verrückt* (mad), so if I want to get off anything all I have to do is put on a standard nonplussed look, which I have perfected after arduous practice, and say, '*nickt verstehn*' (no understand) and I am automatically forgiven anything I do.
>
> One of the things I like about this place is that I can do all the things I have always wanted to do at school, and never had time for; i.e. go for long walks, catch up on my reading, etc. Though I go to many of the local

classes I don't have to do their preps, in order that I should be able to get on with my own syllabus.
Much love,
Stephen

At the end of the holiday, after a single term in Salem, Stephen went back to Gordonstoun, from where he wrote: 'This is such a beautiful place when the sun is shining, the countryside and the colours are beautiful and they remind one of the idyllic Gainsborough pictures. I now understand why the English talk so much about the weather.'

Guy had decided some time ago to buy a house in London and make money by renting out flats. On 29 May he signed the contract and we became the proud owners of 34 Palace Gardens Terrace, in a very central but fairly quiet location near Hyde Park. The house had a basement and four floors, which meant that it divided into two maisonettes and one flat. We had a wonderful time finding furniture for them at auctions in Yorkshire; then Ila and I went down to London to arrange everything, make curtains, and so on.

I always enjoyed my stays in London. I felt free and unobserved. Just to watch what people were wearing in the streets and on the underground was entertaining. And how that changed over the years! In the early days, people were somehow uniform – you could pretty much tell where they came from. But times changed, and everybody began to dress just as they pleased, wearing anything from long dresses and mini skirts to trousers of all kinds. There were also hairstyles of every variety, from long, flowing locks to clean shaven pates, and in all colours from bright red or green to gold or silver. Now one could get an idea what people's inner characteristics might be like, from their outer appearance.

At the beginning of August Stephen and I sailed to Portugal; Guy remained in London to finish decorating the flats and hopefully find tenants. By the time I returned in October he had rented out all three.

We heard that Bunny Fry, whom we had known at the British Embassy in Lisbon, had been posted to the British Legation in Budapest as Minister, so Guy wrote to him to find out whether he could visit him there. He not only wanted to get to know the country, but also to try and see whether he could help my family. I did not think it was a good idea, but did not interfere. We promptly got a long letter back from Bunny, saying that he understood Guy's wish but that the snags were blindingly obvious: 'I don't doubt that the regime is perfectly aware of your marriage, and for you to come here in person would be to put the cat among the pigeons. I do not think that you would stand the least chance of getting a visa, so the question hardly arises. I am sorry.

Anywhere else in the world I should be delighted to have you to stay – as you know.'

However, there was at least some refreshing news from Hungary: Mátyás Rákosi – whom we called the Hungarian Stalin – resigned and left for Moscow in July, no doubt because there was just too much opposition to his reign of terror. Ernő Gerő replaced him, with Soviet backing. Would he be any better? At least he started to release prisoners.

Then, in the autumn, we learnt of the tremendous things that were happening, first in Poland and then in Hungary.

On 22 October we heard the news about Gomulka's election in Poland, in a move against the Communist leadership. And the next day we heard that in Budapest the university students were demonstrating – it seemed that we were not going to lag behind the Poles.

By 24 October telephone communication with Budapest was cut off. There was fighting and some dead. Interference by Soviet troops rapidly inflamed the whole country and the revolution became a freedom fight. Imre Nagy was made prime minister, and at first thought he could turn to the Russian troops for help; but when he realised that he had been deceived by the Soviets he sided completely with the freedom fighters. The news was heart-rending. We were glued to the radio and television and I could not sleep at all. It was difficult for me not to be with Miklóspapa and Magdamama at such a time. We were writing to each other almost every day and occasionally telephoning. We were also daily receiving letters and phone calls of support from other people.

The rebellion continued in Budapest. Kádár appeared instead of Gerő, and promised that troops would be withdrawn if order was established, but the fighting went on. Children played a big part in it. They had been taught at school how to be good Communists, to denounce their parents and fight for the revolution. They now put what they had learned into practice, making 'Molotov cocktails' with bottles of petrol and a wick, which they threw at the Russian tanks. Their parents tried to keep them off the streets but without success. It was said that some children were hiding in a doorway, getting ready to confront a tank with a bottle, when one of them shouted, 'Look out, mother's coming,' and they all fled.

I went to church and asked Father Macmillan to say mass for the Hungarians on Sunday. It was incredible that they were still holding out, but there were many dead. It was obvious what a deep-rooted feeling of despair there was in the country, as despite knowing what retribution they could expect, they just went on fighting. If only the world would learn from all this that not everything was golden in the 'Communist Paradise'. I received a letter from Magdamama saying:

'We are anxiously awaiting the West's reaction to the events in Hungary, although from past experience we haven't much hope.'

At first, I thought that with all the Russian troops in the country the sacrifice of all those people would be in vain and the situation afterwards still worse; but now it seemed that, although the sacrifice was enormous, whatever happened it would not be in vain. Gerő was thrown out and the people were promised that the Soviet troops would soon leave.

I wrote to Lady Edwina Mountbatten of Burma, who had been a good friend of Pista's, and asked her as head of the British Red Cross to organize a collection of medicine and food to send to Hungary. I received a very kind answer from her assuring me that the government and the Red Cross were donating money for this very purpose.

Guy, Ila and I listened avidly to the radio – Béla Kovács and Zoltán Tildy were in the government, which sounded good; but another report said that Russian troops were approaching from the north. We expected at every minute to hear that resistance had ended and that Soviet tanks had 'restored order'. But miraculously this had not happened, and by Sunday 28 October the government seemed to be fulfilling more and more of the insurgents' conditions. People who had escaped were beginning to bring news about this 'decent' revolution. There was no looting, and people were helping each other. Inevitably there was some retribution, but it was a reaction to the incredible cruelty of the AVO (the secret police). It had been announced that Soviet troops had started leaving the capital! I did not dare believe this and listened to the news endlessly. I would not have a moment's peace until I had news of my family.

The television news was fantastic, showing pictures from the Austrian border and from inside Hungary itself. Guy watched all this with tears in his eyes and would have liked to go there to help – so would I. I felt that the whole free world was with us.

News came to us every day from Estoril. In her letters and telephone calls Mama told me how active Papa was. He had sent several cables, to the US president, General Eisenhower; the British and French prime ministers, Anthony Eden and Guy Mollet; and also to the secretary general of the United Nations, Dag Hammarskjöld. He asked them to do everything in their power to save and give freedom to Hungary. With Tibor Bartheldy and Nicky, he went to the Patriarch of Lisbon and asked for the celebration of a memorial high mass for those who died in Hungary. Papa had also asked for an audience with Prime Minister Salazar, which was due shortly, and he intended to ask for a nationwide collection to aid Hungary with food and clothing. The telephone in Casa San José was ringing from morning till night and Hungarians came and went all day. I wrote to Miklóspapa how close to him I felt, at a time when another White Army was forming at home. There was a great need now for a charismatic leader of the type the *fővezér*[58] had been in 1919.

It was wonderful news that Cardinal Mindszenty, who was arrested in 1948 after his continual protests from the pulpit against the repressions of the Communist regime, had been freed. We could actually see him speaking on TV. It was quite unbelievable what the 'insurgents' had achieved. Hopefully terror would not return again – although it seemed impossible that the Soviets would allow free elections, because then they would have to leave.

By Wednesday 31 October Hungary was unfortunately no longer headline news; the Israeli-Egyptian war got first place in the interest of the media. That day they announced English and French air raids against Egyptian and Israeli troops, who were advancing on the peninsula of Sinai. There was a lot of excitement about Suez.

I was also in constant touch with my parents in Cannes, who sent a cable on 1 November, saying: 'Just received telegram, all families well, love, Papi.' With Ila we fell into each other arms, crying with joy.

But our joy did not last long. Soviet tanks – seventeen Soviet Divisions – descended in full force on Budapest on 4 November, and in a few days crushed all resistance. Our frame of mind and spirit sank to the lowest level. The Communist radio said that Horthy agents and soldiers had been active in this 'fascist counter-revolution'. Nothing could have been further from the truth. After so many years, I can still hear the voice of Prime Minister Imre Nagy pleading over the radio for help from the United Nations; it was being repeated again and again – like a drowning man's cry for help. His last message was, 'We are dying for Europe.' Yes. In the middle of Europe we were left alone, none of the central European states came to our aid; nobody had the courage to halt what was now happening. Why was this happening to us?

Ex-Prime Minister Kállay suggests an answer in his memoirs: '... The totalitarian slogan of unconditional surrender made peace impossible and made freedom unattainable.'[59] The British tried to get the United Nations to put up a police force to implement decisions – surely too late for Hungary!

It was difficult to concentrate on other things; I was constantly thinking of the horrors that were happening at home. We had so recently seen on television the opening up of the notorious AVO jails in 60 Andrássy Street and the staggering prisoners emerging; one could hardly believe that they might again go back there. Many people fled to the Austrian border and got out in time, but Budapest is a long way from the border and I was afraid that my poor sisters might have missed the opportunity. Would Sya, after her ordeal, ever try to leave the country again?

News came that Prime Minister Nagy had taken asylum in the Yugoslav Legation. But when he got solemn promises of safety he had left the Legation, since when he had disappeared. How could he believe the word of those bandits!

Mama told me that after the news of 4 November, Papa did not turn on the radio, did not read the papers – I thought it might be better that he avoided listening to the horrible news. Not long afterwards I got a letter from him, and it was noticeably changed in both handwriting and expression from his former style. I was not surprised that he was shattered and shaken, but wished for him not to give up all hope, as hoping for the best had always been his strength.

We were now trying to get Stephen a British passport, which now I was a British subject I could apply for. While we were in London two officials from Scotland Yard, investigating on behalf of the Home Office, came to interview me. They were very friendly, but asked me a lot of questions about Stephen. They particularly wanted to know whether he was interested in politics, and I assured them that he had never shown any interest in the subject. They left saying that they would send someone to Gordonstoun School to interview him.

You can imagine my shock when the next day I received a letter from Stephen in which he enclosed an article he had just written on the recent events in Hungary, at the request of the School Editor, mainly to encourage donations for the Hungarian Relief Fund. They thought it so good that it had been displayed on the wall for everyone to see. The official who would go to see Stephen would probably think that I had deliberately lied. Later I heard that the officer had been there and had not made any comment; either he had not noticed, or had understood the purpose of the article.

There was, however, a strange incident much later, when Guy was alone in the flat. Someone rang the doorbell and said that he was from Scotland Yard. Guy invited him in, and he explained that he was following up on our request for a British Passport, which would not be granted unless the Horthy money was handed over; also, he would be requesting the Home Office to investigate Guy's bank account.

'You don't have to do that, I have got it right here,' said Guy. And he took out his bank statement from his desk, which showed him to be £394 in debt. 'If you want to know anything about the Horthy family's financial circumstances,' he added, 'talk to Winston Churchill's former private secretary, Mr Jock Colville. When he was at the British Embassy in Lisbon he lived almost next door to the Horthys and knows them well.' After that we heard no more, and eventually Stephen was granted a passport.

Meanwhile Guy's posting at Catterick camp had come to an end; he had been told that for the time being he would not get a transfer, he should just stay easily available. This suited us, as it meant we were able to visit my parents in Cannes for a while and then go on together to Portugal.

It was at this time that our Ila finally left us. She had been helping out our friends the Burburys, who had a small baby, and now she went to work for them permanently. Ila was happy to be going back to her real profession; she was after all a perfect nanny, and not meant to be a cook-cum-companion. (Ila stayed with the Burbury family for many years before eventually retiring to an old people's home in Darlington, (in) County Durham. I visited her there, and we spent most of the night talking of all that we had shared over the years. She died shortly afterwards, sitting in her chair; the vicar found her there when he came to take her to church.)

Soon after we arrived in France we received news from Vienna that every member of our family in Budapest was alive. This was almost a miracle, as there had been no food in Budapest since 3 November and Mongolian soldiers were conducting a house-to-house search for freedom fighters. We heard later about the tragic deaths of my cousin Elly Blanckenstein (Pejacsevich) and her husband Lajos, who were senselessly both shot down in their home by Russian soldiers. The same happened to Sya's in-laws, Alice Esterházy and her husband Miklós Szécsen. There are no adequate words to describe these awful tragedies.

We had been in touch with friends in Vienna who were able to assist people in escaping from Hungary. There were guides who knew how to get through the border and made money by escorting people to Austria. They demanded $1,000 for an adult and $500 for a child. How could we get all that money together quickly? Fortunately we had friends who were willing to help. Sir Oliver Duncan immediately sent the half of the necessary sum by cable and King Zog with Queen Geraldine loaned us the remainder – most of which I was later able to repay on my return to Portugal, with money I received from generous Portuguese friends. The dollars were deposited in a bank in Vienna and would be paid out only once people had arrived safely. I sent a note in my own handwriting for the 'guide' to take with him, as proof that we had sent him. For days we were left in suspense – Geraldine, her sister Virginia and many friends came to share our anxiety. Finally, on 20 November, Sya and József telephoned from Vienna. They had arrived one hour ago, with their two sons and Józsi's brother, Lajos.

Sya did not want to leave Vienna before doing something for our two other sisters, because now was the most opportune time to escape – in a week's time it might be too late. But the European countries had pledged to take a certain number of refugees only, so we told Sya not to wait but to join the Swiss quota before it was filled. They got on the last Swiss transport and were due to arrive in Locarno. This was only 500 kilometres from us in Cannes, so Guy and I decided to meet them there.

Words cannot describe the joy of this meeting. Sya was looking quite well, but Józsi was very thin and emaciated. The Swiss authorities were very generous and well organized; the refugees were all given forms to fill in, and could choose where they wanted to settle and what kind of work they wanted to do. Józsi eventually got a good job in a factory near Zürich, and a flat nearby.

Then we received news from Vienna that Éva's son Péter had arrived and was waiting for his mother to come out any day. So we went there in order to offer whatever help might be necessary. Éva arrived on 27 November, followed by Myro and György with their children Magdi and Dudi. We laughed when Guy said that every week a new sister-in-law was born to him. It was like a delightful dream. I remembered the candles I had lit so hesitatingly every month in Fatima, asking Our Lady to keep them safe. As soon as possible I would go on a thanksgiving pilgrimage to Fatima. Eventually Éva and her family made their home in Belgium, and Myro and György settled in Köln, Germany.

Magdi, Myro's daughter – and my goddaughter – was given a wonderful opportunity. An Englishman in Vienna, who had come there to help refugees, offered to finance her education in England. They naturally accepted this generous sponsorship, even though it meant a separation, and Magdi went to Farnborough Hill Convent College, a famous girl's school in England. A year later she won an award for her proficiency in English, which was officially presented to her at the Royal Albert Hall in London. After finishing at the Convent she undertook a secretarial course, because she wanted to earn her living and thus help her parents. That was what my goddaughter was like – I was proud of her.

Guy and I now went back to Portugal to join my parents-in-law for Christmas, and soon Stephen arrived from Gordonstoun. He had grown a lot and was now taller than Guy. We had the loveliest Christmas for many years: Guy was with us, and I was able to talk on the telephone to all my sisters both on Christmas and New Year's Eve. Only a year before, this would have been unimaginable.

My brother-in-law Nicky had got married again. He and the Duchess Hema de Cröy were married in Scotland on 22 December, and came back to live in her villa in Estoril a few days later. This delighted me, as it showed the feelings he had expressed for me in the past were no longer a problem for him; he and Hema were clearly very happy.

Our only concern was about Papa. It was clear that ever since the events in Hungary he tired more easily. Although he seemed in good health, he was doing everything rather automatically or mechanically; he did not seem to have any initiative, and no longer read the papers or listened to the radio.

On the morning of 26 January he woke Mama to tell her that he was having difficulty in breathing, he could hardly get enough air. Mama immediately woke me and I managed to call Dr Loureiro, a heart specialist who lived in Estoril. Two injections gave an immediate improvement in his breathing, and the doctor ordered complete bed rest. That same morning they began a thorough medical check-up. They took X-rays and blood and other tests, and established that the sudden insufficient functioning of the heart was due to general exhaustion. The doctor was confident, and Papa was animated and grumbling about having to stay in bed.

This, Papa's final illness, lasted two weeks; I nursed him during all but the last two days. After the first week I realized that he would not recover, and in spite of the doctor's assertions to the contrary, I felt that the end could come at any moment.

On the seventh day I managed to convince Mama to sleep in another room so that she could rest and I could sit or lie on her bed all night beside Papa. As his sleep was very restless I had to be there to cover him up, but the main reason why someone had to be at his bedside at night was because he would suddenly get out of bed saying that he had to dress to 'go home'. He would say, 'We have to hurry, the carriage is at the door.' I would then gently lead him back to bed saying, 'Not yet Papa, you must be patient, I will tell you when we can go.' His breathing difficulty increased, and on the second week we had an oxygen cylinder standing by, which we sometimes used. Fortunately Papa seemed unaware of the seriousness of his condition and did not suffer at any time.

I have never known anyone bear illness with more politeness and patience; he thanked me for everything and allowed me do whatever was needed, tolerating it without question and as if he did not even notice. Only when the doctors gave an injection or took blood for a test, did he say to me in Hungarian, 'When you do it I don't mind, but these I don't like.' Then bronchitis developed, and although we managed to keep the fever down for two days it worsened, with the result that he was less and less aware of his surroundings. But when he was awake he smiled at family members and seemed to enjoy their presence. Nicky and Hema often came during the day, and Hema made delicious aspics and gelées, which were the only food he ate willingly.

In the morning of 8 February, while I was attending to him he said, 'Bless your soul, when will you get some sleep?' That evening he smiled at all of us, and he did not wake during the night. I could have slept, but I was checking his breathing and his pulse, thinking that I might have to call a doctor at any moment. His hands and feet were very cold and I was trying to warm him up with heated towels.

Before the day-nurse came I gave him a few spoonfuls of hot liquid, which he swallowed in a semi-sleep. When Dr Loureiro arrived, he gave Papa an intravenous injection and said that he could not do any more to help: we should let Papa sleep, and he would come back in the afternoon. He had hardly left the house when Papa's head drooped. The nurse and I immediately gave him the oxygen mask and a sympathol injection. I sent Guy after the doctor and they hurried back. Loureiro then told me not to bother any more; Papa had gone. I felt very peaceful and quiet, and hoped that Papa was the same. I suddenly felt very tired.

Luckily, Mama was dressing in the bathroom; so, with the help of the nurse, I dressed Papa in his admiral's uniform, and put two Hungarian flags with the crown and the crest at the head and the foot of the bed. The only decoration on his uniform was the Maria Theresia Order. I covered his legs with the Austro-Hungarian admiral's flag, and lit four candles in silver candelabra and placed them on either side of the bed. This is how Mama found him when she came in; he lay there looking very peaceful, his expression tranquil and almost content.

Mama was very brave, although she was devastated. I knew that her life had no sense without him; I also knew that I would stay with her as long as she lived. She repeatedly asked me whether she would have to leave the house, because she wanted to stay there, where they had been together. I gave her my assurance that she would not have to leave.

Within a short time the room was filled with flowers, and Papa remained like this with us for about ten hours. In the afternoon many people came to express their condolences. King Umberto came with General Graziani, then Don Juan and Dona Maria, Count and Countess of Barcelona. Don Juan, who had also been a naval officer, stood at attention beside Papa's bed when he entered the room and also before he left. The Archdukes Habsburg and many others continued to come until late at night.

When we were alone we prayed at his bedside – I had put into Papa's hands the little cross he had been wanting to hold all the time over the last few days.

The next morning was a very sad time. With Nicky and Guy we went to Lisbon to choose a coffin and look at the burial place. Guy saw the coffin closed and sealed, and the Anglican Reverend Hewitt and Professor Pap – who had been a priest before he became a doctor – gave a short funeral sermon. Our 'Uncle Doctor' Pap spoke very beautifully.

The coffin was taken to the chapel in the British Cemetery in Lisbon, where our Hungarian friends watched over Papa and kept vigil, changing over every two hours. Guy had accompanied the coffin, and he told us afterwards how beautiful it was: the setting sun illuminating the catafalque through the open chapel door, with the Hungarian flag and all the flowers.

The funeral was on 11 February in the lovely British Cemetery. This walled-in, centuries old cemetery is like a big garden, and is especially lovely in spring with Judas trees and flowering shrubs. One day when we had been walking there with Papa, he'd said to me, 'This is where I would like to be put to rest, until I can be taken home to a free Hungary. If you live to see that, you will take me home, won't you?' I promised that I would.

Guy and I took Mama, Nicky and Hema to Lisbon in our car. Royalty, diplomats, Portuguese state officials and many others came to say farewell: some to the admiral, some to the Regent, and others to a friend, whose life had been extinguished by the news of the suppression of liberty and the crushing of the fight for freedom of his beloved country by Soviet tanks. He no doubt represented an epoch which was now gone. So many lies had been spread about him, but those who knew him well were deeply devoted to him. I have the proof of this in the huge number of letters that came from all over the world, which I have kept.

We arranged for a simple tombstone carved with the Hungarian and the Horthy crest, with a quotation from the Bible which said, 'We may be trampled on but do not get lost'. And before the marble stone was put in place we covered the grave with some Hungarian soil, sent to us by Hungarian refugees.

We now had to look after Magdamama very carefully. Over the next few weeks we helped her answer the hundreds of letters and telegrams that were arriving daily, and I massaged her back every day. Whenever we had some errand in Lisbon she asked to be taken to the British Cemetery to visit Papa's grave. There was a bench in front of the grave and Mama would sit there and pray until we came to pick her up.

Stephen arrived for the Easter holidays in April, looking very well. He was happy to find Guy still here, and together we started to hunt for a house or a 'quinta' (a small farm) where we might eventually make a home. We spent a lot of time looking at various places for sale and also looked on the other side of the River Tagus, where land was cheaper.

This was where we eventually found a property we liked: the Quinta do Farol. Farol means lighthouse, and the house was on an elevation, dominating the valley in a way, so maybe this is why it got the name. It needed a lot of work: except for orange trees the land was just bare sandy soil, and although the house had windows upstairs, the ground floor was a barn; but we both could see its potential.

In June, Guy went to London to look for another flat to rent out. When he returned he brought with him his younger brother David, with whom he had always been very close. We spent a very enjoyable ten days together before David had to return to Nairobi, where he had made his home since the war. During his stay we all went to look at various quintas, but liked none of them better than Quinta do Farol, and so we decided to buy it. Madeleine then unexpectedly gave me as a gift a contribution towards the cost of the property, which was a very welcome surprise.

Over the following months we arranged several picnics at Quinta do Farol, and made the down payment on the property, which was an exciting moment – we now had taken the first step towards acquiring a new home. We employed a *caseiro* (caretaker) called João to live on the place, bought two milking cows and planted some trees. Guy told me that there would be a lawn and a swimming pool, which was difficult to imagine in that sandy desert. But in time Guy was to make it happen.

The latter part of the year seemed to hold a series of tragedies. Archduke Joseph Franz Habsburg died suddenly in Carcavelos on 26 September. We immediately went to express our sympathy to Archduchess Anna and the children, and went to the funeral the next day.

In early October I received a cable from Ellamami, saying that they had just had a call from Switzerland telling them that Józsi had brain thrombosis and his condition was very serious. There was a serious epidemic of Asiatic flu in Europe and Józsi caught it. Remembering his state on his arrival in Switzerland, I realized that his body probably had no resistance. It was hard to believe that this should happen now that they were free at last. I kept in touch by telephone.

On 24 October the news came that 'Józsi left us in the afternoon'. What a devastating situation this was for Sya, to be left without him, in a new country and with no money. Within a few days I went to be with her and help in any way I could.

As the year drew to an end, and I helped Stephen and Guy prepare our first Christmas without Papa, I was sad too for poor Sya, who this Christmas would be without Józsi. And my thoughts kept turning to those who had fought for freedom and were still suffering the consequences of their brave sacrifices. In the Western world the general opinion was that our freedom fight had been marvellous, and many people helped the refugees at that time, but I was appalled by the apparent disinterestedness towards the Hungarian deportees in the Soviet Union. The leaders of Communist Hungary did not ask for their return and the Soviet Union denied their existence. And the authorities in the west either did not care or did not want to annoy the Soviet Union by making controversial demands. These thousands of people who had sacrificed everything for freedom were left to their dreadful fate. May God have mercy on those who suffer, and even more mercy on those who make them suffer ... .

Early in 1958 I took Mama to the doctor, as she had lost weight and often had stomach problems. I had a conference with Professor Pap and Doctor Lima Basto, a world-famous surgeon and cancer specialist, who told me that Mama had an ulcer that was cancerous and near bursting. It was vital that she should undergo an operation within the week. He said he would carry out the operation, and assured me that this would not only prolong her life but that she would not have any pain, even in case of a recurrence; but if she did not have surgery she would suffer a great deal.

This was not an easy task, as Mama had never been in hospital or had an operation in all her life. Her children were all born at home, and she had told us more than once that she would never consent to an operation. Fortunately, she herself suggested going into hospital to make it easier to follow the diet and milk cure she had been given for her ulcer, and once there, Lima Basto was able to perform the operation with great success.

Improvement came very quickly. She could not believe that the next day she was standing up without any pain. It was like a miracle! And it was very gratifying for me when she said that she was grateful for not having been told about the operation until the last minute, as otherwise she would have never gone ahead with it.

In the meantime, my husband was due to go on another general staff appointment. To his horror he was posted as instructor to the British Military Mission in Iraq, which was training that country's armed forces. He had always advised officers not to go there if possible, because of the climate and the general living conditions. And I of course was not able to go with him, as Mama needed so much help and support.

Part Four

23

Subud

In 1958 a change came into my life that turned out to be bigger than
anything that had happened to me before. This is quite a statement
for someone who has experienced as many changes of situation as
I have during my lifetime. But what began now was of a different
nature, as it was mainly an inner development.

Guy had just been posted to Iraq as an instructor to the British
Military Mission, and I was in Portugal looking after Mama after her
operation, when I received a letter from Stephen that set me a problem
I was not sure how to approach.

Let me go back a bit: At the age of twelve, Stephen had subscribed
to a book club in the United States from which he ordered titles by mail.
One of them was Kenneth Walker's book about the teaching of G. I.
Gurdjieff, which explains the significance of human life on earth in
terms of the possibility of developing consciousness to higher levels.
Stephen became fascinated, and having no brothers or sisters and no
father, it was with me that he tried to share his enthusiasm, although I
found the subject difficult to understand or warm to.

In Scotland he continued to pursue this interest, and shared it with
one of his friends, Tim Fryer. Tim, being a year older, left Gordonstoun
School before Stephen did; he promised Stephen that he would go to
Coombe Springs, a house near Kingston-on-Thames in London, where
there was a group practising the Gurdjieff system, and tell him what he
found. He kept his promise and wrote to Stephen saying that he had
been surprised to discover that the people in Coombe Springs were no
longer doing Gurdjieff work but were engaged in something called
Subud. He added that there was no way he could explain Subud in a
letter, but that he had started doing something called the 'latihan',
which was the most extraordinary experience he had ever had.

Stephen told me all this in his letter, and said that upon reading the
word 'Subud' he had the strange feeling that it was not new to him. He

felt a kind of inner certainty that this was what he was looking for and that it would change his life. He had written to Coombe Springs and had been told that people could come and start Subud at any time, but that there was a minimum age limit of eighteen years.

I felt reassured by this reply because Stephen was just seventeen. His question to me was: could he go to Coombe Springs during the coming Easter holidays, just to find out more about Subud? I replied that we would talk about it when he came back and then decide what to do. Naturally I was worried – I was afraid that Stephen would get involved in some kind of a sect, and hoped that I would be able to talk him out of joining whatever it was.

He wrote three very long letters about what he knew and what he felt. In his sensible way he told me that he realized I was responsible for him until he reached the age of twenty-one, and would therefore do whatever I decided was best. I pondered on it and weighed it all up; I was aware that his wish for this was deep and sincere, and knew that he did not just accept things he was told and that nobody had been influencing him. He was just drawn to whatever this Subud was by some inner compulsion. I therefore decided that I should at least give him the chance to find out more about it. Since he was only seventeen, I thought he would have to wait to join in any case, so I agreed for him to spend the second half of his Easter holiday in England, when he could visit Coombe Springs with his friend Tim. His answer was immediate, thanking me for setting his heart at rest, and for 'thinking hard about it and coming to such an objective decision.' He wrote: 'I see that however far we may be from each other, we are nearer than ever, because we completely understand each other. I have been waiting anxiously, and your decision could not have been more just.'

So Stephen went to Coombe Springs; and as he looked older than his age, no one asked him how old he was and he received what they called the 'opening'. He continued to share everything with me, and told me in several long letters what the people and the place were like and what he was experiencing there. He explained that Subud was not like the Gurdjieff work, in which one followed a teacher. This was a spontaneous experience that seemed to come from within, once one had received a certain contact. This contact, which could be passed on from one person to another, was what was called the 'opening'.

I was impressed. It all sounded simple and straightforward and not at all like a cult or a sect that was trying to trap people. He repeatedly suggested that I go to Coombe Springs to find out about Subud for myself, and I developed the firm intention to do that.

For the time being, however, I remained in Portugal with Magdamama. We discussed the very upsetting news that was coming out of Hungary. The retributions against the freedom fighters of the 1956 uprising were still going on. The young people who had been arrested were being kept in prison until they reached the age at which they could be executed. It was hard to believe. In June, Imre Nagy and Paul Maléter, the minister of defence in Nagy's cabinet, were hanged, which resulted in worldwide indignation.

In July some very worrying news came from Iraq. There was a coup d'état in Baghdad, which brought an end to both the monarchy and British influence. King Faisal and his family were killed, and Prime Minister Nuri Said – whom they called the Winston Churchill of the Middle East – was brutally murdered and his body dragged around the streets until nothing remained of it. There was no news of Guy, whose job with the Military Mission was not directly connected with the British Embassy.

I went to London and stayed with Stephen, as I was hoping it would be easier to get news there or even to meet Guy. Eventually he got messages through that he was safe, and was writing to me. The first letter I received was censored, and the next ones gave me the news that he would have to stay in Baghdad until he had closed down the Military Mission. The Soviets had taken over, and were re-equipping the Iraqi Forces with Russian arms and planes.

Later on, he told me about all that had happened. On arrival in Baghdad he had immediately joined the training programmes. He visited the British officers responsible and was not impressed by their standards, a state of affairs he reported to the commander-in-chief, Lord Mountbatten, and to the British ambassador in Baghdad, Sir Michael Wright. Sir Michael asked to see Guy privately at the British Embassy, a lovely old fort that had been given to the British by the Iraqis as thanks for freeing them from the Turks. He said Guy's report had confirmed his own suspicions that things were not right in the Military Mission. He told Guy, 'You are to be promoted, and I insist you stay on to command the Mission.' When Guy asked permission to decline, he was informed that the posting had already been approved.

Some weeks after his arrival he was invited to a party, where the host, a Hungarian bank manager, asked him what was happening about the coup that was 'due any moment'. When Guy replied that he knew nothing, the Hungarian said, 'Nonsense, you are connected with the Embassy and must know!' He went on to say that the prime minister and the Ministry of Defence had arrested a colonel who was planning to kill the King and take control of the government.

Guy went straight to the Embassy. He asked to see the military attaché, who assured him it was just a rumour of the kind that circulated all the time. Thinking that the attaché, who had been in Baghdad for four years, ought to be in the picture, Guy was relieved and left it at that.

Not long afterwards, on 14 July, Guy was woken at four in the morning by a loud bang, like the sound of a bomb going off. The cook was going to the market and Guy decided to take him there in his Volkswagen in the hope of getting some news. They found the roads blocked and some houses burning, and had to take a roundabout route to the Mission. On the way Guy stopped at the new Baghdad Hotel and booked all the available rooms, just in case. At the Mission he found several officers listening to the BBC. The seven o'clock news gave the cricket score, and then added: 'We have some late news from Baghdad, which says that there has been a revolution.' Guy told all the officers to go home, take off their uniforms and stay there until he contacted them.

He tried to get to the Embassy, but it was very difficult as by now all the main roads were blocked by howling mobs, who were overturning cars and burning them. After several diversions down side roads he managed to get within a mile of the compound. Leaving the car, he borrowed the cook's Arab headdress and walked through the crowds.

Outside the Embassy's Park Gate, he found a dense mob of Iraqis shouting, 'Down with the British!' There were Iraqi soldiers guarding the entrance, and Guy asked to be let in, but he was thrown back into the crowd. He then saw an Iraqi colonel, whom he knew to be the prime minister's ADC, standing nearby. When Guy went up to him and said that he wanted to see the ambassador, the colonel replied, 'OK, tell the ambassador everything all right.' He took Guy to the guards, who started arguing, at which the colonel hit the sergeant in the mouth with his Sten gun, knocking out several teeth, and pushed Guy through the iron gates.

As he made his way down to the Residence, Guy could hear the screaming mobs outside the walls and saw that the Chancery was on fire. He walked up the steps of the Residence and opened the door to see hundreds of Iraqis ransacking the place, passing all the pictures and china out of the other side of the building to boats on the River Tigris. He quickly shut the door and went to hide in the shrubbery and trees. There was a howl and an Englishman came running by, his head bleeding. Guy grabbed him and asked what had happened. He said that he was the telephone operator and that the Iraqis had attacked him as he escaped from his burning room. He knew nothing of the ambassador.

Guy was cursing his own stupidity for going there – it was like jumping from the frying pan into the fire – when another Englishman, who escaped through a window, ran up and said, 'I think the ambassador is on the roof.' Guy rushed back to the Park Gates and grabbed the Iraqi colonel, shouting, 'Come! Ambassador being killed.' The colonel gave him a gun, and calling some other soldiers, came back down the road with him, firing into the air as they went. The Iraqis trying to break down the Chancery door fled, and after a few moments Sir Michael and Lady Wright and the Head of the Chancery appeared. The ambassador's ADC, Colonel Graham, had been shot dead. Seemingly in shock, the ambassador asked, 'Where is Nuri?' Guy said he thought that he was probably dead, and took the party off to the shelter of the trees. He asked permission to go and see the new ruler, and despite the stress of the situation they composed a message saying that whoever it was would be held responsible for British lives and property. He then proposed that they all take advantage of the Iraqi colonel's escort to go to the Baghdad Hotel, where he had reserved the rooms earlier on.

After safely delivering them to the hotel, Guy went on to the Ministry of Defence. At the entrance he met an Iraqi general and two Russian officers, whom he later heard had come from the Persian Embassy, where the plot had been planned. By then it was clear that the royal family had been assassinated. The new ruler, Colonel Abdul Karim Qassim – trained in the UK, with pro-Communist leanings and fully supported by the Communist Party – met Guy and told him there was nothing to worry about. He guaranteed the safety of the British party and promised to place a guard around the Baghdad Hotel. There was chaos everywhere; British factories and houses were being attacked and there was no transport or telephones. Guy eventually got the Swiss Chargé to let him send messages to the UK, which was how I finally heard that he was alive.

Guy later received the Queen's Commendation for Brave Conduct for his actions, which I thought he had really deserved. The text of the citation read: 'Awarded to Colonel John Wallace Guy Bowden of the Queen's Own Hussars for bravery when wearing disguise in Baghdad'.[xiv]

It was now three months since Stephen had received the 'opening', and I was determined to find out about Subud while I was in England. On a beautiful sunny evening Stephen and I drove down to Kingston-on-Thames, and I clearly remember a strange experience on the way. I found myself involuntarily praying that God would protect me and only let this happen if it was truly God's will and the right way to Him. I was surprised at this prayer, which came into my mind over and over.

Coombe Springs belonged to Mr John Bennett, who led a Gurdjieff School called 'The Institute for the Comparative Study of History,

---

[xiv] Appendix 13: Newspaper cuttings on Guy's Commendation, and his C.B.E.

Philosophy and the Sciences'. Prior to the appearance of Subud it had already attracted a group of people who were looking for new depth or significance in their lives.

The drive down Coombe Lane led to a large country mansion set back from the road. It had a lovely garden, and well-kept grounds in which there were some ancient springs. When we arrived, Stephen explained that his mother was there to speak with somebody about Subud, and I was taken into a living room to meet three ladies. One of them, Olga de Nottbeck, talked to me, while the other two just sat with half-closed eyes, looking noncommittal.

I told them frankly that I had only come to find out what my son had got into; but then I found I was telling them things about myself that I had never before realized. I told them that although I was a practising catholic and liked my religion, it seemed that things were always the same and it was not getting me anywhere. This was true; I had just never put it into words or admitted it to myself.

Margaret Wichmann, one of the ladies who had been sitting with her eyes closed, suddenly opened them; she gave a radiant smile and, nodding her head slightly to Olga, left the room. Olga then told me that I could be 'opened' if I wished. I asked whether this was what had happened to my son; and when she said that it was, I said that I would like to find out for myself. I was ushered into another room and told to take off my shoes and any jewellery. A friendly-looking lady – Maria Kibble – appeared and told me to close my eyes, relax, and submit my will to the will of God. I did not feel anything in particular, just a peaceful, happy feeling. I had no idea how long it lasted, but after a while I heard her say, 'Finish'. And – do not ask me why – I just knew that whatever happened, I would go on with it.

What I had just experienced for the first time was the 'latihan'; the practice that is at the core of Subud.

I think it will be helpful if I interrupt my story at this point to briefly describe Subud as I understand it today, based on more than forty years experiencing and witnessing its action. This is not an easy task, as Subud is not a teaching but a personal experience, and unlike anything else I know. So, as far as I can, I shall try to define it in terms of my actual experience.

As I just said, Subud is in the first place a personal experience, one in which each person feels a movement or vibration within their body that originates not from their mind or their will, but seems to come from a deeper level of their self. It is spontaneous, not learned, and entirely individual. It is this experience that is referred to as the latihan, an Indonesian word that simply means 'training' or 'exercise'.

The practice of Subud consists simply of submitting to this action of the latihan on a regular basis and following what happens. This is generally done with other members – men and women do it separately. For those who want to join, there is usually a three-month waiting period, so that they can be certain about their wish to be opened. As one goes on, the experience changes and develops; the involuntary movements gradually become more complete, and are often accompanied by singing and so on. Those who have done the latihan regularly for many years report that it gradually brings them to an experience of deep peace and of wide 'inner space'. This can be accompanied by outer changes, including better health and a deeper understanding of life.

I do not want to give the impression that it is always easy however, as these improvements are often preceded by periods of 'purification' that may involve difficulties and suffering. But we all know that suffering is necessary, as without it there is often no progress.

For me it gave the answer to my childhood wish to understand more about why we are in this world, and what happens when we leave it.

Subud started in 1925 with the spiritual experience of a young man, Muhammad Subuh Sumohadiwidjojo, who was living in the suburbs of Semarang, a town in Central Java. He described how he went for a walk late one night to clear his head after studying bookkeeping. Suddenly he was startled by a brilliant white light, which appeared in the sky above him. The light descended and entered his body through the crown of his head. He felt his body shake and was convinced that he was about to die. Not wishing to collapse in the street he hurried home, lay down on his bed and surrendered himself to God. For a short time he saw his whole body full of light, and then he had the first experience of what we now call the latihan – his body moved of its own accord: first he was moved to sit up and then to walk to his study, where he went through the movements of the Muslim prayer but without saying any words. He was then moved to walk back to his bed and lie down.

He told how this experience returned almost every night, and how the movements that accompanied it kept changing – the movements of prayer giving way to dancing and marshal arts. They also gradually became deeper and more complete, involving his feelings and understanding: he found he was being taught about and experiencing all the levels of life in the universe: the material, vegetable, animal, human, and levels higher than that. He knew that what was happening to him was the will of God, but he did not understand its purpose until a culminating experience occurred about eight years after the first one, in which he was finally given the understanding that the gift he had received was not for him alone but could be passed on to whoever might ask for it; and that they in turn would be able to pass it on. He was told that he should make no propaganda, but simply wait for people to ask.

Muhammad Subuh – who came to be known simply as 'Bapak' (pronounced ba-pah), an Indonesian term of respect given to older men – followed these instructions meticulously; and it turned out that the experience he had received could indeed be passed on from one person to another. For the next few years it spread slowly through Java.

The name 'Subud', which has no connection with Bapak's name 'Subuh', was adopted in 1947. It is a contraction of three Sanskrit words, *susila*, *budhi*, and *dharma*, which together are taken to mean 'right living through submission to God's power, which is present within our being'. The use of Sanskrit also confirmed that Subud was not a sect of Islam, but was meant to embrace the whole of humankind.

People sometimes tried to imply that Bapak was someone special; but he often told us that he was a person just like any of us, and he was happy to give the impression of being an ordinary man. I like the description given by Varindra Tarzie Vittachi, a journalist who later became the first international chairman of the Subud organisation: he said that Bapak was the 'most extraordinary ordinary man he knew'. The author Aldous Huxley once told Bapak that he considered him to be the leader of Subud. Bapak replied that people might think so at first, but soon discover that his function was like that of a school servant, who airs the schoolroom, cleans the blackboard and straightens the chairs before the teacher arrives – the teacher being God Himself.

I must explain here that the belief in God is not a prerequisite for joining Subud. Those of my readers who do not believe in God, or object to the word 'God', can substitute the 'Great Life Force' or 'Creator'. I hope they will bear with me and form their own conclusion once they have read the rest of what I have to say.

People who join are not expected to believe in anything in particular about Subud or the latihan; they are advised to believe what they themselves experience. But Bapak did always describe the latihan as the 'worship of God': worship that is not directed by our mind but by God's power. The fact is that most people who follow it sincerely – even when they start off as atheists and agnostics – through their own experience eventually come to accept that its working comes from a higher power. Their faith is therefore based on proof rather than belief.

That has been my own conclusion. And I have come to believe that what we receive in the latihan is something universal – a contact with God's power that is the birthright of all human beings, but with which humanity has increasingly lost touch. Descriptions of a similar experience seem to be at the core of all the revealed religions; in

Christianity for example, it is described in the Acts of the Apostles as the coming of the Holy Spirit to the apostles at Pentecost, and its working is described as being passed on as 'baptism of the spirit'.

As it brings no new teaching, Subud is not a religion; what it seems to be is a new revelation that can revitalize existing religions by providing proof of God's power. It has come to us in an age when human beings are more oblivious of the reality of God than they have been in earlier ages. And, perhaps for that reason, it has come in a more accessible form: one that is free of hierarchy and human intermediaries, free of local cultural forms and, above all, free of human teachers and teachings. The remarkable thing in this process is that one does not become 'holy', but 'normal'. There is no place for faking or imagination. It is able to bring understanding equally to Christians, Muslims, Jews, Buddhists, to people of any religion or none at all, who all do the latihan together. My experiences have shown me that Catholics can become better Catholics, Muslims better Muslims, etc., while there are others who through their worship in Subud can be shown the religion that best suits their nature.

Subud is for those who ask to receive it; it is not permitted to force it on anyone. This is why Bapak said not to use propaganda for Subud; and it also explains why in general people have to wait three months if they wish to take part in this 'way of life'.

As I tell you the rest of my life story I shall also be tracing the effect of this practice on my life and on me as person.

I had only a very short time after my opening before I was due to leave England, and in fact I had just three latihans at Coombe Springs before leaving for Portugal and Iraq, two countries where there was not a single person in Subud at that time. The latihan is normally practised for half an hour twice a week, but because I was now to be entirely on my own I was told that I could do the latihan three times a week.

Before I left I asked Mr B. (as John Bennett was called by everyone) what I should tell my catholic confessor in Portugal about Subud. Father Francisco Pippan was a highly intelligent Italian Salesian priest, who had been my mother-in-law's and my confessor for years. Mr B. told me not to think about it in advance but just tell him the truth of what I had experienced.

I followed Mr B.'s advice and told my confessor what had happened to me in Coombe Springs. I was amazed when he said, 'Listening to you, I would like to go there myself!' I explained that I had not told him about Subud in order to ask whether I should continue or not, because that was not in doubt, I only wanted him to tell me whether, as a practising Catholic, what had happened to me in Coombe Springs was a sin or not. He said that from what I had told him, what I had experienced could not possibly be a sin. I thanked him and left.

Sometime later he said to me that he had been surprised that someone like myself, who had access to a large 'library' – the Church – where I could choose any book I liked, had gone elsewhere to look for another book. I replied that it was he, as my confessor, who should have shown me the right book in that library. He honestly admitted that he did not know where to find 'that' book.

On arriving home I had some very disappointing news from Guy. It had taken him three months to close down the Mission and send the soldiers and their families off to the UK, and he was looking forward to leaving Iraq himself. However, when he was finally ready to go, and went to say goodbye to the ambassador, he was told that Lord Mountbatten had already approved the ambassador's personal request that Guy should immediately return to Baghdad as military attaché. When he got back to England he was told that he could only stay for a few days, which meant that he was not able to come to Portugal and that we would have to spend Christmas without him.

In October I received the first letter from someone in Portugal who was interested in Subud. José Simões Serra was an elderly gentleman who had read Bennett's book *Concerning Subud* and had written to the author for more information. He was told to 'get in touch with Mrs Bowden, who is the only person in Portugal who has attended Subud and who will be able to tell you anything you may wish to ask.' (A surprising statement.) We met, and after explaining as much as I could about Subud I had to tell him that, as men do the latihan only with men and women only with women, I could not open him; he would need either to go to England to receive the contact or else wait until a man 'helper' came to Portugal.

Let me explain what a helper is. A helper is a normal Subud member with a specific function. Usually, they are people who have been in Subud the longest, have attended latihan regularly, and so have more experience. They are the ones who can 'open' people – or rather, 'witness their opening'. They can also give explanations about Subud, thus making it possible for Subud to spread.

On 21 November Mama had a fall in the living room in Casa San José, and when I tried to lift her it was clear that she had broken her hip. I called an ambulance to take her to the British Hospital, where she was immediately operated on and had a pin put in her hip. I was very sad that she had to undergo more suffering, as if she had not experienced enough already.

Luckily she did not have too much pain and gradually began to get better. She sat on a chair while they made her bed, and I combed and arranged her hair. I was the only one she allowed to touch it, so every day I combed her fine, long, snow-white hair. Although ill, she was still beautiful.

Although she recovered quickly from the operation, before Christmas she started getting weaker and it became increasingly difficult for her to get up. But we were still able to spend Christmas Eve together in a happy, joyful atmosphere. We took a lovely fir tree to her hospital room, and Stephen sprayed it with some white 'snow'. We sat around her bed, Nicky, Hema, Stephen and I, and lit a lot of sparklers, which made the whole occasion very festive. She was very lively and obviously enjoyed the evening.

As the days passed, her weakness increased. We called in two specialists, but they were unable to help; they told us frankly that there was no hope and that Mama could not last long. During that time I left her only at night, and would have stayed on at the hospital then as well, if it would not have shown her how seriously ill she was.

On 6 January 1959, she suddenly and intuitively became fully aware of the situation. I was sitting next to her when she said, 'I now understand everything. My operation a year ago was for cancer – thank you for hiding it from me at the time. I know that this is the end, and I am glad to go. There has been nothing for me to do here since Papa left.' She asked me to write down who she wanted to leave her few tokens of value to – her ring, her bracelet, and so on; she did not forget anything. I was happy when she asked me to tell her confessor, our dear Father Francisco, to come and see her because she wanted to make a life-confession. None of this was said in a sad or tragic way, just simply and naturally. I felt no sadness either – it was as if we were discussing the weather.

I called Father Francisco immediately, and left him alone with Mama while I guarded the door outside for about half an hour, until Mama called me in again. She asked Father Francisco not to hurry away, but stay with us for a while. We had quite an animated conversation during which she asked him to perform her burial, and then she suddenly repeated something once or twice, looked at me and said, 'Ily, I am repeating myself.' Those were her last words to me. That night the nurses insisted that I go home for a rest, and they promised to ring me if there was any change in her condition.

At eight o'clock the next morning, just as I was leaving the house, the hospital telephoned to say that Mama was unconscious. She did not regain consciousness all day, and the priest came to give her the last sacrament. I managed to convince Hema and Nicky to go home, but

Stephen would not leave. Professor Pap came at ten and sat with us. Suddenly Mama's pulse got faster and her breathing heavier, and at eleven o'clock in the evening, on 8 January, without any struggle her breathing stopped; it was as if she had fallen asleep.

When it was the time for her to go, Magdamama died beautifully, in the same way as she had lived. Mine was the saddest responsibility: to comb her hair for the last time and to dress my dear, angelic Mama. I could not let anyone else do that. She had asked me to put her little cross into her hand and, like Papa, had asked me not to remove her wedding ring.

On 11 January, Father Francisco laid her beside Papa in the British Cemetery. The funeral was very moving. King Umberto was there along with many others including of course our faithful employees Guilhermina and Maria, who were devastated.

Prime Minister Kállay wrote a beautiful letter, and other letters and telegrams came pouring in.[xv] Although it was a sad task to reply to them, it was wonderful to see how many people had loved Mama. Unfortunately, Stephen had to leave immediately after the funeral because he had been accepted by Oxford University and now had to take the 'house' examination. So I remained alone in what was now a very empty house. Everything was so full of memories that my last task was very hard to complete. I had to close down Casa San José, which Mama had transformed into such a cosy home – a little world of its own, which had now come to an end. I cannot describe the pain I felt. It seemed to me that it was not just the door of Casa San José that had closed for ever, but an epoch: one that, with its two World Wars, its precious events, tragedies and sad memories, was perhaps more varied and richer than most others in our history.

What helped me come through was the gratitude I felt towards the people whose help had allowed us this sunny, joyful 'Rodosto',[60] and that had lightened as much as anything could the bitter exile and the suffering we felt for our country. My thoughts were with our benefactors all the time, as bit by bit I took this special world apart. I hoped that they would know and feel that it was not only I who was grateful to them with all my heart, but that there were certainly countless other nameless, grateful Hungarians as well. I entrusted Papa's letters and other documents, their clothes and especially Papa's uniforms, to friends for the time being; and hoped to be able to leave for Baghdad in a month's time.

I had a long letter from Stephen, all about his journey by boat to England and, suddenly switching into English, he ended by saying:

[xv] Appendix 14: letters from Miklós Kállay and Ferenc Chorin.

I was very depressed, thinking that it wasn't right for me to leave you, taking care of my own affairs while you over-exert yourself doing everybody else's work – but when I read your letter and saw that you seriously seem to be trying to look after yourself, then I stopped worrying. But don't imagine, Mama, that everything will change and you will feel independent just because Grandfather and Grandmother no longer have to be looked after. I think that you have to give up this constant attention to the needs of others, because otherwise you will always feel dependent on everyone and it will tie you down. I know I am like that, and I think you are the same.

One thing that cheered me was Sya's marriage to Eugen Schelling. Her husband József had met this kindly man, a wealthy Swiss industrialist, soon after they settled in Switzerland, and they had become friends. After József died, Eugen came and tried to help Sya wherever he could, and fell in love with her. When he asked her to marry him she was hesitant at first, but I had met him several times and knew that he was a very good, kind-hearted person who loved Sya very much. In my opinion József had brought them together, as if intending to put her in Eugen's care.

I still often went across the river to our farm, where the builder had started work. I had acquired a detailed description of how to build a fireplace and although the builder had never made one before, between us we managed it. It was a big moment when we first lit the fire and found that it had enough draw – we both felt very proud. I also designed a winding, stone staircase that, despite the major challenge I had faced in calculating the right height and width of the winding steps, was another success.

I managed to leave for England as planned. Stephen was in London, preparing for his Oxford examination, and I stayed with him for a week. We naturally went out to Coombe Springs together. It was an extraordinarily happy feeling to be with Subud brothers and sisters in such a relaxing atmosphere.

We discovered that Éva Bartók was living at Coombe. She was a Hungarian-born film actress, whose story was the first to get Subud into the national papers. She had been following the Gurdjieff method for years; and in 1957, when Bapak first came to England at Mr Bennett's invitation, she was both pregnant and seriously ill. The doctors advised an urgent operation, and she flew from Hollywood to England as she wanted to be operated on there. The surgeons in

London also advised an operation without delay, explaining that if she had the operation she would lose her child, but that without one she would not live to give birth to her child anyway. Mr Bennett told her about the latihan and Bapak's forthcoming arrival, and she decided to delay the operation so as not to miss him.

When Bapak arrived, his wife Ibu Siti Sumari witnessed Éva Bartók's opening and she continued regularly with the latihan. Her condition gradually improved, and finally her surgeon declared that she did not need an operation after all. They could not make out what had happened. Four months later she gave birth to a strong, healthy little girl: Deana. As she was a famous film actress, the papers got hold of the story and reported that she had been miraculously cured.

Mr Bennett later wrote: 'Several months later, a distinguished prelate who asked for information about Subud, affirmed that his interest had been aroused by the unmistakable spiritual transformation that was revealed by the photographs he had seen of Miss Bartók before and after she came to Subud.'[61]

Stephen and I sent word that we would like to visit her, and she received us in her small rented house. It was a very strange and wonderful meeting, considering that had we met under any other circumstances we would probably never have spoken to each other. I would not have been keen to meet her, as she was a film actress about whom many scandalous things had been written; and she would never have cared to meet us, as she was Jewish and her father had died in a labour camp, which she had at first associated with the name Horthy.

We became very good friends. Later that year, when I visited her on one of my trips to London, she mentioned that Bapak had advised her to have her two-year-old daughter Deana baptised, as it was important for her to have a religion. She therefore asked Mr Bennett whether he would be Deana's godfather, and asked me to be Deana's godmother, to which I very happily agreed.

24

Baghdad

On 5 March 1959 I flew to Cyprus, where I had to spend a day and a night before continuing my journey to Baghdad. I had been told in Coombe Springs that the cashier in Barclays Bank was a Subud member called Sami Jorgnacibachi. I went up to the man behind the cash desk and pushed my Subud membership card towards him. He looked at it, closed the counter and said, 'Please wait ten minutes'. Ten minutes later a car drove up and two Subud members introduced themselves as Mustafa and Güzin. They said it was quite unnecessary for me to stay in a hotel, as their family would gladly put me up. I felt their loving intention and accepted the offer.

Mustafa could speak some English, but his wife Güzin spoke nothing but Turkish. Even though we did not speak the same language, to my surprise I felt very much at home during my overnight stay with them. Their simple, sincere hospitality was free of any fuss and was really wonderful. We hugged each other when I left as if we were friends of long standing. This was the first time that I experienced the magic inner bond with those who practised the latihan.

In Baghdad, Guy was there to meet me at the airport and take me to the house that would be my home during the next four years. It had a small garden surrounded by a very high wall for security, and a clever dachshund called Shahan, whom Guy had inherited from his predecessor. The houses there were all detached, with a lot of date palms between and around them. We had a cook called Ramatullah and a boy servant called Maki.

Despite the many months that had passed since the revolution, I was aware that the situation was still very disturbed. A main feature of the times was the truckloads of people who were paid to come into the city from the desert to demonstrate. They rode standing up in open lorries, rhythmically shouting and jumping about. This went on almost all day and night; and we had to be very careful where we went, because foreigners had been dragged out of their cars and killed.

Guy drove me around to show me the city, which had an area of new, taller buildings in the middle called New Baghdad. One day we were driving over one of the many bridges over the Tigris when we saw a howling mob coming towards us on foot. They were running with their fists held high, shouting. Guy stopped the car, and when the crowd came close he opened the window and leant out with his arms outstretched, shouting something which sounded similar to the noise they were making. I was petrified, because we were so obviously foreign and I knew that was dangerous, but when the crowd reached us they laughed at my husband and banged the car with their hands in approval.

Once they had gone and we had driven on, I slowly recovered from the shock and asked Guy how he had known what to do. He said that the Iraqi people reflect what you show them: if you laugh, they laugh, but if you are afraid or angry they can get aggressive. I was amazed.

I have never experienced a place like Baghdad. I found the heat very hard to bear, as temperatures could reach around 52 degrees centigrade for two-thirds of the year – a dry heat, which made one feel barely alive. During this period most people slept on the roof, where they could get a bit of breeze and the temperature was a few degrees lower. During the day the heat poured down, while at night it oozed out. The winters were the opposite – bitterly cold weather invaded the country from the north, and the temperature could drop to freezing point. I was sorry for the Iraqi people, because they really suffered. It seemed to me that the weather helped explain their violent and irresponsible character, and that it had much to do with their inclination to cruelty. They baked in the scorching heat for nine months and were then miserably cold for the remaining three, thanks to the poverty that prevented most of them from being able to buy warm clothes.

Nobody can imagine what it was like driving a car there. There were no rules, or if there were, nobody bothered about them. Cars overtook on your right or left and at hair-raising speed, but it was advisable not to pass an Iraqi driver, because he would then step on the accelerator and overtake you in turn, waving his fist. The ambassador's English driver jokingly told me that when he got home he would have to take another driving test.

Our daily diplomatic life in Baghdad was fascinating but generally very tiring. There was mostly more than one reception, cocktail party or dinner every day; and as military attaché, Guy had to go to all of them because they were the best places in which to get information about the situation in the country. I went with him, except when he visited the Hungarian and Russian Embassies. I felt unable to set foot in either for as long as Hungary was occupied by the Soviet Union and so many of my countrymen were enduring terrible tortures, deportation and other forms of suffering.

Guy told me that when he was first introduced to the Hungarian ambassador, Guy asked him, 'How are things in Hungary?'

The ambassador replied, 'Oh, marvellous, much better than under that bandit Horthy.'

So then Guy asked, 'Then why is it that more than one hundred and twenty thousand of them have fled to England, Australia, Canada and other countries?'

'They were all bandits!' was the reply; and the ambassador went to find the person who had introduced them and complained that the British military attaché had been very unpleasant to him.

On another occasion he managed to corner the Hungarian ambassador once again, and to tease him said, 'Look into your heart – you are surely not a Communist. True Hungarians cannot possibly be Communists.' The ambassador was very embarrassed, and after looking around in the hope that no one was listening, he fled.

At the various receptions we were expected to attend, it was easy to tell the Communist representatives from the others. They were uniformly grey people, and there was a noticeably hushed atmosphere around them. They did not raise their voices, let alone laugh. I never had any trouble finding Guy at any party because he had a very hearty, loud laugh and I just followed the sound of it. He used to get shocked, indignant looks at receptions held at the Communist Embassies.

On Sundays I liked to go to the Catholic Church of Our Lady of Fatima in Baghdad. It was interesting to see Muslims coming to do their prayers there because it bore the name of the Prophet's daughter. I also tried to do the latihan three times a week by myself as I had been told. Actually, what kept me doing it regularly was something I'd been told that Bapak had said, 'Be diligent with your exercise and everything else will be given to you.' I never forgot this, and it made me carry on regularly – and after many years of latihan I can say that I believe it to be true.

The latihan has shown me many truths, which has sometimes been painful; but it has also given me the gift of being happy without any obvious reason, a state I describe as 'singing inside'. When I am in this latihan state, it seems as though everything I say or do turns out to be right. I even say things which I have not thought about or decided beforehand, but which produce much better results than if I had made up my mind about them in advance.

I also noticed a change in the way I loved others. At first I was alarmed when I sensed a seeming emptiness in the place where emotion, passion, possessiveness, etc., had once been. Did I not love my family any more? What had happened to my longings and my worries about those I cared for? In the place of those feelings came something different, which was hard to explain; something that neither hurt feelings nor time could influence; something much deeper and unfocused; something all-embracing.

Every year Guy sent me back to Europe for the hottest months – July and August. It was a welcome break, and I was glad to miss the 14 July celebrations to mark the anniversary of that grim revolution. I could spend time with Stephen, and do whatever was necessary for the upkeep of our flats in London.

That first year we went to Coombe Springs several times, and enjoyed the company of a girl called Josephine Chamberlain – in whom I could see Stephen was very interested. It was a special joy for me to be with Margaret Wichmann, who emanated such a happy, loving feeling. She told me out of the blue one day that it had been confirmed by 'testing' that I could become a helper in Subud.

I should explain the meaning the word 'testing' has in Subud. It is a process of using the latihan to ask specific questions, either to broaden our experience of our spiritual journey or to ask for guidance about a specific issue that is affecting our lives. This can be done alone, but it is usual for two or more people to do it together. In a state of latihan, one person asks the relevant question out loud. Those present take note of the question but do not think about it. They then just surrender and continue to do latihan. What they then receive in their latihan may convey an answer or clarification about what was asked.

I realized that it was unusual for someone to be asked to become a helper after only one year in Subud, and I told Margaret that I did not think I was qualified just yet. She explained that if we take on a task in Subud in a humble and sincere way we are given the strength to do it. Also, that the reason I was being given this responsibility was because I was going back to a far-off country where there were no long-term Subud members yet, and I might meet people who wanted to join.

1959 was also the year that the first Subud World Congress was organized, and it was being held at Coombe Springs. I could hardly believe my luck – or whatever it was – that circumstances allowed me to be there before going on to Portugal.

People were arriving from all over the world, and Bapak had been invited from Indonesia. Thirty-five countries were represented, and a total of 450 members attended the Congress. The latihans and the plenary sessions were held in the 'Djamichunatra', a lovely hall John Bennett had built for the Gurdjieff work, and here Bapak also gave a lot of explanations.

Bapak spoke in Indonesian, his words being translated by Mr Bennett. He spoke spontaneously, without notes, and with authority. He also answered questions that were put to him.

Bapak's explanations revealed and clarified so many things that had been hidden from me. One of the most important for me was his explanation that the worship of God ought to be integrated into everything we do.

All this was very new to me and I was observing myself as if I were someone I still did not know. I particularly remember two incidents, which I experienced first-hand.

The first occurred when we were all sitting in the Djamichunatra during one of Bapak's talks; I recall it very clearly, as if it were today. Two long windows were open, one on my side of the hall and the other facing me. I had already noticed what an unusually quiet night it was – there was no breeze and everything was very still. In answer to a question that had been put to him, Bapak was giving an explanation about money, saying that if we ask God for money we may receive only wind. The moment Bapak said the word 'wind', the trees I could see through the window started going 'shshshsh', as if moved by a strong wind. They were waving fiercely and I could also feel the air moving inside the hall. I sat bolt upright and stared around in amazement. I looked at Bapak, who just laughed. One of the other people who reacted as I did was Ronimund von Bissing. I talked to him about it years later, and he remembered the incident just as I did. He was sitting quite far from me at the time, but we looked at each other as if to say, 'What is this?'

The second incident was when Éva Bartók was asked to answer questions about Subud on television. She went to Bapak and asked him what to do. He said that she should not worry or think about it at all, but just go to the interview and leave the rest to God. She asked me to go to the little television room (which was in Bapak's quarters) and watch the show, so that I would be able to tell her how it went. Before the programme started I went into the little room and sat down on the sofa. Shortly afterwards Bapak and Ibu Siti Sumari came in, and Bapak sat next to me with Ibu on the other side. As soon as he sat down I felt an inner vibration, which was so strong that at first I thought I would not be able to watch the interview.

The reporter who asked the questions was a well-known and unpleasant talk-show host. He seemed nervous, whereas Éva looked very relaxed. He spent most of the time asking her about her film career, then suddenly said, 'Oh! I have forgotten to ask you about Subud, and our time is almost over. What is Subud for?' The camera turned to Éva, who closed her eyes for a second and then calmly said,

'Subud is for those who need it.' The presenter then said, 'I'm sorry, our time is up.'

I left at that point, but I was still vibrating strongly inside. I could not sleep at all that night and the vibration only stopped at midday the next day. Later on I had the good fortune to be in Bapak's company quite often, but I never again had as strong a reaction as I did that first time.

Bapak and Ibu's eldest daughter, Rochanawati, came with them to attend the congress. She was one of our most experienced helpers, and was much loved by all who knew her. Sadly, she died just seven years later, but the clarity of her sayings and much of the advice she gave us remains, thanks to people like Margaret Wichmann and to my daughter-in-law, who both came to know her well and wrote down these 'jewels'. Let me give you just a few of them:

Patience is the key to heaven. Without patience you cannot make progress.

Even if everything is taken away from you, your worship of God cannot be taken away.

If you feel worried or hurt by people, or pleased if they admire you, or angry with someone, or sad, this eats into your heart and makes wounds. But for heaven you must have a whole, pure heart. So when someone hurts you, don't let it get into you, but leave it on the outside.

Don't listen to gossip. When you hear something about a person that is not good, just notice it, and then lock your hearing with a key, like in a door. Don't pass it on. When you see something, just notice it, and lock your eyes with a key; the same with your mouth. For such knowledge is given by God for your own guidance, not to be passed on to others.

If you love yourself, you will not readily besmirch yourself by doing things like talking about other people.

It is important for you to be happy in this world, otherwise you will not be happy after you die. Even if you are ill and you suffer, you must be happy inside. When you are ill it means God is scraping some dirt off you.

It is important not to be afraid. What you are afraid of can enter into you. Submit to God under all conditions, sincerely, 100 per cent, and God will protect you.

By the time Guy arrived to join me for a fortnight's holiday in Portugal I had bought a big bed for Quinta do Farol, and we moved into an otherwise empty house. It was fun to be in our own home with its staircase and fireplace, and we soon bought chairs and a dining table. We still had no electricity, and the lamps we carried around reminded me of my great-grandmother's home in Hungary. Guy helped the builder to design the plans for a swimming pool, and I spent my time planting trees. We bought another cow; and later I bought a sow, that soon gave birth to her first nine piglets.

The previous year, the Belgian owner of the neighbouring quinta had died, and people had thrown things out into a ditch next to us. I'd picked up some sticks that looked to me like raspberry canes, and had planted a lot of them. This was a wonderful investment: over the following years they produced the most marvellous raspberries, which I sold to the best grocery shops in Lisbon. Nobody had ever seen such large and tasty raspberries in Portugal – they must have been brought from Belgium.

Stephen and Jo Chamberlain arrived for a visit and booked into a small hotel. I could see that things were becoming serious between them, and they were starting to hint about getting married. Although she did not look it, Jo was nine years older than Stephen – a big difference in age. I knew it was Subud that had brought them together and that it formed a real bond between them, but Guy naturally did not understand this and strongly disapproved. Stephen was only eighteen, although he seemed older in every way.

I finally got back to Baghdad on 13 November. I felt as if I was on another planet as I plunged back into the hectic diplomatic life: cocktail parties, receptions, dinners; working with the Red Crescent; and when I could, riding in the desert. The desert was full of birds, and I delighted in watching them. One day we were driving north when we saw some very dark rain-clouds gathering ahead of us; I noticed eagles appearing from every direction and quickly asked Guy to stop the car so that I could watch through my binoculars. What I saw next was really remarkable – the eagles were flying towards the rain-cloud from all sides to enjoy the uplift caused by its approach. From my past gliding experience, I immediately knew what they were doing. When they got to the right spot, they circled round and were lifted up so high that some of them became mere specs in the sky, hardly visible even with the binoculars. I counted fifty-two eagles, but there were more than that enjoying the ride.

We were very lucky to have Sir Humphrey Trevelyan as our ambassador. We got on very well with him and his wife Peggie, and Guy and I went on several wonderfully interesting excursions with them. We visited the marvellous excavations at Babylon and Nimrud and also went north to Mosul, Niniveh and Kurdistan. I was also able to visit some fascinating archaeological digs with Sigrid Kahle, the Swedish wife of the counsellor at the German Embassy.

On my next yearly absence from the intense heat of Baghdad, I went to London. Here I had some serious talks with Stephen, who was studying theoretical physics at Christ Church in Oxford. He asked my permission to marry Jo – who had recently changed her name to Henrietta (which I felt suited her much better).

This too needs a bit of explaining. Some Subud members, who for one reason or another were not happy with their original names, were asking Bapak to tell them which first name suited them best. They had heard that as a child, Bapak had been cured of a serious illness when his name was changed, and they asked him to explain why names seem to be so important. He gave the following explanation:

> A name does in fact have a strong influence on a person, because when someone is called by their name they will move in response, and such a movement comes from their whole being. So the entire self, when called by name, feels as though it were being woken from sleep or started up again having been stopped. If an adult or a child has the wrong name, when their inner feeling is aroused in this way it becomes adjusted to a name that does not correspond to their individuality. As a result, in their behaviour, in their ways and actions, the inner is not in harmony with their heart and mind.[62]

Bapak also emphasized the fact that people certainly do not have to change their name if they do not wish to do so, all the more so because our name is normally given to us by our parents or by someone they trust, and changing it could offend them.

This was naturally strange to us in the West, but much more importance is attached to names in the East, where it is widely accepted that a name can influence a person. There are many examples of this in history – we know that Jesus changed the names of his apostles; and monks and nuns change their names when they enter an order.

I was rather apprehensive that Stephen also might ask Bapak about his right name. I had always let him do whatever he felt was right, but it was well known that every first-born son in the Horthy family had been named Stephen for the last nine generations, out of reverence for Saint Stephen, the first King of Hungary; I was therefore rather concerned about what my family and many Hungarians might say about a change of name. Later, Stephen did indeed go and ask Bapak about his right name, and Bapak said that he already had the right one – Stephen.

I naturally gave Stephen's request for my consent to his marriage a lot of thought. I was certain that if I did not give my consent he would marry Henrietta anyway, as soon as he was twenty-one; and in the meantime it might disrupt his studies if he were to go up to London all the time. They might also start living together without being married. I therefore told him that I would give my consent to their marriage on one condition: that they find a flat in Oxford. I knew that it was hard to find accommodation there, but I felt that it was definitely a pre-condition for their marriage that Stephen should live where he studied.

The next day, Stephen and Henrietta went to Oxford to search for a flat. As they were driving down the main street a woman came out of a house, and stuck a 'Flat to let' sign on her door. They went straight in. The rent was reasonable and the woman was delighted to get such a pleasant young couple as tenants. They even had a garden in which they could grow vegetables. In the six weeks it took me to sort out our flat in London, they did up theirs in Oxford. We fixed the date of the wedding for September, and I left for Portugal to meet Guy at the quinta.

As I mentioned earlier, Guy did not approve of my allowing Stephen to get married so soon, and tried to persuade me to change my mind. I fully understood his reasons: Stephen was very young and Henrietta that much older. But I knew that I had no choice, and stuck to my decision. In September, Guy left for Baghdad and I went back to England for the wedding.

25

Stephen's Wedding – Islam

On 17 September 1960, Stephen and Henrietta were married in a lovely little church in Hampstead, very near to the house in Redington Road where Henrietta lived. It was a warm, sunny day and many Subud members assembled in front of the church.

There was a sad moment for me when we entered the church and the family of the bride – Henrietta's mother and sisters – were ushered into the front seats on the left, while I sat alone on the right in the seats reserved for the bridegroom's family. I imagined how it would have been if Stephen had got married in Hungary. But these thoughts soon vanished, as there was a lovely, happy atmosphere in the church. I also knew that all my family would be meeting Henrietta very soon. Stephen's best man was Tim Fryer, and John Bennett gave Henrietta away, as her father had died the previous year. When the ceremony ended and they turned towards the congregation, tears were pouring down Henrietta's face – she told me later that she felt such a wave of good wishes washed over her that she could not keep the tears back.

It was the newly-weds decision that I should accompany them on a tour in Europe so as to introduce Henrietta to my family, some of whom Stephen himself had not seen since leaving the Palace in Budapest when he was only three years old. So the couple spent the first part of their honeymoon in Germany, Belgium and Switzerland – in the company of their mother and aunts! They then went off to the Black Forest to have some time to themselves.

At the end of November I returned to Iraq. On my arrival in Baghdad, Sigrid Kahle came to ask me to give her the Subud contact. I was happy to witness her opening, and it was wonderful to be able to do latihan with her regularly.

Early in 1961 she and I had the most marvellous excursion to the ancient site of Uruk, now known as Warka, in southern Iraq. We drove south in a Land Rover, through desert lined with palm orchards, along the river Euphrates, and were welcomed at Warka by a team of German archaeologists headed by Professor Heinrich Lenzen.

Professor Lenzen had been working at the site for thirty years. He had the most fascinating stories to tell and could bring the past to life. He told us that when he first went there the Bedouin had told him legends of the past, and had asked him strange things, like: 'Do you see the spirits around you?' When he answered that he did not, they said, 'That is strange, because you are doing what they want you to do.' He added sadly that now, thirty years later, the same workmen did not remember any of it. He thought it was the result of coffee and radio having been introduced to this part of the world; before, when they were drinking tea made of desert herbs, their perception of the spiritual world was very clear.

The archaeologists lived in neat mud huts, and had built some for guests too. Each had a tiny window and contained a simple bed, a small table with an oil lamp, and some hooks on the wall for clothes. I will never forget the first night in Warka. I had a strange experience when I did a short latihan before going to bed. It seemed as if I was imploring God for something in a strange language, and I fell to my knees in a sort of lamentation. The words I uttered were so clear that afterwards I was able to write down three that I had been repeating (unfortunately they are now long-since lost). This experience was not upsetting, but it took some time before I was able to fall asleep. Next morning, Professor Lenzen told us the story of Uruk and started by explaining that because women gave birth to life, at first God had been represented by a woman. There were priestesses, not priests; and it was only later, when it was realized that woman cannot have a child without a man, that the deity was changed into a male figure. This led to a huge upheaval and a war. Uruk was besieged, and the city's women prayed non-stop, asking the goddess to save their men.

He also explained that although they had deciphered the ancient cuneiform writing, of course no one would ever know what it sounded like. Naturally I did not say anything, but I had the strange feeling that I knew what the language had sounded like, and that the night before I had received the lamentation of the women of Uruk. Heinrich Lenzen might have believed me if anyone would, but I did not talk about it because I myself could hardly believe or understand what I had 'picked up' or received.

There followed a series of happenings to which at the time I did not attach much importance. It started with a diplomatic reception at the Indian Embassy, where a Mr Kazmi, the UNESCO delegate from India, came up to me and asked whether I would like to go to his house on

Fridays, where he was teaching some of his compatriots how to pronounce the Arabic of the Holy Quran, after which they discussed its meaning in English. I thanked him for the invitation but gave it no more thought.

However, his request did make me aware of one thing – that being in an Arab country it was important to know something about the Quran. My only knowledge of the Islamic holy book was that, at the time, the Catholic Church forbade its members to read it. I discovered that one could ask one's confessor for permission to read the Quran, so I wrote to my confessor in Portugal, our dear Father Francisco, and put the case to him. The answer came promptly: 'You can read anything you like!'

Hardly had I received this letter when I again met Mr Kazmi at a diplomatic reception. He came straight up to me and asked why I had not come to the Friday meetings at his house, and whether I would come to the next one, which happened to be the next day. 'Yes,' I said. And off I went the next morning – still wondering why I was doing so. I will never understand why he picked me out of such a big crowd of people.

On arrival at Mr Kazmi's house I found myself the only Christian and the only woman in the gathering, which consisted of nine young Indian Muslims and our host. One after the other they read the same *Surah*, or chapter, of the Quran aloud, and Mr Kazmi corrected their pronunciation, after which the meaning of the passage was discussed in English. I was fascinated by what I heard. They asked me questions on Christianity, and I asked them about Islam. They translated for me some of the things the Quran says about the Virgin Mary. I had no idea that Moslems felt a special devotion to Mary and acknowledged the Immaculate Conception and virgin birth of Christ. I was told that some mosques even have a niche devoted to Mary.

Still not knowing at all what I was doing there, I went back every Friday, and to my utter amazement found I was able to repeat some of the *Suwar* correctly, even though I did not know the meaning of the words I was saying. The sound and rhythm of the Quranic language simply fascinated me; it obviously worked through my 'inner' and not through my brain.

In the evenings my husband and I sometimes went for a walk on the banks of the River Tigris; we would hear the muezzin's call to prayer: 'Allahu Akhbar,' from the minaret of the mosque. I stood still to listen and Guy asked, 'Why have you stopped?' I answered, 'Don't you hear the call to prayer? It's so beautiful.' He looked at me in astonishment, and I admit that I was also a bit surprised at my own reaction.

At that time it could be dangerous for Iraqis to be seen with or be visited by Western diplomats. Indeed, the British military attaché – Guy – and the American attaché, were two people who were always tailed by an Iraqi motorcyclist and were not supposed to leave Baghdad. There were checkpoints everywhere and we had to show our papers. It was easier for me, being a woman and therefore less important in this Islamic world. When I passed a checkpoint and showed my papers, they would ask, 'Where is your husband?' and when I said that he was at the Embassy, they would just wave me on. Even so, when I visited an Iraqi friend I would never telephone them from home, and would park my car two blocks away from their house and go on foot. This surprised people, and they asked me how I knew what to do. I told them that being Hungarian I'd had my share of experiences of living under foreign occupation, so I knew all the 'tricks'.

I was officially allowed to go to the Red Crescent, the Iraqi Red Cross Society, and it was there that I made many friends. The head of the organisation, Suad al-Radi, was a very charming woman; she, her sister Naira Abbas, the gynaecologist Dr Amnah Murad and many others, all became my friends. The educated women of Iraq were already quite emancipated. They could take up professions and there were many women doctors and lawyers, etc.

In the city women often dressed in European clothes, but outside Bagdhad, in the countryside and desert, women still wore lovely loose robes, some of which were very colourful rather than just being black. When we rode out into the desert on horseback we would often come across isolated little settlements, where behind each mud hut there was always a mud oven in which the local inhabitants baked unleavened bread. I will never forget a beautiful, tall and slender woman in bright green robes, who hurried back to hide in her mud hut when she saw us coming.

Thanks to my upbringing I could speak several languages, I therefore did not feel at all happy being in a country where I could not speak the local tongue. Sigrid Kahle and I started to take Arabic lessons but found them very difficult. Yet while I was struggling with colloquial Arabic, I found I could recite bits of the Quran effortlessly. I amazed myself when, following a morning at Mr Kazmi's house, I recited the *Ayat al Kursi* prayer to my friends from beginning to end from memory. They asked whether I knew what I was saying, and when I told them that I hadn't got a clue, they started to help me understand.

Because of all this, my Iraqi friends seemed to be fond of me and often took me on excursions. They dressed me up in black Arab clothes with a black scarf over my head, and told me to cover my face in the holy places and look down so that people could not see my blue eyes. They said that I did not have to be afraid of anything because they would always surround me and if anyone asked me a question, they would answer for me. At the time I had no idea why we had to take so many precautions.

Inside the mosque I followed and copied everything they did. It was interesting to note the difference between the mosques belonging to the Sunni and the Shia Muslims. Sunni mosques were lovely – they just had beautiful carpets and nothing else for decoration. I felt a strong atmosphere of worship there. Shia mosques, on the other hand, were hung with all kinds of offerings that people had brought. The ceilings and walls were covered with clocks and all sorts of objects. There was usually the tomb of an Arab saint in the middle and a cordoned-off space into which people threw offerings of jewels or money.

When we discussed these trips back at the Red Crescent, I heard one of the ladies ask the others how I had behaved when we were in the mosques. 'Oh,' they said, 'she behaved much better than we do!' I found that quite funny and very reassuring.

Naturally, I did not mention my escapades in diplomatic circles, so as to prevent my friends from getting into trouble, but one day I was taken aback when I overheard a conversation between two ambassador's wives: they said that anyone could go into a Sunni mosque, but that it was very dangerous for a Christian to go into a Shia mosque, as the Shias believed that this would desecrate their holy place. There were cases where Christians who had 'intruded' had been killed. Now I understood why my Iraqi friends had been so anxious that I should not be noticed, and had surrounded me when we were in a Shia mosque.

Guy and I, together with Ambassador Humphrey Trevelyan and his wife Peggy, made plans for a trip to Amman, Jerusalem and Petra in Jordan. I prepared myself weeks ahead, having found a lovely book on the life of Christ in the Embassy library. I read it avidly, and marked the parts that I intended to read on the spot in Jerusalem.

Driving up the River Jordan valley was wonderful. It seemed to me to be just as it must have been in the days of Christ – it was not built up and nothing had been spoilt. As we drove I said a little prayer to myself, asking God that my husband should somehow be touched and feel something of the inner anticipation that I was experiencing: 'Even if it has nothing to do with me, just let him be touched somehow,' I found myself saying.

When we arrived at the hotel in Jerusalem, Humphrey said that we should ask for a guide to show us around. I hesitantly said that I did not want a guide, as I knew exactly what I wanted to see, but that they should find one while I went around on my own. I was actually hoping to do just that, but to my surprise Humphrey was delighted, and said that I should be the guide and that they would follow me wherever I wanted to go.

We started off at Saint Stephen's Gate, and as we walked along we saw a notice on our right that read: 'The Convent of the Sisters of Sion, where you can see the pavement where Christ stood when condemned to death.' This seemed to be fairly new, as I had not read about it in the guidebooks. We went in, and an English speaking nun then told us that, while staying at the convent, a priest had received a revelation that 7 metres below the building were the pavement and the place in front of Pilate's house where Jesus had been condemned to death. They dug down 7 metres and found a pavement, which archaeologists had been able to confirm was indeed from that period.

The nun then led us in single file down some steep, narrow stairs. As I was going down I felt tears running down my cheeks, but I quickly brushed them off and lagged behind so that the others would not notice. When we reached the bottom we found a large space, with an ancient stone pavement and nothing else in it besides the columns that held up the ceiling. In the centre of this hall there was a mat, covering part of the pavement. As we approached, the nun lifted up the mat. At that moment I fell forward prostrate on the ground with outstretched arms and no notion of what was happening to me. This lasted for a minute or two at the most. Peggy later told me that Guy moved to pick me up, but the nun stopped him and said, 'Don't touch her. Things like that happen here.' When I came to and got up, I was ice-cold from the tips of my fingers down to my toes. The ambassador appeared embarrassed and was looking at the wall, not knowing what to do, while the nun asked me if I wanted a glass of water. I said that I was all right and did not want anything, and we all walked on as if nothing had happened. The nun went on to explain that this was the spot where it was thought that Jesus Christ was probably standing when he was condemned to death. She told us how it had been excavated and so on, but I cannot remember any of the details of what she said. We went back to the stairs but had to wait because people were coming down. As I looked at them I noticed that everyone coming down those stairs had tears in their eyes. Some seemed to notice it and some did not. It was strange – or perhaps significant.

We spent the rest of the day seeing the sights of Jerusalem; and Guy, who was obviously a bit anxious, never left my side. I felt like a sounding board as I went around the city, as in some places I felt an inner vibration. But I was careful, and when I again felt the urge to prostrate myself on the ground I resisted it and no one noticed.

When we got back to our room at the hotel, Guy asked me to tell him what had happened to me in the Convent of the Sisters of Sion. He said that he had seen many ecstasies and strange things when he was in India, but he knew me to be a well-balanced, practical person, so he wanted to know what I had felt.

The moment he asked, it suddenly became very clear to me what had actually happened – up until then, I myself had not realized. I told him that something so powerful had happened on that spot that if we could fully feel it, it would be too much for us and perhaps we would even die. Awareness of it depended on the person's degree of openness, and I seemed to have felt just a little of it. I told him that I'd had tears running down my face when we came down the stairs, and that I had seen the same thing happening to other people. To my amazement he said, 'If you had not said that, I would never have remembered, but I also had tears in my eyes as I came down the steps. Of course, I didn't understand why.' To me this was the answer to my prayer in the Jordan Valley, and I felt immensely grateful to the Almighty.

From Jerusalem we drove further south to Petra, built in the first century BC, which also lay in the Kingdom of Jordan. It was in a fabulous valley, which could only be entered through a very narrow slit between huge rocks called the Siq. We had to leave the car behind and ride through this slit in the rock walls on mules. When we emerged from the narrow passage we were confronted with an unbelievably beautiful sight. Facing us were a monumental arch and columns, like the front of a temple, carved out of a huge pink rock. This long valley, flanked by enormous sandstone rocks, was something very different from the rest of the world.

Inside the pink temple we found two small niches, one on each side of the hall. I stepped into one of them and spontaneously began singing a melody, which caused a tremendous echo and sounded like singing in a cathedral. I was delighted with this effect and continued to sing, wondering how the acoustics worked. Humphrey, Peggie and Guy passed the niche, looked in and walked on. I was expecting them to comment on my singing and was surprised that they did not seem to hear it. I followed them and could not refrain from asking Guy, 'Did you hear me singing in there?' He answered with a very vague 'Yeess,' and talked about something else. They had obviously not heard anything. I would have liked to have gone back and tried again with one of them, but I did not want to make myself conspicuous after my strange behaviour in Jerusalem.

These things were all very strange to me and I had no idea what they meant. At the time I just accepted it and, although it surprised me, I did not think very much about it. But the memory has never faded, and as I write I feel just as if I were there. I realise now that if I had not been opened and had not received the latihan, I probably would never have had these experiences.

I felt very lucky, and would not have missed our trip for anything. I saw the difference between those who sincerely lived Islam and those who did not. For example, in Baghdad some official people drank alcohol when they were with foreigners but piously refused an alcoholic drink when other Muslims were around. The Arabs of the desert were different. One day we had lost our way, when we saw some sheep and found a shepherd asleep on the ground. We woke him up and asked him which way to go. Guy offered him some cold beer from the boot of the car. He took it avidly, looked at it more closely and handed it back. In spite of his thirst he would not touch an alcoholic drink. Luckily I had some water, which he happily accepted.

Things were still perpetually exciting in Baghdad. President Qassim continued to rule with the support of the Communist Party, but was coming up against the opposition of the Baathist Party. To curry favour with the people he started a campaign claiming that Kuwait should be returned to Iraq. He invited the diplomatic corps to state receptions, where he would rant against the British for as long as three hours at a time and lay claim to Kuwait, which had originally belonged to the Turks and was liberated by the British at the end of World War I.

It got to the stage where Guy told me that he thought the situation was dangerous and he sent a signal to the commander-in-chief, Lord Mountbatten, suggesting that Qassim might attempt to take over Kuwait. He received an answer that asked: 'How could Qassim do it?' Guy's reply was that he could do it on a camel, but that he had tanks and could be in Kuwait in four hours.

I was with Guy at a reception when his driver came in and whispered to him that the ambassador wanted him at the Embassy 'Now!'. Guy came to me quietly and said where he was going and that I should stay at the reception, he would be back later.

He found the ambassador in an agitated, angry mood. He said, 'You have ruined three years of hard work trying to improve Anglo-Iraqi relations. We are invading Kuwait tomorrow.' He asked whether it was not possible to hold the troops offshore as a threat, rather than actually land. Guy explained that from a military point of view this was not feasible due to the likely cost in lives. He then came back to the reception.

The British troops landed the next morning and in a matter of hours Kuwait had been taken over. The Arab World naturally screamed abuse about Britain's 'old world, Victorian gun-boat tactics', but eventually things quietened down and we tried to rebuild a good relationship with 'The Leader'. And so it went on, with never a dull moment during the years that we were there. There were civil disturbances, attempted assassinations, and rumours of coups, following which Qassim would arbitrarily shoot the officers involved.

As usual, on 12 June we celebrated the Queen's Birthday in the Embassy gardens. People were ringing up congratulating us before Guy even told me that he had been included on the Birthday Honours List. He had been made a Commander of the Order of the British Empire (C.B.E.). So this time, for us, it was a double celebration!

At the end of June I went back to Portugal and then on to London to deal with our flats and to see Stephen and Henrietta, who were expecting their first child. We had a delightful time together, preparing their home for the baby's arrival. We had latihan regularly with the members in Hampstead and also went to Coombe Springs. There was always a happy, inner peace after doing the latihan, about which Bapak once jokingly commented, 'Now you aren't worrying about your bank account!'

Henrietta's birth-pains began on 30 August and, after a couple of false alarms, on 1 September a lovely, healthy baby boy was born and given the name Leonard István. Henrietta was utterly exhausted and remained in the hospital for another week, while I looked after their home and cooked for Stephen before a happy homecoming with the new addition to our family.

I went back to Portugal for two months of hard work on our farm, and Guy managed to come for a short holiday. The previous year we had dug a borehole, which had been successfully located for us by a water-diviner; this gave us an abundance of water and we now installed overhead watering. Our *caseiro* João thought it was a miracle that we arranged our own rain whenever it was needed! We were growing lucerne for the cattle, and my raspberries were superb.

Each year there was a Military Attaché's Conference in Cyprus, which we attended. During the 1962 conference, one of the participants gave me the famous book *Exodus* by Léon Uris, which I was keen to read but which I knew was banned in all the Arab countries. I had it in my handbag on our return to Baghdad, and while Guy was dealing with the passports at the airport customs control a customs official came up to me and said, 'Open your bag.' For a moment I panicked. I realized that if they found the book on me Guy would get into a lot of trouble. I heard myself say, 'You have no right to ask me that, as I have diplomatic immunity.' The man went on insisting and I went on flatly refusing, but when he saw Guy coming back the man disappeared. I told Guy about it and he scolded me for having brought the book to Iraq. But my Iraqi friends were delighted – they all wanted to read it and it was passed on from one to another.

In June the next year I again left Baghdad and, after stopping off in Zürich to visit Sya, went to see my mother near Geneva. She had been in touch with my Subud friend Ronimund von Bissing, and his wife had then witnessed her opening. This was a great and unexpected joy for me. There were now three generations of us doing the latihan, which I felt was a great blessing.

Our time in Baghdad was coming to an end. The last three months were hectic, with National Days, Army Days, Republic Days, Independence Days, plus another wonderful excursion to Warka, this time with Suad al-Radi of the Red Crescent. Once again I stayed in my little mud-hut room with the tiny window. Just before dawn I looked out of it and saw an Arab approaching. He went up to the outside water tap, which was very near my window, and I watched him put a piece of cloth on the ground, wash his face, hands and feet, and perform his prayers. It was done with great calm and reverence, and made a deep impression on me. He could not see me and there was no one around – he was alone with God.

1963. On the first day of the year I went to the Church of Our Lady of Fatima for the last time. The next day Mr Kazmi left Baghdad to return to India; and, on 17 January, Guy and I left Baghdad for good.

Sir Roger Allen, the ambassador who had replaced Humphrey Trevelyan at the end of 1961, told Guy that he would have liked him to stay but realized that he had already been there longer than any other military attaché, and that if he did not let Guy go now he would never be able to leave, as the next ambassador would inevitably need his help. He gave us a farewell dinner party and made a speech praising Guy's services, the like of which Guy said he had not heard in his thirty-eight years in the army. Even the press reported that no one had ever been given such a farewell.

Three weeks later, on 8 February, there was a coup in Baghdad, during which Qassim was killed. Despite the fact that the new military attaché was already in place, Guy was immediately recalled. But to my relief he was unable to travel, as Baghdad Airport was closed.

We stayed in London for a month, and I used the time to take cookery lessons. I signed up for all the lessons I could get, and although I learned a lot I had quite a hard time. After preparing breakfast for Guy and doing the washing up I went off to one cookery course, at the end of which we had to wash up. Then I cooked lunch for Guy and washed up, went to the afternoon course and washed up, and finished my day by making supper and washing up! With the exception of weekends I did this full time for four weeks. It was not much fun, but I learned a great deal.

I want to say something here about my first meeting with Varindra Tarzie Vittachi, which happened during this stay. Varindra, who came from Ceylon (now Sri Lanka) was a Subud friend of Stephen's, and very fond of him. One day, when I was having tea with Stephen and Henrietta at their home, he called in and we were introduced. He sat down and we were chatting when he suddenly hit the table with his fist and said, 'By Jove, she's colour-blind!' (alluding to his own dark skin). We became lifelong friends. He told me later that he had avoided meeting Stephen's 'aristocratic mother' so as not to be disappointed, which he had presumed he inevitably would be.

It is difficult to describe Varindra in just a few words. He was highly intelligent, a brilliant journalist, a captivating storyteller, and a sceptic who always exposed feelings of superiority, pomposity or 'holiness'. He started out with communist tendencies, but his search for inner truth led him to study the Gurdjieff system, which in turn brought him to Subud. He became convinced that there was 'a force in the latihan and that I had made contact with it'. He became one of Bapak's most trusted ambassadors. ' "You courier," Bapak said. "Take job so you can visit many Subud centres." '[63]

When I first knew him, Varindra had just been made chairman of the World Subud Association, a position he was chosen to occupy repeatedly until his retirement in 1993, just before his death. In his role as Bapak's messenger he would always pass on to us the understandings that he gained from Bapak; these always contained valuable lessons, such as 'It is easier to renounce your faults than your virtues!' I found these of immeasurable value, because Bapak's clarifications were often the key to understanding what I received in the latihan. And I remember a few of Varindra's own very perceptive remarks that so often hit the spot: 'A helper is someone who needs help.' 'It is not global warming that will destroy us, it is gullibility.' 'Subud is not a teaching, but it is a great learning.' (I can warmly recommend his book *A Reporter in Subud*, a trilogy comprising his experiences over the years in Subud, as it gives one the essence of Subud in an amusing, readable way.)[64]

Luckily it turned out that Guy could not return to Baghdad, which left me feeling greatly relieved. And in fact, in that same year, Guy retired from the army in order to look after our quinta. It now seemed that we were going to settle down in our new home and farm, buying and selling cattle, raising pigs and growing vegetables and fruit. Guy turned out to be a born farmer – a talent that most of his brothers also seemed to have – and over the next seven years he and I worked very hard at Quinta do Farol. Never before had we led such a healthy life. We grew practically all our own food; we also had a milking cow and I made our butter. Four women came to pick the raspberries and I went to the two best shops in Lisbon twice a week to sell them. They were of such first class quality that now they were never put in the shop windows but were sent straight off to embassies instead.

To my sorrow I received news one morning that Madeleine Apponyi had died in hospital in Boston. I had the feeling that I should have been beside her during her last days. For quite a while I had not received any answer to my letters and I had written to her lawyer, who answered briefly that she was not allowed to have visitors and that anyway there would be no point in travelling such a long way to visit her as she did not recognize anyone. The telegram telling me of her death was from her lawyer, and I could not understand why he had informed me immediately – after all, I was not a relation. I only found out later that in her will – made some years before – she had left all her belongings to me and her money to Stephen. I am grateful that she had never told me of this intention, as it would have been embarrassing to accept.

She once explained to me that her father had created a trust that provided an allowance for his five daughters for life, but that when they died the whole fortune went to some sort of institute. I had not paid much attention to some of her stories, but knew that her two daughters had died young and her only son had been a drug addict who went from one hospital to another. He had died only a short time before his mother. Poor Madeleine had a tragic life, and she had been infinitely good to me.

What began then was like a fairy tale. Many parcels arrived for me from the United States: barrels full of porcelain, boxes full of silver, a mink coat, the most beautiful embroidered bed linen, Persian rugs. Madeleine had very good taste, and I suddenly had more lovely things than I ever had in Hungary. It was unbelievable!

On 4 August I received the following telegram: 'Smashing grand-daughter born 7lb 12oz – 3,509 gr.' Stephen and Henrietta's second child, Helena Linda, had arrived. She had been born at home, and I went over to London to meet my new granddaughter, play with my grandson Leonard, and help with the christening.

Over the next few years my life went in much the same way; working with Guy on the quinta, visiting Stephen and the family when I could, and of course continuing my Subud life.

Out of curiosity, I went to two ecumenical meetings in Lisbon, where all the religions in Portugal were represented. I found that everybody proclaimed their goodwill but actually just tried to put over their own point of view. I do not see how ecumenical cooperation will ever be possible without something like the latihan, which sweeps away our preconceived feelings. I have done latihan together with Protestants, Catholics, Jews, Moslems, Buddhists and even atheists; we worship the same Creative Power – Almighty God – and after the latihan we can each go back to our respective religions, but continue to love each other with a close family feeling. This can only be achieved through God's power; we can never do it alone, even with the best will in the world.

Our little Subud group in Portugal received a major addition – Robert Lyle, a Scot, came to settle in the Lisbon area. So at last we had a man helper and I had someone in Subud to share things with. We worked together in harmony for years, which was a real blessing.

It was always a wonderful experience to do latihan with a large group of people, and even more so to be at an event when Bapak was present, which happened in the summer of 1964. Bapak had once again been invited to visit Subud groups around the world, and I joined Stephen, his family, and some 250 other Subud members from the UK for a long weekend in Paris, where we listened to Bapak talk and had several latihans.

Henry, my third grandchild, was born on 29 July 1965, at home in 9 Redington Road, and it was a lovely, happy occasion, welcoming him into the world.

In 1966 we had a happy holiday with Stephen, Henrietta and my three grandchildren in Norfolk. A little hesitantly, Stephen told me that he wanted to embrace Islam. He was obviously expecting me to say, 'You can't do that! What about family tradition? What would your grandfather say?' and so on. But this was not the answer he got. Instead I said, 'Let me tell you how beautiful it is,' and I started reciting the *Ayat al Kursi* to him. As I had never talked to him about my experiences, this came as a complete surprise and he could hardly believe it. I now felt that all that happened to me in Baghdad must surely have been a preparation for me to be able to accept this decision by my son. Otherwise, even if I had not opposed it, I could never have accepted it in my heart.

When Stephen told me about his decision, he explained that he had gradually come to understand what Bapak meant when he said that Subud is not a religion and that we each need our own religion. What happens in Subud is that we regain our natural state; our soul is reconnected and enlivened by the Power of God, from which it was separated by the influences of this world. But these powerful influences continue to act on us whether we like it or not, constantly trying to separate us from God's guidance. And Subud, having no teaching, cannot really provide us with practical help in how to face such influences. That guidance is in the teachings that were revealed in the various religions. He went on to say how grateful he was that the latihan had guided him towards Islam. First of all, Islam contained practical help that could be used in daily life: the five daily prayers, which constantly bring one back to a clean inner state. Moreover, Islam did not conflict with the reality that he had experienced in Subud: that every creature of God is connected directly to God's power. Soon after that holiday he left for Indonesia, where he embraced Islam. He received the name Sharif – thus keeping the initial letter 'S'.

At the end of July I was back in Portugal and facing a difficult situation. For some time Guy had become increasingly antagonistic towards my participation in Subud. It seemed to be connected with his drinking, as it was at those times he became so critical. All this had started a year earlier, and as time went on I found it more and more stressful, until now I was in a rather strange state. I was not feeling well and there was no real reason for it; I had headaches and could not sleep – something I had not experienced before.

I decided I needed to stay away from home for a while. Olga de Cadaval, head nurse of the servitas at Fatima, had a cottage in her garden in Colares in the Sintra hills, and she kindly let me stay there. I moved into the little house, and Guy occasionally came to visit me. I knew that I had reached a sort of crisis, and I did not want to see anyone; I needed to be alone. I remember, when I went shopping, enjoying the lovely Sintra hills and driving along that winding, romantic road, the air filled with bird song. I cooked simple meals and cleaned the cottage. I listened to Bapak's talks on my little tape-recorder and did latihan. My headaches ceased and I slept well again.

In December Sharif came to see Guy, who had asked for his opinion about my strange behaviour. Sharif told him that because the latihan is a process, sometimes we go through a difficult period if something within us is being purified. He said that what I was going through might be such an experience, and in that case it might be best to let things take their course. Sharif had recently been to the main Subud centre in Indonesia and, from his own experience there, felt it might help the situation if Guy were to let me go to Jakarta to be near Bapak for a while. Guy answered that he was prepared to do anything that could be of help. So they decided that as soon as possible they would ship me off to the Far East.

Sharif then came to see me and told me about his visit to Guy. I accepted their decision, but I remember that even as I was preparing for my journey I had no great desire to go. I had never planned to go to Indonesia, and was just letting things happen.

On 14 January 1967 – my birthday – a KLM plane flew me to Indonesia. It was evening when I arrived in Jakarta and there was no one to meet me. There were telephones but they did not work. I was utterly lost, but thought it best to take a taxi to Cilandak, the suburb of Jakarta where Bapak and many Subud members lived. I had no idea that Subud members had been advised not to take taxis from the airport at night. When I was already in the car, another man got in beside the driver; they started questioning me in broken English about how much money I had, and the situation became scary. I was desperately wondering what I should do, when I had an idea: I told them that I had no money but only a chequebook – which was not true – and I asked them to stop at a big hotel so that I could get some dollars to pay them. They fell for this ruse, and when we stopped at the Hotel Indonesia, in the middle of Jakarta, I hurried to the reception and asked them to ring Cilandak. I was put through to Mas Usman, Bapak's secretary, who told me to wait and he would pick me up. With the help of the hotel porter I got my bags out of the car, paid the taxi and, with a sigh of relief, waited for my lift.

26

Cilandak

Mas Usman arrived and we drove to Cilandak. I was taken straight to the latihan hall, where a lot of smiling people were gathered around Bapak and Ibu. Bapak said I was welcome. This turned out to be my longest stay in Cilandak, a never to be forgotten four months.

In 1967 Cilandak was a quiet countryside full of orchards – it was the fruit-growing district of the capital, Jakarta. Bapak had made his home here, and the Subud community had built a house for him and his family. Called Wisma Subud, it was a walled-in compound with a porter's lodge at the gate. With Bapak's permission, foreigners came to settle there too and built houses. There were shops and little dwellings along the road outside, and the traffic consisted of few cars but many pedestrians, bicycles, betjaks (the two-wheeled, two-seater carriages, pulled by one man) and all kinds of vendors with baskets hanging from either end of a pole across their shoulders. Later it became part of the spreading capital, and the road alongside the Subud compound was constantly filled with heavy, polluting traffic.

In those days things were rather primitive, and foreigners used to go shopping in Singapore – an hour away by air – just to get toilet paper and other such necessities. But all this was rapidly changing, and a few years later you could get all you needed in Jakarta.

The evenings in Cilandak were delightful. People sat in chairs outside their houses enjoying the coolness of the evening and smoking Kretek cigarettes. I smoked an occasional cigarette in those days and enjoyed a Kretek in the evening, as they gave off the smell of cloves, which then filled the air and kept the mosquitoes away. One typical sound we got used to was the 'tshik tshik' of the lizards (which were therefore called tshik-tshaks). They came into our rooms, where they were welcome because they kept them free of mosquitoes. My childhood passion for taming animals was awakened and, by putting down crumbs of bread and patiently waiting with my hand beside it, I finally persuaded one of the tshik-tshaks to take the crumbs from my fingers.

I was lucky enough to share a room with Maria Kibble, who had been one of the first Subud members in Europe. She had witnessed my opening in Coombe Springs and I felt very close to her. She had just embraced Islam and was now using the Arabic version of her name, Maryam. She knew of my experiences in Baghdad and asked me to help her with the pronunciation of the Islamic prayers. We therefore did the prayers together every day and I was gradually learning them by heart. They are very beautiful and we felt greatly helped by them.

During my stay, Margaret Wichmann arrived from England to settle in Wisma Subud. She also had a new name, Mariamah, as she too had become a Muslim. (It may be worth re-iterating here that there is no direct connection between Subud and Islam. Bapak never stopped stressing that the latihan was for all humankind, whatever their race or colour, or whether they followed a religion or not. He did however often say that it was helpful to have a religion, as all the great religions give us the framework for living as human beings should in this world.)

It was now nine years since I had joined Subud and it had never occurred to me to change my name. Then one day I started thinking about who I really was, and the thought bothered me for two days. So I decided to ask Bapak about my name. I wrote a letter to him in which I asked for my right name and whether I should use it with my husband and family, who might not easily accept it. The answer came: my name was Rahmaniyah and I should inform my husband and family, but use it only with my brothers and sisters in Subud. I was stunned, as this seemed a powerful name – maybe I would grow into it. From then on I always used it with my Subud brothers and sisters. I took the courage to write straight away to my parents, my sisters and my husband, telling them of my new name and explaining why it was sometimes necessary to change. It naturally came as a shock to them, but in a few months it was forgotten and they went on calling me Ily, a diminutive of Ilona (which I had never really liked).

I remained in Cilandak while Bapak and Ibu went on another world tour, but just before Bapak left Indonesia I received a letter from Guy, in which he said that when I came back he wanted me to stop doing latihan for one year. This was a shock to me and I went to Bapak for advice. Bapak said that God comes first, then oneself, then one's husband and then the rest. He told me to do latihan when my husband was not at home, or at night. I wondered how I could do that without lying to Guy. But, as I had asked Bapak's advice, I told myself just to go ahead and do what Bapak said, and not think about it in advance.

At home, some months later, I found a letter from John Bennett tucked inside a book. It was an answer to a letter Guy had written to him. Guy had met him in Baghdad, when he had stayed with us on his way back from Nepal. Apparently, Guy had now turned to him for advice on how to join Subud, for Bennett's letter stated that he could not be of assistance and that Guy should ask a Subud helper. Guy must also have told him about my indisposition and journey to Cilandak, because the letter referred to it and advised Guy to stop me doing latihan for a year 'because the latihan is beneficial at first, but then it loses its utility'. (I had suspected that it could not have been Guy's idea!) What Guy did not realize was that Bennett had withdrawn from Subud; he was creating a new school with some of his old pupils who wished to continue with Gurdjieff work – although I later heard that he came back to the latihan. The letter was a shattering revelation. I was afraid that Bennett's words had thwarted any chance that Guy might share my Subud life.

What followed was interesting. As Guy did not mention his correspondence with Mr Bennett, I said nothing about it either. He took it for granted that I had accepted his request and was not doing latihan, and never asked me about it. Thus I did not have to lie to him and could easily follow Bapak's advice. For many months I did latihan at night or when Guy was not at home. I also arranged to take the raspberries to Lisbon on Mondays and Thursdays, and joined the group for latihan at the same time. Guy never found out, and the raspberries worked wonders. From the month of May, when I returned from Indonesia, the raspberries went on producing fruit until Christmas! Raspberries had never been available in Portugal after August, so it was also a successful business. When they finished, I took eggs to Lisbon to sell – and so it went on without any problem.

On 14 July my fourth grandchild was born, and was given the name Marianne. I went to London two days later to see her, and to hear about the family's plan to move permanently to Indonesia. When Bapak had come to the UK he had stayed with Sharif and Henrietta, and had invited them to go and live in Cilandak. At the time Sharif was working as a construction engineer with Ove Arup & Partners in London, but three Subud architects had asked him to join their enterprise in Indonesia, and he had accepted their offer.

Father Manuel Cosme, the priest in Paio Pires – a small town near our quinta – asked me if I would give regular talks about marriage and life in general to the young girls of his parish. I told him that as I was not Portuguese it would perhaps be better if he asked one of the local ladies to take on the task. He firmly disagreed and said he felt that I was the best person for the job. I hesitated, but finally accepted his request.

Between six and twelve girls used to come to the Parish Church to listen to what I had to tell them, and I in turn listened with interest to what they had to say. I always started with a moment of quiet and then the Lord's Prayer – which one of them had to say out loud, slowly and clearly, not rattling it off without a thought as they normally did. We ended our conversations with the 'Hail Mary'. The girls seemed to enjoy coming and we felt close to each other.

I had an interesting experience during the first of these sessions, when I started to say the prayer 'Hail Mary'. Instead of saying, 'Holy Mary, Mother of God, pray for us sinners,' – which was what I was used to, having prayed many rosaries – I heard myself say, 'Holy Mary, Mother of Christ ... '. I then realized that the original wording was strange, as how could God have a mother. From then on I just could not make myself say the original words, and was surprised that nobody mentioned it or apparently even noticed. These are remarkable things, coming from an inner receiving that we do not control, when the heart and the mind are switched off or are directed by our inner.

It was becoming increasingly difficult to get people to work on our farm. A big steel factory had been built between our quinta and the town of Seixal, and many of the local inhabitants started going there to work; this meant Guy was now regularly driving the tractor. One day, when I had gone into Lisbon, Guy was driving the tractor up a steep road with a high bank on both sides. He had just driven past four men who were walking down the road, when the tractor's engine failed. He started sliding backwards, and to his horror the brakes did not work either! He was gaining speed and, looking back, he saw that the four men were unaware of his rapid approach.

So as not to hit them and in order to reduce the tractor's speed, Guy aimed it at the bank. It turned over and buried him underneath, crushing him in the process. The men heard the noise and rushed up to the tractor, but could not move it. They ran to the nearest houses and called more men. Guy was still conscious as they lifted the tractor to pull him out, but then, not being able to hold it up, they dropped it on him again. When they finally got Guy out he was unconscious. They carried him up the hill to the main road, but instead of calling an ambulance, they stopped a small Volkswagen and crammed Guy into the back seat.

When I came home from Lisbon I had to search for Guy, as nobody knew where he had been taken. I found him in a small hospital on our side of the river, which belonged to a Dr Elvas. When I saw Guy it was a terrible shock, as he was ash-grey and covered in black oil from the tractor. He looked dead. Dr Elvas X-rayed his chest, and discovered that both his collarbones and all his ribs were broken. I was told that he could not be moved, and after a few days he seemed a little better. Dr Elvas then told me that he was going to operate and join the two broken collarbones.

I could feel that this was wrong, as Guy was too weak and might possibly not survive an operation. Dr Elvas was very angry when I told him that Guy had to get stronger before the operation and that I would not consent to it yet. When I arrived at the hospital the next morning Guy was unconscious again and I thought he was dying. The nurses said that the doctor had told them to put Guy in a chair to begin to recover, and that when they had done so Guy had lost consciousness. This was the last straw. I got an ambulance, took Guy to the British Hospital and asked Professor Pap to get the best specialist to see him.

Professor Belo Morais came immediately, and the first thing he did was to have X-ray pictures taken of Guy's whole body. He showed me that Guy's pelvis was broken on both sides. His lower body had not even been X-rayed at the other hospital – and he had been made to sit in a chair! Dr Morais later told me that from the evidence on the X-ray film, Guy ought to have been dead.

Except for a tight bandage around his chest to heal the ribs, he was not put in plaster, and the collarbones healed by themselves!

I will forever be grateful for the help I received from Robert Lyle, the Subud helper in Portugal, during this time. He mixed all kinds of strengthening drinks for Guy, and I took them to the hospital every day. I knew that they contributed to Guy's quick recovery, which amazed all the doctors and nurses: five weeks later he sat up for the first time; and in six weeks he was back home, walking with crutches, though still looking frail.

1969. Around this time a book by Gordon Brook-Shepherd was published, with the title *The Last Habsburg*. It would be wrong for me not to comment on it, as I can personally testify to some of the very serious distortions it contains, including a number of historical errors and many malicious comments aimed at my father-in-law, Admiral Horthy. I discuss just a few examples of the book's false statements and inaccuracies in the appendices.[xvi]

When the book was published, Mr Brook-Shepherd received a number of letters of protest from people like Tibor Eckhardt[65] and Gusztáv Hennyey, explaining the errors in his book in detail. They sent me copies of their letters to the author as well as of one to Archduke Otto. They also sent me some of the answers they received. All these letters are in my possession.

[xvi] Appendix 15.

Meanwhile our little Subud group in Portugal was slowly growing. As I had been the first Subud member in Portugal, I became the first helper, then national helper, and eventually I was chosen as a 'spiritual councillor'. This sounds rather grand, but was only a temporary function to represent the country at the Subud World Congress and act as a coordinator nationally and internationally. The appointment lasted for four years – from one World Congress to the next. Every country where Subud was established appointed two councillors – a man and a woman – for the spiritual side, plus a councillor for the organisation. A certain amount of organisation was very necessary, as we needed places for latihan; we also had to start preparing for creating the homes for disabled children and the elderly, and the schools and hospitals that Bapak was hoping we would initiate. Money was obviously needed for all this; and, as there was no compulsory membership fee, Bapak advised us to create Subud enterprises, which would contribute 25 per cent of their net profits to a fund: in this way Subud would be able to fulfil its purpose in the world – because the latihan was not just for ourselves, it was for the whole of mankind.

I continued to go to church and to communion, and at the same time I was doing the Islamic prayers, which had become important to me. I knew that in the past the Catholic Church had also had several daily calls to prayer – like the Angelus, which was said three times a day – but to my knowledge nobody was practising them any longer. I was beginning to wonder whether I was right to mix all this together ... should I be worshipping in both the Christian and the Islamic way?

I was soon to be given an answer. Now that Sharif, Henrietta and my grandchildren were living in Indonesia, Guy very kindly paid for me to go to visit them for five weeks every year. Being near my family in Cilandak was the most wonderful thing that I could have wished for; it was a particular delight to be with my four grandchildren, whom I missed very much. I chose to go during the Islamic month of the Ramadan fast, although I did not explain this to Guy, who probably would not have understood.

Cilandak was completely full with visitors from abroad, as more and more Subud members of all religions were choosing to come here for Ramadan. Even though many were not Muslims they seemed to have good inner experiences, gaining discipline and other advantages from doing the fast along with the latihan.

There were many experiences for me during my first Ramadan fast, which I will not even try to describe, as they are very personal. But I would like to share a couple, the first of which was important and decisive for my future.

In Islam, the twenty-first night of the fast is called a 'night of power'.

Bapak was in the latihan hall with the men, and his wife Ibu assembled the women in the hall of Bapak's house. She explained to us that this was a special night and that we should just sit quietly in latihan; some of us might receive something special, but it did not matter if nothing happened. As I was sitting quietly, my upper body began to move backwards and forwards, and then sideways, right and left. This went on involuntarily all the time we sat there, and I just let it happen. I wondered if this had any purpose at all.

The next day I was attending a councillors' meeting. I sat at the end of the table and there was an empty chair next to me. Suddenly the door opened and Bapak came in and sat down on the chair beside me. He gave us a short talk, in the middle of which he stood up, moved his body backwards and forwards, and said, 'This is Islam' (vertical). Then he moved his body right and left – just as I had done – and said, 'This is Christianity (horizontal); it is the cross, and it is all one.' Well, this was the answer to my concerns about mixing Christianity and Islam. It felt so simple and so right. The Catholic shrine in Fatima, my connection with Islam in Baghdad – for me it was all one inner indication.

Bapak gave a talk on most of the nights of power, and he sometimes asked members to come forward and sing; it could be anything they liked, as long as they sang 'from the inner'. At the end-of-fast celebration, known in Indonesia as Lebaran, we were all in the big hall in Bapak's house, which was packed not only with the residents of Cilandak, but also with many Indonesians from outside the compound. One after another, many people were called to the centre of the hall to sing. Bapak was calling on the different nationalities present to sing in their own languages. There were Germans, French, Ceylonese, Spaniards – a great variety of people. I was sitting at the back, enjoying every minute of the evening, when suddenly I heard Bapak's interpreter Usman calling me to sing something in Hungarian. It was totally unexpected and a shock, but when Bapak called it was not possible to remain seated. I was, so to speak, pushed out of my chair, and while going towards the centre of the hall I feverishly tried to think of a very short little Hungarian song, so that I would quickly finish with it, but having thought of one I forgot the melody. For a few moments, which seemed endless, I stood paralysed, until – as I was told later – Sharif silently came from the back and stood behind me. The melody then emerged and the short little song was quickly over. One would have imagined that I would go happily back to my seat. But no! I turned to Bapak and said, 'Would Bapak like to hear a Portuguese song?' 'Ya, ya,' said Bapak. And then with a strong voice – which amazed me – I sang the Coimbra Fado in Portuguese, as I have never sung it before or since.

In other countries this song was widely known as 'Avril au Portugal', and the whole audience murmured the melody to my singing. When I finished, there was a great ovation and I went back to my seat with tears of joy on my cheeks. Sharif told me afterwards that it was he who had suggested to Bapak to call me, as he wanted 'the cork to come out'. Well, can you beat it, it did!

It was a strange experience and it showed me that, because there was no Subud in Hungary at the time, in Subud I was Portuguese. Somebody had recorded the evening's songs and I took a copy with me to Portugal. The members were delighted.

Early in 1970 I had a strange dream, in which Guy and I were driving on the road from Portugal to Spain and had a serious car accident. The car swerved off the road into a ditch, where it hit a large rock and then turned upside down, rolled over sideways and landed with its wheels in the air. I was kneeling in broken glass, but neither of us was hurt. In the dream I also knew that if Guy had gone alone he would have died. When I woke up I was amazed at the clarity of the dream, but as we were not going to Spain in the foreseeable future I did not attach much importance to it.

After Guy's accident on the tractor we did not want to risk any more misadventures, so we resolved to sell Quinta do Farol and begin looking for a new home on the other side of the Tagus. Guy had started to work for Cicerone, the oldest real-estate agency in Estoril, and in fact he later took over the whole enterprise. He was very clever at putting funny advertisements in the *Anglo-Portuguese News*, which most foreigners read. They seemed to appeal to people, and the agency soon became known. Through his work he of course knew which houses were for sale in the area, and showed me a number of them with a view to finding us a new home.

By now I was fully aware that houses could give one a good or a bad feeling. One day Guy drove me up the road beside the Marinha woods to show me a house that was for sale. Even before we arrived I said to him, 'Yes! This is it!' There was quite a big garden, but it was full of trees. Its name was Casa do Outerio, which we changed to 'Casa do Farol', meaning the house of the lighthouse. We were used to the name and there was a lighthouse nearby.

We were lucky enough to sell our quinta for a good price to a Swedish shoe-factory owner, and we moved to Casa do Farol on 24 March. Guy felled the trees around the house himself and had a swimming pool put in. Inside the house we had some walls removed to make larger rooms. It was a lot of work, but I felt happy that we had found a lovely home.

Two months had passed since my strange dream, when Guy told me he had to go to Spain the following Sunday. I immediately remembered the dream. Guy added that since the workmen were coming that Sunday to do a job in the house, it was important that I should stay at home to supervise the work. I did not know what to do – I did not want to attach too much importance to the dream, but I clearly remembered that Guy should not go alone. I said nothing, as I was afraid he would think it ridiculous and make a point of doing just that – but I 'said' to God that He had given me the dream, therefore He had to do something about it.

On the Saturday, Guy came to tell me that the workmen had rung to say they could not come the next day, so it was all right if I wanted to go with him to Spain. The next morning we set off to Merida, just over the Spanish border, and I completely forgot about the dream. On the way back we had to take a diversion due to some road works. As Guy was driving along a rather narrow road he pointed to something that had caught his attention. At that moment a car appeared over a small hill ahead, coming very fast and straight at us. I grabbed the steering wheel and pulled it to one side. If I had not been there, there would have been a head-on collision. The other car narrowly missed us, but we started to swerve … and then the dream came true: we slid into a ditch, and would have run along and stopped if there had not been a big rock in the middle of it. The car hit the rock at full speed, turned over lengthways and then sideways and landed upside down. It was fascinating, as I knew each move that was coming and was not frightened. We had both slid down to the floor of the car, and I was kneeling in broken glass but without a single scratch. I said to Guy, 'I'm fine, how are you?' In a shaky voice, Guy said that he was all right. The people in the other car had seen the accident in their mirror, and came to help us out, amazed to find us alive. Guy was naturally very pale and shocked, and the woman asked me, 'How come you don't even seem shaken or dazed?'

The car was a write-off. I waited there while the others took Guy to the nearest garage to get a taxi. When we were finally on the way home Guy said, 'This is terrible, I could have killed you.' I told him that would not have been his fault, as he did not want to kill me; but denying me the latihan for the last year and a half was really serious, and it could not go on. Guy was taken aback, and then said, 'All right, once a week for two months, and then we shall see.' After two months, I said to him that from now on it would be twice a week, and this was accepted without another word.

1971 started well; everything seemed to be going smoothly. I was doing latihan with Guy's consent, Subud Portugal had hosted a visit from

Bapak the previous year which had been a truly blessed time, and now we rented a place for latihan and the group was continuing to grow.

In February the news came that Ibu Siti Sumari, Bapak's wife, our beloved Subud mother, had passed away peacefully in her sleep in Cilandak. She was only sixty-four years old. Bapak said no one should be sad but that we should rejoice and be happy for Ibu. She had been unwell with diabetes for some time and was gradually distancing herself from this life, happy to go over to 'that other life'. It was difficult for me to imagine Cilandak without her.

People go and people come: On 28 May, my fifth grandchild, Stewart, was born in Indonesia. How I was longing to be there, but I knew that in three months I would have the opportunity to see him.

For the moment we were leading a full life in Cascais. Having demonstrated his talent for farming, it was amazing how Guy now took to the real-estate business like the proverbial duck to water. Cicerone had become a success. Portuguese lawyers came to him for advice; and besides financial advice, his clients often asked his opinion on the most varied personal subjects. Many retired English couples lived in the area, and Swedes, Norwegians, Dutch, Canadians, Swiss, etc., also preferred to deal with an English agent whom they could trust. One could write a book on his dealings with film stars like Gloria Swanson, as well as some international crooks and dubious arms or drugs dealers.

This year held an important event for me – it was the year of the fourth Subud World Congress, which was held every four years and this time to be held in Indonesia. I flew out with the other delegates from Europe, and we got an enthusiastic welcome from Subud members on our arrival at Jakarta airport.

The whole of Wisma Subud had been transformed for this occasion. The beautiful new latihan hall, designed by the firm of architects Sharif worked with, was the centrepiece of the effort. It was in the middle of the compound and could seat hundreds of people. Light shone from its white cupola. The extraordinary part of the hall was the dome, which Sharif designed. It was 7 centimetres – barely 3 inches – thick, and it was the first shell concrete dome in Indonesia. To house the fifteen hundred foreigners, who came from fifty different countries, seven 2-storeyed bamboo and thatch long-houses were built, each accommodating about two hundred people. Bamboo restaurants, coffee houses, waiting spaces and even a bamboo bank and a post office had been installed. There was a security watchtower with a permanent watchman in case of fire.

President Suharto came to the opening ceremony, where Subud members sat together in national delegations, many of them in their national costumes. There were Bavarian dirndls, Indian saris, Swiss lederhosen, Japanese kimonos, Chinese cheongsams, African robes,

Javanese sarong kebayas, Sumatran jackets and even Cowboy costumes. Mr Malik, the Indonesian Foreign Minister, remarked to Varindra Vittachi that it was the 'prettiest meeting' he had ever seen.

Sharif was Bapak's official interpreter for the whole congress. Since coming to live in Indonesia three years ago he had studied and fully acquired the Indonesian language. When I heard him interpret one of Bapak's talks for the first time, I could not figure out how he was able to do it. I knew about simultaneous translation, but this was different. Bapak would speak uninterruptedly for twenty or thirty minutes – sometimes even longer – and when he stopped, Sharif would render the English translation from beginning to end. After the talk I asked him how he did it. His answer was, 'Oh, Mama, I do nothing at all, I just sit quietly and it all comes – it is the latihan.' His voice carried well, and his English was very clear.

We received a lot from Bapak to take away with us. He again warned us not to imitate him or anyone else. He said that we would receive what we need for ourselves from the latihan – that which corresponds to our own nature. In that way we would not become like someone else but become our true selves; we would become what we were intended to be.

At the beginning of 1972 Guy took me on a trip to Madeira. We went on some lovely excursions and I made a point of visiting and praying at the tomb of King Charles IV of Hungary, the father of Otto Habsburg, who had died of pneumonia on the island. I felt that he also was a victim of the absurd Treaty of Trianon, which tore apart the Austro-Hungarian monarchy – an entity that could have kept Russian or German expansion in check. Had he not been so poorly advised as to attempt his hasty and premature return to Hungary, he might have remained in Switzerland and not died so young. I was wondering why it had all happened as it did.

In March that year Bapak started another extensive world journey from Indonesia, and Sharif was again one of the party. Besides doing his own engineering work in Indonesia, Sharif had become Bapak's permanent interpreter and secretary. He asked me if I could join Bapak's party in June, on the European leg of the tour, to help him with correspondence, because it was very difficult for him to work with a different secretary in each place they visited. Naturally I was delighted, and over those fifteen days I did a lot of typing. The work was fascinating, as mostly I had to type Bapak's answers to people's questions, which was very instructive. And working so closely with Sharif was a great joy. We went to France, Holland, Switzerland, Italy and Norway. Our journey ended at Wolfsburg in Germany; here I said goodbye to Bapak and his party as they left for Indonesia, and I returned home with rich memories.

Later that year I went for my annual visit to stay with Sharif and the family in Cilandak. Mariamah Wichmann was staying with them too, sadly having had to undergo an operation. I loved her and liked to look after her. Her room was downstairs and mine was on the first floor so I gave her a small bell to ring when she needed something. One night I woke up to the sound of the bell ringing, and rushed downstairs to find Mariamah sitting up in her bed, obviously in great discomfort. I brought her something to drink and said that I was glad she had rung the bell. She looked at me in surprise and said that she hadn't. This happened more than once; it was a wonderful inner link that we seemed to have.

My beloved Mariamah died peacefully on the morning of 28 February 1973. I miss her greatly. At times something in her reminded me of Magdamama – it was not just her snow-white hair and big dark eyes. She had been my friend, adviser and helper, especially in my first years in Subud. It was to her that I could always turn for advice about my Subud work in Portugal, where I was entirely on my own. She had a vivid sense of humour, and a quick, hearty laugh – and a no nonsense approach to life. Everything she showed me was of great benefit to me in the years to come.

At the end of the year Guy and I flew to Nairobi to spend Christmas and New Year with his brother David and his family. After spending Christmas together in Mombassa, with its delightful setting of palm trees, looking out over the Indian Ocean, we returned to Nairobi. David was the president of the Jockey Club and was the organizer of the Charity Sweepstake, which he had instigated in Kenya. So we began our year by winning a little money at the picturesque racecourse, which was bordered by bougainvilleas that David had planted. It was a truly memorable holiday.

27

Revolution in Portugal
Christianity and Islam

On 25 April 1974: BANG! – revolution in Portugal! The first we knew was when Sya's husband Eugen telephoned from Switzerland to say that he had heard about it on the news. We then listened to the announcements over the radio: freedom fighters had taken over the radio station, and government leaders were under arrest. Everyone had to stay in their homes and anyone found on the streets would be shot: 'Keep your radio on for further announcements.'

The whole of the capital had been taken over; the airport was closed and no one was allowed to leave the country. Tanks were in Rossio Square and were hailed by big crowds, which gathered despite the announcements. The banned Communist Party came out in the open, and its members were to become very active in the new government. The people were offered a better life, freedom, liberty, a high standard of living … .

Guy went to his office, where he was swamped by foreigners all wanting to sell their property and leave the country. Guy explained to them that at this stage there was no way to sell property, because of the coup d'état. He assured them that there was no danger and virtually no blood had been spilt – one man had been found dead. Nevertheless many of Guy's clients left the keys of their houses with him with instructions to sell whenever possible.

Banks were taken over, and some of our Portuguese friends fled to France. People asked me why I was not afraid and why I did not leave. I had to explain that this coup was nothing compared to what had happened in my own country. People had no idea of the reign of terror my compatriots in Hungary had had to suffer at the hands of the Soviets and the Communist secret police.

It was painful to watch television, where even the head of the

Church, the Cardinal Patriarch of Portugal, was ridiculed. But on 1 May, Labour Day, the Communists made a big mistake. They put up a big poster saying 'There is no God, long live Communism'. This was unacceptable for most of the religious Portuguese people, who then realized what Communism stood for.

It is always easy to destroy and pull down, but difficult to put things right again. What happened next was disastrous for the economy. Wages were doubled and employers were not allowed to dismiss their staff; business became static and there was no investment – and this went on for eight years. Like many others, we suffered the consequences of this. With no income from sales or rents – we had sold all our assets in England to start the business here – we had to live on our pension from England while still having to pay our employees at Cicerone. It was a miracle that the business survived.

Thanks to the kindness of two friends, I was able to fly to Indonesia at the end of August to stay with Sharif and the family for Ramadan. A few years previously my daughter-in-law had joined Islam, taking the Muslim name of Hartati. Having taken this step mainly for the sake of family unity, she had not given much time to it or learned the prayers. One day during my stay she came to tell me about a dream she'd had that morning. She had been standing on a hill holding her two youngest children in her arms, and all around her black waters were rising rapidly. Some people with her told her to jump into the water and get it over with quickly – it was a terrifying situation. She then looked up and saw a beautiful mosque with nothing but lovely carpets in it, and in the middle she saw me doing my prayers. At that point she looked down and the black waters had disappeared. As a result of this experience she had come to ask me to teach her the prayers, which she wanted to do with me from now on. This made me very happy.

Having been led to Islam by an amazing series of events and not from my own volition, I had no intention of giving up the many valuable lessons I had learned over the years as a Catholic. I felt that I still belonged to Catholicism, as I now also belonged to Islam – after all, where was the difference? In both religions we worship the same One and Only Almighty God, Sustainer of All. I am aware of the apparent incompatibilities between the two faiths, but I am deeply convinced that all of these were added by human beings and not by God.

Through the latihan God had led me to Islam. I know that this might be difficult for those who have not shared my experiences to understand, but I wanted to go on belonging to both religions; I deeply felt the reality of Bapak's explanation to me of 'the cross': the vertical being Islam, the horizontal Christianity – meaning that the two are one.

My five years working in Fatima had been the first inkling of a deep connection between Christianity and Islam, and I felt that Our Lady of Fatima had led me to appreciate Islam and Christianity alike.

Oh, the senseless divisions within all the great religions! Edward van Hien reflects my own feelings very clearly and simply in his book *What is Subud*:

> For some time I have had the difficulty, experienced by many others, of not being able to understand the extraordinary number of divisions within the Christian Church of which the Catholic/Protestant split is perhaps the deepest. A further difficulty has been that, even if Christendom were united, what of the 'salvation' of those who follow the other great religions? What of those who lived before Christ or have never heard of him? The more tolerant answers given to this sort of question usually take some such form as 'God is merciful'; but this is said with the implied intonation that, while we will each have our cloud and harp, anyone who is not a Christian might conceivably sit on a lower second-class cloud but would certainly be without a harp. They would, in other words, not be 'saved'. Some Muslims are just as bad. ... Even though few people these days believe such assertions literally, for me, personally, the conclusion has been inevitable that any exclusive claim to salvation by any one religion must contain some very fundamental error somewhere.
>
> Speaking for myself, I had reached the conclusion that the right answer must somehow embrace the following:
>
> 1) The path of the Spirit must be simple to enter (which is not the same as saying that it will be easy to tread).
>
> 2) The road signs must be as easy to understand for a beggar as for a king; for the illiterate as for the highly educated.
>
> 3) The path must be open to those of all religions and not only to Christians or only to Muslims, etc.
>
> Many religious people believe in (1) and (2), but few will accept (3).
>
> It is not difficult to reach the above conclusions, which are in no sense original. Having reached them, however, what does one do about it? Usually nothing.

It is at this point that my wife and I encountered Subud. We very soon gathered that, in some way, a new miracle or dispensation was at work in the world. It seems almost too good to be true that here is a means of worship which is pure content and has no form of its own. Like water it is therefore able to fill the shape of the Christian vessel, the Muslim jar, the Buddhist flask and even the pagan pot. [66]

At the beginning of October I flew back to Lisbon. My mother came and stayed with us for a month. While she was with us there was a rather strange incident. I received a letter from a Hungarian acquaintance who had been a friend of Gyuszi Tost – the Regent's ADC who had shot himself in the Gestapo Headquarters in Budapest. She sent me a photograph of Tost and wrote some complimentary things about him, which I read out to Guy and my mother.

That night – or rather in the early hours of the morning – I had a vivid dream, in which I saw Tost sitting in an easy chair, dressed in the clothes he was wearing in the photograph. I entered his house, and was received by a Mr Tolong, who was very friendly, and talked alternately to me and to Tost. The dream was so strong and clear that I told my mother and Guy about it during breakfast, saying that I had probably had the dream because of receiving the letter the day before, but that I could not make out why this Mr Tolong had come into it. As the word sounded a bit Indonesian, I went to look it up in the dictionary. The word *tolong* meant 'please help', which made quite an impression on all of us, especially when I discovered that I had had the dream exactly thirty years to the day after Tost had committed suicide! We were stunned. And we were even more amazed when, shortly after this, I was lent a book of old wisdom in which I found a statement that people who commit suicide can be redeemed after thirty years have passed.

All I could do was to have holy mass said for him. I also wrote to Sharif in Cilandak to enquire what should be done in a case like this, and if there was anything else I ought to do, inasmuch as Tost's plea for help had come to me. Bapak's daughter, Ibu Rahayu, answered that after the latihan, when I was really quiet inside, I should pray to God to bless and help Gyuszi Tost to his right place.

In early January 1977 the news came that my mother had died at her home in Vevey, in the south of Switzerland. Towards the end of her life, after having been opened in Subud, my mother had mentioned to me several times that she asked God only for one thing – she prayed that she should never be a burden to anyone but rather just drop down dead one day. Her prayer was wonderfully answered on 7 January when, at the age of eighty-three, she returned from visiting a friend and on opening the door of her flat in Vevey, she dropped down dead in front of the door.

I flew to Zürich, and drove with Sya to Vevey to attend the holy mass for my mother and the reception afterwards at the Hotel du Lac. All my sisters were there and my half-sister Harry had arranged everything very beautifully. I had a lovely experience during the mass: I felt that my mother was happy, and felt so light and joyful myself that I had to control my expression so as not to shock my sisters and the others who were present. Everybody had their sad funeral faces on, and I had to hide the smile which kept returning to mine. I prayed for her, but strangely not as if for a mother, rather as I would for a very dear friend.

In 1978, there was alarming news from Hungary. It was with shock that Hungarians all around the world received the news that the Carter administration in the USA had handed the Holy Crown of Hungary over to the totalitarian Hungarian Communist regime. In 1952 their demand for its return had provoked worldwide protests, and had been refused. It was difficult to believe that now the US government had gone ahead in spite of this, and despite the fact that during his visit to America in 1974, Cardinal Mindszenty had begged the American Nation to keep the Holy Crown in the free world until such time as Hungary was free from foreign occupation and had a freely and democratically elected government. I could only hope that those now responsible for the Crown would keep it safe.

28

Subud International Helper
Return to Hungary

In 1979 we moved once more; this time to Quinta de Janes, a lovely place with a fabulous view of the sea. I now had my own room at the back of the house with its own entrance from the garden, which I made into my latihan and writing room. The garden, besides being beautiful had an added bonus. When I was in London the year before, I had been shown a Thai way of making lampshades with real flowers and had decided to start a lampshade enterprise. The shades were made with pressed, fresh flowers placed within many layers of acid-free silk paper that were glued together; the effect was like porcelain and the flowers kept their colour. They were attractive and very unusual, and sold extremely well. I soon had seven Subud sisters working with me and we started selling the shades in shops. We called the enterprise 'Flora Mulia' (Indonesian for 'noble flower'). Now, I was able to make use of the abundance of flowering shrubs in our new garden to add to my supply of pressed flowers. The yellow hibiscus in particular looked lovely on the shades, and kept their colour well.

Four years had passed since the previous Subud World Congress, which had been held in Wolfsburg; we were now coming together for another one, in Toronto, Canada. It was clear to most of us by now that the latihan was not just for us. If the world were ever to become a better place the latihan had to be available to all of humankind. This by no means meant that Subud was the 'only way', but it was one way which could really bring people and religions together – an essential need in the world, then as now.

During the congress, Bapak chose a group of helpers who were to exercise the function of international helpers and travel to groups and members all over the world. From the many helpers present, Bapak appointed four women and four men – and to my utter surprise I was one of them. I felt very grateful, I had benefited so much myself that I was willing and keen to help in any way I could.

Bapak said that the international helpers work required sincerity, submission and absolute trustworthiness. We could not be swayed by friendship or closeness to anyone but must be objective in our judgement. We were also to assume the responsibility of replying to questions concerning spiritual matters sent by members from all over the world.

Over the next ten years, in our role as international helpers in Subud, I and others visited more Subud members and travelled to more countries than I could have imagined – Mexico, South America, Spain, Malaysia, Singapore, Sri Lanka and Pakistan amongst others – in some cases several times. I was very fortunate to have such outstanding dedicated partners to work with on these trips. Raphael Hoegh-Krohn from Norway and I in particular worked very closely together. His deep gratitude to Bapak for having brought us this gift of the latihan was very moving: 'this true feeling of love that makes everything possible.' I was very saddened by his sudden death from a heart attack in 1988.

When I got back to Quinta de Janes, I told Guy about my commitment and the amount of travel and time it would probably entail. He said that he had no objection, as long as he did not have to pay for my trips. I could assure him that was not expected. At first he found my being away on Subud trips difficult, and tended not to communicate with me at all while I was away. But I came to realise that if I cooked a batch of his favourite food to put in the freezer before I left, he could see that I still cared for him even though I was involved in my Subud travels. He eventually became amazingly tolerant and kind about all my travelling, even reminding me to get my tickets in time.

Guy and I spent our Christmas holidays in Kenya, where I found a wonderful new friend, 82-year-old Marie Louise Mange. She was living near my brother-in-law's bungalow not far from Mombasa, and we walked to her house to pay her a visit. After we left her, I was told her full name and realized that a Subud sister in France had asked me to try to find her address when I was in Kenya. I went back and told her why I had returned. She asked me how I had met her friend in France and I explained that it was because we both were in Subud. 'Oh yes,' she said, 'she sent me a book about it, but I never read it.' She then asked a lot of questions and whether she could receive this Subud 'contact'.

At her age she could be opened without waiting, and here in Kenya she might never meet another Subud member again … . I witnessed her opening and after two more latihans together she was able to continue on her own. I stayed in touch with her, writing to her and sending her Subud literature. She received strongly in the latihan and developed an amazing understanding and faith in the latihan, so complete and fresh it seemed she was twenty-eight and not eighty-two. Her letters were so special that I still enjoy re-reading them today.

1980 was the year I received news about the Horthy family crypt in Kenderes. An attractive building, set among big trees in a small garden between the Catholic and Protestant cemeteries and surrounded with an iron fence, it was in serious need of restoration. The possibility of repairing the crypt arose quite unexpectedly. We heard from Kristóf and Vera Kállay in Rome that the Hungarian government had widely advertised in the US papers that Hungarians abroad would be permitted to repair their families' graves in Hungary. The Communists obviously needed dollars; and this proved to be a clever way of obtaining some, as most Hungarians living abroad were keen to take up this opportunity.

Kristóf and Vera were in touch with the friendly parish priest in Kenderes, Father Antal Pálos – they had met him when he visited Rome to see the Pope – so they were able to arrange matters between us. Kristóf forwarded to us an estimate for the repair. It was expensive, but Sharif and I decided to go ahead with it. Father Pálos visited a friend in Germany every year, and so we were able to correspond with him freely using that address. In this way we were able to keep appraised of how work was progressing.

Bapak often reminded us of the need to carry out social work if we in Subud were to achieve our objective of advancing the welfare of human beings everywhere; we needed to aspire to build schools, homes for disadvantaged children, homes for the elderly, hospitals and so on. All kinds of Subud projects were therefore being started. In Portugal, a Pre-school Refugee Project got the go-ahead with the help of the Norwegian overseas aid agency NORAD – recognising the urgent need to help the young Timorese refugee children. The official inauguration took place on a lovely sunny Sunday and was attended by representatives of the local authorities. It was a big day for me and touched me deeply, as it was the first time that Subud Portugal was publicised. When the representative of the town council thanked Subud Portugal for all its help, and hoped that in the future there would be more opportunities to work with us, I realized that we had begun to understand what Bapak had been telling us: that we would only be able to talk about Subud when we could show some proof through our activities in the outside world.

Although Bapak had said in 1975 that he would only make short journeys in the future, in 1981 he was once again undertaking an immense world tour. He arrived in England in March and, after going to Germany and Austria, came to Portugal before going to a council meeting in Brazil.

While Bapak was in Lisbon I received a telegram saying that my father was dying and that my three sisters had already arrived in Cannes to be with him. I asked Bapak whether it would be better for my father if I stayed here with Bapak, or whether I should go there to be with him. Bapak said that I should go there and that I could open my father. He added that this was the only occasion when a woman could witness the opening of a man (her dying father), or a man could witness the opening of a woman (his dying mother).

I took the first plane to France. On arrival in Cannes my sisters told me that the doctor had just said that Papi had improved and might live for another few months. It was impossible to say whether my father was conscious or not, as he was not visibly reacting to anything. I asked to be allowed to spend the night at his bedside. During the night I felt very heavy and could not feel the latihan. Finally my eyes came to rest on a framed picture of my grandmother; I took a painting of two leopards – that Ellamami had given to my father – off the wall above his bed, and hung grandmother's picture there instead. It is difficult to describe what happened, but at that moment everything changed. The heavy feeling disappeared and I felt the latihan strongly. I do not know how long that lasted, but it must have been about two hours later that my Papi passed away. I was alone with him, and I do not know if it is true, but I felt that his mother was waiting for him. I had the impression that Grandmother was smiling at me from her picture.

I asked Ellamami to let me keep Grandmother's framed photograph, which I have cherished ever since. Strangely, I did not feel that I had lost my father; on the contrary, I felt closer to him than ever, as if something had united us. I had always been very close to my Papi and I know that we had a lot in common. I missed him terribly but I did not feel sad.

I flew back to Portugal where Bapak's visit was in full swing, and afterwards flew to São Paulo with Bapak and his party to attend the Council Meeting. When Bapak left Brazil, I began an extensive South American journey in my role as international helper with Efrain and Judith Gemesio. We visited Argentina, Chile, Peru, Ecuador, Venezuela, Colombia and Mexico. People were wonderful to us. All the national committees paid our expenses while in their country as a matter of course. I was surprised how close I felt to the members – especially to those who shared their problems and thus created a special bond with us. This feeling is still very alive many years later.

I finally got back to Portugal in time for the 'Remembrance Sunday' activities in Lisbon, which were extended over a whole long weekend in November. Since Guy had begun to take an active part in running the

British Legion in Portugal the donations for disabled and wounded servicemen had risen considerably. We had a party where we sold poppies and raffled things. It concluded on the Sunday with a service in the Anglican Church and a reception at the British Embassy.

Our first Subud visit to Zaire[67] was then planned. When finally we had our visas and tickets, Raphael Hoegh-Krohn and I paid the first international helpers' visit to Africa.

As I was watching the seemingly endless Sahara from the plane, I suddenly remembered that as a very small child of about four or five I had asked my parents for a black doll. There were no black people in Hungary at the time and nobody understood this wish of mine. Maybe it originated from the book *Uncle Tom's Cabin*, which our English governess 'Missy' used to read to us when we were children. With some difficulty my parents obtained one for me, and I remember cherishing it. I was about ten years old when I saw a black person for the first time – it was Josephine Baker, who was touring Europe and came to perform in Budapest. She gave only one matinee performance for children, and I begged my parents to take me to see her. I can still see her walking through the audience to the stage. I ran up to her to give her a small package of chocolates. A plain-clothes detective grabbed it from me, looked at it and handed it to Josephine, who smiled and thanked me. On the stage she still had it in her hand, waved to me and held the parcel to her heart. It made me happy and it was a big moment in a child's life.

I was met in Kinshasa airport by a tall, long-faced, very black African, who stood at the entrance of the building with a sheet of paper across his chest with 'Rahmaniyah' written on it in large letters. I went up to him, but before I could say anything he put his hands on my shoulder and touched his cheeks to mine three times on both sides, saying 'ma soeur, ma soeur, ma soeur' (my sister) each time. It felt so sincere and I found it very moving. His name was Kumbu-ki-Mabiala. He took Subud extremely seriously; and as the Subud helper he had worked hard to keep the group together and growing.

It would be difficult to describe with a few words what was for Raphael and myself an unforgettable visit – the first to an African country, where they had hardly had any contact with the rest of the Subud world, and where we received such a warm reception. Their deep faith and true wish to follow on the right path made a deep impression on us. We left already looking forward to our next visit.

From Kinshasa we flew to South Africa, where we were greeted equally warmly in Johannesburg, and then on to Cape Town and Durban. In Cape Town we received a great reception from a very large group. They had their own Subud premises with two large latihan halls. It was the only group in South Africa where the majority of the Subud people were Moslems of Malaysian origin, the others being Christians. We had a meeting with all the members, in which the issue of Christianity and Islam in the group was brought up. I told them about my experiences and views, and when the ladies went to do latihan, one of the Christian members asked in front of all the others, 'Rahmaniyah, please help us to overcome this division between us. It is nice to share the latihan, but once we are outside this hall the Moslem and Christian members are completely separate and do not mix.'

I told them that only God could help them, and that all I could try to do was to suggest a 'test' that we could all do together. I had not realized before that the two oldest active helpers in the group were both called Mary – one was the Moslem Maryam, and the other the Christian Mari. I heard myself ask the two Marys to stand facing each other in the centre of the group, while all the others were asked to be very quiet, in a state of latihan. I asked Maryam to receive and show in her latihan how Mari worshipped God as a Christian. Maryam's receiving was very beautiful, and entirely Christian. Then I asked Mari to show how Maryam worshiped God as a Moslem. There was the strongly Christian Mari, lifting her hands saying, 'Allahu Akhbar' and going down on her knees and prostrating herself in the Moslem way of worship. The feeling and content of both receivings were very affecting. When Maryam finished, the two of them fell into each other's arms; everybody was crying. Tears were running down my face, and I could only thank God for the experience and for having put the right words in my mouth. After we left I was told that the problem was eased for a while, but when I went back a year later, there was sadly still a separation to be felt between the members of the two religions.

1982 was a very busy Subud year for my colleagues and me. Our plans for this year included trips to Spain in May; Malaysia, Singapore, Sri Lanka and Pakistan; back to South America again in September; and a return to Zaire and South Africa with Raphael in November.

I had just arrived home from one of these trips when I received a telephone call from the English Priest in Palma de Mallorca, who told me that my brother-in-law Nicky had locked himself in his flat for days, and he was seriously worried about him. Nicky's wife had died a year earlier and he had been very depressed and lonely ever since. I had been to see him before, but this time Guy did not want me to go, and he went to bring Nicky back to Portugal himself. When I went to pick them up on arrival in Lisbon, I found Nicky being pushed in a wheel chair and Guy looking pale and utterly exhausted. What Guy had done was wonderful, but I did not want to burden him with having Nicky stay in our house, especially since I would be travelling for much of the year.

So we rented a flat for Nicky and I looked in every time I went shopping in Cascais to make sure he had everything he wanted.

I travelled less in 1983; it was good to be able to stay at home for a while. Guy had joined me for Christmas in Durban, and I'd been shocked to see how very lame he was, due to a lot of pain in his hip. He had already undergone one operation for an artificial hip replacement, but now it appeared that there was something amiss. During our stay he'd had daily treatments with an osteopath, and I now turned our guest room into a treatment-room with a hot lamp hanging from the ceiling, and started giving him the same kind of massage that I had seen the doctor do in Durban.

Guy eventually decided to go to London for another hip operation. He had begun to suffer so much that it was almost unbearable, as he could hardly walk, even with crutches. The surgeons found that his artificial hip joint was cracked, so they removed the pieces and replaced it with a new one. When at last he came home, his hip was healing well. He felt no pain at all and walked in a way he had not been able to do for years.

At the end of the year, thanks to the generosity of the members there, the opportunity came for a follow-up visit to Zaire, Zimbabwe and South Africa. I travelled with Muchtar Martins, another international helper who also came from Portugal, and we were delighted to hear we would be joined by Wilbert Verheyen, sent on behalf of UNICEF to see what could be done to best help children in Africa. Wilbert was the chairman of Susila Dharma International (SDI), the welfare wing of Subud; he had a wealth of experience in this area, having worked as a missionary in New Guinea for twenty years before moving to Indonesia, where he helped set up Yayasn Usaha Mulia (YUM) the body that developed and coordinated numerous welfare projects for children. We knew we would learn a lot from him.

While we were in South Africa, in Cape Town, I asked the members why there were no African Subud members in all the groups. They told us that one African couple, Micky and Miriam, had been opened in Cape Town but had not been to latihan, because they lived in Langa, the segregated African district. I immediately said that I wanted to go and look for them, so as to meet black South African members at last. In spite of everybody advising us not to go there, we went by car, accompanied by two members. It was a strange feeling driving into this African township with no other cars in sight. Everybody just walked past us without looking at the car, which was a bit disconcerting. There were no streets and the houses were not in any sort of line, they just had numbers. This meant we had difficulty in finding the right one, but we finally did so and, as we got out of the car, Micky came out of the house with his four children and hugged us. He could not believe that we had come to see them. His wife Miriam arrived later and was also very pleased to see us.

I tried to convince them to come to the latihan the next day. They said that they would try, and told us where to meet them. It had to be outside the district, as they were afraid to be seen with us in the car – Africans had been badly beaten up for being seen with white people. I am glad to say that the arrangement worked out well and they were able to come to the latihan.

On my return to Portugal I found Nicky was considerably better, so Guy and I decided to fly to Kenya for Christmas. We drove to the Mombasa Beach Hotel on the coast. I immediately called my cherished friend Marie Louise Mange, and was shocked to hear from her daughter Marie Claude that, according to the doctor, her mother had only a few more days to live. She had undergone an operation for cancer, but it had advanced too far. She also had a tumour in her head, which caused her terrible headaches, and she could not sleep or keep food down. But when I went to see her the next day I felt somehow that she could not be as ill as they thought. She had not been up for some time and was in pain, but what concerned me most was her bitterness. She complained that it was unfair that she should be struck down like this: 'Why?' she kept repeating, 'Why these terrible headaches?'

I did latihan beside her and talked to her very quietly, suggesting that she should try to accept what God was giving her, and that such a difficult trial was probably a test for her. I explained that this process might well be very necessary for her, and that if she could accept it then her suffering would be a blessing. I was surprised to see how she really listened and understood what I was trying to say.

When I went back the next day, Marie Claude told me that her mother was feeling better, and that during the night she had heard her repeat the word 'acceptez' out loud several times. For the twelve days that we were at the coast I went to do latihan with her every day. Her health rapidly improved, her headaches stopped and she started to eat again. It was a great joy to me to see her condition improve so much – the change was incredible. Her acceptance through the latihan completely changed her. Another doctor came to examine her and found that she did not have a tumour. By the time I left she could sit on the terrace, which meant a great deal to her, and when I visited her for the last time she was waiting for me at the entrance to her house, after having eaten a good meal. Her daughter was overjoyed.

Of course, Marie Louise still had cancer, and there was nothing that could be done about that. She lived only another few months and still suffered pain, but those headaches never came back. I had grown to love Marie Louise. It was a privilege to have known her, and I pray she may be taken to the place that is right for her – in other words, to heaven.

Conditions in Hungary had begun to be relaxed in a number of areas. In 1983 the Baptist preacher Billy Graham was allowed to preach there; and following President George Bush and Prime Minister Margaret Thatcher's visits, Concorde was allowed to land in Budapest. Perhaps the biggest change for my poor compatriots was that at last they were allowed to travel abroad.

Now, in 1985, although Hungary was still occupied by the Soviet Union, the occupying forces were no longer so conspicuous. We heard that tourists could move about freely. Guy suddenly declared that he wanted to go there to visit the country I had told him so much about, and asked whether I would like to go with him. At first I was undecided; but I could not resist the temptation and so we decided to go on a trial trip. Guy invited Ronnie and Jean Hersov – the couple whose house we had bought – to come along with us. We flew from London to Munich, then took a coach to Passau, where we boarded the beautiful *Danube Princess*. We had a most enjoyable boat trip down the Danube to Budapest, where our boat would stay for one day before returning to Passau.

Sailing into Budapest was an exhilarating experience. I was standing on the prow of the boat, with Guy and the Hersovs behind me. It is difficult to describe how I felt as we sailed slowly past Margaret Island – it was May and the chestnut trees and the lilacs were all in bloom – returning after an absence of forty-one years to the city that for me is the most beautiful capital in the world. I had forgotten how stunning Budapest was. As we sailed on, I pointed out the uniquely lovely Houses of Parliament – one of the few buildings that had not suffered from the war – then the church in which I was married, the Fishermen's Bastion, the Royal Palace, and all the lovely bridges. I noted how well the ruins of Budapest had been rebuilt, and cherished memories flooded back to me. Guy later told me that the Hersovs were amazed at the joy I displayed, and the absence of resentment or feelings of revenge for all that I had lost. In truth I had none of those feelings.

The boat anchored beside the Elizabeth Bridge at eleven o'clock in the morning and was due to leave again early the next day. We were able to move about freely – nobody seemed to bother about us or ask questions. It was a relief not to be noticed or followed. We spent the whole day on a guided bus tour, which we left at the top of Buda Hill. I led the way to the house that had belonged to my father, the place where I had been born on the second floor. The front of the building was unrecognisable – I had already seen photographs and knew that it had been bombed – but when we entered the inside courtyard I became speechless with emotion; it was unchanged. Facing us on the ground floor was the lovely glass door with its huge brass handles, and even the curtains behind it were the yellow they had been in my youth. While I was standing there dumbstruck, a woman called to me from the first floor balcony, asking if she could be of help. I thanked her and said that we were just wondering who was living in this house. Putting her hands on either side of her mouth to direct her voice to me alone, she told me in a loud whisper that it had been the home of Count Edelsheim Gyulai, whose youngest daughter had married the Regent's eldest son. I thanked her for the interesting information; and although Guy was nagging me from behind to tell her who I was, I did not want to do that. Ronnie Hersov kept telling me that this was my house and that I had to claim it, as he had had property returned to him in Russia. But I just shook my head and smiled, knowing that it would be of no avail.

We walked over to the Royal Palace, which had been a complete ruin at the end of the war. Although it had been very wonderfully rebuilt I found it different; but when we walked through the Lion Gate, the Palace's inner courtyard was unchanged and brought back many memories. Looking at the corner where I used to park my car, it was almost as if I were back in the forties and could walk inside and go up to my room. However, inside the main entrance nothing reminded me of the past – the uncarpeted white marble staircase was new and cold.

Guy told me that he was determined to come back for treatment at Budapest's thermal baths, which was a pleasant surprise. And indeed, the following year saw our return to Budapest for a two-week cure. We had a big room at the Hotel Gellért, and made use of the thermal and mud baths, physiotherapy, and swimming facilities. The management was very welcoming. Treatments were in the mornings and there was much to see and do in the afternoons.

The first thing I wanted to do was to go and see our faithful valet Mihály Tornyi, who was our driver at the Palace and remained mine until we were taken to Germany. He took me to his home on the outskirts of Budapest, where his wife Juci gave me a warm welcome. Mihály had collected articles and photographs about us, which he gave me. He had also invited the widow of Miklóspapa's driver, Ili Szarka, who had been born and lived in the Royal Palace up until the end of the war, and was a living lexicon of everything about it and everybody who had lived there. A friend of István Boldizsár – the famous artist who had painted a number of portraits of us – also came, and to my surprise gave me a lovely painting of Pista. It was a wonderful gift.

One day they drove us to Kenderes, where I was able at last to see the work that had been done to the family crypt five years before. Our friend Father Pálos had now retired, and the new young priest was a bit bewildered to see me, but kindly opened the crypt for us. It was all very well arranged and the interior was exactly as I had last seen it forty-two years earlier. I stood quietly in front of Pista's grave for a long time. How deep the love still was for him within me. We also went to our old home – the Horthy residence – now an agricultural school. The building had been well kept up, but inside nothing reminded me of the lovely family home. The beautiful trees in the park had disappeared and there were trucks parked all over the place. I had to keep my feelings closed tight and not think of the past.

My yearly visit to Indonesia for the month of Ramadan took place in May. It was good to be back in Sharif's house in Cilandak, The economic situation in Indonesia had resulted in a bit of a slump, office rents had dropped and things were difficult; Sharif and Hartati were working hard. Hartati was amazing. She had decided to make some money and was giving lessons all day long: singing, piano, English, and riding lessons, and people seemed to enjoy her teaching, as she always had more prospective pupils than she could take on.

Quite some time previously, I had received an invitation from the Hungarian Historical Research Society in New York, in conjunction with the American Foundation for Hungarian Literature and Education, to give a lecture on 'Regent Miklós Horthy and the events between 19 March and 15 October 1944'. It was arranged by George Rédey, who was the founder of the Research Society and been working as an engineer in New York for seventeen years. We had a long preliminary correspondence before I finally agreed to the invitation. It was not an easy decision for me, as I had always disliked speaking in public; but I was also aware of my responsibility to make the truth known when I had the chance. My nephew Péter Kendeffy, my sister Éva's son who lived in New York, was a wonderful help and go-between in all this.

The invitation itself was to an exclusive dinner in one of the large reception rooms at the Waldorf Astoria Hotel. Cocktails were to be followed by my lecture, then dinner, and finally an hour and a half of 'conversation', during which previously approved questions would be put to me. The invitation also said that 'we could be said to be living in the era of the falsification of history, and this was why the presence of the vice-regent's widow, an eyewitness to the events in question, was so important'.

So, on 2 October, two weeks after my return from a Subud visit to Zaire, I embarked on a very different expedition. There were about seventy people at the cocktail reception, and I was especially delighted to see Alexander Páthy, who had been one of the generous contributors to the fund collected for the Regent during his exile.

Although I only drank water, the cocktail conversations gave me a disturbed feeling and I felt that I needed a moment of quiet before the lecture started. I left the hall unobserved and went down the large corridor looking for a quiet place, but every door I tried was locked. A hotel employee appeared and asked me what I was looking for. I told him that I just wanted ten minutes alone in an empty room. He unlocked the door in front of us and let me into a huge and beautiful ballroom, where he left me, shutting the door behind him. This was a Godsend. Here I was in an empty ballroom, with ten minutes to do latihan before my lecture! When I got back, we settled into our seats at small round tables and a microphone was placed in front of me. (Oh, how I hate them!) This was my first experience of giving such a lecture and I found it very hard. However, I gained experience for the future; and when the Hungarian communities in Canada, and later in Belgium, also called for a similar talk, I found it easy.

The next night I spent a special evening with our benefactor Alexander Páthy and his wife Susan at their home. They took me out to an oyster dinner and we had a fascinating conversation about their lives, my parents-in-law and my new life. It was a wonderful occasion and they amazed me by showing real understanding for what Subud is. What a blessing it is to have such friends.

My diary showed me that this year I had been to thirteen countries, to five of them twice, and three times to the United Kingdom. It came as quite a surprise.

29

Bapak's Passing

There was interesting news from Hungary in 1987. I had been wondering and worrying what would be the outcome of Premier Gorbachev's visit to the country. It was a great relief when he acknowledged and supported reform. God bless him for that.

This year Ramadan started at the end of April, and as usual I flew to Jakarta to spend it at Cilandak. While I was there Sharif and I had some long talks about his life, as he and Hartati were thinking of living apart, and considering the possibility of a divorce.

The Indonesian members had built a new house for Bapak at Pamulang, about 20 kilometres from Cilandak. At the entrance they were completing a large, glass-walled 'pendopo', a traditional Javanese open-sided hall, which was used for latihan and for meetings. One day, when many of us had travelled out there to see it, Bapak quite unexpectedly walked into the large living room and, with people crowding in, gave an informal talk. He called Sharif, who was standing at the back, to interpret. Sharif's translations were always excellent, but this was a very special occasion and it was perhaps the best I ever heard from him, perfectly translated and beautifully spoken.

The talk contained hints about death, but strangely enough none of us picked them up. Bapak said that he had wanted to greet us in the new pendopo, but the glazing around the sides was not yet finished, so it was too windy for someone who was now almost eighty-nine years old by the Muslim calendar. He said that he was now at a point when it could be said that he was facing death; that his life contained two currents: life in this world and life in death. He felt at peace, but it was more than peace. He told us that he did not want to say too much about it, as his wife would get worried. That afternoon was a tremendous gift for me.

This year especially, Bapak paid a lot of attention to us all: over the last ten days of the fast he gave four evenings of latihan and 'testing', interspersed with talks and explanations – little did I know that it was the last Ramadan at which he would be physically present.

On my return to Portugal I received the news of Ellamami's passing. I flew to Zürich to meet my sisters, Éva, Myro and Sya. We all stayed at Sya's flat in Küssnacht and prepared lunch for the many people who attended Mami's funeral on 17 June. At last she was at rest. I was grateful for all that she had done for us, and I prayed that she might be at peace.

I stayed with Sya for two days, then flew back to Lisbon on 22 June – Bapak's birthday. As usual, the Portuguese Subud group had a dinner that evening to celebrate the occasion. It was only later that we found out Bapak had died at about that time. At midnight I received a telephone call from Muchtar Martins, who had heard the news from Spain of Bapak's sudden and unexpected passing.

I immediately rang Sharif in Indonesia, and he told me that Bapak had died in his car on the way to the hospital. I experienced a deep latihan until 4 a.m. and felt very much at peace. Then I went to bed and slept until the morning. When I woke up I sobbed uncontrollably at the realisation that I would never see our dear Bapak again.

I soon received descriptions of the day's events from several people who had been present. Bapak's house had been busy with preparations for his eighty-sixth birthday celebration, but people had heard that he was unwell and were wondering whether he would be able to attend. Hundreds of Subud members from around the world as well as from Indonesia were assembled in the pendopo and the surrounding gardens. Bapak's son Mas Haryono had asked everyone to forgive Bapak for not being with them. However, refusing a wheelchair, Bapak walked from his bedroom to the interior balcony overlooking the hallway.

This was announced without warning, and people were told that Bapak wanted to greet everybody from the balcony and that they could go into the house and sing 'Happy Birthday'. At such moments people would normally have hurried to get to the house first, but not this time. Everyone moved forward very slowly, singing Happy Birthday – each in their own language. Many of them told me afterwards that they could hardly sing because they started to cry when they saw Bapak sitting there and smiling at everybody, looking so frail and fragile.

Bapak was told that it was advisable for him to go to the hospital, and he agreed. It was a long journey and they drove fast on the empty roads. Bapak was getting weaker, and by the time they reached the hospital he was unconscious. The doctors tried to revive him but it was too late.

It is difficult to find the words to explain what Bapak meant and continues to mean for me and to many others. Anyone who has not met him could not possibly understand the all-encompassing love and understanding that emanated from him. There is simply no human measure for it. I was certain that he could see into the depths of one's being; it was a blessing to be near him – a light and cheerful blessing.

Later that year I flew to Canada, where the Hungarian community in Toronto had invited me to give the same kind of lecture as I had given in New York the year before. István and Irén Vörösváry, who were the publishers of *Kanadai Magyarság*, the largest Hungarian weekly in the Western world, looked after me wonderfully while I was there. 150 Hungarians gathered at the Old Mill restaurant for cocktails and dinner, after which I spoke for an hour. This time was very different from my first attempt in New York, as I felt much more confident. I had a good feeling and knew that it had been a success, and I mixed and chatted with many people afterwards.[xvii]

I then flew to Boston, where Sharif had just arrived on a short business trip from Jakarta. My grandson Leonard was working there, and my granddaughter Marianne was studying economics at nearby Wellesley University. This family get-together was the culmination of an eventful journey. In addition to everything else I had been lucky with the weather – the sun had been out everywhere I went, even though in Boston there'd been a snowstorm only a few days earlier.

1988 was my last year as an international helper. The Subud World Congress was to be held the following January in Sydney, Australia, and new international helpers would be chosen at the same time. For me it was another year full of travel, once each to Ireland, Germany, Indonesia, Italy, America, Poland, Hungary, Belgium, Holland, New Zealand and Australia, and twice to Spain, Zaire and England.

Just after Easter I made my yearly journey to Indonesia. Sharif met me at the airport and we drove home to a now empty house. The two of us were alone there, as he and Hartati were now living apart and she had rented a smaller house in Cilandak.

It was a momentous evening for the family when, two days later, Sharif went to see Hartati and they agreed on a divorce. Sharif had told me that early on in their marriage he had realized that they were not suited to each other. In the normal way they might have divorced after a few years, and it was really Subud that had enabled them to live together for twenty-eight years and to provide a stable and loving home for their children until they were old enough to be on their own.

I went to visit Hartati the next day. We had a walk and a long, useful talk. I was happy that they had finally put an end to the uncertainty and

xvii Appendix 16: newspaper report about the Toronto lecture.

My father-in-law writing his memoirs

My mother-in-law, a master at knitting

At Fatima

*My parents-in-law on their
golden wedding anniversary*

Countess Madeleine Apponyi

*Coming out from Westminster Cathedral with
my second husband, Major Guy Bowden, after
our wedding*

*Visiting Stephen (István) at Gordonstoun
with his grandfather*

The Admiral's eighty-eighth birthday celebration

Reunited in Vienna after so many years
(Magdi, Guy, Éva, the author, Myro, Gyuri, Dudi)

Bapak Muhammad Subuh Sumohadiwidjojo

Bapak and Sharif (Stephen) in Germany

Maria (Maryam) Kibble

Margaret (Mariamah) Wichmann

Eva Bartók

In Baghdad, on the Arab stallion Wadi Jabr

*Visiting the Nedjev mosque with my
Iraqi friends*

Guy with the Russian Military Attaché

*The first meeting of the first international helpers, Kenfield Hall,
September 1979*

Sharif, Hartati (Henrietta) and their children in Jakarta, 1975

Returning to my father's home in Dísz Square, where I was born

My first visit to Budapest since the war, with Guy, May 1985

...h Varindra Vittachi at a Subud gathering in Quito, 1990

With Sharif and his second wife, Tuti, in their house in Boston 1991

The photo of the oranges that led to m
arrest in Kinshasa

Sharif speaks at the reburial of his
grandparents at Kenderes

Receiving my decoration from President Á
Göncz, with General Kálmán Kéri; Oct 1

Surrounded by my family
Back row: Leonard; Marianne & Jim Banks; Helena & Mitchell Cox; Henry; Merna & Stewart Ho
Centre row: Tuti; Leilani & Rhyland Banks; Sharif; Loren Cox; the author; Hartati
Front row: Dexter Horthy; Garrett Cox; Matthea, Aveline & Rosabel Horthy

the difficult situation. It was clear that nothing could bring them together again, and it was a blessing that they had at least parted in friendship. They had pursued entirely different interests for a long time, and seemed always to go separate ways. Sharif once wrote to me to say that they had just passed each other in the air, with Hartati coming from Indonesia while he was going there!

After Ramadan my travels began again, with visits to Italy, Poland and Budapest. It was good to get back to Lisbon and find Guy waiting for me. I had to prepare a lecture I'd been requested to give to the Hungarian community in Brussels. I flew there and went to stay with Éva. Myro and Nicolette, Nicky's daughter, also joined us for the occasion. We all went together to the 'Hungarian House', which was packed full, and I read my hour-long story. There were a lot of questions by a truly appreciative audience, and the evening ended with a happy dinner with our friends Rozann and Giselbert Schmidburg.

When I got home, Guy and I had a long discussion about Nicky's situation, as he was not happy where he was. I was very touched by Guy's suggestion that we should bring Nicky to live with us. I would never have suggested this, as I did not want to disturb Guy's privacy with my brother-in-law's sometimes difficult presence. But Guy had now decided to give Nicky a home with us, and said that he felt ashamed not to have done so earlier. The situation was easier to manage now, as Nicky rarely left his room and we had a spare room and bathroom at the back, which once had been the servant's quarters. The room had two windows with a view of the ocean in the distance, and Guy had it completely redecorated. He put in a new bed and a built-in wardrobe, and I ordered a special leather easy chair for Nicky in his favourite red colour, with a television set and a good reading lamp.

When everything was ready we told Nicky, and he accepted happily. It proved to be an excellent decision, as Nicky changed the moment he was settled in. He was satisfied with everything, loved the food, and even thought that he was in his own home. I only realized this when he asked me how far I had to go to get to my house. I said, 'I am in my house here, Nicky.' He replied, 'Oh, no, this is my house.' I naturally left it at that, and simply told him that I lived very near.

At the end of the year Guy arranged for us to fly to New Zealand via Hong Kong and spend Christmas with my granddaughter Helena, followed by a holiday in Australia. I would then stay on in Sydney for the Subud World Congress, which was to be held in the last two weeks in January. I was very touched by Guy's thoughtfulness.

We first spent three fascinating days in Hong Kong, had excellent Chinese food, and I was amazed at the friendliness and happy air of the people, and the fast and efficient way everything worked. We then flew to New Zealand. It was such fun going shopping with Helena and meeting her husband Mitchell's delightful family. To be able to decorate a Christmas tree for my great grandson Loren was a special treat. But the happiest day for 'granny' was when we went with granddaughter Helena to the Subud House for latihan. The week went by in a flash, and then Guy and I flew via Sydney to the north of Australia, and spent a very restful eleven days discovering this fascinating country.

We eventually returned to Sydney, from where Guy took a flight back to Portugal and I took a taxi to St John's College at the city's University to register for the eighth Subud World Congress. It was a great joy to greet members from all over the world, and added to that, my grandchildren Marianne and Leonard joined us. There was a wonderful Viennese Ball organised one evening, and I felt so proud to walk in on the arm of Leonard, looking so handsome in his full evening dress.

This was the first Subud World Congress without Bapak's physical presence, and most of us were wondering how it would work. Bapak had set an example of how these congresses should be run, but this time if anything it went even better, in the sense that we took responsibilities and initiatives without waiting for Bapak's guidance.

When the new international helpers were chosen by testing, my own mandate ended. I had seen international helpers who were very sad and even upset to leave this work, with all the travelling and a kind of special status. I was therefore relieved and even surprised to note that I had no regrets and was not at all sad. My feelings were unchanged. Although I loved and had been committed to my work, had learned a lot and made many life-long brotherly and sisterly relationships over ten years, I felt it right and natural to go back to Portugal as a local helper.

It would be difficult to make an assessment of those ten years, but the strength and the validity of the latihan was proved to me over and over again; and furthermore, I saw the effect of the latihan on people of many different origins and faiths.

On 14 February 1989, in a quiet ceremony in Indonesia, Sharif married Isni Astuti Wirjohudojo, who we all knew as Tuti. Even I was only told after the event – although they knew that they had my full blessing. Anyone could see that Tuti and Sharif were ideally suited to each other and deserved a happy life together. Now, ten years later, they are still truly happy and fulfil each other. They have also remained good friends with Hartati, who has a wonderfully active, full life of her own and is loved and respected by all of us.

A few months after their wedding, Sharif rang me from Indonesia to say that he and Tuti intended to go to Hungary because he needed to get a birth certificate, his original one having been left behind when we were taken to Germany. But he did not want to go without me. It was his first visit back to his homeland and a big event for both of us to be there together. We all stayed at the Hotel Gellért, a place that always reminded me of a beautiful past. We were touched by the reception we got from the management. Sharif and Tuti were led into a suite, and when Sharif said that he had ordered just a double room, he was told that the manager felt that a suite was more suited to a Horthy, and the management wished to put one at his disposal.

To walk with Sharif and Tuti around Buda Hill, to show them the Royal Palace and the house on Dísz Square, and to eat delicious curd, poppy seed and morello cherry strudels at the Russwurm patisserie together, was a delight and seemed almost unreal to me.

We hired a car, and in beautiful weather drove to Kenderes to see Sharif's grandfather's home and the family crypt. The caretaker, the devoted Piroska, told us that she was often asked to open the crypt and show the graves to people who came there especially, sometimes from far away.

I was excited to hear that the publishing firm Európa wanted to publish the Regent's memoirs in Hungary. Európa's director, Levente Osztovits, and the serial editor, László Antal, came to see me while we were there to discuss the contract. We had a long, fruitful discussion, and little did I imagine that through our work together on this book of mine, he would become one of my truest, most valued friends.

Back in Portugal, Guy and I listened to the most moving news from Hungary: at twelve thirty on 16 June, everything stopped for five minutes. Church bells began to ring, factory sirens sounded and vehicles and pedestrians stopped in silence wherever they happened to be, as Prime Minister Imre Nagy and another 250 martyrs executed by the Communists and dumped into unmarked, common graves in 'plot 301', were reburied. About two hundred and fifty thousand people paid homage, and as the flowers and wreaths were laid, the names of Hungarians who had come from places as far away as Australia and New Zealand were announced. Then came the roll of honour of the executed innocents – I held my breath as each name was followed by 'lived twenty ... twenty-six ... thirty ... thirty-five ... years'. Most were simply workmen, teachers, university students; there was a reformed pastor, a journalist, and others whose names were unknown. People were asked to hold hands with those beside them – the way the peaceful crowd of demonstrators did on 23 October 1956 when the uprising started. Then the huge multitude sang the second Hungarian national anthem, 'Szózat', which ends with the words, 'We swear never to be captive again'. Most of the martyrs were Communists, but they had realized that they had been misled by false ideologies, and it was their own comrades who put them to death. My heart will always bleed for the nameless brave youths and children who stood up against the Soviet soldiers and tanks on 4 November, running away only when their mothers came to stop them.

In August I went back to Hungary for discussions about Miklóspapa's book. I was contacted by Pista's valet, Gyuri Farkas, and we met for the first time in over forty years. It was a very moving encounter, during which he told me about his diary and put it at my disposal. I have already explained how I later managed to publish the contents in a Hungarian edition. (Several years later, in 1998, it was also published in English, with the title *The Tragic Death of Flight Lieutenant Stephen Horthy, Vice-Regent of Hungary.*)[68]

Géza Andrássy, the brother of my nursing companion Ilona, took me to Kenderes to pray beside Pista's tomb on the eve of the forty-seventh anniversary of his death. We then drove back to Budapest to join the big Saint Stephen's Day mass in the Cathedral, where the 'holy right hand' of Saint Stephen was carried in the procession, as it had been in the old days. To be able to witness this again was a great experience. From the Cathedral we walked over to the Forum Hotel and watched the fireworks over the Danube and the Gellért Hill from a balcony. The embankment promenade and the bridges were packed with onlookers – locals and tourists alike – and although I have seen many fireworks, I had never seen a display like this one. It was incredibly beautiful.

At the end of the year Guy and I met Sya in London and flew with her to Miami, where we embarked on a Caribbean cruise. On the boat, I sometimes read Bapak's talks, and in one of them Bapak said that people who do the latihan for some time ought to have a certain spark, which others would notice. I wondered where my spark was after thirty-odd years of latihan; I truly saw no evidence of one. But on the last day of the year I was given a glimmer of hope by our dinner-table partners, a young couple who were leading actors in the evening shows. In the middle of dinner they suddenly asked Guy to tell them frankly who I was, because they thought that I had something special, 'a kind of spark'. I was dumbfounded. God is great.

The following year, when I returned to Hungary with Sharif and Tuti to sign the contract for the publication of Miklóspapa's memoirs, we had no idea that we were arriving just one day before the general elections. It was exciting to be there when the elections turned out so favourably and produced the first freely elected government for forty-six years. We hardly even dared say it, but there was real hope that nothing would now be able to prevent the last step to freedom: the departure of the Soviet troops from the country!

No longer being an international helper, it had been an unexpected thrill to be asked in 1989 to accompany the new international team on their first trip to Zaire. Now, in 1990, they asked me to accompany them again on a visit to this fast-growing Subud community. I was happy to go, and to work once more with Léonard Lassalle, a truly inspired, dedicated helper. At that time there were 700 Subud members in Zaire, of whom 380 were known to be active.

One day when we were in Kinshasa we walked over to a nearby market, and I took a photograph of a colourful woman vendor who was wearing an orange-coloured dress and selling oranges. I was immediately surrounded by several plain-clothed policemen, who promptly arrested me. I was standing with two of the local Subud helpers, Ruagasore and Lusijah, and they were also taken along to the nearby police station. The other Zairian Subud members stopped the rest of our party from following us, saying that they could not help and would only be arrested too.

It was lucky that I could speak French, and I replied to all their questions by repeating that I had done nothing wrong and that they could not keep me there. I was told that taking photographs was forbidden (this proved to be untrue), and they took my camera to have the film developed and see what was on it. They said they had a cell next door and would keep me there overnight. Ruagasore was wonderful. He sat beside me without saying a word, deep in latihan – I could feel it.

The heat was intense. After six hours of cross-questioning, police from Kinshasa Headquarters arrived, packed us into a car and drove us to the main station in the centre of town. On the way one of the police officers told us that they had picked us up because we had been in danger, as the local police had mainly wanted our money. At Headquarters they were much more polite, even friendly. We were told that we could go back to the Catholic Mission where we were staying, but that I would have to come back next morning at eight with my passport. By then the copies of my photographs would be ready and my camera would be returned. They said I should bring a large sum of money with me. I tried to argue that we had come to help the poor people of Zaire and would not be able to do so if I had to give away our funds. Their answer was simply, 'We too are in need of money!'

You can imagine how happy the others were to see us back. It was a nasty experience, to say the least, and we had to pool the cash we had to pay the 'fine'. Luckily we had brought extra dollars for emergencies – and this was one.

Next day everything went smoothly and the money was handed over in exchange for the camera and the photographs. This experience made it clear that foreigners were not safe in Zaire. Unfortunately for me, everyone else had flight reservations for a day earlier than I did; there was no way of changing them and the others told me not to leave the Mission until I went to the airport the next day. In the morning a Subud brother picked me up, as I had a meeting with UNICEF – we were seeking assurances about help in getting material into Zaire for our doctors. On both the way there and back we saw lots of soldiers everywhere, and even more police. The political situation was deteriorating and the situation was becoming increasingly tense. For the first time there were open demonstrations in the streets against President Mobutu. People were singing a spontaneous sort of national anthem in the streets, blaming him for the country's woes.

Guy met me in Lisbon at 6 a.m. and I do not think I have ever appreciated a hot bath and a quiet rest more. After that trip, our Subud visits to Zaire were suspended for several years, as things got worse instead of better and it became increasingly dangerous for foreigners. Subud members there went through terrible hardship; we kept in contact as much as possible, although letters sometimes went astray.

Sharif and Tuti had moved to Boston, where Sharif was working at Hamilton Helmer's management consultancy company. They had bought a small bungalow in beautiful woodland surroundings, with houses scattered among trees – typical of that area. This was their first home together and was full of harmony and happiness. It was more obvious than ever that in each other they had found real life partners. Nothing could make a mother's heart happier. Over the next four years I always spent the month of Ramadan with them, and I felt very much part of the Boston group.

On my visit in 1990 we attended my granddaughter Marianne's graduation from Wellesley University. She was one of only 18 girls who passed with 'summa cum laude'. The service in the chapel, which we watched on television from a big tent, was outstanding. The ceremony was deep and moving; there was beautiful singing as well as Muslim, Christian and Jewish prayers. While we were waiting for lunch we sat opposite a Korean family. The mother was a lively lady, who asked which of us were Marianne's parents. When she heard that Hartati was Sharif's ex-wife and Tuti his present one, she asked Hartati, 'How can you stand this? Don't you hate her?' When Hartati replied, 'Oh, no, she is my best friend!' the Korean lady threw up her hands in amazement.

30

Admiral Horthy's Reburial in Hungary

I n 1991, I heard that the last Soviet troops had crossed the Záhomy Bridge in the early hours of 19 June, leaving Hungary for good – praise be to God!

I had promised Miklóspapa that if I was still alive when Hungary's freedom was restored I would take his remains there, so now I had to start thinking about how and when this might be done.

Members of the Hungarian Seamen's Association, which had been founded by the Regent, unexpectedly approached me with the same idea, offering their help. The first person to suggest this was Captain Miklós Szimon, and the idea was then enthusiastically taken up by Captain András Dávidházy, who contacted me. He had met the Regent several times in the past and was devoted to him. I was certainly happy about their interest, but even so, I was in no hurry. The transfer had to be well and carefully planned, so that I could fulfil Miklóspapa's wishes in the best possible way.

Four months later I went to Hungary to have talks with László Antal about the book I planned to publish on the circumstances of Pista's death. I wanted it to come out the following year, on the fiftieth anniversary of his death. We met in Captain Dávidházy's flat, and he and I spoke again about the possibility of re-burying my parents-in-law.

Sharif and Tuti joined me in Budapest, and László Antal arranged a meeting between Sharif, myself and President Árpád Göncz. We had tea with the president and his wife at his residence, in a very friendly atmosphere. He asked us about our plans for the reburial, and I told him the same as I told everyone else: that we wanted a family funeral and would not be sending out any invitations. We also went to the family crypt in Kenderes and had a pleasant meeting with the mayor, Mihály Baranyi, who assured us of his full cooperation.

In August 1992 Sharif and I returned to Hungary to attend a ceremony at Kenderes to commemorate the fiftieth anniversary of his father's death on Saint Stephen's Day. I arrived in Hungary first, as I had to sign the contract for Miklóspapa's memoirs with Európa Publishers. *The Tragic Death of Flight Lieutenant István Horthy* was also due to come out on this day.

Our visit had engendered a lot of publicity. I was asked to attend a press conference together with Gyuri Farkas, whose diary was the most important part of the book. He was brilliant, and made people laugh when he told the story of how the police had searched his flat without finding the diary, which was hidden under the floor beneath the wardrobe. He held up a large picture of me for everyone to see and said that he had covered it up with a picture of Lenin, which he also produced.

Sharif and Tuti arrived, and we were invited to visit Dr József Antall, prime minister of the first Central government, in his office at the Houses of Parliament. I was deeply touched by Antall's thoughtful and friendly attitude; he even gave me a signed English book, about the British Royal Family and their links to Hungary, for Guy.

It was now that my friend László Antal also started to take an active part in the preparations for my parents-in-law's reburial. Before I arrived he had met Kristóf Kállay, ambassador of the Order of the Knights of Malta and son of the late Prime Minister Kállay, and had suggested that the reburial of Admiral and Madame Horthy should take place under the aegis of the Order of Malta and the Order of St John. Not only had my parents-in-law both held passports issued for them after the war by the Maltese Order, but Miklóspapa was 'Bailli Grand Croix d'Honneur et de Dévotion' – the same rank as an ambassador – and Magdamama was 'Dame Grand Croix d'Honneur et de Dévotion'. They were also members of the Order of St John.

László Antal met Kristóf and his brother Miklós, and they both approved the idea. I was delighted at the proposal. My idea was to make the funeral a family event, although naturally anyone who might want to express their love or respect by being present would be welcome. People tried to persuade me to hold the reburial that year, but I was against it – I do not know why. I told them that I was not in a hurry and asked them to be patient.

On Saint Stephen's day we were driven to Kenderes, where we attended a silent mass for Pista. Mayor Mihály Baranyi gave us lunch, which was followed by a touching ceremony outside the former Horthy home. We listened to very moving speeches by the priest, the mayor and the government representative Dr Ildikó Tota, who made a big impression on me with her really deep, humane and moving words. Some women and children from Kenderes sang and danced. We felt sorry for them because of the heat, which was stifling.

After the ceremony we drove back to Budapest, and Sharif, Tuti and I went to watch the famous fireworks from one of the balconies of the Hotel Intercontinental. After a long and tiring day, we sat on the cool balcony with its wide view of the bridges, the Royal Palace, Gellért Hill and the thousands of people on the Danube Promenade. It was an unforgettable hour and I again wondered how I had deserved it.

Sharif and Tuti had organised a visit Kiev in the Ukraine, and as a surprise had bought me a ticket too. Subud had been introduced there a month before, quite suddenly, one could almost say like an explosion. It had been initiated by an American member, Seth Aronie, giving a six-minute talk on Subud at a 'Healing and Arts' workshop in Kiev. A request had now gone out for helpers to go there, as there were many people waiting to be opened. I felt quite an emotional connection with Kiev. It was where I had spent the last happy days with Pista, even though the circumstances had been difficult. Over the last few days I had talked about Kiev and seen many photographs of the city – and now I was on my way there!

We enjoyed some wonderful hospitality. People are very poor in the Ukraine and they have very little to eat, but we were not allowed to go to restaurants, and partook of very simple but delicious meals with Subud members. The two days were over all too quickly, but a permanent link had been established with our new brothers and sisters. We experienced the lightness, generosity and love of people who have nothing and yet give so much.

Some time after my return home I went to Nicky's room one night to see if everything was all right, and found him on the floor beside his bed with a broken hip. After an appalling experience in one of the local hospitals, where he had to wait six days for an operation, only to have the hip break again two days after he came home, poor Nicky was finally operated on successfully at the Hospital de Jesus in Lisbon.

Sadly, the outcome of all this was that he was now completely bedridden, and it became increasingly difficult for me to look after him. I had help during the day, but at night I had to cope alone. Sometimes I had to get up to him two or three times, which left me very tired. Then I heard of Mira Fonte, a nursing home for elderly patients, and situated just 6 kilometres from our house. It was run by a lady called Anita Mendes. I visited the home and met her, and I immediately knew that this was the solution. The house was clean and comfortable, there were doctors and nurses on call, and Anita was friendly and good to her patients, who obviously loved her. We moved Nicky there on 1 December.

I do not know why, but in 1993 I suddenly decided that the reburial of my parents-in-law should take place this year. Some people argued that it would be better to postpone it until after the forthcoming 1994 elections, hoping that the atmosphere would then be more favourable. I could not argue my case but I just felt that the time was now right. Sharif shared my feelings. As we now know, the 1994 elections brought back the socialist/left wing government, and I was often told afterwards that the reburial took place at the only possible time. I too am convinced that is true.

Since the beginning of 1991 a great many articles had been appearing both for and against the funeral – it was actually causing quite a stir. Péter Gosztonyi always made a point of sending me the critical or nasty articles about our family. He maintained that I knew the good things anyway, but that it was important for me to be aware of the opposing views. I have kept all these articles, both pleasant and unpleasant, as they may be of some interest to the family or a historian one day.

It is not surprising that opinions were divided. We have to remember that, following the Communist take-over in 1945, the regime did not allow anything good about the Regent to be printed. His memory was consistently smeared, and from then onwards he became the 'fascist dictator'. This also suited the governments of the neighbouring countries, which adopted the same policy, and so it spread to the West, where people had no knowledge of the background and no one was interested in defending him. A large part of the Jewish community in the United States still believes that Miklós Horthy persecuted the Hungarian Jews.

In spite of all the stir, I decided to go ahead with the plans for the funeral. I was very grateful for the support I was given by the naval officers and others; I don't know how I could have done it without them. They formed a committee, calling themselves the 'Horthy Committee of the Hungarian Seamen's Association', and told me to refer everybody to them. At the same time they asked my opinion before every decision, and sent me the minutes of all their meetings. It was an invaluable feeling for me to be able to rely on such trustworthy advisers.

I certainly needed help and protection, not only from adversaries but also from those who wanted 'our good'. I received letters with endless suggestions: that the coffins should be transferred to Vienna and from there to a boat, stopping at every town on the Danube with celebrations in each place; that there should be a gala performance at the Opera House; that my parents-in-law should lie in state at the Coronation Church and the Calvinist Church in Budapest. I wanted none of these things, although if the government had suggested them I might have considered it. I got persistent telephone calls and it was a relief to be able to say that the committee in Hungary was making all the decisions and please to contact them with any suggestions.

I had just returned from spending Ramadan with Sharif and Tuti when I received a message asking me to go to Mira Fonte immediately, as Nicky was rapidly declining. When I got there he was very quiet, but still conscious. He died the next day at 9.50 a.m. I was the only family member able to keep vigil beside him. After his long, helpless wasting away, I prayed that he should be at peace at last.

Nicky's body was cremated, as he had wished, and his ashes were carefully stored by the agency that was also going to arrange the transport of his parents' coffins to Hungary.

On 6 April a beautiful memorial service was held at the Protestant St Paul's Church in Estoril. It was jointly conducted by Canon John Humphreys and the Hungarian priest Father Luis Kondor, with Hungarian prayers and the national anthem. I received many telephone calls of sympathy, as well as inquiries from Hungarian television.

There was a lot of work to do and many decisions to make about taking Magdamama, Miklóspapa and now also Nicky's remains to Hungary. Dr László Zeley from Hungarian Radio came to Portugal for two days to conduct a long interview with me – the first for Hungarian Radio. I had already met him in Budapest, and agreed to the interview because he seemed a decent, friendly person, who was easy to talk to.

In May I went to Hungary for ten days in order to decide things on the spot. In Kenderes, Mayor Baranyi seemed to have arranged everything perfectly, but wanted me to approve the plans. He told me that public interest was surpassing all imagination, and that he had therefore had to prepare three large parking areas on the outskirts of Kenderes. He said he was planning to accommodate up to one hundred and fifty thousand people (actually it turned out to be about half that number according to helicopter counts). The coffins were to lie in state under a baldachin, and the ecumenical service was to take place behind the crypt. We measured out the space required for the four hundred seats for the family, the VIPs and the elderly, etc. The Ministry of the Interior had said that it would provide security services, first aid vehicles and mobile toilets.

A large sum of money was anonymously collected, and I also received donations from the Maltese Order and the Order of St John, to help me with my expenses. They generously also offered two mini-buses to take my family to Kenderes and to show them more of Hungary. Hungarian Radio offered me four adjoining apartments in the centre of Budapest.

I also gave several short interviews, which I thought were important so that some false rumours could be corrected. This is what I told the newspaper *Pesti Hirlap*, for example:

> In relation to the 'reburial' in the crypt in Kenderes, which will take place on 4 September, I have heard that there are voices that would like to mix politics into this event. I would like to take this opportunity to clarify the facts and emphasize that in accordance with my father-in-law's wishes and in fulfilment of my promise to him, I am simply taking the remains of the Regent and his wife to the family crypt in their hometown of Kenderes.
>
> The Horthy family considers this to be a family ceremony and we have not sent invitations to anyone. On the other hand, we will happily welcome anybody who would like to demonstrate their love and respect by their presence.
>
> I am deeply touched by the number of letters I have received and the general reaction to the funeral, and I would find it entirely inexplicable if, in a country that calls itself democratic, people could not come to a funeral if they so wish. Why are some people afraid of the remains of a head of state, who served his country in the way he thought best throughout his whole life, who believed in peaceful solutions, who was abducted by the Nazis and who ended his life in exile. An exile where he was only able to live modestly – and then only thanks to others – because during his long regency he did not enrich himself and ended up without even a pension for his services.
>
> I would like to ask everyone who comes to Kenderes on 4 September to bring only love, understanding, peace and unity in their hearts. Then we will receive them with great love.

On 21 August, Peter Feledy interviewed Prime Minister Dr József Antall on television in connection with the planned funeral. I was deeply moved when Mr Miklós Deák from the Hungarian Embassy in Lisbon handed me a sympathetic and considerate letter from the prime minister with the full text of his interview attached. This attention was unexpected, especially just before the reburial, and I will always be grateful to this humane politician. Of course the interview created great controversy in certain quarters, particularly amongst some people who called themselves 'historians'. In fact, they were former party-historians, and whenever the prime minister said something they did not like, they simply proclaimed that he had no right to make historical declarations and should solely concern himself with current politics. I found this attitude absurd.

In his interview the prime minister expressed his own opinion clearly. He said that the negative echoes in the press and among certain political groups certainly did not disturb him, as he simply wished to tell the truth. He would not be able to be present at the reburial in person, but half the government would be there – including the ministers of the interior and defence – in their official roles, and he himself would be represented by his wife and son. The reason for his absence was not the 'yelping' packs of critics, but the fact that he was due to chair an international conference in Budapest, plus the physical restrictions imposed by his health. He hoped that everything would take place as we all hoped and said he would like to assure us of his sincere sympathy. I will give just a few extracts from the text of his interview:

> I wish to point out that I consider Miklós Horthy a Hungarian patriot who had every right and moral grounds to want to rest in Hungarian soil. ... Had there not been so many unjust assessments made about Miklós Horthy, the situation in which so many people are now scrutinising the burial for political overtones would not have developed. We have been in touch with the Horthy family since 1990. We have done our utmost to ensure that the reburial is an act of reverence. ...
>
> It is my personal conviction that there was no alternative to Miklós Horthy's regency in 1920–21, irrespective of what possibilities may have been available in theory. Thus it was the only option left open for Hungary. One can argue about what might have been done better, but Miklós Horthy's regency was the only possibility capable of stabilising the country from the foreign and domestic policy aspects. This is undeniable ...
>
> In rendering historical justice to Miklós Horthy's actions and putting him in his due place, it is not with the intention of carrying out a kind of 'Horthyist programme. ... Miklós Horthy never acted against the constitutional implementation of the law or the constitutional monarchy. He consistently stuck to a ministerial form of government. He never attempted to force – like a dictator or a chief of staff – the kind of

policies for which Pilsudski is known onto the administration, and yet Pilsudski is seen as much more progressive.[69] ... The role he played was truly that of maintaining constitutional order, as far as both the right and the left were concerned; he was both sharply anti-Communist and anti-Nazi at the same time. ... Miklós Horthy was clearly the regent of a monarchy that he never transgressed, nor did he abuse his power. ... In Hungary, Anna Kéthly, Endre Bajcsy-Zsilinszky and others were able to make speeches in Parliament that only members of the opposition in the most democratic of parliaments could have delivered ...

As for entering the war, the move itself was opposed by Horthy, as it was by many members of the government. ... The deportations, which must be wholeheartedly condemned, were carried out following the German occupation. But as soon as Miklós Horthy had the smallest independent scope for action in the summer, he saved the Budapest Jews from deportation by ordering Colonel Ferenc Koszorús to Budapest. ...

Ultimately it must be acknowledged that Miklós Horthy was not put on trial in Nürnberg, although there were some who made efforts to the contrary. The leading powers – including the British and Stalin – had their reasons for not considering Horthy a war criminal. Thus I think that those who wish to exaggerate his role after Nürnberg do poor service not only to historical justice but also to Hungarian history. ...

Refugees would not have been officially accepted in Hungary were it not for the good offices of Miklós Horthy. He did not demand reports on everything, nor did he interfere in the details. But no sober-minded person can imagine how it would have been possible to make Poles, Frenchmen, Britons – if need be, Russians and Jews – safe in Hungary if Miklós Horthy had not extended his protection at the top of the political tree. Nor could opposition politicians have pursued their policies if Miklós Horthy had not been around. ...

When the Gestapo arrested members of the government, opposition and other politicians – including my father – in 1944, Horthy could no longer help them. In the autumn of 1944, when the Lakatos government was in office, Horthy's influence increased somewhat. He was able to speak out in favour of prisoners held by the Gestapo and did his best to get them freed. This is how Endre Bajcsy-Zsilinszky, Ferenc Nagy and others, including my father, were released from prison. Horthy was instrumental and personally involved in this. And I can never forget this.

The last question put to the prime minister was, 'There are a few days left before the reburial. What do you hope will happen?' His reply was:

It must be an act of reverence. And anyone – on whichever side of the political divide they may be – who tries to forge political capital out of the event or seeks to attach a different approach or meaning to the reburial is someone without honour. In accordance with the wishes of a committed Hungarian patriot, Hungary will bury a head of state who governed the country for a quarter of a century. Anyone who wants to use this for any other purpose is in the wrong, and his intentions run counter to the wishes of the family, and to our wishes.

At the same time I hope that, after the unjust distortions of the Horthy image, such an event will help us to form a reasonable picture of Miklós Horthy. ...

Everyone should accept that Miklós Horthy must be appropriately laid to rest with full honours, not only in the family crypt, but also in his place in Hungarian history. That place must be acknowledged, not only by us but by neighbouring countries as well. They will also do right if they do not use the reburial for propaganda purposes, but instead acknowledge that we are seeking to resolve these issues about our history once and for all.[70]

I flew back to Budapest on 1 September. Unfortunately it was not possible for Guy to accompany me, as the pain in the hip that had been operated on was getting so bad again that he had difficulty walking and he was due for another operation in a month's time.

Captain András Dávidházy was waiting for me and drove me straight to Kenderes, where I was put up in our old home – now an agricultural school. I spent two days looking at all the arrangements with Ildikó Tota, the district government representative.

We heard that people who did not view the Regent and the period hallmarked with his name in a positive light were planning a demonstration. It was going to be held on the eve of the ceremony, at the Vérmező, the parade ground behind the Royal Palace. This was not directed against the reburial, but was rather intended to say a 'final goodbye to the Horthy era'.

I went to Budapest to meet all the members of my family as they arrived, one after another. On 3 September we picked up the two mini-buses and drove to the airport to await the coffins. We were all gathered in an airport building, waiting for the arrival of Swissair flight 466, when suddenly there was a huge, torrential downpour. We realized that the demonstration planned on the Vérmező must be taking place about now, and some people were amused that it must be being washed out by the downpour. But I begged them not to laugh or be malicious, because the same thing could happen to us the next day. I later found out that the demonstration had consisted of about a hundred people with umbrellas, who quickly dispersed because of the heavy rain.

At nine thirty on the morning of 4 September we left for Kenderes in sixteen cars, with a police escort ahead of and behind us. This did in fact prove to be necessary, as thousands of cars were trying to park and masses of people were moving towards the cemetery. There was a little drizzle on the way, but by the time we got to Kenderes the sun was out. The family assembled at the Town Hall and then proceeded to the crypt, where thousands of people were already waiting. The fence around the crypt was bedecked with the most beautiful wreaths, and the garden was also full of them. Microphones set up by Hungarian Radio and Television relayed messages, and then from a raised platform, transmitted the ceremony to the huge gathering (seventy thousand people were counted from the air) for an hour and a half. The excellent television announcer Ferenc Börzsöny, whose voice was strong and melodious, provided the commentary.

By this time the weather was just perfect, and when the sun began to get too hot an occasional small cloud and a slight breeze would appear to cool us.

Under the baldachin, Nicky's urn lay between Miklóspapa's and Magdamama's coffins, all three covered in flowers. A guard of honour of eight naval officers surrounded Papa's coffin, and eight young men from Kenderes guarded Mama's. Behind them was an honour guard of boy and girl scouts.

To the left of the catafalque the front rows of chairs were reserved for the family; in all there were about thirty of us. At my request our former valet and driver Mihály Tornyi and his family, and Pista's valet Gyuri Farkas were included. On the right were the ministers, VIPs and the prime minister's wife and son, who represented him and had brought a lovely wreath in his name.

We had to endure a seemingly endless barrage of photographs before the bugler blew the call to attention. Everybody sang the national anthem, which was followed by a number of speeches.

Finally, I went up to the microphone and read my speech of thanks to all those who had contributed to the realisation of this day. Then Sharif came up. He read out his speech in Hungarian, which was especially appreciated because of the rumour that had circulated that he could not speak his mother tongue.

> Your Excellencies, Hungarian brothers and sisters,
>
> I give thanks to Almighty God that He has made it possible for us to be together here today in our beloved homeland as free human beings in a free country. It is the re-emergence of these two freedoms that have made it possible for us to fulfil today our duty to my grandfather, completing the circle of his life by laying his remains, and those of his beloved wife and their youngest son Nicholas, to rest in this earth of Kenderes they loved so much.
>
> I am deeply moved to see so many of you here today. The only thing I can do to try to repay your devotion in sharing this act of piety with us is to tell you a little about my grandparents and my Uncle Nicky, but especially about my grandfather as I knew him, when he was no longer at the centre of affairs, but living frugally in exile. I had the good fortune to share his house for the first twelve years of my life, to sit at his table and listen to his stories, to play and speak with him every day. At the time I took for granted his kindness and generosity, his cheerfulness, his positive attitude and his deep interest in what was going on around him and all over the world.
>
> It was only later, when I began to understand all he had done and experienced, that I came to appreciate what an extraordinary person he was. He had lost his home, his country, his job, his property and three of his four children, but I never once heard him complain or give vent to self-pity – he remained always helpful, positive and deeply engaged, right up to the last few months of his life. I can still remember him in Weilheim after the war, helping my grandmother making the beds and doing other household chores while my

mother was commuting across Germany to work at the Red Cross to provide us with basic necessities.

He was a simple, modest man, and in spite of his great natural dignity he was always accessible to others and never aloof. I remember some extraordinary acts of kindness on the part of both my grandparents towards those less fortunate than themselves.

The great motive forces in his life were a deep love of his country and his devotion to doing his duty to the best of his ability. Acquisitiveness was not one of them. The property he lost after twenty-four years as head of state was no more than he had at the beginning.

Being an only child, I was at home in the adult world and listened to innumerable family discussions that were not intended for my ears. In all those years I never heard Grandfather express hatred or say bad things about others, even about those with whom he had sharp differences of opinion. I have been asked whether my grandfather was anti-Semitic. For me that is unimaginable. He evaluated human beings on their merits – I never heard him express a hint of racial or social prejudice.

I have not shared these observations with you because I want to idealise my grandfather. He was a human being, and therefore made mistakes. But I believe it is in the values exemplified by his personal qualities, and not the politics and issues of the inter-war years, that hold lessons for us today.

I know that we are going through a period of debate in charting a course for our new Hungary, and it is tempting to look for solutions and analogies in our recent history. But the problems and solutions of the inter-war years are no longer relevant to Hungary today. The world has completely changed, not just from what it was before the war, but even in the last ten years. Power and prosperity today have less to do with borders and armies than with transparency and access to the electronic highways linking markets; less to do with confrontation than shrewd cooperation. Just as important, today there are for once no paranoid empires on our doorstep.

To take advantage of today's opportunities, more than ever Hungarians need to be united in their feelings. Debate is very necessary because it can lead to better solutions, but it must not be allowed to lead to hatred and isolation. Given how much my grandfather loved Hungary, it is very important to me that our work today should not create divisions and hatred between Hungarians, but rather lead to a healing of old wounds.

For this reason, I would like us all here today to reach out to those of our countrymen who are not here today because they have a different interpretation from us of my grandfather's historical role. I want to include them in our feelings with love and mutual forgiveness as we proceed with rebuilding our country, thinking more of the opportunities the future holds than of the catastrophes of the past.

In any case, it is not our job today to judge how well or how badly my grandfather performed his job as Regent. I for one believe that it is not given to us as human beings to know what might have been if things had been done differently, nor of the real constraints he was subject to, nor what was in his heart.

I cannot close without saying something about my grandmother and my uncle. I remember grandmother as a strikingly beautiful person, inwardly and outwardly, a really devoted wife, mother and grandmother. Most people who saw her loved her. When she died I was amazed to receive a letter from one of my school friends who used to come to our house to play when we were about ten. He wrote that my grandmother had made such a deep impression on him that he had never been able to forget her. My Uncle Nicky was also an important friend to me as I was growing up. I remember his great charm and wit and his enjoyment of life, and this is my opportunity to thank him for all his kindness and companionship.

May God forgive them their sins and give them a place in the hereafter commensurate with their good deeds in life. Amen.

Sharif's words were greeted with such huge applause that it seemed it would never end. He returned to his place and we just waited.

After that came the ecumenical church ceremony. The coffins were then transported to the crypt. First Magdamama, carried by the young men of Kenderes and followed by the whole family except Sharif. Captain Dávidházy brought Nicky's sepulchral urn; and finally the naval officers carried Miklóspapa's coffin, covered by the Viribus Unitis naval flag. Sharif brought up the rear. There was only space for the family to be present inside the small crypt while the coffins were put into place and Captain Dávidházy recited the navy's Funeral Prayer; this part was also transmitted by the radio and TV. The flag that I had kept all those years was taken off the coffin, folded up and given to my eight-year-old great-grandson Loren to hold. Afterwards, I presented it to the War Museum in Budapest.

The ceremony was now over, but when we emerged from the crypt we were met by an amazing scene. A small detachment of Honvéd (home guard) soldiers presented arms as a farewell to their commander-in-chief. These young men had used their leave to come here at their own expense, in uniform, disregarding the ban on state and army participation in the funeral. It was a silent demonstration, as was that of the representatives of the Jewish survivors who had been saved from the holocaust, who brought flowers and wreaths to the crypt.

People's attitudes were infinitely touching. The crowd had pushed up to the garden fence and everybody was extending a hand, asking for autographs from Sharif and myself, mostly on the remembrance cards they had received on arrival, but also on books, newspapers and so on. We went on signing our names for a long time, and it could have gone on for hours if the naval officers had not put an end to it.

The family and invited guests proceeded to the Town Hall, where we were served a buffet lunch and could meet and talk to more friends. From there we walked over to the garden of the 'Horthy Mansion' for the inauguration of a bronze bust of Admiral Horthy in his naval uniform, commissioned by the Order of Vitéz. We were then taken to the Csárda restaurant, out in the countryside – famous for its delicious Hungarian cooking – where we were the guests of Captain Dávidházy.

When I shared my feelings with Sharif that evening, we found that they were identical. Everything had worked out in an amazing way – even the weather – and whatever I had touched or tried had turned out right. However, I do not deserve credit for this, it was as if things had been 'arranged'. But perhaps the strangest experience was that during the funeral ceremony I had felt such peace and quiet within me, as if I were not even there. I felt no excitement, I was not nervous, and despite the seventy thousand people and the barrage of photographers I felt utterly unperturbed, as I would if I had been alone in my room at home. There was an inner peace inside me that could not be disturbed. I have always hated microphones, but this time it did not bother me and I was able to read my speech out calmly and quietly, with a strong voice. This was surely the work of the latihan, and beyond understanding.

It so happened that my sister Éva's eightieth birthday fell on the day of the reburial and we had decided to celebrate it the next day. We first went to Kenderes to walk around the Horthy Mansion with my grandchildren, and had a quiet look at the crypt and the sea of flowers. Then we went to the Csárda, where I had ordered a birthday lunch and reserved the whole restaurant just for us. The owner and the staff surpassed themselves on our behalf. They made a three-tier birthday cake with eighty candles, which we had to take back to the hotel, as we were too full to eat it.

That evening Éva cut her cake to the accompaniment of gypsy music, after which I showed them archive films of my parents-in-law and Pista, lent to me by kind István Szakály of Hungarian TV. I had translated the Hungarian text of the film into English – a big job – and I read it out to accompany the screening for my English-speaking family. It was very moving to see Pista and his parents come alive.

Most of the next day was spent at the crypt, making a list of the names on the beautiful wreaths and the touching bunches of flowers covering the garden. We also collected the many letters that had been left behind. It was interesting to talk to the police, who said that they had never dealt with a crowd like the one that had attended the funeral – there had been no thefts or disturbances of any kind.

The opposition press reaction to the funeral was surprisingly moderate in comparison with earlier articles. This was clearly due to the effect Sharif's speech had had. One of the most vitriolic reporters wrote that there were 'two humane Europeans present at the funeral and these were Mrs Horthy and her son'. During the next few days Sharif and I gave two more interviews, to the Hungarian and Austrian television. Then the family all dispersed to their far-flung destinations once more and I returned home with two enormous bags full of letters and telegrams, which took me several months to answer.

Only now did I receive my last but greatest present from God in connection with the reburial. When I arrived home, Guy said in a very serious tone that he had to talk to me. This was a bit unusual. He made me sit down quietly and then described to me what had happened to him on the day of the funeral. He had been sitting on the balcony of his room, which has a breathtaking view of the Atlantic Ocean, and was waiting for the time at which the ceremony in Kenderes was due to begin. He looked down at his watch and thought, 'They must be starting now.' When he looked up again the whole sky was full of angels clapping! He thought he had gone mad and quickly shut his eyes. Then he slowly opened them again and they were all there, still clapping. That such a thing should happen to a person like Guy, who was not spiritually inclined and had seemingly never really believed in the latihan, was indeed strange. He was now forced to accept it, as he had seen it with his own eyes. It certainly was a huge gift for me, because from then on he knew I was not talking humbug.

It has indeed been fascinating to note how the latihan has worked in connection with my husband. Bapak told me that as I got stronger inside, everything around me would change, but I had never imagined that this could also apply to Guy. At first the forces in him affected me, and I suffered from this, but gradually things changed and he was obviously touched by the latihan through me. He became more patient, and was no longer irritable but understanding and loving. And now he was even granted his own vision of angels! I could never have expected such a thing in my wildest imaginings.

I received a huge bag of unopened letters and telegrams forwarded by the mayor of Kenderes to add to the hundreds of unanswered letters, telegrams, poems, books, old photographs and newspaper articles that were already waiting at home. Sharif and I published our thanks in two newspapers to everyone who had sent messages of sympathy. Nevertheless I still wanted to send a personal word of thanks to most of them. Time permitting, I worked on them every day and sometimes I was reduced to tears, amazed at the devotion and love that my parents-in-law had engendered and which now flowed towards Sharif and myself.

It was sad that in the British and American press – *The Times*, *The Financial Times*, the *Economist* and the *New York Times* – the reburial was reported in statements obviously based on ignorance of the facts, and on lies spread by Nazi Germany and Communist Hungary that were unfortunately widely believed, especially in the United States. I, my sister, cousins in England and many others responded to these articles, but although acknowledged, none was published – with one exception: the astute letter my son Sharif wrote to the editor of the *Economist*:

Horthy Reappraised

Sir – Your article on Hungary (September 11th), does a disservice not only to Miklós Horthy but also to your readers, by its uncritical acceptance of a Communist version of Horthy's role and its resulting failure to contribute to a proper understanding of the significance of the seventy thousand who turned out for his burial.

Only a tiny fraction of the crowd had much to do with the Extreme Right. A little thought experiment may help understand what is going on.

Let us pretend that Hitler won the war. After forty-four years as a satellite of the Third Reich, Britain becomes free in 1998, as the German Empire collapses under the weight of its own incompetence. Four years later the remains of Winston Churchill, who died in exile, are repatriated for reburial in a churchyard near Blenheim Palace (which has been turned into a college of agricultural workers). Lots of people turn up for the funeral in spite of the stricture of the foreign, and much of the local, press. *Der Volkswirt*, a famous Zürich-based weekly news magazine, is particularly incensed, pointing out that Churchill was an archconservative imperialist, and was even an ally of Stalin (they find a picture of them together). But for those who attend, the funeral represents something different. They are trying to figure out for themselves after forty-four years in limbo, what it means to be British.

Hungary is no more exempt than other European countries from extremists of the Far Right. In Hungary they tried to acquire legitimacy by trying to associate themselves with Horthy (who gave short shrift to their predecessors under Szálasi). Please don't help them.

Sharif Horthy
Wayland, Massachusetts

In October I was surprised to receive a letter from Prime Minister Antall congratulating me on getting a decoration, which he had successfully recommended to the President. The next day the chief of the Presidential Office sent me the following notification:

I am happy to inform you that the president of the Hungarian Republic has granted you a decoration in appreciation of your resistance activities during the Second World War, your support of the policy to end the war, and your outstanding activities in the Hungarian community in Portugal. This high acknowledgement will be bestowed on you by Mr Árpád Göncz, in the Munkácsy Hall in Parliament on Friday 15 October 1993 at 11.30 a.m.

Guy insisted that I go to Budapest to receive the decoration personally, although he was unable to come with me, as he was due to fly to London for his third hip operation. He again refused to let me to go

with him, saying that there was nothing I could do. And so I flew to
Hungary without him, but spoke to him on the telephone every day.

On 15 October – the forty-ninth anniversary of that fatal day in 1944
– I arrived at the Parliament Building. The ceremony was to take place
in the beautiful big hall with the large, historic Munkácsy paintings.
György Szabad, the head of the National Assembly, several ministers,
the army chief of staff and the prime minister's wife, were all present. I
was briefed beforehand by the head of the President's Office, and was
told that it was customary for people to say a few words of thanks.

When the medals had been presented, I said what I felt was
important: After expressing my thanks for the honour, I mentioned my
brother-in-law Nicky and ADC Gyuszi Tost, who had worked with me
at the time. I said that it would make me happy if I could say 'thank
you' for this honour also in the name of all the women who had not
been at the centre of events in October 1944, as we had in the Royal
Palace, but who, unknown and abandoned, many of them humiliated
because of their race, had stood their ground unrecognized.

I was surprised to see a tear running down György Szabad's cheek.
He came up to me afterwards and said that he had assisted at many
decoration ceremonies, but that he had never heard anyone say such
moving words of thanks.

In 1994, Easter Sunday fell on 3 April. This was the day when I started
to write this book about my life. So I have now reached the day when
my story began. Remember? 'Easter Sunday, 1994. The day has come –
I never imagined that it would – I am starting to write down the story
of my life.'

Epilogue

A s I look over these pages telling the story of my life, I can't help but remember a time when, as a child, I fell ill during a journey with my mother in Italy. She took me to an elderly local doctor; he was very kind and gave me some medicine. Then, as we left, he looked at me gravely and said to my mother, 'Your daughter will surely live to be ninety years old.' I was just nine years old, and wondered what it would feel like to be ninety! I did not like the idea very much, as I figured that such very old people would be quite helpless.

And now I am eighty, and it does not seem such a bad idea after all, as long as I am not a burden to anyone and the Almighty grants me health. I am infinitely grateful that I am still fit and do not feel old. I have just learned to use a computer and communicate on the internet – though I will not pretend that it was easy. (To my grandson Leonard I am his 'electronic granny'.) I can still climb a tree to get the lemons and oranges from the top, and also get up on the roof when a tile is broken or the TV aerial needs adjusting. I have an ever-deepening appreciation for life itself, the simple pleasures of God's creations. The beautiful flowers and the birds in my garden, and the view of the ocean stretching out in front of me – I do not know whether it is more beautiful during the day or at night – all overwhelm me and give me a wide feeling of praise towards God.

I am deeply grateful to my husband Guy, who with his untiring work has given me such a beautiful home. Here I found inspiration to write my story, with the aim that my descendants would know the truth.

Looking at my beloved Hungary: the situation there after forty years of Communism was somewhat similar to the aftermath of the First World War, which had resulted in despondency and weariness. Then, Miklós Horthy appeared and brought a new energy, which someone called a 'blood transfusion'; that kind of energy is again needed now, and I hope that it will come about through individuals being moved to help each other and their country.

Miklós Horthy's words to the officer corps in 1919 are still appropriate today. He advised:

> Dig deep into your hearts and destroy the very seed of old misunderstandings and dissension. ... There were those who fled abroad and there were also those whom circumstances compelled to serve in the Red Army. We have found each other, so let us understand one another! Perhaps there has never been a greater and holier aim awaiting us than that which we face today.

In Hungary, people have had a history of helping and supporting each other in tragic circumstances as was so vividly demonstrated during the revolution of 1956. Surely we can find it within ourselves to do so again, so that Hungary in its current rebirth will prosper in decency and tolerance. This is what I wish for my country.

I have the same wish for my second beloved home, Portugal. I feel a special long-standing love for my third country too – the United Kingdom, my second husband's country, which accepted me as its citizen and to whose Queen, Elizabeth II, I swore allegiance when I received my passport.

There is only one burning wish in my heart, and that is to be with my family more often – to enjoy and hug them, and to see my great-grandchildren growing up. I know they are on their own journeys, and I give thanks to the Almighty that they have found the latihan. This is a great comfort to me, as I know what a great blessing the latihan will be for them as they face their own life challenges.

For it has been my experience that it is all too easy – given the demands of modern life – to become inwardly stale, because the material pressure in this world weakens our capacity to feel an inner peace. I cannot help feeling that this, together with the scale on which humanity is polluting the earth, is a great danger to humankind today; and that natural disasters such as tidal waves, floods and earthquakes, are a warning to us. We need more and more to rediscover a source of wisdom and morality within ourselves, to keep renewing our commitment to God all the time. For me the best way to do this is through receiving the Subud latihan. I also find prayer very important, as it is a reminder to turn inwards; it relieves oppressing thoughts and opens the way to receive that 'all-encompassing energy', the Power of God.

I hope that people everywhere can reach out to this Almighty Creative Power, so that they can be shown the right way. The truth is with that power, not with us; we just have to knock for the door to be opened. For those who choose the path of Subud, I hope that the latihan remains convincing, so that they will increasingly be guided by the Power of God and not by their passions and desires.

It is here that my story ends – a story of eighty years of tremendous joys and deep sorrows, hopes and disappointments. I praise God for all the truths I have been shown, for the real values that I have discovered, for all the blessings, and for the son He gave me. And I especially give thanks for the deep inner love I feel towards all God's creation: rocks, trees, flowers, birds, animals of all kinds, and human beings of every colour and creed. It is the depth of that love that brings tears to my eyes at the suffering, disbelief, mistrust, self-pity, abuse and hatred that people needlessly have to endure because those who make these things happen are not aware of God's compassion, guidance, protection and blessing, which through the Power of God I have received in the latihan.

Appendices

Appendices

Appendix 1.   Tribute of Jenő Markotay-Velsz, managing director of MÁVAG

During the night of the 19–20 August 1942, something extraordinary happened which affected me for a long time and which I will never forget.

I slept very restlessly, and kept dreaming about our late vice-regent. Even now, I can almost hear the words he spoke to me in my dream: 'Don't go thinking the Russians shot me down, I just crashed.'

In the morning I woke up feeling very depressed. I tried to forget the bad dream, but it was impossible. It was in the afternoon that I heard the shocking news of this great tragedy, and I realised with alarm that in my dream I had experienced what had actually happened. This incident seemed incomprehensible, and the only explanation I can give for it is something I was once told by a very erudite Chinese gentleman.

The human body and soul are probably a big transmission centre which emits waves just as a radio broadcasting station does. But it does not just emit waves, it can also receive waves transmitted by others. However, just as the transmitted waves can only be received on a radio receiver if it is set to the wavelength of the transmitting waves, so the human soul can only receive the messages transmitted by others if it is able to set itself to the same wavelength. The things which enable us to do this are a long time spent together with, and a true love and devotion for, the other person.

We worked together for seven years ... our desks were next to each other, we had lunch together every day, and very often we did not part company until late at night. I have so many happy memories of this long period that I was very pleased and honoured to be asked by the Hungarian Transport Science Society to write a commemoration of vitéz István Horthy de Nagybánya: the man, the engineer, the factory manager and the leading expert on, enthusiastic supporter of, and tireless worker for, transport and related issues.

His Majesty's government appointed me managing director of the Hungarian State Iron, Steel and Engineering Works, with effect from 1 January 1933. The next morning at nine o'clock a three-man delegation from the MÁVAG branch of the Hungarian Technicians' Fraternal Society arrived, led by vitéz Stephen Horthy de Nagybánya, chief engineer in MÁVAG's car workshop and the society's branch leader, who welcomed me on behalf of the branch. I was moved by the devotion and affection he showed for the company, and could see that he deeply cared about the welfare of the factory and its employees. Shortly afterwards there was a branch meeting which he chaired. All the engineers in the factory were present. Here I could see that he was a born leader, and the engineers liked and respected their young colleague very much. So in the interest of MÁVAG, which was in a critical situation, I appointed vitéz Stephen Horthy de Nagybánya to be deputy managing director and my closest colleague. I was touched by his protests that he was too young for the post and that he had not yet merited such a promotion. It took a lot of persuasion to convince him that the scope of a workshop engineer's duties was too narrow for someone with his abilities. ... Each time he was promoted I had to reassure him that he was not being promoted because he was the son of Hungary's Regent, and prove that he was being singled out on merit.

His modesty was rivalled by his disciplined behaviour. ... He never sought his own comfort and knew no personal interests, all that mattered to him was to carry out the task he has been set. He was obliging and obedient to his superiors, and with his subordinates there was nothing he disapproved of more than undisciplined behaviour. He carried out instructions precisely and was strict in demanding that his own instructions should also be carried out to the letter. He was never late and never kept anyone waiting. ...

His famous flight to India was also not a publicity stunt: he did it out of a sense of duty. In seven years he took only three holidays of a fortnight each.

Nobody could compete with Stephen Horthy in loyalty to his colleagues. He was with his fellow workers through thick and thin, and shared in all their worries and problems. But his best quality was the boundless love he showed his parents. It is impossible to put into words the charm, the respect and the devotion he expressed in a few words of greeting to his mother. He looked up to his father as the most perfect man, and all he wanted was that his father should be pleased with him. Once he and I had an audience with His Highness the Regent in which we thanked him for the favour he had shown us in bestowing an honour on us. I looked with admiration at the boundless respect he showed to his father, and could see on his face the happiness which filled him at the thought that his father considered him worthy of an honour.

However, Stephen Horthy was not only called to be an example for millions to follow as a man; as an engineer he was also one of the best.

His knowledge of engineering, his skill, and his powers of judgment were amazing. He used all his spare time to increase his knowledge of engineering. With all the work he had to do, it was beyond me how he found the time to study technical books and periodicals. ... But he was not just a man of theory: his practical knowledge and flair were also quite extraordinary. He frequently astonished a workshop engineer or worker by himself demonstrating how to do the job. More than once he came up from the workshop grimy and oily, reporting with pleasure that one or other of his experiments had been a success.

However, his real speciality was forms of transport and in particular the engine. He had a complete mastery of shipping and railways, both technically and in terms of transport, but with the engine he was definitely one of the country's leading experts. ... He knew of all innovations, wherever they had occurred, and assessed them with a sure and relevant critique. Every year he attended the European motor shows, and absorbed all he saw and learned like a sponge. ...

The task which had to be accomplished in 1933 was unbelievably difficult. MÁVAG, one of Hungary's largest factories, was in deep trouble. Its equipment was outdated and deficient, and it had no work to speak of. The company's locomotive factory was the only one in the country, but it was on the verge of closing down due to lack of orders. The first task was to prevent the locomotive factory from closing down completely. The government wanted to stop the manufacture of locomotives because of the deficit. Negotiations continued for months, and during the course of these negotiations Stephen Horthy fought with youthful ardour and great enthusiasm for the maintenance of locomotive manufacture. But all this would have been to no avail if we had not been able to secure foreign orders for the locomotive workshop: Stephen Horthy went to London and, as a result, the first order – locomotive boilers for India – arrived. However, in Hungary the trend away from locomotives and towards motorcars continued. So the factory management decided to design a locomotive which would be able to compete with motorcars. Thus the first Hungarian streamlined locomotive was born, and Stephen Horthy played a major part in its design and construction. He was delighted when the streamlined locomotive was ready, and often drove it himself on the test runs. ...

Car manufacture was in an even more desperate state in 1933 ... MÁVAG's car works were completely outdated and ill equipped, which made it impossible to produce cars economically. ...

Stephen Horthy himself planned equipping the new car works, as he had the most detailed knowledge of car manufacture. How happy he was when the arrival of a new machine tool was reported to him, how he could admire modern processing machines, and how enthusiastically he started them operating! Within a year the new car factory was complete, and its work increased so much that in six years it needed to be extended twice. I do not need to say just how much a productive, large car factory means to the country today. ...

Stephen Horthy's achievements in boosting road haulage are also outstanding. He negotiated constantly to sell the existing lorries, and it is entirely due to him that within a short time the four hundred lorries were boosting motor vehicle traffic in Hungary. ...

At the time of the economic crisis in 1933, MÁVAG's iron and steelworks in Diósgyőr were under threat as well. ... Orders had to be obtained from abroad. A great opportunity for this arose in the winter of 1933-34 in connection with railway building works in Persia. Direct negotiations were needed, and somebody had to travel to Teheran. Stephen Horthy readily volunteered to do the job. I did not want to let him go, I did not want it to be him who had to travel through Russia. When I saw that his mind was made up, I wanted at least to send an engineer with him so that he would not have to make the long and dangerous journey alone. He did not want to take anybody with him, because he considered it unnecessary as well as expensive for the company. He spent six weeks in Teheran, gained a great deal of experience, and made MÁVAG a well-known and respected name. Years later the manager of a large French concern stated that they had made a very costly mistake in not recognising early enough the threat that Stephen Horthy's negotiations in Teheran posed to them.

Almost single-handedly he started up aircraft manufacture in Hungary. The development of aircraft manufacture encountered difficulties and obstacles so severe that anyone else would have been unable to overcome them. The task of starting up aircraft manufacture on a large scale was beset by constraints which only Stephen Horthy was able to tackle. ... He knew instinctively that the Hungarian army would only be able to carry out its duties in the coming ordeal if the aeroplane, the most up-to-date weapon, was available to it. ...This firm conviction, together with his ardent patriotism, gave Stephen Horthy the strength and persistence to lay the foundations of aircraft manufacture in Hungary. The eagerness with which he served the cause of aviation is illustrated by the fact that one afternoon he took the factory engineers out to Buda's airport and took them each for a ten-minute flight. In this way he wanted to give them a liking for flying and win them over to the cause. ...

He was not destined to enjoy the fruits of this tiring and stressful work, a time when the murderous price war and ferocious struggle between factories to win work would end – and how he longed for this time, and what plans he made for it! He took part in the hard work of sowing, but could not enjoy the happiness of the harvest.

God has many secrets which we may never be able to explain. The life and death of our vice-regent is probably one such secret, since human understanding cannot fathom how it is possible for someone to live his life as though he knows he does not have much time on Earth and has to hurry in order to become worthy of apotheosis in the short time available. We cannot help believing that God intended him to he a model for all Hungarians, to show the people he passionately loved the road on which they must travel in order to arrive.

(The author, vitéz Jenő Markotay-Velsz, is a chief government adviser and managing director of the Hungarian State Iron, Steel and Machine Works (MÁVAG).)

The text is taken from *Vitéz Nagybánya Horthy István élete és a magyar közlekedés* [The Life of Vitéz István Horthy de Nagybánya and Hungarian Transport] edited by Olaf Wulff and Jenő Maléter (Budapest, 1943), pp. 89–96.

Appendix 2.   György Farkas: 'By sports plane to India'. (From *The Tragic Death of Flight Lieutenant Stephen Horthy Vice-Regent of Hungary*)

I once read in a newspaper article that Stephen Horthy flew in his own plane to Bombay, in order to make himself popular. How naive! If the journalist doesn't know the subject, why does he write about it? And most of all, why does he write things that are not true, thus deceiving the reader? Well, of course, not so long ago the author of such writings could publish them without any problem – in fact he could gain credit for them. On the other hand, if he had written the truth, he would hardly have been praised for it – if indeed he had been allowed to publish it at all.

Well, the truth is that even Stephen Horthy's father, the Regent of Hungary, found out about this plane journey at the last moment, and not from his son – who had made preparations for the flight in the most secrecy – but from the commander of the air force, who felt it was his duty to report the matter to the Regent, who was away from Budapest at the time.

Although my master prepared for the journey in secret, I still had to know about it, since I took part in the rapid preparations. And of course Oszkár Hille, who was head of deputy managing director Stephen Horthy's secretariat at MÁVAG. But apart from this, the important journey was surrounded by the deepest secrecy even within MÁVAG.

So what really happened, and why was the journey so important? The year was 1939. It was summer, the end of June. The Second World War had not broken out yet. It was hot. There were just the two of us in the Palace, because the Regent and his family usually spent the summer months in Gödöllő or Kenderes. Then my master Stephen Horthy said to me:

'Tomorrow I am going to Munich on the morning flight. Pack the essential things in my small flying bag. If everything goes well, I will be back in the afternoon. I will bring the plane, or if not my plane, then another one on loan.'

My further orders were that while he was away I was to go to the Foreign Ministry, take his diplomatic passport with me and have it prepared for him to travel to India. Through the Military Office I was to get hold of maps from the Army Cartographic Institute. I was not to breathe a word about what he wanted them for. I knew someone in the Military Office personally, and if I asked him for something for my master, he could arrange it without any questions being asked.

The next morning we went out to Budaörs, which was where the civil airport was then. My master left, and I got on with the arrangements. ... By the time I got everything done it was time for me to go back to the airport to await his arrival. He got back in the early evening. After we had duly admired the plane, we put it in MÁVAG's hangar and then went home.

That was when the hard work started. ... My master plotted the route on his maps. It was midnight by the time we got to bed. I asked the guards to wake us at 4 a.m. By five o'clock we were in the hangar at Budaörs. I helped start the plane, and soon Stephen Horthy took off for Bombay. All he said before he left was, 'You will be informed of my arrival. If my mother asks where I am, just tell her I have gone abroad.' ...

The Regent found out the details of his son's journey to Bombay from foreign reports, but by that time the aim of the journey had been achieved: the contract had been signed. He got home safely. The Regent met his son at Budaörs airport. Of course the general public still didn't know the real reason of this arduous journey. Its novelty value was blurred by other events: the war was starting; the papers had enough to write about. However, it was certainly a bold undertaking. It's not comfortable or even safe to travel between the sky and the ground in the hot sun, to sleep under the plane on airfields, and to land in the tropical heat of Bombay with the temperature at 52 °C. Not many people would undertake such a journey even in today's modern planes with all their safety equipment. So why did he go? Very few people knew that, even after his return home – apart from his closest colleagues.

In 1939, India invited bids for the delivery of one hundred 424-type express steam locomotives. There were two companies in Hungary which manufactured locomotives:

one was MÁVAG, owned by MÁV, and the other was GANZ (Ganz & Co. Electrical, Machine, Wagon and Shipbuilding Company) The two giant factories were neighbours, and both manufactured the world-famous 424s. An order from abroad for one hundred such locomotives was a deal of enormous significance. Naturally it was those high-level managers who were authorised to sign the contract who had to travel to the negotiations.

In order to secure an advantage in the business negotiations, GANZ had bought up the available seats on the flight to Bombay well in advance. It's important to know that at that time there was only one flight per week between London and Bombay, and generally only one or two seats could be reserved in Budapest. When the plane landed in Budapest it could only take those passengers with reservations, so despite his prestige and good personal connections, Stephen Horthy couldn't get a ticket for the flight. This annoyed him immensely. He could see that he couldn't travel to the negotiations as a competitor on equal terms. In addition it mattered to him whether it was the Hungarian company he led which could deliver the hundred locomotives, or GANZ, which was a partly German concern. He knew that if he couldn't travel there now – and his business competitors had done everything to prevent him from doing so – then the deal would certainly be lost.

It was these reasons that induced him to undertake the perilous journey in a private plane. By the time GANZ's delegation arrived in Bombay on the scheduled flight, the contract had already been signed with MÁVAG.

This is the genuine and true story of the flight to Bombay: there was never any question of making himself popular, though it's undeniable that the outstanding achievement popularised the sportsman.

Appendix 3.   Stephen Horthy's letter to his father from the front

Letter from Kiev, 17 August 1942

Dear Papa,

Apologies for writing this in pencil and for my bad writing (perhaps it will be best if Mama reads it out to you) but I have no ink and it seems my writing will never improve now. Many thanks for your kind letter; I'm pleased to hear that you are all well, though Ily has told me that too. Ily and I have spent a few very pleasant days here in Kiev and I'm sorry we will already have to part tomorrow afternoon.

How right you are when you say that it is the upper classes who acquit themselves well out here: the cavalry, armoured and artillery units are good, and it is mainly the infantry which is weak. The position is the same with those gentlemen who hold positions of authority. Officers coming from below develop *petit bourgeois* attitudes amid comforts to which they are unaccustomed, they develop paunches etc, and *petit bourgeois* men aren't good soldier material.

It's certainly pleasing that there are some among the commanders who are excellent in every respect and well suited to the task, such as Lieutenant General vitéz Lajos Veress, the commander of the Armoured Division; Major-General György Rakovszky, the former chief of staff, now an army corps commander; Colonel Makray, the quartermaster general, and Colonel Kovács, the current chief of staff.

I also have to mention that I have been shown the utmost respect and kindness both by Jány and by all the other gentlemen with whom I have had dealings.

Our losses have been fairly heavy recently because of a lack of momentum. If I may give you some advice: let's not send reinforcements but rather concentrate our forces. If we constantly replenish our units then we will just bleed to death in terms of both men and equipment. The Russians won't by any means be beaten by the end of this year; they are fighting very strongly and are well supplied with munitions and food, so in my opinion they won't be any weaker next year, in fact just the opposite.

I don't know whether this is true, but apparently another two divisions are coming out to act as occupying forces. This news disheartened me greatly because we already have many more troops out here than we can afford. How reassuring it would be if Bartha were no longer in the minister's seat; I feel he's the evil spirit behind this.

One more sad topic, the Jewish companies: I gather there are twenty or thirty thousand Jews out here who are completely at the mercy of the sadists. It makes my stomach turn; it's revolting. It's awful that this could happen even in the twentieth century … I'm afraid we will have to pay a heavy price for this sometime. Couldn't they be taken home to work there? Otherwise few of them will survive the winter.

I'm sorry I can't give you just good news, but I hope you won't mind.

Your respectful and grateful son,

Pista.

Appendix 4.   Sándor Horváth's account of the death of Flt Lt Stephen Horthy

Following the publication of the first volume of my book *Becsület és kötelesség* (Honour and Duty), I received the following account from Sándor Horváth, former dive bomber and fighter pilot, unit leader, rehabilitated lieutenant pilot officer – which for me represents the final truth in connection with the death of Stephen Horthy.

The story of the tragic death of Flight Lieutenant Stephen Horthy, Vice-Regent of Hungary

When the radio broadcast news of the death of Flight Lieutenant vitéz Stephen Horthy de Nagybánya on 20 August 1942, in addition to shock, sorrow and sympathy, doubts were also felt.

The population of Hungary and members of the army and the air force, particularly pilots, greeted accounts of the accident with disbelief. But subsequent events and even greater loss of lives as the war continued led people to forget this incident; the official records of the tragedy were placed in the military archive. For this reason the official view remains that Flight Lieutenant vitéz Stephen Horthy's death was due to pilot error, in that he made a too tight turning, which led to his fatal spin and crash. In other words, he is regarded as having been responsible for the tragedy.

This view was merely reinforced by the appearance in 1998 of Captain Mátyás Szabó's book *Horthy István repülőtiszt halálá* [The death of Flight Lieutenant Stephen Horthy]. He wrote the book from memory but his view of the tragedy remained the same: 'His Highness the Vice-Regent was the victim of his own flying error. Nobody else can be held responsible.' This was his final conclusion on the tragedy.

I found discrepancies in Mátyás Szabó's book, but could not see any breach in his well-written account. I felt that something was not right but could not find any evidence. It was then that I came across the book written by Stephen Horthy's widow. Reading this book, I came to understand how the accident had happened, but I still needed to see the official record of the interview with his duty officer companion.

I managed to obtain the record of this interview in the spring of 2000, and my assumption was proved correct. Flight Lieutenant vitéz Stephen Horthy made no flying errors during his final flight and did not cause his fatal accident. To back up my assertion I will make use of the official records made at the time and of the accounts given in the books written by Stephen Horthy's widow and Mátyás Szabó, adding my own explanations.

The events of that early morning were as follows: At 05.00 on 20 August 1942, two pairs of fighters were sent on a sortie: their mission was to protect two tactical reconnaissance aircraft. The squadron leader had given the commanding officer of each pair detailed orders concerning the mission the previous evening. Flight Lieutenant György Bánlaky, accompanied by Sergeant István Szabó, would protect the reconnaissance aircraft which was to work in the northern zone, while Flight Lieutenant vitéz Stephen Horthy, accompanied by Sergeant Zoltán Nemeslaki, was to protect the one bound for the southern zone. The height difference between the reconnaissance aircraft and the fighters escorting them was to be between 300 and 500 metres.

The record of the interview with Nemeslaki reads:

> After taking off, we made a wide sweep left to arrive over the reconnaissance airfield, where I spotted the reconnaissance plane to be escorted by our fighters. When I saw the reconnaissance plane, it was about 1 kilometre ahead of us, at a height of 200 metres, flying in a roughly easterly direction. We flew in a roughly north-easterly direction at a height of 300 metres in order to catch up with the reconnaissance plane. We caught up with and overtook the reconnaissance plane at a speed of 300 km/h, and my feeling is that His Highness intended to circle to the left in order to position his

fighter correctly in relation to the reconnaissance plane.

There is some logic in Nemeslaki's reasoning, but we must take another factor into consideration here. The reconnaissance plane was flying ahead of them. The two fighters had to identify themselves, but the leading aircraft of the pair did not adjust its position, did not turn off to the right, did not confirm that they were the escorts, and did not gain height.

What happened next took place at a distance of 1,000–2,000 metres from the reconnaissance airfield. I cannot work out the precise distance because I do not know the size of the reconnaissance plane's turning circle. The reconnaissance plane turned, showing itself, and headed south; i.e. to the right. The fighters should have gone in the same direction, but instead the leading plane turned left.

When he did not follow the reconnaissance aircraft, did not turn right, did not fly to the designated zone and did not gain height, the pilot of the leading fighter was not following the orders he had been given because *he was already in an emergency situation*. He turned left because a fault had occurred in the engine of his aircraft. The engine lost power and the aircraft's speed fell from 300 km/h to virtually zero. The leading pilot now attempted the most expedient solution and began a tight left turn. The reconnaissance airfield was closer and he intended to make an emergency landing there.

The next event was the one on which the Accident Investigation Committee based its findings and its judgment of the tragedy. Mátyás Szabó recalled it as follows: 'The reconnaissance plane was flying lower than he was, and he attempted to line up behind it, while still over the airfield, by performing a tight turn. With a full payload, his plane was not travelling fast enough to make the turn. The nose dropped to the left and so the plane slipped down ... he could not bring the plane out of the dive, as a result of which it hit the ground at a steep (70 degree) angle.'

At this point the accident investigators went off on the wrong track. I do not know why and how, but they misinterpreted the official record.

Flight Lieutenant Stephen Horthy did not crash out of this tight left turn but stayed airborne.

Sergeant Nemeslaki recalled what happened next: 'I tried to follow His Highness as he circled to the left, but during the turn my plane started to vibrate because it was stalling, so I eased the angle of my turn, while continuing to watch His Highness' plane constantly.'

Sergeant Nemeslaki was to the left of his commander, but in the old no. 2 position, not on the Rotte line. His plane was travelling at 15–20 km/h less than the other, which was why it started vibrating first. He eased the angle and pulled out of the turn in time, otherwise he would have crashed. Since the two planes were identical, if they had been travelling fast enough, the second plane – which was flying the tighter circle – would have been able to follow the leader no matter how tight the turn, could have turned out onto the right-hand side of the leader, or stalled and dived like a Stuka. In this case, their speed was too low.

Mátyás Szabó continued his observations as follows: 'The plane was carrying a full payload and its speed was far below what was required to perform the turn; his escort, who was flying right next to him, realised this and was forced to open the throttle and pull his plane out of the turn.'

Mátyás Szabó's book does not even mention the two observers, when it is their observations which are crucial. Zoltán Nemeslaki was first and foremost an escort and he was concentrating on his task. He did not give a precise location for the accident, but we can draw conclusions from the events.

Despite the difficulties, Flight Lieutenant vitéz Horthy managed to pull off the tight turn and head for the reconnaissance airfield. From there, observer Acting-Pilot Officer Gyula Szabó followed the course of the flight. He was standing at the edge of the reconnaissance airfield and had a good view of what happened. 'One of the planes was approaching the airfield in a straight line from the direction of Nikolayevka.' This was the plane flown by Sergeant Nemeslaki, who was now unable to escort his commander and could only follow at a safe distance. He was unable to return to his proper position because his commander was flying at the lowest possible speed and it was impossible to fly alongside him.

Meanwhile, the other plane flew to the right of Nemeslaki's, roughly following the line of the river, demonstrating the pilot's outstanding expertise.

As a mechanical engineer, Flight Lieutenant vitéz Horthy was well aware of the gravity of his predicament from the symptoms his engine was displaying. (The Piaggio PIRC 40 air-cooled aircraft engine had already been the cause of several tragedies.) When his speed dropped from 300 km/h to virtually zero, he pulled off a tight turn without losing height – no mean feat. He hoped to be able to reach the airfield where he could deploy his undercarriage and wing flaps to make an emergency landing. But it was not to be. It was not possible to recover the plane from the rapid loss of speed. This is why all Captain Mátyás Szabó's assessment is so painful and unjust, particularly his final judgment: 'His Highness the Vice-Regent was the victim of his own flying error.'

I want to back up my statement regarding an engine fault with the account of an outside observer, so I think it is important to mention the statement made by Captain Elek Baranyi. He reported seeing a 'trail of stars' leaving the aircraft and took them to come from the firing of the flare gun. But when his plane stalls, a pilot is subjected to an enormous pressure and is unable to move, so he would be unable to reach for his flare gun and fire it. The 'trail of stars' could only have come from combustion products being forced out of the engine, or more likely from an attempt to smother a smouldering ignition cable. This would also indicate an engine fault.

I would also refer to the observations of Corporal Rafael Mészáros, who saw the following: 'A Hungarian fighter was approaching the airfield from east to west. I recognised it easily with binoculars but also with the naked eye. It was three minutes past five; I looked at my watch. I couldn't believe my eyes: the plane was on fire, I could see yellow flames on the side, but no shot had been fired. Why was the side of the plane on fire? Where was the yellow trail of flame coming from?'

The observation of the corporal on duty is accurate. He saw the plane of the commander in the section between the river and the place of the crash.

He immediately reported his observation to his commander, but the probability is great that Captain Miklós Fraknói did not pass it on. In the literature I found no description of it. If the corporal's report had reached the investigators a different decision would have emerged. Unfortunately it did not happen.

Summoning up the above, I think I can state with a clear conscience that Flight Lieutenant vitéz Stephen Horthy made no flying error during the course of his last flight. He was not the cause but the victim of the fatal accident, which he suffered in the end and which led to the sacrifice of his life.

In writing this account, I have sought to draw attention to events that have been disputed for nearly six decades. I hope I have removed the uncertainty that surrounded this tragedy. As a former soldier, I think every mother, wife, sibling and child has a right to know what happened to the lost, beloved soldier, the father or the son.

With this account I have merely sought to inform the family and the nation of the circumstances in which Flight Lieutenant vitéz Stephen Horthy de Nagybánya, then vice-regent of Hungary, met his death in a flying accident.

Sándor Horváth   21 November 2000
Former dive-bomber and fighter pilot,
Unit leader, rehabilitated lieutenant pilot officer

Appendix 5.   Report by Jean de Bavier, March 1944; quoted in
**   *Hungarian Premier* by Miklós Kállay, vol. II p. 86**

Extracts from the report written by the International Red Cross delegate Jean de Bavier
on a personal investigation in December 1943 of the situation of refugees and prisoners
of war in Hungary. The report appeared in the *Revue de la Croix Rouge Internationale*
in March 1944.

We visited many well-organised camps between 2–17 December 1943. This is just a very
brief account of what we saw.

Pesthidegkút camp: It should be noted that Magyar Viscosa, a textile factory set up
near Esztergom, employs thirty Polish and three French internees. All are very content;
they are accommodated in the factory's brand new hostel in excellent circumstances: the
Poles in a big dormitory and the Frenchmen in a nice room. They are paid the same as
Hungarian workers.

Ipolyhídvég camp: The camp is in the barracks of a former border guard post.
Eighty officers, about twenty privates and one woman live here in conditions identical
to those in other Polish camps. The camp doctor is a very cultured man; the mood of the
internees is excellent. Their only complaint is that they receive only enough paraffin to
provide lighting for three hours per day. The delegate helped to improve this situation,
though Hungarian peasants' paraffin ration is the same. The camp commander is
friendly and very understanding.

Süttő camp: Actually a large village where about sixty internees work in the fields.
Most of them live with peasants, very comfortably; the rest are accommodated in a small
house in conditions identical to those in any camp in Hungary. Their only complaint is
that food is expensive. Some of the internees prefer to eat their own food; they receive
food from their hosts at official prices. The population is very friendly towards the
internees.

Mosonmagyaróvár camp: An enormous aluminium factory in which about fifty
Polish internees work, their accommodation is excellent, ... we can say that the situation
of the Polish internees is particularly favourable. On the other hand, due to the
properties of the mineral being processed, the work is very hard. Health care provision
is very good.

Gencsapáti camp: A picturesque palace, which the government bought before the
war to set up a holiday home for officers. It is now occupied only by Polish officers.
When the International Red Cross delegate visited, there were about a hundred officers
there, with eleven women and three children. The large living rooms have been
converted into comfortable bedrooms. The camp also has nice outbuildings: kitchens,
bathrooms, sick rooms, etc. Nobody complained, though living together with so many
others has its disadvantages.

Várpalota camp: The camp serves to accommodate several hundred Polish
internees working in the bauxite factory and the five Polish officers who supervise them.
The internees have the use of a large kitchen and sitting room, and they are treated the
same as Hungarian workers in every respect.

Dömsöd camp: A less significant officers' camp on the bank of the Danube, in a
village built in varying styles. As in the other camps, the internees have freedom of
movement within three kilometres of the camp; if they want to go further afield they
have to ask permission, but officers can go as far as Budapest. The mood of the internees
is good, which is due primarily to the excellent Polish commander. The officers have
even organised a school for their children.

The International Red Cross delegate sums up his report by saying that he received an
extremely good impression of the camps he visited and that the circumstances in which
the internees were living were outstanding in every respect.

Appendix 6. Text of Declaration signed by Dr Ernő Pető, Samu Stern, Dr Károly Wilhelm. Budapest, 3 February 1946

Declaration

We the undersigned, Samu Stern, who was president of the Council of Hungarian Jews after the German occupation on 19 March 1944, and Dr Károly Wilhelm and Dr Ernő Pető, who were leading members of the council up to 16 October 1944, hereby confirm that Dr Dezső Ónódy, a secretary in the Cabinet Office, was in constant contact with us. He personally took memoranda we wrote on behalf of Hungarian Jews up to Ambassador Nicholas Horthy junior, with whom he worked, and Nicholas Horthy junior was kind enough to pass these requests on to the Regent. On many occasions Dr Dezső Ónódy secretly took the undersigned lawyer Dr Ernő Pető, one of the leading members of the council, to see Nicholas Horthy junior, and through him we were able to inform the head of state about the matters which had such serious implications for the Jews, and thereby prevent in many cases the atrocities planned by the Germans against Hungarian Jews.

It was also in this way that we were able to thwart the German Gestapo's plan to deport Budapest's Jewish population starting on 26 August. With their help we were able to obtain an order from the head of state that military force should be used to resist the Gestapo's intentions (the Esztergom Armoured Division was ordered to go to Budapest and orders were given to police commanders). It was this resistance that saved Budapest's Jews from deportation.

When the Council of Ministers gave the head of state the power to grant exemption certificates to those Jews who merited it, we submitted countless requests through Dr Ónódy for Jews to be saved. Dr Ónódy reported on these in Mr Horthy junior's office and submitted them to the head of the Cabinet Office, recommending in every case that the certificate be granted; the head of the Cabinet Office then gave a report on them to the head of state. In this way the lives of countless of our co-religionists were saved up to 15 October 1944.

Dr Dezső Ónódy was always known for his democratic ideas and humanitarian feelings, and this was one reason why he was arrested by the Gestapo on 16 October, imprisoned, and then deported to Germany.

We are prepared to give oral testimony of the above under oath before any Hungarian or Allied authority at any time.

Signed: Dr Ernő Pető, Samu Stern, Dr Károly Wilhelm
Budapest, 3 February 1946

Each signatory gave his address, and the document was officially stamped on behalf of the leaders of the Israelite Community in Pest by the managing secretary in confirmation that they had witnessed the signatures and that the signatories were competent to make the declaration.

**Appendix 7. Reasons for the failure to implement a ceasefire.
From Lieutenant General Aggteleky's collection: III/2 p. 3**

The failure of the attempt to implement a ceasefire on 15 October 1944 after the Regent's proclamation was not due to the things which happened in the capital: the mistakes and omissions of, or crimes committed by, either the civilian or the military leadership or by individuals there; or the success with which the Germans and the Arrow Cross seized power. The success or failure of the attempt depended above all, in fact almost exclusively, on how contact could be made with the Russians on the front line, first and foremost by the First and Second Armies, and how the change of sides could be implemented. If all this had been done successfully, then the following events would have had no bearing on achieving a ceasefire: the capture of the commander of the First Army Corps in Budapest by General Hindy, which allowed the Germans and Arrow Cross to seize military control of Budapest; and the occupation of the radio by the Arrow Cross and the broadcast of Szálasi's counter-proclamation.

Nor would the situation have been changed by the fact that Vörös' explanatory order went out after he yielded to German pressure, whereas the covering order did not go out. Even the government's passive and weak behaviour after the broadcast of the Regent's proclamation, their lack of resolute action and their retreat before the Germans would not have prevented a ceasefire being achieved. The fact is that the government should not have given up its decision to implement a ceasefire at the first sign of problems, just an hour or two after the Regent's proclamation was broadcast (the arrest of the commander of the First Army Corps, the loss of the Radio, the appearance of Vörös' explanatory order) or omitted to take any countermeasures, simply slumping into passivity. Instead it too should have worked with all its might to secure a ceasefire as quickly as possible.

It was a mistake for the government to continue negotiating with Rahn and the German ambassador in the afternoon and night of 15 October, offering conditions for restoring German-Hungarian links and finally discussing handing over control of the state to the Germans – when the Arrow Cross were already in the process of seizing power, supported by the Germans. As a consequence, Rahn and the German ambassador gained the upper hand and were able superciliously to ask for proposals to be submitted in writing and to demand as a condition for continuing the negotiations that the mines surrounding the Palace (and thereby also the German Embassy) should be removed. Thus they regained the ability to communicate freely with their forces which carried out the coup and brought Szálasi to power, and with the Arrow Cross. ...

All these many mistakes, omissions and crimes would not have prevented the ceasefire being achieved if the commanders of the First and Second Armies had forcefully and resolutely carried out their task – one which confronted them with an almost superhuman moral dilemma.

The implementation of the change of sides would not have encountered significant difficulties. The Russian troops opposite were prepared for it. Lieutenant General Béla Lengyel, then commander of the Eighth Army Corps fighting along the line of the river Tisza, wrote the following account as an eye-witness and active participant in the events: 'On 15 October 1944, groups of Russian officers and men carrying white flags came across to the Hungarian positions in front of the Fifty-first Infantry Regiment and drank with our men. Lengyel personally had to ask a Russian colonel, who was already in high spirits, that they should return peacefully to their own positions.'

Nor, it seems, would we have encountered too many difficulties with the Germans, either at the front or in the capital. Their position had become catastrophic and they would have had neither the resources nor the time to attack us with significant forces. The two army commanders bear an even greater responsibility by virtue of the fact that they knew about the planned ceasefire and the conditions for implementing it at least four to five days earlier and would have had time to prepare at least mentally and spiritually for their serious task.

But an objective assessment of the events requires us also to note that just as the unfavourable reports arriving from the fighting troops had a detrimental influence on the government in its decisions and actions, so the news of damaging events in the capital (the order from Vörös, the chief of general staff, which led to confusion; Szálasi's counter-proclamation on the radio) had a paralysing effect on the actions of the army commanders.

As a result of this, it is my firm and unshakable conviction that the Hungarian soldiers, the armed forces as a whole, are guilty neither of disloyalty nor of betrayal in connection with the events of October 1944. Though there were – unfortunately – exceptions, omissions and crimes committed by a few, their number is relatively speaking insignificant and it is irresponsible slander to state that such behaviour was prevalent.

I am convinced that on 15 October the importance of the events, of the decision, lay with the First and Second Armies. If the armies had really managed to carry through the changeover to the Russian side on 15 October, then the events of that day in Budapest would have paled into insignificance. However successful the German coup, there is no doubt that the combined Hungarian and Russian forces would have swept the Germans and their Arrow Cross lackeys out of the capital within 48 hours. The bad news from the capital only started to reach the fighting troops in the evening of the fifteenth; but contact should have been made with the Russians immediately after the proclamation had been broadcast because the Germans would definitely prevent this happening on the sixteenth.

In his proclamation the Regent said, 'I have given appropriate instructions to the commanders of the Hungarian Army. Bound by their oath, the troops are still obliged to obey their commanding officers, whom I appointed.' But the orders of the commanders who had been 'appropriately' instructed never arrived. The troops waited in vain for these orders on 15 October and also on 16 October. Then in the evening of 16 October the Regent's second proclamation was broadcast, which ordered the troops to 'continue fighting with determination'.

The Regent is not responsible for anything that happened after the early hours of 16 October. I saw the Regent three times between 7–13 October. In the struggle for a ceasefire he stood out among all his colleagues in terms of determination, decisiveness and persistence. But he had no principal colleague who would do anything, take responsibility, be prepared to act, overcome all obstacles and be dynamic, above all with regard to military matters. However, we must acknowledge that the situation was desperate, almost catastrophic, and would have required almost divine qualities in such a principal colleague who would accept joint responsibility ...

There was a complete lack of unity in the military leadership in the preparation and implementation of the ceasefire. This in itself was enough to pose a serious threat to a successful outcome. It was almost impossible for the Regent to succeed in taking everything into his own hands and leading the implementation process in a professional manner, attending to every detail – particularly amid the whirl of an accumulation of events each of which in itself was decisive.

The necessity to be objective requires us to point out the circumstance that forced him to take this step. General János Vörös was appointed to the post of chief of general staff in the Sztójay government as a result of definite German pressure. As Vörös and I were born in the same town, I have followed his career with more than a passing interest. He was not a paid agent of the Germans, nor indeed pro-German; the simple fact was that – in common with many others accused for no good reason – at that time he was convinced that it was in Hungary's interests to continue fighting alongside the Germans. The circumstances of his appointment naturally resulted in the Regent not having full confidence in him. But because of the Germans the Regent could not replace him, at least not for the time being. But regardless of all this, it was Hungary's fate that János Vörös, though his intellectual abilities may have been above average, was sadly lacking in strength of character and the moral and other military virtues which were essential in the responsible position of chief of general staff, particularly in the whirl of decisive events which had an almost catastrophic effect on the destiny of the nation.

Appendix 8.   Letter from General vitéz Géza Lakatos

Your Highness,

It is with immense pleasure that I take the first available opportunity – with Your Highness' permission – to communicate at least in writing: I have been preparing to do so in vain for the last eighteen months. I am prompted to write not only by my old loyalty and sincere respect but also by a very special reason, which I will set out in detail below. The fact is that on the night of 15–16 October 1944, the night of that unfortunate turning point for the state, something occurred the full truth of which Your Highness could not have known, just as I only found it out last February from the witness statements of Ambrózy and Lázár in the Szálasi trial. This revealed to me a shocking turn of events of which I had no inkling and which I feel it is my moral duty to bring to Your Highness' attention.

Your Highness may know that Ambrózy and Vattay came to see me at the prime minister's residence at eleven o'clock on the night of the fifteenth to say that they considered Your Highness' life to be under threat. Vattay was the spokesman and said he thought the only solution was to place the security of Your Highness' and the family's lives under the protection of the German Reich. I replied that if he thought that, then it was up to him to put forward the proposal. He was happy to do so and left straight away with Ambrózy. Others present during this discussion were the ministers Iván Rakovszky, Gusztáv Hennyey, the late Lajos Csatay and Baron Péter Schell, and also the state secretary, István Fáy.

About an hour later, at midnight, Vattay came back – this time Ambrózy was not with him – with the response that His Highness had completely accepted the solution proposed, on one condition: that he could take his closest colleagues with him in order not to leave them exposed to the vengeance of the Arrow Cross. These colleagues were Ambrózy, Lázár and – of course – Vattay. The colleagues listed above, i.e. Rakovszky, Hennyey, Csatay, Schell and Fáy were present again. At the time I never suspected or even presumed that the adjutant general's account was so terribly at variance with the truth that I later discovered from the witness statements of Ambrózy and Lázár, which was that Your Highness did not want to hear of it.

On the basis of a decision that we believed had been made by the highest authority, I had the task of informing the German Embassy, and this was then the basis of all subsequent developments. These were the ending of resistance at half past five in the morning, Your Highness being taken away from the Palace on the pretext of being taken to a place of safety, and then in the afternoon the intermediary role I was forced to play in connection with forcing Your Highness' resignation by blackmail. That is to say, on the basis of Vattay's story and my report, essentially, as far as the Germans knew, Your Highness had already given way completely at midnight and had surrendered both politically and militarily. I now know that this was not true, but at the time I never suspected that it might not be.

I do not know what led the adjutant general to take this ill-considered step – perhaps it was consideration for Your Highness? – but even so I feel that in this way he did terrible damage to the cause, because it was this that gave impetus to subsequent developments, the significance of which in every regard is almost incalculable. This applies to the fate of the whole country, to the awkward position of the government and not least to Your Highness personally, whose legendary and courageous past made this act incomprehensible to everyone. But I myself would also have acted quite differently on 16 October, when the Germans threatened Your Highness with the lives of Nicky and the whole family in demanding after the oral surrender a formal written resignation; after all, this seemed logical in view of what had gone before.

I have not spoken to Vattay about the matter since then, indeed we have not met since we were in the 'Khida prison, but any reproaches after the event would be illusory anyway. I do not want to start making accusations, though I could include the inadequate military preparations. My only aim was to set out for Your Highness a true account of the events – if only as a potential historic record – and to report on an important circumstance of which Your Highness could have had no knowledge.

I am extremely concerned and interested in what happened to Your Highness and the whole family, but I cannot write about that or related matters now. My family and I are well. My son returned from France more than a year ago, but my son-in-law is still a prisoner of war in England. I have retired to our heavily looted and much reduced estate, I run the estate and take no part in politics.

I ask for God's blessing on Your Highness, the whole family, and our poor homeland. Please pass on my good wishes to Her Highness.

I remain Your Highness' loyal and humble servant,

Géza Lakatos

Budapest, 9 June 1947

Appendix 9.   Legal opinion of Dr. Géza Töreky on the statement signed by the Regent vitéz Nicholas Horthy on 16 October 1944

My legal opinion on Regent Nicholas Horthy's written statement dated 16 October 1944, which contains his alleged resignation, is as follows. I will base my opinion on the facts as stated by the Regent in his memoirs, which are public knowledge.

The Regent, who had been detained in the Grassalkovics (Hatvany) palace in Verbőczy Street since six o'clock in the morning, returned to the Royal Palace at six o'clock in the evening with a German escort in order to pack his belongings. There he was accompanied wherever he went by three German soldiers armed with machine guns. It was in these circumstances that he was visited in the bathroom of his ransacked apartment by Prime Minister Lakatos, accompanied by the German ambassador, Veesenmayer. Lakatos gave him the document written by the Germans in German which contained the Regent's resignation and the appointment of Szálasi as prime minister. When the Regent asked what this meant, Lakatos replied that the freedom and life of the Regent's son, Nicholas Horthy junior, depended on the Regent signing the document. It is well known that Nicholas Horthy junior had been lured into a trap, injured, and captured by the Germans the previous day. When Veesenmayer gave his word of honour that, if the document was signed, the Regent's son would be set free, the Regent made the following statement: 'I am neither resigning, nor appointing Szálasi prime minister, but I will sign the paper in order to save the life of my only remaining child. A signature forced from me by blackmail when I am surrounded by machine guns cannot have constitutional validity.'

These facts are in agreement with the information contained in the records of the Nürnberg court, and make it quite clear that the written statement did not agree with the Regent's wishes and that the written statement was not signed through the Regent's own free will.

Now as in the interpretation of any legal statement it is not the literal meaning of the expressions used which is authoritative but the intention of the person making the statement – and the statement reserving his rights which the Regent made openly at the time of signature shows beyond doubt that the Regent's true wishes were the opposite of what was written in the document – this alone renders the written statement of resignation null and void.

But all the circumstances which contributed to the signature being given also indicate that the Regent did not make a valid statement of resignation. At the time of signature the Regent was personally under duress for the following reasons: after his proclamation announcing Hungary's request for a ceasefire, German soldiers had surrounded and besieged the Palace containing his residence; they had taken him away from the Palace to the SS Headquarters in Verbőczy Street and then only allowed him to return with armed guards to fetch his most essential belongings from his apartment, which had been ransacked in the meantime; at the time of his signature in the Palace he was surrounded by three guards armed with machine guns; and finally, after signing the document he was hurriedly taken abroad and held captive there until the end of the war. All these facts prove that the foreign power occupying the country had forced its will to prevail with ruthless determination and by force of arms, despite the wishes of the Regent, who opposed this.

The fact that he was taken away as a matter of urgency also indicates that the occupying power was well aware that the text of the written statement the Regent had signed was the opposite of his true wishes, and it was for this reason that it thought it had to prevent the Regent by force from publicising his own standpoint. If the Regent had really resigned there would have been no need for all these forceful measures.

In addition to the direct physical threat applied to the Regent personally, the occupiers also used psychological duress by luring his only surviving child into a trap and capturing him in order to use him to blackmail his father. That this act threatened the life of the Regent's son is clearly shown by the fact that they wounded him at the time of his capture. The effect of this situation was exacerbated by Prime Minister

Lakatos making a specific reference, at the time he handed over the written text, to the threat to the life of the Regent's son if the Regent refused to give his signature. This was also a use of duress, which precludes the statement of resignation being valid.

There can be no doubt that when he handed over the written text and informed the Regent of the threats mentioned above, Lakatos was not acting on his own initiative, nor indeed on behalf of the Hungarian government: he was himself under pressure and was following the instructions of the German ambassador Veesenmayer, who had accompanied him to the Palace and was present at the time. The fact that the text was in German clearly shows that its origin was in German, not Hungarian law, something which is also proved beyond doubt by the personal participation in the events of the ambassador Veesenmayer, the representative of the occupying power. Thus it was exclusively the will of the foreign occupying power that prevailed through the signature of the document.

A statement which was originally null and void was not given legal force subsequently by the fact that Hungarian constitutional bodies which had been misled and also intimidated acknowledged it. The Regent himself never withdrew the statement reserving his rights, which he made when he signed the document under duress.

On the basis of all this, my opinion is that the Regent Miklós Horthy did not resign from the office of head of state.

Signed: Dr Géza Töreky, Royal Hungarian Privy Councillor, retired president of the Royal Hungarian Supreme Court.
Alpnachdorf, Switzerland, 3 October 1953

Appendix 10. A letter from John Flournoy Montgomery

John Flournoy Montgomery sent me a copy of the following letter he wrote, requesting help for Admiral Horthy in April 1948.

I am sending you an autographed copy of my book *Hungary – The Unwilling Satellite*, which I hope you will have time to read. My object in writing this book was to bring a better understanding of Central Europe to the American people, which seems to me to be very important.

At the same time, it gives a picture of Admiral Horthy that is quite different from the Communist-inspired portrait which is cherished by our government despite overwhelming evidence to the contrary. This has resulted in Admiral Horthy having received treatment that is impossible to understand.

As you will see in my book, Admiral Horthy was a firm friend of the Allies. He stayed as Regent under difficult conditions so that he would be in a position to help the Allies. When he found we had no intention of coming through the Balkans he made a speech on the radio, which is given in an appendix of my book, denouncing the Nazi regime and stating his position unequivocally.

As a result, the Royal Palace was attacked by the German army. He and his family were taken off to prison where they remained until the arrival of the American troops. However this wasn't a rescue. He was sent to Nürnberg as a criminal. They could find nothing on him there but to all intents and purposes he is still a prisoner. All efforts of friends to help him were for a long time unavailing. For some months he and his family, including a young grandson, suffered greatly. Since that time CARE packages and so forth, sent by friends in America, have enabled him to exist, but he and his family are still under restraint and unable to leave the country.

His son Nicholas, who shot at the SS when they arrested him, spent many months at Mauthausen as a result, was refused a visa to the United States because of the clamour of the Communist press, whereas Hungarian Communists have no difficulty even to this day in getting visas to come the United States.

It is difficult to understand all this; particularly so in the case of the Regent, since he is the only head of a satellite country, or enemy country, who revolted when it was not safe to do so. He is the only head of any of these countries who spent any time in a German prison and the only one who can be certified as a friend throughout the whole period by every member of the American Legation in Budapest. He is likewise the only head of a country who has been treated as a criminal.

Young Michael has just been received by our president and, as far as I am concerned, there is no reason why he should not be, but he was the head of an enemy country just the same as the Admiral but he did not revolt against the Germans until it was safe to do so. He remained with the Communists until he was put out. Why has Admiral Horthy been singled out for such treatment?

The answer seems to be that the Communists have hated him ever since he overthrew the Béla Kún Communist Revolution in Hungary and because he told the world constantly the truth about Communism. In this connection, my predecessor, Nicholas Roosevelt, who reviewed my book for the *New York Times*, said of the admiral: 'It is interesting to see how Hungary's Regent, Admiral Horthy, stands out head and shoulders above all others in this book as a man of integrity and hard common sense. That was the impression which the admiral made on me during the three years that I was Mr Montgomery's predecessor at the American Legation in Budapest. This, incidentally, is quite different from the impression of him built up in this country by political refugees – particularly by those of a leftist tinge.

The old admiral used to hold forth to me for hours on the dangers to Hungary of Soviet Russia; so often, in fact, and so long, that I felt that he was hipped on the subject. Yet in retrospect it is clear how very right he was in regarding Communist Russia as the greatest menace to his people.'

There are reports from time to time that Admiral Horthy is going to be handed over to Tito to be butchered. It would seem incredible that such a thing should be seriously considered, but apparently it is still a possibility.

I might add that the admiral's life has not been made any easier for him by the American authorities in Germany. Possibly it is the first time the army ever had a top admiral completely at its mercy, and they are enjoying it. Whatever the reason may be, he is still a prisoner to all intents and purposes and does not have the perquisites of a prisoner; that is, the right to be fed and taken care of. Certainly if we are going to restrain his movements, common decency would seem to demand that we supply him with his needs.

The great question is: Why is he still under restraint?

Appendix 11. Telegram in *Hungaria*

The telegram from Miklós Horthy and the Churches, sent to the London Conference.

The Conference of the Foreign Ministers of the United States of America, Great Britain and France. London:

Under the Soviet occupation, Hungary cannot give news of itself. It is therefore the duty of the historical Churches and those parts of our nation living in exile to draw attention to those without any protection, the hundreds of thousands languishing in Soviet captivity for the past five years.

Through destructive Asian tactics, six hundred thousand people were driven out of Hungary in 1945. Most of these prisoners were not even soldiers. They were grabbed in the streets, from their flats, their workshops, their peaceful lives. As well as the masses of men, many women, the elderly and young children were driven ahead of them. Mass graves indicate the road out of Europe.

Cardinal Mindszenty, through his 'Pro captivis' prayer campaign and his efforts to care for those left behind, has tried to find healing for the nation's worst pain. Through the family welfare work of the Catholic and Protestant clergy it was possible to establish that out of the six hundred thousand who disappeared over the years, around two hundred and fifty thousand got back to their homeland. There are therefore approximately three hundred and fifty thousand people missing. Out of these, two hundred thousand belong to the present Hungarian territory. One hundred and fifty thousand belong to the Hungarian parts of the successor states; Of the situation of these the Hungarian religious agencies have no data. It is certain that within the territory that is today's Hungary, two hundred thousand families are waiting for the return of their next of kin from the Soviet Union; and it is also certain that for the last year and a half the Soviets have completely put a stop to the return of Hungarian prisoners.

Until the collapse of the sovereignty of the Hungarian state, it fought with unstinting energy for the preservation of the human rights of its citizens. It protected these rights to the utmost, against all ideological and military attacks.

The efforts of the Regent, and the conduct of Prince Primate Serédi and the Hungarian catholic and protestant bishops at the time, checked the deportation of the Jews; and in this way about two hundred thousand Jews in Budapest were saved. This was during the most turbulent time of the war. Now, five years after the end of the war, we must speak up for the two hundred thousand Hungarian prisoners.

Today Hungary fights perhaps its most difficult battle in its thousand-year-old history. Its resistance and survival means the victory of Western thought in the Danube Basin. But this struggling nation is waiting for a sign and for ideological support from the West. The case of the prisoners of war is a serious test of this expectation.

With the Hungarian people's deep confidence in the West's solidarity, we turn to the prestigious Council to adopt as their own the case of the multitude of Hungarian prisoners-of-war. The foundation of a future real, deep and wise peace depends on a noble action now.

Nicholas Horthy   Estoril, 10 May 1950

The Roman Catholic Church 'Mindszenty Pro Captivis' prisoner-of-war service
The Hungarian Reformed Church's spiritual welfare centre
The Hungarian Ágost Church's spiritual welfare centre
The Hungarian Unitarian Church's spiritual welfare centre
The MHBK Hungarian Combatants Fraternal Community prisoner-of-war service.

München, 9 May 1950

Appendices

Appendix 12. Field Marshal Lord Ironside's letter to Admiral Horthy

Hingham, Norfolk, 19 May 1956

My dear Admiral,

How good of you to send me your book. Both my wife and I have been in hospital once more, but we are now out and hope neither of us will go back again. My wife is walking well and I can get about to see all my old veterans from the South African and First Great War. We are just going to have a big parade at St Paul's for the Old Contemptibles – those who fought in the first three months of 1914.

What a wonderful work you have produced. I have read it over two or three times. What a story you had to tell and how well you have told it. It has been beautifully translated into English.

You have told me so many things I wanted to know, after I had met you for my two months in Hungary at the beginning of your regency. How you managed to guide your country in the conditions which of two great wars, perhaps the second was the most brutal. Hungary had so little to make her wish to fight, except to combat Communism. And there we were fighting so that the Russians might become stronger than they had ever been. How we regret it now. Should we ever have defeated Hitler unless Russia had been attacked and so came in with us?

I was much touched when I saw the picture which you painted of the Emperor Franz Joseph. It is a masterpiece. How did you ever find the time to learn to be such an artist? I could never have been one if I had worked for a lifetime.

What a united family you have had and how you must enjoy having them with you from time to time. I also have been happy in my family, so I know your feelings.

I felt it very much when I heard that you were arrested after the second war. What a triumph for you to know that not even your enemies could find any accusation to bring against you. I watched the papers carefully to see what was happening.

I heard a very good report on your grandson from the Duke of Edinburgh. They are proud to have him at Gordonstoun. I hope his mother is glad that it was decided to send him there. I shall see him again one of these days and see how he has opened up into a man. When I saw him at lunch in my Club he seemed too old for his years, and I was not surprised at that after what you had all been through. Anyway, he can be proud of his forbears, his parents and his grandparents.

One of the things I honoured you so much for was that you refused to be crowned a king. I think the people who offered you the title did not understand what a Regent in Hungary was. Something so important in Hungarian life yet so simple and so loyal to the people.

I am a Scotsman and, like you, a Magyar. I've felt that the reigning Sovereign of both England and Scotland often forgets the importance of the smaller country. The Scots and the Magyars have very much the same dear characters. Simple but obstinate. Loving freedom more than anything else. Loyal to their leaders. ...

Again, thank you for the book. I sent round four copies to various friends and told them to circulate them to the younger officers so that they may realise the true story of Hungary. So many people know nothing about it.

My best love to both you and Madame Horthy, in which my wife joins.
Yours ever,
Ironside.

Appendix 13. Newspaper cutting on Guy's Commendation

THE BRAVE MAJOR OF BAGDAD

HE GOT PAST THE ARABS IN DISGUISE

Colonel John Bowden

"Evening News" Reporter

THE Queen's Commendation for Brave Conduct has been awarded to Colonel John Wallace Guy Bowden of The Queen's Own Hussars, for bravery when wearing disguise in Bagdad.

It happened when the British Embassy was attacked by an armed mob during the army coup in Irak last year.

The citation says that on July 14, and the following days, Colonel Bowden, then a major, "maintained communications between Her Majesty's Ambassador and the members of his staff."

They were separated by streets filled with armed mobs.

He Went Back

Colonel Bowden, knowing he would have been lynched if he were recognised, travelled many times between the Ambassador's house and his staff, in disguise, and each time managed to escape the mob.

Colonel Bowden, aged 42, was in Baghdad helping to train Iraki soldiers. He has since returned to Irak as Military Attache.

He was formerly military attaché at the British Embassy in Lisbon, and instructor at the Staff College, Quetta.

In 1954 he married Countess Ilona de Horthy, daughter-in-law of Admiral Nicholas Horthy, the former Regent of Hungary.

COL. BOWDEN GETS C.B.E.

Colonel J.W.G. Bowden, Military Attache at the British Embassy, was awarded a Commandership of the Order of the British Empire (C.B.E.) on the occasion of Queen Elizabeth's birthday, according to the Honours List published on Thursday.

Others honoured are: The Most Reverend Angus Campbell Macinnes, Archbishop in Jerusalem, (CMG); Arthur Craig-Bennett, British Council Representative in Libya and formerly in Baghdad, (OBE); Norman Darbyshire, lately First Secretary, Political Residency, Bahrain, (O.B.E.); Ahmad Mohammed Hassan Hijazi, judge of Her Majesty's Court, Kuwait, (O.B.E.); David Lister, Senior Master, New Mansour Primary School in Baghdad, (M.B.E.); Mohammed Abdul Latif, Account and Administration Officer, British Consulate-General, Basra, (M.B.E.)

(See also Page 13)

Appendix 14. Letters of condolence

a) From former Prime Minister Miklós Kállay

New York, 13 January 1959

Dear Ily,

I was worried in the weeks after Christmas when we didn't get any news from you. I was afraid something was wrong and was concerned about Her Highness, but I dismissed such pessimistic thoughts because her death would be as if everything that was beautiful and noble had left this world. Please accept Márta's and my own deepest condolences, we are with you in your great pain. Please also tell István what we feel about his loss.

And Ily, you were wonderful, both when you stood by His Highness and now in your dedication during these last years. I know no example of anyone showing such devotion to duty and such love through a succession of tragedies as you have. If there is ever a country, a people, justice and gratitude again, this will be legendary.

The sympathy and love that have been shown here are moving. I asked for a requiem mass to be said at eleven o'clock on Saturday the seventeenth in St Stephen's Hungarian Parish Church. We are sending out notices, which Mrs Erzsébet Ráth has volunteered to do. There will be no sermon; I will write and tell you about the mass. If you would let me know István's address, I will write to him.

With much love,
Miklós Kállay

b) From Mr Ferenc Chorin.

New York, 9 January 1959

Dear Ily,

We were deeply shocked and greatly saddened by the news that Her Highness had departed this life. The news was not unexpected, her last letters and the news arriving here were not encouraging, but still we were profoundly depressed by the sad news. With her one of the last memories of the old Hungary has gone; we all vividly remember her radiant appearance, which gave a particular sparkle to every festival. I think it must be deeply comforting for you to know that you stood by the Regent and his wife with such admirable loyalty and steadfastness in the difficult days of their lives, and if Hungarian life still survives or is reborn, I think your wonderful selflessness will always be remembered. Please tell Nicholas that we think fondly of him, and pass on our condolences to him.

With true friendship and respect,
Your old friend,
Ferenc Chorin

Appendix 15. My observations on the content of *The Last Habsburg* by Gordon Brook-Shepherd

Mr Brook-Shepherd starts by emphasising his authoritative sources, and introduces his book by saying:

> It was in discussion with his eldest son, Archduke Otto ... that the idea of writing a definitive biography of the Emperor Charles first arose ... unexpectedly and unasked on my part, his widow, the former Empress Zita of Austro-Hungary, had agreed to give her personal assistance in the re-telling of the story of her husband's life and struggles ...

I will point out just a few of the many false statements that Mr Brook-Shepherd made. First of all it is important to mention the text of the Emperor's hand-written resignation, dated November 1919 (reproduced in the book on page 341). The English translation on page 219 is somewhat inaccurate. It reads:

> I do not wish to stand in the way of the evolution of the Hungarian nation, for whom I still feel the same unchanged love. Consequently I resign my part in the business of state and accept this decision as regards the new form of government in Hungary

A more correct translation of the essential part is as follows:

> I do not want my person to be a hindrance to the free development of the Hungarian nation, towards which I am filled with unchanging love.
>
> Consequently I resign from any part in conducting the affairs of the state and accept in advance Hungary's decision to establish its future government.

Page 253 is full of inaccurate and malicious remarks such as: 'On hearing that he [Horthy] was alive, Charles had him appointed, through the Bethlen Committee, as minister of war in the Szegedin 'counter-government' – a post which Horthy subsequently exchanged for that of commander-in-chief of the incipient anti-Communist army. The Emperor had unwittingly placed the asp in his own breast.'

How could King Charles have possibly appointed Horthy in May 1919, following his renunciation of any part in affairs of state in November 1918?

Mr Brook-Shepherd writes the following about Admiral Horthy's entrance into Budapest in November 1919: 'The admiral turned soldier-of-fortune entered the city in triumph at the head of 'his' monarchist army. He had marched thus far as the Emperor's man and it was on the shoulders of the dynasty that he now climbed much higher.'

How can anyone say that a man who was liberating his country from murder and terror had 'turned soldier-of-fortune', or call the army 'his monarchist army', when it was clearly a nationalist one. It was certainly not on the 'shoulders of the dynasty' that he 'climbed higher'; it was the Hungarian nation that elected him Regent. But the author says that he 'was appointed to this curious post. His was the classic case of the absolute corruption of absolute power.'

It is wrong to say that he was 'appointed', as he was elected by the National Assembly – by 131 votes out of 141. Only the author himself knows what he means by 'curious post' and 'absolute corruption'.

Page 255: 'Thus when Horthy coolly bestowed upon himself the title of Duke, Charles swallowed the impertinence and even brought himself indirectly to sanction it by addressing his self-ennobled Regent as 'Your Grace' in his next message to Budapest.'

If Horthy bestowed the title upon himself, why then did he never use it? The Regent explained the situation very clearly in his memoirs. A year before, on 2 February 1920, an Ambassadorial Conference had already issued a formal veto against any restoration of the Habsburgs in Hungary, because it felt that it would 'rock peace to its foundations' and would therefore 'neither be recognised nor tolerated' by the Allies. On 27 March 1921, King Charles secretly entered the country and suddenly appeared unannounced in Budapest. The Regent wrote in his memoirs:

> It was Easter Sunday, a day of brilliant sunshine, the trees were in blossom and the whole of Hungary was celebrating the resurrection of Our Lord, grateful that the signs of better times were visibly multiplying. King Charles, wearing a Hungarian officer's uniform, expressed the hope that he could once more take his place as head of the state. He gave me a graphic account of his life in exile. I assured His Majesty that, were I able to recall him, our crowned King, whose legitimate claims I recognised and was prepared to defend, it would be the happiest termination of my present office. In Hungary, I told him, his estates had been left unsequestered and the income deriving from them was at his disposal. I begged him to believe that I still felt myself bound by the oath I had sworn to the Emperor, and I had no wish to retain my office as Regent … 'But Your Majesty should consider, that the very moment I hand the reins of state over to the King, the armies of the neighbouring states will cross our frontiers. We have nothing with which to oppose them in the field. Your Majesty will then be forced to return to Switzerland, Hungary will be occupied by foreign troops and the evil resulting from renewed occupation will be incalculable.' …
>
> The tide of nationalism was running high in our neighbour states and their governments would not permit a restoration of the Habsburg symbols.
>
> As attempts have since been made to place this two-hour discussion between His Majesty and myself in a false light – for it was, as I held then and still hold today, a discussion on the outcome of which depended the very existence of our Fatherland – I must add that, before he departed, his Majesty expressed his profound thanks to me and invested me with the Grand Cross of the Military Order of Maria Theresia, creating me Duke of Otranto and Szeged. And I must add further that I have neither worn the Grand Cross nor used the ducal title. This gesture of His Majesty, however, shows better than words that he, at any rate, was convinced of my good faith and that my attitude sprang from my sense of responsibility and duty. [pp.146–152]

Mr Brook-Shepherd says that pages 266–267 of his book tell 'Charles' own account' to which the Empress has also added 'a few extra details'. However, it is very different from the Regent's account. The Regent never said anything about the King's version, but would never have wished to suggest that the King was lying. He believed in Charles' sincerity and attributed all the distortions to his entourage. He gave his own version and left it at that.

That year the King made a second attempt at restoration, without giving any prior warning to the Regent. Page 290: 'To every garrison commander between Győr and Budapest, Horthy sent orders to fire on this railway cavalcade. In fact hardly a shot was fired.' This of course cannot be proved, and the author does not even bother to say where he got this information. I have heard so much about this episode, and all of it convinces me that this story is untrue. The Regent never gave that order, and if one was given at all, it can only have been issued by someone else.

Page 298: 'When he tried to betray his Nazi ally as he had betrayed his sovereign.' An extraordinary statement and a strange comparison. Hitler had severed all ties, broken all promises and invaded Hungary, and yet the Regent still tried to play fair and let him know his intentions. 'Horthy, who had taken over from Communism in 1920, now fled for his life from it twenty-five years later.' The truth of course was that he was arrested and taken out of the country.

On the same page, 298: 'He died in exile in Portugal in 1957, taking a troubled conscience with him to the grave.' Footnote: 'At the dying man's insistent pleading, the Emperor's oldest son, Archduke Otto, visited Horthy shortly before his death. The former admiral and Regent begged for political 'absolution'.

This is a complete distortion of what had actually happened. Archduke Otto's visit was the result of an agreement they made in July 1949 to first exchange letters and mutual visits later. The Regent did not initiate the process. I have described the agreement and the visits in detail in Chapters 20 and 21. The Regent visited Archduke Otto on 22 May 1950, and Archduke Otto returned the visit on 15 April 1953. The Regent was not a dying man at the time – he was in excellent health. He died four years later after the Hungarian revolution in 1957.

I was amazed that Mr Brook-Shepherd made the following statement in his answer to Mr Eckhardt's letter of 16 September 1970: '... I would like to direct your attention to my footnote on page 298, in which I record Horthy's own search for 'absolution' in a talk with Otto Habsburg, shortly before the Regent's death. I have this on the authority of the Archduke himself, who has been a personal friend of mine some twenty-five years.'

For the Archduke's sake, I hope that this is another of Mr Brook-Shepherd's errors.

Appendix 16. Newspaper article on the lecture by the widow of Stephen Horthy, Toronto, 1997

Last Sunday, 8 November, the widow of Stephen Horthy gave a very successful and historic lecture in a function room at The Old Mill in Toronto. The room was packed to overflowing by an audience who assembled in one of the banqueting rooms in this fine old building from five thirty in the evening. The lecturer was introduced by István Vörösváry, who had organised the event. Soon afterwards a dinner, which easily satisfied even the most refined of palates, was served.

After the dinner Dr György Nagy introduced Mrs Stephen Horthy, who stepped onto the podium to give her eagerly awaited hour-long lecture. In her introduction, she stated that she had decided to publicise a detailed account of the events of 1944 after seeing an American-produced film about Wallenberg on television. There were so many lies and so much false information in this film that the truth now had to be told. She emphasised that the Regent had never met Eichmann in his life, and did not hold any reception in 1944 in honour of him or anyone else.

In the main body of her lecture Mrs Horthy gave an account of her personal experiences of the election of the vice-regent, the tragic death of Stephen Horthy, and the events leading up to the German invasion in March 1944. She told us the part the Regent played in the appointment of the Lakatos government, about the secret negotiations that took place then, and the circumstances in which negotiations were started with Moscow. She told us many previously unknown details of the events leading up to 15 October, about the final outcome, and about the Regent's family being taken away to Germany.

What fascinated the audience most was perhaps Mrs Horthy's account of their internment in Germany and then the Regent's life and last days in Portugal, which was very direct and based on her own moving experiences. The great love and devotion she felt for her parents-in-law shone from every word she spoke: this was a testimony to her true Christian and warm human nature. After the lecture Mrs Horthy talked for a long time with her audience, who didn't want to let her leave.

Notes

[1] 'Baron Edelsheim Gyulai, Saviour', *Neues Politisches Volksblatt* [New Political Popular Press], 27 March 1893.

[2] *Budapesti Ujság*, 21 November 1888, p. 1.

[3] József Mittuch, *Adatok Elefánth történetéhez* [Information on the story of Elefánt] (Booklet published privately in Nyitra [now Nitra] 1904).

[4] *Vitéz nagybanyai Horthy István élete és a Magyar Közlekedés* (Budapest, Fővárosi Nyomda Rt., 1943), republished (Ontario, Vörösváry Publishing Co. Ltd, 1976).

[5] (Budapest, Auktor Publisher, 1992).

[6] György Barcza, *Diplomata Emlékeim* [My Diplomatic Memories] (2 vols., Budapest, Európa-História, 1994), vol. I, p. 208.

[7] Miklós Horthy's memoirs have been published in eight editions:
Horthy Miklós Emlékirataim
(Buenos Aires, Talleres Graficos Cagnasso y Cía, 1953).

Admiral Nikolaus von Horthy, Ein Leben für Ungarn
(Bonn, Athenaeum Verlag, 1953).

Almirante Nikolaus von Horthy Memorias (Barcelona, Editorial AHR, 1955).

Nikolaus von Horthy Muistelmat (Helsingissa Kunstannusosakeyhit Otava, 1955).

Horthy Memorie (Corso Roma, 1956).

The Admiral Horthy Memoirs (New York, Robert Speller & Sons, 1957).

Horthy. Emlékirataim (Toronto, Weller Publishing Company Ltd, 1957).

Horthy Miklós Emlékirataim (Budapest, Európa-História, 1992).

All the quotations in this book have been translated from the 1992 Hungarian edition.

[8] Lajos Dálnoki Veress, *Magyarország Honvédelme a II. világháború előtt és alatt* [Hungary's national defence before and during the Second World War] (4 vols., Munich, Deutsch Druckerei GmbH, 1972), vol. I, p. 113.

[9] Péter Gosztonyi, *A magyar honvédség a második világháborúban* [The Hungarian army in the Second World War] (Rome, Katolikus Szemle, 1986), p. 30.

[10] Dálnoki Veress, *Magyarország Honvédelme a II. világháború előtt és alatt*, vol. I, pp. 229–230.

[11] The coded telegram can be found in the Tibor Eckhardt-Legacy, New York. Text of telegram translated from G. Hennyey, *Magyarország sorsa Kelet és Nyugat között* [Hungary's destiny between East and West] (Budapest, Európa-História, 1992), pp. 261–62.

[12] Lujza Esterházy, *Szivek az ár ellen* [Hearts against the tide] (Budapest, Püski, 1991), p. 122.

[13] As in Germanic and Latin languages, in Hungarian there are two pronouns that can be used when addressing somebody, one formal and one informal. It was normal for the aristocracy to use the informal address with their friends, but the formal one with their families.

[14] Miklós Kállay, *Magyarország miniszterelnöke voltam 1942–1944* [Prime Minister of Hungary 1942–1944] (Budapest, Európa-História, 1991), pp. 44–47.

Notes

[15] István Jánosy, *Vitéz Horthy István a Repülő* [Vitéz Stephen Horthy the Pilot] (Budapest, A Magyar Repülő Sajtóvállalat & Stádium Sajtóvállalat Rt., 1943), p. 87.

[16] *Horthy István Repülő Főhadnagy Tragikus Halálá* (Budapest, Auktor Publisher, 1992). English edition: (New Jersey USA, Universe Publishing Co., 1997).

[17] 'Mátyásföldtől Bankstownig. Egy öreg sas emlékezik' [From Mátyásföld to Bankstown. An old eagle looks back]
Unpublished manuscript written in Budapest, 1954, p. 125.

[18] 'An unusual witness: former corporal Rafael Mészáros' in *Horthy Istvan Repülő Főhadnagy Tragikus Halálá*, pp. 99–100.

[19] *Vitéz Horthy István a Repülő* [Vitéz Stephen Horthy the Pilot].

[20] *Vitéz nagybanyai Horthy István élete és a Magyar Közlekedés* [Life of vitéz Stephen Horthy and Transport in Hungary].

[21] Gosztonyi: *A magyar honvédség a második világháborúban*, p. 137. (Gyula Kádár, *Emlékezés* [memoirs] p. 90).

[22] Gosztonyi: *A magyar ellenállási mozgalom és visszhangja a német iratok tükrében* [The Hungarian resistance movement and its echoes in German documents] A pamphlet produced privately by Gosztonyi, p. 11.

[23] *Ibid* p. 12.

[24] *The Admiral Horthy Memoirs* (New York, Robert Speller & Sons, 1957), pp. 7–9.

[25] Sándor Szenes, *Befejezetlen Múlt, Keresztények és Zsidók, sorsok* [Unfinished Past, Christians and Jews, their fates] (Budapest, Sándor Szenes, 1986).

[26] Gosztonyi, *A magyar honvédség a második világháborúban*, pp. 219–220.

[27] Gosztonyi, *A magyar ellenállási mozgalom és visszhangja a német iratok tükrében*, p. 18. (The quotes from the unpublished 1944 diary of János Vörös come from a copy in Gosztonyi's possession.)

[28] Dr Ernő Pető's letter to Dr Lajos Marton, *Tekintet* Magazine 1989/4.

[29] *Ibid.*

[30] A novena is an act of devotion over nine days, in which an individual or group of people pray with a particular aim or wish in mind.

[31] From the private collection of Dr Péter Gosztonyi.

[32] From the private collection of writings gathered by Béla Aggteleky: Recollections of Adjutant General Antal Vattay, based on notes made in 1944/1945. (In the author's possession.)

[33] *Ibid.*

[34] Memoirs of Antal Vattay, deposited in the Museum of Recent History in Budapest, 25 November 1965.

[35] The text of this note is quoted by Macartney in *October Fifteenth: A History of Modern Hungary* (2 vols., Edinburgh, University Press, 1961) vol. II, p. 351.

[36] Dálnoki Veress, *Magyarország honvédelme a II. világháború előtt és alatt*, vol. III, pp. 159–160.

[37] C. A. Macartney, 'Ungarns weg aus dem zweiten Weltkrieg' [Hungary's way out of the Second World War](*Time History Quarterly*) 1066 (14), pp. 88–89.

[38] *Ibid.*

[39] Private collection of Lieutenant General Aggteleky: G/42, p. 7, (14 September 1973).

Notes

40 Lieutenant General Aggteleky quotes this in a letter to General L. Székely, 6 Sept.1966. Private collection of Lieutenant General Aggteleky: vol. II. (6.IV/2), p. 3.

41 Private collection of Lieutenant General Aggteleky: vol. II. *Észrevételeim Lakatos 1044 okt.28-i ön- vallomásához* [my observations on Lakatos' account] (1071.1.6), p. 10.

42 General Gusztáv Hennyey, *Magyarország sorsa Kelet és Nyugat között* [Hungary's destiny between East and West] (Budapest, Európa História, 1992), p. 130.

43 Private collection of Lieutenant General Aggteleky: *Összefoglalóm' Lakatos Géza 1944 október 28-án kelt beszámolójához* [My summary of Géza Lakatos' account dated 28 October 1944] (8 January 1971).

44 Géza Lakatos, *Ahogy Én Láttam* [As I saw it] (Englewood USA, Universe Publishing Company, 1993), p. 160.

45 G. Hennyey: *Magyarország sorsa Kelet és Nyugat között* [Hungary's destiny between East and West] (Budapest, Európa-História, 1992,) p. 117.

46 Private collection of Lieutenant General Aggteleky: vol. II, *Észrevételeim Lakatos Géza 1944okt.28-án kelt beszámolójához.* [My observations on Géza Lakatos' account of 29 October 1944] p. 2–3 (8 January 1971).

47 Private collection of Lieutenant General Aggteleky: notes on the protocol taken by parliamentary secretary István Bárczy.

48 Private collection of Lieutenant General Aggteleky: Colonel Imre Pogány's letter E/5, p. 6, 13.02.1972, and Comments G10, p. 6, (18 December 1972).

49 Gosztonyi, 'The Private War Diary of the Chief of the Hungarian General Staff in 1944' *Wehrwissenschaftliche Rundschau* [Journal of Military Affairs] vol. II (1970).

50 Private collection of Lieutenant General Aggteleky: Colonel Imre Pogány's comments G/10, p. 6, (18 December 1972).

51 'Elfogatásom Története' [The story of my capture], Lajos Dálnoki Veress, in Gosztonyi, *A magyar honvédség a második világháborúban*, p. 49.

52 Gosztonyi, *A magyar honvédség a második világháborúban*, p. 211–212.

53 This was the property of Baron Hirschberg, rented by the banker Bleichröder until the state took it over. The previous year, Mussolini had spent three days there.

54 The questions and answers quoted are my translation from the German Military Tribunal's protocol of 4 March 1948.

55 My own translation of Miklóspapa's message.

56 Lujza Esterházy, *Szivek az ár ellen* [Hearts against the Tide] (Budapest, Püski, 1966).

57 The original copy of this letter is in my possession.

58 The Regent's title as commander-in-chief.

59 Miklós Kállay, *Hungarian Premier 1942–1944* (New York, Columbia University Press, 1954), p. 503.

60 Rodosto (now Tekirdag) in Turkey was where Ferenc Rákóczi, the then Prince of Transylvania, lived and died in exile in the eighteenth century.

61 J. B. Bennett, *Concerning Subud* (London, Hodder & Stoughton, 1958), p. 68.

62 *Bapak's Talks* (to date: 12 vols., Rickmansworth UK, Subud Publications International, 2003), vol. 10, p. 5.

Notes

Varindra Tarzie Vittachi, *A Reporter's Assignment in Subud*, 2nd edn. (Rickmansworth UK, Subud Publications International, 1971) p. 22, p. 86.

[64] Varindra Tarzie Vittachi, *A Reporter in Subud,* (Rickmansworth UK, Subud Publications International, 2003).

[65] Tibor Eckhardt was the Smallholder Party leader from 1932 until he left Hungary for the United States in order that, when the need arose, he could set up a functioning émigré government.

[66] Edward van Hien, *What is Subud* (London, Rider & Company, 1963), pp. 21–2.

[67] Zaire: formerly the Belgian Congo, since 1998 the Dem. Rep. of Congo.

[68] (New Jersey USA, Universe Publishing Co.).

[69] Josef Pilsudski, Polish marshal, statesman (1867–1935).

[70] Published by the Press Department of the Ministry of Foreign Affaires of the Republic of Hungary.

Index

Index

Index

Index